FoxPro 2:
The Complete Reference

FoxPro 2:
The Complete Reference

Edward Jones and David Nesbitt

Osborne **McGraw-Hill**
Berkeley   New York   St. Louis   San Francisco
Auckland   Bogotá   Hamburg   London   Madrid
Mexico City   Milan   Montreal   New Delhi   Panama City
Paris   São Paulo   Singapore   Sydney
Tokyo   Toronto

Osborne **McGraw-Hill**
2600 Tenth Street
Berkeley, California 94710
U.S.A.

For information on translations or book distributors outside of the U.S.A., please write to Osborne **McGraw-Hill** at the above address.

FoxPro 2: The Complete Reference

1234567890 DOC 998765432

ISBN 0-07-881688-2

Publisher ——————
    Kenna S. Wood

Acquisitions Editor ——————
    Elizabeth Fisher

Associate Editor ——————
    Scott Rogers

Technical Editors ——————
    Paul Sevigny
    John Levy

Project Editor ——————
    Kathy Krause

Copy Editor ——————
    Paul Medoff

Proofreading Coordinator ———
    Nancy McLauglin Pechonis

Proofreaders ——————
    K.D. Sullivan
    Audrey Baer Johnson
    Valerie Haynes Perry

Indexer ——————
    Richard Shrout

Illustrator ——————
    Susie C. Kim

Computer Designers ——————
    Helena Charm
    Lance Ravella
    Marcela Hancik

Word Processors ——————
    Lynda Higham

Cover Designers ——————
    Bay Graphics Design, Inc.

Contents at a Glance

Contents

II
Programming in FoxPro

14
The Basics of FoxPro Programming 251

15
Using Memory Variables 265

16
Process Control in a FoxPro Program 279

17
Programming for Data Entry, Editing, and Reporting 293

24

FoxPro System Memory Variables 747

V
Appendixes

Acknowledgments

We would like to offer our thanks to a number of individuals, without whom this book would not have been possible. Thanks to Liz Fisher and her editorial expertise in juggling the demands of busy schedules (and in dealing with a transcontinental move for one of the authors), and to Paul Sevigny and John Levy for much hard work in providing the technical review. Also, many thanks go to Scott Rogers, Kathy Krause, Nancy Pechonis, and Paul Medoff for all of the behind-the-scenes work of coordinating, production, and copy editing that is necessary to bring a good book to the marketplace.

Introduction

From its more humble beginnings as FoxBASE, Fox Software's relational database manager for the PC has grown into FoxPro 2, a product that many agree sets the standard for database management in the DOS world. FoxPro 2 gives you speed, dBASE compatibility, a powerful applications development environment, and much more. FoxPro also provides relational query-by-example and implementation of SQL commands for fast, simple retrieval of data. You'll find details on all these features and many more in this book.

About This Book

This book is designed to meet the needs of both beginners and intermediate to advanced users of FoxPro. Overall, you will find material that leans toward beginners in the front half of the book, while material that appeals to advanced users is primarily in the back half of the book. Throughout this text, you will find exercises and real-world examples that you can follow to see how you can most effectively use FoxPro. And while you will be better off with the features in the latest version of FoxPro, the book is designed to be used with all versions of FoxPro, up to and including version 2.0.

How This Book Is Organized

This book is divided into five sections. Part I covers the basics of FoxPro and is written in a demonstration-by-example style. Part II covers programming with FoxPro; this section contains numerous examples of program code that you can adapt to your specific tasks. Part III details the use of FoxPro on a network and how applications can be written for use on a network. Part IV contains a detailed reference to all commands, functions, and system memory variables used by FoxPro, as well as a chapter on how to optimize the FoxPro application. Part V consists of four appendixes containing tables of information helpful to all FoxPro users.

Chapter 1 introduces new users to FoxPro, providing coverage of system requirements, installation, and the menu and command structure of the program. In Chapter 2, FoxPro's user interface is detailed and all menu options are explained, along with instructions for using dialog boxes in FoxPro. Chapter 3 starts off the actual use of databases by showing you how to design database files, how to add and list data, and how to change the structure of a file. Chapter 4 builds on these concepts by showing how data can be rearranged through sorting and indexing.

Chapter 5 shows how you can structure various types of queries to retrieve the data you need. Chapter 6 continues this subject through the use of Relational Query By Example (RQBE), a feature of FoxPro 2. Chapters 7 and 8 deal with getting your desired data on paper, in the form of reports or mailing labels. In Chapter 9, you learn how you can use macros to automate your work, and Chapter 10 shows how you can use FoxPro's power to manage relational databases.

Chapters 11, 12, and 13 are more advanced in nature than the chapters that precede them. In Chapter 11, you'll learn how you can use the screen design tools in FoxPro 2 and in earlier versions of FoxPro to design screens for viewing and editing data. Chapter 12 shows how you can use various FoxPro tools and the Editor in FoxPro, which is used extensively when writing programs. Chapter 13 details the use of the Menu Builder and the Project Manager, tools unique to FoxPro 2 that aid in developing sophisticated applications.

Chapters 14 through 19 cover programming in FoxPro. These chapters contain detailed information on how you can control events within FoxPro programs; how you can handle data entry, editing, and reporting needs; how you can tailor a user interface using FoxPro's powerful commands; and how you can use the more advanced commands and functions within FoxPro for programming needs.

Chapters 20 and 21 specifically deal with the needs of the FoxPro user or programmer on a network: Chapter 20 details the use of FoxPro on a network, while Chapter 21 provides tips and techniques needed when programming applications for use on a network.

In Chapters 22 and 23 you will find a detailed command reference and function reference. These chapters are extensive, so you will have an excellent reference to all FoxPro commands and functions once you are familiar with the program. Chapters 24 and 25 round out the book with coverage of FoxPro's system memory variables and tips on optimizing FoxPro.

The appendixes provide listings of file types and system functions used by FoxPro, along with an ASCII table.

Conventions Used in This Book

Throughout this book, we have attempted to follow style conventions to make your understanding of the various elements of FoxPro use and programming as clear as possible. For example, any items that you are asked to type in will appear in **boldface** type. Key presses are indicated with small caps (ALT-D, for example), variables in syntax statements are set in italic type (*exp1*, for example), and FoxPro commands and functions are set in uppercase (QUIT, for example). (Note that FoxPro will accept commands typed in either upper- or lowercase. We have chosen uppercase for consistency and readability.)

Part *I*

Using FoxPro

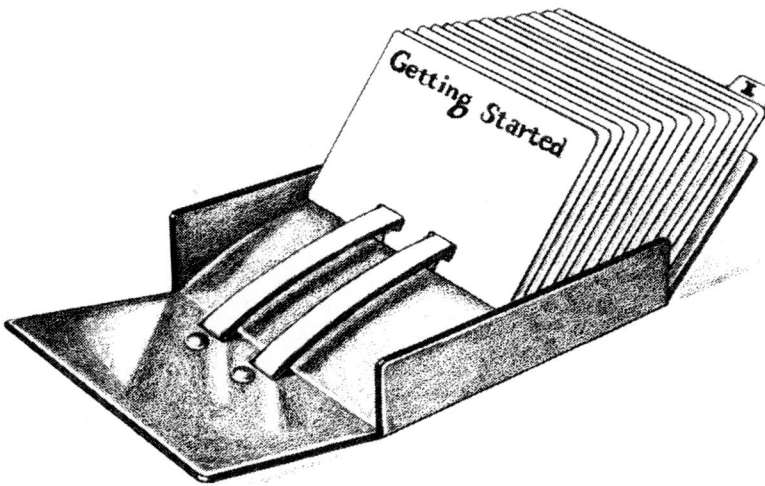

Chapter *1*

Getting Started with FoxPro

FoxPro, Fox Software's most recent implementation of the dBASE dialect, offers many improvements over its predecessor, FoxBASE+, as well as dBASE III PLUS and dBASE IV. Beginners can get up to speed quickly, performing routine tasks using FoxPro's interactive user interface. Experienced application developers will find a powerful set of tools for developing key components such as screens, menus, and reports, along with a robust programming language.

System Requirements

To use FoxPro, you need an IBM-compatible computer with a minimum of 512K of memory and at least one floppy drive and one hard disk drive. A mouse is not required, but is recommended for ease of use. You must be using DOS 2.1 or later or OS/2 version 1.0 or later. FoxPro can be used with either a monochrome or color monitor and with any compatible printer.

To use FoxPro on a local area network, you need workstations with a minimum of 640K of memory, any combination of disk drives (or no drives), and DOS 3.1 or later or OS/2 version 1.0 or later. The operating system can be any of the following:

- Novell Advanced NetWare
- IBM PC network or Token Ring network with IBM PC Local Area Network

- 3Com 3Plus network with 3Com 3Plus operating system

- Any other network configuration that is 100 percent NETBIOS compatible with DOS 3.1 or above and with the networks just listed

Conventional-Memory Requirements

All the IBM PCs (XT, AT, and PS/2) and compatibles contain up to 640K of conventional memory. FoxPro requires a minimum of 512K of conventional memory with at least 400K free. If you are using a machine with only 512K of installed memory, you should remove all memory-resident programs before installing or using FoxPro.

On a 512K machine, FoxPro will need to access the disk much more often than when it has more memory to work with. For better performance, you should increase the conventional memory to 640K in your machine and avoid using memory-resident programs while using FoxPro (unless those programs are designed to use extended or expanded memory that you may have installed above 640K).

Extended and Expanded Memory

FoxPro is designed to take advantage of expanded memory (EMS) or extended memory configured as EMS. FoxPro can use AST RAMPage, Intel Above Board, or any other memory card meeting the LIM 4.0 (Lotus-Intel-Microsoft) memory specifications.

Installing FoxPro

FoxPro comes with an installation program and a booklet entitled *Getting Started*, which contains detailed information for installing and starting FoxPro. Because versions of FoxPro change and the instructions may change along with software updates, this text will provide only some general tips regarding installation. You should refer to your latest FoxPro documentation for detailed specifics on installing the program.

Before the Installation

There are a few simple steps you'll need to perform before you'll be ready to install FoxPro on your system:

1. Check your FoxPro documentation to verify that you have all of the 5 1/4-inch floppy disks necessary to install FoxPro. You should also locate the *Getting Started* booklet supplied with your FoxPro documentation. At the time of this writing, FoxPro provides a phone number to call if you need 3 1/2-inch disks. The phone number is on a sheet packed with the documentation.

2. Check your hard disk for at least three megabytes of free disk space. (Use the DIR command; the description "*xxxxx* bytes free" that appears at the bottom of the directory listing indicates the amount of free space remaining.) This is important because the program itself requires between one and two megabytes of disk space for installation.

3. Create a directory in which to store the program files for FoxPro and another directory to store your data files. For example, if the hard disk is C, use the following commands:

```
C:
MD C:\FOXPRO
MD C:\FOXPRO\FOXDATA
CD C:\FOXPRO
```

The last command in the example makes FOXPRO the current directory.

Installation Procedure

You can install FoxPro in the current directory by performing the following steps:

1. Insert the Installation Disk into drive A.

2. Change the default drive to A by typing **A:** and then pressing ENTER.

3. Enter the following command:

```
INSTALL C:
```

where C is the drive on which you want to install FoxPro. (If your hard disk uses a letter other than C, substitute the letter for your hard disk in this example.)

Refer to the *Getting Started* booklet supplied with your FoxPro documentation, and follow the instructions within to complete the installation process.

Creating a Batch File for FoxPro

You can create a batch file to make starting FoxPro and changing to the desired subdirectory an easier task. If you have installed FoxPro in a subdirectory named FOXPRO on drive C of your hard disk and have installed a subdirectory in it named FOXDATA, the commands shown here can be used to accomplish this task. If your hard disk is not C, substitute your drive letter in the following commands. If your subdirectories are named something other than FOXPRO and FOXDATA, substitute your names for these.

To create the batch file, first enter the following commands from the DOS prompt, pressing ENTER at the end of each line:

```
CD\
COPY CON FOXPRO.BAT
```

When you complete the second command, the cursor will move down a line and will wait for additional entries. Type the following lines, pressing ENTER after each line:

```
CD\FOXPRO\FOXDATA
FOXPRO
```

Then press F6, followed by ENTER. You should see the message "1 File(s) copied."

You'll need to perform one more step to make the batch file work properly: You'll need to modify the PATH statement in your AUTOEXEC.BAT file so that FoxPro is included in your PATH statement. Use your word processor (any word processor that can save files as ASCII text can be used) to open the file named C:\AUTOEXEC.BAT. (This assumes that your AUTOEXEC.BAT file is stored on drive C. If it is not, substitute your drive name for C.) Find the statement that starts with PATH= and add an entry for FoxPro at the end of the line. For example, an existing PATH statement that reads as follows:

```
PATH=C:\DOS; C:\PERFECT
```

should be modified to read like this:

```
PATH=C:DOS; C:\PERFECT; C:\FOXPRO
```

If no PATH statement exists in your AUTOEXEC.BAT file, add one that looks like the following (substitute the appropriate drive letter if your hard drive is something other than C):

```
PATH=C:\DOS; C:\FOXPRO
```

When you have made the necessary changes to your AUTOEXEC.BAT file, save the file as ASCII text. (See your word processor's documentation for specifics on saving files as ASCII text.) Then restart your computer by pressing CTRL-ALT-DEL so that the new AUTOEXEC.BAT file will take effect. From this point on, you can always start FoxPro and switch to the FOXPRO\FOXDATA subdirectory simply by typing **FOXPRO** at the DOS prompt.

Starting FoxPro

Start your computer in the usual manner. If you created a batch file by following the directions in the previous section, you can enter **FOXPRO** and press ENTER to switch to the proper directory and load the program.

NOTE: OS/2 users should be aware that if you are using FoxPro for DOS, you will need to run the program through the DOS Compatibility Box of OS/2; see your OS/2 documentation for details.

If you are not an OS/2 user and have not set up the batch file, switch to the subdirectory that contains the FoxPro program and type **FOXPRO** from the DOS prompt. Once you are in FoxPro, you will need to manually choose your data directory from the Files list box whenever you open files. For example, if your hard disk is drive C and the program is stored in a subdirectory named FOXPRO, you could start the program by entering the following commands from the DOS prompt:

```
CD\FOXPRO
FOXPRO
```

Once the program starts, you will briefly see an introductory screen and a copyright message. In a moment, the FoxPro menus and Command window will appear, as shown in Figure 1-1. The screen contains a menu bar with seven menu options, a Command window, and the working surface (the remainder of the screen). You can enter FoxPro commands or you can select menu options that have the same results as entering FoxPro commands.

FoxPro's Options and Features

The following sections cover some of the major features and enhancements found in FoxPro 2.

System   File   Edit   Database   Record   Program   Window

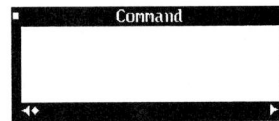

Command

Figure 1-1.   *FoxPro menus and the Command window*

Language Enhancements

FoxPro is a superset of FoxBASE+, with over 200 commands and functions beyond FoxBASE+ and over 140 beyond dBASE IV. Both FoxBASE+ and dBASE III PLUS programs will run without any changes under FoxPro.

Mouse Support

The use of the mouse adds another level of convenience to the FoxPro environment. If you have written a FoxBASE+ program, you can add mouse support to your applications without changing a single line of code.

Rushmore Technology

FoxPro uses an optimizing technique known as Rushmore to access data in indexed files very efficiently. In fact, the technique is so effective that Fox Software is currently seeking a patent for the technology. Rushmore Technology enables some complex database operations to run hundreds (in some cases thousands) of times faster than in prior versions of FoxPro and FoxBASE+.

SQL Language

FoxPro supports the SQL SELECT command, which allows you to develop and execute complex queries against one or more databases. If you are unfamiliar with the format for the SELECT command, you can use the RQBE facility, described in the next section, to generate the SELECT command for you.

Relational Query By Example

The RQBE facility, shown in Figure 1-2, allows you to interactively create and execute complex queries using single or multiple databases. All queries are interpreted as SQL SELECT commands, which can be incorporated in programs or used on an *ad hoc* basis. You can save your queries by selecting Save from the File menu and specifying a filename.

The User Interface

FoxPro's user interface lets you use direct commands, keyboard-driven menu options, or mouse-selected options. In fact, you can switch between these methods without having to change from one mode to another; menu choices and direct commands are available simultaneously. If you begin typing, FoxPro assumes that you prefer direct commands, and the entry you type appears in a Command window. If you instead use an ALT-key combination or the mouse, FoxPro selects the appropriate item. Also, all FoxPro commands used to perform a menu operation are displayed in the Command window. When you start FoxPro, the FoxPro menus and the Command window appear, as shown previously in Figure 1-1.

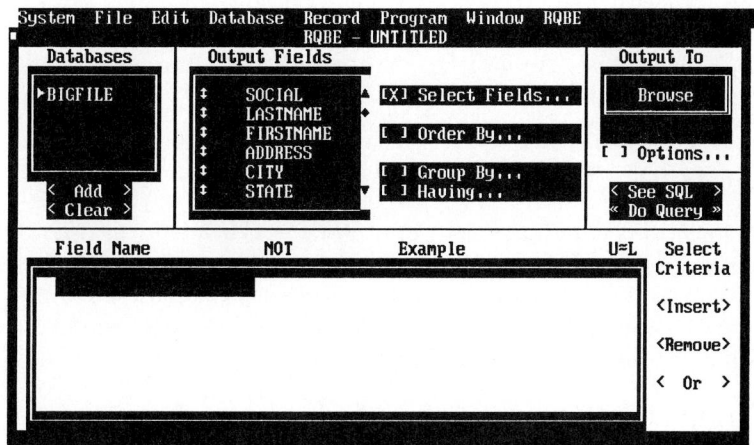

Figure 1-2. The RQBE facility

FoxPro's Menus

The FoxPro menus are an integral part of the user interface. When you start FoxPro you are presented with a main menu, containing the submenus detailed below.

System Menu

The System menu provides access to online help, macros, and desktop accessories (filer, calculator, calendar/diary, special characters, ASCII chart, capture utility, and puzzle). Online help on subjects ranging from basic database concepts to the use of programming commands and functions may be accessed by selecting the Help option or by pressing F1. The Macro option gives you the ability to define a series of keystrokes under a CTRL-key, ALT-key, or function-key combination that will trigger a command or series of commands.

File Menu

The File menu gives you the ability to create, open, and save a wide variety of file types on your hard disk, including databases, database indexes, program files, text files, reports, and labels. This menu also includes options for setting up your printer, printing files, and quitting FoxPro.

Edit Menu

The options on the Edit menu are used for performing editing functions on a variety of data, such as text files, program files, and memo fields within databases. With the FoxPro Editor you can cut and paste blocks of text between files, edit multiple files, and search and replace. Other nice features are the Undo option, which reverses the most recent text-editing action, and the Redo option, which reverses the most recent Undo command.

Database Menu

Options found on the Database menu allow you to perform operations on the entire database. For example, data found in one file can be appended to another. You can also copy data from one file to another and perform sorting operations on a data file, storing the results in another file. The Database menu also includes utilities for producing reports and labels.

Record Menu

The Record menu gives you the option of working with individual records of a database file. The Append and Change options let you add a new record or edit an existing record. Also included are options that give you the ability to move around the database using the Goto, Locate, and Seek options; replace the values of records; delete records; and recall deleted records.

NOTE: The Record menu is not available unless you have already opened a database file.

Program Menu

The Program menu includes options you'll find useful for running and debugging your FoxPro programs. The topic of programming is discussed in detail in Chapters 12 through 19.

NOTE: The contents of the program menu will differ between FoxPro version 2 and FoxPro version 1.x.

Window Menu

The Window menu contains various commands that let you manipulate windows. You can move or resize windows or zoom between a reduced size and the full screen. You can also cycle between multiple open windows.

While FoxPro can display as many windows as you can comfortably work with at the same time, only one window will be active. The window that contains the cursor is the active window. On most monitors, the top line of the active window is also highlighted.

NOTE: Most options in this menu have CTRL-*function-key equivalents, discussed in more detail in Chapter 2, "The FoxPro User Interface."*

The Command Window

The Command window is where FoxPro commands normally appear when you enter them. If you open the Window menu and choose the Command option or press CTRL-F2, the Command window will be the active window. The Command option and its CTRL-F2 equivalent can also be used to display the Command window if it has been hidden.

All commands that you type appear in the Command window. (FoxPro is not case-sensitive; you can type commands either in upper- or lowercase.) By means of the Command window, you can control FoxPro operations when in the "interactive" or Command mode. You can scroll through the Command window by pressing the UP ARROW or DOWN ARROW key. Mouse users can scroll by clicking on the up or down arrows in the scroll bar at the right edge of the window. All the commands you see in the Command window are remembered by FoxPro, so you can repeat a command by moving the cursor up to that command and pressing ENTER.

This capability of remembering commands can be quite useful for correcting mistakes. If you make an error when entering a command, simply move the cursor back up to that line; then use BACKSPACE, DEL, and the cursor keys to correct the error. When done with the correction, press ENTER to repeat the command.

Like all windows, you can resize the Command window. You may find this helpful, as many of the more complex commands that you enter will extend beyond the visible width of the default Command window size. Note that you are not restricted by the size of the Command window as to the length of the command you type; when you enter a long command, it simply scrolls to the right when you reach the right side of the window. Mouse users who make a mistake in entering a long command can go back to the incorrect line and use the left or right arrow in the scroll bar at the bottom edge of the window to scroll horizontally in the window. Keyboard users will have to settle for the use of the cursor keys; however, you can use CTRL-LEFT ARROW and CTRL-RIGHT ARROW to move left or right a word at a time.

If you hide the Command window or close it by mouse-clicking on the close box or choosing Close from the File menu, you can still enter commands. However, you will, in a sense, be "flying blind" because you will not be able to see the commands you enter. The CTRL-F2 key combination can be used to quickly restore the Command window to view.

Dialog Boxes

FoxPro makes extensive use of *dialog boxes*, which are boxes designed to accept various responses. Many menu options and some commands will result in the appearance of a dialog box. Although different dialog boxes contain different options, navigating through the dialog boxes is similar in all cases. If you now open the File menu with ALT-F and choose Open, you will see the File Open dialog box, as shown in Figure 1-3. The use of this dialog box will be detailed in Chapter 2, but you should become familiar with the overall design of a dialog box.

A dialog box contains various objects, including menus, check boxes, list boxes, and pushbuttons. Here is a brief summary of how these objects work.

Menus   The rectangles next to the words "Drive," "Directory," and "Type" in Figure 1-3 are *menus*. You can open menus by mouse-clicking on them or by pressing TAB to move to the item and pressing ENTER. You can move in the reverse direction through the choices with SHIFT-TAB.

Check Boxes   *Check boxes* can be selected by tabbing to them and pressing the SPACEBAR or clicking the mouse between the brackets.

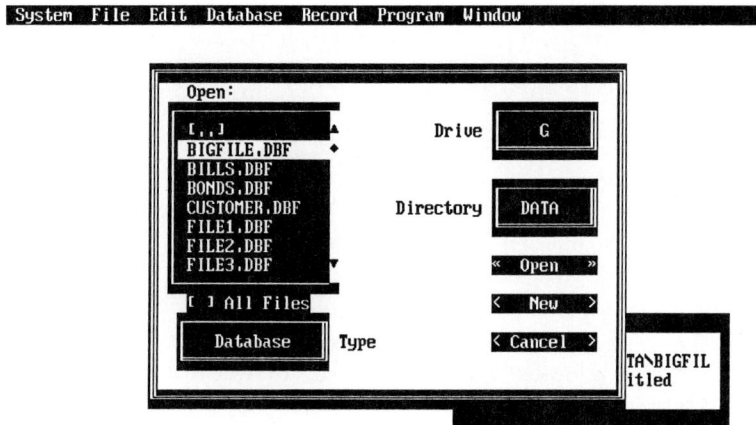

Figure 1-3. *The File Open dialog box*

List Boxes   A *list box*, like that occupying most of the left side of this dialog box, contains a list of items that is sometimes called a *pick list*. In this example, a list of database files appears; if none have been created yet, the list box will be empty. You can press UP ARROW and DOWN ARROW to scroll among items in the list box, and you can select an item by pressing ENTER. Mouse users can click on an item in a list box to select it. If more items are in the list box than are visible at one time, mouse users can use the scroll bar in the list.

Pushbuttons   *Pushbuttons* are used to perform a particular action, such as opening the selected file or canceling the use of the dialog box. In the dialog box in Figure 1-3, the available pushbuttons are labeled Open, New, and Cancel. Keyboard users can select a pushbutton by tabbing to it and pressing ENTER. Mouse users can select a pushbutton by clicking on it.

The Application Development Tools

Using FoxPro's new development tools (available in version 2), it is possible to create an application without writing a single line of code. The following sections provide a brief summary of the new tools available to application developers in FoxPro 2.

Project Manager

The Project Manager gives application developers the ability to keep track of the key components associated with their application. This includes programs, screens, menus, reports, labels, queries, and formats. FoxPro stores all information related to your project in a database with a .PJX extension. FoxPro uses this information to build your application when you select Build from the Project Manager dialog box.

Screen Builder

The Screen Builder gives you the ability to design application screens, including many of the objects found on screens in FoxPro's environment, such as pushbuttons, check boxes, list boxes, and text-edit regions. All information related to your screen is stored in a database file with an .SCX extension and is used to generate FoxPro code with the Screen Builder. The generated code can be inserted into your application or executed directly.

Menu Builder

The Menu Builder gives you the ability to design menus for your applications. All information related to your menu is stored in a database file with an .MNX extension and used to generate FoxPro code using the Menu Builder. The generated code can be inserted into your application or executed directly.

Chapter 2

The FoxPro User Interface

This chapter covers FoxPro's user interface. Areas covered will include keyboard techniques; mouse techniques; the use of menus, windows, and dialog boxes; and how various objects can be positioned on the screen.

Using the Mouse with FoxPro

There are three basic operations you can perform with the mouse. These are pointing, clicking, and selecting (also called dragging). The mouse controls the location of a special cursor, called the *mouse pointer*. In FoxPro, the mouse pointer takes on the shape of a small rectangular block.

Pointing   *Pointing* refers to positioning the mouse pointer directly on an object. Simply roll the mouse in the direction of the object. As you do so, the mouse pointer will move in the same direction on the screen.

Clicking   *Clicking* refers to pressing the left mouse button once. By pointing to different objects and clicking on them, you can select many of the objects while in FoxPro.

Double-Clicking   *Double-clicking* refers to pressing the left mouse button twice in rapid succession. This is commonly the equivalent of selecting an item and pressing ENTER.

Selecting or Dragging   *Dragging* refers to pressing and holding the left mouse button while moving the mouse. This is commonly done to choose menu options within FoxPro.

Mouse Tips

If you have just purchased your mouse for use with FoxPro, here are a few helpful tips to keep in mind.

Software Drivers   Most mice require software drivers to be installed before they will work properly. Refer to the instructions packed with your mouse for details on installing the mouse software.

Mouse Surface   When you are manipulating a mouse, you will find that a surface with a small amount of friction seems to work better than a very smooth desk. Commercial pads are available if your desktop is too smooth to provide good results.

Cleaning   If you turn the mouse upside down, you will probably see instructions which indicate how the ball can be removed for cleaning. A cotton swab dipped in alcohol works well for cleaning the ball. If your mouse uses an optical sensor instead of a large ball underneath, you should refer to the manual that accompanied the mouse for any cleaning instructions. Some mice do not require regular cleaning, so check your manual to be sure.

Using the Keyboard

Any operation accessible with a mouse can also be performed on the keyboard. FoxPro offers keyboard users three methods: hot keys, control keys, and function keys. *Hot keys* are letters within the text of a menu option that are highlighted. Some hot keys are used in combination with another key. For example, holding down the ALT key and the letter S key will pull down the System menu. You can then use the letter H hot key to access the Help option.

Control-key combinations (referred to as shortcuts) let keyboard users choose certain menu options without displaying the pulldown menu first.

Function keys are the keys F1 through F10 or F12 on your keyboard. FoxPro assigns default values to function keys F1 through F10. You can change the value of function keys F2 through F9 (and F11 and F12, if your keyboard has them) using the Macro menu option found on the System menu. Table 2-1 lists some of the major control keys and function keys.

Shortcut Key	Action	Menu Pad
ALT	Activate the menu bar	
ALT-S	Open	System menu
ALT-F	Open	File menu
ALT-E	Open	Edit menu
CTRL-U	Undo	
CTRL-R	Redo	
CTRL-X	Cut	
CTRL-C	Copy	
CTRL-V	Paste	
CTRL-A	Select All	
CTRL-F	Find...	
CTRL-G	Find Again	
CTRL-E	Replace and Find Again	
ALT-D	Open	Database menu
ALT-R	Open	Record menu
CTRL-K	Continue	
ALT-P	Open	Program menu
CTRL-D	Do	
CTRL-M	Resume	
ALT-W	Open	Window menu
CTRL-F7	Move	
CTRL-F8	Size	
CTRL-F9	Zoom Up	
CTRL-F10	Zoom Down	
CTRL-F1	Cycle	
CTRL-F2	Command	

Function Key	Action	Menu Pad
F1	Help	System menu
F2	Resume	
F3	List	
F4	Directory	
F5	Display Structure	
F6	Display Status	
F7	Display Memory	
F8	Display	
F9	Append	
F10	Activate the menu bar	

Table 2-1. *FoxPro 2 Shortcut and Function Keys for Keyboard Users*

The FoxPro Menu System

The FoxPro menu system, shown in Figure 2-1, is composed of four main parts: the menu bar, menu pads, pulldown menus, and menu options. Note also that menu options may also contain hot keys, letters within the menu option that are either underlined or highlighted. You can make a selection by pressing this letter in the menu option.

Menu Bar   The *menu bar*, located at the top of the screen, displays the names of the pulldown menus.

Menu Pad   The *menu pad* resides on the menu bar and is actually the name of the pulldown menu. Certain menu pads may appear dim because they have been disabled. Menu pads may be added or deleted, depending on the current operation being performed.

Pulldown Menus   *Pulldown menus* (also called *popup menus*) are lists of options related to the menu pad. Certain menu options may be disabled (appearing dim), indicating they are not available.

Menu Options   *Menu options* are the options you will select to perform FoxPro operations. Options followed by an ellipsis (...) present dialog boxes when chosen. *Dialog boxes* present you with more choices and allow you to specify

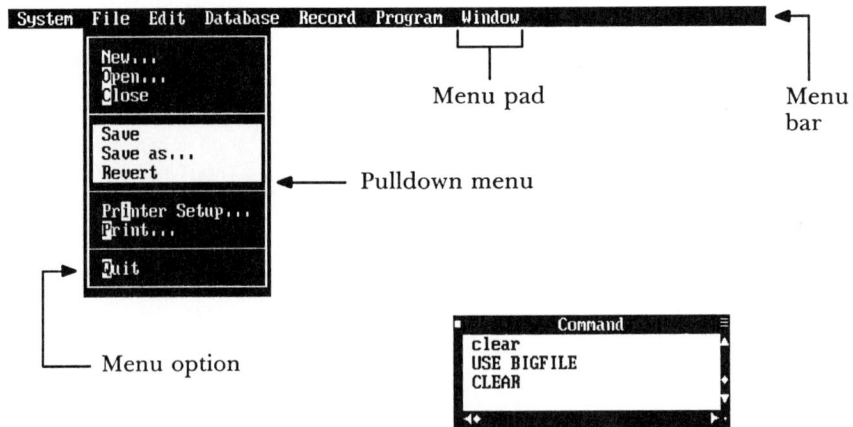

Figure 2-1.   *The FoxPro menu system*

additional information about the menu option selected. Some menu options also contain control-key combinations that can be used as shortcuts to choose menu options without displaying the pulldown menu.

Making Menu Selections

You can access the FoxPro menus using the mouse or the keyboard. While mouse users will find the interface quick and intuitive, keyboard users will enjoy the flexibility of performing the same operation using different methods.

Mouse   To use a mouse to select a menu option, point to the desired menu, click on its name with the left mouse button and hold it down, move the pointer to the desired option, and release the left mouse button.

Keyboard   To select a menu option using the keyboard, press ALT and the first letter of the desired item on the menu pad. Use the UP ARROW or DOWN ARROW key to highlight your choice and press ENTER or the SPACEBAR.

Canceling a Menu Selection

The methods listed below can be used to exit from almost any option in FoxPro without performing the operation. There are certain operations, like copying files, that cannot be canceled once the operation has begun.

Mouse   Move the mouse pointer to the open work area and click the left mouse button to cancel an option.

Keyboard   Press ESC to cancel a menu selection.

Summary of Menu Options

The following is a brief summary of the FoxPro menus and their options. A summary of keyboard techniques, including the shortcuts, was also listed in Table 2-1 earlier in this chapter. As you review FoxPro's menus and options, keep in mind that an option followed by an ellipsis (...) indicates that a dialog box will be displayed when that menu option is chosen.

The System Menu

The System menu, shown in Figure 2-2, contains a useful set of desktop accessories for performing general tasks. You can access FoxPro's online Help facility and the Macro option, which gives you the ability to define a series of keystrokes under a CTRL-key, ALT-key, or function-key combination. Following is a summary of the options in the System menu.

About FoxPro...   This option displays information about your copy of FoxPro, such as the version and serial number.

Help...   When selected, this displays FoxPro's Help window, which contains an extensive list of commands and keywords, listed alphabetically. You can obtain online help on subjects ranging from basic database concepts to the use of programming commands, and you can access functions using the Help option. The Help facility can also be accessed by pressing F1.

Macros...   When you select this option, the Keyboard Macros dialog box is displayed, giving you the capability to record a series of keystrokes and assign them to a single key combination, such as CTRL-key, ALT-key, or certain function keys. The key combinations you define are called *macros*.

```
 System  File  Edit  Database  Record  Program  Window
┌─────────────────────┐
│ About FoxPro...     │
│ Help...        F1   │
│ Macros...           │
│                     │
│ Filer               │
│ Calculator          │
│ Calendar/Diary      │
│ Special Characters  │
│ ASCII Chart         │
│ Capture             │
│ Puzzle              │
└─────────────────────┘

                                   ┌─── Command ───────┐
                                   │ clear             │
                                   │ USE BIGFILE       │
                                   │ CLEAR             │
                                   │                   │
                                   └───────────────────┘
```

Figure 2-2.   *The System menu*

Desktop Accessories

The utilities making up the desktop accessories are the Filer, Calculator, Calendar/Diary, Special Characters, ASCII Chart, Capture, and Puzzle.

Filer   The Filer can be used for DOS file management, such as erasing and renaming files.

Calculator   The Calculator, when selected, provides a desktop calculator. Modeled after a pocket calculator, its operation is fairly obvious. You can use the numeric pad (after pressing NUM LOCK) to enter numbers, or you can use the numbers at the top row of the keyboard. The ENTER key may be used to complete the entry of numbers or math symbols.

Calendar/Diary   The Calendar/Diary, when chosen, displays the current month (based on the computer's clock), along with a Diary area where you can type notes of your choosing. To enter a note, press TAB and begin typing. When you close the Calendar (by clicking on the close box at the upper-right corner with the mouse or by choosing Close from the File menu), the note will be saved automatically. You can repeatedly press UP ARROW or DOWN ARROW to move from month to month, and you can press the T key (for "Today") to return from anywhere to the current date.

Special Characters   The Special Characters option displays a chart of foreign characters and special graphics characters.

ASCII Chart   The ASCII Chart option displays a chart of all ASCII characters in the ASCII character set. These options are of interest to programmers, who may need to refer to the list from time to time.

Capture   The Capture option lets you capture a block of information on the screen and paste it into the Editor.

Puzzle   The Puzzle option displays an entertaining puzzle on the screen that resembles a child's number puzzle. You can either use the cursor keys or click on the numbers with the mouse to move them around. Pressing the S key or clicking on < Shuffle > will cause the numbers to be remixed in a random order; the object of the game is to attempt to align the numbers in order from 1 through 15.

File Menu

The File menu, shown in Figure 2-3, gives you the ability to create new files; open and save a wide variety of file types, including databases, programs, text files, indexes, and labels, on disk; and print files. You can also end your FoxPro session through the File menu.

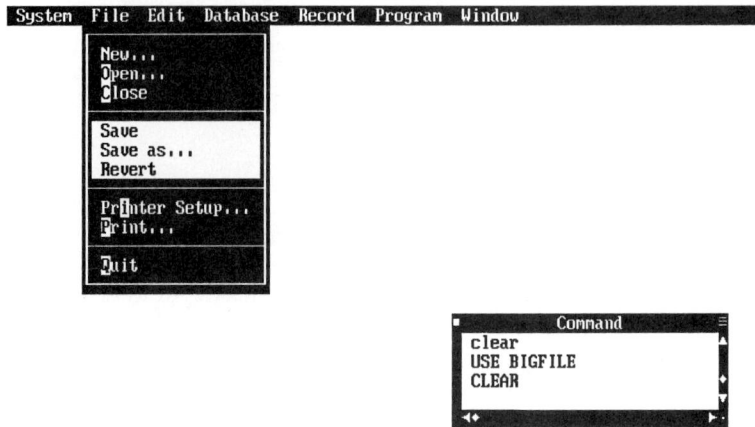

Figure 2-3.   *The File menu*

New...   The New option lets you create a new file. When you choose this option, the New dialog box appears. If you do not have a database open in the currently selected work area (sections of memory allocated to an open database), you can create a database file, program file, or text file. When a database is open in the current work area, you can create any one of the available file types: database, program file, index, report, label, screen, menu, query, or project. FoxPro allows up to ten work areas.

Open...   Selecting Open displays the Open dialog box, allowing you to open existing files. A selection can be made from the scrollable list within the dialog box. The file types are listed in the order of their extensions.

Close   Selecting Close closes the active file. If you have made changes to a file (with the exception of database files), FoxPro will ask if you want to save the changes. Changes to database files are always saved automatically.

Save   Changes made to the active file are stored without closing the document. When multiple edit windows are active, only the contents of the frontmost window are stored to disk.

Save as...   Save as displays the Save as dialog box, enabling you to save a file under a different name or to a different directory or drive.

Revert   Revert returns you to the last saved version of a file. Before doing so, FoxPro asks if you want to discard the changes to the current file.

Printer Setup...   Printer Setup specifies printer settings for printing files, such as left and right margins and the choice of the print device.

Print...   Print displays the Print dialog box, enabling you to print files and set parameters such as line numbering and page ejects.

Quit   Quit ends your FoxPro session and returns you to the system prompt.

Edit Menu

FoxPro uses the same editor for text files, program files, and memo fields within databases. When using a mouse, you'll find navigation is quite easy. However, the keyboard can be used as well. The Edit menu is shown in Figure 2-4.

Undo   Undo reverses your last editing command.

Redo   The action that was previously reversed using the Undo Command can be redone using Redo. Redo is the opposite of Undo.

Cut   Cut removes selected text from the field or file you are currently editing and places it into a section of memory called the *clipboard*, from which it can be quickly recalled.

Copy   Copy places a copy of selected text from a field or file into the clipboard without removing it from the current location.

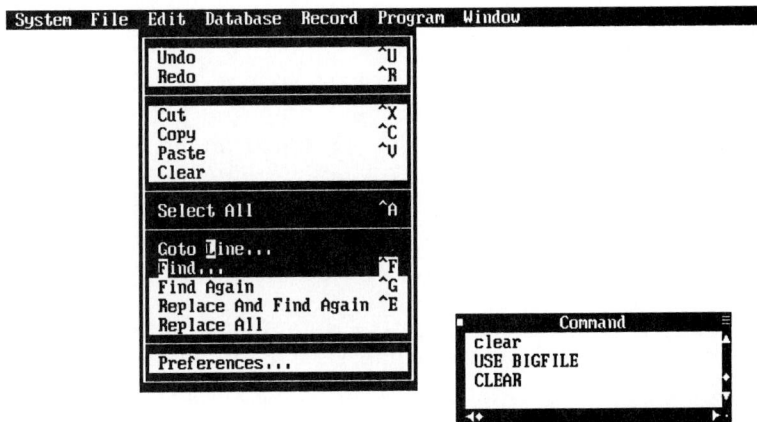

Figure 2-4.   The Edit menu

Paste   Paste places a copy of the contents of the clipboard into the current file or field at the cursor location. If you choose Paste while a piece of text is selected, the contents of the clipboard replace the selected text.

Clear   Clear removes selected text or data without placing it on the clipboard.

Select All   Select All selects all lines of text in the current editing window. Choosing Select All within a Browse window causes all text in the current field to be selected for successive cut-and-paste operations.

Goto Line...   Goto Line moves the cursor to a designated line number.

Find...   Find locates a specified text string.

Find Again   Find Again locates the next occurrence of the string found previously with the Find option. The search continues forward from the cursor position. Find Again is enabled only after you have specified the string initially with the Find option.

Replace And Find Again   Replace And Find Again replaces the string specified in the Look For box with the string in the Replace With text box, then continues to search for the next occurrence of matching text.

Replace All   Replace All replaces every occurrence of the string specified in the Look For text box with the string specified in the Replace With text box without pausing to ask about replacing the text each time it encounters a match. This option is only available after you have used Find.

Preferences...   This option allows you to change the default settings of the Editor in the Preferences dialog box. You apply your preferences to a single file or to all subsequent program files, text files, and memo fields.

Database Menu

The Database menu, shown in Figure 2-5, contains options that allow you to perform operations on the entire database. The menu also includes utilities for producing reports and labels.

Setup...   Setup allows you to set up the current work area. If no database is open in the current work area, an Open dialog box appears, allowing you to select a database to open. Once a database is open, the Setup dialog box appears.

Figure 2-5. *The Database menu*

Browse Browse displays the contents of the database in tabular format within the Browse window. FoxPro's Browse window is unique in that you can split it into two partitions and examine different parts of your database at the same time. In addition, you can edit field data, delete and append records, move and resize fields, and more.

Append From... Append From adds records to the active database from another database.

Copy To... Copy To displays the Copy To dialog box, which allows you to copy the contents of a database. In this dialog box you can set the conditions that records must meet to be copied from the open data file to a new file, as well as setting the type for the new file.

Sort... Sort creates a new sorted database from an existing database.

Total... Total displays the Total dialog box, allowing you to compute numeric-field totals for records in the active database.

Average... Average displays the Average dialog box, allowing you to compute numeric-field averages for records in the active database.

Count... Count returns a count of the records in the active database based on a specified condition.

Sum...   The Sum dialog box is displayed when you choose the Sum option, giving you the ability to add the contents of numeric-field variables in the active database.

Calculate...   Calculate displays the Calculate dialog box, enabling you to perform financial and statistical operations on fields in a database or on expressions involving fields.

Report...   Report is used to print or display reports developed with FoxReport, the FoxPro report writer. Report files that are created with FoxReport can be stored on disk with the default extension of .FRX.

Label...   The Label dialog box is displayed when you choose the Label option, enabling you to produce labels in predefined label formats. Labels created in FoxPro have an .LBX extension.

Pack   Pack causes all records that have been marked for deletion to be permanently removed from the active database. All open index files associated with the database are rebuilt automatically when the database is packed.

Reindex   Reindex rebuilds any open index files associated with the active database.

Record Menu

The Record menu, shown in Figure 2-6, gives you the option of working with individual records of a database file.

NOTE: This menu is not enabled unless a database file is already open.

Append   Append allows you to add records to the end of the active database.

Change   Change allows you to edit existing information in the active database.

Goto...   Goto displays the Goto dialog box, which allows you to move the record pointer to a specified record in the database.

Locate...   The Locate dialog box is displayed when you select this option, enabling you to look for a record in the active database that matches the specified conditions.

Continue   Continue causes FoxPro to look for the next record in the database, matching conditions specified previously using Locate. Continue is disabled until you perform a Locate.

```
 System  File  Edit  Database  Record  Program  Window
                              ┌──────────────┐
                              │ Append       │
                              │ Chang█       │
                              │              │
                              │ ▓oto...      │
                              │ ▓ocate...    │
                              │ Continue  ^K │
                              │ Seek...      │
                              │              │
                              │ Re▓lace...   │
                              │ ▓elete...    │
                              │ ▓ecall...    │
                              └──────────────┘

                         ┌──────────Command──────────┐
                         │■ clear                   ▲ │
                         │  USE BIGFILE               │
                         │  CLEAR                   ♦ │
                         │                          ▼ │
                         └◀♦─────────────────────▶──┘
```

Figure 2-6.   *The Record menu*

Seek...   Seek searches the active database based on an open index file. For Seek to be enabled, the active database must be indexed and the index must be open.

Replace...   Replace displays the Replace dialog box, allowing you to change field information in one record or in a range of records.

Delete...   Delete marks records for deletion. The records are not physically deleted; to physically delete records you must use Pack, on the Database menu.

Recall...   Recall unmarks records previously marked for deletion. Records marked for deletion are not removed until the Pack option, on the Database menu, is used.

Program Menu

The Program menu, shown in Figure 2-7, contains options to aid in the development and running of FoxPro programs.

Do...   Selecting Do displays the Do dialog box, listing FoxPro program files that can be executed. When a program is executing, FoxPro is no longer in interactive mode, and the menu bar disappears. To interrupt program execution press ESC and choose Cancel from the dialog box that appears.

```
 System  File  Edit  Database  Record  Program  Window
                                      Do...      ^D

                                      Cancel
                                      Resume     ^M

                                      Compile...
                                      Generate...
                                      FoxDoc
                                      FoxGraph...


                                          Command
                                   clear
                                   USE BIGFILE
                                   CLEAR
```

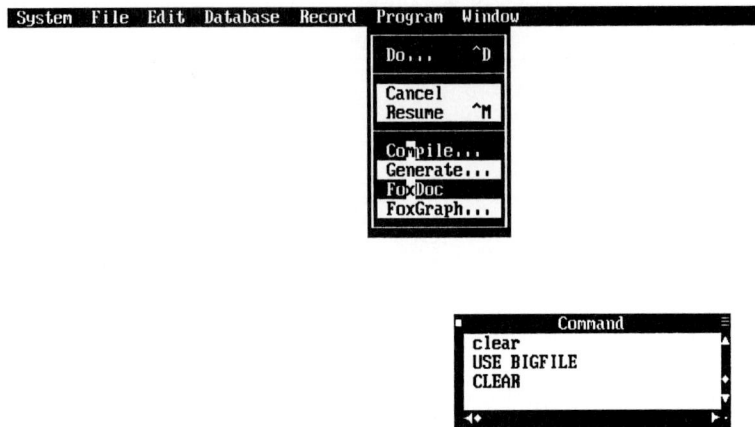

Figure 2-7.   *The Program menu*

Cancel   Cancel ends execution of a FoxPro program file. This option is available only after choosing Suspend (available in the dialog box that is displayed when program execution is interrupted with the ESC key) to pause program execution.

Resume   Resume continues execution of a program at the line in the program file where execution was paused.

Echo   Echo opens the Trace window, displaying the lines from the program file as it executes. This option appears only in FoxPro version 1.*x*, and therefore is not shown in Figure 2-7, which is a screen from FoxPro 2.

Step   Step causes the program file to pause after executing each statement. To continue program execution at the point where it was interrupted, choose Resume. To abort program execution choose Cancel. This option appears only in FoxPro version 1.*x*.

Talk   Talk displays responses to FoxPro commands. Choosing this option causes responses to be displayed in the current output window. This option appears only in FoxPro version 1.*x*.

Compile...   Compile displays the Compile dialog box, allowing you to compile FoxPro program files. Complied program files have an .FXP extension.

Generate... Use this option to generate FoxPro code for various objects created with FoxPro's application development tools.

FoxDoc FoxDoc starts FoxDoc, the automatic application-system documenter for FoxPro programs.

FoxGraph... FoxGraph is an optional utility designed to generate business and scientific graphics for data in a corresponding database file. This option is disabled until you purchase and install FoxGraph on your hard disk.

FoxView FoxView, found in FoxPro version 1.*x*, is a utility for designing screens and generating applications.

Window Menu

The Window menu, shown in Figure 2-8, is used to manipulate FoxPro's windows.

Hide Hide removes the currently selected window from sight, adding the name of the window to the bottom of the Window menu. When you hide a window, it is not closed; the contents will appear the same when the window is restored. You can restore a window by choosing its name from the Window menu.

Clear Clear clears the current window. It is the equivalent of entering **CLEAR** at the command level.

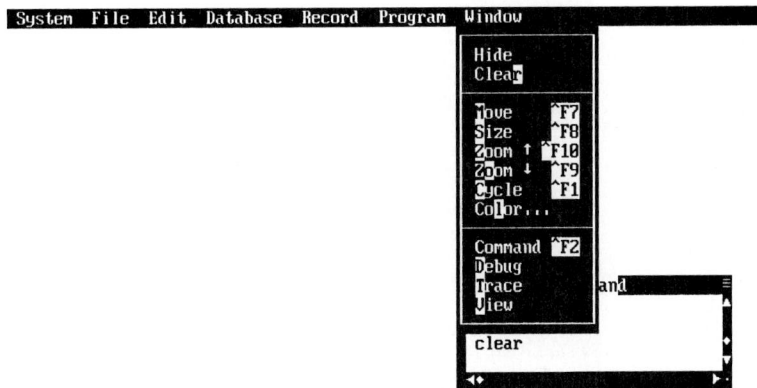

Figure 2-8. The Window menu

Move   Select Move to move a window to a new location. When you choose Move, the border of the current window flashes. Press the arrow keys to move the window. When the window is at the desired location, press ENTER, and the window border stops flashing.

Size   Size allows you to adjust the size of the currently selected window. When you choose Size, the border of the current window flashes. Press the arrow keys to adjust the right and bottom borders of the window. When the window is the desired size, press ENTER, and the window border stops flashing.

Zoom↑ and Zoom↓   There are two Zoom options, Zoom↑ and Zoom↓. Zoom↑ expands the current window to fill the entire screen. Choosing Zoom↓ when the currently selected window is already at full size causes the window to revert to its original size.

Cycle   Cycle causes the current window to move to the bottom of the stack of open windows, making the next window the current window.

Color...   Color gives you the ability, through the use of the Color Picker dialog box, to control the colors in FoxPro's menus, pulldowns, windows, dialog boxes, alerts, and more. The intensity and contrast of monochrome monitors can also be adjusted.

Command   Command displays FoxPro's Command window.

Debug, Trace, and View   The Debug, Trace, and View options are used to display the Debug, Trace, and View windows, respectively. The Debug and Trace windows are programming tools; see Part II for details on programming. The View window is covered in Chapter 10, "The Relational Powers of FoxPro."

Working with Windows

Windows are an integral part of FoxPro's interface. As you perform operations with the user interface, you will notice that you perform the operations in a window. While you can open more than one window at the same time, you can only work in one window at a time. The window in which you are working is the *active window*, which usually has window controls drawn on it. These controls allow mouse users to easily manipulate FoxPro's windows. Figure 2-9 shows several windows, with the active window in the front containing controls.

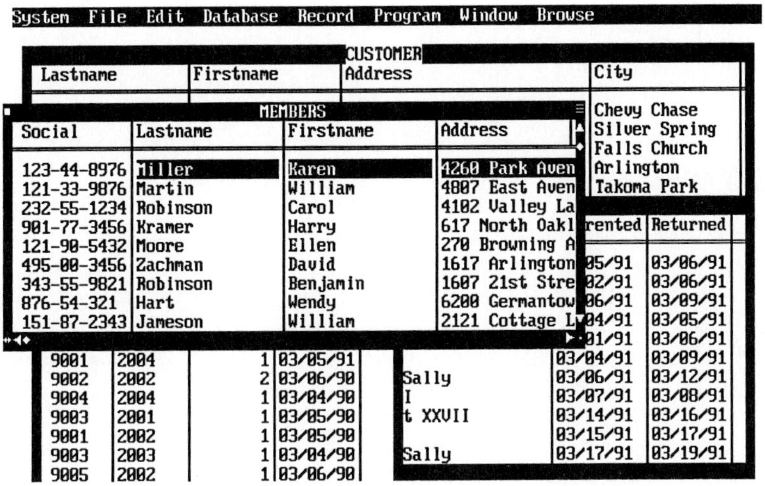

```
System  File  Edit  Database  Record  Program  Window  Browse
                              CUSTOMER
   Lastname        Firstname   Address                    City
                     MEMBERS                            Chevy Chase
   Social     Lastname      Firstname      Address      Silver Spring
                                                        Falls Church
   123-44-8976 Miller       Karen        4260 Park Aven Arlington
   121-33-9876 Martin       William      4807 East Aven Takoma Park
   232-55-1234 Robinson     Carol        4102 Valley La
   901-77-3456 Kramer       Harry        617 North Oakl rented Returned
   121-90-5432 Moore        Ellen        270 Browning A
   495-00-3456 Zachman      David        1617 Arlington 05/91  03/06/91
   343-55-9821 Robinson     Benjamin     1607 21st Stre 02/91  03/06/91
   876-54-321  Hart         Wendy        6200 Germantou 06/91  03/09/91
   151-87-2343 Jameson      William      2121 Cottage L 04/91  03/05/91
                                                        01/91  03/06/91
      9001  2004      1 03/05/91                        03/04/91 03/09/91
      9002  2002      2 03/06/90      Sally             03/06/91 03/12/91
      9004  2004      1 03/04/90      I                 03/07/91 03/08/91
      9003  2001      1 03/05/90      t XXVII           03/14/91 03/16/91
      9001  2002      1 03/05/90                        03/15/91 03/17/91
      9003  2003      1 03/04/90      Sally             03/17/91 03/19/91
      9005  2002      1 03/06/90
```

Figure 2-9. Examples of windows

Opening a Window

There are many ways to open windows in FoxPro. Some windows are implicitly opened by simply performing certain operations, like choosing Browse from the Database menu. The Command window is displayed when you start a FoxPro session. Other windows can be explicitly opened from the menus with the mouse or the keyboard using the following techniques.

Mouse   From the Windows menu pad, position the pointer over the option and click the left mouse button.

Keyboard   Press ALT and the first letter of the desired item on the menu pad. Use the UP ARROW or DOWN ARROW key to highlight your choice, and press ENTER or the SPACEBAR.

Adjusting the Size

The techniques for adjusting the size of a window also differ according to whether you are using a mouse or the keyboard.

Mouse   To resize a window, position the pointer over the size control (shown as a white dot in the lower right-hand corner of the active window in Figure 2-9), then press and hold down the left mouse button while dragging the border. When the window is the desired size, release the left mouse button.

Keyboard   Select the Size option from the Window menu or press CTRL-F8. The window border will flash, indicating that it is ready to be sized. Use the arrow keys to adjust the window to the desired size and press ENTER. The border will then stop flashing.

Moving a Window

Windows can also be moved a variety of ways using the mouse or the keyboard.

Mouse   Position the pointer over the title bar of the window you wish to move and press and hold down the left mouse button, dragging the entire window to the desired position. Release the left mouse button when the window is where you want it.

Keyboard   Select the Move option from the Window menu or press CTRL-F7. The window border will flash, indicating that it is ready to be moved. Use the arrow keys to move the window anywhere or use the PAGEUP (PGUP), PAGEDOWN (PGDN), HOME, or END keys to move the window to the extreme left, right, top, or bottom of the screen. Press ENTER when the window is positioned where you want it. The border will then stop flashing.

Hiding a Window

When you hide a window, the contents remain intact. The name of the window is added to the bottom of the Window menu with an assigned number in the order in which it was hidden.

Mouse   If there are already several windows visible on the screen, bring the window you wish to hide to the front by clicking on it once. Select the Hide option from the Window menu, and the window will disappear. To hide all windows, press SHIFT while opening the Window menu and select Hide All. To restore a window, open the Window menu and select the name of the desired window. The window is displayed with its original contents. Restore all windows by pressing SHIFT and selecting the Show All option.

Keyboard   Select the Hide option from the Window menu and the window will disappear. To hide all visible windows, open the Window menu by pressing SHIFT-ALT-W. Next, select the Hide All option from the Window menu to hide all windows. To restore a window, press ALT-W to open the Window menu and press the number assigned to the window name. The window is displayed with its original contents. To restore all windows, open the Window menu with SHIFT-ALT-W and select the Show All option.

Changing Windows

Often you will need to jump from one window to another when you are working in FoxPro. Again, there is one method for mouse users and another for those using the keyboard.

Mouse   Position the pointer over any visible portion of the window and click the left mouse button.

Keyboard   Select the Cycle option from the Window menu or press CTRL-F1. Continue pressing CTRL-F1 or selecting the Cycle option until the desired window is brought to the front.

The Zoom Option

NOTE: All system windows can be zoomed except the View window.

Mouse   Position the pointer over the Zoom control in the upper-right corner of the window and click the left mouse button. The window will expand to fill the screen. If the window is already fully expanded, it will contract to its previous size.

Keyboard   Select the Zoom ↑ option from the Window menu or press CTRL-F10. The window will expand to fill the screen. To contract the window to its previous size, select the Zoom ↓ option from the Window menu or press CTRL-F9.

Closing a Window

NOTE: The ESC key does not close the Command window.

Mouse   Move the mouse pointer to the close box in the upper-left corner of the window and click the left mouse button. The window will disappear. To close all opened windows, hold down the SHIFT key, open the File menu, and select the Close All option.

Keyboard   Close the active window by pressing ESC or selecting the Close option from the Window menu and pressing ENTER. To close all opened windows, open the File menu with SHIFT-ALT-F and select the Close All option.

Dialog Boxes

The purpose of a dialog box is to specify further information about a selected operation in FoxPro. Many menu options—those that are followed by an ellipsis (...)—and some commands will result in the appearance of a dialog box. Dialog boxes contain various controls that are used to designate, confirm, or cancel actions. Although different dialog boxes contain different options, navigating through the dialog boxes is similar in all cases. You can move forward in the dialog box using TAB and backward using SHIFT-TAB. As you move through the dialog box, the controls will be highlighted. A summary of keyboard techniques for navigating through dialog boxes is listed in Table 2-2.

If you select the File menu and choose Open, you will see the File Open dialog box, shown in Figure 2-10. This dialog box contains various controls, including buttons, menus, a check box, and a pick list. Here is brief explanation of each of these controls.

Check Boxes

Check boxes are designated by square brackets. The line in the File Open dialog box labeled "All Files" is a check box. In some dialog boxes, check boxes are presented as lists of options from which more than one can be selected. When an "X" is present between the brackets, this means the option has been selected. If you are using a mouse, you select a check box by simply moving the cursor between the brackets and clicking the left mouse button. Keyboard users can use TAB or SHIFT-TAB to move to the check box. Press the SPACEBAR and an "X" will appear in the brackets.

List Boxes

A list box contains a list of items that is sometimes called a pick list. In the File Open dialog box, shown in Figure 2-10, a list of database files appears. If no files have been created yet, the list will be empty. You can use the UP ARROW and DOWN

Key	Action
ESC	Leave the dialog box before taking action
CTRL-ENTER	Select the default text button and exit
TAB	Move forward within the dialog box
SHIFT-TAB	Move backward within the dialog box
UP ARROW/DOWN ARROW	Scroll up or down through a list box
HOME/END	Move to the top or bottom of a list box
PGUP/PGDN	Page forward or backward within a list box

Table 2-2.   *Keyboard Techniques for Navigating Within Dialog Boxes*

Figure 2-10. *The File Open dialog box*

ARROW keys to scroll among items in the list box and select an item by pressing ENTER. Mouse users can click on an item in a list box to select it and then press ENTER, or they can double-click on the item. If more items are in the list box than are visible at one time, mouse users can use the scroll bar in the list.

Pushbuttons

Pushbuttons are used to perform a particular action, such as opening the selected file or canceling the use of the dialog box. In the dialog box in Figure 2-10, the available buttons are labeled "Open," "New," and "Cancel." Pushbuttons can be recognized by the angle brackets surrounding text. Keyboard users can select a button by tabbing to it and pressing ENTER. Mouse users can select a button by clicking on it.

Radio Buttons

Radio buttons are not used in Figure 2-10, but can be recognized as options with a pair of parentheses to their left. Radio buttons are used when more than one option is presented, but only one can be selected. Keyboard users can select a button by tabbing to it and pressing ENTER. Mouse users can select a button by clicking on it.

Pulldown Control

When you select this control, you are presented with a menu of options. In Figure 2-10, the pulldown control "Drive" would display a list of available disk drives, enabling you to choose the databases from a different drive. To use a pulldown control, tab to the control and press the SPACEBAR. Make your selection and press ENTER. If you are using a mouse, point to the pulldown control, hold down the left mouse button, move to the choice, and release the left mouse button.

Chapter 3

Creating and Adding Information to Databases

This chapter focuses on techniques for creating database files using FoxPro. Other areas discussed include data entry and editing, deletion of records, and modification of databases. The chapter will also cover techniques for using the Browse mode, editing data while in Browse mode, entering data into memo fields, and appending data from other files.

What Is a Database?

A *database* is a collection of related information organized in a specific way. There are many everyday examples of databases in the business world. A good example would be a personnel file for a small company. The personnel file may contain entries for each employee, along with categories related to the entry, such as the social security number, address, and phone number.

FoxPro organizes information in tables containing rows and columns. The rows are called *records* and are of fixed length while the columns are called *fields*. A field is similar to a category in the personnel file. FoxPro allows you to name a field, such as social security number or phone number, and assign attributes, such as data type and length. FoxPro uses six data types, which are described in the following section.

Data Types

When you create a database using FoxPro, you must decide how the data will be stored on a field-by-field basis. You do this by assigning a data type to each field. FoxPro uses the following six field types.

Character Fields   *Character fields* are used to store characters, which may include letters, numbers, symbols, or spaces. A character field has a maximum size of 254 characters.

Date Fields   Use *date fields* to store dates. The default format for entering dates is *MM/DD/YY*, but you can change this format from the command level with the SET DATE command. FoxPro automatically inserts the slashes when you enter all six digits of a date into a date field. (You must include any leading zeros for the day and month. If you omit leading zeros, you must enter the slashes yourself.)

Numeric Fields   Enter numbers, with or without decimal places, into *numeric fields*. You can enter numbers up to 20 digits in length, and you can enter the minus sign for negative numbers. FoxPro is accurate to 15 decimal places.

Float Fields   *Float fields* are numeric fields, but with a floating decimal point. As with numeric fields, you can enter numbers or the minus sign, and the entries are accurate to 15 decimal places.

Logical Fields   In a *logical field*, enter a single letter representing a true or false value. The letters "T" and "Y" represent true, and "F" and "N" represent false.

Memo Fields   *Memo fields* are used for the storage of large blocks of text. An unlimited amount of text can be stored in a memo field (limited only by available hard disk space).

Creating a New Database

To get a better understanding of the methods used to create a database, you can create the personnel database that will be used throughout this chapter. The personnel database will contain the following field categories:

First Name	State
Middle Name	ZIP Code
Last Name	Department
Social Security Number	Job Title
Street	Date Hired
City	Emergency Contact

To create a database in the FoxPro environment you must first open a file, identifying it as a database file, and then define its record structure. To open the file, enter the CREATE command followed by the name of the new database

CREATE *filename*

and press ENTER. Because the CREATE command is only used to create databases, you don't have to specify the new database name with a .DBF extension. FoxPro will do this for you.

You can also open a file in FoxPro using the File menu. Use the mouse or ALT-F to open the File menu, and select the New option. When you do this, the New dialog box shown in Figure 3-1 appears. Select the Database option and choose the OK button or press ENTER. If you have already created a database, there will be additional options in the dialog box. Unless an existing database has already been opened for use, the Index option is unavailable; hence it is dimmed.

Let's create our personnel database using the CREATE command by entering the following:

```
CREATE PERSONL
```

Pressing ENTER causes the database's Structure dialog box to appear, as shown in Figure 3-2. Note that the Database, Record, Program, and Window menus in the menu bar at the top of the screen are replaced with the Structure menu. When the File menu is used to create a database, the CREATE command is generated followed by UNTITLED as the filename in the Command window. The database will be given an actual name when a structure is defined for it.

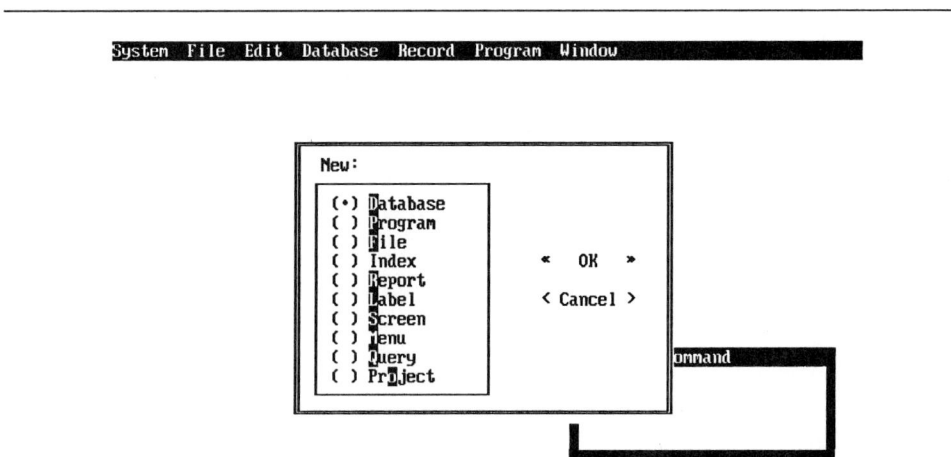

Figure 3-1. The New dialog box

```
 System  File  Edit  Structure
```

```
 Structure: Untitled
          Name        Type    Width Dec
 ┌──────────────────────────────────┐       Field
 │                                  │     ┌──────────┐
 │                                  │     │ <Insert> │
 │                                  │     │ <Delete> │
 │                                  │     └──────────┘
 │                                  │
 │                                  │        « OK »
 │                                  │      <Cancel>
 └──────────────────────────────────┘
  Fields:   0      Length:    1    Available: 3999
```

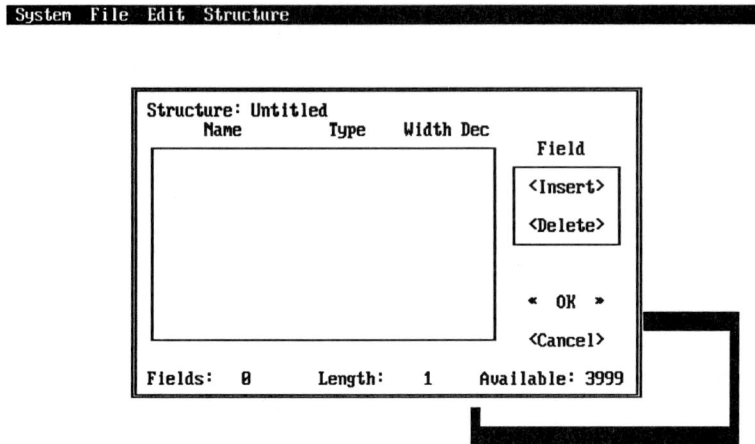

Figure 3-2.   *The Structure dialog box*

The Database Structure Dialog Box

There are four columns in the Structure dialog box for entering field names,
field types, fields widths, and the number of decimal places for numeric fields.
Here is the complete structure for the personnel database.

Field	Field Name	Type	Width	Dec
1	Firstname	Character	15	
2	Middle	Character	15	
3	Lastname	Character	15	
4	Ssn	Character	11	
5	Street	Character	30	
6	City	Character	15	
7	State	Character	2	
8	Zipcode	Character	10	
9	Dependents	Numeric	2	
10	Department	Character	20	
11	Jobtitle	Character	30	
12	Startdate	Date	8	
13	Emergency	Memo	10	

Using this as an example, type the name of the first field into the Name column. When naming a field, use a name that best describes the contents of the field. Field names can consist of letters, numbers, and underscores, but must start with a letter. Spaces are not allowed. Field names can contain up to ten characters. FoxPro will not allow the entry of field names that are too long or that contain illegal characters. When ENTER is pressed, the cursor will automatically move to the Type column.

When the cursor is in the Type column of the Structure dialog box, you can either enter the first letter of the desired field type or press ENTER to display a pulldown menu showing the available field types. When this menu is visible, you can press the first letter of the desired field type followed by ENTER, or you can use the mouse to select the desired field type.

There are some interesting statistics listed at the bottom of the Structure dialog box. In the lower-right corner is the number of available bytes remaining in the current record. This number is calculated by adding the numbers in the field's Width column and subtracting the total from the maximum of 4000 bytes (characters) per record. Memo fields count as ten spaces, but since the actual text of a memo field is stored in a different file, the 4000 character-per-record limit will not affect the amount of text you can store in memo fields. If you are following this example, enter the width of the first field and press ENTER. Use the same procedure to enter the remaining fields in the structure.

Correcting Mistakes

If you need to correct a mistake, use the mouse or the cursor keys to move to the field name or field type you wish to correct and use BACKSPACE and the character keys to make any desired corrections. You can also use the arrow keys to move left, right, up, or down in the form. To insert new characters between existing characters, place the cursor at the desired location and then type the correction. Pressing INS takes you out of *Insert mode* and into *Overwrite mode*. When not in Insert mode, any characters that you type will overwrite existing characters. A more complete list of FoxPro editing keys is shown in Table 3-1. These editing keys also work with the Editor when editing memo fields.

Inserting, Moving, and Deleting Fields

There may be times when you will want to make changes such as inserting, moving, or deleting fields within the database structure. Here are some keyboard techniques for doing so.

Inserting Fields   To insert a new field, use the mouse or the TAB key to position the cursor on the row where you want to insert the new field, and then choose the Insert button (or press CTRL-I). This action causes FoxPro to create a field with the name Newfield, a character type, and a width of ten. You can then modify the field name and type as desired.

Key	Action
LEFT ARROW	Move cursor left one character
RIGHT ARROW	Move cursor right one character
UP ARROW	Move cursor up one line or one field
DOWN ARROW	Move cursor down one line or one field
INS	Toggle insert mode on/off
DEL	Delete character at cursor
BACKSPACE	Delete character to the left of the cursor
ESC	Abort operation
TAB	Move cursor right one field
SHIFT-TAB	Move cursor left one field
CTRL-W	Save changes and exit

Table 3-1.   *Keyboard Shortcuts for the Structure Dialog Box*

Moving Fields   To move a field with the mouse, move the pointer to the double-headed arrow to the left of the field name, hold the left mouse button down, and drag the field to a new position. If you are using the keyboard, use the TAB key to move the cursor to the double-headed arrow and press the SPACEBAR to highlight the entire field line, then use LEFT ARROW or RIGHT ARROW to move the field. When you have finished moving the field, press the SPACEBAR to complete the operation.

Deleting Fields   If you are using a mouse, position the pointer on the desired field, double-click, and choose the Delete button. Keyboard users can tab the cursor to the field targeted for deletion and then choose the OK button or press CTRL-D to delete the field. This action will remove the field and move all of the fields that come after it up one position.

The Structure Menu

There are only two options on the Structure menu: Insert Field and Delete Field. These menu options are equivalent to the Delete and Insert buttons found in the Structure dialog box.

Saving the Database Structure

To complete the database definition process, use the mouse or the TAB key to move to the OK button in the dialog box and press ENTER. If you leave the field name blank and press Enter, the cursor will automatically move to the OK button, and you can press ENTER. An alternative method is to press CTRL-W. If you use the FoxPro menus to create your database structure, the dialog box shown in Figure 3-3 will appear.

Enter the name of your database in the field on the left side of the dialog box, tab over to the Save button in the dialog box, and press ENTER or click on the Save button. The name you use must not exceed eight characters. FoxPro automatically puts an extension of .DBF on the file. If the database contains memo fields, a corresponding file with an .FPT extension will also be created by FoxPro. Once you have done this, you will see this message in a new dialog box that appears.

```
Input data records now? (Y/N)
< Yes >        < No >
```

You can choose Yes or No. Choosing No completes the database-definition process, while choosing Yes completes the process and leaves the file open for adding new records. If you are following this example on your computer, select Yes to enter the first record into the personnel database.

Adding Information to the Database

Now that we've defined the structure for the personnel database, it's time to enter data. In the previous section, when you completed the definition process, FoxPro prompted you with the question, "Input data records now? (Y/N)." If

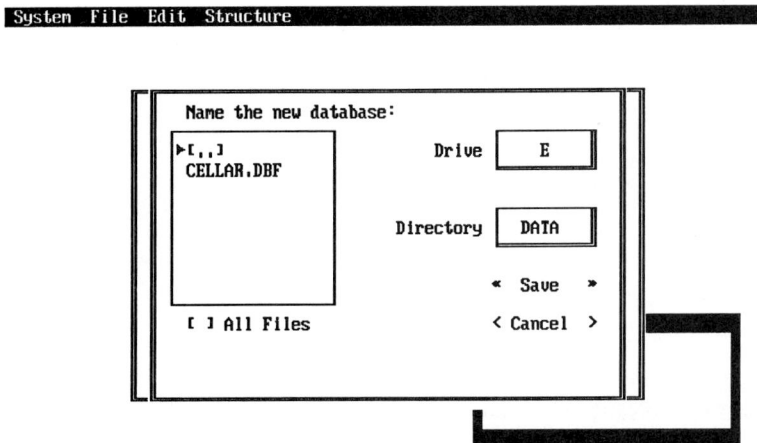

Figure 3-3. A dialog box for naming a database file

Figure 3-4.   *A data entry form*

you responded with a "Y," you should have a simple entry form, shown in Figure 3-4, on your screen right now, with blank spaces beside each corresponding field name. The layout of the screen form should match the structure of your personnel database.

NOTE: *If we had not just set up this database and started adding records immediately, we would have had to open an existing database using commands or the FoxPro menus. To do this from the menus, open the File menu, select the Open option, and choose the filename you want from the dialog box that appears. Once the desired database file has been opened, open the Record menu and choose the Append option from the menu to begin adding data.*

At the command level, you can add data to a database with the APPEND command. If you are following the example, the personnel database is already open. However, if you wished to open it for the first time, you would enter the following commands:

```
USE PERSONL
APPEND
```

If you are following the example on your computer, enter the following information, pressing ENTER after each entry is completed.

Firstname	**Maryann**
Middle	**L**

Lastname	**Saeedi**
Ssn	**525-77-7723**
Street	**1200 Lawrence Avenue**
City	**Rockville**
State	**MD**
Zipcode	**23022-9999**
Dependents	**1**
Department	**Sales, Marketing**
Jobtitle	**Sales Manager, Western Div.**
Startdate	**11/02/88**
Emergency	

To correct mistakes made during the data entry process, use the cursor keys and the BACKSPACE key to correct and retype the entry. Once you have completed the data entry process, the cursor should be at the start of the memo field.

Adding Data to Memo Fields

To add or edit data in a memo field, move the cursor to the memo field and press CTRL-PGDN or double-click on the memo field with the mouse. The entry form will be covered by a window, and you will be editing inside the window with the FoxPro Editor. When using the Editor, it isn't necessary to press ENTER at the end of every line; the Editor will automatically move the cursor to the next line. Here also, you can use cursor keys for navigation and the BACKSPACE and DEL keys for corrections. Make the following entry in the Emergency memo field:

```
In case of emergency call (703) 555-7900 Ext. 7910 or (301) 555-1156
```

When you have finished editing the memo field, choose Close from the File menu or click on the close box at the upper-left corner of the window. You can also use the CTRL-W key combination to close a memo field. Table 3-2 shows some useful keyboard shortcuts for editing memo fields.

Use the PGDN key or the DOWN ARROW key to move to the next blank record in our personnel database. To continue with the example, enter the next seven records, using CTRL-W to complete the memo field entry and the PGDN or DOWN ARROW key to move to the next record upon completion of the current one.

Firstname	**Debra**
Middle	**P**
Lastname	**Jackson**

Key	Action
CTRL-PGDN	Activate the Memo Editor when the cursor is in the memo field
CTRL-HOME	Move cursor to the top-left corner of the window
CTRL-END	Move the cursor to the bottom-right corner of the window
CTRL-LEFT ARROW	Move cursor left one word
CTRL-RIGHT ARROW	Move cursor right one word
CTRL-W	Save changes and exit
CTRL-A	Select all text within the window
CTRL-U	Undo
CTRL-R	Redo
CTRL-X	Cut
CTRL-C	Copy
CTRL-V	Paste
CTRL-F	Find
CTRL-G	Find again
CTRL-E	Replace and find again
UP ARROW	Move cursor up one line
DOWN ARROW	Move cursor down one line
INS	Toggle Insert mode on/off
DEL	Delete character at cursor
BACKSPACE	Delete character to the left of the cursor
ESC	Close memo field after prompting you to save changes
SHIFT-ARROW	Select a block of text

Table 3-2.   *FoxPro Memo Field Editing Keys*

Ssn	**525-57-5723**
Street	**6311 Arwen Court**
City	**Rockville**
State	**MD**
Zipcode	**25022-9999**
Dependents	**0**
Department	**Customer Service**
Jobtitle	**Shift Supervisor**
Startdate	**11/02/90**
Emergency	**In case of emergency, call spouse at (703) 555-8312**
Firstname	**Phillip**
Middle	**L**

Lastname	**Jackson**
Ssn	**525-55-7723**
Street	**124 Lake Drive, Apt. 102**
City	**Rockville**
State	**MD**
Zipcode	**23022-9999**
Dependents	**2**
Department	**Customer Servce**
Jobtitle	**Shift Supervisor**
Startdate	**11/02/88**
Emergency	**In case of emergency, call spouse at (703) 555-8442**

NOTE: *The misspelling of "Service" in the above record is intentional for now.*

Firstname	**Joseph**
Middle	**W**
Lastname	**Ballou**
Ssn	**525-67-6723**
Street	**1200 Sunrise Valley Drive**
City	**Reston**
State	**VA**
Zipcode	**23022-9999**
Dependents	**2**
Department	**Engineering**
Jobtitle	**Project Manager**
Startdate	**10/01/89**
Emergency	**In case of emergency, call spouse at (703) 555-3312**

Firstname	**Mildred**
Middle	**M**
Lastname	**Shelorson**
Ssn	**525-71-7123**
Street	**1250 Morgan Avenue**
City	**Leesburg**
State	**VA**
Zipcode	**23022-9999**

Dependents	2
Department	**Finance**
Jobtitle	**CFO**
Startdate	**11/02/89**
Emergency	**In case of emergency, call Daniel Shelorson at (703) 555-3103**
Firstname	**John**
Middle	**M**
Lastname	**Murray**
Ssn	**765-37-7737**
Street	**1300 Morgan Avenue**
City	**Leesburg**
State	**VA**
Zipcode	**23022-9999**
Dependents	**2**
Department	**Quality Assurance**
Jobtitle	**Team Leader**
Startdate	**11/02/89**
Emergency	**In case of emergency, call Rosslyn Murray at (703) 555-3367**
Firstname	**Joseph**
Middle	**M**
Lastname	**Tahan**
Ssn	**525-81-8123**
Street	**1265 Cedar Lane**
City	**Fairfax**
State	**VA**
Zipcode	**22021-9999**
Dependents	**0**
Department	**Engineering**
Jobtitle	**Project Manager**
Startdate	**11/02/89**
Emergency	**In case of emergency, call (703) 555-3103**
Firstname	**Scott**
Middle	**E**
Lastname	**Lord**

Ssn	**566-72-8723**
Street	**1250 South Lake Drive**
City	**Reston**
State	**VA**
Zipcode	**23022-9999**
Dependents	**1**
Department	**Public Relations**
Jobtitle	**Director**
Startdate	**11/02/90**
Emergency	**In case of emergency, call (703) 555-3103**

Using the Edit Mode

To enter the Edit mode, shown in Figure 3-5, open the Record menu and choose Change. Edit (or Change) mode in FoxPro displays as much of a record as will fit on the screen. You can use the cursor keys to move the cursor to any location in the record. While in Edit mode, you can also use PGUP and PGDN to move forward or backward through the database, one record at a time.

NOTE: You can add records while in the Edit mode by using the Append option from the Record menu.

Let's make a change to the Department field for the employee record for Phillip L. Jackson in our personnel database. Since the file is already in use, enter the CHANGE command or choose the Change option from the Record menu. Next, use PGUP to find the record for Phillip L. Jackson. To make the correction to the Department field, place the cursor on the Department field, use RIGHT ARROW to move the cursor to the front of the misspelled word "Servce," and make the correction. Once you make the change, you can save it by pressing CTRL-W or by moving to another record with either the mouse, the arrow keys, or PGUP and PGDN. When you have finished, save your changes and quit with CTRL-W.

The Browse Mode

Before considering Browse mode, we'll need a database containing more records than the sample one created earlier. Use the following commands to create a new file based on the existing one, and copy records from the existing personnel database into the new file four times.

```
COPY STRUCTURE TO BIGFILE
USE BIGFILE
```

```
 System  File  Edit  Database  Record  Program  Window  Browse
                            PERSONL
  Firstname  Scott
  Middle     E
  Lastname   Lord
  Ssn        566-72-8723
  Street     1250 South Lake Drive
  City       Reston
  State      VA
  Zipcode    23022-9999
  Dependents 1
  Department Public Relations
  Jobtitle   Director
  Startdate  11/02/90
  Emergency  Memo
                                                  ommand
                                                 ml
                                                 om employee.asc
                                         browse
                                         CHANGE
```

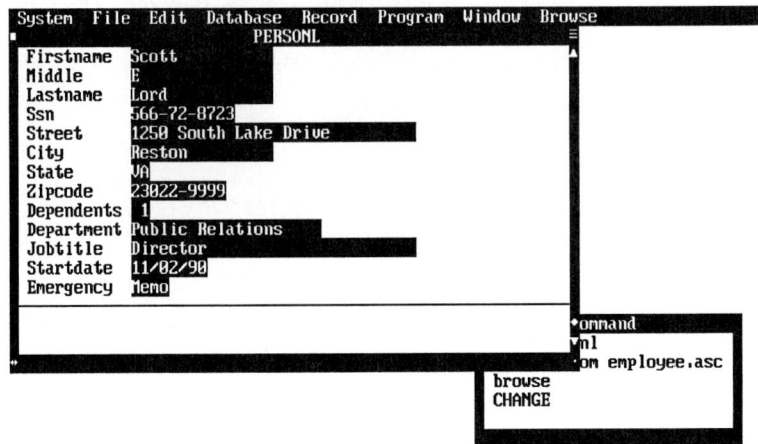

Figure 3-5.   *Edit mode*

```
APPEND FROM PERSONL
APPEND FROM PERSONL
APPEND FROM PERSONL
APPEND FROM PERSONL
```

This will create a file with 32 records, enough to fill a screen while in the Browse mode. Type **BROWSE** to get into Browse mode now.

The *Browse mode* displays records in a tabular format, allowing you to see more than one record at a time. At any time, you can enter the Browse mode by typing **BROWSE** at the command level, or by opening the Database menu and choosing Browse. (Note that unless you are already appending to or editing a file, the Browse menu does not appear as a menu option.) Figure 3-6 shows, in the Browse mode, the large personnel database you just created.

When in Browse mode, you can use PGUP and PGDN to move up and down a screen at a time. UP ARROW and DOWN ARROW move the cursor between records. Use TAB and SHIFT-TAB to move the cursor between fields. Mouse users can click on any desired field or record to place the cursor at the desired location.

Mouse users can also use the scroll bars to navigate within the window by clicking on the left, right, up, or down arrows in the window's scroll bars. You can click on the up and down arrows (triangular in shape) at the right edge of the screen to scroll through the the database vertically. You can also drag the diamond-shaped indicator anywhere in the scroll box; this provides a vertical movement relative to the location of the indicator. For example, if you drag the indicator halfway down the scroll bar and release it, you will be positioned roughly halfway down the personnel database.

```
 System  File  Edit  Database  Record  Program  Window  Browse
                           BIGFILE
 Firstname      │Middle    │Lastname    │Ssn        │Street          │
 Maryann        │L         │Saeedi      │525-77-7723│1200 Lawrence Ave│
 Debra          │P         │Jackson     │525-57-5723│6311 Arwen Court │
 Phillip        │L         │Jackson     │525-55-7723│124 Lake Drive, A│
 Joseph         │W         │Ballou      │525-67-6723│1200 Sunrise Vall│
 Mildred        │M         │Shelorson   │525-71-7123│1250 Morgan Avenu│
 John           │M         │Murray      │765-37-7737│1300 Morgan Avenu│
 Joseph         │M         │Tahan       │525-81-8123│1265 Cedar Lane  │
 Scott          │E         │Lord        │566-72-8723│1250 South Lake D│
 Maryann        │L         │Saeedi      │525-77-7723│1200 Lawrence Ave│
 Debra          │P         │Jackson     │525-57-5723│6311 Arwen Court │
 Phillip        │L         │Jackson     │525-55-7723│124 Lake Drive, A│
 Joseph         │W         │Ballou      │525-67-6723│1200 Sunrise Vall│
 Mildred        │M         │Shelorson   │525-71-7123│1250 Morgan Avenu│
 John           │M         │Murray      │765-37-7737│1300 Morgan Avenu│
 Joseph         │M         │Tahan       │525-81-8123│1265 Cedar Lane  │
 Scott          │E         │Lord        │566-72-8723│1250 South Lake D│
 Maryann        │L         │Saeedi      │525-77-7723│1200 Lawrence Ave│
 Debra          │P         │Jackson     │525-57-5723│6311 Arwen Court │
 Phillip        │L         │Jackson     │525-55-7723│124 Lake Drive, A│
 Joseph         │W         │Ballou      │525-67-6723│1200 Sunrise Vall│
```

Figure 3-6. *The Browse mode displaying a large personnel file*

The scroll bar at the bottom edge works horizontally in a similar manner. Clicking on the triangular-shaped left and right arrows will move the database columns horizontally, and dragging the diamond-shaped indicator within the scroll box provides a horizontal movement relative to the location of the indicator. Other mouse features work the same in Browse as they do in other windows: You can resize the window by dragging on the size indicator (lower-right corner), and you can zoom the window to full-screen size and back by repeated clicking on the zoom indicator in the upper-right corner.

The Browse Menu

While you are in Browse mode, an additional menu, Browse, shown in Figure 3-7, appears on the menu bar at the top of the screen.

The Browse menu options are detailed here.

Change   Selecting Change displays a database in the Browse window, but in full-screen (Edit) format, like the display that appears when using the CHANGE or EDIT command.

Grid Off   Selecting Grid Off hides vertical lines that normally appear between columns. Once you select it, the name of the command changes to Grid On, and you can reselect it to display the lines.

```
 System  File  Edit  Database  Record  Program  Window  Browse
                           BIGFILE
 Firstname      Middle       Lastname     Ssn      Change           I
                                                   Grid Off
 Maryann        L            Saeedi       525-7    Unlink Partitions  E
 Debra          P            Jackson      525-5    Change Partition ^H
 Phillip        L            Jackson      525-5                       A
 Joseph         W            Ballou       525-6    Size Field        1
 Mildred        M            Shelorson    525-7    Move Field        u
 John           M            Murray       765-3    Resize Partitions u
 Joseph         M            Tahan        525-8
 Scott          E            Lord         566-7    Goto...           D
 Maryann        L            Saeedi       525-7    Seek...           e
 Debra          P            Jackson      525-5    Toggle Delete    ^T
 Phillip        L            Jackson      525-5    Append Record    ^N A
 Joseph         W            Ballou       525-6                      1
 Mildred        M            Shelorson    525-71-7123  1250 Morgan Avenu
 John           M            Murray       765-37-7737  1300 Morgan Avenu
 Joseph         M            Tahan        525-81-8123  1265 Cedar Lane
 Scott          E            Lord         566-72-8723  1250 South Lake D
 Maryann        L            Saeedi       525-77-7723  1200 Laurence Ave
 Debra          P            Jackson      525-57-5723  6311 Arwen Court
 Phillip        L            Jackson      525-55-7723  124 Lake Drive, A
 Joseph         W            Ballou       525-67-6723  1200 Sunrise Vall
```

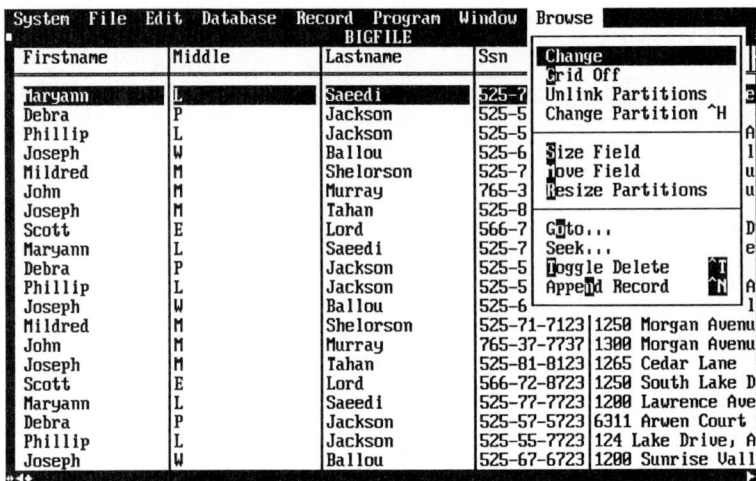

Figure 3-7.   *The Browse menu*

Unlink Partitions   Selecting Unlink Partitions unlinks the two portions of a window that has been split in two (see Resize Partitions), allowing independent movement in each. This choice is unavailable unless the partition has already been split.

Change Partition   Selecting Change Partition deactivates an active partition and activates an inactive partition of a window that has been split into two partitions. This choice is unavailable unless the partition has already been split.

Size Field   Selecting Size Field resizes the field containing the cursor. Tab to the desired field, select the option, and use the arrow keys to change the size. Then press any key except the arrow keys to complete the resizing.

Move Field   Selecting Move Field moves a field to a new location. Tab to the desired field, select the Move Field option, and use LEFT ARROW or RIGHT ARROW to relocate the field. When you have finished, press any key except LEFT ARROW or RIGHT ARROW.

Resize Partitions   Selecting Resize Partitions lets you split a window into two parts. If the window is already split, this lets you change the size of the partitions. Also use this option to change a split window back to a single window. Choose the option, then use LEFT ARROW or RIGHT ARROW to open, close, or change the size of the partitions. When you have finished, press any key except LEFT ARROW or RIGHT ARROW.

Goto...   Selecting Goto displays a dialog box that lets you move to a different record in the database. From the dialog box, you can choose Top or Bottom (to go to the top or the bottom of the database), or you can choose Record, then enter a record number in the Recno box to go to a specific record by number. You can also choose Skip to skip a given number of records.

Seek...   Selecting Seek displays a dialog box in which you can enter a search term. The database index will then be searched for the desired expression.

NOTE: The Seek option is only available if a file is indexed.

The use of the Seek option is detailed further in Chapter 5, "Performing Queries."

Toggle Delete   Selecting Toggle Delete lets you mark a record for deletion while in Browse mode. Place the cursor at the desired record and choose Toggle Delete to mark the record for deletion. You can use CTRL-T to select this option.

Append Record   Selecting Append Record adds a blank record to the end of the database. You can select this option with CTRL-N.

Splitting the Browse Window and Using Edit

You can use the Change option from the Browse menu to display a record in the Edit mode while in a Browse window. This can be particularly useful for seeing records in both tabular form and a full-record form at the same time, which you can do once you split a window. You can first split the Browse window in two by choosing Resize Partitions from the Browse menu and using the arrow keys to adjust the size of the partitions. When you finish resizing the partitions, press ENTER. Then choose Change from the Browse menu. The screen display in the active partition will change to the Edit mode. A sample Browse window split into two parts is shown in Figure 3-8.

With this type of display, you can easily find records in the left partition and see all the fields for that record in the right partition. Note that once you are using the Edit style of display in Browse, the first command of the Browse menu changes to Browse when the Edit partition is the active partition. You can then use the menu option to change the display back to a Browse display.

Adjusting Field Sizes and Positions

While in Browse mode, you can modify the widths of columns or rearrange field positions.

NOTE: Changing column widths and field positions in the Browse display does not affect the actual location and field widths in the database file.

```
 System  File  Edit  Database  Record  Program  Window  Browse
                            BIGFILE
 Firstname       Middle        Lastname        Firstname  Maryann
                                               Middle     L
 Maryann         L             Saeedi          Lastname   Saeedi
 Debra           P             Jackson         Ssn        525-77-7723
 Phillip         L             Jackson         Street     1200 Laurence Avenue
 Joseph          W             Ballou          City       Rockville
 Mildred         M             Shelorson       State      MD
 John            M             Murray          Zipcode    23022-9999
 Joseph          M             Tahan           Dependents 1
 Scott           E             Lord            Department Sales, Marketing
 Maryann         L             Saeedi          Jobtitle   Sales Manager, Weste
 Debra           P             Jackson         Startdate  11/02/88
 Phillip         L             Jackson         Emergency  Memo
 Joseph          W             Ballou
 Mildred         M             Shelorson       Firstname  Debra
 John            M             Murray          Middle     P
 Joseph          M             Tahan           Lastname   Jackson
 Scott           E             Lord            Ssn        525-57-5723
 Maryann         L             Saeedi          Street     6311 Arwen Court
 Debra           P             Jackson         City       Rockville
 Phillip         L             Jackson         State      MD
 Joseph          W             Ballou          Zipcode    25022-9999
```

Figure 3-8.   *A Browse window split into two parts*

To change column widths, you use the Size Field option of the Browse menu. To
resize a field, place the cursor in the field and choose Size Field from the Browse
menu. Use LEFT ARROW or RIGHT ARROW to resize the field as desired, then press ENTER
to complete the resizing.

To change locations of fields, use the Move Field option from the Browse
menu. To move a field, tab over to the desired field and choose Move Field from
the Browse menu. Relocate the field using LEFT ARROW or RIGHT ARROW and press ENTER
to place the field in the desired location.

Unlinked Partitions

Whenever the Browse window is split between a Browse display and an Edit
display, both partitions display corresponding movement as the cursor is moved
between records. This happens because partitions are *linked* (tied together) by
default with respect to records. If you prefer independent control over the
partitions, choose Unlink Partitions from the Browse menu. After choosing
Unlink Partitions, you can switch between partitions with CTRL-H or the mouse
and independently move around in each partition. Mouse users will note that
when partitions are unlinked, a second vertical scroll bar appears. The center
scroll bar now controls movement in the left partition, while the right scroll bar

controls movement in the right partition. Also, the Browse menu option changes to Link Partitions. Choose Link Partitions to restore the link between the partitions.

Displaying Multiple Databases in Browse Mode

FoxPro also gives you the ability to display multiple databases in different windows simultaneously. For example, to display the original personnel database beside the larger database that is in use at the moment, enter the following commands:

```
SELECT 1
USE BIGFILE
BROWSE
```

and then press CTRL-F2 to switch from the Browse window back to the Command window.

You could then use commands like

```
SELECT 2
USE PERSONL
EDIT
```

to display the original database file in an Edit window. Before proceeding, enter **CLEAR ALL** to close any databases currently open.

Using the LIST and DISPLAY Commands

You can view selected portions of your database with the LIST or DISPLAY command. When you type **LIST** by itself and press ENTER, you are shown the entire contents of the database for each field. You can limit the display to certain fields by including the field name after LIST. If you specify more than one field, separate them by a comma. For example, if you wanted a list of all employees with their social security numbers from the personnel database, you could enter the following:

```
LIST Lastname, Ssn
```

FoxPro shows only the last names and the social security numbers contained in the database.

```
Record# Lastname      Ssn
      1 Saeedi        525-77-7723
      2 Jackson       525-57-5723
      3 Jackson       525-55-7723
      4 Ballou        525-67-6723
      5 Shelorson     525-71-7123
      6 Murray        765-37-7737
      7 Tahan         525-81-8123
      8 Lord          566-72-8723
```

If you had entered **LIST** without any field names, you would have seen a list of all the fields.

The DISPLAY command is different from the LIST command because, by default, it allows you to view the current record only. To see more than one record with DISPLAY, you must add an optional clause, such as ALL or NEXT 5. For example, when you enter the following:

```
GO 4
DISPLAY
```

the fourth record in the personnel database will be displayed. (The GO command, followed by a record number, tells FoxPro to move to that record.)

If you try the following commands

```
GO 5
DISPLAY NEXT 3
```

you will see three records, beginning with record 5.

You can see an entire database by entering

```
DISPLAY ALL
```

When you use DISPLAY ALL instead of LIST, the screen will pause every 20 lines, and you can press any key to resume the scrolling. The LIST command will cause the contents to scroll up the screen without stopping.

You can also use the DISPLAY command to search for specific information if you follow it with a specific condition. As an example, you could display only the last name and social security number for employees with more than one dependent by entering

```
DISPLAY FIELDS Lastname, Ssn FOR Dependents > 1
```

You can find more detailed coverage on performing selective queries in Chapter 5, "Performing Queries."

Searching Within a Field

The DISPLAY command can also be used to search for information that is contained within a field. This is useful when you need to find a record, but only know a portion of the information contained in the field. The format for this command is

DISPLAY FOR *"search text"* $ *fieldname*

where *"search text"* are the actual characters that you want to look for, and *fieldname* is the name of the specific field that you wish to search. To find the employee in our example with a last name of Jackson, enter the following command:

```
DISPLAY FOR "Jackson" $ Lastname
```

The employee records for Phillip L. Jackson and Debra P. Jackson will be found. To search for data within the text of the memo field, enter the following:

```
DISPLAY FOR "spouse" $ Emergency
```

This will display all records containing the word "spouse" anywhere in the Emergency field.

Deleting and Recalling Records from the Database

You can delete records with the Delete and Pack menu options or with their equivalent DELETE and PACK commands. The DELETE command, or the Delete option of the Record menu, can be used to delete the record. Later, the PACK command, or the Pack option of the Database menu, can be used to permanently remove all records that have been identified for deletion with the DELETE command or Delete menu option.

Deleting Records

The Delete option of the Record menu, or its command equivalent, DELETE, marks a record for deletion but does not actually remove the record from the database. You can use the DELETE command or the Delete menu option to delete as many records as desired. Later, you use the PACK command or the Pack menu option to permanently remove the records. An advantage to this two-step method of deleting records is that you can change your mind any time before performing the pack. You can "undelete" deleted records that have not yet been removed with a PACK command by using the RECALL command.

To illustrate, list the Lastname and Ssn fields in the personnel database by entering

```
LIST Lastname, Ssn
```

which will result in the following display:

```
Record# Lastname       Ssn
      1 Saeedi         525-77-7723
      2 Jackson        525-57-5723
      3 Jackson        525-55-7723
      4 Ballou         525-67-6723
      5 Shelorson      525-71-7123
      6 Murray         765-37-7737
      7 Tahan          525-81-8123
      8 Lord           566-72-8723
```

Now let's mark a single record for deletion. First, you should be at the record in the database that you want to delete. Type **GO 1** to get to the first record.

Open the Record menu with ALT-R and choose the Delete option. In the dialog box that appears, the Scope option lets you choose a group of records for deletion. You can choose All records; Next n, where n is a number (such as 5, for the next five records); Record n, where n is the record number of the record to be deleted; or Rest, which deletes all records from the current record to the end of the file. To delete the first record, tab over to the Delete button, then press ENTER to delete the record. List the personnel database again, by the Lastname and Ssn fields.

```
Record# Lastname       Ssn
      1*Saeedi         525-77-7723
      2 Jackson        525-57-5723
      3 Jackson        525-55-7723
      4 Ballou         525-67-6723
      5 Shelorson      525-71-7123
      6 Murray         765-37-7737
      7 Tahan          525-81-8123
      8 Lord           566-72-8723
```

FoxPro identifies all records marked for deletion with an asterisk. The deleted records remain in the database until you use the PACK command or the Pack option of the Database menu. Keep in mind that because a pack operation involves copying all undeleted records into a temporary file, it can be time-consuming with large databases.

You can also delete records with the DELETE command. As an example, try the following commands now:

```
DELETE RECORD 5
LIST Lastname, Ssn
```

You can see by the results of the LIST command that record 5 is now also marked for deletion.

Recalling a Deleted Record

If you delete a record by mistake, you can use the RECALL command to undo the damage. The format for the RECALL command is

RECALL RECORD n

where n is the record number you wish to recall. The confirmation "1 record recalled" appears.

Let's recall the first record (Saeedi) that was marked for deletion earlier by entering

```
RECALL RECORD 1
```

Use the LIST command again to verify that the record has been unmarked for deletion.

```
Record# Lastname      Ssn
      1 Saeedi        525-77-7723
      2 Jackson       525-57-5723
      3 Jackson       525-55-7723
      4 Ballou        525-67-6723
      5*Shelorson     525-71-7123
      6 Murray        765-37-7737
      7 Tahan         525-81-8123
      8 Lord          566-72-8723
```

Let's try a shortcut here: Press UP ARROW and move the cursor within the Command window to the commands you entered earlier. You can place the cursor on the desired command, then press ENTER to repeat the command. Try this with the previous command. Once you do so, the database will be listed again, showing only the Lastname and Ssn fields.

NOTE: If you wish to recall all records marked for deletion, use the RECALL ALL command.

Using the SET DELETED Command

Since records marked for deletion are still in the database, various operations, such as SUM and COUNT, will still use the record in calculations as if it had never been deleted. Also, the deleted record may appear in your reports, which is often undesirable. To avoid displaying and using records that are marked for deletion, use the SET DELETED command. The SET DELETED command "hides" records marked for deletion, making them unavailable for most database operations. As an example, enter the following:

```
SET DELETED ON
LIST Lastname, Ssn
```

When the LIST command is used, records marked for deletion do not appear. To make the deleted records visible again, enter

```
SET DELETED OFF
LIST Lastname, Ssn
```

When you try the LIST command again, the record marked for deletion will again be visible in the database.

Deleting and Recalling Multiple Records

You can mark more than one record for deletion by specifying the number of records to be deleted. For example, enter the command

```
GO TOP
DELETE NEXT 2
LIST Lastname,Ssn
```

In this example, GO TOP moves the pointer to the first record; then DELETE NEXT 2 marks records 1 and 2 for deletion.

The results are shown here.

```
Record# Lastname     Ssn
      1*Saeedi       525-77-7723
      2*Jackson      525-57-5723
      3 Jackson      525-55-7723
      4 Ballou       525-67-6723
      5*Shelorson    525-71-7123
      6 Murray       765-37-7737
      7 Tahan        525-81-8123
      8 Lord         566-72-8723
```

The RECALL command can be used in the same manner. To do so, enter

```
GO TOP
RECALL NEXT 2
LIST Lastname,Ssn
```

and records 1 and 2 will be unmarked. For now, enter **RECALL RECORD 5** to recall the record deleted earlier.

Modifying the Structure of a Database

After a database has been in use, you may wish to make changes to its structure, perhaps deleting, adding, or enlarging a field. When you change the structure of a database, FoxPro creates a new empty database according to your instructions, then copies the old database into the new database. From the command level, this is done with the MODIFY STRUCTURE command. From the menus, you choose the Setup option of the Database menu. When the dialog box appears, you select Structure - Modify. The methods for making changes have already been discussed under "Inserting, Moving, and Deleting Fields." However, the changes made will affect how your data will be saved.

When a database is modified, data is only returned from fields of the temporary file to fields in the modified database structure if FoxPro can make sense of the data transfer. If the field names and field types match between the old and new databases, data is transferred. If you change the type of a field, FoxPro may or may not be able to transfer the data, depending on the types. As an example, if you change a character field to a numeric field, any valid numeric entries that were stored in the character field will be transferred to the numeric field. However, if you were to change a logical field to a numeric field, all data in the field would be lost, as there is nothing in common between a logical and a numeric field.

If you change the name of a field and change its location in the database structure at the same time (by adding or deleting fields), FoxPro will not transfer the data in that particular field, since it doesn't know where to find the data. FoxPro uses either the field name or the position of the field in the database structure to transfer existing data. If both are changed, the existing data is lost.

If you need to change both the name of a field and its existing location in a database structure, perform the task in two steps. Change the field name and exit the MODIFY STRUCTURE process. Then, repeat the MODIFY STRUCTURE command and change the field location in the file structure.

Saving the Changes

Once you have completed your desired changes to the database structure, tab to or click on the OK button in the dialog box. You will see the following confirmation prompt:

```
Copy old records to new structure?
<< OK >>              << Cancel >>
```

This indicates that FoxPro is ready to copy the data from the old file into the modified database. Select OK from the prompt, and after a short delay (during which FoxPro automatically rebuilds the database), the Structure dialog box will disappear. You can tab to the OK button in the remaining dialog box to exit the operation.

Chapter 4 will discuss techniques for arranging and viewing your data.

Remember to always use the QUIT command when exiting FoxPro. FoxPro speeds its operation by keeping large amounts of data in memory. If you exit FoxPro without quitting (by just turning off the computer, for example), data in memory will be lost.

Chapter *4*

Sorting and Indexing a Database

When you first enter information into a database, typically the concern is for accuracy. A client's company name, address, and purchase-order number must be correct for billing purposes. On the other hand, when you need to view information, perhaps in the form of a report, you usually desire accurate information arranged in a specific order: perhaps numerically by invoice number for a client database, or alphabetically by name for an employee database. Databases generally contain records that have been entered randomly, with each new record added to the end. You can use sorting and indexing to arrange your database in a way that best fits your need at the time. The first portion of this chapter covers how to sort and discusses some disadvantages that accompany the sorting process. The second portion of the chapter covers indexing, which offers some advantages over sorting while accomplishing the same overall result.

In this chapter, most commands will be executed at the command level, rather than through the menus. You can perform sorting and indexing tasks with either method, but many of the more complex sorting and indexing operations can be performed more quickly with commands. Once you become familiar with the syntax of the commands, you can use them within your FoxPro programs. Since it is good to have an idea of both methods, however, the chapter will include coverage of both methods; use whichever method you are comfortable with for your own use.

Sorting

When you perform a sort using FoxPro, you do not overwrite the database that you are currently working with. Instead, a new database is created containing the records in the desired order. If you were to sort a database of names in alphabetical order, the new database would contain all the records that were in the old database, but they would be arranged in alphabetical order, as shown in Figure 4-1.

From the command level, the format for the SORT command is

SORT ON *fieldname* [/A/C/D] TO *newfile*

To sort a database from the FoxPro menus, open the Database menu, choose the Sort option, and then fill in the desired fields for the sort order in the Sort dialog box. A new file by the name of *newfile* is created, sorted by the field specified. To sort in ascending order, choose the Ascending button under field options or specify /A at the command level. This order places character fields in alphabetical order, numeric fields in numerical order, and date fields in chronological order, earliest to latest. If you choose the Descending button under Field Options or specify /D at the command level, character fields are sorted in descending order ("Z" to "A"), numeric fields from highest to lowest,

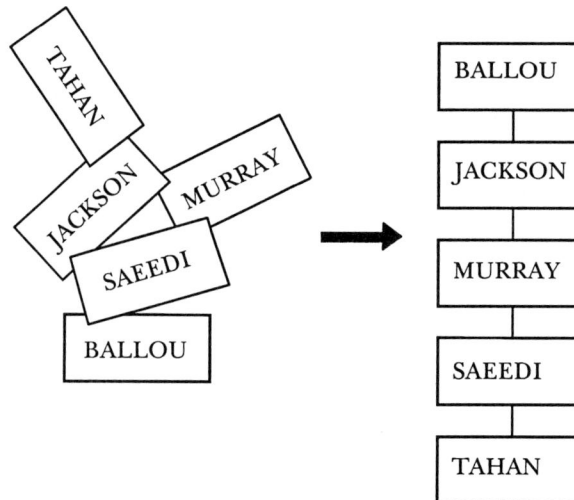

Figure 4-1.   *The process of sorting*

and date fields in reverse chronological order, latest to earliest. You cannot sort on memo fields. If you do not specify ascending or descending order, FoxPro assumes that ascending order is your preference.

Sorts are also normally in *ASCII order*, with uppercase letters treated differently than lowercase letters. ASCII order ascending specifies "A" through "Z," then "a" through "z." ASCII order descending specifies "z" through "a," then "Z" through "A." If you want uppercase and lowercase letters treated equally in the sorting order, include the /C option.

Selecting a Sort Field

A sort can be performed using the SORT command or through the FoxPro menus. From the menus, open the Database menu with ALT-D and choose Sort. Figure 4-2 shows the contents of the Sort Order dialog box, which appears next. In the upper-left part of the dialog box is the Database Fields list box, which lets you choose desired fields that the sort will be based on. The center portion of the dialog box contains a Field Options box, which lets you select ascending or descending order and whether FoxPro should ignore case (sorting uppercase and lowercase letters together) or sort uppercase before lowercase. When you select fields from the Database Fields list box, they are added to the Sort Order box on the right side of the dialog box.

You can limit the number of records included in the sorted file by adding a Scope, For, or While clause, found in the bottom-center in the Input box. The Output box at the lower-right corner of the dialog box contains a Save As entry

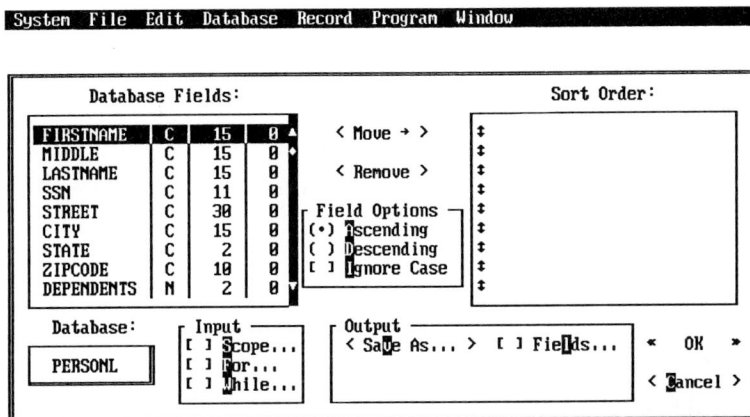

Figure 4-2. The Sort Order dialog box

for the filename to be assigned to the sorted file, along with a Fields option. The Fields option, when chosen, lets you specify a list of fields that will be included in the sorted file. When this option, the default, is checked, all fields are included in the sorted file.

As an example, we will sort on the employees' start date. Tab to the Database Fields list box and select Startdate with the cursor and ENTER key. Once selected, the field name, preceded by the database name (PERSONL. in FoxPro 2 and later, PERSONL−> in FoxPro 1.*x*), appears in the Sort Order list box. Ascending order, which is the default shown in the Fields Option box, is fine for this example. No Scope or For clauses are needed, since all records are desired. Tab to the entry space after the Fields button and enter **PERSONL2** as the filename. Then select OK from the dialog box. In a few moments, you'll see a message indicating the completion of the sorting process.

To see the results, enter

```
USE PERSONL2
LIST Lastname, Startdate
```

You will then see the following:

```
Record# Lastname      Startdate
      1 Saeedi        11/02/88
      2 Jackson       11/02/08
      3 Ballou        10/01/89
      4 Shelorson     11/02/89
      5 Murray        11/02/89
      6 Tahan         11/02/89
      7 Jackson       11/02/90
      8 Lord          11/02/90
```

which shows that the records in this new file are arranged in the order of start date, with the earliest dates first.

Enter **USE PERSONL** to close this database and reopen the original. Next we'll look at some examples using the SORT command. For an example, use the SORT command to alphabetize the personnel database by employees' last names. Enter the following:

```
USE PERSONL
SORT ON Lastname TO PERSONL3
```

To see the results of the sort operation, we must close the old database and open the new database. Try the following commands

```
USE PERSONL3
LIST Lastname
```

The results are shown below:

```
Record# Lastname
      1 Ballou
      2 Jackson
      3 Jackson
      4 Lord
      5 Murray
      6 Saeedi
      7 Shelorson
      8 Tahan
```

The old file, PERSONL, still exists in its unchanged form. The sorting operation has created a new file, called PERSONL3, that is in alphabetical order. Remember, the file that is currently in use cannot be overwritten during the sort process; each time a sort is performed, a new file must be created. Enter **USE PERSONL** and try the SORT command with the /D option (for descending order) on the Lastname field by entering

```
SORT ON Lastname /D TO PERSONL4
```

To see the results, you need to list the new file you created. Enter

```
USE PERSONL4
LIST Lastname
```

The results should be

```
Record# Lastname
      1 Tahan
      2 Shelorson
      3 Saeedi
      4 Murray
      5 Lord
      6 Jackson
      7 Jackson
      8 Ballou
```

Now let's try a sort on a numerical field. In this example, we will sort on the number of dependents for each employee. Return to PERSONL by entering **USE PERSONL** and enter

```
SORT ON Dependents TO PERSONL5
```

When the sorting process is complete, if you enter

```
USE PERSONL5
LIST Lastname, Dependents
```

you should then see

```
Record# Lastname        Dependents
      1 Jackson         0
      2 Tahan           0
      3 Saeedi          1
      4 Lord            1
      5 Jackson         2
      6 Ballou          2
      7 Shelorson       2
      8 Murray          2
```

showing the records arranged by the contents of the Dependents field in ascending order.

Before going on to consider the topic of sorting on multiple fields, you may want to perform some housekeeping by deleting the example files you just created. This can easily be done from the command level. First, enter **USE PERSONL** to close the file you are currently working with and open the original PERSONL database. (Database files must be closed before you can erase them.) Then, enter

```
RUN DEL PERSONL2.*
RUN DEL PERSONL3.*
RUN DEL PERSONL4.*
RUN DEL PERSONL5.*
```

to erase the database and accompanying memo-field files.

Sorting on Multiple Fields

When you want to sort on more than one field at the command level, you can list multiple fields separated by commas. Here is the general format for this type of sort:

SORT ON *field1*[/A/C/D], *field2*[/A/C/D],...*lastfield*[/A/C/D] TO *newfile*

For example, sorting the database on the Lastname field may reveal duplicate last names. To arrange the last names in the proper order, it would be necessary to sort using the last and first names. You can do this from the command level by listing the fields as part of the SORT command. To sort by last name and first name, enter

```
SORT ON Lastname, Firstname TO PERSONL2
```

Enter **USE PERSONL2** and then **LIST Lastname, Firstname** to see the results of the sort.

```
Record# Lastname       Firstname
      1 Ballou         Joseph
      2 Jackson        Debra
      3 Jackson        Phillip
      4 Lord           Scott
      5 Murray         John
      6 Saeedi         Maryann
      7 Shelorson      Mildred
      8 Tahan          Joseph
```

In this example, the Lastname field is the *primary field*. A primary field is the field that will be sorted first by the SORT command. After the database has been sorted by the primary field, if there is any duplicate information in the first field, SORT will sort the duplicate information by the second field listed in the command. This field is known as the *secondary field*. Enter **USE PERSONL** before continuing.

To do this from the menus, Open the Database menu with ALT-D and choose Sort. When the dialog box appears, tab to the Database Fields list box, highlight Lastname, and press ENTER. Then highlight Firstname and press ENTER. The Lastname and Firstname fields will appear in the Sort Order list box at the right side of the dialog box.

Tab to the Output portion of the dialog box and enter **PERSONL2** as the filename. Then, select OK. When the sorting process is complete, choose Open from the File menu and choose PERSONL2 as the name of the new file to open. Next, open the Database menu and choose Browse. You will see the data, sorted in order of last name and first name, as shown in Figure 4-3. When you've finished viewing the data, press ESC to get out of the Browse mode.

You are not limited to two fields. In fact, you can sort with all fields in the database. As an example, the commands

```
USE PERSONL
SORT ON State, City, Dependents, Lastname TO MASTER
```

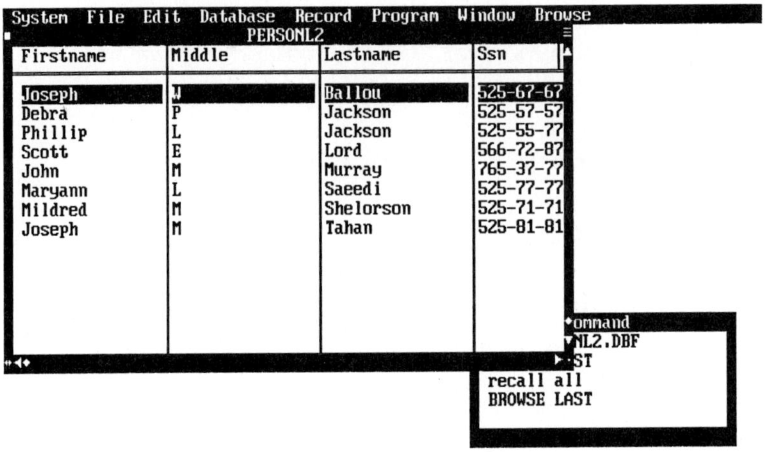

Figure 4-3. *A personnel file sorted by last name, then first name*

would create a database called MASTER that would alphabetize employee records by states, within each state by city, and within each city by number of dependents. If there are any duplicate entries at this point, the last names will be sorted in ascending order. In this example, State is the primary sort field, while City, Dependents, and Lastname are secondary sort fields.

Using Ascending and Descending Sort Orders Together

Sometimes it is necessary to combine ascending and descending sorts into a single operation. Suppose you want to print a report showing employees with the most dependents within each state and city. To do this enter the following:

```
USE PERSONL
SORT ON State/A, City/A, Dependents/D TO PERSONL3
```

Enter the following to see the resulting sort:

```
USE PERSONL3
LIST Firstname, Lastname, State, City, Dependents
```

```
Record# Firstname  Lastname  State    City       Dependents
      1 Phillip    Jackson   MD       Rockville  2
      2 Maryann    Saeedi    MD       Rockville  1
      3 Debra      Jackson   MD       Rockville  0
      4 Joseph     Tahan     VA       Fairfax    0
      5 Mildred    Shelorson VA       Leesburg   2
      6 John       Murray    VA       Leesburg   2
      7 Joseph     Ballou    VA       Reston     2
      8 Scott      Lord      VA       Reston     1
```

The display shows that in all cases where there are matching states and cities, the records are arranged starting with the greatest number of dependents.

Using the FOR Clause to Sort Selected Records

To produce a sorted file that contains only a specific subset of the records in the database, use the "FOR" statement with the SORT command. The format for the SORT command when used in this manner is

SORT ON *fieldname* [/A/C/D] TO *newfile* FOR *condition*

For example, to produce a new database sorted by employee last names and containing only those records with Virginia addresses, enter

```
USE PERSONL
SORT TO PERSONL4 ON Lastname FOR State = "VA"
USE PERSONL4
LIST Lastname, State
```

and the results appear as

```
Record# Lastname    State
      1 Ballou      VA
      2 Lord        VA
      3 Murray      VA
      4 Shelorson   VA
      5 Tahan       VA
```

Because of the use of a qualifying FOR condition, the new database contains only the records of employees located in Virginia.

Using the FOR Clause to Sort Selected Fields

You can create a new file containing only selected fields from a database by including a list of fields with the SORT command. This is useful when you need to extract specific types of information from large databases. You might want to create a file in alphabetical order containing only names and addresses and excluding all other fields. The syntax of the SORT command when used in this manner is

SORT TO *filename* ON *expression* FIELDS *list of fields*

As an example, you could create a file with only the names and addresses from the PERSONL database with a command like the following. Note that due to typesetting limitations, the command appears here on more than one line, but you would enter it as a single line in the Command window.

```
SORT TO MYFILE ON Lastname, Middle, Firstname FIELDS Lastname,
Middle, Firstname, Address, City, State, Zipcode
```

The sorted file, MYFILE, would contain only the Lastname, Firstname, Address, City, State, and Zipcode fields.

A Caveat

Sorting may be quite time-consuming, particularly in version 1.*x* of FoxPro. With version 2, sorting is much faster, although it still is somewhat slower than indexing. Sorting also uses considerable disk space, since each sort essentially duplicates the original database. You can accomplish the same result of keeping databases in order and use considerably less disk space if you use index files.

Indexing

An *index file* allows you to define the order of the records in your database without changing the database. Whenever you need to arrange the information in the database for reports or mailing labels, simply build a different index file. An index file consists of at least one field from a database. The field is sorted alphabetically, numerically, or chronologically. With each entry in the field is the corresponding record number from the parent database. The record number is used to reference the record in the parent database. In effect, an index file is a virtual sort of the parent database, since none of the records in the parent database are sorted.

To get a better understanding of an index file and its use, consider the index in the back of this book. If you wish to find information on a specific subject, you can hold your page and look for the subject and corresponding page number in the back. Just as a book index is a separate section that indicates where information is located, a FoxPro index file is a separate file that contains information regarding the location of individual records in the parent database. When the database file is opened along with the index file, the first record to be retrieved is not the first record in the parent database; instead, it is the first record listed in the index. The next record retrieved will be the second record listed in the index, and so on. Remember, indexing does not affect the order of the parent database.

In FoxPro 2, you can have two basic types of indexes: index files and index tags. Index files are files containing a single index; these are created with the INDEX ON . . . TO variation of the INDEX comand. (This is also the only type of index you can have in FoxPro 1.*x*.)

By comparison, *index tags* are tags that are added to a compound index file. With *compound index files,* FoxPro can maintain information on the different indexes that you create in a single index file. (By comparison, FoxPro's predecessor, FoxBASE, required a different index file for each index.) In FoxPro 2, you can have multiple index tags in the same compound index file, and you can have a special type of compound index file called the *structural compound index file*. The structural compound index file is a compound index file that has the same name as the database file, but with the compound-index-file extension of .CDX. When FoxPro 2 opens a database, it looks for a structural compound index file (a compound index file having the same name as the database). If one is found, FoxPro opens it automatically, and the index file is updated automatically as the database changes.

Indexing with the INDEX Command

From the command level, the general format of the INDEX command is similar to the format of the SORT command:

INDEX ON *expression* TO *index-file name* [FOR *condition*] [UNIQUE]

If you are using FoxPro 2, you can also use the format

INDEX ON *expression* TAG *index-file name* [OF *.CDX filename*] [FOR *condition*] [UNIQUE] [COMPACT] [ASCENDING] [DESCENDING] [ADDITIVE]

When you use the INDEX command with the TO clause, FoxPro produces a single .IDX index file containing the index information. The extension .IDX is added to all noncompound index files. When you use the TAG clause, FoxPro adds the index tag to the named compound index file (or, if none is named, to the structural compound index file). The basic format for the INDEX command is

INDEX ON *fieldname* TO *index-file name*

or with version 2, you can also use the basic format of

INDEX ON *fieldname* TAG *index-file name*

The first format creates an index file based on the named field, with all records included in the index. The second format creates an index tag, and because no compound index file is named, the tag will be added to the structural compound index file (the one with the same name as the database file).

When you use the UNIQUE clause you are telling FoxPro to create an index that will exclude all duplicates. For example, if a social security field were used to build the index, and two records contained the same social security number, the second occurrence would be omitted from the index. The FOR expression lets you build a selective index that contains only those records that meet the condition specified by the FOR clause.

To illustrate the use of the INDEX command, here we will create an index for the personnel database. As an example, use the following commands to index the personnel database by city.

If you are using FoxPro 2, enter

```
USE PERSONL
INDEX ON City TAG CITIES
```

If you are using FoxPro 1.*x*, enter

```
USE PERSONL
INDEX ON City TO CITIES
```

The index you just created will arrange the personnel database in order by city. Enter **LIST Lastname, City**, and you will see the result of the new index file:

```
Record# Lastname     City
      7 Tahan        Fairfax
      5 Shelorson    Leesburg
      6 Murray       Leesburg
```

```
4 Ballou        Reston
8 Lord          Reston
1 Saeedi        Rockville
2 Jackson       Rockville
3 Jackson       Rockville
```

Notice that the record numbers that indicate the order of the records in the database itself are not in order. The command you entered creates an index containing the index information. Any index you create is automatically made active immediately after its creation. Hence, the order of the records displayed with the LIST command is now controlled by the new index.

It's good practice to give index files or tags a name related in some manner to the field that has been indexed. This helps you and others keep track of how the database file was indexed and what field was used.

Indexing with the FoxPro Menus

To index a file using the menus, open the File menu and choose the New option. When the dialog box appears, choose Index, then choose OK. The Index On dialog box appears, as shown in Figure 4-4. (Note that there will be fewer options in the dialog box you see if you are using version 1.*x* of FoxPro.) You can base your index on a field by making a selection from the Field list box on the left, or base the index on an expression (such as a combination of fields), by entering the expression in the Index Expression window. The expression can be manually typed in, or you can tab over to < Expr... > and press ENTER to bring up the Expression Builder to create the index expression. Expressions can become complex, including field names, functions, and/or operators. (Examples of indexing with complex expressions are provided later in this chapter.) After the entry of the expression used to build the index, choose OK from the dialog box to exit the Expression Builder and return to the Index On dialog box.

The dialog box that appears with FoxPro 2 and above offers some additional options. At the lower center of the dialog box is an area with output options. This controls what type of index is created. You can select .IDX (normal) or .CDX (compound) index files, and you can choose compact-type index files by checking the Compact check box. Compact indexes take up less space, but are not compatible with versions of FoxPro prior to version 2. If you choose compound (.CDX) type files, you can also choose whether the tag will be added to the structural compound index file (the .CDX file having the same name as the database).

The Unique check box in the Options window lets you select a *unique index*, in which duplicate entries of the indexed field or expression are ignored. This is the equivalent of the UNIQUE clause when used with the INDEX ON command.

```
 System  File  Edit  Database  Record  Program  Window
        8 records sorted
┌──────────────────────────────────────────────────────────────────────┐
│    Database Fields:                              Index On:             │
│   ┌────────────────┐  ┌─ Options ─────────┐  ┌───────────────────┐    │
│   │ FIRSTNAME  │ C │▲│ (•) Ascending      │  │                   │    │
│   │ MIDDLE     │ C │◆│ ( ) Descending     │  │                   │    │
│   │ LASTNAME   │ C │ │ [ ] Unique         │  │                   │    │
│   │ SSN        │ C │ │ <For...>           │  │                   │    │
│   │ STREET     │ C │ │ Tag Name           │  │                   │    │
│   │ CITY       │ C │ │                    │  │                   │    │
│   │ STATE      │ C │ │    <  Move →  >    │  │                   │    │
│   │ ZIPCODE    │ C │ │                    │  │                   │    │
│   │ DEPENDENTS │ N │ │    <Remove/Edit >  │  └───────────────────┘    │
│   │ DEPARTMENT │ C │▼│                    │                           │
│   └────────────────┘  └────────────────────┘                         │
│   ┌─ Index Expression ─┐  ┌─ Output ──────────────┐                   │
│   │  <Expr...>         │  │ ( ) IDX [X] Compact    │   «   OK   »     │
│   │                    │  │ (•) CDX [X] Structural │                  │
│   │                    │  │ <Save As...>           │   < Cancel >     │
│   │                    │  │ E:\FOXPRO\DATA\PERSONL  │                 │
│   └────────────────────┘  └────────────────────────┘                 │
└──────────────────────────────────────────────────────────────────────┘
```

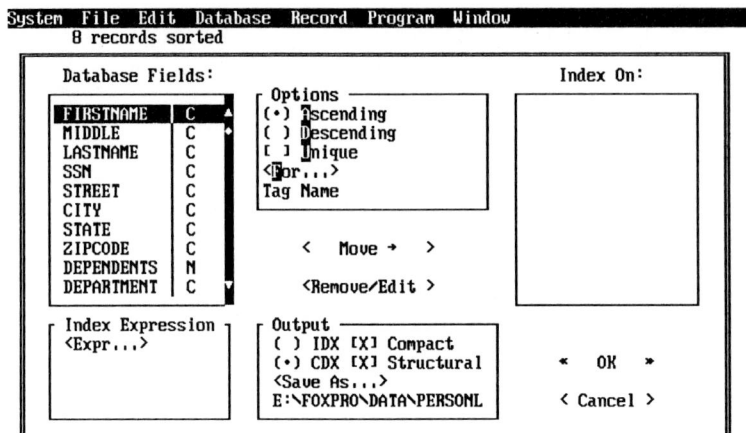

Figure 4-4. *The Index On dialog box*

The <For...> entry lets you specify an expression to limit records that are
stored in the index. This is the equivalent of adding the FOR clause to the
INDEX ON command. For example, entering an expression like

```
State = "VA"
```

in the <For...> window would limit the resultant index to those records with
"VA" in the State field.

As an example, let's build an index using the menus.

FoxPro 2 Users   To try indexing with the FoxPro 2 menus, choose New from
the File menu. When the dialog box appears, choose Index and then choose OK.
In a moment, the Index On dialog box will appear. Tab to or click on Lastname
in the Database Fields list box at the left side of the dialog box. When you
highlight the name and press ENTER, you will see the field name appear in the list
box at the right side of the screen. You may also notice that Lastname appears
by default as a tag name within the Options area of the dialog box. While you can
change this to any tag name that you desire, you can leave the tag name as it is
for this example.

At the lower-center area of the screen, you may notice that a compact,
structural compound index file (.CDX) is chosen as the default. You can leave the

options in this area as it is for now. Select OK to create the index. When the indexing is completed, choose Browse from the Database menu to view the file. It will appear in order by last name. Before continuing, press ESC to leave Browse mode.

FoxPro 1.x Users   Open the File menu with ALT-F and choose the New option. When the dialog box appears, choose Index, then choose OK. In a moment, the Index On dialog box will appear. Choose Lastname from the Field Names list box. Once you select Lastname, it will appear in the <Expr...> window. Tab to the OK button and press ENTER to accept the index expression; the dialog box will vanish and another dialog box will appear, prompting you for a filename.

Enter **LNAMES** as the filename for the index and select OK to create the index. When the indexing is completed, choose Browse from the Database menu to view the file; it will appear in order by last name. Before continuing, press ESC to leave the Browse mode.

Selective Indexing with the FOR Clause

You can limit the records stored in the index by using the FOR clause along with the INDEX ON command or the <For...> expression window of the Index On dialog box. When used from the command level, the syntax for the index command in FoxPro 2 becomes

INDEX ON *expression* TAG *filename* FOR *condition*

In FoxPro 2 and 1.x, it becomes

INDEX ON *expression* TO *filename* FOR *condition*

where the condition used with FOR is any expression that evaluates to a logical true or false. This is a powerful FoxPro option that can, in effect, filter the database of unwanted records while placing records in order at the same time.

The SET FILTER command along with a simple use of the INDEX command would accomplish the same result, but assuming an updated index already exists, using FOR with INDEX ON is faster than the use of SET FILTER. As an example, if you wanted to produce a report of employees in the database who lived in Maryland or Virginia, indexed in ZIP code order, you could use a command like

```
INDEX ON Zipcode TO ZIPCD FOR State = "MD" .OR. State = "VA"
```

to accomplish such a task.

To do the same thing from the FoxPro menus, open the File menu with ALT-F and select New. When the dialog box appears, choose Index and choose OK; then tab to the <Expr...> window and enter

```
State = "MD" .OR. State = "VA"
```

and choose OK. A moment later, another dialog box will appear, prompting you for a filename.

Indexing on Multiple Fields

The process for creating indexes based on several fields is similar to sorting on multiple fields. There is a limitation, however: You cannot directly index on multiple fields that are not of the same field type. For example, you could not index by Lastname and Dependents, because Dependents is a numeric field, while Lastname is a character field. There is a way around this, and it will be discussed later in the chapter.

To see how indexing on multiple fields works and to be sure the LNAMES index file that you created earlier is still active, look at the Lastname and Firstname fields by entering **LIST Lastname, Firstname**. Notice that Phillip Jackson is listed before Debra Jackson, which is not correct. Because you indexed the file on last names only, the order of the first names was ignored. To correct the situation, enter

```
INDEX ON Lastname + Firstname TO FULLNAME
```

In the index, records having the same last name are now indexed by last names and then by first names.

Now enter **LIST Lastname, Firstname** to see the results:

```
Record# Lastname      Firstname
      4 Ballou        Joseph
      2 Jackson       Debra
      3 Jackson       Phillip
      8 Lord          Scott
      6 Murray        John
      1 Saeedi        Maryann
      5 Shelorson     Mildred
      7 Tahan         Joseph
```

This technique can be used to create an index file on a number of fields. Use the plus (+) symbol along with the INDEX command to combine the fields. For example, the following INDEX command,

```
INDEX ON Zipcode + Lastname + Firstname TO ZIPNAMES
```

would index the database three ways: by ZIP codes, by last names (where records have the same ZIP code), and by first names (where records have the same last name *and* the same ZIP code). Multiple indexes are useful aids when you are working with large databases and must organize them into comprehensible groups.

Indexing on Fields of Different Types

You cannot index directly using multiple fields of different types (such as character and numeric), as noted earlier. To get around this problem, make use of the FoxPro functions to convert fields that are not character data into character data. *Functions* are used to perform special operations that supplement the normal FoxPro commands. (Functions will be explained in greater detail in the programming section of this book.) For indexing, you will need to use one of two functions: the DTOS (Date-To-String) function, or the STR (String) function. The DTOS function converts the contents of a date field into a string of characters that follow a year-month-day format. The STR function converts the contents of a numeric field into a string of characters. You can use the DTOS and STR functions in combination with your index commands to accomplish the result of indexing on combinations of different types of fields. The normal format for an index command, when combined with these functions, would be

INDEX ON *character field* + STR(*numeric field*) + DTOS(*date field*)
TO *index-file name*

To build an index file that is indexed in alphabetical order by state and in numerical order by dependents within each group of states, for example, enter this command:

```
INDEX ON State + STR(Dependents) TO TEST
```

Enter **LIST Lastname, State, Dependents** to see the results of the index file; they should resemble the following:

```
Record# Lastname      State  Dependents
      2 Jackson       MD     0
      1 Saeedi        MD     1
      3 Jackson       MD     2
      7 Tahan         VA     0
      8 Lord          VA     1
      4 Ballou        VA     2
      5 Shelorson     VA     2
      6 Murray        VA     2
```

Now let's use the DTOS function to build an index file that is indexed in chronological order by Startdate and in alphabetical order by Lastname. Enter the following:

```
INDEX ON DTOS(Startdate) + Lastname TO HIREDATE
```

Enter **LIST Lastname, Startdate** to see the results of the index file; they should resemble the following:

```
Record# Lastname     Startdate
      3 Jackson      11/02/88
      1 Saeedi       11/02/88
      4 Ballou       10/01/89
      6 Murray       11/02/89
      5 Shelorson    11/02/89
      7 Tahan        11/02/89
      2 Jackson      11/02/90
      8 Lord         11/02/90
```

NOTE: *You can also use these functions within the menus by manually entering the functions along with the field names in the index expression window.*

Opening Databases with Index Files

You can open a database with one or more index files simultaneously by adding the word "INDEX" and the index filenames after the USE *filename* portion of the command. Only one index file can be active at a time. The syntax for the USE command, when used with the INDEX option, becomes

USE *filename* INDEX *index name 1*[, *index name 2*]

For example, you could simultaneously open the PERSONL database along with the CITIES and FULLNAME index files with a command like

```
USE PERSONL INDEX CITIES, FULLNAME
```

NOTE: *The last index file you list is the controlling index. In the above example, the FULLNAME index file would control how the records are displayed or printed in a report.*

If (in version 2 or above) you are working with a compound index file with the same name as the database (or the structural compound index file), you need not worry about specifying the index filename along with the USE command. The structural compound index file, if it exists, is automatically opened by FoxPro whenever you open a database. If you choose to add index tags to compound index files that have other names, you can activate such an index file at the same time that you open the database with this variation of the USE command:

USE *filename* INDEX *.CDX filename*

The compound index file named as part of the command will then be opened along with the database.

Using the SET INDEX and SET ORDER Commands

As noted earlier, a database can be opened with more than one index. However, the order in which the records appear or are printed is controlled by only one index. For an index to control the order of the records, it must be active. You can easily tell which indexes are in use at any time by using the LIST STATUS and LIST DISPLAY commands. An index that has just been created is active, and the SET INDEX command makes a dormant index active. The SET INDEX command is the command-level equivalent of choosing Open from the File menu and selecting Index from the Type button in the dialog box that appears.

Suppose that you need two lists from the PERSONL database. The first list must be in order by dependents and the second by last name. To create the indexes from these fields, enter the following commands:

```
INDEX ON Dependents TO CHILD
INDEX ON Lastname TO NAMES
```

These commands create two indexes on your hard disk: CHILD and NAMES. Each index file contains the appropriate field from each record and the corresponding record numbers. NAMES, for example, contains last names in alphabetical order and the matching record numbers for each last name. Since NAMES was the last index created, it is the active index.

By using the SET INDEX command you can activate any index. For example, to activate and display the database organized by number of dependents instead of by last name, enter

```
SET INDEX TO CHILD
LIST Lastname, Dependents
```

The display should appear as follows.

```
Record#  Lastname     Dependents
      2  Jackson      0
      7  Tahan        0
      1  Saeedi       1
      8  Lord         1
      3  Jackson      2
      4  Ballou       2
      5  Shelorson    2
      6  Murray       2
```

The records have been indexed numerically by dependent using the CHILD index.

You can also activate an index using the SET ORDER command. With SET ORDER, you use numbers, for example, SET ORDER TO 2. The number indicates the order in which the index file was originally opened. When using FoxPro 2, you can enter the command,

SET ORDER TO TAG *tagname*

where *tagname* is the name for the index tag. If, for example, you entered **USE PERSONL INDEX NAME, CHILD** to open the files, the CHILD index would be the second index opened; therefore, entering SET ORDER TO 2 would make CHILD the active index file.

Using REINDEX

When you open the database to make changes, you also open the index file. If you forget to do so, you can update the index with the REINDEX command. For example, if you add a new employee to the personnel database without opening the index, the record will be omitted from your reports. Use REINDEX to reindex the file and add the new record to the index.

Using CLOSE INDEX

If you decide that you do not want to use any index file, the CLOSE INDEX command will close the index file while leaving the associated database open. To execute the command from the command level, enter

CLOSE INDEX

There is no CLOSE INDEX command from the menus, but FoxPro will close an index if you open another index from the menus.

Chapter 5

Performing Queries

The ability to access information selectively in your database is essential when making decisions. For example, when providing service to a customer on the phone, you usually need quick access to information. Producing reports or mailing labels may require you to search the database for a subset of information based on certain criteria, for example, all employees over 25 years of age. In FoxPro, accessing needed information involves performing *queries* on your database using expressions that represent your search criteria.

You usually query a database using an *expression*. Therefore, the first portion of this chapter discusses the anatomy of an expression in FoxPro. Next, we'll explore how expressions are used with the LOCATE, SEEK, FIND, and SET FILTER commands. This will be done from the FoxPro menus and the command level.

The Anatomy of an Expression

In FoxPro, a query must include a *logical expression*; that is, an expression that evaluates to either true or false. In Chapter 4, "Sorting and Indexing a Database," logical expressions were used to build indexes and perform sorts. For example, the command

```
INDEX ON Zipcode TO ZIPCD FOR State = "MD" .OR. State = "VA"
```

was used to create an index for all employees living in Maryland or Virginia, arranged by ZIP code. The expression used is

```
State = "MD" .OR. State = "VA"
```

FoxPro will first look at the State field in each record to see if it contains the characters "MD". If the characters are not found, it will look at the record to see if the characters "VA" are found. If either set of characters is found, the expression is evaluated to true. Otherwise, the expression is false.

Expressions may contain one or more functions and operators. *Functions* are used to perform special operations that supplement the normal FoxPro commands. *Operators* are symbols used to indicate the performance of an operation. In the above example, the = operator is used to symbolize equivalency. FoxPro uses four types of operators: relational, logical, arithmetical, and string.

Relational Operators

Relational operators are used in expressions to make comparisons on various types of data, such as numerical, character, or date data types. For an expression to be valid, the comparison must be made on the same data type. For example, using the following expression with the numerical field Total

```
Total > "SIXTY"
```

would produce an error message in FoxPro, telling you that there was a type mismatch. This is because you were attempting to compare a numerical field and a character string.

In the above expression, the > operator is used to indicate greater than. Table 5-1 lists the relational operators used in FoxPro.

While you cannot mix two different data types when using an operator, all of these operators (except $ and ==) can be used with numerical, character, or date fields. The $ and == operators can only be used with character fields.

You can use the $ operator to search for a substring within a field. If you wanted to find all of the employees in our example who lived on Reston Avenue, you could use this expression:

```
"Reston Avenue"  $ Street
```

In this case you are looking for all records that contain "Reston Avenue" in the Street field. This operator is also useful for searching memo fields.

=	Equal to
<> or #	Not equal to
<	Left operand is less than right operand
<=	Left operand is less than or equal to right operand
>	Left operand is greater than right operand
>=	Left operand is greater than or equal to right operand
$	Substring comparison
==	Character string comparison (trailing blanks are significant when EXACT is ON)

Table 5-1. *FoxPro Relational Operators and Their Meanings*

The == operator tells FoxPro that you are looking for a character string exactly like the one specified. This is different from the = operator. For example, the following expression, using the = operator,

```
Lastname = "WILL"
```

would return all last names whose first four characters match the characters within the quotation marks:

```
Record# Lastname
    1  WILL
    7  WILLIAMS
   11 WILLSTON
```

However, the same expression using the == operator

```
Lastname == "WILL"
```

finds only the first record shown above. While this operator is useful for finding exact matches, FoxPro offers another way to accomplish this as well. This will be discussed later on in the chapter.

Logical Operators

Logical operators are used to build complex expressions. For example, to determine the number of employees at least 25 years of age, you would use the following expression:

```
AGE >= 25
```

But what if you needed to determine the number of employees at least 25 years old, but less than 45? The following complex expression would be appropriate:

```
AGE >= 25 .AND. <= 45
```

Keep in mind when using these operators that .AND. will generally narrow your search and .OR. will expand it.

Table 5-2 contains a list of the logical operators used by FoxPro. Note that, with the exception of ! and (), these operators begin and end with dot delimiters.

Arithmetical Operators

Arithmetical operators can be used to construct numerical expressions. Here are some examples of numerical expressions.

```
WEIGHT = 2 * 75
WEEKLY = (20 * 160) / 4
Total = ((50 + 90) / 3) * 5
```

Table 5-3 shows the complete list of arithmetical operators and their meanings.

String Operators

There are only two string operators in FoxPro, and both are used to perform string concatenations. The first operator, plus (+), joins two strings together, regardless of trailing blanks in the first string. For example, the expression

```
"Audrey  " + "Lake"
```

would appear as

```
"Audrey  Lake"
```

()	Used to group expressions
.NOT.	Must not meet condition
!	Must not meet condition
.AND.	Must meet both conditions
.OR.	Must meet either condition

Table 5-2.   FoxPro Logical Operators and Their Meanings

()	Used to group expressions
**	Exponentiation
^	Exponentiation
*	Multiplication
/	Division
+	Addition
−	Subtraction

***Table 5-3.** FoxPro Arithmetical Operators and Their Meanings*

The second operator (−) is used to concatenate strings, removing any trailing blanks from the first string. In the above example, replacing the + with −, would produce the string: "AudreyLake".

Functions

FoxPro uses functions to perform a variety of operations, from converting data types to performing math operations. When a function is used to perform an operation it usually returns a value. For example, in Chapter 4, "Sorting and Indexing a Database," the STR() function was used to convert a number found in the Dependents field to a character string. In this case, the value returned is actually the converted data.

Functions are also used to return system information, such as the date or time. For example, enter the following into the command window:

```
? TIME()
? DATE()
```

You should be presented with the current system date and time. Note that all functions end with parentheses, but some functions do not require expressions between the parentheses. Note also the use of the ? command. This command evaluates an expression and prints the result.

FoxPro uses another group of functions to test certain conditions and return a value of true (.T.) or false (.F.). They are called *logical functions* and can also be used at the command level. The DELETED() function is a good example. This function returns true (.T.) when a record has been marked for deletion.

Now that you are familiar with the anatomy of an expression, it is time to use some expressions with the FoxPro commands.

Performing Queries

Querying the database will usually involve one of two scenarios: the selection of a single record or the isolation of a subgroup of records (a process often followed by the printing of a report). If you wish to retreive a single record, the Locate and Seek commands, found on the Record menu, and also accessible at the command level, are what you want. To follow along with the examples in this chapter on your computer, enter **USE PERSONL** in the Command window to open the personnel database.

Locate

Locate will find the first occurrence of a record. To locate a record, open the Record menu with ALT-R and choose Locate. The dialog box (shown in Figure 5-1) that appears next contains three options: Scope, For, and While. The Scope option reveals yet another dialog box with four options: All, Next, Record, and Rest. The optional use of a scope lets you define a limit to the operation of Locate. You can choose All (to specify that the use of Locate should span all records; this is the default). You can choose Next and then enter a number, which specifies a group of records starting with wherever the pointer is now located (for example, entering **10** would tell FoxPro to limit its use of Locate to the next ten records). You can choose Record and enter a number, which again selects a specific record by its record number. Or you can choose Rest, which limits the use of Locate to all records located between the pointer and the end of the file.

If you select either the For option or the While option, the Expression Builder dialog box appears. In Figure 5-2, the For option has been selected, as indicated by the FOR Clause window in the upper portion of the dialog box. Field names, which are normally used to build search expressions, can be selected from the Field Names box at the lower-left corner of the dialog box. Once a name is selected, it appears in the FOR Clause or WHILE Clause window. As an alternative, you may choose to enter the field name in the FOR Clause or WHILE Clause window by typing it.

You can select an operator, such as =, by clicking on the Logical box and selecting the operator from a pulldown menu. However, it is usually faster to simply type the symbol into the FOR Clause box. Figure 5-3 shows the Expression Builder dialog box with the Logical pulldown menu open. Note that logical functions as well as operators are listed on the menu. FoxPro groups the functions and operators on these menus by data type.

Enter the desired search value. Text expressions are always entered surrounded by quotes, numbers are entered exactly as they are stored in the numeric field, and dates may be entered using brackets ({}) or the CTOD function. For example, CTOD("12/20/90") would be evaluated as a date value of 12/20/90. You can also use memo fields within your conditions when searching for a value.

System File Edit Database Record Program Window

```
[ ] Scope...          « Locate »
[ ] For...            < Cancel >
[ ] While...
                           ommand
                      use person1
                      recall all
                      use person1
                      clear
```

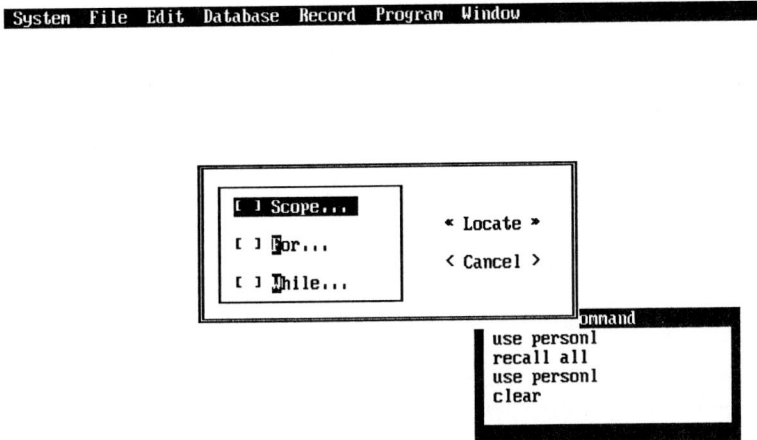

Figure 5-1. *The Locate dialog box*

You can check your expression for correct syntax, if desired, by tabbing to or clicking on the Verify button. If the expression is a valid one, FoxPro will display an "expression is valid" message. Tab to or click on the OK button to finish your entry. The Locate dialog box will reappear, with the For option selected. You can

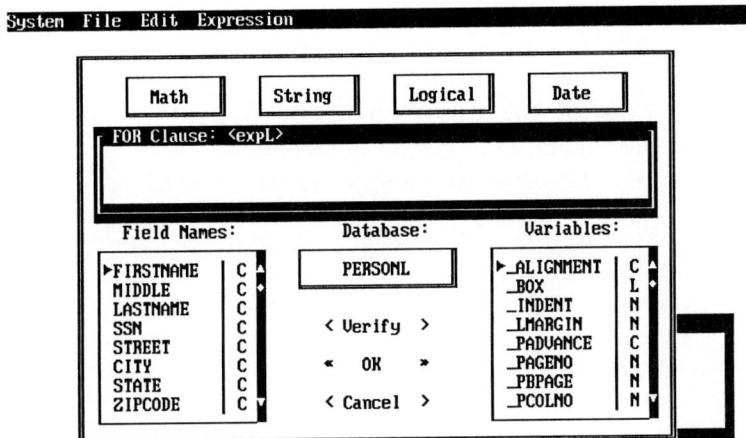

System File Edit Expression

```
   Math        String      Logical       Date
 FOR Clause: <expL>



   Field Names:      Database:       Variables:
►FIRSTNAME  C        PERSONL      ►_ALIGNMENT  C
 MIDDLE     C                      _BOX        L
 LASTNAME   C                      _INDENT     N
 SSN        C      < Verify >      _LMARGIN    N
 STREET     C                      _PADVANCE   C
 CITY       C      «  OK   »       _PAGENO     N
 STATE      C                      _PBPAGE     N
 ZIPCODE    C      < Cancel >      _PCOLNO     N
```

Figure 5-2. *The Expression Builder dialog box*

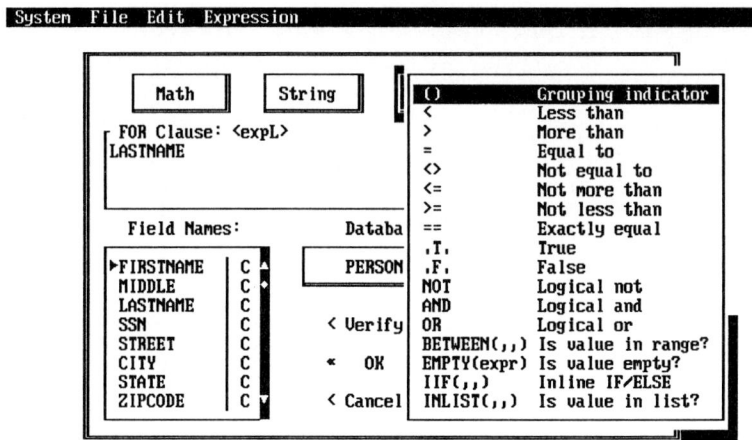

Figure 5-3.   The Expression Builder with the Logical pulldown menu open

now tab to or click on the Locate button to implement the search. Remember that the process only locates the record but does not display it. You can now choose the Change option of the Record menu to view the record.

As an example, let's locate Ms. Saeedi, an employee in our personnel database. Assuming the database is open (if it is not, type **USE PERSONL** and press ENTER to open it), you can open the Record menu with ALT-R, choose Locate, and select the For option when the Locate dialog box, shown earlier in Figure 5-1, appears. Type the following expression into the FOR Clause window:

```
Lastname = "Saeedi"
```

Another way to do this is to select Lastname from the list of fields, type an equal sign or choose one from the pulldown menu that appears when you tab to the Logical menu and press the SPACEBAR or click on the Logical menu, then type **"Saeedi"** (you must include the quotation marks). For mouse users, an alternative to typing the quotation marks is to click on the String box and select "text" from the pulldown menu that appears, then type the name. Again, it is usually faster to just type in the quotation marks manually.

Next click on the OK button, and the Locate dialog box reappears. Finally, click on the Locate button in the Locate dialog box to implement the search. When the first occurrence of the record is found, FoxPro prints the record number on the screen. To view the record, type **EDIT** in the command window and press ENTER.

The Continue Option

To find the next occurrence of the same search term, use the Continue option on the Record menu. This option is helpful because the first record located may not be the record desired. Choosing the Continue option will continue the search, seeking the next record that meets the condition you specified when using Locate. If no further records meet the specified condition, you will see an "End of Locate scope" message on the screen. (You will see the same error message if an initial use of Locate fails to find a record.)

The LOCATE FOR Command

You can also find the first occurrence of a record using the LOCATE FOR command. The syntax for the command is

LOCATE [*scope*] FOR *condition*

where *condition* is a logical expression, such as Lastname = "Shelor", which defines your search. *Scope*, which is optional, can be used to limit the number of records searched. You can enter **ALL** to specify that the use of LOCATE should span all records. If the scope is omitted, FoxPro assumes that you want to search all the records in the file. You can enter **NEXT** and then enter a number, which specifies a group of records starting with the current pointer location. For example, entering **NEXT 10** as the scope would tell FoxPro to limit its use of LOCATE to the next ten records, starting with the current record. You can also enter **REST**, which limits the use of LOCATE to all records from the current pointer location to the end of the file.

If you wish to find the next occurrence of the record, use the CONTINUE command. This command performs the same operation as Continue on the Record menu; it searches for the next record that meets the condition you specified when using Locate. LOCATE and CONTINUE will carry on a sequential search until a record is found or you reach the end of the database. If a LOCATE or CONTINUE command is unsuccessful, you get the message, "End of Locate scope." For example, a simple search can be entered in the Command window to search the City field of the personnel database,

```
LOCATE FOR City = "Reston"
DISPLAY
```

and the result, shown partially below,

```
8 Scott E Lord 566-72-8723 1250 South Lakes Drive Reston VA...
```

shows that the record found indeed contains "VA" in the State field. If this is not the desired record, the search can be continued with the CONTINUE command. By entering these commands as examples,

```
CONTINUE
DISPLAY
```

the result, shown below,

```
4 Joseph W Ballou 525-67-6723 1200 Sunrise Valley Drive Reston VA...
```

shows that the CONTINUE command found the next occurrence of the desired record.

When using LOCATE, keep in mind that FoxPro searches by examining the characters in your search term from left to right. Therefore, you need only enter as much of the term as necessary to find the proper record. For example, the command

```
LOCATE FOR Lastname = "Bal"
```

would be enough to find a person named Ballou, if there were no other names with "Bal" as the first three letters of the name. If you know exactly what you're looking for and want FoxPro to look for your precise search term, you can first enter the command,

```
SET EXACT ON
```

then enter the desired LOCATE command. The SET EXACT command tells FoxPro to execute any LOCATE, FIND, or SEEK operations using the same length for the search term and the actual data. You can later enter **SET EXACT OFF** to disable this effect.

The Seek Option

Records can be found faster than the LOCATE command can manage if you use the Seek option. The Seek option is available from the Record menu only if an index is active. When you open the Record menu and select Seek, the Expression Builder appears, containing a Value to Seek window. You use the Expression Builder in the same manner as you did with the For option: Just enter the desired expression into the Value to Seek window. However, you only need the expression itself and not the field name, because FoxPro knows which field (or fields) the index is based on. For example, if we needed to find Mr. Murray (an employee in our database), we could first index the database by last name by entering

```
INDEX ON Lastname TO LNAMES
```

and then opening the Record menu with ALT-R and choosing the Seek option. When the Expression Builder dialog box appears, enter **"Murray"** into the Value to Seek window.

*NOTE: Instead of entering **Lastname** = **"Murray"**, as was done with Locate, you would only enter **"Murray"** in the Value to Seek window, assuming the active index is based on Lastname. Remember that since Seek is designed to work with an index, you must search for data based on the index. (You could not, for example, use Seek to search for a last name if the database were indexed only by social security number.)*

After entering the search value, tab to or click on the OK button, and the seek will take place. You then enter **EDIT** in the command window to view the desired record. Keep in mind that the Seek option finds the first occurrence in the index. If there are duplicate occurrences of that index expression, such as more than one Murray in a file indexed on last name only, you may want to use Browse to aid you in finding the desired record.

The SEEK Command

The SEEK command is similar to the Seek option on the Record menu—it is only necessary to enter the search value. The format of the SEEK command is

SEEK *expression*

Expression can be a number, a character string (which *must* be surrounded by quotation marks), or a variable (variables are covered in Chapter 14, "The Basics of FoxPro Programming"). The expression can also be a combination of constants, variables, and operators (including functions). The SEEK command will search the active index file and find the first record matching your specifications. The record itself will not be displayed; the SEEK command will simply move the record pointer to the desired record.

The FIND Command

The FIND command is only accessible at the command level. Like the SEEK command, it, too, does an index search, making it necessary to open an index file before using it. When you use the FIND command you must specify a *constant* with it. A constant is a number, date, or character string that is used for its literal meaning. The format of the FIND is

FIND *character string*

where *character string* is a group of characters that do NOT need to be surrounded by quotation marks. For example, if you want to search for someone in the personnel file with a last name of Lord, enter

```
INDEX ON Lastname TO LNAMES
FIND Lord
```

Enter **DISPLAY** to look at the record that follows.

```
8 Scott E Lord  566-72-8723  1250 South Lake Drive  Reston VA...
```

REMINDER: When using the FIND command, make sure that an index is open first. Also keep in mind that you do not have to put quotes around a character string with the FIND command.

Using the SET FILTER Command to Select Subsets of Data

Up until now, we have talked about queries involving individual records. However, producing a report or mailing labels often involves selecting a group of records. One way to do this is to create and set a *filter*. When you set a filter, only records meeting the conditions specified will be affected by commands issued.

The syntax for the SET FILTER command is

SET FILTER TO *condition*

where *condition* is a logical expression, such as Lastname = "Murray," that defines your search. Once the command is entered, other database commands, which would normally use records from the entire database, will use only those records that meet the condition specified by the filter. In effect, this lets you work with a subset of a database as though it were the entire database.

A command like

```
SET FILTER TO CITY = "Rockville" .AND. State = "MD"
```

limits a database to those records located in Rockville, MD. The SET FILTER command is the equivalent of the Filter option available from the Database/Setup menu choices. You can isolate a group of records by issuing a SET FILTER command, and then you can use the LIST or BROWSE command to view the data, or the REPORT FORM command (covered in Chapter 7, "Reports") to produce a printed report. For example, let's create a filter for employees living in Maryland with two or more dependents. Enter the following commands:

```
CLOSE ALL
USE PERSONL
SET FILTER TO State = "MD" .AND. Dependents >= 2
LIST Lastname, State, Dependents
```

The SET FILTER command in this example restricts the listed records to only those with addresses in Maryland and with two or more dependents. The output appears as

```
Record# Lastname        State Dependents
      3 Jackson         MD    2
```

You can enclose parts of the expression in parentheses to build very complex expressions. For example, the command

```
SET FILTER TO ( Expiredate >= CTOD("01/01/91") .AND.
Expiredate <= CTOD("12/31/91") ) .OR. State = "MD"
```

would limit the records available to those with an expiration date in 1991 or with the letters "MD" in the State field.

You can see whether a filter is in effect at any time by using LIST STATUS or DISPLAY STATUS. The listing that results from either of these commands will include the filter condition for any filter that is in effect.

You can cancel the effects of an existing filter by entering

```
SET FILTER TO
```

without including any condition in the command, as shown above. If you duplicated the earlier example, use the SET FILTER TO command now to clear the effects of the filter.

Now that we know how to search and retreive information from a database, the next step is to present it in a desirable format in a report. Chapter 7 will cover the subject in detail.

Chapter 6 looks at how you can perform queries using the RQBE window, a feature available to users of FoxPro 2.

Chapter *6*

Creating Queries with RQBE

For users of FoxPro 2 and later, FoxPro offers another method for performing queries: the RQBE (Relational Query-By-Example) facility. When you use the RQBE facility to create your queries, your selections are interpreted as SQL SELECT commands. SQL, or Structured Query Language, was originally implemented on mainframe computers in the 1970s by IBM. The SELECT command is powerful because it allows you to specify the desired information to FoxPro without defining the retrieval method. FoxPro determines the best way to retrieve the desired information.

About Rushmore

In addition to the flexibility of the SQL SELECT command, FoxPro automatically utilizes a special optimizing technique called *Rushmore* for faster execution of your queries. Rushmore is a data retrieval technique, unique to FoxPro, that provides very efficient access to sets of records. With Rushmore, many complex database operations run hundreds of times faster than with comparable database managers using the dBASE language. The SQL statements generated by FoxPro's RQBE facility will automatically take advantage of Rushmore. This is a significant advantage over the types of queries detailed in Chapter 5, which are done with FOR clauses or SET FILTER statements. When you construct your own queries using FOR clauses of various commands or the SET FILTER command, Rushmore only works if you happen to have an index active that supports your type of query. For example, if you entered a LIST command with a FOR clause based on the contents of a Lastname field, Rushmore would speed the results of your query only if the file were indexed on the Lastname field. By comparison, you do not need to do any indexing to take advantage of Rushmore when you use the RQBE facility or SQL SELECT command to construct your queries. Rushmore handles any needed indexing automatically.

Using the RQBE Window

You can access the RQBE window by choosing New from the File menu. When the dialog box appears, you can select Query and then choose OK. From command level, simply enter **CREATE QUERY** and press ENTER. Either method results in the display of the RQBE window. Note that if a database has not been opened, the next box appearing will be a box listing available databases. If a database is already open, it is chosen by default. Select a database and choose Open. The RQBE window will appear, and you can define your query.

In brief, there are just a few basic steps to follow when creating queries:

1. Open the RQBE window, either by choosing New from the File menu and then choosing Query, or by entering **CREATE QUERY** from the command level.

2. Select the database(s) for use in the query. (If a database is already open, it is chosen by default.)

3. Specify any desired join conditions if you are opening two or more databases.

4. Select the fields you want to see in the results of the query.

5. If desired, change the order of the fields for results.

6. Select the desired destination for the results. (By default, the output is to a Browse window.)

7. Specify any selection criteria for the records.

8. Perform the query.

9. If desired, save the query for reuse later.

At the upper left of the RQBE window is a list box for databases to be used by the query, as shown in Figure 6-1. The upper-center portion of the window contains a list box named Output Fields. You will use this box to determine the fields that should be included in the results of the query. At the upper-right side of the window, the Output To pulldown menu is used to determine where the results of the query appear. By default, the results appear in a Browse window, but you can have them appear in the form of a printed report or store them as a new database file.

The lower portion of the window contains the Select Criteria area. In this area, you enter the conditions that limit the records provided by the query, such as "all employees living in Virginia" or "all employees with 0 dependents."

When the RQBE window is visible, a new menu pad, the RQBE menu, appears on the FoxPro menu bar. The RQBE menu contains the same options that are shown as selection buttons in the RQBE window. You can either select the desired button or choose the option from the menu. The various buttons and their equivalent RQBE menu options are discussed in the section that follows. Also included in this chapter are examples that use the sample database created in earlier chapters to demonstrate the use of the RQBE window.

Once you have chosen the desired options in the RQBE window, select the Do Query button at the right side of the window, and the query will be performed. Depending on your selection at the Output To menu, your results will either appear on the screen, be printed, or be stored in a new database file.

Choosing Databases for Use with the Query

If a database is already open when you open the RQBE window, that database name appears by default in the Databases list box. All of the fields of the database are listed by default in the Output Fields list box. You can specify additional

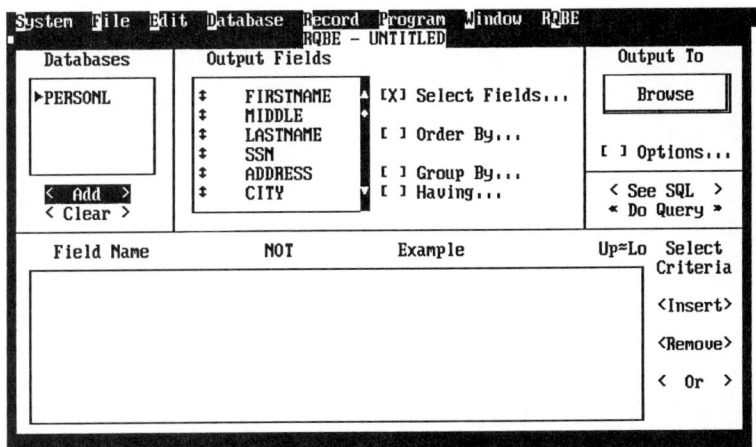

Figure 6-1. The RQBE window

databases for use with the same query; this is necessary when you need to perform a relational query. (The use of the RQBE window to perform relational queries is discussed in Chapter 10, "The Relational Powers of FoxPro.")

To select a database for use in the query, choose the Add button in the RQBE window or choose Add from the RQBE menu. When the Open File dialog box appears, choose the desired database from the list box and choose Open. The name of the database will then be added to the Databases list box in the RQBE window.

NOTE: Each time you open an additional database, the RQBE Join Condition dialog box appears. You can use this dialog box to specify the common fields that link multiple databases. See Chapter 10 for more on this topic.

Choosing Fields for the Query Results

By default, all fields of the first open database are selected as output of the query. You can control the fields made available in the query's results. To do so, choose the Select Fields button in the RQBE window or choose Fields from the RQBE menu. This causes the RQBE Select Fields dialog box to appear, allowing you to specify the desired fields. To add fields, select the desired field(s) in the Database Fields list box, then choose Move to move the chosen field(s) to the Selected Output list box. To remove field(s) from the query output, select the desired field(s) in the Selected Output list box, then choose Remove to remove the chosen fields from the query output. An example near the end of this chapter demonstrates the use of these techniques.

Choosing an Order for the Query Results

You can determine a sort order for the results of the query by choosing the Order By option or by choosing Order By in the RQBE menu. When you do this, the RQBE Order By dialog box appears, and you can specify the desired sort order for the records. Select a desired field in the Selected Output list box, choose the Ascending or Descending option, then choose Move to move the field name into the Ordering Criteria portion of the dialog box. You can repeat this step for additional fields; the first field chosen establishes the first level of sorting, the second field establishes the second level of sorting, and so on. Again, an example near the end of this chapter demonstrates the use of these techniques.

Grouping the Query Results

You can group the records in the query based on the values in a particular field. To do so, turn on the Group By option. This causes the RQBE Group By dialog box to be displayed, and you can then choose the field or fields that will control how the query results will be grouped. If you want to specify conditions that groups must meet before they are included in the results, turn on the Having option in the RQBE window, or choose Having from the RQBE menu. This causes the RQBE Search Conditions dialog box to appear. You can choose selection conditions for the groups in this dialog box by entering the desired conditions (such as **Age > 17** or **Lastname < "Mz"**).

Specifying the Output Destination

To control where the results of your query are sent, use the Output To popup in the RQBE window. This popup provides choices of Browse, Report/Label, Table/DBF, or Cursor. The default choice, Browse, causes the query results to appear in a Browse window. The Report/Label choice can be used to print the query results using a stored report file or label file. The Table/DBF option lets you store the query results in another database. The Cursor option lets you store the query results in a temporary database that you can then browse or base reports on. For more details on all of these options, see "Changing the Query Output" near the end of this chapter.

Sample RQBE Window Queries

If you've created the PERSONL database (first mentioned in Chapter 3, "Creating and Adding Information to Databases"), you can use it now to perform a few simple queries using the RQBE window. In the first example you'll select all employees living in the state of Virginia. Open the File menu with ALT-F and choose New. From the dialog box that appears, select Query and choose OK. Remember, if the PERSONL database has not been opened, the next box that appears will list available databases; choose PERSONL and then choose Open if this dialog box appears.

When the RQBE window appears, as seen previously in Figure 6-1, note that PERSONL appears in the Databases box. (Remember, any open database will appear by default.) Also, note that all fields in the personnel database appear by default in the Output Fields box. Later you'll learn how to change this, but for now, leave the field selection for this example.

At this point, you need to specify the selection criteria. To do so, tab to (or click on) the Field Name box and press ENTER; a menu of fields appears, as shown in Figure 6-2. To specify a field to control the selection criteria, simply pick the desired field from the menu of fields. In this case we are looking for all records for the state of Virginia, so choose PERSONL.STATE from the menu. When you do so, notice that the Like clause automatically appears beside the Field Name entry.

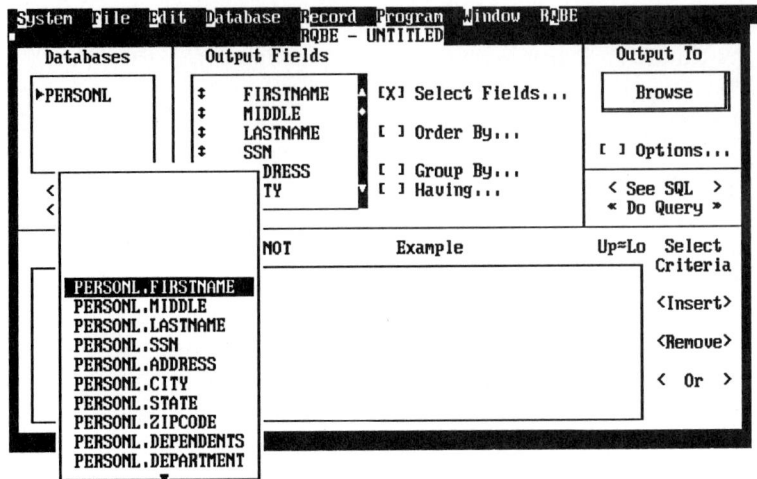

Figure 6-2. *A menu of fields in the RQBE window*

Move over to the Like entry column by pressing TAB. Pressing ENTER will reveal five other choices for refining your selection criteria: Exactly Like, More Than, Less Than, Between, and In. If you wish to specify the inverse of the condition (Not Like, Not Exactly Like, Not Less Than, etc.) simply move to the Not check box and press ENTER. This tells FoxPro to select every record that does not meet the specified criteria. For now, leave the Not check box blank and use the Like clause, since you want a selection criteria that identifies all employees in Virginia. Press ENTER to move to the Example column, and enter **VA** for the state of Virginia. At this point, your query should resemble the example shown in Figure 6-3.

To perform the query, tab to or click on the Do Query button at the right side of the window. Doing so causes a Browse window like the one in Figure 6-4 to appear, containing the names of only those employees residing in the state of Virginia. Press ESC to close the Browse window.

Examining the SELECT Command

To see the SELECT command generated by this query, press ESC to clear the Browse window, then tab to or click on the See SQL button above the Do Query button. You should see the following:

```
SELECT *;
    FROM PERSONL;
    WHERE PERSONL.STATE="VA";
    INTO CURSOR QUERY
BROWSE NOMODIFY PREFERENCE QUERY
```

The WHERE command tells FoxPro to select all records from the PERSONL database where the State field contains "VA". The INTO clause tells FoxPro to put the results of the query into a temporary database called CURSOR. After the SELECT command has been executed, the temporary database remains open. However, when this database is closed, it is deleted. The NOMODIFY option is used to prevent modification of the results of the query.

Examining the SQL command can help you become familiar with the SQL data retrieval language (which is the subject of a book in itself). It can be useful within FoxPro, because you can enter the same SQL command that you see into the Command window, and FoxPro will perform the same query. Within your programming, you can use SQL SELECT statements to retrieve desired data. Programming in FoxPro is detailed in Part II of this book.

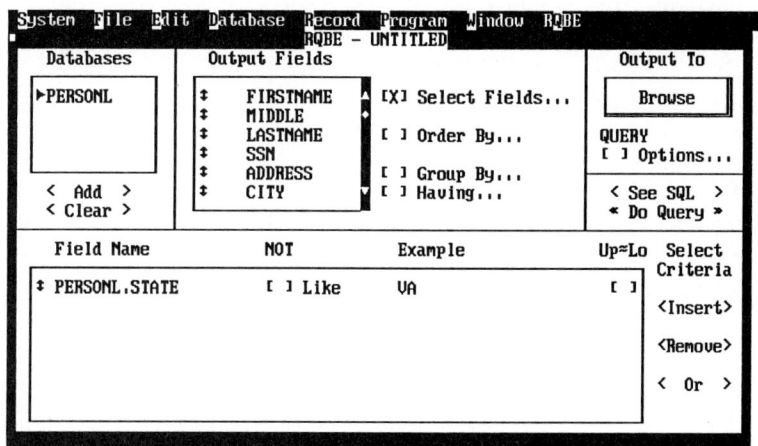

Figure 6-3. A sample query

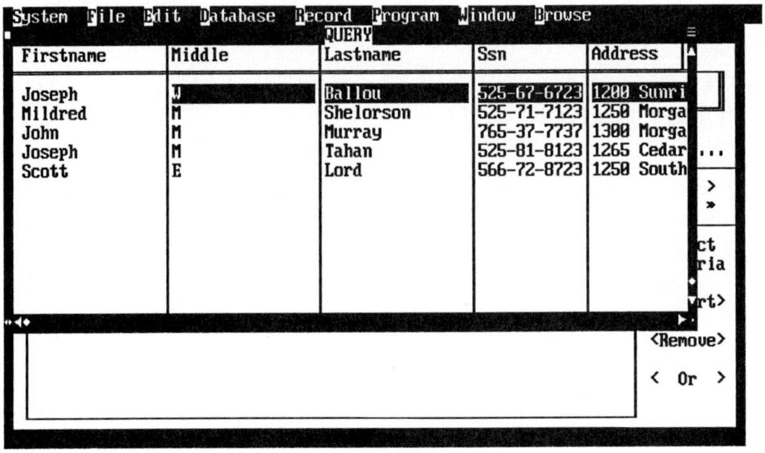

```
┌─────────────────────────────────────────────────────────────────┐
│ System  File  Edit  Database  Record  Program  Window  Browse     │
│                             QUERY                              ═   │
│ ┌──────────────┬──────────────┬─────────────┬──────────┬────────┐ │
│ │ Firstname    │ Middle       │ Lastname    │ Ssn      │ Address │ │
│ ├──────────────┼──────────────┼─────────────┼──────────┼────────┤ │
│ │ Joseph       │ J            │ Ballou      │525-67-6723│1200 Sunri│ │
│ │ Mildred      │ M            │ Shelorson   │525-71-7123│1250 Morga│ │
│ │ John         │ M            │ Murray      │765-37-7737│1300 Morga│ │
│ │ Joseph       │ M            │ Tahan       │525-81-8123│1265 Cedar│...│
│ │ Scott        │ E            │ Lord        │566-72-8723│1250 South│ │
│ │              │              │             │          │        │ > │
│ │              │              │             │          │        │ » │
│ │              │              │             │          │        │ct │
│ │              │              │             │          │        │ria│
│ │              │              │             │          │        │rt>│
│ └──────────────┴──────────────┴─────────────┴──────────┴────────┘ │
│                                                         <Remove>  │
│                                                         <  Or  >  │
└─────────────────────────────────────────────────────────────────┘
```

Figure 6-4.   *The results of a sample query in the Browse window*

Inserting and Removing Selection Criteria

There are two methods for removing the existing selection criteria:

1. Tab to or click on the Remove button to remove the selection criteria.

2. Highlight (by tabbing to or clicking on the field name) the selection criteria you wish to delete, and press DEL.

To insert multiple lines of selection criteria, use one of the following methods:

1. Tab to or click on the Insert button to insert the selection criteria.

2. Highlight (by tabbing to or clicking on the field name) the selection criteria, and press INS. This will open a blank line just above the highlighted selection.

Using Logical Operators in Queries

Chapter 5, "Performing Queries," discussed the use of *logical operators*, such as .NOT., .AND., and .OR., in queries. You can also use logical operators in the RQBE window to specify conditions for your queries.

The .AND. Condition

When you place multiple entries in the RQBE window, FoxPro assumes that a query based on an .AND. condition will be created; this is a query where all of the named conditions must prove true in order for the record to be in the results. As an example, let's narrow our search to all employees living in Reston, Virginia. Tab to the right side of the Selection Criteria box, and press ENTER to add a new row. Press ENTER again to display the list of fields. Choose PERSONL.CITY from the list, press TAB twice to move to the Example column, and enter **Reston**. Now let's examine the generated SELECT command by tabbing to the See SQL button and pressing ENTER. You should see the following:

```
SELECT *;
    FROM PERSONL;
    WHERE PERSONL.STATE="VA";
    AND PERSONL.CITY="Reston";
    INTO CURSOR QUERY
BROWSE NOMODIFY PREFERENCE QUERY
```

To perform this query, tab to the Do Query button and press ENTER. Your results should resemble those shown in Figure 6-5.

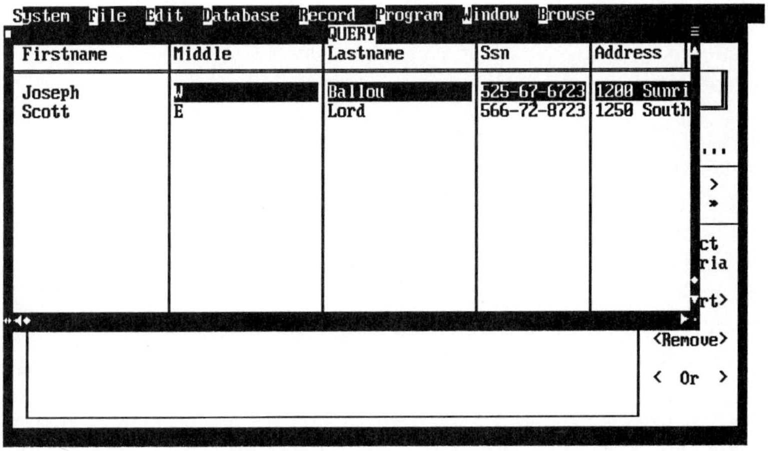

Figure 6-5. *A sample query using the .AND. condition*

The .OR. Condition

The RQBE window also makes the .OR. logical operator available to you. When you include .OR. in your query, only one of the named conditions has to prove true for the record to be included in the results. To illustrate this, let's add the .OR. clause to the existing selection criteria. Press ESC to clear the Browse window of the previous results.

To specify an .OR. condition you use the Or button in the lower-right side of the window. Click on the Or button or press the O key. In a moment, you should see a line with the designation "OR" appear under your existing selection criteria.

Next, with the cursor in the space below the Field Name box, press the ENTER key. Choose PERSONL.STATE from the list of fields, press TAB twice to move to the Example column, and enter **MD**. Now let's examine the generated SELECT command by tabbing to the See SQL button and pressing ENTER. You should see the following:

```
SELECT *;
    FROM PERSONL;
    WHERE PERSONL.STATE="VA";
    AND PERSONL.CITY="Reston";
    OR ( PERSONL.STATE="MD" );
     INTO CURSOR QUERY
BROWSE NOMODIFY PREFERENCE QUERY
```

To perform this query, press ESC to clear the window, then tab to the Do Query button and press ENTER. Your results should resemble those shown in Figure 6-6. Press ESC to clear the Browse window for the next example.

Using Date Ranges in Queries

It is also possible to create queries based on *date ranges*. For example, to see a list of all employees with a start date after 11/02/88, first clear all existing criteria by choosing Remove (click repeatedly on the Remove button, or press R repeatedly). Then, tab to or click on the Field Name area and press ENTER. Choose PERSONL.STARTDATE from the list of fields, tab to the column containing the Like entry, press ENTER, and choose More Than from the menu. In the Example column, enter **11/02/88**. Finally, choose Do Query. Your results should resemble those shown in Figure 6-7.

Specifying the Sort Order for Your Results

To specify the order in which your results appear, use the Order By button or select Order By from the RQBE menu. When you do this, a dialog box appears and you can select the field or fields that will control the order of your results. If

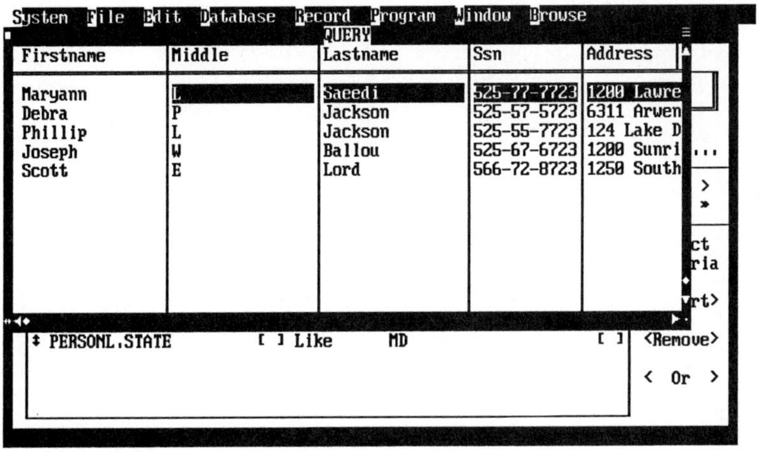

System File Edit Database Record Program Window Browse

		QUERY			

Firstname	Middle	Lastname	Ssn	Address	
Maryann	L	Saeedi	525-77-7723	1200 Laure	
Debra	P	Jackson	525-57-5723	6311 Arven	
Phillip	L	Jackson	525-55-7723	124 Lake D	
Joseph	W	Ballou	525-67-6723	1200 Sunri	...
Scott	E	Lord	566-72-8723	1250 South	

‡ PERSONL.STATE   [ ] Like   MD   [ ]   <Remove>

< Or >

Figure 6-6.   *A sample query using the .OR. condition*

you have been following the previous example, press ESC to clear the Browse window, open the RQBE menu with ALT-Q, and choose Order By. You will see the Order By dialog box, as shown in Figure 6-8.

Select the PERSONL.LASTNAME field in the Selected Output box at the left side of the screen (you can also highlight the field using the cursor keys followed

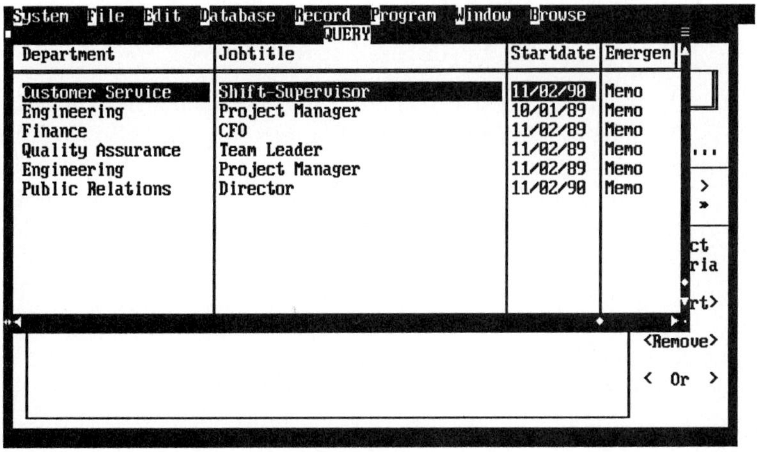

System File Edit Database Record Program Window Browse

		QUERY		

Department	Jobtitle	Startdate	Emergen	
Customer Service	Shift-Supervisor	11/02/90	Memo	
Engineering	Project Manager	10/01/89	Memo	
Finance	CFO	11/02/89	Memo	
Quality Assurance	Team Leader	11/02/89	Memo	...
Engineering	Project Manager	11/02/89	Memo	
Public Relations	Director	11/02/90	Memo	

<Remove>

< Or >

Figure 6-7.   *A sample query using a date range*

```
  System  File  Edit  Database  Record  Program  Window  RQBE
                            RQBE - UNTITLED
      Databases          Output Fields                    Output To
  ┌─────────┐     ┌────────────────────────■┐      ┌──────────────■┐
  │   ┌─────────────────────────────────────────────────────────────┐
  │   │  Selected Output                      Ordering Criteria      │
  │   │  ┌─────────────────────┐ ▲        ┌────────────────────────┐ │
  │   │  │ PERSONL.FIRSTNAME    │ ▲ ‹ Move → › │‡                   │ │
  │   │  │ PERSONL.MIDDLE       │ ●           ‡│                    │ │
  │   │  │ PERSONL.LASTNAME     │   ‹ Remove › ‡│                   │ │
  │   │  │ PERSONL.SSN          │             ‡│                    │ │
  │   │  │ PERSONL.ADDRESS      │ ┌ Order Options ┐ ‡│              │ │
  │   │  │ PERSONL.CITY         │ (•) Ascending   ‡│               │ │
  │   │  │ PERSONL.STATE        │ ( ) Descending  ‡│               │ │
  │   │  │ PERSONL.ZIPCODE      │             ‡│                    │ │
  │   │  │ PERSONL.DEPENDENTS   │             ‡│                    │ │
  │   │  │ PERSONL.DEPARTMENT   │   «  OK  »   ‡│                    │ │
  │   │  │ PERSONL.JOBTITLE     │             ‡│                    │ │
  │   │  │ PERSONL.STARTDATE    │ ▼ ‹ Cancel › ‡│                   │ │
  │   │  └─────────────────────┘         └────────────────────────┘ │
  │   └─────────────────────────────────────────────────────────────┘
```

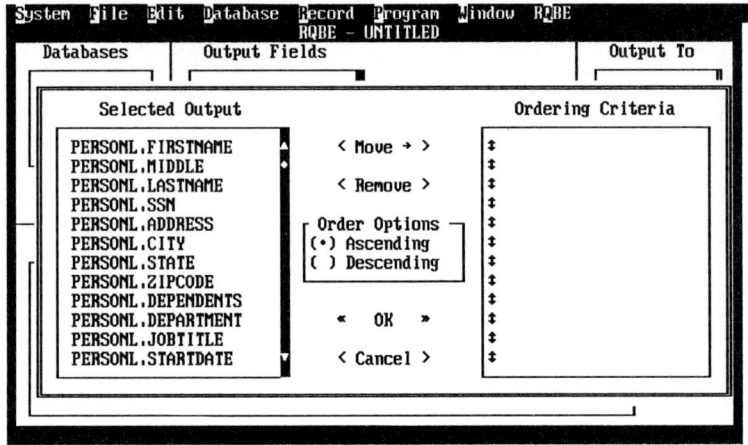

Figure 6-8. *The Order By dialog box*

by ENTER, or you can click on the field name and then click the Move button). PERSONL.LASTNAME will appear in the Ordering Criteria box on the right side of the screen.

Tab to or click on the OK button. When the Order By dialog box disappears, choose Do Query from the RQBE window to display the results in the Browse window. The records are displayed in alphabetical order by last name.

Creating Queries Using Selected Fields

To create queries based on selected fields, choose Fields from the RQBE menu, or click on the Select Fields button. A dialog box appears, allowing you to add or remove fields that will appear in the results. For example if you want to display the first and last names of all employees living in Virginia, open the RQBE menu using ALT-Q and choose Fields from the menu. A dialog box appears showing fields selected for output, as shown in Figure 6-9.

Remove all selected fields from the right side of the dialog box by pressing L. Next, tab to or click on PERSONL.LASTNAME in the Database Fields box and press ENTER to move the field to the Selected Output box. Repeat this step to move the PERSONL.FIRSTNAME field to the Selected Output box also. Finally, tab to or click on OK and choose Do Query. The resulting Browse window will display only the selected fields.

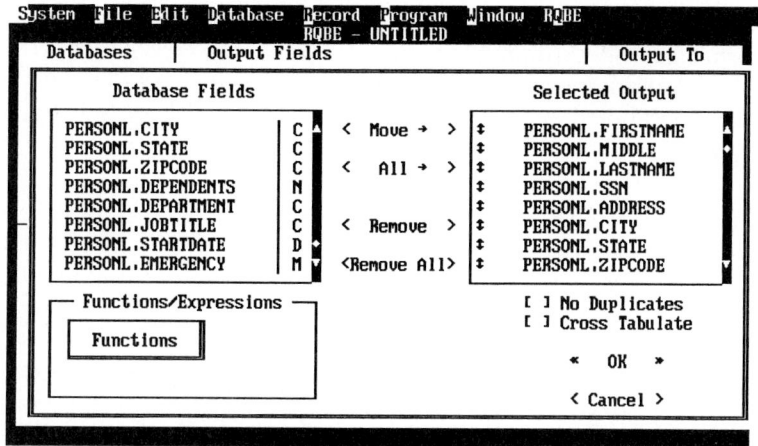

Figure 6-9. *Fields selected for output*

Changing the Query Output

While it is often helpful to see the results of a query in the form of a Browse window, there will probably be times when you want to get your query results in other forms. The popup menu in the Output To area (at the upper-right corner of the RQBE window) lets you specify the output of a query; by default, this is set to Browse.

When you tab to or click on the Output To popup, it displays these options: Browse, Report/Label, Table/DBF, and Cursor. You can choose the desired option from this list.

- Use Browse to display the results in a Browse window, as the examples in this chapter have demonstrated.

- Use Report/Label to send the data to the screen or the printer in the form of a report.

- Use the Table/DBF option to store the results of the query to another database file. When you choose this option, an Open File dialog box appears, and you can select an existing database where the results should be stored from the list box, or you can enter a name for a new database file.

- Use the Cursor choice to store the results in a temporary database. The database appears in the View window, and you can use the temporary database for browsing or reporting as desired. Once you close the temporary database, it no longer exists. If you want to store the results of the query permanently, use the Table/DBF option rather than the Cursor option.

The Report/Label choice offers a wide range of options regarding the query's output. You can send the query results to the screen in report form, or to the printer as a report or as mailing labels. Choose Report/Label from the Output To list box and then choose Options. This causes the RQBE Display Options dialog box to appear, as shown in Figure 6-10.

The Formatting Options box in the dialog box has Screen Display chosen as a default; if you leave this choice selected, the query's output is sent directly to the screen in a simple columnar format. Change this selection to Report to have your query output in the form of a stored report. Change the selected option to Label to generate mailing labels using the query. (See Chapter 7 for information on designing reports, and Chapter 8 for information on designing mailing labels.)

In the Output Destinations box, you can specify additional output options. Check the To Printer box to send the results to the default printer port. Check the To File box to send the results to an ASCII disk file. If you turn on the To

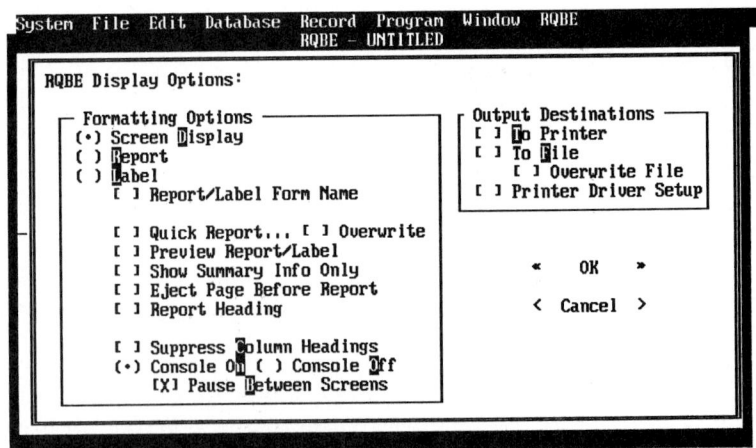

```
 System  File  Edit  Database  Record  Program  Window  RQBE
                          RQBE - UNTITLED

 ┌──────────────────────────────────────────────────────────────┐
 │  RQBE Display Options:                                        │
 │  ┌─ Formatting Options ─────┐    ┌─ Output Destinations ─┐    │
 │  │ (•) Screen Display       │    │ [ ] To Printer        │    │
 │  │ ( ) Report               │    │ [ ] To File           │    │
 │  │ ( ) Label                │    │    [ ] Overwrite File  │    │
 │  │     [ ] Report/Label Form Name  │ [ ] Printer Driver Setup │ │
 │  │                                                            │
 │  │     [ ] Quick Report... [ ] Overwrite                      │
 │  │     [ ] Preview Report/Label                               │
 │  │     [ ] Show Summary Info Only        «    OK    »         │
 │  │     [ ] Eject Page Before Report                           │
 │  │     [ ] Report Heading                <  Cancel  >         │
 │  │                                                            │
 │  │     [ ] Suppress Column Headings                           │
 │  │     (•) Console On ( ) Console Off                         │
 │  │         [X] Pause Between Screens                          │
 │  └────────────────────────────────────────────────────────┘  │
 └──────────────────────────────────────────────────────────────┘
```

Figure 6-10.   *The RQBE Display Options dialog box*

File option, you can also turn on the Overwrite File option. If the file exists and Overwrite File is turned on, the existing file is overwritten; otherwise, the query output is added to the end of the existing file.

The remaining options within the Format Options dialog box further refine your selection:

- Report/Label Form Name is available when you choose Report or Label under Formatting Options. Checking Report/Label Form Name causes the Open File dialog box to be displayed, so you can either choose an existing report or label file or enter the name for a new report file or label file.

- Quick Report is available when you choose Report and specify a new report using the Report/Label Form Name check box. When you choose Quick Report, the Quick Report dialog box appears (see Chapter 7), and you can choose the desired options for the report's design.

- Overwrite is available when you choose Quick Report. Selecting the Overwrite option will cause any existing report with the same name to be overwritten by the new report design.

- Preview Report/Label is available when you select Report or Label under Formatting Options. If you select Preview Report/Label, a visual representation of the report or label is sent to the screen, based on the query's output. If you later want to print the report or the labels, you must turn off this option and again select Do Query.

- Show Summary Info Only is available when you choose Report under Formatting Options. If this option is turned on, detail lines are omitted from the report; only summary lines appear.

- Eject Page Before Report is available when you choose Report under Formatting Options. If this option is turned on, a page eject (form feed code) is sent to the printer before the report begins printing.

- Report Heading is available when you choose Report under Formatting Options. If this option is turned on, you can specify an additional heading, one line in length, to be added to the report. When you choose Report Heading, the Expression Builder appears. You can then enter the heading in the window of the Expression Builder and choose OK.

- Suppress Column Headings is available when you choose Screen Display or Report under Formatting Options. If this option is turned on, headings are omitted from the screen display or from the report.

- Console On and Console Off determine whether output appears on the screen. If Console On is chosen, output appears on the screen. If Console Off is chosen, output does not appear.

- Pause Between Screens is available only if Screen Display is chosen under Formatting Options. By default, the option will be turned on, causing FoxPro to pause after each screen of data. If you turn off this option, FoxPro will display the data continuously on screen without pausing.

Saving and Reusing Queries

You can save your queries for later use under FoxPro in one of two ways. You can choose Save As from the File menu and enter a name for the query when prompted, or while you are in the RQBE window you can press ESC or click on the Close box. If you have made any changes while in the RQBE window, FoxPro always asks if you want to save the query before exiting.

For example, if the RQBE window is still open on your screen, press ESC now. The following prompt appears.

```
Do you want to save changes to
C:\FOXPRO\DATA\UNTITLED.QPR?

<Yes>        <No>        <Cancel>
```

If you choose Yes, another dialog box appears, prompting you for the name of the query file. (Queries are saved with an extension of .QPR.) If you choose No, the current query is discarded without being saved. If you choose Cancel, you are returned to the RQBE window. For now, choose Yes and enter **QSAMPLE** for the query name.

Reusing Saved Queries

To reuse a stored query, from the Command window use the command,

DO *queryname*.QPR

where *queryname* is the name of the stored query file. For example, you could repeat the results of the query you just stored by entering **DO QSAMPLE.QPR** in the Command window.

To modify an existing query, you can use the command,

MODIFY QUERY *queryname*.QPR

where *queryname* is the name of the stored query that you want to modify. Upon entering the command, the existing query will appear in the RQBE window. You can make any desired changes to the query, and save it (with the same name or a different name) using the Save As option from the File menu.

Chapter 7

Reports

Generating reports is one of the most frequent operations performed with a database. In this chapter we'll focus on techniques for creating, modifying, and printing reports. This will include a detailed discussion of FoxReport, FoxPro's Report Generator. As in previous chapters, we will also cover methods for producing reports from the command level.

The Report Creation Process

The process of creating a report in FoxPro involves defining how the report will look and saving this definition to a file. You can do this using FoxPro's Report Generator (FoxReport), an integrated feature of FoxPro. The report you design can be stored to a file, which is given an .FRX extension when saved.

Before starting the Report Generator it is important to establish the environment necessary to create the report. This involves opening all relevant databases and index files. Before going into greater detail about the Report Generator, let's consider the various types of reports that can be created.

Types of Reports

There are two basic types of reports that can be produced with the Report Generator: quick reports and customized reports. When you create a quick report there are only a few decisions to make. You select the format for the report, the fields to be displayed, and an optional title.

When you have a special format in mind, a customized report is what you want. FoxPro offers a variety of tools for creating and customizing reports to fit your needs. The following sections discuss both reports in greater detail.

Quick Reports

You can create reports from the command level with the CREATE REPORT command. The format for the command is

CREATE REPORT *filename*

This can also be done from the menu by opening the File menu and choosing New. When the dialog box appears, select Report as the file type. When you do so, FoxPro adds the Report menu to the right of the Window menu. Also, a special window for defining the report layout is displayed, as shown in Figure 7-1. This window will be discussed in greater detail later in the chapter; for now, open the Report menu with ALT-O and choose Quick Report.

The Quick Report dialog box now appears. One of the first decisions to be made concerns the format of your report. The dialog box offers two choices: Column and Form. A report displayed in a *columnar format* usually contains data

Figure 7-1. *The Report Layout window*

for each specified field arranged in columns, with an optional title for each column. The following is an example of a report in a columnar format.

Lastname	Firstname	State	Dependents
Saeedi	Maryann	MD	1
Jackson	Debra	MD	0
Jackson	Phillip	MD	2
Ballou	Joseph	VA	2
Shelorson	Mildred	VA	2
Murray	John	VA	2
Tahan	Joseph	VA	0
Lord	Scott	VA	1

The second choice (Form) produces a report that resembles a paper-based form, with field names displayed to the left of the contents of the fields. Here is an example of the form format.

```
Firstname:    Maryann
Lastname:     Saeedi
State:        MD
Dependents:   1

Firstname:    Debra
Lastname:     Jackson
State:        MD
Dependents:   0

Firstname:    Phillip
Lastname:     Jackson
State:        MD
Dependents:   2

Firstname:    Joseph
Lastname:     Ballou
State:        VA
Dependents:   2

Firstname:    Mildred
Lastname:     Shelorson
State:        VA
Dependents:   2
```

```
Firstname:    John
Lastname:     Murray
State:        VA
Dependents:   2

Firstname:    Joseph
Lastname:     Tahan
State:        VA
Dependents:   0

Firstname:    Scott
Lastname:     Lord
State:        VA
Dependents:   1
```

Use the Titles option when you want to include a title for each field name. When you use the form format, the title is placed to the left of the field. When the columnar format is in use, the title appears at the top of the field.

Use the Fields option to specify the fields to be included in the report. If you do not use this option, FoxPro includes all the fields in the database in the report. Select the OK button, choose Save from the File menu or press CTRL-W, and enter the name of the report in the dialog box that appears next. Exit the Report Generator by choosing Close from the File menu, and the stored report is ready for use.

When you produce a quick report containing selected fields, one or more columns of data may be cut off at the right margin. You can solve this problem by changing field widths or moving the locations of columns in a customized report. The right margin is set at 80, so you can't fit more data in the report by printing in compressed mode or using wider paper. You can, however, change the right margin, as detailed later in this chapter. If you don't want all the fields in the report, another way to obtain a quick report with the selected fields you desire is to use the SET FIELDS command. Briefly, the syntax of this command is

SET FIELDS TO *field1*, *field2*, *field3*,...*fieldn*

The command makes the database appear to have only those fields that you specify in the list of fields. Therefore, if you wanted a quick report of the Personnel database with only the name, city, state, and starting-date fields included, you could first open the database and use the command

```
SET FIELDS TO Lastname, Firstname, City, State, Startdate
```

and then proceed to create and save the report. The report would contain only the fields of your choice. After creating the report, you can make the rest of the fields available for use again by closing and reopening the database or by entering **SET FIELDS TO ALL** without any list of fields after the command.

A Sample Quick Report

You can see how a quick report can be designed, using the sample personnel database, by performing the following steps.

1. From the Command window, type **USE PERSONL** to open the personnel database.

2. Type **CREATE REPORT** in the Command window or choose New from the File menu, choose Report, and choose OK.

3. When the Report Layout window appears, open the Report menu with ALT-O.

4. Choose Quick Report from the menu.

5. In the Quick Report dialog box, choose Form Layout by pressing F.

6. Choose OK. The field names and field masks will appear in the detail area of the Report Layout window.

7. Open the File menu with ALT-F and choose Save. When prompted for a name for the file, type **RSAMPLE1**. Then choose Save from the dialog box to save the report. If asked whether you want to save the environment information, answer Yes to the prompt. (When you save a report with FoxPro 2 or later, FoxPro automatically saves the current environment, or a record of the open database, index files, and any filter in effect.)

8. Press ESC to close the Report Layout window.

9. From the Command window, enter

```
REPORT FORM RSAMPLE1
```

to see the report on the screen. You could enter **REPORT FORM RSAMPLE1 TO PRINT** to cause the report to be printed (using the default printer port). The REPORT FORM command is detailed later in this chapter.

HINT: If you are using the RQBE window to design a query that will produce a report, be sure to design and save the report before designing and implementing the query.

Customized Reports

There are times when you need to create reports with special formats. This may require placing fields in various locations, adding custom headers and footers, and changing formatting attributes. FoxPro offers formatting features that go well beyond those offered for doing quick reports. Depending on how complex your needs are, the precise steps involved in the report's design will vary in complexity. In the following sections, we'll examine some of the tools provided by FoxPro for customizing reports.

Examining the Report Layout Window

One of the most important features of the Report Generator is the Report Layout window, in which you design the layout for your report. Open the File menu now, and select New. Choose Report as the file type from the dialog box that appears next. (An alternate method for starting the process is to enter **CREATE REPORT** *filename*.) At this point you are presented with the Report Layout window (shown earlier in Figure 7-1).

The Report Layout window contains a status line at the top. Cursor movement is tracked using the Row (R:) and Column (C:) indicators in the upper-left corner. The box next to the column indicator displays the current action being performed. The last box on the status line displays the area in the window that the cursor is on. Something else that you'll notice is the addition of the Report menu.

Another feature of the Report Layout window consists of the three major sections within the window. These are called *bands*, and they identify placement areas for specific types of information. Within these bands you can place fields, text, and simple graphics, such as boxes. The page header (PgHead) and page footer (PgFoot) are used to place information that will appear at the top and bottom of every page of the report. You use the Detail band to show how data will be displayed for each record. The page header and page footer bands are optional.

There are three additional bands that are also optional: Title, Summary, and Group. Information contained in the Title band is displayed once for the entire report. The Summary band is also displayed only once and is used to summarize the data in your report; it can include totals, averages, or even a concluding paragraph. You'll find the Group band useful because it gives you the ability to display your data in specific groups, with corresponding headers and footers for each group. Figure 7-2 shows an example of a Report Layout window with bands.

You can display bands of information, such as Title and Summary, on a separate page. It is also possible to display groupings of data on separate pages. Lines can be added or deleted from the bands using the Report menu. A band can contain as many lines as you wish, up to the limit of 255 lines for the entire report. Remember that the Report Layout window, like other windows in FoxPro, can be manipulated (resized, moved, and scrolled through).

```
System  File  Edit  Database  Record  Program  Window  Report
                              CELLAR.FRX
R:  0 C:  0 ‖  Move ‖   Page Header ‖
PgHead
PgHead
PgHead                           Eduardo's Wine List
PgHead
Detail
Detail   Winery     winery
Detail   Type       type
Detail   Flavor     flavor
Detail   Origin     origin
Detail   Dpurch     dpurch
Detail   Rating     r
Detail   Dcork      dcork
Detail   Cost       cost
Detail   Pvalue     pvalue
Detail   Comments   comments
PgFoot
PgFoot
PgFoot
PgFoot   DATE()
```

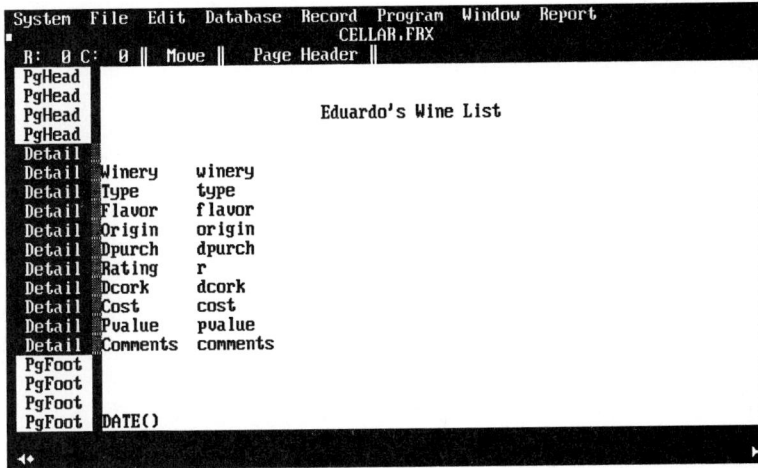

Figure 7-2. An example of a report layout

Manipulating Objects in the Report Layout Window

Anything entered into the Report Layout window is considered an *object* by
FoxPro. These objects can be selected, moved, and deleted. The following are
some techniques for doing this using the keyboard and the mouse.

- To delete an object, select the object by placing the cursor anywhere on
  the object and pressing the SPACEBAR, then DEL. (If you're using a mouse,
  click on the object to select it.) Then, press DEL or open the Edit menu with
  ALT-E, and choose Cut from the menu to delete the object.

- To move an object, place the cursor anywhere on the desired object and
  press the SPACEBAR to select the object. Once selected, the object will appear
  highlighted. Use the cursor keys to move the object to its new location,
  and press ENTER to complete the movement. Mouse users can simply click
  and drag the desired object to its new location.

*NOTE: An alternative method for moving objects is provided with the Cut and
Paste options on the Edit menu. Place the cursor anywhere within the object and
press the SPACEBAR to select it. (If you're using a mouse, click on the object to select
it.) Next, choose Cut from the Edit menu to remove the object from its existing
location. Then place the cursor at the new location and choose Paste from the Edit menu
to insert the object at the new location. (The Paste option of the Edit menu always inserts
whatever was last deleted with the Cut option or copied by the Copy option.)*

- To copy an object, select the object by placing the cursor anywhere on the object and pressing the SPACEBAR; then choose Copy from the Edit menu. Place the cursor where the duplicate of the object is to appear, and choose Paste from the Edit menu.

The Report Menu Options

The Report menu contains options that give you the ability to add, rearrange, or move fields; add new lines; add boxes or text; and in general change the layout and/or format of the report. If you press ALT-O while the Report Layout window is visible, the Report menu will open, as shown in Figure 7-3.

Page Layout

The Page Layout option lets you change specifications that affect the layout of the printed page. When you choose this option, the Page Layout dialog box, shown in Figure 7-4, appears. Use the Page length option to change the length of the printed page. The default value of 60 allows 6 blank lines at the end of a normal 8 1/2 x 11-inch sheet of paper. Legal-size (14-inch) paper works well with a setting of 82. For the various European paper sizes, you may need to experiment to obtain the best results.

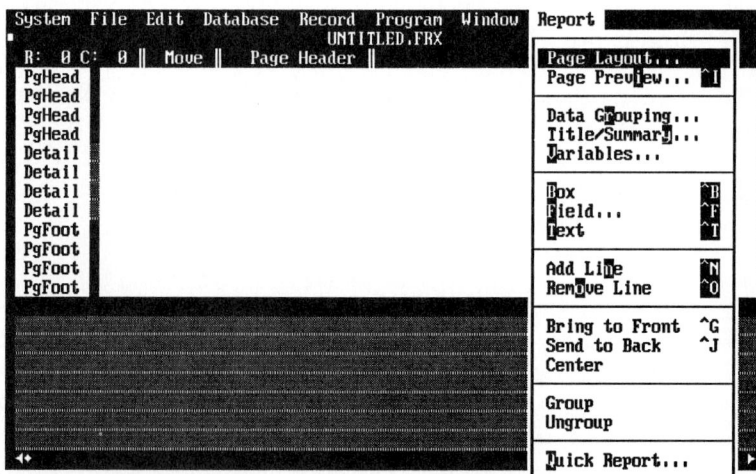

Figure 7-3.   *The Report menu*

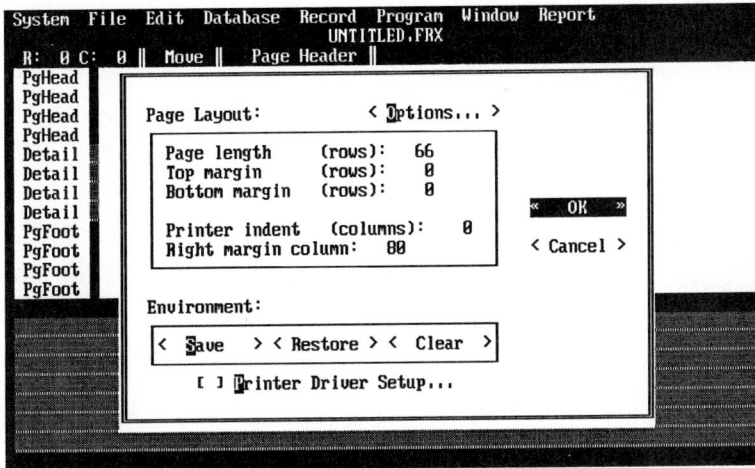

Figure 7-4. *The Page Layout dialog box*

The Top margin option lets you specify a top margin, or the number of lines down from the top edge where printing will begin. Laser printer users should note that this will be in addition to the default top margin set internally by your printer; see your printer manual for details on the printer's default top margin.

In a similar fashion, the Bottom margin option provides a setting for a bottom margin, or number of lines up from the bottom edge. Data will not appear beyond this setting.

The Printer indent option lets you enter a number of spaces by which all data in the report should be indented.

The Right margin column option lets you specify a number for the right margin. This is particularly useful with printers that allow compressed print. When using the compressed-print mode of most dot matrix printers, you can enter **132** as a margin when using 8 1/2-inch-wide paper, and you can enter **240** as a margin when using the larger computer fanfold paper. Once all your desired options have been entered, select the OK button to exit the dialog box.

Page Preview

This option lets you see what a report will look like, before saving the report and exiting the Report Generator. After laying out the desired fields and other data, choose Page Preview from the Report menu, and a visual representation of the printed report, shown in Figure 7-5, will appear on the screen. Two options, Done and More, appear at the bottom of the screen. Choose More to view successive pages of the report (if there are any). Choose Done to exit back to the Report Layout window. This option is quite useful for checking your design; you

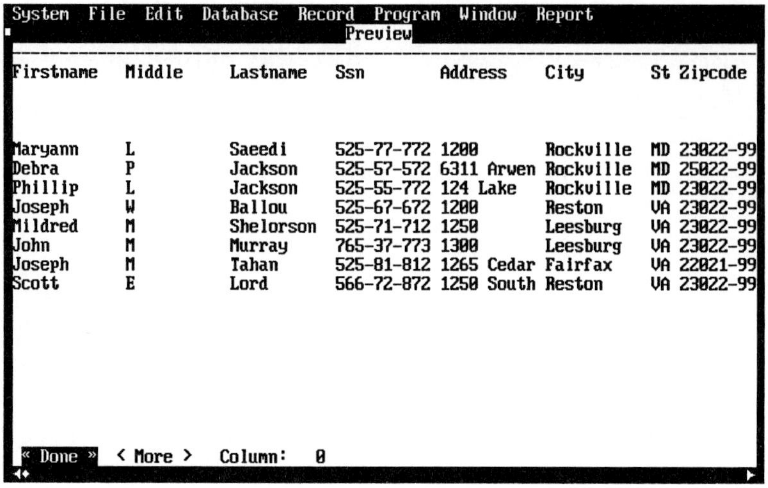

```
 System  File  Edit  Database  Record  Program  Window  Report
                              Preview
 Firstname   Middle    Lastname    Ssn          Address     City        St Zipcode


 Maryann     L         Saeedi      525-77-772 1200          Rockville   MD 23822-99
 Debra       P         Jackson     525-57-572 6311 Arwen    Rockville   MD 25822-99
 Phillip     L         Jackson     525-55-772 124 Lake      Rockville   MD 23822-99
 Joseph      W         Ballou      525-67-672 1200          Reston      VA 23822-99
 Mildred     M         Shelorson   525-71-712 1250          Leesburg    VA 23822-99
 John        M         Murray      765-37-773 1300          Leesburg    VA 23822-99
 Joseph      M         Tahan       525-81-812 1265 Cedar    Fairfax     VA 22821-99
 Scott       E         Lord        566-72-872 1250 South    Reston      VA 23822-99







 « Done »   < More >   Column:    0
```

Figure 7-5.   *An example of Page Preview*

can go back into the Report Layout window, make changes to the report, and try Page Preview again until you are satisfied with the design of the report.

Data Grouping

You can use the various group options of the Report menu to work with groupings of records within a report. Most likely, you will need to arrange reports broken down by groups. For example, you might like to see all employees divided into groups by state of residence. By utilizing the ' Data Grouping option of the Report menu, you can define multiple levels of grouping.

While many more than three levels of groups may seem like overkill to some, it is nice to know that FoxPro is accommodating when you must base a complex report on a large number of subgroups. Multiple groupings can be quite common in business applications. In something as simple as a national mailing list, for example, you might need to see records by groups of states; within each state, grouped by city; and within each city, grouped by ZIP code. That represents three levels of grouping alone. Cut the data in the table more specifically, such as by income levels, and you can quickly come to appreciate FoxPro's ability to perform effective grouping.

When you choose the Data Grouping option from the Report menu while designing a report, the Group dialog box seen in Figure 7-6 is displayed.

Use the Add, Change, or Delete button to add, change, or delete group bands from a report. When you choose Add, you then see the Group Info dialog

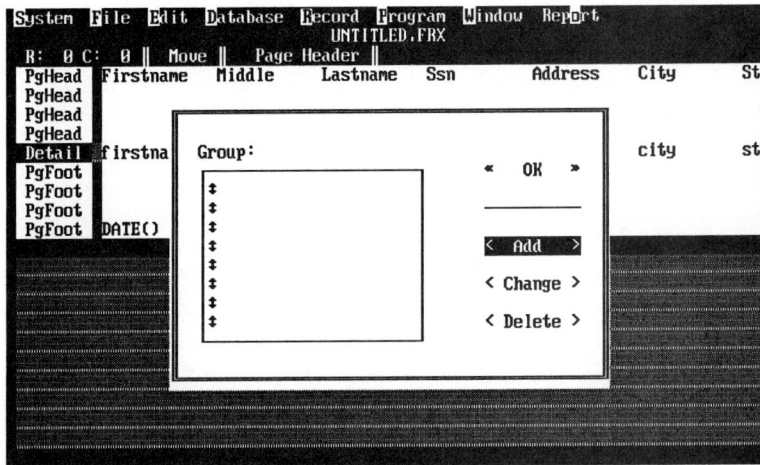

Figure 7-6. *The Group dialog box*

box, shown in Figure 7-7. You can use this dialog box to enter a field name (or other expression) to base your group on.

If you want to establish the group by field name (such as groups of records from the same state or with the same assignment), you would enter the name of that field. You can also group records based on a valid FoxPro expression. As an

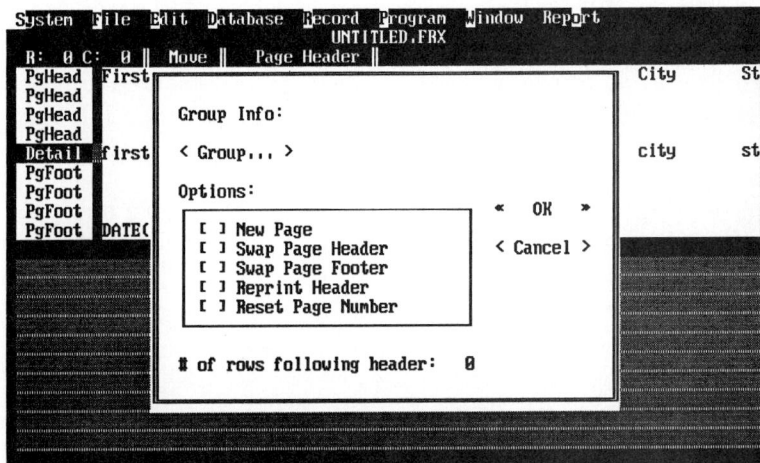

Figure 7-7. *The Group Info dialog box*

example, if you were using an index based on a combination of Lastname + Firstname to control the order of records, you could enter the expression **Lastname + Firstname** to define the grouping. Once you add a group band, you can then enter desired text or fields into that band within the report specification. After selecting the desired type of grouping, FoxPro will insert a new starting Group Band and a new ending Group Band for the group. Group bands must fall outside of the Detail Bands.

The Swap Page Header option tells FoxPro to place group headers instead of page headers on all pages where the group header appears. The Swap Page Footer option does the same for footers. When chosen, each page containing a group footer prints the group footer at the bottom of the page in place of the page footer.

Once you've placed the desired group, you can check to see if the results are what you desire by pressing ALT-O from the Report menu and choosing Page Preview from the menu. The resulting report will be divided by group. Note that the file must be sorted or indexed on the field you are grouping by to get the records in the proper group order; you may need to save the report, index, or sort the file from the menus or at the command level and then run the report. When you are satisfied with the results, save the report specification by pressing CTRL-W.

REMINDER: *You must create or activate an index or sort the file before a report containing groups will print properly. If the report will be generated as part of a query in the RQBE window, you can use the Order By option of the RQBE window to add a sort order to the file.*

Title/Summary

This option lets you add Title bands or Summary bands to a report. When you choose this option, the Title/Summary dialog box shown in Figure 7-8 appears. You can check the desired boxes that affect both the Title band and Summary band. Selecting Title Band adds the Title band, while selecting Summary Band adds the Summary band. The bands, once added, are empty; you must add any desired text or fields to the bands.

The New Page option tells FoxPro to start the band on a new page. Once you check the desired boxes and choose OK, you are returned to the Report Layout window.

Box

Selecting this option from the Report menu causes another menu to be displayed, offering a choice of Single, Double, or Char(acter) boxes. You can add boxes composed of a single line, a double line, or another character you select.

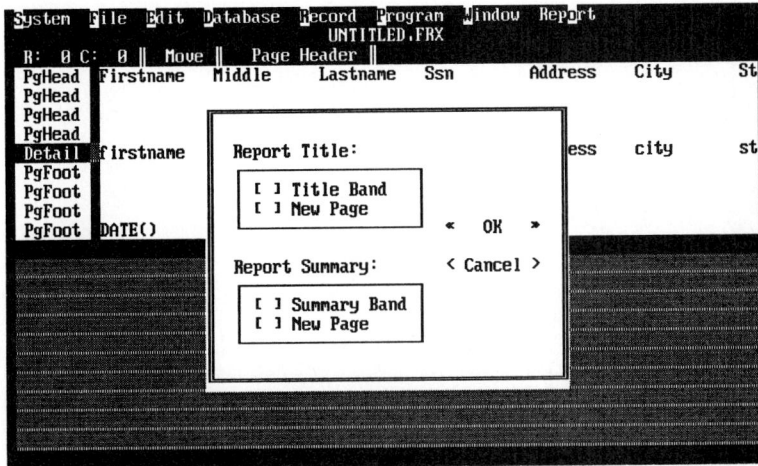

Figure 7-8. *The Title/Summary dialog box*

If you choose Char, a pulldown menu appears displaying all possible characters. Keyboard users can move the cursor to the upper-left corner for the box, choose Box from the Report menu, and select the box type, stretch the box with the cursor keys, and press ENTER to complete the box. Mouse users can select the desired type of box, then click at the upper-left or upper-right corner of the box and drag to the desired diagonal corner.

Field

Use this option of the Report menu (or its shortcut key, CTRL-F) to place fields at the cursor location or to place expressions (such as combinations of fields or calculations based on fields) at the cursor location. Choosing Field from the menu causes the Report Expression dialog box shown in Figure 7-9 to be displayed.

In the Report Expression box, you enter the name of the field or expression that you want to place at the cursor location. If you need help in building the expression, tab to < Expr... > and press ENTER to bring up the Expression Builder. You can enter a calculation based on a field as an expression. An example, in the case of a numeric field named Cost, might be

```
COST*.06
```

which would result in a "sales tax" figure that is 6 percent of the value contained in the Cost field.

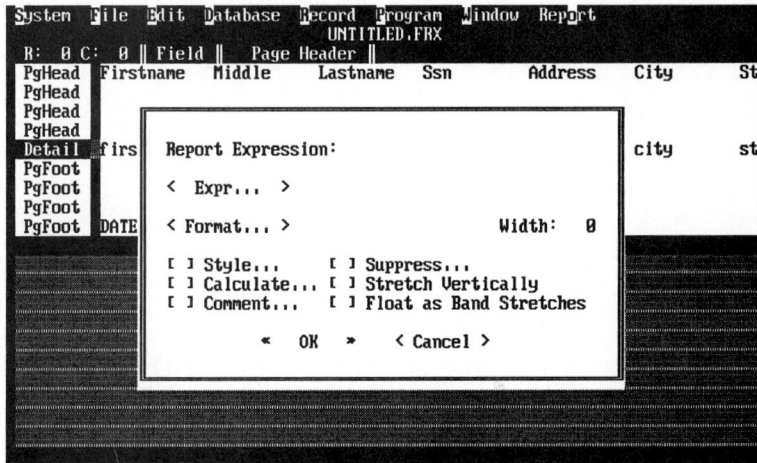

Figure 7-9. *The Report Expression dialog box*

Text

This option of the Report menu is used to add text to the report. The added
items will then appear in the report in accordance with the band where you add
them. For example, adding text in the Detail band will cause it to appear once for
each record of the report; adding an item in the PgHead band will cause it to
appear once each time the page header prints, and so on.

Add and Remove Line

Use the Add Line option to add lines to the bands in the layout window.
Remember, you can add as many lines as you want; as long as the total number
of lines for the report does not exceed 225. The new line will be added just before
the current position of the cursor. Use the Remove Line option to delete the line
that the cursor is located on. If the line is not empty, FoxPro will prompt you
before deleting the line.

Bring to Front and Send to Back

These options are used when, for one reason or another, you choose to overlay
one object (such as a box) with another object (such as a field). For example, it is
possible to drag a field so it partially covers a box or a title you have entered as

text. If you then select one of the objects (such as the text) with the TAB key and choose Bring to Front from the Report menu, the selected object appears over the object it partially covers. If you select Send to Back, the selected object is placed under the other object. You may find these options useful when combining text labels and boxes. For example, you might type a few words as a descriptive label and later add a box whose position covers the label. By selecting the box and choosing Send to Back from the Report menu, the text would overlay the box.

Center

This option allows you to center an object between the left and right edges of the report.

Quick Report

This option provides an immediate report based on either a columnar or a form layout, as detailed earlier in this chapter.

The Report Expression Dialog Box

When you position the cursor within an expression or field located in the Detail band and press Enter, the Report Expression dialog box appears. When you select < Format... >, you can press ENTER to display the Format dialog box, shown in Figure 7-10. This provides various formatting options, which you can select by checking the boxes. One of the Character, Numeric, Date, and Logical options will be chosen based on the field type; however, if your field is based around an expression, you may want to change this option according to your preference. The list of available formatting options that you see will vary, depending on the data type. The Editing Options may be checked according to your wishes for that field.

Tables 7-1, 7-2, and 7-3 show the various formatting options. Once you choose the desired options and select the OK button, the Report Expression dialog box reappears.

In the Width box of the Report Expression dialog box, you can enter a maximum width for the field. This is useful if you have a long field and you want to restrict its length in a particular report.

The Style option, when chosen, displays another dialog box with choices for any of eight printing styles: normal, bold, italic, underline, superscript, subscript, condensed, and double. Choose any of these styles by checking the desired box

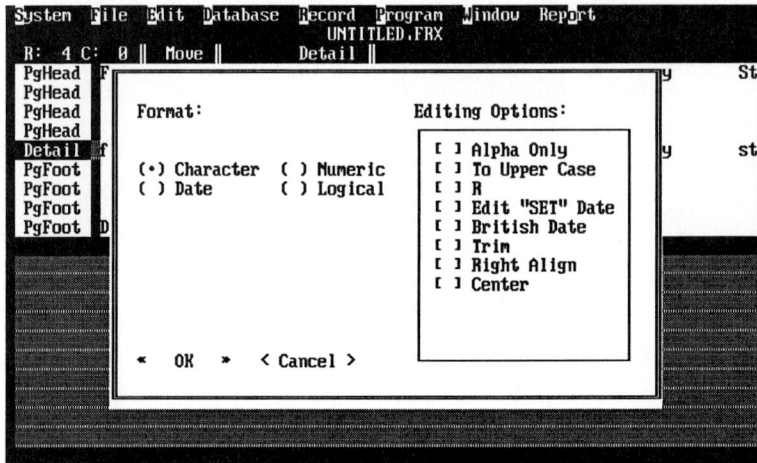

Figure 7-10.   *The Format dialog box*

and selecting OK. You can choose more than one option at a time. (Note that your printer must support the chosen options.)

The Stretch Vertically option of the Report Expression dialog box lets you stretch the contents of a long character field or a memo field vertically. This permits the wrapping of text past more than one line in the report, which makes this option quite useful with memo fields. If you do not select this option, a memo field placed in a report will not take more than one line per record printed—any excess text gets cut off when the field ends at the width you specify. If you select the Stretch Vertically option, FoxPro will take as many lines as are necessary to print the complete contents of the memo or character field.

Option	Action
Alpha Only	Permits only alphabetic characters
To Upper Case	Converts all characters to uppercase
R	Displays but does not store characters
Edit "SET" Date	Prints data as date in the current SET DATE format
British Date	Prints data in the British (European) date format
Trim	Removes leading and trailing blanks
Right Align	Prints data flush right in field
Center	Prints data centered in field

Table 7-1.   *Formatting Options for Character Data*

Option	Action
Left justify	Aligns numeric data flush left in field
Blank if zero	Does not print output if field contents contain zero
(Negative)	Encloses negative numbers in parentheses
Edit "SET" Date	Prints data as date in the current SET DATE format
British Date	Prints data in the British (European) date format
CR if positive	"CR" (for credit) appears after a number if the number is positive
DB if negative	"DB" (for debit) appears after a number if the number is negative
Leading zero	Prints leading zeros
Currency	Prints value in currency format
Scientific	Prints value in scientific notation

Table 7-2.   Formatting Options for Numeric Data

The Totaling option, when chosen, reveals a choice of totals. This option allows you to define a numeric summary field. Once you check the Totaling box, FoxPro allows you to select whether the total will be a Count (of the number of records), Sum (of the numeric data), an Average, Lowest (which displays the lowest value in any of the records), or the Highest (the maximum value in any of the records). Also shown when you select the Totaling option is a Reset option, which determines when the totaling field will be reset. Tab to this menu and press ENTER, and you are provided a choice of End of Report, End of Page, or by the name of the field or expression you are using. (In other words, each time the value of that field or expression changes, the total will be printed.)

The Suppress Repeated Values option of the Report Expression dialog box will tell FoxPro not to print repeated values within the report. If this option is selected, and the field value is the same for more than one consecutive record, the value is printed for the first record, but not for successive records.

Option	Action
Edit "SET" Date	Prints data as date in the current SET DATE format
British Date	Prints data in the British (European) date format

Table 7-3.   Formatting Options for Date Data

Once you have chosen the desired options within the Report Expression dialog box, select OK, and the dialog box will close, revealing the Report Layout window underneath.

> **NOTE:** *You can modify the format and style settings for an existing field at any time. Just place the cursor anywhere in the field, and press* ENTER. *Doing so will redisplay the Report Expression dialog box. You can make the desired modifications to the formatting and style options, and then choose OK to implement the changes.*

Printing and Displaying Reports

The new report can be displayed on the screen or printed at any time with the REPORT FORM command. If you wish to display the report on the screen, enter

REPORT FORM *filename*

To send a report to a printer, enter

REPORT FORM *filename* TO PRINT

The same operation can be performed from the menus by opening the Database menu and choosing Report. Next, enter the name of the stored report in the dialog box, check any desired options from the Report dialog box that appears, and select the OK button to produce the report. In addition to the < Form... > window, the Report dialog box has some other features. The Environment check box tells FoxPro to use any environmental settings that were in effect while the report was designed.

The Scope, For, and While options are used to limit records that will appear in the report. Scope can be used to limit the number of records that qualify for the operation. When Scope is selected, another dialog box appears containing three options: All, Next, and Rest. You can enter **Next** and then a number, which specifies a group of records starting with the current pointer location. For example, entering **Next 10** as the scope would tell FoxPro to limit its selections to the next ten records. Or you can enter **Rest**, which limits the operation to all records from wherever the pointer is located to the end of the file. When Scope is not selected, FoxPro assumes that you want to see all records in the file (defaulting to a scope of All).

The For and While options are used to further limit your records, as described in Chapter 5, "Performing Queries." The While option works best with an index, but the For option can be easily used on any field, whether an index exists or not. (FoxPro 2 users should keep in mind that the Rushmore technology present in FoxPro 2 will speed the results if you have an index open to support your For options.) When you choose For from the dialog box, the Expression Builder (covered in detail in Chapter 5) appears. Using the Expression Builder, you can enter an expression that will limit the records available to the report. The use of the While option will also result in the display of the Expression Builder, which can be filled in the same manner.

The Plain box produces a plain report, with no headings. The No Eject option tells FoxPro not to send a page-eject (formfeed) code before printing the report. The Summary option tells FoxPro to produce a summary report only. Individual records do not appear in the report—only summary totals appear. (This option makes sense when you have included summary fields in your report, a subject covered later in the chapter.) Checking the To Print option routes the report to the printer, while checking the To File option and entering a filename in the corresponding text box stores the report output in the form of an ASCII text file. Such files can be read by most word processors and all popular desktop publishing packages.

The Heading option, when chosen, causes the Expression Builder to appear, this time containing a window for a heading. You can use this window to enter a custom heading of your choice, or you can build an expression that results in a desired heading. If you want to enter text in your heading, surround the text in quotes. Fields are normally used as headings with multiple groupings in reports, a topic covered later in the chapter.

Once you enter the name of the report form, check the desired options, and select the OK button, the report is produced in accordance with your chosen options.

A Sample Custom Report

By performing the following steps, you can use the sample personnel database to see how a custom report can be designed.

1. From the Command window, enter **USE PERSONL** to open the personnel database.

2. Enter **CREATE REPORT** in the Command window (or choose New from the File menu, choose Report, and choose OK).

3. Move the cursor to row 1, column 50. (You can tell the cursor locations from the R and C designations shown in the upper-left corner of the Report Layout window.)

4. Open the Report menu with ALT-O, and choose Field. Press ENTER to open the Expression Builder, tab over to the Date popup, press ENTER, and select DATE() as the desired function from the list. Then choose OK from the Expression Builder and choose OK again from the remaining dialog box.

5. Press HOME to get back to the left margin, and move the cursor down to row 4, the first line of the Detail band. Type

   Name:

   and press ENTER to complete the entry of text. Then move the cursor over to column 6. Press CTRL-F to display the Report Expression dialog box and press ENTER. (You can also get to this dialog box with the Field choice of the Report menu.)

6. Enter **Lastname** in the window as the desired field name and choose OK twice.

7. Move the cursor to row 4, column 22. Press CTRL-F, press ENTER, type **Firstname** in the window for the desired field name, and choose OK twice.

8. Move the cursor to row 5, column 0. Type **Address:**, press ENTER, and move the cursor to row 5, column 9. Press CTRL-F, press ENTER, type **Address** in the window for the desired field name, and choose OK twice.

9. Move the cursor to row 6, column 0. Type **City:**, press ENTER, and move the cursor to row 6, column 6. Press CTRL-F, press ENTER, type **City** in the window for the desired field name, then choose OK twice.

10. Move the cursor to row 6, column 22. Type **State:**, press ENTER, and move the cursor to row 6, column 29. Press CTRL-F and ENTER, type **STATE** in the window for the desired field name, and choose OK twice.

11. Move the cursor to row 6, column 33. Type **Zip:**, press ENTER, and move the cursor to row 6, column 38. Press CTRL-F, press ENTER, type **ZIPCODE** in the window for the desired field name, and choose OK twice.

12. Move the cursor to row 7, column 0. Press CTRL-N twice, to add two new lines to the Detail band. Move the cursor down one row, to row 8, column 10. Type **Job Title:**, press ENTER and move the cursor to row 8, column 22. Press CTRL-F and ENTER, type **JOBTITLE** in the window for the desired field name, and choose OK twice.

13. To add a calculated summary field that shows the total number of employees in the database, move the cursor to row 11, column 0. Type **Total Employees:**, press ENTER, and move the cursor to row 11, column 17. Press CTRL-F and ENTER. Since this is simply a count of records, you could use any field as the basis for this summary (totals) field. Enter **SOCIAL** as the desired field name and choose OK. When the Report Expression dialog box reappears, choose Calculate. In the Calculate dialog box, which appears next, choose Count and choose OK. Tab over to the Width entry in the Report Expression dialog box, and enter **3**. Then choose OK.

If you want to see how the report will look on paper without wasting paper, open the Report menu with ALT-O and choose Page Preview. A visual representation of the report as designed will appear on the screen.

14. Open the File menu and choose Save to save the report. In the dialog box that appears, enter **RSAMPLE2** as a name for the report file and choose Save from the dialog box. If FoxPro asks if you want to save the environment information, choose Yes.

15. Press ESC to close the Report Layout window.

16. From the Command window, enter

```
REPORT FORM RSAMPLE2
```

to see the report on the screen. (You could use the variation of the command, **REPORT FORM RSAMPLE2 TO PRINT** instead to cause the report to be printed using the default printer port. For more details on the REPORT FORM command, see the following section.)

Producing Reports at the Command Level

From the command level, the LIST command is useful for printing data as well as examining data on the screen. To direct output to the printer, use the TO PRINT option with the LIST command. This avoids having all your command words print on the page along with the desired data. The normal format of the command with this option is

LIST [*field1*, *field2...fieldn*] TO PRINT

To try this command, enter

```
LIST Lastname, City, State, TO PRINT
```

to print all the name, city, and state fields for each record in the database. If you are using a laser printer, you may also need to enter an EJECT command to cause the printed sheet to feed out of the printer.

You can get selective by specifying a FOR condition with the LIST command and still send output to the printer with TO PRINT. For example,

```
LIST Lastname, Firstname, City FOR Lastname = "Jackson" TO PRINT
```

prints the last names, first names, and cities of both employees named Jackson. The command

```
LIST Lastname, City, State, Dependents FOR Dependents > 0 TO PRINT
```

provides a printed listing like the one that follows, with the last names, cities, states, and dependents for all employees with one or more dependents.

```
Record#     LASTNAME   STATE   CITY         DEPENDENTS
      2     Lord       VA      Reston       1
      3     Saeedi     MD      Rockville    1
      4     Shelorson  VA      Leesburg     2
      5     Murray     VA      Leesburg     2
      6     Ballou     VA      Reston       2
      7     Jackson    MD      Rockville    2
```

You can use the curly braces surrounding a date to tell FoxPro that the enclosed set of characters should be read as a date value. That date value can then be used to form a conditional command for printing a report. This is a very handy tool for printing activity within a certain time period. For example, the command

```
REPORT FORM INCOME FOR Startdate <= {10/01/87} TO PRINT
```

will produce a report of all records with hire dates earlier than November 2, 1987. A report of all employees with hire dates within a particular month could be produced with a command like this one:

```
REPORT FORM INCOME FOR Startdate > {09/30/87} .AND. Startdate < {10/31/87} TO PRINT
```

You can also generate stored reports with commands. The REPORT FORM command uses the following syntax:

REPORT FORM *filename* [*scope*]
    [FOR *expression*]
    [WHILE *expression*]
    [TO PRINT/TO FILE *filename*]
    [PLAIN] [SUMMARY] [NOEJECT]
    [HEADING "*character expression*"]
    [ENVIRONMENT]

The *scope*, FOR, and WHILE options work as discussed earlier in this text; see Chapter 5 for a full discussion of these options.

If the TO PRINT clause is added to the command, the report is routed to the printer and to the screen. If TO PRINT is omitted, the report is displayed only on the screen. If the TO FILE option is included, the report will be sent to a file, in the form of ASCII text. You can use either TO PRINT or TO FILE, but you cannot use both options in the same REPORT FORM command.

The PLAIN option prints a plain report, without the standard headings. The SUMMARY option prints a report with summary fields only. The NOEJECT option suppresses the normal page-eject (formfeed) codes that are sent to the printer. The HEADING option lets you add a custom heading; character expressions must be enclosed in quotes.

The ENVIRONMENT option can be used to specify a *view file* that can control records available for processing, which fields appear, and any relationships between other files. (View files are covered in Chapter 10, "The Relational Powers of FoxPro.") When you save a report, FoxPro automatically saves the current environment to a view file under the same name as the report. Adding this clause to the REPORT FORM command, therefore, saves you the trouble of opening a database and index file if they are not already open. For example, you could load FoxPro from DOS or OS/2 and enter one command such as **REPORT FORM MYFILE ENVIRONMENT** to open the database and any index files and produce the report.

Commands for Margin Settings and Manual Ejects

You can change your printer's left margin with the SET MARGIN command. FoxPro normally defaults to a printer margin value of zero. Entering **SET MARGIN TO 12**, for example, would cause the printer to indent 12 spaces at the beginning of each line. (This command affects only the left margin. The right margin cannot be set with a command in FoxPro, but by monitoring the field widths assigned to any one band in a report, you can in effect control the right margin.) The EJECT command, as mentioned earlier, causes the printer to perform a form feed to advance to the top of the next sheet. The EJECT command is not available from the menus; it must be entered as a command. An alternative is to use the Form Feed button on your printer to accomplish the same task.

Chapter 8

Designing Labels

FoxPro's label-generation facility is extremely flexible, giving you the ability to design your own layout or choose from nine predefined layouts, including Rolodex and envelope sizes. When you are ready to print your labels, they can be produced in the common "three-across" or "four-across" format, where the labels are placed on the label sheets in rows of three or four labels each. Label designs are stored on the disk with an .LBX extension.

   This chapter will cover how to create labels using FoxPro's Label Generator and how to add and move fields within a label design. The chapter will also cover using expressions in a label design, saving a label design, and printing labels.

Creating Labels

The initial process for creating labels in FoxPro is similar to the method followed when creating reports. From the menus, you choose New from the File menu and select Label from the dialog box that appears.

   From the command level, you use the CREATE LABEL command, specifying an optional filename as shown here

   CREATE LABEL [*filename*]

where *filename* is the name assigned to the label file. When you use either method, the Label Design screen, shown in Figure 8-1, appears next. (Remember to open your database before starting the label design process.) When you use the CREATE LABEL command without first opening a database, FoxPro will present you with a dialog box from which to make a database selection. If you are using the menus, you'll find that the Label button on the File Type dialog box is disabled until a database is opened.

Using the menus also produces a Label Design screen with the filename of UNTITLED.LBX. The Label Design screen, which will be discussed next, is an essential tool in the label-creation process.

The Label Design Screen

The center of the Label Design screen contains an area representing the contents of the label. In this area you place the field names or expressions that will provide the data when the labels are printed. At the top of the screen is a Remarks window, which can contain an optional description of the label. When you are creating a new label, this window contains the default label size of 3 1/2 × 15/16 × 1. This is the most commonly used size and matches standard peel-and-stick labels available in office supply stores.

You can select a different label size by opening the Label menu (using ALT-L) and selecting Layout. You would then make your selection from the resulting menu that appears to the left of the Label menu.

There are six parameters within the Label Design screen that allow you to control the overall dimensions of the labels: Margin, Number Across, Width, Height, Spaces Between, and Lines Between. Figure 8-2 shows the relationship between the various parameters that make up the label dimensions.

You'll use the Margin parameter to set the distance between the beginning of the leftmost label and the left edge of the sheet of labels. This value is set to zero

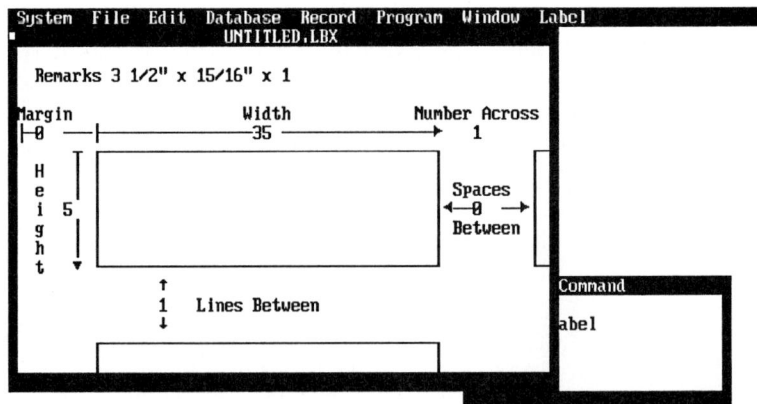

Figure 8-1.   *The Label Design screen*

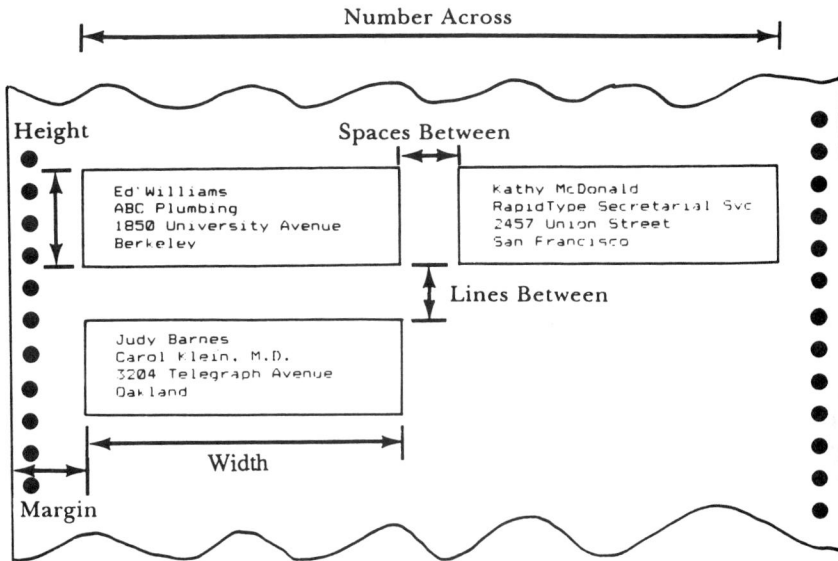

Figure 8-2.   *The relationship between label dimensions*

by default because most labels are attached to the underlying paper at the left edge of the label sheet. Use the Height and Width settings to change the height and width of the label. The default values of 35 characters for the width and 5 rows for the height will match the 3 1/2-inch × 15/16-inch label size commonly used by dot matrix printers, assuming you are printing at the standard of 10 characters per inch and 6 lines per inch.

Use the Number Across parameter to define the number of labels printed across a sheet of labels. With roll-fed labels, this is usually 1, but with the popular sheets of "three-across" labels used in laser printers, this value would be set to 3. The Spaces Between parameter controls the number of spaces between the labels. You only need to make an entry here when the Number Across value is set at more than 1. Finally, the Lines Between parameter controls the number of blank lines that appear between labels. Depending on your labels, you may need to play with this option to prevent data from printing across the breaks in the labels.

Table 8-1 lists some suggested settings for common label sizes. The suggested settings in the table assume that your printer is printing 6 lines to the inch and 10 characters per inch. This is the default setting for many printers, including most Epson-compatible dot matrix printers, and most laser printers when using a 10-point standard Courier font. If you use compressed printing, different size fonts, or different line spacing on your printer, you will need to experiment with the values until you find a set of values that works for the labels you've designed. While designing the label, you can use the TAB key or the mouse to move between the different settings on the Label Design screen.

Type of Label	Width	Height	Number Across	Margin	Lines Between	Spaces Between
3½ × ¹⁵⁄₁₆ × 1 across	35	5	1	0	1	0
3½ × ¹⁵⁄₁₆ × 2 across	35	5	2	0	1	2
3½ × ¹⁵⁄₁₆ × 3 across	35	5	3	0	1	2
4 × 1⁷⁄₁₆ × 1 across	40	8	1	0	1	0
1⁷⁄₁₆ × 5 × 1 across	50	8	1	0	1	0
Xerox Cheshire Labels	32	5	3	0	1	2
Rolodex 3 × 5	50	14	1	0	4	0
Rolodex 2¼ × 4	40	10	1	0	1	0
No. 7 Envelope	65	14	1	0	8	0
No. 10 Envelope	78	17	1	0	8	0

Table 8-1.   *Common Label Sizes and Settings*

HINT: *If your printer offers the use of proportional fonts, you should avoid these when printing labels and use monospace fonts instead. Characters printed using proportional fonts will not appear in aligned columns due to the differences in the size of the characters.*

The Expression Builder

You can use the Expression Builder to add fields or expressions in the design area. To get to the Expression Builder, place the cursor at the desired location and choose Expression from the Label menu or simply press CTRL-E. Using either method, the Expression Builder appears, as shown in Figure 8-3.

Enter the desired expression in the window. The expression can be a single field name or a combination of field names. Reports commonly combine multiple fields to form an expression. For example, an expression such as

```
TRIM(Firstname) + " " + Lastname
```

would result in a printout of the first name, followed by a space, followed by the last name.

You can also use calculations you create based on fields. With a numeric field called Taxes, you could enter the expression

```
Taxes * .12
```

to calculate an amount that is 12 percent of the amount contained in the Taxes field.

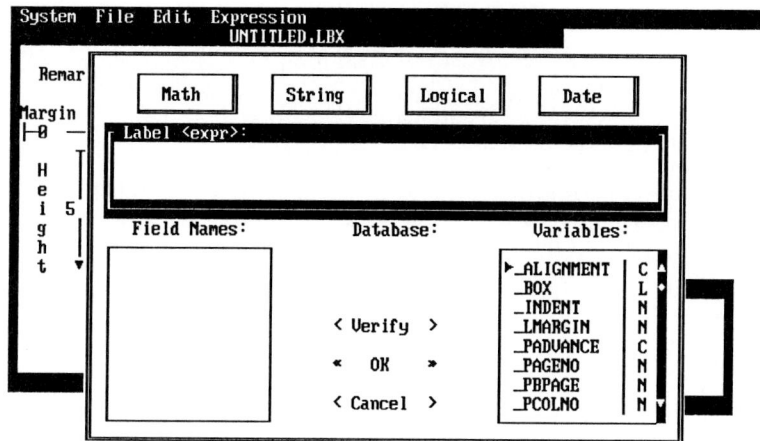

Figure 8-3.   *The Expression Builder*

Page Preview

You can review your work any time during the design process (or afterwards) using the Page Preview option on the Label menu. When you open the Label menu with ALT-L and choose Page Preview, or simply press CTRL-I, a visual representation of the label appears, as shown in Figure 8-4. Choose More to see

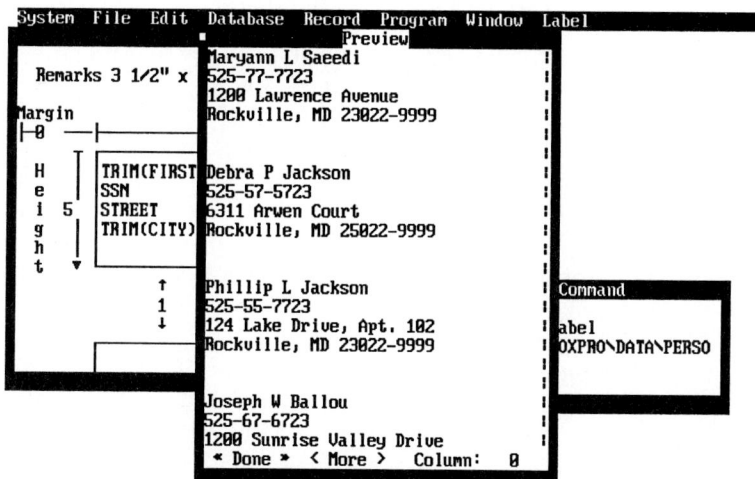

Figure 8-4.   *Labels shown in Page Preview mode*

additional labels or choose Done when you have finished with the Page Preview option.

Saving a Custom Label Layout

If you've created a unique layout for a special label, you can add it to the list of standard layouts available to you when you open the Label menu and choose Layout. To do this, simply open the Label menu, choose the Save Layout option, and enter a description for the new layout.

Saving the Label Form

After entering the needed field names or expressions within the design area, choose Save from the File menu or press CTRL-W to save the label design. If no name for the label was entered when you began the process, FoxPro will ask for a filename. When the label file has been saved, you are returned to the command level.

Printing Labels

You can print labels by choosing Label from the Database menu or by using the LABEL FORM command. If you choose Label from the Database menu, the dialog box shown in Figure 8-5 appears.

Press TAB to get to the < Form...> window, then enter the name of the label between the window brackets. (You could also click on the Form button and choose the desired form from the list box that appears.) You can select Scope, For, or While to limit the number of records which will appear as labels.

Selecting Scope causes another dialog box to appear containing four options: All, Next, Record, and Rest. All is the default scope and specifies that all records will be affected by this operation. You can choose Next and then enter a number, which specifies a group of records, starting with the current pointer location. For example, entering **10** would tell FoxPro to only print labels for the next ten records. You can choose Record and enter a number, which selects a specific record by its record number, or you can choose Rest, which tells FoxPro to print labels for all records from the current pointer location to the end of the file.

When you select either the For or the While option, the Expression Builder appears. The differences between the FOR and WHILE commands were discussed in Chapter 5, "Performing Queries." Remember that when you choose the For option, every record in the database will be tested to see if the expression is true. If the expression is true, the label will be printed. Choosing While causes

System File Edit Database Record Program Window

```
Label:
  <For]... >     [X] Environment      [ ] Scope...
                                      [ ] For...
  [X] Set Printer Driver              [ ] While...

  [ ] Sample                          «   OK   »
  [ ] To Print
  [ ] To File                         < Cancel >
  (•) Console On ( ) Console Off                  TA\PERSO
```

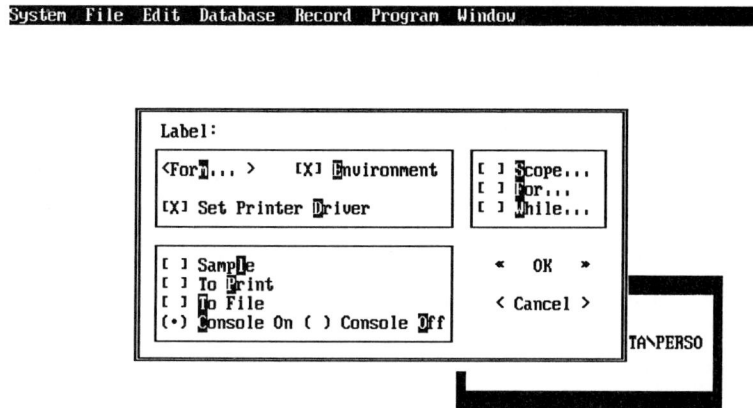

Figure 8-5. *The Print Label dialog box*

labels to be printed as long as the logical expression is true—if a record is found where the logical expression evaluates to false, the printing will be discontinued, even though there may be additional records that meet the specified condition later in the database.

Turn on the Sample option if you want to print a sample label (containing rows of Xs) before the actual printing of data begins. This is often helpful in aligning labels in your printer before printing. Turn on the To Print option to route the labels to the printer; otherwise, they only appear on the screen. The To File option can be selected to store the output in an ASCII text file. If you choose this option, enter a name for the file in the window beside the To File option. When you've finished selecting the options, choose OK to begin producing the labels.

From the command level, use the command

LABEL FORM *filename* [*scope*] [FOR *condition*] [WHILE *condition*] [SAMPLE]
[TO PRINT/TO FILE *filename*]

As with other commands, all clauses within the brackets are optional. The SCOPE, FOR, and WHILE clauses are used to limit records printed, as discussed previously.

For example, the command

```
LABEL FORM  EMPLABEL FOR State = "VA"
```

would produce the following results:

```
Joseph W Ballou
525-67-6723
1200 Sunrise Valley Drive
Reston, VA 23022-9999

Mildred M Shelorson
525-71-7123
1250 Morgan Avenue
Leesburg, VA 23022-9999

John M Murray
765-37-7737
1300 Morgan Avenue
Leesburg, VA 23022-9999

Joseph M Tahan
525-81-8123
1265 Cedar Lane
Fairfax, VA 22021-9999

Scott E Lord
566-72-8723
1250 South Lake Drive
Reston, VA 23022-9999
```

In the example above, the label will be sent to the screen only. To send the label to the printer, add the TO PRINT clause:

```
LABEL FORM  EMPLABEL FOR State = "VA"  TO PRINT
```

HINT: *If you are using the TO PRINT option, add the SAMPLE clause to print a sample label (composed of rows of Xs) before printing of the data begins. This often helps in aligning labels in the printer before actual printing begins.*

To send the labels to a file, enter

```
LABEL FORM  EMPLABEL FOR State = "VA"  TO FILE LABLFILE
```

NOTE: *When you use this method, the specified file is created with a .TXT extension. You can use either the TO PRINT clause or the TO FILE clause, but you cannot use both at the same time.*

Tips for Printing Labels

If you want the labels printed in a certain order, simply index or sort the database first. Then use the LABEL FORM command or the Label option of the Database menu. It is usually wise to print a test run of labels on plain paper first and to visually align the printout with a sheet of blank labels. If the alignment looks correct, you can proceed to print on the labels themselves. To print labels selectively, you can use the SET FILTER or INDEX ON...FOR command.

Keep in mind that if a given record does not contain data in a certain field that is included in your label design, FoxPro will not automatically compress the printed lines. Instead, a blank space will appear on the label representing that field.

An Example Label

As an example, try creating a label for use with our sample personnel database. Open the personnel database and begin the process by entering

```
USE PERSONL
CREATE LABEL EMPLABEL
```

The Label Design screen, shown earlier in Figure 8-1, appears.

With the cursor on the first line of the design area, press CTRL-E to open the Expression Builder. For this example, the first line will contain a combination of first name, middle initial, and last name, each separated by a space. Enter the following expression in the window now.

```
TRIM(Firstname) + " " + TRIM(Middle) + " " + TRIM(Lastname)
```

Then choose OK from the dialog box to insert the expression.

Move the cursor down to the second line of the design area. Press CTRL-E again and enter **Ssn** in the window of the Expression Builder. Select OK from the dialog box to place the expression, and move the cursor down to the third line. Open the Expression Builder and enter **Street** into the window, then select OK.

Position the cursor on the last line of the label. Open the Expression Builder one more time with CTRL-E, enter the expression

```
TRIM(City) + ", " + State + " " + Zipcode
```

and select OK from the dialog box. Save the label with CTRL-W. To review the label form select Page Preview from the Label menu with CTRL-I.

Print the labels to the screen by entering

```
LABEL FORM EMPLABEL
```

If you want to see a printed version of the labels, enter the command

```
LABEL FORM EMPLABEL TO PRINT
```

The results should resemble the following:

```
Maryann L Saeedi
525-77-7723
1200 Lawrence Avenue
Rockville, MD 23022-999

Debra P Jackson
525-57-5723
6311 Arwen Court
Rockville, MD 25022-9999

Phillip L Jackson
525-55-7723
124 Lake Drive, Apartment 102
Rockville, MD 23022-9999

Joseph W Ballou
525-67-6723
1200 Sunrise Valley Drive
Reston, VA 23022-9999

Mildred M Shelorson
525-71-7123
1250 Morgan Avenue
Leesburg, VA 23022-9999

John M Murray
765-37-7737
1300 Morgan Avenue
Leesburg, VA 23022-9999

Joseph M Tahan
525-81-8123
1265 Cedar Lane
Fairfax, VA 22021-9999
```

```
Scott E Lord
566-72-8723
1250 South Lake Drive
Reston, VA 23022-9999
```

You can also make changes without the use of the Expression Builder. For example, let's include a title in front of the social security number. Place the cursor on the second line of the layout and insert **"SSN: "** + before the social security field.

```
"SSN: " + Ssn
```

The labels should now resemble the following:

```
Maryann L Saeedi
SSN: 525-77-7723
1200 Lawrence Avenue
Rockville, MD 23022-999
```

```
Debra P Jackson
SSN: 525-57-5723
6311 Arwen Court
Rockville, MD 25022-9999
```

```
Phillip L Jackson
SSN: 525-55-7723
124 Lake Drive, Apartment 102
Rockville, MD 23022-9999
```

```
Joseph W Ballou
SSN: 525-67-6723
1200 Sunrise Valley Drive
Reston, VA 23022-9999
```

```
Mildred M Shelorson
SSN: 525-71-7123
1250 Morgan Avenue
Leesburg, VA 23022-9999
```

```
John M Murray
SSN: 765-37-7737
1300 Morgan Avenue
Leesburg, VA 23022-9999
```

```
Joseph M Tahan
SSN: 525-81-8123
1265 Cedar Lane
Fairfax, VA 22021-9999

Scott E Lord
SSN: 566-72-8723
1250 South Lake Drive
Reston, VA 23022-9999
```

Modifying Existing Labels

When you want to change an existing label, use the command

MODIFY LABEL *filename*

where *filename* is the name that the prior label design was stored under. Or, from the File menu, choose Open, and in the dialog box that appears, select Label. In the list box that next appears, choose the existing label to modify by name.

Either method will cause the Label Design screen, containing the existing label, to appear. You can proceed to make the desired modifications and save the changes with CTRL-W. Remember that you can make changes to a field by placing the cursor within the field and pressing ENTER to bring up the Expression Builder.

Chapter *9*

Macros

In previous chapters you've seen how the use of keyboard shortcuts can provide flexibility to your environment and give you quicker access to many of FoxPro's features. You can develop your own shortcuts using FoxPro's macro facility. When you create a *macro*, you record the actions needed to perform a desired task and assign these to a single key combination. You can save the macro and later use it to play back those sequences by pressing the same key combination.

When the macro is played back, FoxPro behaves as if you had manually performed the actions contained in the macro. In addition to keystrokes, you can also store frequently used phrases, names, or complete paragraphs of text in a macro. You are not limited to using a single key for the macro; you can use various combinations of letter keys and function keys.

Third-Party Macro Facilities

While you can use commercial keyboard redefiners to perform the same functions as FoxPro macros, there are good reasons for avoiding external keyboard redefiners. First, they consume memory that could be utilized by FoxPro. FoxPro requires a minimum of 512K of memory. Unless your keyboard redefiner can utilize extended or expanded memory, you may run into "insufficient memory" messages when trying to use it along with FoxPro. Second, keyboard redefiners, which are by nature memory-resident, may interfere with the operation of FoxPro.

Assigning Macros to Keys

In FoxPro, a macro can be assigned to key combinations that use CTRL or ALT with letter keys, or CTRL, ALT, or SHIFT with function keys. You can also assign macros to function keys F2 through F9 (and to F11 and F12 if your keyboard has these keys). F1 is reserved for the Help facility, and F10 activates the menu bar. You cannot use SHIFT-F10, as it is reserved to call up the Macro Key Definition dialog box. You can, however, use SHIFT-F1. While function keys F2 through F9 already have commands assigned to them, you may find it easier to use the menus. Table 9-1 lists predefined function keys and their assignments.

Many of the key combinations also have assignments. Table 9-2 shows some of the assigned key combinations that use CTRL keys. Before assigning a macro to a key combination, you may want to check the list to avoid overriding an existing keyboard shortcut. For example, if you assign CTRL-A to a macro, you will not be able to use CTRL-A to select text in the Editor while your macro is loaded.

Creating a Macro

To create a macro, choose the Macros option from the System menu and then choose New from the dialog box that appears, or simply press SHIFT-F10. Either method will cause the Macro Key Definition dialog box, shown in Figure 9-1, to appear.

To record a macro, press the combination of ALT or CTRL and the function or letter key you want to assign to the macro. If that key was used earlier, FoxPro

Key	Assignment
F1	Help
F2	Set
F3	List
F4	Directory
F5	Display Structure
F6	Display Status
F7	Display Memory
F8	Display
F9	Append
F10	Activate/Deactivate Menu Bar

Table 9-1. Function Key Assignments

CTRL-**Key**	**Assignment**
CTRL-A	Select All
CTRL-C	Copy
CTRL-D	Do
CTRL-E	Replace and Find Again
CTRL-F	Find
CTRL-G	Find Again
CTRL-K	Continue
CTRL-M	Resume
CTRL-R	Redo
CTRL-U	Undo
CTRL-V	Paste
CTRL-W	Exit and Save
CTRL-X	Cut
CTRL-F1	Cycle Windows
CTRL-F2	Display Command Window
CTRL-F7	Move Window
CTRL-F8	Size Window
CTRL-F10	Zoom Window

Table 9-2.   *CTRL-Key Assignments*

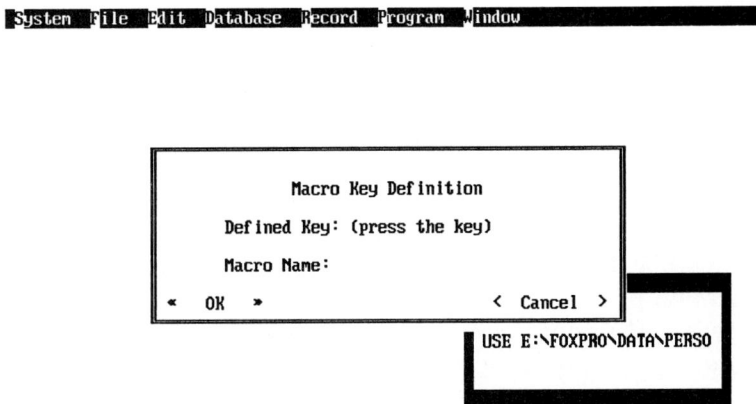

```
 System  File  Edit  Database  Record  Program  Window

                    ┌──────────────────────────────────────┐
                    │          Macro Key Definition          │
                    │   Defined Key: (press the key)          │
                    │   Macro Name:                           │
                    │ «   OK   »                  < Cancel >   │
                    └──────────────────────────────────────┘
                                    USE E:\FOXPRO\DATA\PERSO
```

Figure 9-1.   *The Macro Key Definition dialog box*

will ask for confirmation before overwriting the old assignment in memory. After pressing the desired key, you can proceed to perform the actions desired in the macro. When you have finished, press SHIFT-F10 and choose OK to stop the recording.

To summarize, the overall process for creating a macro involves these four steps:

1. Press SHIFT-F10 or choose the Macros option of the System menu and choose New from the dialog box that appears. This causes the Macro Key Definition dialog box to appear.

2. Press CTRL or ALT along with the letter key or function key that you want to use for the macro. You can use CTRL or ALT plus any of the 26 letters, or CTRL, ALT, or SHIFT along with any of the 12 function keys (but remember, you cannot use F1 or SHIFT-F10).

3. Enter the keystrokes that will make up the macro. If you make an error, press SHIFT-F10 and choose Discard from the dialog box to end the recording and start again.

4. Once all the keystrokes have been entered, press SHIFT-F10 and select OK to stop the macro recording.

After the macro has been recorded, you can press the CTRL-, ALT-, or SHIFT-key combination assigned to the macro to play back the macro whenever needed.

The Keyboard Macros Dialog Box

When you choose the Macros option from the System menu, the Keyboard Macros dialog box, shown in Figure 9-2, is displayed. The center of this box contains a list of all macros currently in memory, along with the keys assigned to them. The upper portion of the list displays the macros that are assigned to the letter keys, while the lower portion of the list shows the macros that are assigned to the function keys.

The Save and Restore options let you load a set of macros into memory or save the current macros in memory to a *macro file*. Macros exist in memory; if you do not save macros to disk before leaving FoxPro, they are lost. When you save your macro, FoxPro adds an extension of .FKY to the end of the filename. The command-level equivalents for these options are RESTORE MACROS FROM

```
 System  File  Edit  Macros
```

```
                        Keyboard Macros

    ┌─────────────┐   ┌──────────────┐  ┌─────────────┐
    │             │   │▶F2         ▲ │  │             │
    │  <  Save  > │   │ F3         ◆ │  │  < Record > │
    │             │   │ F4           │  │             │
    │  < Restore >│   │ F5           │  │  <  New   > │
    │             │   │ F6           │  │             │
    │  <Set Default>  │ F7           │  │  <  Edit  > │
    │             │   │ F8           │  │             │
    │  < Clear All >  │ F9           │  │  <  Clear > │
    │             │   │ SHIFT_1    ▼ │  │             │
    └─────────────┘   └──────────────┘  └─────────────┘  SO

                        «   OK   »
```

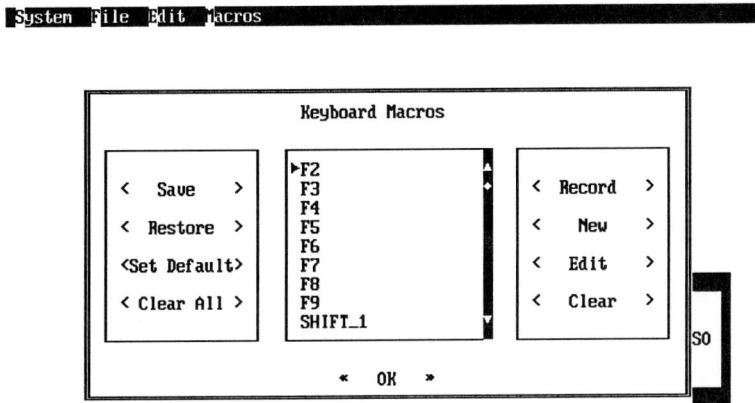

Figure 9-2.   *The Keyboard Macros dialog box*

macro filename, which loads the macro file, and SAVE MACROS TO *macro filename*, which saves the current macros to the named file.

NOTE: *When you restore macros, you are actually adding to the list of macros already in memory. If you restore a macro file containing a new definition for a frequently used function key, such as F9 (Append), the second definition of F9 will replace the first.*

The Set Default option stores the macros currently in memory to a *startup macro file*. The macros stored in this manner will be automatically loaded into memory whenever FoxPro is started.

The New option, discussed earlier, begins the creation of a new macro and causes the Macro Key Definition dialog box requesting the key combination for the new macro to appear. Another way to achieve the same option is to press SHIFT-F10.

The Clear option clears the highlighted macro from memory. To use this option, first highlight the unwanted macro in the list box. Then choose Clear to clear the macro. The Clear All option clears all existing macros from memory.

The Edit option lets you edit an existing macro, while the Record option lets you begin recording a macro.

Since you can save different sets of macros under different filenames, this gives you an unlimited number of possible macros. One helpful hint in keeping track of your macro files is to give them the same name as the associated database file.

A Sample Macro

To get an idea of the power of macros, let's create a macro to aid us in editing the Personnel database. Suppose that you regularly update records by opening the database file in a window on the screen, and you zoom the window to full size so that you can view as much of the file as possible. You could create a macro to perform this task with the following steps.

1. Press SHIFT-F10. The Macro Key Definition dialog box appears, asking which key you want to define for the macro.

2. Press CTRL-A to designate the CTRL-A key combination as the macro key, then choose OK. In the upper-right corner of the screen, you will see the message, "Recording Ctrl_A. Shift-F10 to stop."

3. From the File menu, choose Open. If database files are not visible in the list box, choose Database from the Type list box. In the list box of databases that appears, choose PERSONL, then choose Open.

4. From the Database menu, choose Browse.

5. From the Window menu, choose Zoom [↑].

6. Press SHIFT-F10 to halt recording of the macro. In the dialog box that appears, choose OK.

To try the macro, press ESC to exit the Browse mode and enter **CLEAR ALL** in the Command window to close the database file. If you now want to open the file, enter the Browse mode, and zoom the window, you can use the macro to carry out all of the steps needed. Press CTRL-A now to play back the macro. All the keystrokes are entered from the macro, and the database file appears in the Browse window.

Before proceeding, press ESC to exit the Browse mode.

Saving Macros

If you want to reuse macros, you'll need to save them to a disk file so they can be reloaded later. To save macros, open the System menu with ALT-S, then choose Macros. In the Keyboard Macros dialog box, which appears next, choose Save. Enter a DOS name of your choosing for the file when prompted for a name.

Once the macros have been saved, you can exit FoxPro. When you later get back into FoxPro, you can restore saved macros to memory by choosing Macros from the System menu and choosing Restore from the Keyboard Macros dialog box.

Tips for Creating and Using Macros

When recording a macro, it is a good idea to avoid using the cursor keys to move to an option or filename whenever possible. Not only will this mean fewer overall keystrokes in the macro, there will also be less chance of error during playback caused by a list of available options being different than it was during recording. This type of error can be a particular problem when using a macro to choose filenames from a pick list, because the list changes as files are added to or deleted from your directory.

Before using a macro, remember to move to the area where the macro will be used. For example, if you create a macro to supply a frequently entered character string to a text field in a dialog box, you must position your cursor within the field before using the macro.

Adding to Existing Macros

You can add to the end of an existing macro by pressing SHIFT-F10 to start a macro, and then pressing the same key combination as the existing macro. For example, if you have already defined CTRL-A as a particular macro and you want to add more keystrokes to the end of that macro, you can press SHIFT-F10, which reveals the Macro Key Definition box. Press CTRL-A as the key to define, and choose OK. The following dialog box now appears, as shown in Figure 9-3.

System File Edit Database Record Program Window

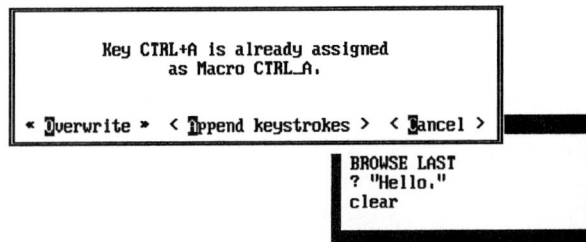

```
          Key CTRL+A is already assigned
               as Macro CTRL_A.

 « Overwrite »   < Append keystrokes >   < Cancel >
                                    BROWSE LAST
                                    ? "Hello."
                                    clear
```

Figure 9-3. *A dialog box warning of an existing macro*

The dialog box presents you with three options: Overwrite, Append keystrokes, or Cancel. You can now choose Append keystrokes to add your keystrokes to the end of the existing macro. Selecting Overwrite clears the old macro and assigns a new macro to the key combination you picked, while Cancel exits the macro definition without adding any changes.

Inserting Literals and Adding Pauses in Macros

FoxPro lets you insert literals and add pauses into a macro. When you are in the process of recording a macro and you press SHIFT-F10, the Stop Recording dialog box that appears provides you with five choices: Insert Literal, Insert Pause, OK, Discard, and Continue.

The Insert Literal option tells FoxPro to record the literal value of the next keystroke, rather than the value assigned by a different macro. For example, if you redefined the ALT-F key with a different macro and you wanted to use the original definition of ALT-F (File menu) within the macro you were creating, you could use the Insert Literal option. The OK option saves the macro to memory as it currently exists, and the Discard option discards the macro from memory.

The Insert Pause option can be useful for allowing a user to enter an item that will change from day to day. FoxPro provides the opportunity to add pauses to a macro when you press SHIFT-F10 while recording a macro. To cause the macro to pause during execution, select the Insert Pause option. Then select the Continue option to continue the current macro-recording process. The resulting macro will pause during execution at the point specified to let the user enter any desired text. When the user again presses SHIFT-F10, the macro continues with its operation.

Limitations of Macros

Do not attempt to make a macro a part of itself. For example, if you can call a macro with the Macros menu's Play option followed by the letter "J," you cannot call up the Macros menu, choose Play, and enter the letter "J" within the macro. Such a technique would set up an anomaly known in programming as a *recursive loop*, where the program chases its own tail. FoxPro will let you get away with this, but only to a point. The macro will repeat itself until an internal limit is reached, and an error message will then result.

Also remember that key combinations permitted for assigning macros include CTRL or ALT plus any of the 26 letters, or CTRL, ALT, or SHIFT along with any of the 12 function keys with the exception of F1 and SHIFT-F10.

Chapter 10

The Relational Powers of FoxPro

It is often necessary in business to establish relationships between multiple databases to obtain accurate information. For example, an engineering firm may use the same employee for several different clients, keeping employee information in one file and client information in another. To effectively invoice all clients, a relationship must be established between the employee database and the client database. As a *relational database manager*, FoxPro gives you the ability to use more than one database file at a time and to define relationships between two or more database files.

FoxPro is a relational database manager. It is surprising how often this fact gets ignored and how often the full relational capabilities of FoxPro aren't taken advantage of. Some simple applications, like the mailing list with less than a dozen fields, do not demand relational capabilities. (Such applications make you wonder why FoxPro was needed in the first place, but that's a topic for another discussion.) It is the complex applications that present a relational challenge to the FoxPro user.

This chapter describes a number of ways you can take advantage of FoxPro's relational capabilities. The chapter further discusses ways to produce reports based on multiple databases. Many of the examples in the chapter will make use of the PERSONL database created in Chapter 3, along with a new database called HOURS.DBF. The HOURS database will be used to store a record of hours worked during a given week for each employee in the PERSONL file.

Understanding Relational Databases

As an example of the needs of a relational application, consider the following databases, one for personnel and one for a record of hours worked. The HOURS database will contain records of the number of hours worked by each employee, and of the client for whom (or assignment at which) the employee performed the work. However, the HOURS database will not contain the names of the employees; it will refer to each employee only by social security number. The PERSONL file, on the other hand, contains the full name of each employee, but no record of the hours worked by that employee.

If you are using two database files like these and you need a report showing employees' names, assignments, and numbers of hours worked, you need a *relational report*. Such a report is called "relational" because it draws on information from more than one database file. The PERSONL file contains the last name and first name fields. The HOURS file contains the assignment and the hours worked fields. In order to produce a report based on these fields, you must either use SET RELATION to link the files or you must produce a query (through the RQBE window) that will retrieve data from both files and link them into a single "virtual table." That table can then be used from the RQBE window to produce a report.

The key to retrieving data from a relational database is to link records on some sort of matching, or *common,* field. In this context, the term "common field" is used to indicate a field or a combination of fields common to both database files. In the case of the PERSONL and HOURS databases, each will contain a field, Ssn, for the social security number. This field will be used in the examples to form the basis for a relationship between files. Unless you have a field (or combination of fields) that is common between the files, a relational link is not possible. This is one important reason why the design process behind relational databases is not to be taken lightly.

Ways to Relate Databases in FoxPro

FoxPro is quite flexible in the ways in which it lets you draw relationships between database files. Some products (like Ashton-Tate's dBASE III PLUS) let you relate files at the command level through the use of the SET RELATION command. Other products (like Borland's Paradox) let you relate files by building queries within a Query-by-Example design screen. Still other database products (particularly some in the Macintosh environment) let you relate files by drawing a link between the files in some type of a "view" window. FoxPro is unique in that it lets you use all three of these methods. You can relate files through the RQBE window, detailed in Chapter 6, "Creating Queries with RQBE"; you can use the SET RELATION command, popular with those who have programmed in the dBASE or the FoxBASE+ programming language; or you can use FoxPro's View window to relate the files. If you are new to all three methods, you are likely to find the use of the RQBE window to be the easiest. The View window will primarily appeal to users of FoxPro prior to version 2. If you are using FoxPro 2 or later, you will find that any relationship that can be established in the View window can be established with more flexibility through the RQBE window. However, for those who have not upgraded, the View window will be covered in this chapter.

HINT: If you are working with large databases, there is an inherent speed advantage in using the RQBE window to relate your files. As mentioned in Chapter 6, the RQBE window produces SQL SELECT commands, which automatically make use of FoxPro 2's Rushmore technology for optimizing queries. From the command level, you can utilize Rushmore by opening index files that support your FOR statements used after the SET RELATION command. However, you must take the time to make sure this is done. With the RQBE window, the optimization is done automatically.

Creating the HOURS Database

Since relational tasks require the use of more than one database file, this chapter uses a sample database called HOURS, which contains a record of hours worked by employees. If you plan to duplicate the example, enter

```
CREATE HOURS
```

to create this database before proceeding. In the database definition screen, duplicate the structure shown here:

Field Name	Type	Width	Dec
Assignment	Character	20	
Ssn	Character	11	
Weekdate	Date	8	
Workhours	Numeric	4	1

Choose OK when done, and respond with **Yes** to the "Input data records now?" prompt. Enter the following records:

Assignment	Ssn	Weekdate	Workhours
National Oil Co.	525-57-5723	10/18/91	35.0
National Oil Co.	525-81-8123	10/18/91	37.5
National Oil Co.	566-72-8723	10/18/91	40.0
City Revenue Dept.	525-77-7723	10/18/91	38.5
City Revenue Dept.	525-55-7723	10/18/91	40.0
City Revenue Dept.	525-71-7123	10/18/91	38.0
Smith Builders	525-67-6723	10/18/91	40.0
Smith Builders	765-37-7737	10/18/91	40.0
National Oil Co.	525-57-5723	10/25/91	37.0
National Oil Co.	525-81-8123	10/25/91	40.0
National Oil Co.	566-72-8723	10/25/91	38.0
City Revenue Dept.	525-77-7723	10/25/91	39.5
City Revenue Dept.	525-55-7723	10/25/91	40.0
City Revenue Dept.	525-71-7123	10/25/91	40.0
Smith Builders	525-67-6723	10/25/91	39.0
Smith Builders	765-37-7737	10/25/91	35.0

Querying from Two Databases

You can easily design a query based on multiple databases by using the RQBE window. The following paragraphs describe the overall process; after the description is an example you can follow using the PERSONL.DBF and HOURS.DBF database files.

To query from two databases, first bring up the RQBE window, either by entering **CREATE QUERY**, or by choosing New from the File menu, selecting Query in the dialog box that appears, and choosing OK. If you are asked to select a database, choose the first database that you will be working with. If a database is already open, you will not be asked this question.

Once you select the database, the RQBE window appears. The first database that you are working with appears by name in the Databases box in the upper-left corner of the RQBE window. To add a second database to form a relational query, use the Add button (either click on it, or tab to it and press ENTER). The Select Database dialog box will again appear, and you can choose the next desired database from the list box of databases in the dialog box. Once you choose Open, a new dialog box appears, asking you for the RQBE Join Condition, as shown in Figure 10-1. In this dialog box, you must specify the condition that will be used to link the files together—that is, the basis of the relationship.

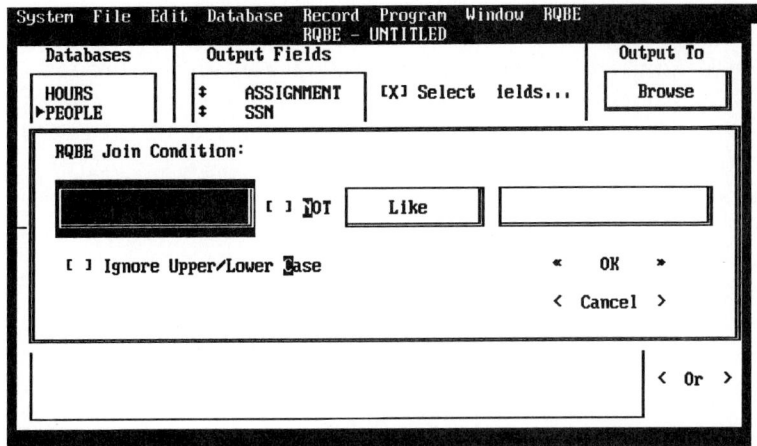

Figure 10-1.   *The RQBE Join Condition dialog box*

Tab to or click on the first list box, and a list of fields from the first database will appear. Choose the field that will be used to establish the link. The list box in the center assumes that the "Like" condition is desired. Unless you are linking files based on a very unusual relationship, this default will be what you desire. Tab to or click on the list box at the far right to display a list of fields from the second database. Choose the desired field in the second database that will link to its equivalent field in the first database. Then tab to or click on the OK button.

At this point, you can select the desired fields that are to appear in the query. By default, all fields from the selected database (whichever database has the arrow beside it in the Databases box at the upper-left corner of the RQBE window) will appear in the query. However, when working with relational queries, you will often want to pick and choose fields from both databases. To do so, choose the Select Fields option, and when the Select Fields dialog box appears, use the list box of fields along with the Move, Remove, and Remove All options to place the desired fields in the Selected Output area. When the desired fields are visible in the Selected Output area of the dialog box, choose OK.

At this point, you can choose any other desired options in the RQBE window and then choose the Do Query option to produce the query results. Remember that you can specify where the query appears with the Output To option in the RQBE window; see Chapters 6, "Creating Queries with RQBE," and 7, "Reports," for specifics on using the Output To options and for details on designing reports to be used with your queries.

A Sample Relational Query

To get a listing containing each employee's name, assignment, week ending date, and number of hours worked with both databases linked through the common (Ssn) field, try the following steps. In the Command window, enter **CLEAR ALL** to close any databases that may be open. Then, enter **USE PERSONL** to open the personnel file. Enter **CREATE QUERY** to open the RQBE window and begin a new query.

Click on Add or press A. When the Select Database dialog box appears, choose HOURS.DBF from the list box, then choose Open. In a moment, the RQBE Join Condition dialog box appears, as shown earlier in Figure 10-1.

Press ENTER or click on the list box at the left side of the screen to display the list of fields in the HOURS file. Choose HOURS.SSN (the social security field) from the list box. Since this is the common field between both files, this field will be used as the basis of the relational link.

Tab over to the list box at the right side of the dialog box and again press ENTER or click on the list box to display the list of fields in the PERSONL file. Choose PERSONL.SSN from the list box. Finally, choose OK. The complete expression needed, "HOURS.SSN Like PERSONL.SSN," appears in the Select Criteria area at the bottom of the RQBE window, as shown in Figure 10-2.

Click on the Select Fields button (or press F). When the Select Fields dialog box appears, click on Remove All (or press L). Doing so will remove all fields from the Selected Output area.

One by one, choose the following fields in the Database Fields list box (at the left side of the screen), and press ENTER (or choose Move) when a field is

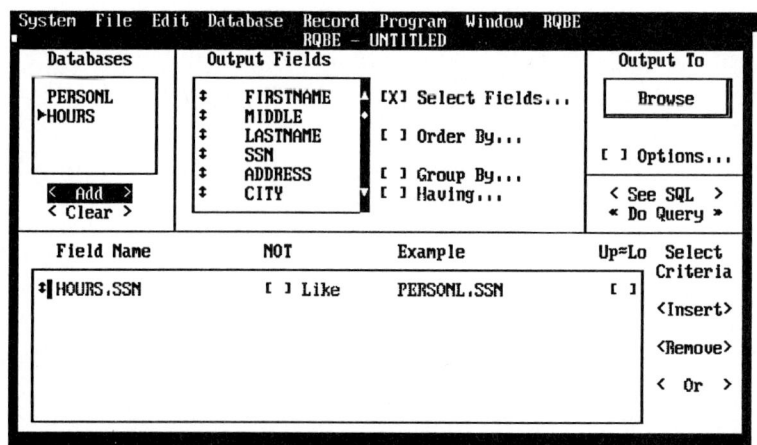

Figure 10-2.   *An RQBE window containing criteria needed to relate files*

highlighted to move the field into the Selected Output area: PERSONL.LAST-NAME, PERSONL.FIRSTNAME, HOURS.ASSIGNMENT, HOURS.WEEK-DATE, and HOURS.WORKHOURS. When all these fields are visible in the Selected Output area at the right side of the dialog box, choose OK.

Click on the Do Query option (or press Q). The results of the relational query will appear in a Browse window, assuming that Output Options is set to Browse. Your results should resemble those shown in the example in Figure 10-3.

Keep in mind that you can use any of the techniques discussed in Chapter 6 to further refine your relational queries. You can specify conditions for the selected records that are to appear in the query and specify a sort order. Refer to Chapter 6 for more details on these techniques. See Chapter 7 for details on designing reports that can be used with the Output option of the RQBE window.

The View Window

Another way you can relate files is by using the View window. This method is not quite as simple as using the RQBE window to build a query, because with the View window, your files must be indexed on the fields that are the basis of the relationship. (The RQBE window takes care of this requirement automatically.) Nevertheless, you may prefer to link files using the View window, especially if you have used it with earlier versions of FoxPro. If you are going to duplicate the examples that follow, first close (without saving) any open queries by pressing ESC, and enter **CLEAR ALL** in the Command window to close any open files.

Lastname	Firstname	Assignment	Weekdate	Workhours
Saeedi	Maryann	City Revenue Dept.	10/18/91	38.5
Saeedi	Maryann	City Revenue Dept.	10/25/91	39.5
Jackson	Debra	National Oil Co.	10/18/91	35.0
Jackson	Debra	National Oil Co.	10/25/91	37.0
Jackson	Phillip	City Revenue Dept.	10/18/91	40.0
Jackson	Phillip	City Revenue Dept.	10/25/91	40.0
Ballou	Joseph	Smith Builders	10/18/91	40.0
Ballou	Joseph	Smith Builders	10/25/91	39.0
Shelorson	Mildred	City Revenue Dept.	10/18/91	38.0
Shelorson	Mildred	City Revenue Dept.	10/25/91	40.0
Murray	John	Smith Builders	10/18/91	40.0
Murray	John	Smith Builders	10/25/91	35.0
Tahan	Joseph	National Oil Co.	10/18/91	37.5
Tahan	Joseph	National Oil Co.	10/25/91	40.0
Lord	Scott	National Oil Co.	10/18/91	40.0
Lord	Scott	National Oil Co.	10/25/91	38.0

Figure 10-3. *The results of a sample relational query*

To relate databases using the View window, first open the View window by choosing View from the Window menu. The View window appears, as shown in Figure 10-4.

In the View window, you see ten work areas, lettered from "A" through "J." A database file can be opened in each of these work areas. The text buttons that appear at the left side of the View window are labeled View, On/Off, Files, Misc, Setup, Browse, Open, and Close. The top four buttons—View, On/Off, Files, and Misc—display windows by the same names when chosen. The View window button is used to get back to the View window from one of the other windows. The On/Off button displays a window of environmental settings, such as the bell and the use of the ESC key, that can be turned on or off. The Files button displays a Files window that you can use to set the default drive and path. The Misc (for "miscellaneous") button displays a window where you can change assorted settings in FoxPro, such as the symbol used for currency, and the tone used for the bell.

The bottom buttons—Setup, Browse, Open, and Close—relate to files you are using through the View window. Use Setup to display the Setup dialog box. From here, you can decide which index files should be used with a database or you can change the structure of a database. Use the Browse button to display the currently selected database in a Browse window. Use Open to display the Open File dialog box, so that you can open a particular database file in the chosen work area. The Close button, when available, is used to close the database that is open in the currently selected work area.

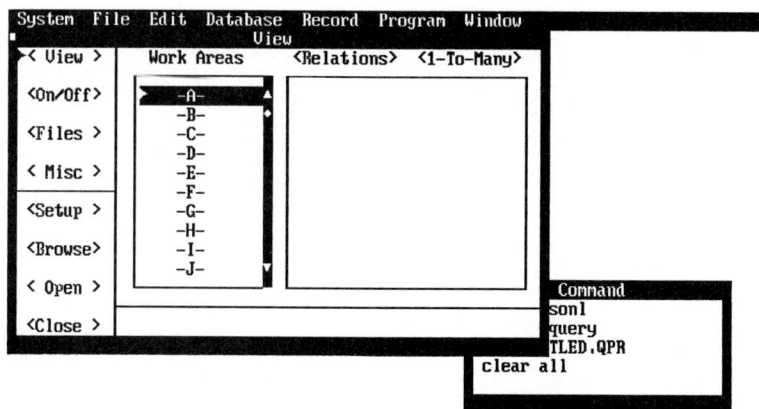

Figure 10-4.   *The View window*

Setting Relations Through the View Window

Once the View window is visible, you must open all needed files in their own work areas. To open a file, first tab to or click on the desired work area; then choose Open (click on Open or press P) to display the Select Database dialog box. From the dialog box, choose the desired database, then choose OK. If you have duplicated the sample databases in this book, tab to or click on work area A, then press P to display the Select Database dialog box, choose HOURS.DBF from the list box, and finally, choose Open. In a similar manner, tab the cursor over to (or click on) work area B, then press ENTER to display the Select Database dialog box, choose PERSONL.DBF from the list box, and choose Open. At this point, the View window will show both files open in work areas A and B, as shown in Figure 10-5. The triangle beside PERSONL indicates that it is the active file. You can make any file the active one by clicking on it, or by highlighting it and pressing ENTER followed by ESC (to close the Browse window that appears).

If you are following the example, the PERSONL file is currently the active file in the Work Areas list box. Since the file must be indexed, first choose Setup (click on it, or press S). At the right side of the dialog box that appears (in the Index area), choose Add (press A) to add an index. Choose New, highlight the Ssn field in the list box, and press ENTER. Choose OK to accept the index as a tag to the compound index file. Choose OK again to return to the View window.

The next step is to select the database that will be the parent database. With relationships, one database is the *parent database*, and the other is the *child database*. The parent database controls the child, so that whenever you move the record pointer in the parent database, the record pointer in the child database

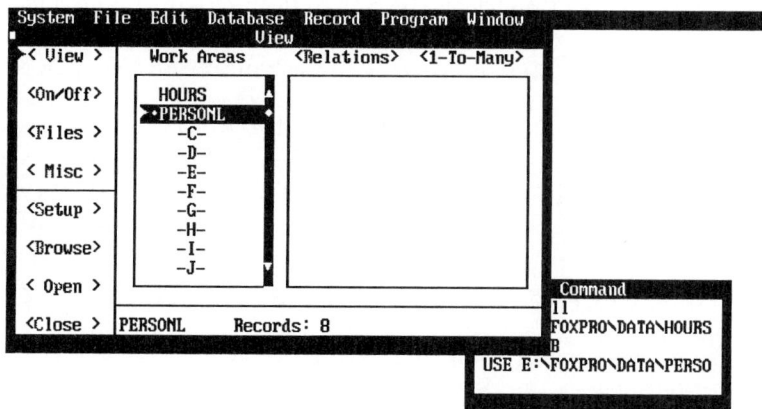

Figure 10-5. *Multiple files open in the View window*

moves accordingly. Once you have highlighted the parent database in the Work Areas list box, choose the Relations pushbutton at the top of the View window. The name of the parent database will appear in the Relations list (at the right side of the View window), and an arrow will be pointing from it. If you are following the example, highlight the HOURS file in the Work Areas list box and press ENTER and then ESC. Next, click on Relations (or press R). The name HOURS will appear in the Relations box and an arrow will appear pointing below and to the right of the HOURS name.

Next, you must choose (in the Work Areas list box) the child database that will be related to the parent database. The child database must be indexed on the basis of the relation. If the child database is already indexed, the Expression Builder appears, and if the indexed field matches a field in the parent database, FoxPro uses this field name as the default in the Expression Builder. (You can change it to anything you want.) If the child database is indexed but the order has not been set, a Set Index Order dialog appears, so you can choose the desired order. Note that if the child database has not been indexed, FoxPro assumes that you want to establish a relationship based on record numbers. This is rarely practiced, so you'll probably want to index your files before establishing relationships through the View window.

If you are following the example, highlight PERSONL in the Work Areas list box and press ENTER. When you do this, the Set Index Order dialog box appears, and the field name Ssn appears by default in the list box. Because the child (PERSONL) database is indexed on the Ssn field, and an equivalent field exists in the parent (HOURS) database, FoxPro assumes that this is the field that should be used for the link.

Choose OK from the dialog box, then choose OK again from the Expression Builder dialog box that appears. At this point, the arrow coming out of the HOURS filename points into the PERSONL filename in the View window, as shown in Figure 10-6. Also note the dot that appears beside the filename PERSONL. In the View window, the dot indicates that the file is indexed.

With HOURS still chosen in the Work Areas list box, you can click on the Browse button (or press B) to display a Browse window for the HOURS file. Press CTRL-F1 until the View window is again visible, and select PERSONL in the Work Areas list box. (Click on it and press B for Browse or move the cursor to PERSONL and press ENTER.) Another Browse window will appear for the PERSONL file. If you use the usual sizing methods to move and size the windows so you can see both at the same time, you will see that the relationship has been established. As you move the cursor within the HOURS file, you will see that there is a corresponding movement to the appropriate employee name in the PERSONL file.

With the relationship established, you can use a combination of alias name and pointer (*filename-* >) along with the field name to retrieve data or to indicate fields within reports you design. For example, the expression

```
PERSONL->Firstname
```

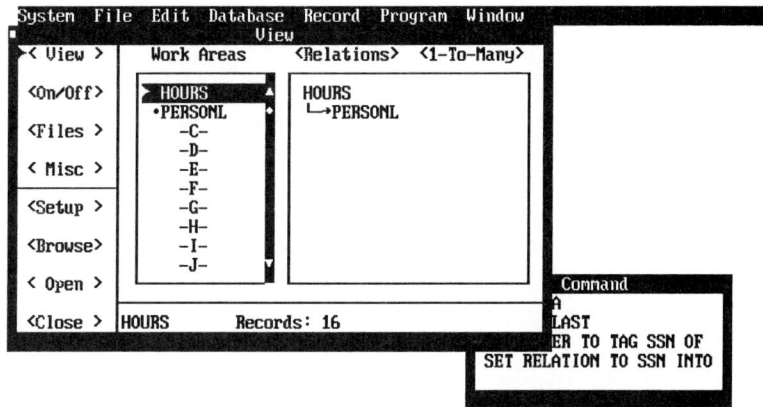

Figure 10-6.   *The View window showing the established relationship*

indicates the Firstname field from the PERSONL database, where PERSONL is the *alias*, Firstname is the *field name*, and a hyphen and a greater-than sign make up the *pointer*. As an example, first close both the Browse window and the View window by pressing ESC repeatedly, so you can see the screen. Then, try these commands:

```
SELECT 1
LIST PERSONL->Lastname, HOURS->Weekdate, HOURS->Workhours
```

Your results should resemble the following:

Record#	PERSONL.LASTNAME	HOURS.WEEKDATE	HOURS.WORKHOURS
1	Jackson	10/18/91	35.0
2	Tahan	10/18/91	37.5
3	Lord	10/18/91	40.0
4	Saeedi	10/18/91	38.5
5	Jackson	10/18/91	40.0
6	Shelorson	10/18/91	38.0
7	Ballou	10/18/91	40.0
8	Murray	10/18/91	40.0
9	Jackson	10/25/91	37.0
10	Tahan	10/25/91	40.0
11	Lord	10/25/91	38.0
12	Saeedi	10/25/91	39.5
13	Jackson	10/25/91	40.0
14	Shelorson	10/25/91	40.0

```
15   Ballou                  10/25/91              39.0
16   Murray                  10/25/91              35.0
```

You can use the same technique of alias name, pointer, and filename to indicate desired fields in the reports that you design. Remember, when producing relational reports you must establish the needed relationship before you attempt to generate the report. See the next section, "Relating Files with SET RELATION," for more details about the use of commands when a relationship has been established. Also, see "Creating Relational Reports" later in this chapter for specific tips on designing relational reports for use once you have established a relationship.

Relating Files with SET RELATION

The relational powers provided by FoxPro are also available from the command level. Databases can be linked through the use of the SET RELATION command, which establishes a relationship based on a common field (or combination of common fields). The example that follows uses a relationship based on the common social security number (Ssn) field, which exists in both the HOURS .DBF and the PERSONL.DBF database files. Once a link has been established with the SET RELATION command, whenever the record pointer is moved in the HOURS database, the record pointer in the PERSONL database will move to the record containing the same social security number as is contained in the HOURS database. This link lets you display matching data from both files with a LIST command. You can also design reports or labels that are based on a relational link between files.

The syntax for the SET RELATION command is

SET RELATION TO *key expression* INTO *alias* [ADDITIVE]

Key expression is the common field or fields present in both databases. The *alias* is usually the name of the other database that the active database will be linked to. Note that ADDITIVE is an optional clause, needed only when you are setting a relation into more than one file at a time.

The overall process of linking two databases using a common field involves the following steps:

1. Open the file from which you want to establish the relation in one work area.

2. In another work area, open the file that you wish to link to the first file.

3. Activate an index file based on the field (or expression) that is the basis of the relationship.

4. Use the SET RELATION command to establish the link.

Once the link exists, moving the record pointer in the active file results in a corresponding movement of the record pointer in the related file. The nature of such a relationship is evident from the following example.

An important requirement of the SET RELATION command is that the related file must be indexed on the common field. In the case of this example, the PERSONL database must be indexed on the Ssn field. Enter the following commands to create an index file for the PERSONL database, based on the social security field.

```
CLEAR ALL
USE PERSONL
INDEX ON Ssn TO SOCIALS
```

You can work with multiple database files by opening more than one database file at a time. You do this by using different work areas; each work area contains a different database file. You choose the desired work area with the SELECT command; for example, entering **SELECT 2** at the command level would choose work area 2. (When no SELECT command is used, work area 1 is chosen by default.)

Open the HOURS and PERSONL database files by using the following commands:

```
CLOSE DATABASES
SELECT 1
USE HOURS
USE PERSONL IN 2 INDEX SOCIALS
```

NOTE: The USE PERSONL IN 2 portion of the command line tells FoxPro to open the database file PERSONL, but to open it in work area 2 without actually changing work areas. The INDEX SOCIALS option tells FoxPro to open the SOCIALS index file you just created.

Now you can use the SET RELATION command to establish a link based on the common Ssn field. The HOURS database is currently active, so you can link the PERSONL database to the HOURS database. Enter

```
SET RELATION TO Ssn INTO PERSONL
```

The change is not yet visibly apparent, but FoxPro has established a relationship between the files. To see the results, enter the commands

```
GO 4
DISPLAY
```

and you will see the fourth record in the HOURS database. The record indicates that an employee having the social security number 555-77-7723 worked 38.5 hours for the City Revenue Department.

To determine the name of this employee, enter

```
SELECT 2
DISPLAY
```

The PERSONL database (open in work area 2) will become the active database. The record pointer will be at record 1 (the record containing the social security number 555-77-7723), and you can see that the employee is Maryann L. Saeedi. Because of the relation, FoxPro has automatically found a matching social security number in the PERSONL database.

Wherever you move the record pointer in the HOURS database, FoxPro will try to move the record pointer to a matching social security number in the PERSONL database. If FoxPro cannot find a match according to the relationship you have established, the record pointer will be positioned at the end of the database. At the end of a file, all fields are blank. You can use this fact to test for failures to find a match by listing key fields from both databases.

You can retrieve data in the related file by including the alias name and pointer (*filename->*) along with the field name. In the expression

```
PERSONL->Firstname
```

the filename PERSONL is the alias, and Firstname is the field name. The combination of the hyphen and greater-than symbol make up the pointer. To see how this works, try the following commands:

```
SELECT 1
LIST PERSONL->Lastname, Weekdate, Assignment, Workhours
```

The results,

```
PERSONL.LASTNAME WEEKDATE  ASSIGNMENT          WORKHOURS
Jackson          10/18/91  National Oil Co.       35.0
Tahan            10/18/91  National Oil Co.       37.5
Lord             10/18/91  National Oil Co.       40.0
Saeedi           10/18/91  City Revenue Dept.     38.5
Jackson          10/18/91  City Revenue Dept.     40.0
Shelorson        10/18/91  City Revenue Dept.     38.0
Ballou           10/18/91  Smith Builders         40.0
```

```
Murray          10/18/91   Smith Builders            40.0
Jackson         10/25/91   National Oil Co.          37.0
Tahan           10/25/91   National Oil Co.          40.0
Lord            10/25/91   National Oil Co.          38.0
Saeedi          10/25/91   City Revenue Dept.        39.5
Jackson         10/25/91   City Revenue Dept.        40.0
Shelorson       10/25/91   City Revenue Dept.        40.0
Ballou          10/25/91   Smith Builders            39.0
Murray          10/25/91   Smith Builders            35.0
```

demonstrate that the SET RELATION command, combined with the use of the alias and pointer, can be a powerful tool for obtaining relational data. You could add the TO PRINT option at the end of the LIST command to generate a printed list like the one shown above.

When working with related files, remember that you can test for mismatched records (such as an entry in the HOURS file with no matching social security number) by listing the common field from each of the related files. For example, the command

```
LIST HOURS->Ssn, PERSONL->Ssn, PERSONL->Lastname
```

should produce a listing with a matching member for each entry in the HOURS file. If an employee name and social security number turns up blank next to an entry in the HOURS listing, it is clear that a mismatch exists. Such a mismatch could be caused by a social security number entered incorrectly into the HOURS file.

A Warning About Relationships and Indexes

When working with related files, you must make sure that the indexes that support the use of the SET RELATION command are kept current. If someone opens a database without using an accompanying index file and adds or edits records, the resulting incomplete index files can cause incorrect results when you are trying to establish relationships or generate relational reports. When in doubt, use REINDEX to rebuild any indexes you are using.

Using View Files to Store Relationships

If you are going to establish relationships from the command level (as opposed to creating them by running a program), you'll likely find the CREATE VIEW FROM ENVIRONMENT command to be a useful one. This command lets you take a "snapshot" of all open databases and index files and of any existing relationships. You can avoid a considerable amount of repetitive typing by saving the relationship as part of a view file, then using the SET VIEW command to open the database files and index files and establish the relationship at the same time.

You save the environment, including the relational link, by entering

CREATE VIEW *filename* FROM ENVIRONMENT

where *filename* is the name you want to give the view file. At any time later, you can reopen the databases, the index files, and the relational link by entering

SET VIEW TO *filename*

where *filename* is the name that you gave to the view file when you saved it.

Creating Relational Reports

As mentioned earlier, once the SET RELATION command (or the View window) has been used to establish a relationship, you can use the LIST . . . TO PRINT command to generate simple listings of relational data. You must include the filename and pointer when you are retrieving data from the related file. The same technique can be used when designing relational reports. When entering a field name or an expression into the Expression window during the creation of the report, you must again include the filename and pointer symbols to indicate a field in a related database. You can use this same technique with labels, if desired. Just include the filename and pointer whenever you are referencing a field that is not in the active database.

REMINDER: *All needed files must be open and the relationship established before you can generate a relational report or label. If all needed databases are not open and you try to print a relational report, you will get an "ALIAS NOT FOUND" error message. This indicates that, because the related file has not been opened and the relationship has not been established, the report cannot locate the data it needs.*

Analyzing Types of Relationships

Before you delve deeply into working with relationships between multiple files, you may find it necessary to do some analysis on paper and determine the relationships that need to be drawn between the fields. For example, when one field in a record of a database relates in a unique manner to a field in another record in a different database, you have a one-to-one relationship. For example, you may be managing a personnel system that contains employees' medical benefit information in one file and salary information in another file. Each database contains one record per employee, meaning that for every record in the medical file, there is a corresponding record for the same employee in the salary file. The relationship between the files is a one-to-one relationship.

By comparison, if one field of one record in the first file relates to a field in one or more records in the second file, you have a one-to-many relationship. The example used with the SET RELATION command in this chapter is that of a one-to-many relationship, as one record in the PERSONL file can have many records associated with it in the HOURS file.

Last is a type of relationship that is not as common as the first two: the many-to-many relationship, which occurs when a field of several records in one database will relate to a field of several records in another database. A common example of a many-to-many relationship is that of student tracking at a high school or college, where many students are assigned to many different classes. To set up this or any many-to-many relationship, you will need at least three database files. (The third file serves as an intermediate, or "linking," file between the two files that contain the "many" data.)

When relating files, it is often advantageous to have a field that will always contain unique data for each record in the database, such as the Ssn field used in our examples. (Unless an incorrect entry is made, no two employees will ever have the same social security number.) Customer numbers, employee ID numbers, and stock numbers are other types of data routinely used for the purpose of unique identification. In some cases, a single field with unique data may not be available; for example, you may have a list of customers, but your company may not assign customer numbers as a practice.

If you can't convince management to change the way it tracks customers, you have the alternative of creating a link based on more than one field. In the case of customers, you could index on a combination of Lastname + Firstname + Address and establish the relation on the expression with a command like

```
SET RELATION TO (Lastname + Firstname + Address) INTO MYFILE
```

This would provide a workable alternative, assuming you never have two customers with the same name living at the same address.

Chapter *11*

Creating Screens

When you are using APPEND, CHANGE, or EDIT to add data or make changes to a database, FoxPro presents you with an onscreen form that lists the various field names alongside highlighted areas that contain the actual data. While this provides a workable approach to adding and editing data, it has its limitations. One drawback is that the screen presented to the user may not be the friendliest possible; cryptic field names may make it difficult for new users to understand the purposes of the fields. Another drawback is the lack of control during an editing operation. If you want to restrict the editing of a particular field, you are very limited as to what you can do with the CHANGE or EDIT command. To overcome such limitations, FoxPro provides a means of designing screens, which can then be used for adding or editing data.

Differences Between Versions of FoxPro

The methods you'll use to create data entry screens differ greatly between FoxPro 1.*x* and FoxPro 2. If you are using FoxPro 2 or later, you can use FoxPro's built-in Screen Painter to design screens. If you are using FoxPro 1.*x*, you'll use a utility called FoxView (provided with your copy of FoxPro) to design screens. Because there are substantial differences between the two methods, they are discussed separately. If you are using FoxPro 1.*x*, you should refer to "Creating Entry Forms with FoxView" in the second half of this chapter. If you are using FoxPro 2 or later, you can continue reading and ignore the section discussing FoxView.

The FoxPro 2 Screen Painter and Format Files

If you've used earlier versions of FoxPro, FoxBASE+, dBASE III PLUS, or dBASE IV, you're probably familiar with the use of screen-design tools, or *screen painters*. The screen painter provided with FoxPro 1.*x* and FoxBASE+ is known as FoxView. With a screen painter, what generally happens is this. You start the screen painter, and you are presented with a (mostly) blank screen that serves as a drawing or design surface. You use various key combinations to place desired fields on the screen, and you can add descriptive text anywhere in the screen. When you save the screen design, a *format file* is generated. This format file contains program statements that control the layout of the data entry screen. Later, when you need to add or edit data using the screen's design, you can open the database and put the screen into effect with a SET FORMAT TO *screen filename* command. All further data entry and editing then follows the design of the screen.

What's important to note is that the Screen Painter in FoxPro 2 does things differently. You still lay out your screen using a design surface, and you can still move fields around on the screen, place descriptive text where needed, and save the results to a screen file. But you cannot directly generate a format file for use with the SET FORMAT TO command. What FoxPro's screen painter can generate is a "code snippet," or a portion of a program, that can be integrated into your FoxPro programs (assuming you have some knowledge of programming). If your programming experience is limited, there is a way to use the code that the Screen Painter generates. This chapter will show how you can design and save screens for use in your FoxPro programs, and how the results of saved screens can be used to enter and edit data.

Starting the FoxPro Screen Painter

You can start the process of designing a new screen in one of two ways: choose New from the File menu, choose Screen in the dialog box that appears, and choose OK or enter **CREATE SCREEN** in the Command window. Using either method, the Screen Painter appears, as shown in Figure 11-1. Note that a new menu called Screen is added to the menu bar when you are using the screen painter; in the figure, the menu is shown open.

The Screen Menu

The various commands on the Screen menu can be used to place objects at desired locations on the screen and to bring up dialog boxes that control additional aspects of the screen. The Screen Layout option causes the Screen Layout dialog box to appear; this dialog box contains options for defining a window and will be covered in further detail later. The Open All Snippets option

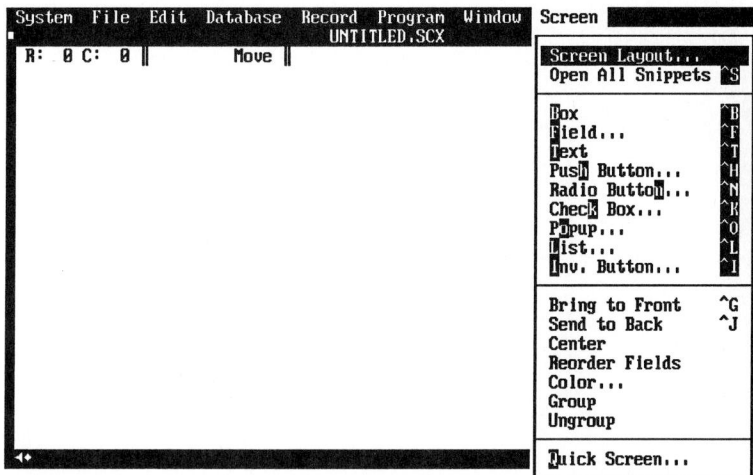

Figure 11-1. *The FoxPro Screen Painter with the Screen menu visible*

relates to opening code snippets, a feature of programming (see Part II of this book for a detailed discussion of programming). The next portion of the menu contains the choices for the types of objects you can choose to insert at the cursor location; you can insert boxes, fields, text, pushbuttons, radio buttons, check boxes, popup menus, list boxes, and invisible buttons. (Invisible buttons are regions of a screen you define, which a user may click on to select an option.)

Below the menu choices for the desired types of objects appear a number of menu choices that control how the objects appear, or are placed. These include Bring to Front, Send to Back, Center, Reorder Fields, Color, Group, and Ungroup. The last choice in this menu, Quick Screen, lets you quickly create a default screen based on all the fields in a database file.

Once you have started the Screen Painter, you can design the data entry screen by placing fields at the desired location with the Field option of the Screen menu or with the CTRL-F key combination, as described shortly. You can place text where desired by typing the text and pressing ENTER. You can also create a default screen quickly by opening the Screen menu with ALT-C, and choosing Quick Screen from the menu. When you do this, the Quick Screen dialog box appears, as in Figure 11-2.

In the dialog box, you can choose By Column Layout to arrange the database fields in columnar form, or you can choose By Row Layout to arrange the fields by rows.

The Titles option, when checked, causes titles based on the field names to appear beside the fields.

The Fields option, when checked, displays a Field Picker dialog box. From this dialog box, you can choose specific fields to be included in the screen. By default, the Quick Screen option includes all fields.

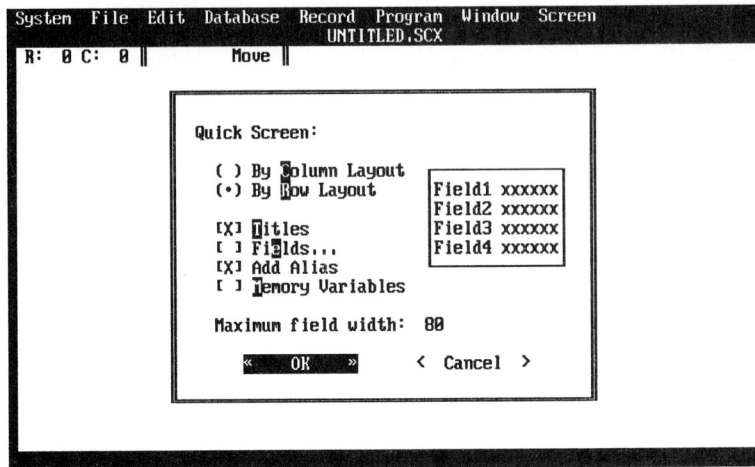

Figure 11-2.   *The Quick Screen dialog box*

The Add Alias option, when checked, tells FoxPro to add any alias names to the field names within the program code generated by the Screen Painter. This is useful if you are planning to use the screen design in a relational application.

The Memory Variables option, when checked, tells FoxPro to create memory variables for all the fields. This may be useful in programming, as many programmers write data entry and editing programs that make use of variables, as discussed in Part II of this book.

Use the Maximum field width option to specify the maximum displayed width of any field in the form. If a field is longer than the maximum displayed width, the Screen Painter will create a field in which the contents can scroll from left to right.

Once you have chosen the desired options in the Quick Screen dialog box, choose OK, and a default screen is created for the database in use. Figure 11-3 shows an example of a default screen created with the Quick Screen options of the Screen menu.

Placing Fields

If you prefer not to use the Quick Screen option, you can place the desired fields at the cursor location manually by choosing Field from the Screen menu or with the CTRL-F key combination. Place the cursor at the desired location for the field, and press CTRL-F. This causes the Field dialog box to appear, as in Figure 11-4.

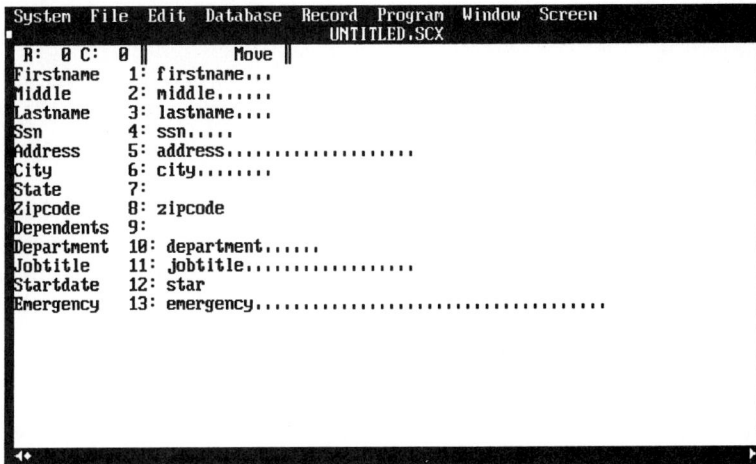

Figure 11-3. Sample results of the Quick Screen menu option

You can choose the desired type of field: Say, Get, or Edit. The default choice, Get, is most often used; this tells FoxPro to display the field in reverse video. The field can be edited by the user. In the programming code produced by Screen Painter, FoxPro uses an @ . . . GET command to display and allow editing of the field.

Figure 11-4. The Field dialog box

The Say choice specifies a display only field. If you choose this option, the code for the screen contains an @ . . . SAY command to display the field and prohibit editing.

The Edit choice causes FoxPro to create a data entry area that is larger than the field; the user can then scroll through this area when editing. If you choose this option, the code for the screen contains an @ . . . EDIT command to display the field.

Depending on the choice made, the entry box immediately below the Say, Get, and Edit buttons displays the name Say, Get, or Edit, along with a text box where you can enter the name of the desired field. You can type the field name or choose the pushbutton (Say, Get, or Edit) to display a list box of fields. Choose the desired field name from the list.

Also, depending on your choice of the type of fields, you can use the options at the bottom of the dialog box to specify a range for editing of the field or to add optional clauses that further control editing of the field. The When clause allows editing of a field only when a specified logical expression is true. The Valid clause permits validity checking of an entry. The Message clause lets you add a help message that appears at the bottom of the screen when the cursor moves into this area. The Error clause lets you display a custom error message whenever the clause specified by VALID is invalid. The Comment option lets you add a comment about the object. The Disabled option disables the field, so it is skipped over during editing. The Refresh option is available only when you choose Say as the type of field. You must check this box if you want the value displayed by the field to change automatically as the record pointer is moved to another record. The Scroll bar, Allow tabs, and Length options are used only when you choose Edit as the type of field. These options let you determine whether a scroll bar appears with the editing region, whether tabs in the editing region will be allowed, and the desired length for the editing region.

Placing Text

To enter descriptive text, such as titles and headings for fields, place the cursor at the location where the text is to begin. Type the desired text and press ENTER to complete the text entry. You can use the Text option of the Screen menu and begin typing, but it is easier to simply type the text at the desired screen location. Once you press ENTER after typing the text, all typed characters become a single object that you can move around the screen.

Moving and Deleting Objects

Like most screen painters, the Screen Painter in FoxPro 2 is *object oriented*. This means that any fields or text you place on the screen are considered objects. You can move objects around on the screen and delete any unwanted objects. To move an object (whether it is text or a field), place the cursor anywhere on the object, and click on it or press the SPACEBAR. The object will be highlighted, indicating that it has been selected. Use the cursor keys or the mouse to drag the object to its desired location. If you use the cursor keys, you must press ENTER to anchor the object in its new location; with the mouse, the object is anchored as soon as you release the left mouse button and click elsewhere.

To delete an unwanted object, first select the object by using the selection methods just described. Then press DEL.

Placing Boxes

To place a box, first place the cursor in the upper-left corner for the desired box. Then, choose Box from the Screen menu or press CTRL-B; a small blinking box will appear on the screen. Use the arrow keys or the mouse (click on a corner of the box and drag) to stretch the box to the desired size, then press ENTER.

Placing Pushbuttons

Pushbuttons are multiple-choice buttons that resemble those used by the FoxPro dialog boxes. You normally use pushbuttons in a screen when you want to present the user with one of several possible options. To place a pushbutton, first place the cursor in the desired location for the pushbutton. Then choose Push Button from the Screen menu (or press CTRL-H). The Push Button dialog box appears, as shown in Figure 11-5.

In the Push Button Prompts area at the left side of the dialog box, you enter the desired prompts for the various buttons. At the right side of the dialog box, you can use the Horizontal and Vertical options to specify whether the buttons should be laid out horizontally or vertically. The Terminating option determines whether the user choosing any of these pushbuttons will terminate the editing

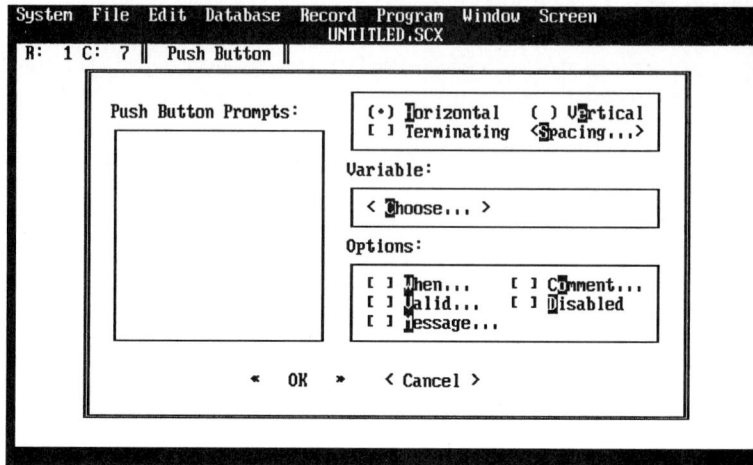

```
 System  File  Edit  Database  Record  Program  Window  Screen
                              UNTITLED.SCX
 R:  1 C:  7 ║  Push Button ║

        Push Button Prompts:      (•) Horizontal    ( ) Vertical
                                  [ ] Terminating   <Spacing...>
      ┌─────────────────────┐
      │                     │     Variable:
      │                     │     ┌──────────────────────────┐
      │                     │     │  < Choose... >           │
      │                     │     └──────────────────────────┘
      │                     │
      │                     │     Options:
      │                     │     ┌──────────────────────────┐
      │                     │     │ [ ] Then...    [ ] Comment...│
      │                     │     │ [ ] Valid...   [ ] Disabled  │
      └─────────────────────┘     │ [ ] Message...               │
                                  └──────────────────────────┘

                    «   OK   »   < Cancel >
```

Figure 11-5.   *The Push Button dialog box*

operation. In most cases, you would want this option turned off, which is the default. In some cases, such as where you add an OK pushbutton to a screen, you would want such a button to be terminating.

The Spacing option lets you change spacing between pushbuttons; by default, FoxPro puts one line between buttons arranged vertically, and one space between buttons arranged horizontally.

In the Variable text box, you enter the name of the field (or memory variable) that the user's choice will be stored to. You can type in the field name or variable name, or choose an existing field name with the Choose button. If you enter a variable name that does not exist in the current environment, FoxPro adds program code to create a variable by that name.

The When option allows selection of a button only when a specified logical expression is true. The Valid option permits validity checking of the selection of a button. The Message option lets you add a help message that appears at the bottom of the screen when the cursor moves into this field of the screen. The Comment option lets you add a comment of your choosing about the pushbutton. Such comments are purely for your reference, as they are visible in the Comment field whenever you are editing the design of the screen. The Disabled option disables the pushbutton, so it is skipped over during editing.

Placing Radio Buttons

Radio buttons are much like pushbuttons. Like pushbuttons, FoxPro uses radio buttons extensively in its dialog boxes. Like pushbuttons, they provide a list of choices that the user can select from. To place a radio button, first place the cursor in the desired location for the button. Then choose Radio Button from the Screen menu or press CTRL-N. The Radio Button dialog box appears, as shown in Figure 11-6.

In the Radio Button Prompts area at the left side of the dialog box, you enter the desired prompts for the various buttons. At the right side of the dialog box, you can use the Horizontal and Vertical options to specify whether the buttons should be laid out horizontally or vertically. In the Variable text box, you enter the name of the field or memory variable that the user's choice will be stored to. You can type in the field name or variable name or choose an existing field name with the Choose button. If you enter a variable name that does not exist in the current environment, FoxPro adds program code to create a variable by that name.

The When option allows selection of a button only when a specified logical expression is true. The Valid option permits validity checking of the button selection. The Message option lets you add a help message that appears at the

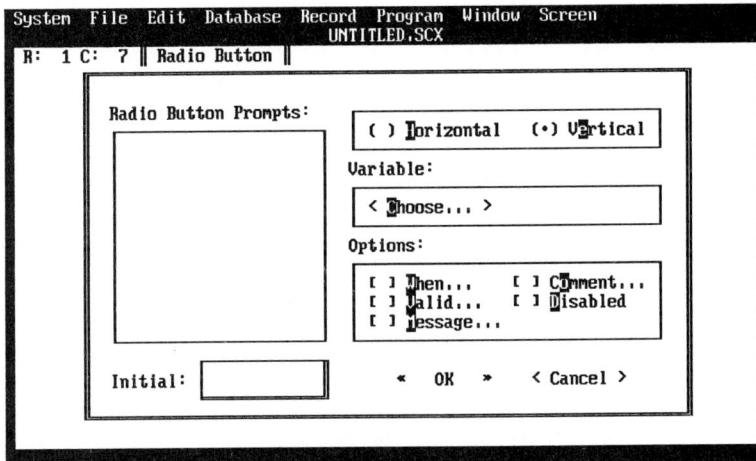

Figure 11-6.   *The Radio Button dialog box*

bottom of the screen when the cursor moves into this field of the screen. The Comment option lets you add a comment of your choice about the radio button. The Disabled option disables the radio button, so it is skipped over during editing. Use the Initial list box to choose which radio button should be initially selected as the default in your screen.

Placing Check Boxes

Check boxes are simple yes/no selections that are shown as brackets on the screen. To place a check box, first place the cursor in the desired location for the check box. Then choose Check Box from the Screen menu or press CTRL-K. The Check Box dialog box appears, as shown in Figure 11-7.

Since a check box provides only one option (yes or no), there is an entry box for just one prompt. Enter your desired prompt for the check box here. In the Variable text box, you enter the name of the field or memory variable that the user's choice will be stored to. You can type in the field name or variable name, or choose an existing field name with the Choose button. If you enter a variable name that does not exist in the current environment, FoxPro adds program code to create a variable by that name.

The When option allows checking of a box only when a specified logical expression is true. The Valid option permits validity checking of the check box. The Message option lets you add a help message that appears at the bottom of

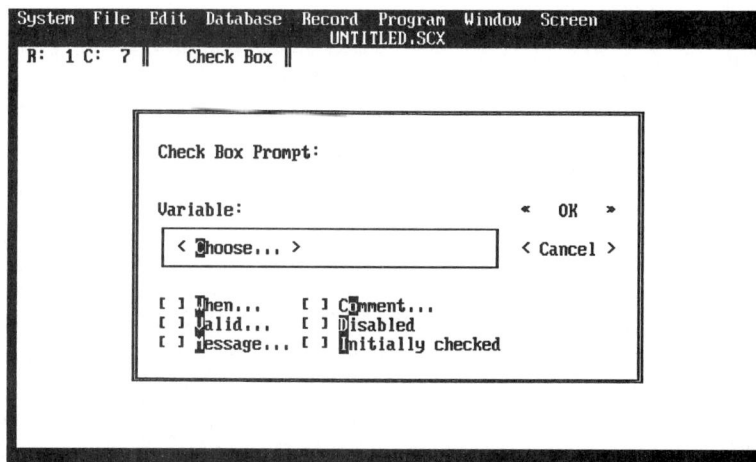

Figure 11-7.   The Check Box dialog box

the screen when the cursor moves into this field of the screen. The Comment option lets you add a comment of your choosing about the check box. The Disabled option disables the check box, so it is skipped over during editing. Use the Initially checked box to determine whether the check box should be initially checked in your screen.

Placing Popups

Popups are the popup menus, or lists of choices, that are also used in many places throughout FoxPro. When you specify the popup, you define all the items that can appear in the popup. To place a popup, first place the cursor in the desired location for the popup. Then choose Popup from the Screen menu or press CTRL-O. The Popup dialog box appears, as shown in Figure 11-8.

In the List Popup area at the left side of the dialog box, you enter the desired prompts for the choices of the popup. At the right side of the dialog box, you can use the Array Popup option to specify the name of an array that the list of choices should be based on. In the Variable text box, you enter the name of the field (or memory variable) that the user's choice will be stored to. You can type in the field name or variable name, or choose an existing field name with the Choose button. If you enter a variable name that does not exist in the current environment, FoxPro adds program code to create a variable by that name.

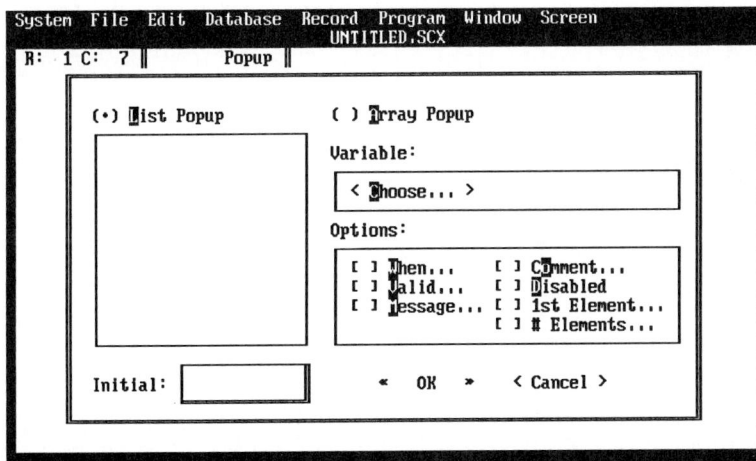

Figure 11-8. The Popup dialog box

The When option allows selection of a popup only when a specified logical expression is true. The Valid option permits validity checking of the selection from a popup. The Message option lets you add a help message that appears at the bottom of the screen when the cursor moves into this field of the screen. The Comment option lets you add a comment of your choosing about the popup. The Disabled option disables the popup, so it is skipped over during editing.

The 1st Element and # Elements options are used only when you choose the Array Popup option. Normally, all elements of an array are used by the popup. Use these options to change that default. You can specify the first element of the array to use for the popup, and the number of elements of the array to include as popup choices. Use the Initial list box to choose which choice within the popup should be initially selected (the default) in your screen.

Placing Lists

FoxPro's Screen Painter also lets you place scrollable lists in a form. These lists can be based on the contents of an array-type memory variable, a popup menu, fields of a database structure, records in a chosen field, or files available on disk. To place a list, first place the cursor in the desired location for the list. Then choose List from the Screen menu or press CTRL-L. The List dialog box appears, as shown in Figure 11-9.

In the List Type area at the left side of the dialog box, you choose the type of object that the list will be based on (Array, Popup, Structure, Field, or Files).

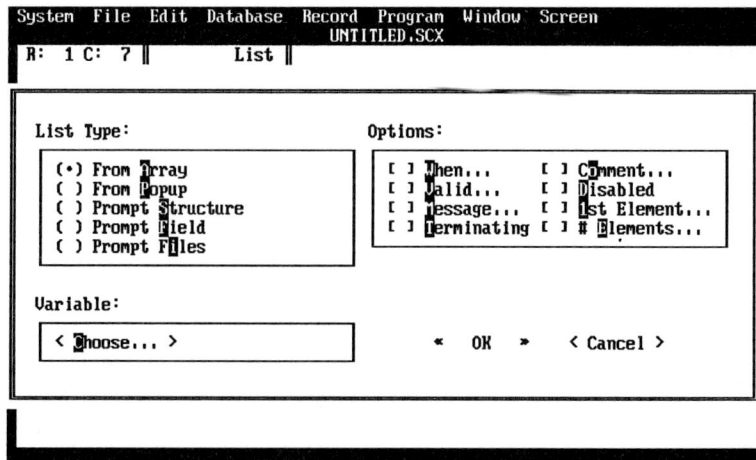

Figure 11-9. *The List dialog box*

Choose Array to base the list on the contents of an existing array-type memory variable. Choose Popup to define the list based on an existing popup. Choose Prompt Structure to base the list on the fields of a database structure. Choose Prompt Field to base the list on existing entries of all records for a particular field in a database. Choose Prompt Files to base the list on available files in the current directory.

In the Variable text box, you enter the name of the field or memory variable that the user's choice will be stored to. You can type in the field name or variable name or choose an existing field name with the Choose button. If you enter a variable name that does not exist in the current environment, FoxPro adds program code to create a variable by that name.

The When option allows selection of a choice in the list only when a specified logical expression is true. The Valid option permits validity checking of the selection from a list. The Message option lets you add a help message that appears at the bottom of the screen when the cursor moves into this list box on the screen. The Comment option lets you add a comment of your choice about the list. The Disabled option disables the list, so it is skipped over during editing.

The 1st Element and # Elements options are used only when you choose the From Array option. Normally, all elements of an array are used by the list. Use these options to change that default; you can specify the first element of the array to use for the list and the number of elements of the array to include as list choices. The Terminating check box can be used to tell FoxPro to terminate the data entry when the user chooses this option.

Further Control of Screen Objects

As mentioned earlier, there are choices in the Screen menu that let you further control the objects you place on the screen. These options include Bring to Front, Send to Back, Center, Reorder Fields, Color, Group, and Ungroup. These options are detailed as follows.

Bring to Front and Send to Back let you change the order in which objects may lie atop one another. Select the desired object and choose Bring to Front to bring that object to the front or select Send to Back to move that object to the back. For example, you might purposely draw a box that passes over a field at some point. You could select the field and then choose Bring to Front to display the field atop the portion of the box. Selecting the box and then choosing Send to Back would accomplish the same result.

The Center option of the menu centers the selected object relative to the screen or window it is in. The Reorder Fields option changes the order that selected fields are accessed on the screen. The Color option of the menu causes the Color Picker dialog to appear; you can then select the desired colors for the object.

The Group option of the menu changes all currently selected objects into a single group, so you can move the selected objects as a single object. You can select multiple objects by moving to each object and pressing SHIFT-SPACEBAR or by holding the SHIFT key while clicking with the mouse. Once a series of objects has been combined into a single object with the Group option, you can select that object and use the Ungroup option to ungroup them, restoring them to individual objects.

Saving Screens and Generating Code

Once you have completed a screen design, you can save the screen with the Save command of the File menu or with CTRL-W. When you choose Save from the File menu or press CTRL-W, the characteristics behind the screen's design are saved to a special file with an .SCX extension. You will need this file if you want to make further changes to the screen's design.

In addition to saving the design of the screen, you will also need to generate program code based on the screen's design if you want to make actual use of the screen. To generate code for the screen, open the Program menu and choose Generate. The Generate dialog box appears, as shown in Figure 11-10.

Many of the options in the Generate dialog box are associated with programming, so they may or may not make sense at this point. (Part II of this book has more details on FoxPro programming.) In the Screens list box at the left side of the dialog box, you can enter the names of all screens to be included in the generated code. Use the Edit button to edit the name of a screen; use the Add and Remove buttons to add or remove screens from the list box.

Figure 11-10.   *The Generate dialog box*

HINT: FoxPro lets you include multiple screens in the code generated by Screen Painter. By default, the screen you have been designing appears by name in the list box, but you can add other screens that will then be included within the generated code. A default screen provided with FoxPro, called CONTROL, may be particularly helpful to include with your screens; this screen provides buttons for movement within a database.

The Code options at the right side of the dialog box let you customize the behavior of the program code produced by the Screen Painter; you can control whether screens automatically open and close files, whether windows are defined and released by the code, and how READ commands within the code are applied. These options may interest you if you are an advanced programmer; if not (or if the options make no sense at this point), you can just leave all the options in their default positions.

In the Output File text box at the bottom of the screen is the proposed name for the screen. By default, this name will be the same name as you opened or saved the screen under, but with an extension of .SPR.

Once you have added any additional screens to the list box and edited the filename (if desired), choose the Generate button at the bottom of the dialog box to generate the screen. The program code will be generated and saved to the filename you indicated with an extension of .SPR.

Using Screens

As mentioned earlier, you cannot use the program code generated by the Screen Painter in FoxPro 2 with a SET FORMAT TO command. However, you can use the program code generated by FoxPro (the .SPR file) within your own programs, or you can move the record pointer to the desired record manually and enter **DO** *filename***.SPR**, where *filename* is the name of the screen file, to edit the record through the screen. For example, if you design a screen and save that screen under the name MAILER and generate the program code using the default extension of MAILER.SPR, you can enter the following command

```
DO MAILER.SPR
```

and the form will appear, displaying the current record for the database. When writing your own programs, you can integrate the program code generated by Screen Painter by entering **DO** *filename***.SPR** at the appropriate location in your program or by using FoxPro's Editor to read the contents of the .SPR file directly into your program. When using .SPR files in your programs, remember that it is the responsibility of your program to find the desired record for editing before calling the screen file with the DO command.

NOTE: *If you prefer to design screens that can be easily used from the command level, consider adding the CONTROL1 screen file, provided with FoxPro 2, to the screens you design. (CONTROL1.SCX is a screen design that is included with the sample Organizer application provided with FoxPro.) Doing so will make it easy to edit records, as buttons will appear in your screen for moving throughout a database.*

A Screen Painter Example

Assuming you've duplicated the example of the PERSONL database, you can create a screen for data entry and editing by performing the following steps.

1. Start FoxPro and enter **USE PERSONL** in the Command window to open the database.

2. Enter **CREATE SCREEN SAMPLE1** in the Command window to start the Screen Painter.

3. Open the Screen menu with ALT-C and choose Quick Screen. With the defaults chosen in the dialog box, choose OK.

4. Select all field names and all fields by holding SHIFT and using the arrow keys followed by SPACEBAR or by holding SHIFT and clicking on each field name and each field with the mouse.

5. With all fields selected, use the mouse or the arrow keys to drag the fields and field names to the center portion of the screen. Press ENTER to anchor the fields in the new location.

6. Place the cursor just above and to the left of the word "Firstname." Open the Screen menu with ALT-C and choose Box. Drag the box with the cursor keys or the mouse until it encloses all the field names and all the fields and press ENTER to complete the drawing of the box.

7. At any blank space in the upper-right corner of the box, type **Press CTRL-W when done** and press ENTER.

8. Open the File menu with ALT-F and choose Save to save the screen design to a screen file. If you are asked if you want to save the environment information, answer yes. If you started this process by entering **CREATE SCREEN SAMPLE1**, the file will be saved under the name SAMPLE1 .SCX.

9. Open the Program menu with ALT-P and choose Generate. The Generate dialog box will appear.

10. Choose Generate. The Screen Painter will generate the code needed to create the screen. The program code will be saved to a file named SAMPLE1.SPR.

11. Press ESC to exit from the Screen Painter.

12. At the Command window, enter **GO 5** to go to record 5. Enter **DO SAMPLE1.SPR**. The current record will appear in the form you just designed. If you wanted to add a record using the form, you could enter **APPEND**, followed by **DO** *screen filename***.SPR**.

Creating Entry Forms with FoxView

NOTE: If you are using FoxPro 2 or later, none of the following applies. Refer to the first half of this chapter for details on creating forms with the built-in Screen Painter provided with FoxPro 2.

To create data entry forms in FoxPro version 1.*x*, use the Forms View mode of FoxView. To start FoxView, enter **FOXVIEW** from the command level or choose FoxView from the Program menu. An introduction screen will appear; press ENTER to continue. In a moment, the FoxView shell appears, as in Figure 11-11.

Because FoxView is a stand-alone program, you must load a database from the FoxView shell before you can begin creating a data entry screen. This is true even if you previously opened a database file while in FoxPro.

```
<D:\>                                   Friday  09/01/89  9:00

Welcome to FoxView 3.0
Press F1 for HELP

FoxView D:>
```

Figure 11-11.   The FoxView shell

Commands Available in FoxView

At the prompt in the FoxView shell, you can use commands for various purposes, such as loading database files to create forms, saving existing form designs, and displaying the structure of a database. The list below provides some of the more commonly used FoxView commands. The first four commands listed perform the same functions they do in DOS; see your DOS manual for more details about the purposes of these commands.

Command	Purpose
drive:	Changes default drive
CD*path*	Changes directory
DIR	Displays directory listing
DIR /W	Displays directory listing in wide format
LIST	Lists database structure for file in use
LOAD *filename*	Loads an existing table (previously saved with a screen form's design)
SAVE *filename*	Saves a current form and the underlying table on which it is based
USE *filename*	Loads a database file to be used in designing a new form
VIEW FORMS	Shows Forms View; same as pressing F10
VIEW TABLE	Shows Table View; same as pressing F10

You can also use certain keys for specific tasks while in FoxView. The F10 key will serve as a toggle to switch between Forms View and Table View. Forms View is a mode that displays the screen design you are working with as a form, while Table View displays an underlying table that the screen form is based upon. The SCROLL LOCK key exits either the Forms View or the Table View and returns to the FoxView shell. The ESC key is used to toggle a series of menus on and off. It may be most helpful to remember that regardless of where you are in FoxView, you can use the SCROLL LOCK key to get back to the FoxView Shell.

A general scenario for using FoxView to create forms is as follows.

1. Enter **USE** *filename* to open a database and simultaneously load the database fields into FoxView. (An alternative way of opening a file is to press ESC for the menus and choose Use Datafile from the Load menu.)

2. Then enter **VIEW FORMS** (or press F10) to switch to the Forms View mode. Here you see a form much like that used so far for entry and editing based on the database you opened with the USE command.

3. Next revise the form as desired, moving fields to new locations and changing the names of fields to more descriptive labels where necessary. You can also add lines and boxes and change colors within the form.

4. When the form changes are complete, save the form and the underlying table it is based on either by pressing SCROLL LOCK to get back to the shell and entering **SAVE** *filename* or by pressing ESC to display the menus and choosing Save Table from the Load menu.

5. You must also use the menus to generate a *format file*, which is used by FoxPro to display the data in your modified screen form. The format file is a text file containing @ . . . SAY . . . GET commands to control the display and editing of data. To do this, press ESC to display the menus and choose Select From Template List from the Gen menu. From the next menu to appear, you choose Format File Generator to create the format file.

When you want to modify an existing screen form, you can enter **LOAD** <*filename*> from the FoxView shell to load the existing file. (An alternative method is to press ESC for the menus and choose Load Table from the Load menu.) Once the existing form has been loaded, you can then enter **VIEW FORMS** (or press F10) to switch to the Forms View mode. You next revise the form as desired, and save the changes using the save techniques outlined in the previous discussion.

Using Forms View to Create a Form

Once you have loaded a database and entered the Forms View mode, the screen resembles the structure of the loaded database; a typical example is illustrated in Figure 11-12. If you accidentally press F10 too many times, you will see a tabular chart containing information about the fields. This is the Table View mode. From Table View mode, pressing F10 again will switch back to Forms View.

Once you are in the work area of Forms View, you can draw your desired data entry form. Fields can be moved around, boxes can be added, colors can be changed, and more descriptive names can be entered to describe the fields. The function keys are used for specific tasks while in Forms View mode of FoxView. Table 11-1 outlines the uses for the function keys in Forms View.

When you first load a database and begin using the Forms View mode, the field names appear at the left side of the screen. The highlighted areas that appear to the right of the field names represent the actual fields, and are called *field templates*. The row and column indicator at the top of the screen tells you the row and column position of the cursor while you are working in the screen. Cursor movement is performed with the same editing keys as in Edit or Change mode.

Pressing INS moves you in and out of Insert mode. When you are in Insert mode, all characters that you type are added to the existing text at the cursor location. When you are out of Insert mode and in Overwrite mode, all characters that you type replace any existing characters.

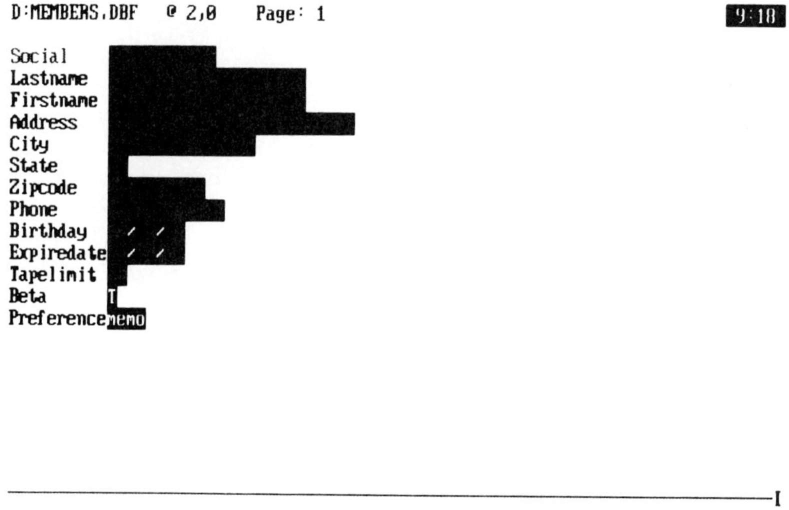

Figure 11-12.   *Forms View mode*

Moving Fields

In FoxView, use DRAG (F3) to drag the currently highlighted area to a different location. To drag one or more fields to a new location, use the EXTEND SELECT (F6) key along with the DRAG (F3) key. You use EXTEND SELECT to highlight as many fields as you wish by pressing F6 and moving the cursor keys until the fields you want to select are highlighted. You then press ENTER to complete the selection. Drag the fields to a new location as a group, by pressing F3, moving the selection with the cursor keys, and pressing ENTER to complete the movement. The fields will still appear highlighted as a block due to the extend select operation. However, as soon as you press any of the cursor keys, the extended selection will be canceled.

When moving fields to new locations, be careful to measure whether there is sufficient room to fit the entire field at the screen location that you choose. If, for example, you attempt to place a field that is 20 characters long at column 62, the field will be placed, but you will cut off the display of the last two characters because the screen ends at the character position 80.

Changing Field Labels

To modify field labels, move to the desired field and press the SPACEBAR. Pressing SPACEBAR puts you in Edit mode, where you can add or delete characters, and insert spaces or remove spaces at the end of the label. Adding spaces at the end of the label will increase the distance between the label and the field, while removing spaces will shorten the distance between the label and the field.

Key	Action	Purpose
F1	HELP	Displays Help screen.
F3	DRAG	Helps to drag (or move) the currently selected area to a different location. Use cursor keys to highlight desired object, press F3, drag the item to the new location with the cursor keys, and press ENTER.
F4	SIZE	Helps to resize the currently selected field or box. Use cursor keys to highlight the desired object, press F4, use the cursor keys to resize the item, and press ENTER. Note that changing the size of a field in a form does *not* alter the field size in the database.
F5	RESEQUENCE	Lets you resequence, or change the data entry order, of the fields in the form. See "Moving Fields and Objects in Table View" for additional information on this key.
F6	EXTEND SELECT	Lets you select more than one field at a time to apply other changes to. For example, you could simultaneously move two adjacent fields in a form to a new location by moving the cursor to the first field, pressing F6, moving the cursor to the second field, and pressing ENTER. Both fields would then be highlighted, and you could use DRAG (F3) to move them to a new location.
F8	COPY FIELDS	Copies the selected field or fields to a new location one row down and eight columns across.
F10	TOGGLE FORMS VIEW/TABLE VIEW	Switches between Forms View and Table View.

Table 11-1.   *Function Key Assignments in Forms View*

Adding Text

You can add text, such as headings or comments, to any location in a form. Text objects can be inserted by pressing CTRL-N. Once a text object is inserted with CTRL-N, it is automatically placed in the Drag mode. You can then use the cursor keys to move the object. Once the words "text object" are in the desired location, press ENTER and enter the text. Note that to add or delete fields, you must switch to Table View (described shortly).

Saving Screen Format Files

To use the data entry screen back in FoxPro, you must save the file as a *screen format file*. You should also save the table that contains the locations FoxView uses to create the screen format file. The format file allows you to use the form, while the table allows you to modify the form. You could save just the screen format file and use the file to add or edit data; however, if you ever wanted to change the design of the screen, you would have to redo the entire screen from scratch. By saving both the screen format file and the table that the screen's design is based on, you can later modify the screen design without starting from scratch.

In FoxView, you must use menu options to save screens, tables on which screens are based, and other objects related to applications design. You can display or hide the menus, shown in Figure 11-13, at any time by pressing ESC.

Most of the options on the four FoxView menus apply to other uses of FoxView, such as generating applications using the Applications Generator. Only the Select From Template List option of the Gen menu and the Save Table option of the Load menu apply to the creation of screen forms.

To save a screen form, open the Gen menu, highlight the Select From Template List option, and press ENTER. The list of available templates appears, as in Figure 11-14.

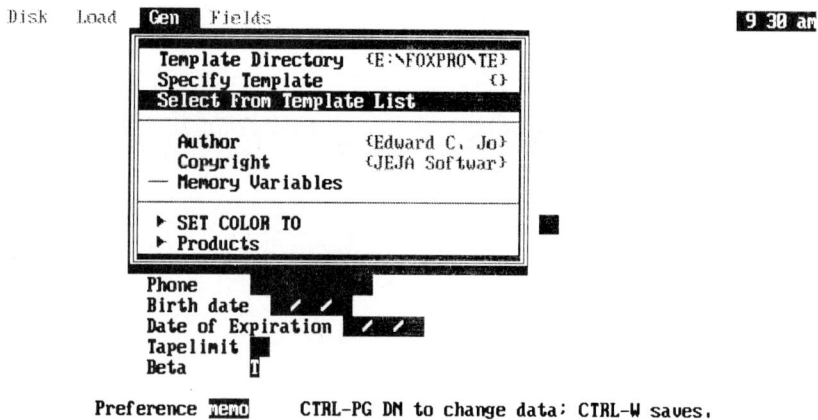

Figure 11-13.   *The FoxView menus*

```
E:MEMBERS.DBF    ⏎ 6,15    Page: 1                          9:30 am

                        ┌─── TEMPLATES ───┐
┌─────────┬──────────────────────────────────────────────────────┐
│ ADVANCED │ FoxPro Advanced Application                          │
│ APPS1    │ File-Maintenance Application                         │
│ FORM1    │ Format File Generator                                │
│ FORM2    │ Driver with FORM/SAYS/GETS/STOR/REPL procedure file  │
│ SIMPLE   │ Simple Database Application                          │
│          │                                                      │
│          │                                                      │
│          │                                                      │
│          │                                                      │
│          │                                                      │
│          │                                                      │
│          │                                                      │
└─────────┴──────────────────────────────────────────────────────┘
                                                              Ins
        Select Template Program with the cursor keys;  RETURN accepts
```

Figure 11-14.   *The list of templates*

Select Format File Generator from the list to tell FoxView that you wish to create a screen format file based on the screen design you have completed. At the bottom of the screen, FoxPro prompts for a DOS filename for the format file. Enter a valid DOS name for the screen form, and FoxPro will create a format file based on the screen design. When the process is complete, the menu will reappear, and a confirmation message will appear at the bottom of the screen.

You should next save the table on which the screen is based so it can be modified later if need be. To do this, open the Load menu and choose Save Table. Again, a prompt for a filename appears at the bottom of the screen. You can either press ENTER to accept the default name (same name as the screen form), or you can enter a different filename. Tables are saved with an .FV extension, while screen format files are saved with an .FMT extension.

Leaving FoxView

To leave FoxView, select Quit FoxView from the Disk menu or press ESC to close any menus that are open, press SCROLL LOCK to exit the Forms View mode, and enter **QUIT** at the FoxView prompt.

Using a Screen Format File

To use a screen format file, first open the database with the USE command. Then, enter

SET FORMAT TO *filename*

where *filename* is the name of the format file you created while using FoxView. Once this is done, any full-screen operations, such as APPEND, EDIT, or CHANGE, will use the data entry screen you designed, rather than the default data entry screen. Also note that if the Browse mode is used, any formatting rules present in the format file will apply to the data entry in the Browse window.

Modifying a Screen Form

To change an existing screen form, enter FoxView by typing **FOXVIEW** as a command or choosing FoxView from the Program menu. When the FoxView shell appears, enter

LOAD *filename*

where *filename* is the name of the table you saved previously in FoxView. Once the file has been loaded, use F10 to get into Forms View mode. If you did not save a table while in FoxView, you will not be able to load the existing screen, even if you saved the format file.

NOTE: *While you can use the DRAG (F3) key to relocate fields, you cannot insert or delete fields in Forms View mode. You can, however, insert or delete fields in Table View mode. (For additional information on Table View, see "More About Table View" in this chapter.)*

Drawing Boxes

Boxes can be drawn with the Box (CTRL-B) key combination. The procedure for doing this is as follows.

1. Place the cursor at the object nearest the spot where you want to position one corner of the box. A precise location is not necessary, as you can drag the box to the desired location later.

2. Press CTRL-B to display the Select Box menu.

3. Pick one of the six available types of boxes from the menu.

4. Press ENTER to create the box and automatically enter the Drag mode.

5. Use the cursor keys to drag the box to the desired location, and press ENTER.

6. If desired, use SIZE (F4) to change the size of the box. With the box selected, press F4, then use the cursor keys to change the box size. Press ENTER when you have finished.

Changing Colors

If you are using a system with a color monitor, you can change colors of selected objects. The procedure for doing this is as follows.

1. Select the object(s) with the cursor keys. EXTEND SELECT (F6) may be used if more than one object will have the same color change.

2. Press the Palette key combination (CTRL-P) to display the Color Palette. If the Color Palette covers the fields or objects you are changing, you can move it with the CTRL-LEFT ARROW and CTRL-RIGHT ARROW keys.

3. If you are working with fields, press the slash (/) key to switch back and forth between the labels and the field templates (highlighted areas of the form).

4. Use the cursor keys to move among the different foreground and background choices of the Color Palette. Once the cursor highlights the desired color choice, press ENTER to assign the color to the selected object.

More About Table View

FoxView lets you work with data entry screens using either Table View or Forms View. Forms View displays the form as it will appear on the screen during data entry or editing. However, all of the underlying data that controls the appearance of the form is contained in a table that you can view through Table View. In effect, Table View is a kind of chart used by FoxPro to contain field characteristics, colors, sizes, locations, and so on. You can use Table View mode to limit the ways in which data is accepted into the fields. You can set rules, such as a maximum amount in a numeric field. You can set formats for a field, such as a format that specifies that entries in a character field will appear as all uppercase letters.

Changes can be made to a screen form while in Table View or Forms View. Any changes you make in Table View appear in the form in Forms View. Likewise, the additions and changes you make to a form in Forms View are stored (and visible in the table's columns when you switch modes) in Table View.

When you press F10 in the Forms View mode of FoxView, the Table View appears. Pressing F10 again returns you to Forms View. An example of Table View is shown in Figure 11-15. There are 20 columns in Table View. Use TAB or SHIFT-TAB to view the various columns. As you press TAB repeatedly, the eight

```
E:MEMBERS.DBF                                                        9 37 am

  #. Als Field      Typ Wid Dec   Label         Hue Row Col Pag (Fld) (Atr) Place
  1.  A  Social      C  11         [Social    ]   4   6  15  1  GET   112  SIDE
  2.  A  BOXOBJECT   B  65   17    [ ▗▙▌▌█▄ ]     4   4   6  1  SAY   112  HOR
  3.  A  Lastname    C  15         [Lastname  ]   4   7  15  1  GET    48  SIDE
  4.  A  Firstname   C  15         [Firstname ]   4   8  15  1  GET    48  SIDE
  5.  A  Address     C  25         [Address   ]   4   9  15  1  GET   112  SIDE
  6.  A  City        C  15         [City      ]   4  10  15  1  GET   112  SIDE
  7.  A  State       C   2         [State     ]   4  10  43  1  GET   112  SIDE
  8.  A  Zipcode     C  10         [Zipcode   ]   4  11  15  1  GET   112  SIDE
  9.  A  Phone       C  12         [Phone     ]   4  13  15  1  GET   112  SIDE
 10.  A  Birthday    D   8         [Birth date]   4  14  15  1  GET   112  SIDE
 11.  A  Expiredate  D   8         [Date of Exp]  4  15  15  1  GET   112  SIDE
 12.  A  Tapelimit   N   2         [Tapelimit ]   4  16  15  1  GET   112  SIDE
 13.  A  Beta        L   1         [Beta      ]   4  17  15  1  GET   112  SIDE
 14.  A  Preference  M  10         [Preference]   4  19  10  1  GET   112  SIDE
 15.  A  TEXTOBJECT  T  40         [CTRL-PG DN]   4  19  30  1  SAY   112  HOR


                                                                       ─Ins
─────────────────────────────────────────────────────────────────────────────
      FIELD:  can be up to 10 alphanumeric characters and underscore
```

Figure 11-15.   *Table View*

rightmost columns are replaced with six additional columns. You can keep pressing TAB to view all the available columns in Table View mode. The columns within the table, and their purposes, are described in the following paragraphs.

This first column contains the field numbers. (Note that field numbers initially follow the order of fields in the database structure.) The field numbers determine the order of data entry in the form; the cursor appears in field 1 first, in field 2 second, and so on. You can move fields to a new position in the table with the MOVE (F7) key. If you do so, the field is renumbered in accordance with its new position.

ALS   This is the work area that the file is opened in. FoxPro can have up to ten database files opened in ten work areas, labeled "A" through "J." By default, any file you open is opened in work area A unless you use the SELECT command to change work areas.

Field   This contains the field name, taken directly from the database structure when you used the USE command to load a database into FoxView.

Typ   This is the field type, which can be C (character), N (numeric), F (float), D (date), L (logical), or M (memo). Two other designations can also appear in this column: B for BoxObject and T for TextObject. Boxes you draw are designated as BoxObjects in the table, while sets of text that you add are designated as TextObjects.

Wid   This column indicates the width of the entry area in the form. Note that this is not necessarily the same as the actual width of the field in the database structure. For example, you might have a 20-character field, but in the form you might want to limit the visible width of the entry area to 15 characters.

Dec   This column indicates the number of decimal places in a numeric field. Note that with BoxObjects, the Wid and Dec columns contain the dimensions of the box.

Label   This contains the name of the label that appears above or to the left of the actual field data entry area. When you enter the USE command in FoxView to open a database file, the default form uses the names of the fields as labels. You can modify these labels as desired to better reflect the purposes of the fields.

Hue   This column controls the color, intensity, and blinking (if any) of the label. Different numeric values between 0 and 255 determine the exact color and whether it is displayed steadily or blinking. Because of the large number of color values, direct entry of the values into the Hue column of the table isn't recommended; it is usually much easier to select colors in the Forms View mode by displaying the Color Palette with CTRL-P. Once you pick a desired color for a label from the Color Palette, you can switch back to Table View mode with F10, and the corresponding color code will appear in the Hue column.

Row   This column indicates the row number where the field is located, from row 0 (the top row) to row 24 (the bottom row) of the screen.

Col   This column indicates the column number where the field begins, from column 1 (the leftmost column) to column 80 (the rightmost column) on the screen.

Page   This column indicates which page of the form a field appears on. You can create multiple-page data entry forms, where certain fields appear on the first page, certain fields on the second page, and so on. Up to 16 pages are permitted on a data entry form. When in Forms View mode, you can use the PGUP and PGDN keys to move between pages. To move a field to a new page while in Table View, change its page number in this column. (You can move fields to another page in Forms View by highlighting the field, pressing DRAG (F3), and pressing PGUP or PGDN.) Note that fields can only be moved as far as the next available empty page. For example, you cannot place an object on page 4 if there are no objects on page 3.

Fld   This column indicates whether the actual field is a GET, a SAY, or a HIDE (hidden) field. Once the cursor is in this column, you can press the SPACEBAR to toggle between the three available options: GET, SAY, and HIDE. In a GET field, the data appears in reverse video, and it can be edited. In a SAY field, the data appears, but it cannot be edited. Contents of hidden fields do not appear in the form, but the field is shown in the table. Hidden fields are useful when you want certain fields to be available for your use, but hidden from other users.

Atr   This column controls the color, intensity, and blinking (if any) of the selected field's GET, or reverse video, area (the actual field, as opposed to the label). This column does for the field's GET what the Hue column does for the field's label. Different numeric values between 0 and 255 determine the exact color, and whether it is displayed steadily or blinking. As with the Hue column, direct entry of the values into the Atr column of the table isn't recommended; it is easier to select colors in the Forms View mode by displaying the Color Palette with CTRL-P. Once you pick a desired color for a field from the Color Palette, you can switch back to Table View mode with F10, and the corresponding color code will appear in the Atr column.

Place   This column controls whether the field template (the reverse video area denoting the actual field) appears beside the label or below the label. Once the cursor is in this column, you can press the SPACEBAR to toggle between the available options: BESIDE, and BELOW. Note that the Place column can also be used with TextObjects. With TextObjects, you are offered two choices: VERTICALLY (for vertical placement of the text) and HORIZONTALLY (for horizontal placement of the text).

Picture   This column lets you specify a Picture clause that will limit data entry to a specific type or format. You enter a template into this area, and the template limits how data is accepted in the field. Table 11-2 shows the possible picture templates you can use.

Range   This column defines an upper and lower boundary for a particular field. Any values outside of the proper range are rejected, and FoxPro displays an error message.

Valid   This column lets you enter an expression that validates the data entered. It differs from the Range column in that you can limit the data to specific values. For example, perhaps only certain states should be accepted in a State field in a database. You could enter an expression such as

```
State $ MD VA DC
```

to limit a field named State to accept entries as only those three states. You could also include complex expressions, such as LEN(TRIM(Social)) > 0, which would force an entry in a field called Social, or Hireday > = DATE() + 366, which would force entries in a date field to be more than one year ahead of the current date.

Symbol	Meaning
	Functions
!	Converts letters to uppercase
A	Displays alphabetic characters only
S	Allows horizontal scrolling of characters
M	Allows multiple choice
T	Trims trailing spaces
B	Left alignment of entry
I	Center alignment of entry
C	Positive credits followed by CR (for "credit")
X	Negative credits followed by DB (for "debit")
(	Uses ( ) around negative numbers
L	Displays leading zeros
Z	Displays zeros as blanks
$	Displays numbers in financial format
^	Displays numbers in exponential format
R	Allows use of literals within a template without having those literals stored in the database
	Templates
A	Allows only letters
L	Allows only logical data (true/false, yes/no)
N	Allows only letters or digits
X	Allows any character
Y	Allows Y or N
#	Allows only digits, blanks, periods, or signs
9	Allows only digits for character data, or digits and signs for numeric data
!	Converts letters to uppercase
format	Used to format the entry; for example, with hyphens and parentheses to format a phone number, as in (999) 999-9999

Table 11-2. *Functions and Templates Used with Picture from Modify Field Options*

NOTE: The fields are not checked for validity until the cursor is moved out of the final field in the form. At that point, if a field entry does not meet a condition specified by the Valid option, an error message will appear, and the cursor will move back to that field. If you desire, you can define a customized error message in the User column; this error message will appear when the Valid condition is not met.

Init This column contains an optional expression used to fill a blank field with initial data.

Calc   This column defines a field as a calculated field or a field whose contents are dependent on calculations based on other fields or memory variables.

User   This column can contain any string of up to 254 characters. It is not normally used by FoxView, and you can store notes about a field in this column. However, if you use the Valid option, any text string in the User column will appear as the error message if the data entered does not meet the conditions specified by the Valid option.

Moving Fields and Objects in Table View

Fields and labels can be moved around in Table View. You can also add fields, delete fields, and change the data entry order of fields. You must use Table View if you want to add any database fields you previously deleted from the form or if you want to add calculated fields. If you attempt to add a field in Forms View, FoxView assumes you wish to add a text object.

To add a new field to the table, place the cursor at the desired location and press CTRL-N. A new field will be inserted below the cursor position. It will be called Noname, and its row and column positions will be directly below the prior field in the table. You can then change the name as desired. You can position the field on the resultant form by changing the Row and Col entries for the new field, or you can switch to Forms View with F10 and drag the field to the desired location. Note that adding a field to the table does *not* cause a new field to be added to any database. You must use MODIFY STRUCTURE to add a corresponding field to the database.

To delete a field from the table, highlight the desired field, and press CTRL-U. The field will be deleted from the table and from its location in Forms View. Using this option does *not* delete the field from the corresponding database; it only means that the field will not be used in the form.

To change the data entry order of fields, you can either move fields to new locations or resequence the fields. You move a field in the table by highlighting the field, pressing MOVE (F7), moving the cursor to the field that you want to come right before your relocated field, and pressing ENTER.

You can also use the RESEQUENCE key (F5) to resequence the data entry order of all the fields. When you press F5, a prompt appears containing the following question:

```
RESEQUENCE fields by Row, Col, or Attribute (R/C/A)?
```

Choosing Row causes the fields in the table to be rearranged based on the row number of each field. The lower the row number, the earlier in the table the field appears. If there is more than one object on a row, they are arranged by column number. Choosing Column causes the fields in the table to be rearranged based on column positions of each field. The lower the column number, the earlier in the table the field appears. If there is more than one object in a column, they are arranged by row number.

Choosing Attribute causes the fields to be placed in order based on whatever attribute in the table the cursor is presently highlighting. For example, if you move the cursor to the Label column, press F5, and choose Attribute, the fields will be arranged in the table in alphabetical order, based on what's in the Label column. If you move the cursor to the Typ column, press F5, and choose Attribute, the fields will be arranged in the table in groups of field type, with box objects first, character fields second, date fields third, floating fields fourth, logical fields fifth, memo fields sixth, and text objects last.

A Note About FoxView and DOS

Because FoxView is a stand-alone program, you do not have to be in FoxPro to run it. You can run it directly from the DOS prompt if you wish. Switch to the subdirectory containing your program files and enter **FOXVIEW** at the DOS prompt to load FoxView.

Chapter 12

FoxPro Tools and the FoxPro Editor

This chapter will detail the use of the various FoxPro tools (also called desk accessories) and the FoxPro Editor, which is used extensively when programming in FoxPro.

Desk Accessories

FoxPro provides a series of desk accessories for various tasks not necessarily related to database management. These include a calculator, filer, calendar and diary, screen-capture utility, ASCII table, and a set of special characters. While memory-resident programs like Borland's SideKick and Central Point Software's PC Tools commonly provide such desktop tools, the ones provided by FoxPro work well with the FoxPro environment and have the advantage of consuming no extra memory.

Calculator

The Calculator, shown in Figure 12-1, provides a desktop calculator with memory. To use the Calculator, choose the Calculator option from the System menu. You can use the keyboard or the mouse to operate the Calculator. The plus and minus keys perform addition and subtraction, and the asterisk (*) and slash (/) keys perform multiplication and division. Special functions can be

Key	Purpose
R	Recall memory (MR)
Z	Clear memory (MC)
A	Store/Add to memory (M+)
S	Subtract from memory (M−)
N	Plus/minus toggle (+/−)
Q	Square root ($\sqrt{\ }$)

Table 12-1. *Calculator Keyboard Equivalents*

accessed with the keyboard equivalents shown in Table 12-1; all other Calculator keys use the equivalent keys on the keyboard. Mouse users can simply click on the desired numbers and symbols on the Calculator.

When performing calculations, the operators (+, −, *, and /) should be placed between the desired numbers you enter. The result appears in the display panel of the Calculator.

You can change some aspects of the Calculator's behavior by choosing Preferences from the Edit menu when the Calculator is active. When you do this, the Calculator Preferences dialog box, shown in Figure 12-2, appears. Options are provided for the status of the NUMLOCK key and for how decimal places are handled.

The first three options control how NUMLOCK behaves.

- **Don't alter NumLock** When this option is selected, the Calculator does not change the state of the NUMLOCK key.

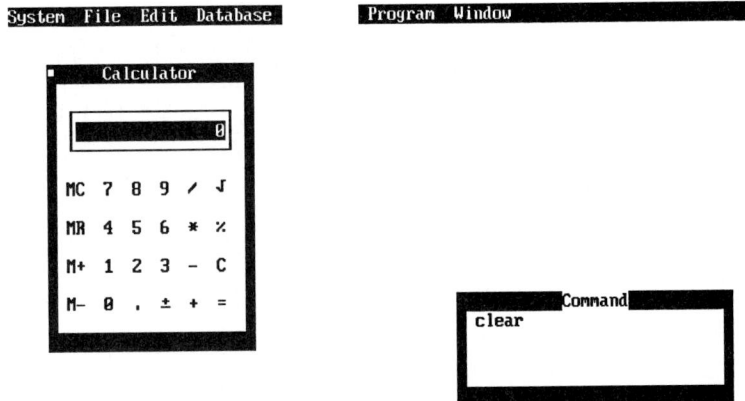

Figure 12-1. *The Calculator*

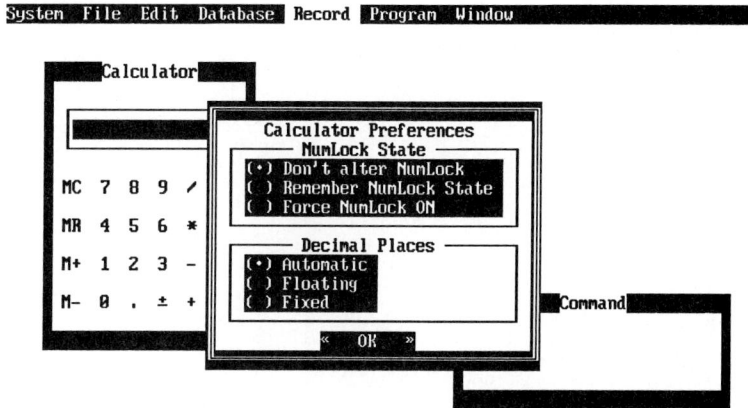

Figure 12-2.   *The Calculator Preferences dialog box*

- **Remember NumLock State**   When this option is selected, the Calculator uses the same NUMLOCK setting that was in effect the last time it was used.

- **Force NumLock ON**   When this option is selected, NUMLOCK is turned on whenever the Calculator is activated.

The final three options control the display of decimal values in the Calculator.

- **Automatic**   When this option is selected, decimal places in results vary depending on the numbers entered and the operation performed.

- **Floating**   When this option is selected, numbers are displayed with as many decimals as needed to show the entire number.

- **Fixed**   When this option is selected, numbers are displayed with a set number of decimal places. (After choosing Fixed, you are asked to enter the desired number of decimal places.)

When you exit FoxPro, any settings made to the Calculator Preferences are saved to the resource file and will remain in effect for further use of the Calculator.

Calendar/Diary

The FoxPro combination Calendar/Diary, useful for keeping track of dates and appointments, is shown in Figure 12-3. To access the Calendar/Diary, choose Calendar/Diary from the System menu.

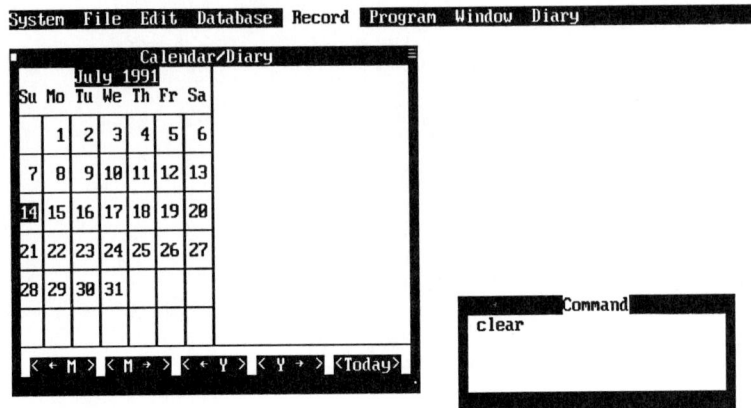

Figure 12-3.   *The Calendar/Diary*

The cursor appears in the Calendar portion of the window. To move to the Diary portion, press TAB or click anywhere in the Diary window with the mouse. To move back to the Calendar, press SHIFT-TAB or click anywhere in the Calendar.

To change the selected day in the Calendar, you can use the arrow keys or click on the desired day. To move backward or forward a month at a time, use the PGUP and PGDN keys or click on the month buttons at the bottom of the window. To move backward or forward a year at a time, use SHIFT-PGUP and SHIFT-PGDN or click on the year buttons at the bottom of the window. When the Calendar/Diary is active, another menu, called Diary, appears on the System menu. This menu contains Back Month, Ahead Month, Back Year, and Ahead Year options you can use to move within the Calendar. You can quickly get back to the current date by pressing T, by clicking on the Today button at the bottom of the window, or by choosing the Today option from the Diary menu.

To make entries in the Diary, first choose the desired day in the Calendar, then press TAB or click in the Diary panel, to activate the Diary portion of the window. Enter text as desired (there is no limit to the amount of text you can enter). You can use standard window techniques to zoom or resize the Calendar/Diary window.

Because diary entries are stored in the resource file, you may want to delete old entries from time to time. To do so, select a day on the calendar prior to which you want to delete all entries. Then open the Diary menu with the mouse or with ALT-Y. Choose Delete from the menu, and you will see the Delete Entries confirmation dialog box, shown here.

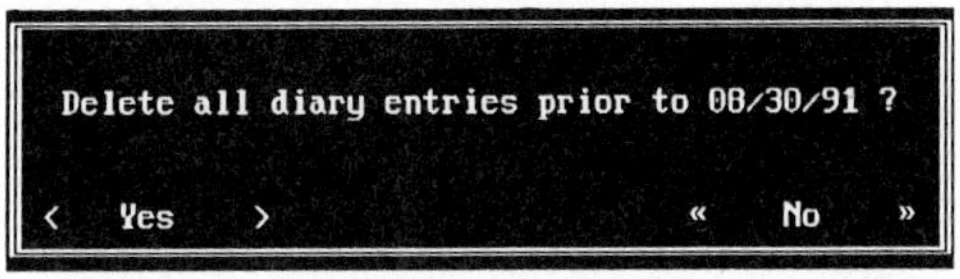

Choosing Yes from the dialog box will cause all diary entries prior to the selected day to be deleted. The No option returns you to the Calendar/Diary without deleting entries.

You can quickly close the Calendar/Diary by pressing ESC. You can also click on the close box of the window or choose Close from the File menu to close the Calendar/Diary.

Special Characters

FoxPro offers the Special Characters accessory, shown in Figure 12-4, which is useful for supplying unusual symbols, such as foreign currency symbols or line-drawing characters. To access the Special Characters accessory, choose Special Characters from the System menu.

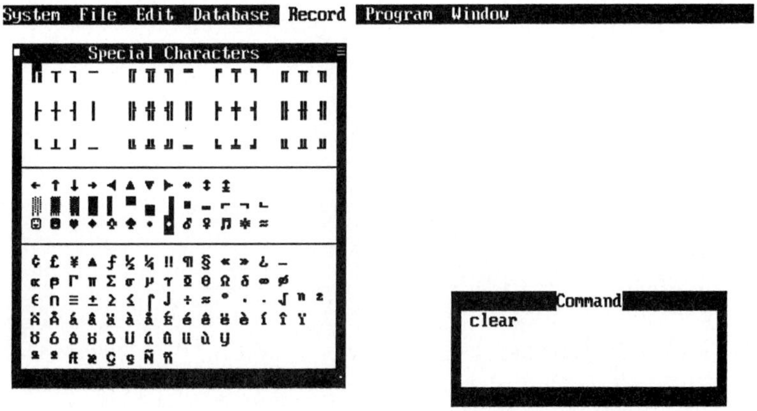

Figure 12-4. *Special Characters*

Special Characters will automatically paste any character that you choose into the window that was last active. To choose a character, simply click on it or move the cursor to the desired character and press ENTER or the SPACEBAR. (Note that for the character to appear in the last active window, the window must be open and must be a type of window into which you can normally paste information.)

HINT: *You may have trouble getting the special character to appear in the window with some hardware. If this is the case, Fox Software recommends that you try holding down* SHIFT *when choosing the special character.*

Suppose, for example, you are designing a report for printing currency amounts and you want to use the symbol for Japanese Yen in the report. While the report design screen is visible, you can position the cursor at the report location where the symbol is needed, bring up the Special Characters accessory, highlight the Yen symbol, and press ENTER. The symbol will appear in the report and will be printed *if* your printer has the capability of handling the extended character set. Figure 12-5 shows the special character pasted into the design of a report.

HINT: *The Special Characters accessory doesn't go away when you press* ENTER. *It remains visible until you close the window. This lets you paste multiple characters from the Special Characters accessory or multiple occurrences of the same character.*

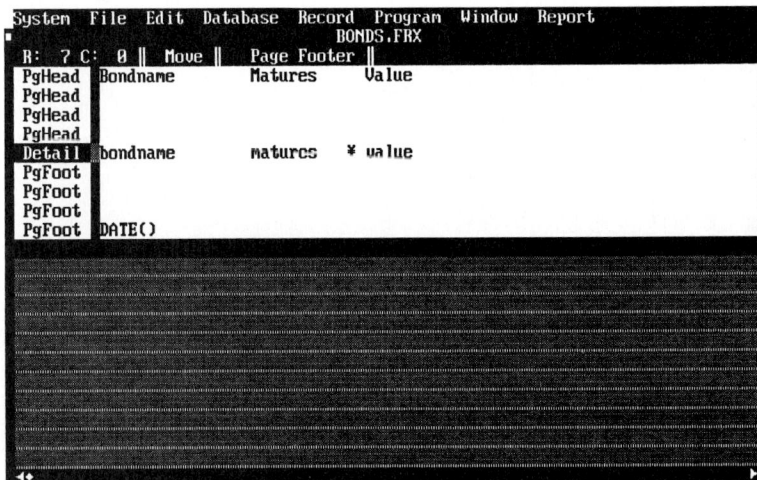

Figure 12-5.   A special character used in a report

To close the Special Characters accessory, press ESC, click on the close box of the window, or choose Close from the File menu.

ASCII Chart

FoxPro's ASCII Chart accessory, shown in Figure 12-6, is useful for serious programmers who often need to find an ASCII value for sending escape codes to printers or for other similar tasks. To access the ASCII Chart accessory, choose ASCII Chart from the System menu.

As with the Special Characters, the ASCII Chart accessory will automatically paste any character that you choose into the window that was last active. To choose a character, click on it, or move the cursor to the desired character and press ENTER or the SPACEBAR. (For the character to appear in a window, the window must be open and must be a type of window into which you can normally paste information.)

HINT: *With some hardware, you may have trouble getting the ASCII character to appear in the window. If this occurs, try pressing SHIFT when choosing the ASCII character.*

To reach the desired character in the ASCII Chart, you can use the cursor keys, PGUP and PGDN, or the mouse with the scroll bar at the right edge of the window. You can also very quickly type the decimal value of the ASCII character if you know it. For example, quickly typing **122** brings up the lowercase letter "z," which has an ASCII value of 122. (This quick-typing method of selecting options may not work in very early versions of FoxPro.)

Figure 12-6. *The ASCII Chart*

To close the ASCII Chart accessory, press ESC, click on the close box of the window, or choose Close from the File menu.

Capture

The Capture accessory can capture any portion of the screen and paste that portion into the clipboard. You can then use the Paste command from the Edit menu to paste the captured screen portion into a window. Note that graphic characters cannot be captured with the Capture accessory.

To use Capture, first make sure the desired text to be captured is visible on the screen (not partially hidden by a window). Then choose Capture from the System menu. A message will appear, telling you to select the top-left corner of the area to be captured. Move the cursor to the top-left corner and press ENTER. Another message now tells you to select the bottom-right corner; move the cursor to the bottom-right corner of the desired area and press ENTER again. The area will be pasted into the clipboard. Mouse users can select the area by clicking and dragging from the top-left corner to the bottom-right corner.

Once the area has been captured, you can place the cursor at the desired area in a window—for instance, when you are editing a text file or program or designing a report—and choose Paste from the Edit menu or press CTRL-V. The contents of the clipboard will then appear at the cursor location.

Filer

The Filer accessory, shown in Figure 12-7, provides numerous options for managing files. To access the Filer, you can choose Filer from the System menu. You can also access the Filer by typing the command **FILER** in the Command window. Access to the Filer by way of the FILER command can be useful if you want to provide users of a FoxPro program with access to file management, although the disadvantage of this is that the Filer can be dangerous in the hands of a novice. You can delete files and entire directories through the Filer, as well as copy files, move files from one directory to another, or edit selected files.

Most of the Filer is occupied by a list box, which shows all files in the current directory. At the bottom of the Filer appear ten text buttons with names like Find, Edit, Copy, and Move. You can select among these buttons by pressing the highlighted letter or by clicking on the desired button.

The list box has five columns, called Name, Ext, Size, Last Modified, and Attr (Attribute). The Name and Ext columns display the filename and extension (if any) for the file. Directories and subdirectories are shown in brackets; in Figure 12-7, the filename [..] at the top of the list denotes the parent directory, G:\DATA.

The Size column displays the size of each file in bytes, and the Last Modified column displays the DOS date and time stamp on the file. The Attr column displays the attributes of the file, as indicated by the operating system. Up to four

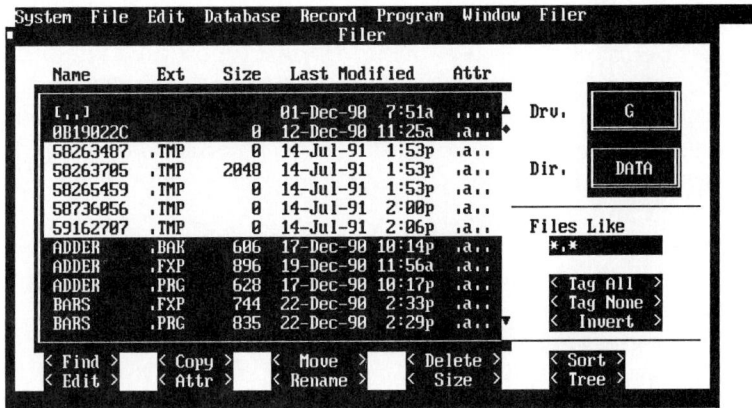

Figure 12-7. The Filer

letters can appear in this column: "a" for archive, "h" for hidden, "r" for read-only, and "s" for system. (For an explanation of file attributes, see your DOS manual.)

The upper-right side of the Filer has two popup menus for your disk drives and directories. You can tab to either menu and press ENTER or click on the desired menu to display a list of available drives or directories. Use these menus to move between drives or directories.

Beneath the menus appears the Files Like text-entry box. You can enter filenames or DOS wildcards to restrict the types of files that appear in the Filer's list box. As an example, typing ***.PRG** in the Files Like box would restrict the files shown to program files.

Navigating in the Files List

The UP ARROW, DOWN ARROW, PGUP, and PGDN keys will move the cursor within the files list. Mouse users can use the scroll bar at the right edge of the files list.

To view a list of files in a different directory, tab to the Dir. menu at the right side of the Filer and press ENTER to display directories above the current one. Highlight the desired directory and press ENTER to switch to that directory, or highlight the drive letter to switch to the root directory. You can highlight any directory in the files list and press ENTER to switch to that directory. Mouse users can click on the desired directory to choose it for viewing.

Tagging Files

Selecting one or more files from the files list is known as *tagging*. You can tag a single file or a group of files. Tagged files are indicated in the files list by the presence of a triangle-shaped marker beside the filename. After a file or files have been tagged, you can use any of the buttons at the bottom of the Filer to perform an operation (such as copying or erasing) on the tagged files.

To tag a single file, tab to the list box and use UP ARROW or DOWN ARROW to highlight the desired file, then press the SPACEBAR. You can tag multiple files by moving to each desired file and holding down the SHIFT key while pressing the SPACEBAR. Note that repeatedly pressing the SPACEBAR causes the file to switch between tagged and untagged.

Mouse users can tag individual files by clicking on the desired file in the List Box. To tag multiple files, hold down the SHIFT key while selecting the desired file with the mouse.

The lower-right portion of the Filer contains buttons labelled Tag All, Tag None, and Invert. Choose Tag All to tag all files and Tag None to remove all tags from files. Choosing Invert reverses the order of any existing tags; tagged files are untagged, and untagged files are tagged. The Tag All option, along with the Files Like entry box, can be useful for tagging groups of files of the same type. As an example, you could delete all backup (.BAK) files by typing **.BAK** in the Files Like box, choosing Tag All, and then choosing Delete.

Deleting Files

Files can be deleted by tagging the files, then choosing the Delete option. When you do this, a dialog box appears, warning you that the file will be deleted. Choose <Delete> from the dialog box to delete the file. If multiple files have been tagged, the dialog box contains two additional options: Skip, and Delete All. You can confirm the deletion or choose Skip to skip to the next tagged file. If you choose Delete All, all tagged files will be deleted without any further confirmation.

Renaming Files

Files can be renamed by tagging the file and choosing the Rename option. When you do this, a dialog box appears, displaying the old name and asking you for the new name. Enter the new name and choose <Rename> from the dialog box to rename the file. If a file by the new name already exists, an error message will appear in a dialog box, warning you that the rename operation cannot be completed.

Finding Files

The Find option lets you find files based on a name or extension, and tag those files. When you choose Find, the Find Files Like dialog box, shown in Figure 12-8, appears.

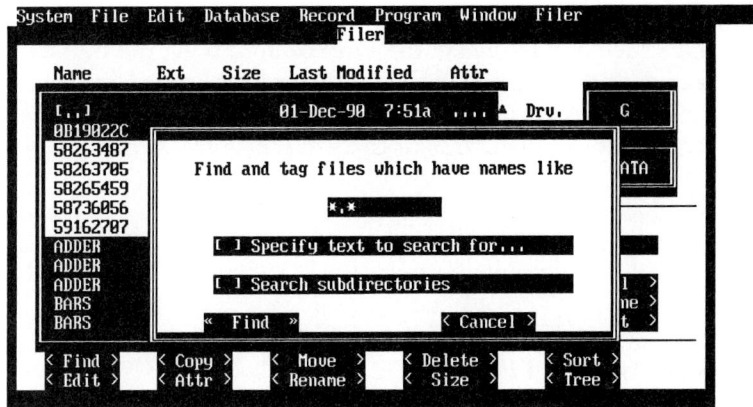

Figure 12-8. *The Find Files Like dialog box*

In the text box, enter the specification for the type of files you want to find and tag. For example, entering ***.TXT** would cause the Filer to find and tag all files with a .TXT extension. Note that you can enter more than one specification at a time by separating the specifications with a semicolon. For example, you could enter ***.TXT; *.COM; *.EXE** in the text box.

The Find Files Like dialog box also contains two options that add to its power: the check boxes labelled "Specify text to search for..." and "Search subdirectories." If you select Specify text to search for..., another dialog box appears, and you can enter up to three text strings (of a maximum of 256 characters each). If you use this option, the Filer will tag only those files found containing the text strings. The Search subdirectories option tells Filer to search all subdirectories in the current directory. Hence, if you start at the root directory, the Find option will search the entire drive. (This may take some time if you have a lot of files on your hard disk.)

When the Filer completes its search, you are placed back in the files list and all files matching your specification will be tagged. If you choose the Search subdirectories option, any directories that contain a file that matched the specification will also be tagged. You can proceed to use the other Filer buttons to choose an option for the tagged files. If you are performing a destructive operation such as a Delete, it may be a wise idea to check the names of the tagged files before performing the operation.

Editing Files

Files can be edited using the Edit option. The Edit option will open an Editor window for every tagged file. (You can find more details on the use of the Editor in a later section of this chapter.) If you have tagged a large number of files, you may run out of memory before enough windows can be opened. An error message will appear, and you must return to the files list and untag some files.

If you have specified strings in the Find option to tag the files for editing, the first occurrence of the search text will appear highlighted in the files that you edit. You can then perform search-and-replace operations on the text using the Editor commands described later in this chapter.

NOTE: *Editing should only be attempted with text files, such as programs you write in FoxPro; nontext files, such as databases or indexes, should not be loaded into the Editor.*

Moving and Copying Files

Files can be copied with the Copy option. To copy a file, tag the desired file or files and choose Copy. A dialog box will appear, asking for a specification for the copied file. Enter the specification and select Copy from the dialog box, and the file(s) will be copied to the new file(s). (Note that you can tab to or click on the <Target Directory> button to pick a different directory from a list box as the destination for the copied file.) You can copy multiple files by using wildcards in the file specification; for example, if you tagged all files with a .PRG extension, you could enter a file specification of *.PBK, and all tagged files would be copied to new files with the same name and a .PBK extension.

Two options in the dialog box, Replace existing files, and Preserve directories, let you specify whether any existing files at the destination having the same name should be overwritten and whether the directory structure, as well as the files, should be copied.

The Move option lets you move a file or files from one location to another. It operates just like the Copy option (see above), with one difference: When the tagged files have been copied to the new location, they are removed from the old location. FoxPro does this quickly, because it does not actually copy and delete the files from the hard disk; it instead performs a sophisticated renaming operation that appears to "move" the files between directories.

Changing File Attributes

The DOS attributes of a file can be changed with the Attr option. When you tag one or more files and select Attr, a dialog box appears containing four attribute choices: Read-Only, Hidden file, Archived, and System. The check boxes for the choices will be selected or deselected according to the file's current status. For example, if you have tagged a read-only file, the Read-Only check box will be filled in with an "X." You can press the highlighted letters of your choice or click on the check boxes with the mouse to change file attributes as desired.

The Change All button at the bottom of the dialog box can be used to tell FoxPro to change the attributes for all tagged files, without stopping to display the dialog box for each file you have tagged.

Size

The Size option can be used to display statistics on the size of a file. Tag the desired files in the list box, then choose Size. A dialog box containing information on the disk space consumed by the tagged files will appear.

Sort

The Sort option can be used to sort files shown in the files list. When you choose the Sort option, a dialog box for selecting sort criteria appears. You can sort by name, extension, size, date, or file attributes. You can also choose whether the list is to be sorted in ascending or descending order. After selecting the desired options, choose OK, and the files in the list box will be sorted. This does not affect the order of the files on the disk; only the appearance of the files in the list box is affected.

Tree

The Tree option can be used to display a *tree panel* (a visual representation of the layout of files within your directories). You can perform operations on entire directory structures from the tree panel. Choose Tree, and FoxPro will take a few moments to scan your entire hard disk. When this is done, the tree panel showing your files and directories will appear, similar to the example shown in Figure 12-9.

To navigate within the tree panel, use the scroll bars and the mouse, UP ARROW and DOWN ARROW, or PGUP and PGDN. You can tab over to or click on the Drv. popup menu to display and select from all available disk drives. For your information,

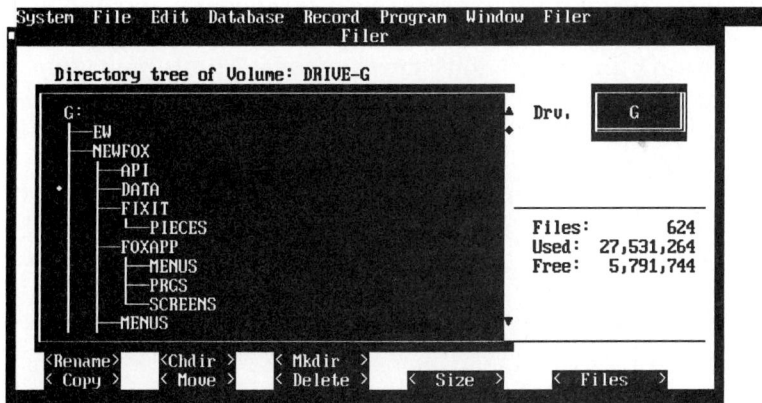

Figure 12-9. *A tree panel*

the lower-right portion of the tree panel shows the number of files on the drive, the disk space used, and the remaining free space on the drive.

You can use the buttons shown at the bottom of the tree panel to rename directories, make directories, or change directories. You can also copy or move directories, delete directories, and determine the size (disk space used) for a particular directory.

Keep in mind that when you are working in the tree panel, you are working with entire directories, so the potential for accidental damage is great. It is a wise idea to back up files before performing any deletions of entire directories. You also should not casually rename directories without considering what effects this could have on other programs on your system. If, for example, you are using Microsoft Windows and you casually rename certain directories using FoxPro's Filer, you could wreak havoc when Windows later looks for directories that no longer exist.

Exiting the Filer

To exit the Filer, press ESC or click on the close box at the upper-left corner of the window. When you exit the Filer, you are automatically placed back in the directory you were in when you started using the Filer.

The FoxPro Editor

If you spend much time developing applications in FoxPro, you are likely to make use of the FoxPro Editor. If you are an experienced user of another dBASE-compatible product like FoxBASE+ or dBASE III PLUS, you should seriously consider the Editor in FoxPro, even if you have grown used to a commercial program editor such as Brief. Many users of FoxBASE+ and dBASE III PLUS used commercial editors because the limitations of the standard editors provided with FoxBASE+ and dBASE III PLUS made them unsuitable for heavy-duty work in applications development. Those limitations are history when it comes to the FoxPro Editor. And the seamless integration with the programming environment offered by the FoxPro Editor is simply not possible with a commercial editor.

FoxPro's built-in Editor rivals low-end word processors in terms of power and flexibility. Because it uses the same windowing environment that FoxPro uses, you can edit multiple documents or files within windows, and you can independently size and move the windows. The number of windows that can be opened at once is limited only by your available memory and the FILES setting in your CONFIG.SYS file.

Because the Editor swaps data between disk and memory as needed, memory limitations will not have an effect on the size of the file you can edit. Note, however, that the number of windows open will have an effect on memory, because each window open in the Editor uses up an additional amount of memory. On machines with minimal memory, it is possible to open so many windows that you run out of memory. Since the Editor is disk based, you should exercise the same common-sense precautions that you would exercise with any disk-based Editor, such as not removing a floppy disk containing a file being edited or not using the Filer to rename or erase a file that's open in an Editor window.

The FoxPro Editor also provides complete support for cut-and-paste, move, and copy operations. This can be particularly useful in programming, where you often want to reuse a portion of existing program code in another part of a program. You can also copy lines of code that have already been entered in the Command window into a FoxPro program in an Editor window. This lets you test lines of code before placing them in a program.

The FoxPro Editor offers full search and replace, a feature not found in most other editors provided with dBASE-compatible products. And the search is fast in FoxPro; you can find any text string in a file of three megabytes in under ten seconds.

You can also change the preferences used by the Editor to match a variety of settings. You can determine whether indentation of lines and compilation of .PRG files is automatic, and whether word wrap and justification should be turned on when you are using the Editor to edit text files. You can even use FoxPro macros to make the Editor behave like your favorite word processor.

Creating a New File

You can create a new file with the Editor in one of two ways. You can choose the New option from the File menu. Then, in the dialog box that appears, you can choose Text if you want to create a text file or you can choose Program if you want to create a program (.PRG) file. Then choose OK, and the Editor will open in a window containing a blank screen. The file will be named UNTITLED (the name appears at the top of the window). When you save the file, you will be asked to supply a name.

The other way to create a new file is to use the MODIFY COMMAND command or the MODIFY FILE command, along with a new filename or with no filename provided. If (in the Command window) you enter **MODIFY COMMAND** *filename*, where *filename* is a new file, or you omit the filename completely, FoxPro assumes you want to create a new program, and the Editor opens in a window containing a blank screen. In similar fashion, if you enter **MODIFY FILE** *filename*, where *filename* is a new file or you omit the filename completely, FoxPro assumes you want to create a new text file and the Editor opens in a window containing a blank screen. In either case, the FoxPro Editor is open, as shown in Figure 12-10, ready for the creation of a new document or program. If you supplied a filename, it appears at the top of the window; otherwise, the name UNTITLED appears at the top of the window.

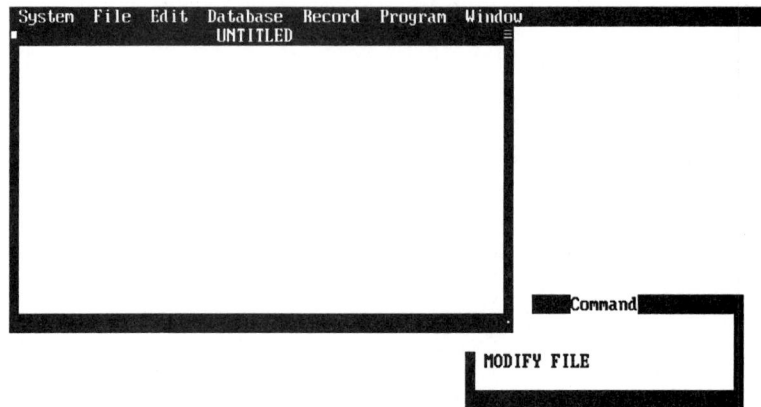

Figure 12-10. *The FoxPro Editor*

Note that the only difference between a program and a text file is how FoxPro handles the preferences for the file. With programs, FoxPro assumes that you do *not* want word wrap turned on. (Word wrap is not normally used when you are writing programs.) With text files, FoxPro assumes that you *do* want automatic word wrap turned on. Of course, you can change either of these preferences if you want; see the "Setting Preferences" section later in this chapter for details.

Opening Existing Files

You can open an existing file in the same two ways; from the menus, or with the MODIFY COMMAND/MODIFY FILE commands. To open an existing program, choose the Open option from the File menu. When the dialog box appears, shown in Figure 12-11, choose File from the Type popup to open a text file or choose Program from the popup to open a program file. You can then choose the file by name from the list box that appears. If the file is in a directory other than the default directory, you can choose another directory from the Directory popup in the dialog box; all files of the chosen type will then appear in the list box.

To open an existing file using commands, enter **MODIFY COMMAND** *filename* or **MODIFY FILE** *filename*, where *filename* is the name of the existing file. Use MODIFY COMMAND to open a program, and use MODIFY FILE to open a text file. Note that you can include a full pathname as part of the filename if desired.

Saving and Closing Files

You can save a file by choosing the Save option of the File menu, by pressing CTRL-W, or by clicking on the Close box in the Editor window. If you did not

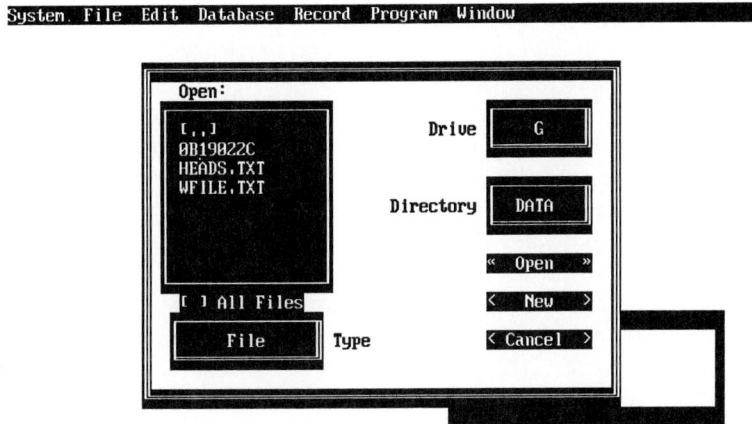

Figure 12-11.   The File Open dialog box

supply a name for the file when you created it, FoxPro will always ask you to supply a name the first time you save a file. Filenames must follow the standard DOS conventions of eight characters or less and no spaces. You can use any extensions you desire, although .PRG is recommended for program files and .TXT is a commonly used extension for text files.

If you use the Save option of the File menu to save a file, you will not automatically exit from the Editor. You must choose Close from the File menu, click on the close box of the window, or press ESC to close the Editor window. If you save a file by clicking on the close box and answering Yes (by typing Y, clicking on Yes, or pressing ENTER) in response to the "Save changes?" prompt that appears, the Editor automatically closes. And if you use the CTRL-W key combination to save a file, the Editor automatically closes after the file is saved.

Note that you can save a copy of an existing file under a different name. To do this, load the file in the manner described. Then choose Save as from the File menu, and when the dialog box appears, enter a new name for the file.

Entering Text

To enter text within the Editor, you type just as you would on most typewriters but with one significant difference. When you are editing a text file (assuming word wrap is enabled in the Preferences window), it is not necessary to press ENTER at the end of each line. If you keep typing as you approach the end of a line, FoxPro will automatically word wrap, or place words too long for one line at the start of the next line. If you are editing a program, FoxPro will not wrap words, unless you have turned on word wrap for .PRG files in the Preferences window of the Editor.

If you are using the Editor to work on a large text file, remember that you can use the CTRL-F10 key combination to quickly zoom a window to full screen. Repeatedly pressing CTRL-F10 will alternately zoom a window back and forth between its initial size and full screen.

Undesired text can be removed with the BACKSPACE or DEL key. The FoxPro Editor imitates most PC-based word processors in that BACKSPACE deletes the character to the left of the cursor and DEL deletes the character at the cursor location. The FoxPro Editor is also normally in an *Insert mode* of operation, meaning that any characters to the right of the cursor are pushed to the right by any new characters that are inserted into existing text. You can switch between Insert mode and Overwrite mode by pressing the INS key. In *Overwrite mode*, new characters typed in existing text replace the existing characters. The mode is indicated by the shape of the cursor. When in Insert mode, the cursor is a narrow underline; when in Overwrite mode, the cursor is a large block.

The FoxPro Editor has a handy Undo option which will undo your prior actions. To undo an action, choose Undo from the Edit menu or press CTRL-U, and the last action you did will be reversed. You can continue to choose Undo to undo repeated actions up to the last time you opened or saved the file during this editing session.

The Redo option of the same Edit menu reverses the most recently undone operation. You can choose Redo from the Edit menu or press CTRL-R.

Cursor Movement

Cursor movement in the FoxPro Editor can be completely controlled with a combination of nine keys: the four cursor keys, PGUP, PGDN, HOME, END, and CTRL. The cursor keys work as they commonly do in other editors, moving the cursor in the direction of the arrow. HOME moves the cursor to the start of a line, and END moves the cursor to the end of a line. PGUP moves the cursor up by one window, and PGDN moves the cursor down by one window. You can also use the CTRL key in combination with RIGHT ARROW and LEFT ARROW or with HOME and END. CTRL-RIGHT ARROW and CTRL-LEFT ARROW move the cursor by one word to the right or left, respectively. CTRL-HOME moves the cursor to the start of a file, and CTRL-END moves it to the end of a file. Table 12-2 shows the keys and respective movement of the cursor.

Mouse users can make use of the scroll bars at the right and bottom edges of the windows to quickly move through text. You can click on any of the arrows in the scroll bars to move in the desired direction; you can also quickly move through a file by dragging the diamond-shaped indicator at the right scroll bar. You can place the cursor at any visible point in the text by clicking at the desired location.

Selecting Text

For various operations involving copying, deleting, or moving text, you will need to highlight, or *select* blocks of text. You select blocks of text with the mouse or

Key	Purpose
RIGHT ARROW	Moves cursor one character right
LEFT ARROW	Moves cursor one character left
UP ARROW	Moves cursor one line up
DOWN ARROW	Moves cursor one line down
PGUP	Moves cursor up one window of text
PGDN	Moves cursor down one window of text
HOME	Moves cursor to start of current line
END	Moves cursor to end of current line
CTRL-RIGHT ARROW	Moves cursor one word right
CTRL-LEFT ARROW	Moves cursor one word left
CTRL-HOME	Moves cursor to start of text
CTRL-END	Moves cursor to end of text

Table 12-2. FoxPro Editor Cursor-Movement Keys

with the SHIFT keys in combination with the other cursor-movement keys outlined in Table 12-2.

To select text, first place the cursor at the start of the text you want to select. Then hold down either SHIFT key and use the cursor keys (or the cursor keys in combination with CTRL) to move to the end of the text that is to be selected. As an example, if you wanted to select three lines within a program, you could place the cursor at the start of the first line and press SHIFT-DOWN ARROW three times. Figure 12-12 shows the results of such an operation.

Mouse users can easily select text to be cut, copied, or moved by moving the mouse pointer to the start of the text, and dragging to the end of the desired text. Note that you can also select a word by positioning the mouse pointer on the word and double-clicking. You can select a line by positioning the mouse pointer on the line and triple-clicking. Another way to quickly select a segment of text is to position the mouse pointer at the start of the text and click, move the cursor to the end, and hold either SHIFT key while clicking.

Cut, Copy, and Paste

You can delete, copy, and move text within the Editor with the Cut, Copy, and Paste options of the Edit menu. You can use the Cut and Copy options after you have selected a block of text with the methods described above. Text that is cut or copied is placed in a temporary area of memory known as the clipboard. After you have cut or copied a selection, you can use the Paste option of the Edit menu to paste the text from the clipboard into another location of the file.

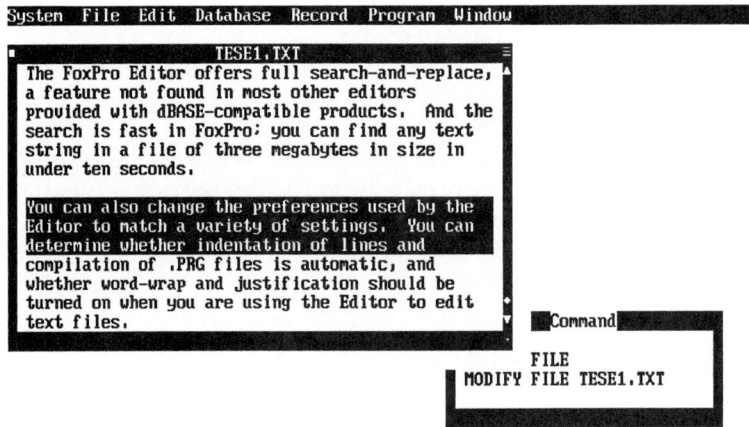

Figure 12-12. *Three lines of text selected in the Editor*

To delete a selection, choose Cut from the Edit menu or press CTRL-X, the hot-key equivalent. To reinsert the selection at a new location, move the cursor to the desired location and choose Paste from the Edit menu or press CTRL-V. Note that you can continue to paste the same text at multiple places in a file by moving the cursor to each desired location and choosing Paste from the menu or pressing CTRL-V again.

To copy a selection, choose Copy from the Edit menu or press CTRL-C. This creates a copy of the text and stores it in the clipboard while leaving the original text unchanged. Move the cursor to the location where the copy is desired and choose Paste from the Edit menu or press CTRL-V. The copy of the text will appear at the cursor location.

One significant advantage to writing programs with the FoxPro Editor is that you can cut, copy, and paste between windows. If you have two programs open in two windows, you could copy a block of text from one program into the clipboard, switch windows with CTRL-F1, and then paste the block into the other program.

Find and Replace

You can access the FoxPro Editor's find-and-replace features by selecting the Find option from the Edit menu or by pressing the equivalent CTRL-F key combination. When you do this, the dialog box shown in Figure 12-13 appears.

Enter the desired search string in the Look For text box. If you want to replace the found text with a different text string, enter the replacement text desired in the Replace With text box. Note that with replacements, FoxPro highlights the text and waits for your instructions; you must press CTRL-E to make

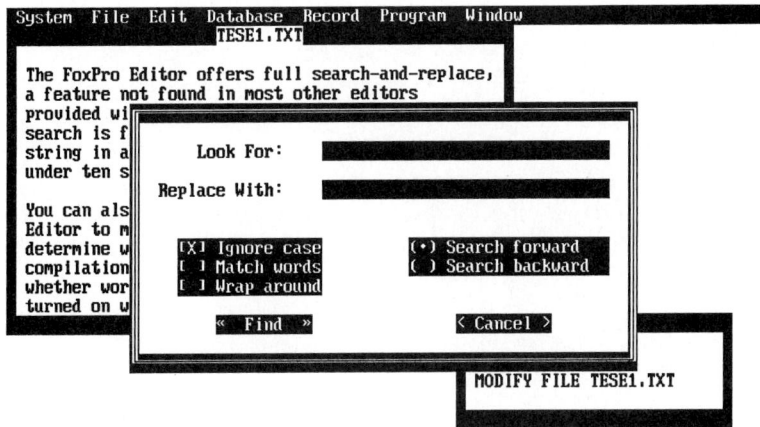

Figure 12-13.   *The Find dialog box*

each replacement or choose Replace All from the Edit menu to tell FoxPro to make all replacements without asking. Tab to the Find button and press ENTER or click on the button to begin your search.

Note the options shown in the dialog box. You can change any of the settings by tabbing to the desired option and pressing the SPACEBAR or by clicking on the desired option. The Ignore case option is selected by default. This tells FoxPro that the case of the letters does not matter in a find operation. Turn this option off if you want case to matter during a search. The Match words option, when chosen, tells FoxPro to look for whole words, and not for the text string when it appears as part of a word. The Wrap around option, when chosen, tells FoxPro to search for the text even if it wraps around the end of a line.

In version 2 of FoxPro, there are two additional options; Search forward and Search backward. You can use these options to choose the direction of the search, which is forward by default.

When you enter the desired text strings in the dialog box and choose Find, FoxPro finds the text just once. If you want to find it a series of times or perform a series of replacements, open the Edit menu again and choose Find Again to find the same text again, choose Replace And Find Again to make a replacement and proceed to the next occurrence of the search text, or choose Replace All to make all replacements in the file.

Printing Files

You can quickly print a file, whether it is a text file or a program, with the Print and Printer Setup options of the File menu. When the desired file is open in the Editor, choose the Print option of the File menu to print the file. The Print dialog box, shown in Figure 12-14, offers you a choice of whether to include line numbers (sometimes useful for debugging programs) and whether a page eject (form feed) should be sent to the printer before or after printing.

Note that FoxPro provides some rudimentary print formatting options through the Printer Setup menu option. Choosing Printer Setup from the File menu causes the Printer Setup dialog box, shown in Figure 12-15, to appear.

You can use the Print to list popup to print to a chosen printer port or to a file. You can also change the left and right margins from the default values of 0 and 80. Enter the desired selections, then choose OK from the dialog box. Then, choose Print from the File menu to print the file.

Setting Preferences

The behavior of many aspects of the FoxPro Editor can be controlled through the settings in the Preferences dialog box, shown in Figure 12-16. From the Edit menu, choose Preferences to open the Preferences dialog box.

You can select or deselect options in the usual manner, by tabbing to them and pressing the SPACEBAR or by clicking on the desired option. The options work as described here:

Wrap words When selected, Wrap words causes word wrap to be on; FoxPro automatically wraps words to the next line as you reach the right edge of the window. This option is normally off when editing program files, and normally on when editing text files.

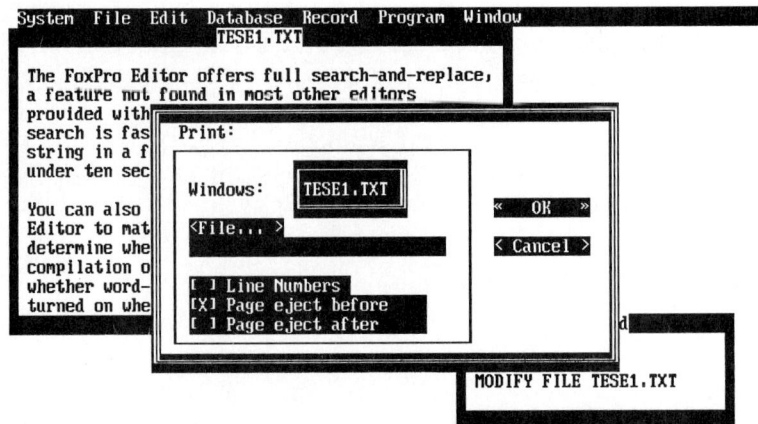

Figure 12-14. *The Print dialog box*

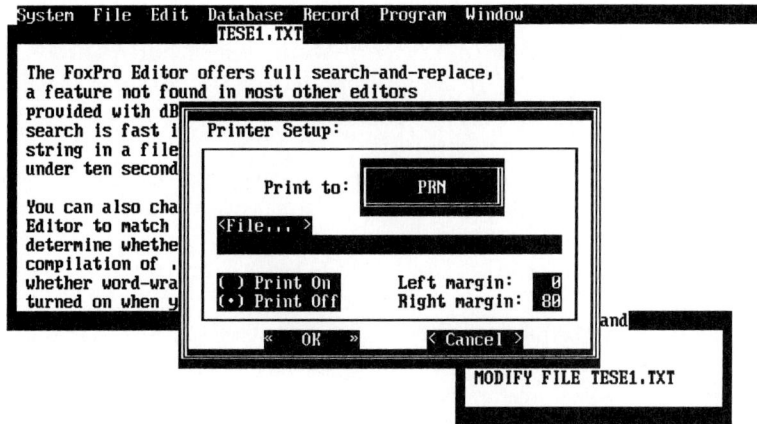

Figure 12-15.   *The Printer Setup dialog box*

Auto indent   When selected, Auto indent automatically indents a new line by the same amount as the previous line. This option is useful when writing programs, assuming you follow the typical programming syntax of indenting lines that fall inside of matched commands.

Make backup   When selected, Make backup causes the Editor to save the prior version of the file under a .BAK extension whenever you save the file.

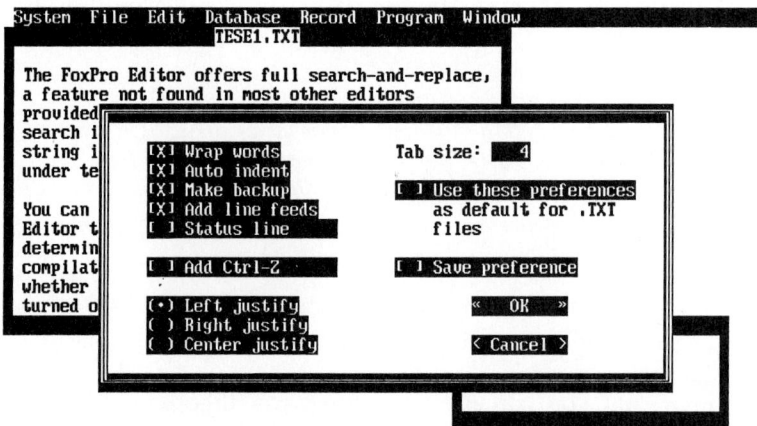

Figure 12-16.   *The Preferences dialog box*

Add line feeds   When Add line feeds is selected, FoxPro saves files using a carriage return and linefeed at the end of each line. This is desirable for program files. For text files, you may or may not want this option turned on. You will probably want it turned off if you intend to read a text file created with the FoxPro Editor into another word processor.

Status line   When Status line is selected, a status line containing the cursor row and column number appears at the top of the Editor window.

Add Ctrl-Z   When selected, Add Ctrl-Z tells FoxPro to assume that any occurrence of the Ctrl-Z character (ASCII 26) marks the end of a file. If the box is not checked, files containing Ctrl-Z characters will be read or written in their entirety.

Left justify   When left justify is selected, FoxPro left-justifies the text.

Right justify   When right justify is selected, FoxPro right-justifies the text.

Center justify   When center justify is selected, FoxPro centers each line of text.

Tab size   The numeric value in the Tab size option specifies the number of spaces inserted when the TAB key is pressed. If unchanged, the default value is 4.

Use these preferences   The Use these preferences option specifies whether the changes you make to the preferences should be used as the default values for all new files created of the type you are currently editing. For example, if you are editing a program (.PRG) file and you turn on the Use these preferences option, the preferences will be used for all .PRG files you create.

Save preference   When selected, Save preference causes the preferences to be saved to the resource file FOXUSER.DBF. Note that the initial window size and position are also saved to the resource file.

HINT: If you don't like the size or placement of the Editor window, move and/or resize the window to your liking. Then choose Preferences from the Edit menu and choose Save preference from the dialog box. Then exit and restart FoxPro. When you next start the Editor, the window size and position will be at the new location you chose.

Redefining the Editor with Macros

Keep in mind that you can use the macro capabilities of FoxPro, detailed in Chapter 9, to make the FoxPro Editor behave like your favorite word processor. Doing so is a simple matter of using the Macros option of the System menu to remap various key combinations so that they imitate the command keys of your word processor. As a simple example, perhaps you use WordPerfect and you are accustomed to using F7 as a save-and-exit key. Since CTRL-W saves changes and exits from the FoxPro Editor, you could use the Macros option of the System menu to remap the F7 key to perform the CTRL-W keystroke. After choosing Macros from the System menu, you would select F7 from the macros list box to start recording a macro for the F7 key. Once the recording dialog box appeared, you could press CTRL-W, press SHIFT-F10, and choose OK from the dialog box to complete the macro. From then on, pressing F7 when in the Editor would cause any changes to be saved and the Editor window to be closed. As detailed in Chapter 9, you will need to save any macros you define to a macro file if you want to be able to use them repeatedly.

Chapter *13*

The Project Manager and FoxPro's Power Tools

If you plan on developing applications in FoxPro, you should make use of FoxPro 2's Project Manager. You can use the Project Manager to combine and coordinate all the different elements used in a FoxPro application. A FoxPro *project* is a special database file that tracks the location of the pieces of an application. The project database also stores object code for an application and tracks the current versions of all files used by the project. The Project Manager is the tool you use in FoxPro to design and update your projects.

You've already been introduced to most of the power tools in FoxPro; the power tools are the utilities that you use to design certain objects like reports, labels, and screens. One more power tool, the Menu Builder, will be detailed in the first half of this chapter. Once you have used the power tools to create all the screens, labels, reports, and menus needed for an application, you can tie these parts together into a single unified application using the Project Manager. At any time during the design of a project, you can add your own programs, in the form of code snippets, to various parts of the application. Projects allow the parts of an application to be scattered across multiple directories, so the use of a project makes it easier to include program routines from libraries of prewritten program code used by multiple applications. The use of projects also makes distribution of the final application easier, as FoxPro's Project Manager lets you combine all parts of the application into a single .APP file. If you purchase the optional FoxPro Distribution Kit, you can use the Project Manager to build executable (.EXE) files that can be run at other machines without FoxPro.

The first half of this chapter covers the use of the Menu Builder, a FoxPro power tool that lets you quickly and easily design menus for use by your application. Typically, the main menu of an application is the starting point, and therefore the main menu is typically the main file used by the Project Manager. Once your menus have been designed, you can use the Project Manager to link the menu choices to the desired uses of the other objects, like screens, reports, and labels. The second half of this chapter will detail the use of the Project Manager and how you can combine the elements of a project into an application. At the end of this chapter, you'll find an example that demonstrates how you can use both the Menu Builder and the Project Manager to design and build an application.

The Menu Builder

FoxPro's Menu Builder gives you the ability to design visually a working model of a desired menu system. When you are satisfied with your design, you can generate the source code (which is stored in a file with an .MPR extension) for your menu. FoxPro stores the details of the menu system in a database with an .MNX extension in case you wish to modify your original design.

As you develop your menu system, functionality may be added using code snippets. The code snippets are actually expressions or procedures that are invoked in response to a user's selection. One of the most important tools of the Menu Builder is the Menu Design window, which will be discussed in the following section.

The Menu Design Window

The Menu Builder can be accessed from the FoxPro menus by pressing ALT-F and choosing Menu as the file type from the dialog box that appears next. You can also enter **CREATE MENU** *menuname* in the Command window. Either method causes an additional menu entitled Menu to appear on the menu bar, and the Menu Design window is displayed, as shown in Figure 13-1. You use the Menu Design window to define all the components associated with your menu system, such as menu pads, menu options, and code snippets.

The first areas usually defined in a menu system are the menu pads, which appear across the top of the menu bar. You enter the text of your menu pads in the text field located in the left portion of the Menu Design window.

Assigning Hot Keys

You can also assign hot keys in the text of your menu pads and menu options. In both cases, the method for doing so is the same; place "\<" before the character that will act as the hot key. For example, to assign "F" as the hot key for the File menu, you would enter the following into the Menu Design window:

```
\<File
```

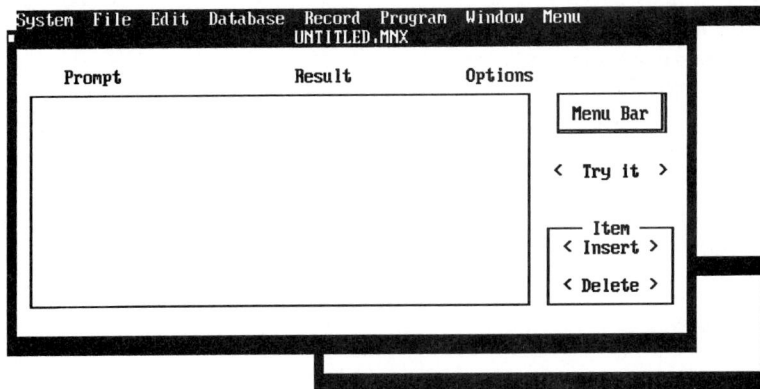

Figure 13-1.   *The Menu Design window*

Keep in mind that you cannot have multiple occurrences of the same hot key within a menu or on a menu bar. If you try this, only the first occurrence of the hot key is recognized.

Responding to Menu Pads

When you are ready to define a response for each menu pad, use the Result popup menu located to the right of the field containing the text for your menu pad. You can respond to a selected menu pad with one of four choices: Submenu, Command, Pad Name, or Procedure (Proc.). Initially, a Submenu is the default choice, with a Create pushbutton displayed to the right. However, if a submenu already exists for the menu pad, an Edit button will appear instead, and you can use it to edit an existing submenu.

To select a response other than Submenu, tab over to the Result popup menu, press the SPACEBAR, highlight your selection, and press ENTER. If you are using a mouse, position the mouse pointer on the popup and press the left mouse button, releasing it when the cursor is over the desired selection. Below is a summary of each response:

Submenu   Choose this option when you wish to create a menu of commands in response to a selected menu pad. Submenus will be discussed in greater detail in the following section.

Command   Instead of a submenu, you can specify any valid FoxPro command.

Pad Name   Choose this option to specify a menu selection from FoxPro's System menu. Refer to FoxPro's Commands & Functions manual for the system names associated with each menu selection.

Procedure   Choose this option to create or edit a procedure or code snippet. If no procedure has been defined, a Create pushbutton appears, and you can choose this button to open an Editor window and begin creating the procedure. If a procedure already exists, an Edit pushbutton appears, and you can choose this button to edit the existing procedure.

Creating a Submenu

As mentioned earlier, the default choice for the Result popup menu is Submenu, with a Create or Edit pushbutton to the right. The submenu defined here will be displayed when the user selects the related menu pad. When you choose either button, another design window similar to the previous one is displayed. In the upper-right corner (above the "Try it" pushbutton), the text of the current menu option is displayed on another popup menu. You use this button to return to the previous design window.

When defining submenus, the process is generally the same as for the menu pads. You enter the text of each menu selection, assigning hot keys using the previously discussed method, in the text box on the far left and assign responses to each menu selection using the Results popup menu.

Creating Divider Lines in Submenus

You can group together menu selections with divider lines. To do so, enter a backslash (\) followed by a hyphen (-) in the text box located on the far left of the Design window.

Saving the Completed Menu

Once you have finished designing the menu, choose Save from the File menu or press CTRL-W. The first time you save a menu, you are prompted for a filename (unless you supplied it in the CREATE MENU *menuname* command).

Generating Menu Code

To generate the program code needed to produce the menu, open the Program menu, and choose Generate. The Generate dialog box will appear, with the default name for the output file. By default, menu code is saved under the same name as the menu design, but with an extension of .MPR. However, you can enter any name you want.

With the desired filename in the text box, choose Generate from the dialog box to generate the menu. FoxPro will display various messages as the menu code is generated, and a completion message will appear when the process is done. You can press ESC to put away the Menu Builder. Refer to the end of this chapter for a complete example of how you can use the Menu Builder and the Project Manager to design an application.

The Project Manager

FoxPro's Project Manager is an organizational tool that lets you combine and maintain all the elements of an application from a single location. With the Project Manager, you can specify the tools that will be needed to create the application, and the project will keep track of the relationships between the parts of the application. This helps you maintain the files as you make changes to the various pieces of the application. For example, an application for managing a mailing list might contain a database file, three different index files, a screen form designed with Screen Painter, two reports, a label design, and a menu system. The Project Manager could be used to build a single project that keeps track of the names and locations of all of these parts. Note, however, that you typically do *not* add a database to a project unless you want that database to be read-only. The Project Manager can also be used to build an application based on the contents of the project. The application contains the program code generated by the menus and screens, in addition to any program code you have written manually and added to the project. If you program in other languages (such as C), you may be familiar with "Make" utilities that are used to recompile programs and their associated parts. FoxPro's Project Manager is similar in function to such utilities.

The Project Manager is typically used by developers, who often need to combine all the needed files of an application into a single unit for wider distribution. Effective use of the Project Manager assumes some knowledge of programming, as applications designed with the aid of the Project Manager make use of code snippets, which are portions of programming code that perform certain tasks throughout your application. In detailing how you can use the Project Manager, this chapter will include some examples of FoxPro program code in the form of code snippets. For additional information on programming in FoxPro, refer to Part II of this book.

A Note About Stand-Alone Programs

The project manager can also create stand-alone executable (.EXE) programs, or FoxPro programs that can be run without having FoxPro installed on a machine; however, you must have purchased the FoxPro Distribution Kit to enable the Project Manager to create stand-alone files. Refer to the documentation that accompanies the FoxPro Distribution Kit for additional information.

Creating a Project

To create a project, choose New from the File menu and choose Project from the dialog box that appears. Enter a name for the project when prompted, then choose OK. From the command level, you can enter **CREATE PROJECT** *project name*. With either method, the Project window appears, and a new menu, Project, is added to the FoxPro menus, as in Figure 13-2.

The Project window contains a list box that shows all files in the project, along with Edit, Info, Add, Remove, and Build buttons.

Choose Add to add a file to the project list. When you choose Add, a Files dialog box appears, and you can choose the desired file to add to the project, as in Figure 13-3.

NOTE: *The Files dialog box includes a Type popup menu; you can use the Type popup to display a specific type of file (such as a database, index, or screen). Also note that the Library option of the Type popup refers to libraries of C routines; you can use routines written in the C programming language in FoxPro if you have the optional FoxPro Library Construction Kit.*

By default, the first file that you add to a project is considered to be the main file, or main module, of an application. A bullet appears beside the filename to indicate that this is the main file.

The Edit button can be used to edit the file currently selected in the list box. For example, if a report or label file is currently highlighted in the list box and you choose Edit, you are taken to the Report Design screen or the Label Design screen, and you can make changes to the report or the label. The Edit button simply saves you the trouble of leaving the Project Manager if you want to make changes to the design of an object used by the project.

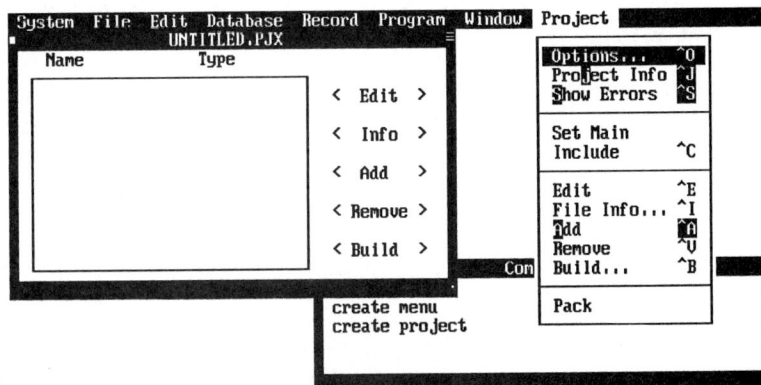

Figure 13-2. *The Project window with the Project menu visible*

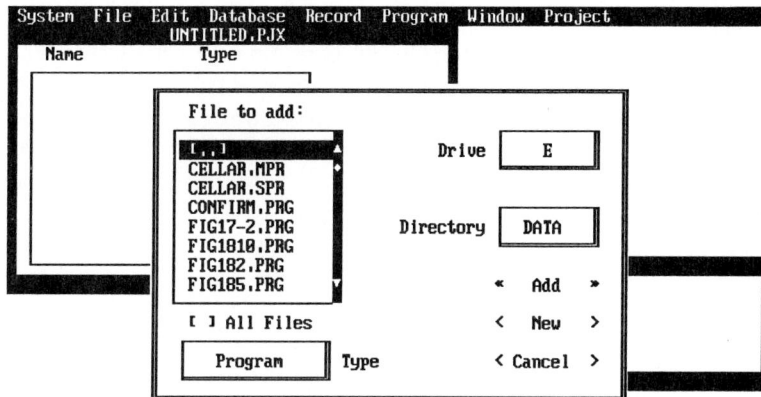

Figure 13-3.   *The Project window with the Files dialog box*

The Info button shows an information dialog box about the currently selected file with information such as the date of the last build by the Project Manager and the creation or modification date of the current version.

The Remove button lets you remove the selected file from the list box, omitting that file from the project.

The Build button displays another dialog box that lets you build the project. Once you have added all the desired files to the list box, choose Build to display the Select Build Option dialog box, shown in Figure 13-4.

You can select the desired options in the dialog box and choose OK. To build (or rebuild) a project, turn on the Rebuild Project option. This causes all files in

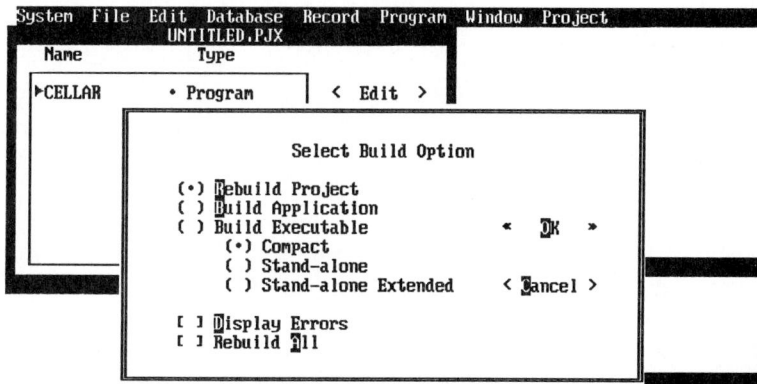

Figure 13-4.   *The Select Build Option dialog box*

the list box to be added to the project database. Also, if any screen or menu designs have been changed since the last build of the project, new program code will be generated for those screens or menus. To rebuild a project and generate an application (.APP) file at the same time, choose Build Application. The Build Executable options, which let you build freestanding .EXE files, are available only if you have purchased the optional FoxPro Distribution Kit. For more details on building an application, see the section, "Creating Applications," later in this chapter.

Two other options in the dialog box are Display Errors and Rebuild All. If Display Errors is turned on, FoxPro displays an error window during the building of the project. Any errors that occur during the project build (often due to referencing a file in program code that cannot be located) will be displayed in the window. Turn on the Rebuild All option if you want FoxPro to update all files in the project, regardless of creation dates and times. Normally, FoxPro compares the date and time of the current version of the file with the date and time of the version last built with the project, and if they differ, FoxPro updates the project for that file.

The Project Menu Options

As shown in Figure 13-2, the Project menu is added to the FoxPro menus when you are working with a project. The Edit, Info, Add, Remove, and Build options of this menu correspond to the Edit, Info, Add, Remove, and Build buttons in the Project window; hence, they perform the same tasks as described earlier. The other options of the Project menu are as follows:

Options   Choose Options from the Project menu to display the Options dialog box, shown in Figure 13-5. You can use the various options shown in this dialog box to change information associated with the project, such as developer information, the style of comments used within program code for the project, the home directory for the project, and where screen and menu program code should be saved.

Project Info   Choose Project Info from the Project menu to display the Project Information dialog box, as shown in Figure 13-6. This dialog box displays information for all files in the project, such as how many of each type of file are currently used in the project.

Show Errors   This option of the Project menu displays any errors detected in the building of the project.

Set Main   This option can be used to reassign the selected file as the main file of the project.

```
System  File  Edit  Database  Record  Program  Window  Project
┌──────────────────────────────────────────────────────────────────┐
│ Name    ┌─ Developer Information ──────────────────────────────┐  │
│         │  Author:                                             │  │
│ CELLA   │  Company:                                            │  │
│         │  Address:                                            │  │
│         │  City:                           St:      Zip:       │  │
│         │                                                      │  │
│         │ ┌─ Comment Style ──────┐  ┌─ Build Options ─────────┐│  │
│         │ │ (•) Box              │  │ [X] Debugging Information││  │
│         │ │ ( ) Asterisk  [    ] │  │ [ ] Encrypt    [X] Logo ││  │
│         │ └──────────────────────┘  └─────────────────────────┘│  │
│         │ ┌─ Screen/Menu Code ───────────────────────────────┐ │  │
│         │ │ [X] Save Generated Code                          │ │  │
│         │ │ (•) With Screen/Menu ( ) With Project ( ) In Directory │
│         │ │ <Directory...>                                   │ │  │
│         │ └──────────────────────────────────────────────────┘ │  │
│         │ ┌─ Home Directory ─────────────────────────────────┐ │  │
│         │ │ <Directory...> E:\FOXPRO\DATA\                   │ │  │
│         │ └──────────────────────────────────────────────────┘ │  │
│         │           [ ] Make these the default settings        │  │
│         │                                                      │  │
│         │            «   OK   »      < Cancel >                │  │
│         └──────────────────────────────────────────────────────┘  │
└──────────────────────────────────────────────────────────────────┘
```

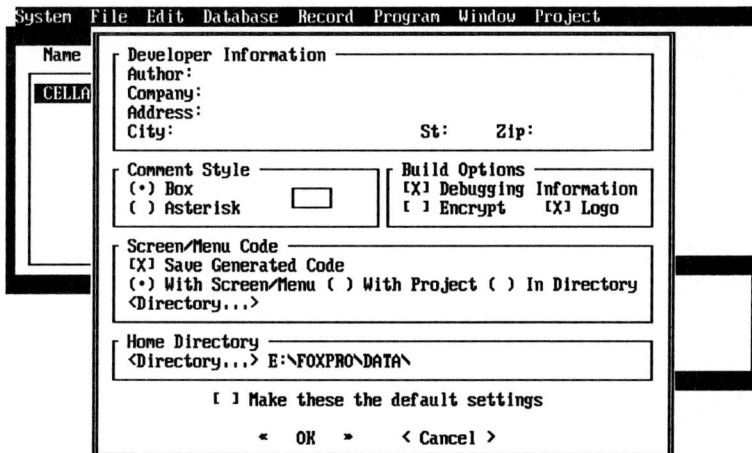

Figure 13-5.   *The Options dialog box*

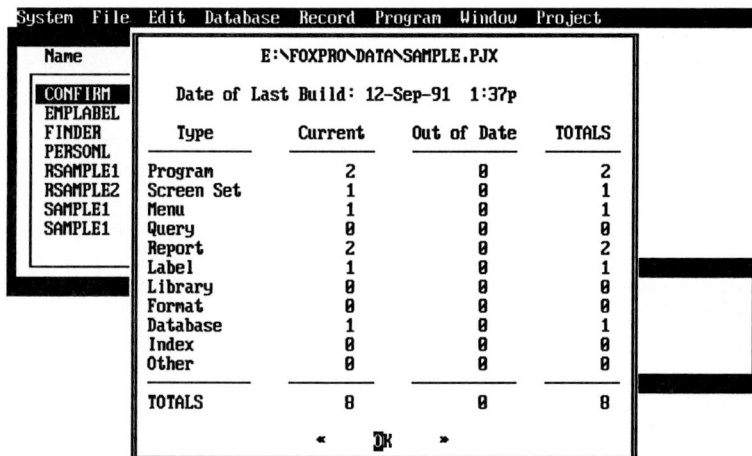

```
System  File  Edit  Database  Record  Program  Window  Project
┌──────────────────────────────────────────────────────────────────┐
│ Name    │           E:\FOXPRO\DATA\SAMPLE.PJX                     │
│         │                                                         │
│ CONFIRM │     Date of Last Build: 12-Sep-91  1:37p               │
│ EMPLABEL│                                                         │
│ FINDER  │     Type          Current    Out of Date    TOTALS     │
│ PERSONL │    ─────────────────────────────────────────────       │
│ RSAMPLE1│     Program          2           0            2        │
│ RSAMPLE2│     Screen Set       1           0            1        │
│ SAMPLE1 │     Menu             1           0            1        │
│ SAMPLE1 │     Query            0           0            0        │
│         │     Report           2           0            2        │
│         │     Label            1           0            1        │
│         │     Library          0           0            0        │
│         │     Format           0           0            0        │
│         │     Database         1           0            1        │
│         │     Index            0           0            0        │
│         │     Other            0           0            0        │
│         │    ─────────────────────────────────────────────       │
│         │     TOTALS           8           0            8        │
│         │                                                         │
│         │              «   OK   »                                │
└──────────────────────────────────────────────────────────────────┘
```

Figure 13-6.   *The Project Information dialog box*

Include   Use this option to include the selected file in the building of an application. You can choose not to include a File when you want to keep the file in a project so it is updated along with the project, but you do not want the file included in any applications you create.

Pack   Use this option to pack the project database. Since a project is a special type of FoxPro database, any files that you remove with the Remove option are still in the database, but they have been deleted. Use the Pack option to permanently remove all record of the files from the project database and thereby recover disk space.

Creating Applications

As mentioned earlier, when you have added all desired files to the project list box, you can proceed to build an application. When building applications, remember to exclude all files that you want the user to be able to modify. Hence, databases and indexes should typically be excluded from the project when you build the application. To exclude a file, select that file in the list box, and choose Exclude from the Project menu. A small circle containing a slash will appear beside the filename in the list box, indicating that it will be excluded from any build. If you later copy the application for general distribution, remember to also copy all excluded files, as they will not be included in the application.

To create an application based on a project, perform the following steps:

1. Use the File Open command or the CREATE PROJECT or MODIFY PROJECT command to open the project in the Project window.

2. Choose Build from the Project window, or select the Build option of the Project menu. The Select Build Option dialog box, as shown earlier in Figure 13-4, appears.

3. Choose Build Application. (Remember, the Build Executable option and its associated choices of Compact, Standalone, and Standalone Extended are only available if you have the optional FoxPro Distribution Kit.)

4. If you wish to see any errors displayed during the building of the application, turn on the Display Errors check box. If all files in the project should be updated regardless of creation dates or times, turn on the Rebuild All check box.

5. Choose OK. If you have made any changes to the project, you will be asked if you want to save the changes to the project database; choose Yes.

6. A Save dialog box now appears, asking for a filename for the application. By default, applications are saved with an .APP extension. Enter the

desired name for the application (or choose an existing name to overwrite from the list box of existing applications) and choose Save.

FoxPro will build the application, which will be saved under the assigned name with the .APP extension. From within FoxPro, you can run the application with the DO *filename*.APP command; for example, if you named the application MAILER, you could enter **DO MAILER.APP** in the Command window to run the application.

Building a Sample Project and Application

If you have duplicated the exercises in the prior chapters of this book, you can see how FoxPro's Project Manager can be used in the building of a simple application. You will need the PERSONL database used throughout this book so far, and you will need the SAMPLE1.SPR screen file created in Chapter 11, the RSAMPLE2 report design created in Chapter 7, and the EMPLABEL label design created in Chapter 8.

WARNING: Since the effective design of an application requires some programming, the following example uses some short programs as code snippets to control the results of various menu selections. If you are not yet familiar with FoxPro programming, the statements used in these code snippets may or may not make sense. The fundamentals of programming are detailed in Part II of this text, so you can refer to that section to learn more about what functions the statements perform. Experienced programmers should note that the code snippets used as examples in this chapter have been designed purposely for simplicity. This chapter is not meant to imply that serious applications should be designed using these techniques. For example, a code snippet called FINDER.PRG uses a LOCATE command to search for a record, but most programmers would prefer to use a FIND or SEEK command for its increased speed. This chapter's examples serve only to demonstrate how your program code and the objects created by the FoxPro power tools can be integrated into an application. The complexity of the program code added to an application is, as always, up to the developer.

The design of this simple application is illustrated in Figure 13-7. The application's menu choices will allow for the adding, editing, or deleting of records in the PERSONL database, and the printing of reports or labels.

Before you proceed to build a menu that will serve as a starting point for the project (and the resulting application), you will need to create two code snippets that will be later used for finding records in the database, and confirming that a

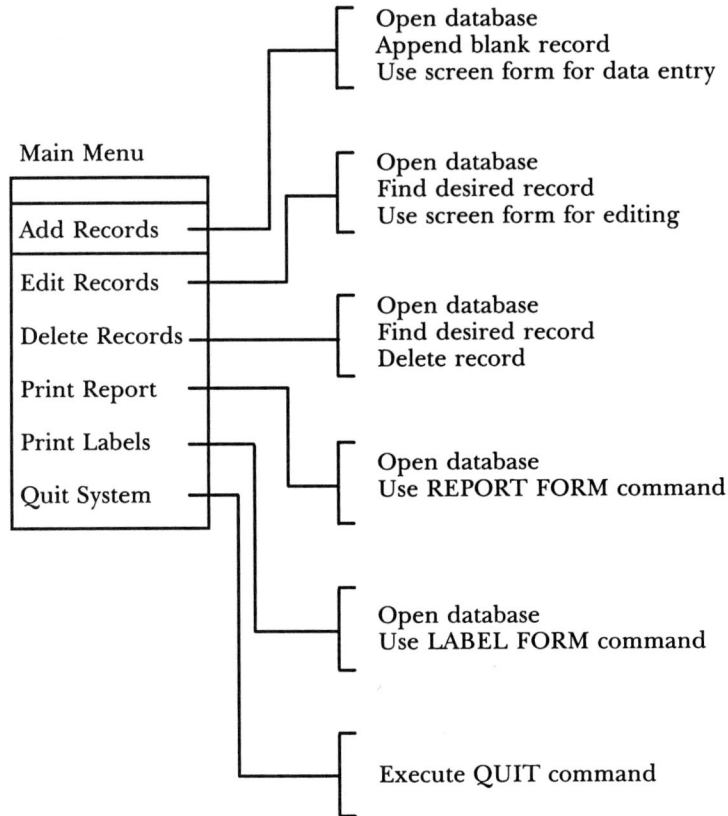

Figure 13-7. *Overall design of the sample application*

record should be deleted. Perform the following steps to create and save these code snippets for later use:

1. In the Command window, enter **MODIFY COMMAND FINDER**. An Editor window appears. Type the following, pressing ENTER at the end of each line. Be sure to check your work for typos before continuing.

```
CLEAR
ACCEPT "Enter social security number of employee: " TO SSFIND
LOCATE FOR SSN = SSFIND
IF .NOT. FOUND()
```

```
    CLEAR
    ? " There is no employee by that number."
    WAIT
    CLEAR
    RETURN
ENDIF
```

2. Save the program by pressing CTRL-W.

3. In the Command window, enter **MODIFY COMMAND CONFIRM**. An Editor window will appear. Type the following, pressing ENTER at the end of each line. Be sure to check your work for typos before continuing.

```
CLEAR
? FIRSTNAME, LASTNAME
ACCEPT "Delete this employee? Y/N:" TO ANS
IF UPPER(ANS) = "Y"
    DELETE
ENDIF
CLEAR
```

4. Save the program by pressing CTRL-W.

You can now proceed to design the menu needed to provide the choices; this can be done using FoxPro's Menu Builder. (See the start of this chapter for overall details about the Menu Builder.) Perform the following steps to construct the menu and the code snippets that support its choices.

1. In the Command window, enter **CREATE MENU SAMPLE1**. In a moment, the Menu window appears.

2. For the first prompt, enter Add Records. Tab over to the Result column and press ENTER to display the menu of results. Choose Proc. (for Procedure). When you do so, <Create> appears beside the Result column.

3. With <Create> highlighted, press ENTER. An Editor window will open, and you can enter the code snippet that will run as a result of the Add Records menu choice. Type the following, pressing ENTER after each line.

```
CLEAR
USE PERSONL
APPEND BLANK
DO SAMPLE1.SPR
CLEAR
CLOSE DATABASES
```

When you have finished entering the program code, press CTRL-W. The code snippet will be saved, and the Menu window will again be visible. Note that the highlighted choice has changed from <Create> to <Edit>. You could press ENTER with this choice highlighted any time you are in the Menu Builder to make changes to the code snippet.

4. Press TAB twice to move to the next prompt (which is currently blank). For this prompt, enter **Edit Records**. Tab over to the Result column and press ENTER to display the menu of results. Choose Proc. (for Procedure). With <Create> now highlighted beside the Result column, press ENTER to open an Editor window. Type the following, pressing ENTER at the end of each line.

```
CLEAR
USE PERSONL
DO FINDER
DO SAMPLE1.SPR
CLEAR
CLOSE DATABASES
```

When you have finished, press CTRL-W to save the code snippet.

5. Press TAB twice to move to the next prompt. For this prompt, enter **Delete Records**. Tab over to the Result column and press ENTER to display the menu of results. Choose Proc. With <Create> now highlighted beside the Result column, press ENTER to open an Editor window. Type the following, pressing ENTER at the end of each line.

```
CLEAR
USE PERSONL
DO FINDER
DO CONFIRM
CLEAR
CLOSE DATABASES
```

When you have finished, press CTRL-W to save the code snippet.

6. Press TAB twice to move to the next prompt. For this prompt, enter **Print Report**. Tab over to the Result column and press ENTER to display the menu of results. Choose Proc. With <Create> now highlighted beside the Result column, press ENTER to open an Editor window. Type the following, pressing ENTER at the end of each line.

```
CLEAR
USE PERSONL
```

```
WAIT "  ready printer, press any key..."
REPORT FORM RSAMPLE2 TO PRINT
CLEAR
CLOSE DATABASES
```

When you have finished, press CTRL-W to save the code snippet.

7. Press TAB twice to move to the next prompt. For this prompt, enter **Print Labels**. Tab over to the Result column and press ENTER to display the menu of results. Choose Proc. With <Create> now highlighted beside the Result column, press ENTER to open an Editor window. Type the following, pressing ENTER at the end of each line.

```
CLEAR
USE PERSONL
WAIT "  ready printer, insert labels, press any key..."
LABEL FORM EMPLABEL TO PRINT
CLEAR
CLOSE DATABASES
```

When you have finished, press CTRL-W to save the code snippet.

8. Press TAB twice to move to the next prompt. For this prompt, type **Exit**. Tab over to the Result column and press ENTER to display the menu of results. Choose Command. With the cursor now in the text box beside the Result column, enter **QUIT**.

9. Open the Program menu with ALT-P, and choose Generate. FoxPro will ask if you want to save the changes to the menu; choose Yes from the dialog box. The next dialog box that appears shows the default filename for the menu code, SAMPLE1.MPR. Choose Generate from this dialog box to generate the code needed for the menu. In a moment, FoxPro will display a progress dialog box showing that the menu code is being generated. When it is done, press ESC to exit the Menu Builder.

With the main menu complete, you are now ready to use the Project Manager to build the application. Perform the following steps to do this:

1. In the Command window, enter **CREATE PROJECT SAMPLE1**. The Project Manager window will appear with the filename SAMPLE1.PJX in the header of the window.

2. Open the Project menu with ALT-O and choose Add. When the files list box appears, tab to or click on the Type popup, and choose Menu. In the list box, choose SAMPLE1.MNX, the menu file that you just created, and

choose Add. The name SAMPLE1 and the type designation "menu" will appear in the project list box.

3. Again, choose Add. This time, from the Type popup, choose Screen. From the list box, choose SAMPLE1.SPX. Choose Add, and from the dialog box that next appears, choose OK to accept the defaults for the screen.

4. Choose Add. From the Type popup, choose Report. From the list box, choose RSAMPLE1.FRX. Choose Add to add the report to the project.

5. Choose Add. From the Type popup, choose Label. From the list box, choose EMPLABEL.LBX. Choose Add to add the report to the project.

6. Choose Add. From the Type popup, choose Database. From the list box, choose PERSONL.DBF. Choose Add to add the database to the project.

7. With PERSONL.DBF still highlighted in the list box, open the Project menu with ALT-0, and choose Exclude. This will tell FoxPro to keep track of the database as part of the project, but to exclude it from the build process. (If this is not done, the user of the application would be unable to modify the database, as it would be read-only while being used by the application.)

8. Open the Project menu with ALT-0, and choose Build. When the Select Build Option dialog box appears, turn on the Build Application option and choose OK. FoxPro will ask if you want to save changes to the project; answer Yes to the prompt.

9. A Save File dialog box will appear asking for a name for the project; by default, SAMPLE1 appears as a name in the text box, because you entered this name when you used the CREATE PROJECT command to start the Project Manager. Choose Save from the dialog box to accept the default name and build the application.

FoxPro will flash various messages on the screen as it builds the project and the application. When it is done, you will see the message, "Build application completed."

Press ESC to close the Project Manager. You can now run the completed application with the DO *application name*.APP command. In the Command window, enter **DO SAMPLE1.APP**.

The FoxPro menus will be replaced by the menus of the application, although the Command window will still be visible. You can close the Command window by clicking on the Close button. Try the various options of the menu to see how the application operates.

For the sake of simplicity, this is a greatly simplified example of an application. However, you can use similar techniques closely matched to your own needs to design FoxPro applications for your own use.

Part II

Programming in FoxPro

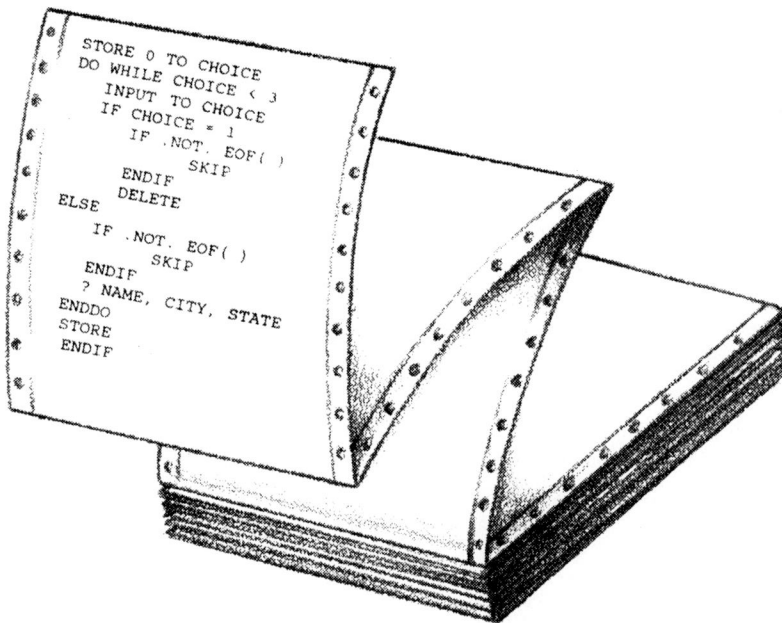

```
STORE 0 TO CHOICE
DO WHILE CHOICE < 3
   INPUT TO CHOICE
   IF CHOICE = 1
      IF .NOT. EOF( )
         SKIP
      ENDIF
      DELETE
   ELSE
      IF .NOT. EOF( )
         SKIP
      ENDIF
   ? NAME, CITY, STATE
ENDDO
STORE
ENDIF
```

Chapter 14

The Basics of FoxPro Programming

This chapter will provide a short introduction to FoxPro programming. If you are already familiar with programming in the dBASE dialect, you might want to skim over this chapter, as much of it will be familiar. For the most part, FoxPro is command compatible with dBASE IV and with dBASE III PLUS, so you can generally use programs written for these products with FoxPro. dBASE IV users should keep in mind, however, that there are some dBASE IV commands and functions, such as SET SQL, that are not supported by FoxPro. If in doubt, compare the command reference from your dBASE IV documentation with that in this book or in your FoxPro documentation.

HINT: *Whenever you run across a command that you're uncertain about, you can find a detailed explanation of the command, along with examples, in Chapter 22 of this book. If you're in doubt about a function, see Chapter 23.*

In FoxPro, a *program* (or command file) is nothing more than a text file containing a series of FoxPro commands. Whenever you run a FoxPro program, FoxPro executes the list of commands stored in that program in sequential order, unless you request otherwise through the design of the program. One program can call and execute another program. Information can be transferred between programs. With programming, complex systems can be efficiently designed by creating a series of smaller programs for individual tasks.

A Sample Program

As an example of a FoxPro program, consider the database structure shown here,

Field	Field Name	Type	Width Dec
1	LASTNAME	Character	15
2	FIRSTNAME	Character	15
3	ADDRESS	Character	25
4	CITY	Character	15
5	STATE	Character	2
6	ZIPCODE	Character	10
7	CUSTNO	Character	4
** Total **			87

whose filename is CUSTOMER.DBF, and the program listing that follows. The program, named SEARCHER.PRG, is designed to locate a particular customer in a database, based on the entry of a desired customer number.

```
*SEARCHER.PRG searches customer database.
USE CUSTOMER
CLEAR
? "ABC Software Customer Base Editing Program"
?
ACCEPT "Enter the customer number:" TO THISNUMB
LOCATE FOR CUSTNO = THISNUMB
IF .NOT. FOUND()
    CLEAR
    ? "No such customer number in the database!"
    WAIT
    RETURN
ENDIF
SET FORMAT TO CustScrn
EDIT
*finished editing, so exit this program.
RETURN
```

The first line of the program is a comment line. This line, which begins with an asterisk to distinguish it from an executable line, is not acted on by FoxPro; it is used purely for explanations to anyone examining the program. While comments are not mandatory, they can help explain a program's operation to a programmer who is unfamiliar with the program; even if you are the only programmer to maintain your programs, notes are helpful when you are trying to remember how a program works months or years after you wrote it.

The second line directs the program to use CUSTOMER.DBF as the database to search.

The third line of the program contains a CLEAR command. This clears the screen of any image that may have been present before the program began running.

The next two lines of the program both begin with the ? command. In FoxPro, the ? command moves the cursor to a new line and prints any expression that follows the question mark symbol on the screen. Hence, the line that reads,

```
? "ABC Software Customer Base Editing Program"
```

prints all of the text enclosed in the quotation marks to the screen. The line that follows, which has only the ? command, serves to place a blank line below the text on the screen.

The next line of the program uses the ACCEPT command to tell FoxPro to accept an entry from the user. The text that appears between quotes after the ACCEPT command is placed on the screen, and the program halts, awaiting the user's response. Once the user types a response and presses ENTER, that response gets stored to a memory variable named THISNUMB. Memory variables are areas of memory containing specific data under names you assign; they are covered in more detail in the next chapter.

The next line of the program, LOCATE FOR CUSTNO = THISNUMB, uses the LOCATE command to search the database for a customer number that matches the value stored to the memory variable by the ACCEPT command.

The next line of the program uses the IF command, along with the FOUND() function, to perform a test for whether the desired record has been located or not. The IF command makes up half of a matched pair of commands known as the *IF...ENDIF commands*. The IF and ENDIF commands are commonly used to evaluate conditions and act upon the results. In this example, if the prior LOCATE command is not successful (the desired record is not found), the four commands between the IF command and the ENDIF command will be executed; the screen will be cleared, the message stating "No such customer number in the database!" will appear on the screen, and a WAIT command will pause the program and ask the user to press any key. Finally, the RETURN command will cause FoxPro to exit from the program.

On the other hand, if the LOCATE command finds the desired record, none of the commands between IF and ENDIF will be carried out. In this case, the command following the ENDIF command, which reads SET FORMAT TO CustScrn, will be carried out. This command places a custom screen form (format file) into effect for the database in use. Next, the EDIT command places FoxPro into an edit mode, so changes can be made to the desired record. Once any changes are made and the user presses CTRL-W to exit the Edit mode, the RETURN command causes FoxPro to exit from the program.

If you are new to programming in any dialect of the dBASE language, some of these commands may seem confusing. However, each of these commands, along with the topics behind memory variables and expressions, will be detailed in this and following chapters.

Creating Programs

You can create programs with the MODIFY COMMAND command, using the form

MODIFY COMMAND *filename*

Entering **MODIFY COMMAND** along with a filename brings up the FoxPro Editor. You then use the Editor to type commands that will be stored as a program. When you use MODIFY COMMAND, the file you create will have an extension of .PRG (PRoGram) unless you enter a different extension. If the filename you enter already exists on the disk, it will be recalled to the screen. If the filename does not exist, a blank screen within the Editor window is displayed.

You can also create programs from the menus by opening the File menu, choosing New, and then choosing Program from the dialog box that appears.

Using the FoxPro Editor

Once you are in the FoxPro Editor, the screen is like a blank sheet of paper. You type the commands that you wish to place in your program, pressing ENTER as you complete each line. If you make any mistakes, you can correct them with the arrow keys and BACKSPACE or DEL. The editing keys available in the Editor are detailed in Chapter 12, "FoxPro Tools and the FoxPro Editor." When using FoxPro's Editor in insert mode, the cursor is shaped like a thin line, and any characters you type will push any existing characters at the insertion point to the right. You can get out of insert mode and into overwrite by pressing INS. When you are in the overwrite mode, the cursor is shaped like a block, and any characters you type overwrite existing characters.

HINT: Use CTRL-F10 to expand the size of the Editor window to full-screen.

One ability of the Editor that will likely come in handy when programming is its ability to delete, move, and copy blocks of text. You can mark a block of text for deletion in the Editor by placing the cursor at the beginning of the text, holding the SHIFT key, and moving the cursor to the end of the block of text while continuing to press SHIFT. The marked text will appear in a different shade. You can then delete the marked text by pressing DEL.

To move or copy text, you mark the block of text in the same manner, and then use the Cut, Copy, or Paste options of the Edit menu. To copy a block of text to another location, first place the cursor at the start of the text, hold SHIFT and move the cursor to the end of the text. Open the Edit menu and choose Copy. Move the cursor to where the copied text should appear, open the Edit menu, and choose Paste. The copied text will appear in the new location.

To move a block of text to another location, first place the cursor at the start of the text, hold down the SHIFT key, and move the cursor to the end of the text.

Open the Edit menu and choose Cut. Move the cursor to where the text is to be moved, open the Edit menu, and choose Paste. The cut text will appear in the new location.

Whenever you finish editing with the FoxPro Editor, choose Save from the File menu or press CTRL-W to save the program. If you want to leave the FoxPro Editor without saving the file, you can choose Close from the File menu or press ESC and then answer No to the dialog box that appears.

Using Another Word Processor

You can also create a program by using other word processing programs. While the FoxPro Editor is convenient and quite powerful, you may prefer to use your favorite word processing program. (If you do use your own editor, be sure to see "Compiling Versus Interpreting," which follows this paragraph.) Any word processor that can save files as *ASCII text* (text without any control codes) can be used to create a FoxPro program. This includes WordPerfect, MultiMate, WordStar, and Microsoft Word. In WordPerfect, save the file with the CTRL-F5,1 key combination. In WordStar, open the file in the "non-document" mode. In Microsoft Word, save the file as "unformatted ASCII." The important points to remember are to save the file as ASCII and to use the .PRG extension when naming the file; otherwise, FoxPro won't recognize the file as a program (unless you include the extension) when calling the program with the DO command.

Compiling Versus Interpreting

Foxpro uses a compiler to run programs on a *compiled* basis, rather than an *interpreted* basis. Interpreters convert each line of a program into machine language each time the program runs. Compilers translate the entire program into what is known as *object code* once, and each time the program runs, it runs using the object code. The use of a compiler offers a significant speed advantage over an interpreter. Earlier versions of Ashton-Tate's dBASE, including dBASE II, dBASE III, and dBASE III PLUS, are interpreter-based. By comparison, FoxPro, FoxBASE+, and dBASE IV all use compilers.

When you run a FoxPro program by entering **DO** *filename*, FoxPro looks for a compiled object-code file with an extension of .FXP. If FoxPro finds the file, it runs the program using the already compiled object code. If FoxPro can't find the file, it looks for a *source-code file*, an ASCII text file of commands with a .PRG extension. FoxPro compiles this file, creating an object code file of the same filename, and then runs the program.

It is important to know this if you use your own editor to modify existing programs. When you change an existing program using the FoxPro Editor, FoxPro recompiles to a new object file when you run the program. If you use your own editor to change a program and the existing object code file is not erased, entering **DO** *filename* will cause the old version of the program to be run. When making changes with your editor, you must erase the old object-code (.FXP) version of the program or use the SET DEVELOPMENT ON command when you start your FoxPro session. Entering **SET DEVELOPMENT ON** will tell FoxPro to compare creation dates and times between source (.PRG) and object (.FXP) files; if they differ, FoxPro will recompile the program before running it.

If you write a program and you want to compile that program without running the program, you can use the COMPILE command. (This command is useful when you want to test new programs for compilation errors.) Enter the command

COMPILE *filename*

where *filename* is the name of the program file to be compiled. FoxPro will compile the program into on object-code (.FXP) file. As the program is compiled, FoxPro looks for any language errors. If you use the SET LOGERRORS ON command before you compile a program, any error messages and their respective line numbers will be written to a text file. The text file will have the same name as the program and an .ERR extension. Note that you can also compile programs from the menus by choosing the Compile option from the Program menu.

Programming Concepts

There are various concepts associated with programming that you should know about before delving into the topic of FoxPro programs: constants, variables, expressions, operators, and functions.

Constants

A *constant* is an item of fixed data whose value does not change. Unlike fields, whose values change depending on the position of the record pointer, a constant's value is dependent on nothing; once established, the constant remains the same. There are numeric, character, date, and logical constants. For example, 5.05 might be a numeric constant, while "a" might be a character constant. All character constants must be surrounded by quotes. Date constants must be surrounded by curly braces, and logical constants must be surrounded by periods.

Memory Variables

A *memory variable*, often simply called a *variable*, is a memory location within the computer that is used to store data. Memory variables are referred to by their assigned names. A variable name must be ten or fewer characters. It must consist of letters, numbers, and underscores only, and it must start with a letter. You cannot use names of commands; and it would be a good idea not to use field names. Because the contents of a memory variable are stored apart from the contents of a database, memory variables are useful for temporary processing of values and data within a FoxPro program. Data can be stored in the form of memory variables, to be recalled for use by the program at a later time. Memory variables will be covered in greater detail in the following chapter, but this brief introduction will benefit readers who are new to programming.

In FoxPro, you can create memory variables directly in two ways; with the STORE command or with an *assignment statement* (=). For example, both of the commands that follow will create a memory variable called AGE and assign the value 21 to that variable:

```
AGE = 21
STORE 21 TO AGE
```

You can also create memory variables indirectly, with the ACCEPT, INPUT, WAIT, and READ commands. These commands are detailed further in this and the next chapter.

Expressions

An *expression* can be a combination of one or more fields, functions, operators, memory variables, or constants. Each part of an expression, whether that part is a constant, a field, or a memory variable, is considered an element of the expression. All elements of an expression must be of the same type. You cannot, for example, mix character and date fields within the same expression unless you use functions to convert the dates to characters. If you try to mix different types of fields within an expression, FoxPro will display an "Operator/operand type mismatch" error message.

The most common type of expression found in FoxPro programs is the *mathematical expression*. Mathematical expressions contain the elements of an expression (constants, fields, memory variables, or functions), usually linked by one or more mathematical operators (+, −, *, /). Examples of mathematical expressions include

```
HOURLYRATE - SALARY
COST + (COST * .05)
HOURLYRATE * 40
```

```
637.5/HOURLYRATE
82
```

Character expressions are also quite common in FoxPro programs. Character expressions are used to manipulate character strings or groups of characters. Examples of character expressions include

```
"Bob Smith"
"Mr. " + FIRSTNAME + " " + LASTNAME + " is behind in ; payments."
```

Operators

Operators, which are represented by symbols, work on related values to produce a single value. Operators that work on two values are called *binary operators*; operators that work on one value are called *unary operators*. Most of FoxPro's operators are binary operators, but there are a couple of unary operators. FoxPro has four kinds of operators: mathematical, relational, logical, and string operators.

Mathematical Operators

Mathematical operators are used to produce numeric results. Besides addition, subtraction, multiplication, and division, FoxPro has operators for exponentiation and unary minus (assigning a negative value to a number, as in −47). The symbols for math operators are as follows:

Operation	Symbol
Unary minus	−
Exponentiation	** or ^
Division	/
Multiplication	*
Subtraction	−
Addition	+

If an expression contains more than one mathematical operator, FoxPro executes the operations in a prescribed order, known as the *order of precedence*. Unary minus will be performed first, followed by exponentiation, then multiplication or division, and finally addition or subtraction. In the case of operators with equal precedence, division and multiplication or subtraction and addition, calculation will be from left to right. When different types of operators are in a single expression, math and string operators are handled first, then relational operators, then logical operators.

You can alter the order of operations by grouping them with matched pairs of parentheses. For example, the parentheses in (3 + 6) ∗ 5 force FoxPro to add 3 + 6 first and then multiply the sum by 5. You can group operations within operations with nested parentheses. FoxPro begins with the innermost group and calculates outward, as in the case of ((3 + 5) ∗ 6) ^ 3, where 3 + 5 is added first, multiplied by 6, and then raised to the power of 3. There is no limit to the amount of nesting, beyond the normal limitation of 1,024 characters for any sort of program line.

Relational Operators

Relational operators are used to compare character strings with character strings, date values with date values, and numbers with numbers. The values you compare can be constants or variables. The relational operators are

Operation	Operator
Less than	<
Greater than	>
Equal to	=
Not equal to	< > or #
Less than or equal to	< =
Greater than or equal to	> =

Any comparison of values results in a logical value of true or false. The simple comparison 6 < 7 would result in .T. The result of 6 < NUMBER depends on the value of NUMBER. You can also compare such character strings as "canine" < "feline" because FoxPro orders letters and words as in a dictionary. However, uppercase letters come before lowercase letters; so "Z" < "a", even though "a" comes before "Z" in the alphabet.

Logical Operators

Logical operators compare values of the same type to produce a logical true, false, yes, or no. The logical operators are

```
.AND.
.OR.
.NOT.
```

The order of preference for logical operators is NOT, then AND, then OR.

String Operators

The *string operator* you will commonly use in FoxPro is the plus (+) sign. The plus sign is used to combine two or more character strings. This is known as *concatenation*. For example, "Orange" + "Fox" would become "OrangeFox" (remember, a blank is a character). Strings inside variables can also be concatenated; for example, if ANIMAL = "Fox" and COLOR = "Orange", then COLOR + ANIMAL would result in "OrangeFox".

Functions

Functions are used in FoxPro to perform special operations that supplement the normal FoxPro commands. FoxPro has a number of different functions that perform operations ranging from calculating the square root of a number to finding the time. Every function statement contains the function name, followed by a set of parentheses. Most functions require one or more arguments inside the parentheses.

For example, the DATE() function returns the correct date, according to the computer's clock. Entering the expression

```
? DATE()
```

results in the current date appearing on the screen at the cursor location. The TRIM() function is another commonly used function, which causes all trailing spaces to be removed from a character expression. For example, assuming that a customer database with FIRSTNAME, LASTNAME, and ADDRESS fields is in use, the commands

```
SET PRINT ON
? FIRSTNAME, LASTNAME, ADDRESS
```

would result in an unattractive printout that looks like this:

```
William      Martin               4807 East Avenue
```

Using the TRIM() function, the large gaps between the fields can be eliminated, as shown in the following example:

```
SET PRINT ON
? TRIM(FIRSTNAME), TRIM(LASTNAME), ADDRESS

William Martin 4807 East Avenue
```

The programming chapters that follow will make use of various functions to perform certain tasks. If you are not familiar with functions, note that a complete list of FoxPro functions can be found in Chapter 23.

Some Commonly Used Commands

Some FoxPro commands are often used within programs but rarely (or never) outside of a programming environment. Since these commands will be used with increasing regularity throughout the next five chapters, they are introduced here.

SET TALK

The SET TALK command determines whether results of certain FoxPro commands or calculations are displayed during execution of a program. When SET TALK OFF is executed within a program, visual responses to the FoxPro commands will halt until a SET TALK ON command is encountered. You can use SET TALK OFF to stop the display of messages such as the "% of file indexed" message during indexing, or the record number displayed after a GO TO or LOCATE command. When you begin a session with FoxPro, SET TALK is on. Note that it's a good idea to place a SET TALK ON command at the end of your programs.

SKIP

The SKIP command moves the record pointer forward or backward. The format of the command is

SKIP [−] [*integer*].

The integer specified with SKIP will move the pointer forward or backward by that number of records. For example, entering **SKIP 4** moves the record pointer forward four records. Entering **SKIP − 2** moves the record pointer backward two records. Entering **SKIP** without an expression moves the pointer one record forward. If you attempt to move the record pointer beyond the end of the file or above the beginning of the file, a "Beginning of file encountered" or an "End of file encountered" error message will result.

RETURN

The RETURN command is used to halt the execution of a program. When a RETURN command is encountered, FoxPro will leave the program and return to the command level. If the RETURN command is encountered from within a program that has been called by another program, FoxPro will return to the program that called the file containing the RETURN command.

?, ??, @, and TEXT

Four commands are commonly used to display or print text: ?, ??, @, and TEXT.

The ? and ?? Commands

The ? and ?? commands will display a single line of text at a time. If ? is used, a linefeed and carriage return occur before the display. A ?? does not include the linefeed and carriage return before the display, so that the subsequent value is displayed on the current line. If the ? or ?? command is preceded by a SET PRINT ON command, output is also routed to the printer. An example is shown in the following program:

```
SET PRINT ON
? "The last name is: "
?? LASTNAME
?
? "The salary per 40-hour week is: "
?? SALARY * 40
SET PRINT OFF
```

You can also add the optional AT clause and a column position to the ? or ?? command to control where on the line the data appears. For example, the command

```
? "Lastname:" AT 26
```

would print the word "Lastname:" starting at column 26 on the current line.

The @ Command

For more selective printing or display, the @ command will move the cursor to a specific location on the screen or page and, when combined with SAY, will display the information there. FoxPro divides the screen into 24 rows by 80 columns. The top-left coordinate is 0,0, while the bottom right coordinate is 23,79. The general format of the @ command is

@ row,column [SAY *"character string"*]

Omitting the SAY clause clears the designated row from the column position to column 79.

To try the use of the @ command, enter

```
CLEAR
@ 12,20 SAY "This is a display"
```

The TEXT...ENDTEXT Command

Using the @ command with the SAY option, you can generate report headings or statements at any required location. Screen formatting with the @ command will be covered in greater detail in Chapter 17, "Programming for Data Entry, Editing, and Reporting."

The TEXT command is useful for displaying large amounts of text. TEXT is commonly used to display operator warnings, menu displays, and notes that appear during various operations of the program. TEXT is followed by the text to be displayed and then ended with ENDTEXT. The text does not need to be surrounded by quotes. Everything between TEXT and ENDTEXT is displayed. The following example will erase the screen with CLEAR and then display a copyright message:

```
CLEAR
TEXT
******************************************************
      FoxPro Copyright (C) 1989 Fox Software
The Legal Staffer Copyright (C) 1990 J Systems, Inc.
For technical support, phone our offices at 555-5555
******************************************************
ENDTEXT
WAIT
```

In the above example, the WAIT command at the end of the program causes FoxPro to display a "Press any key" message and pause until the user presses a key.

The TEXT command must be used from within a program. Any attempt to use TEXT as a direct command will result in an error message.

Chapter *15*

Using Memory Variables

Chapter 14 introduced memory variables, an important topic in FoxPro programming. This chapter will continue coverage of memory variables in further detail. Here we will cover how to create variables of different types, how to save and restore variables from disk, and how to use arrays in FoxPro.

A memory variable is precisely what its name implies: a variable, or changeable, item stored in memory. Unlike a database field, which is relatively permanent, a memory variable is temporary in nature; it remains only until FoxPro is exited and control returns to DOS. Memory variables are commonly used for storing data that is needed on a temporary basis. Three common specific uses for memory variables in FoxPro are for performing calculations, storing data that will later be placed into fields of a database file, and storing and acting on user responses.

As an example of the last task, consider the short program shown below.

```
WAIT "Press C to CANCEL, any other key to print:" TO DOIT
IF UPPER(DOIT) = "C"
    RETURN
ENDIF
REPORT FORM MYFILE TO PRINT
```

In this program, the WAIT command causes the message to be displayed and waits for the user to respond with a keypress. When a key is pressed, that key is stored as a memory variable called DOIT. The IF...ENDIF commands then evaluate the contents of the memory variable. If the uppercase value of the character typed is the letter "C," the report is not run and program control returns to the program that called this program. If the user responds with any character other than the letter "C," the REPORT FORM command is executed, resulting in the printing of a report. (Readers unfamiliar with the conditional nature of the IF...ENDIF statement will find it detailed in Chapter 16, "Process Control in a FoxPro Program.")

As this short program demonstrates, information that is stored in a memory variable can be used later in the program. The information will remain under the name you assigned the variable until it is cleared by a specific command or until program control returns to either a higher-level program or the DOS environment.

Types of Memory Variables

In FoxPro, there are four types of memory variables. They are character variables, numeric variables, date variables, and logical variables. *Character variables* are used to store alphanumeric strings, which can be any combination of characters and numbers. *Numeric variables* are used to store numeric values. *Date variables* store date values, and *logical variables* store logical (true or false) values.

While there are no "memo" variables in FoxPro, the lack of such a specific type of variable will not cause a problem if your application makes use of memo fields. FoxPro has a number of powerful commands and functions specifically designed for extracting and evaluating data contained in memo fields as a series of one or more character strings. You can use these commands and functions to move data between memo fields and character variables.

Creating and Naming Memory Variables

Memory variables can be directly created in one of two ways: with the STORE command or with the assignment (=) statement. With either method, you name the variable and assign a value to it in the same command. For example, both commands shown below will create a memory variable called M_AMOUNT and give it the value of 25.

```
STORE 25 TO M_AMOUNT
M_AMOUNT = 25
```

Names for memory variables can be up to ten characters in length. The names can include letters or numbers, but no spaces. (You can use underscores in memory variables instead of spaces.) FoxPro is not case sensitive when it comes to memory variable names. For example, TEMPNAME and tempname would refer to the same memory variable.

It is a wise idea to avoid using reserved words in the dBASE language as memory variable names. For example, since IF is a reserved command word (part of the IF...ENDIF statement), an assignment statement like

```
IF = 320
```

might cause problems, as under some conditions, FoxPro could try to evaluate the statement as the start of an IF...ENDIF statement.

You should also use names that are different than database field names. If a program encounters a name that can be either a variable or a field, the field name will take precedence over the memory variable. If the variable corresponds to a field in a database file, you can give it a similar name. A common technique in such cases is to precede the field name by the letter "M" (Memory) and an underscore. Hence, Lastname could refer to a field, while M_LASTNAME could refer to a variable.

If you are familiar with other high-level programming languages, one difference between FoxPro and such languages may be apparent; there is no need to apply a specific data type to a variable before creating it with the STORE command or with an assignment statement. FoxPro automatically assigns a data type, based on the information that is stored to the variable. For example, if you enter the command **STORE "hello, there!" TO MSTUFF**, the variable MSTUFF is a character variable, because you have stored a character value (indicated by the presence of the quotation marks). If you enter the command **STORE 257 TO MSTUFF**, MSTUFF becomes a numeric variable, because a number has been stored to the variable.

Table 15-1 shows examples of how all four types of variables can be created.

Creating Character Variables

A *character variable* consists of a character string surrounded by quotes. You can use double quotes (" "), as shown in this book, or single quotes (' ') around the character string. You can also create blank character variables using the SPACE()

STORE Command	Assignment Command	Variable Type
STORE "York" TO M_NAME	M_NAME = "York"	Character
STORE 20 TO M_NUMBER	M_NUMBER = 20	Numeric
STORE {04/30/92} TO M_DAY	M_DAY = {04/30/92}	Date
STORE .T. TO M_CHOICE	M_CHOICE = .T.	Logical

Table 15-1. *Assigning Data Types for Memory Variables*

function. For example, both of the following statements create a blank character variable containing ten spaces.

```
STORE "          " TO M_NAME
STORE SPACE(10) TO M_NAME
```

To accept character data from a user and store it to a memory variable, use the ACCEPT command, the WAIT command, or the @...SAY...GET command. (These are all detailed in Chapter 17, "Programming for Data Entry, Editing, and Reporting.")

Creating Numeric Variables

You can create numeric variables by simply assigning them numeric values. Thus, the commands STORE .065 TO TAXRATE and TAXRATE = .065 both have the same effect. Either command will create a numeric variable with a value of .065. Note that if you must move numbers stored in character fields into numeric variables, you will have to use the VAL() function to convert the character values into numeric values.

You can also create numeric variables indirectly with the AVERAGE, SUM, and COUNT commands. These commands are useful when performing math operations on fields of a database file. As an example, consider the following database file. Note that the first two fields, Salesrep and Repnumb, are both character fields. The last field, Amtsold, is a numeric field.

Salesrep	Repnumb	Amtsold
Jones, J.	1011	350.00
Artis, K.	1008	110.00
Johnson, L.	1002	675.00
Walker, B.	1006	1167.00
Artis, K.	1008	47.00
Williams, E.	1010	256.00
Smith, A.M.	1009	220.00
Allen, L.	1005	312.00
Smith, A.	1001	788.50
Jones, J.	1011	875.00
Shepard, F.	1001	1850.00
Robertson, C.	1013	985.50
Keemis, M.	1007	362.00
Jones, J.	1011	519.00
Artis, K.	1008	617.00
Jones, J.	1011	290.00

The COUNT command provides a count of the number of records meeting a specified condition. For example, you could use the following statement to count the number of sales for J. Jones (sales rep number 1011) and store that value to a variable called SCOUNT:

```
COUNT FOR Repnumb = "1011" TO SCOUNT
```

To provide a numeric sum of the sales for the same sales rep and store the sum in a variable called STOTAL, you could use the following statement:

```
SUM FOR Repnumb = "1011" TO STOTAL
```

In a similar fashion, you could store the average sales for K. Artis to a variable named SAVERAGE by using the following statement:

```
AVERAGE FOR Repnumb = "1008" TO SAVERAGE
```

Creating Date Variables

FoxPro offers various methods of storing dates to variables. You can surround the date in curly braces, as in the following statements:

```
EXPDATE = {12/15/90}
STORE {12/15/90} TO EXPDAY
```

The use of curly braces is command-compatible with dBASE IV.

You can also use CTOD(), which is the character-to-date conversion function. This method is more awkward than using curly braces, but is compatible with earlier software, including FoxBASE+ and dBASE III PLUS. For example, the command

```
STORE CTOD("12/15/90") TO EXPDAY
```

uses the CTOD() function to convert a character string (consisting of a date surrounded by quotes) to a date value.

You can also use the DATE() function to store the current date, according to the computer's clock, to a variable. For example, the command

```
STORE DATE() TO TODAY
```

would store the current date under the memory variable name TODAY.

Date variables can be used in calculations. You can add a number to a date to produce a future date, you can subtract a number from a date to produce a date in the past, and you can subtract an earlier date from a later one to get the elapsed number of days.

Creating Logical Variables

A *logical variable* contains a single true or false value and can be created with the true (.T.) or the false (.F.) symbol. For example, the statement MARRIED = .T. would store a logical value of true to the variable called MARRIED. Note that case is not significant. You can also use .Y. as an equivalent for .T. and .N. as an equivalent for .F.

Viewing the Contents of Memory Variables

The DISPLAY MEMORY and LIST MEMORY commands can be used to show existing memory variables, their contents, and their data types. DISPLAY MEMORY and LIST MEMORY produce the same result, except that DISPLAY MEMORY pauses after each screenful, while LIST MEMORY produces a continuous display. A sample of the result of the DISPLAY MEMORY or LIST MEMORY command is shown in the following program listing. Note the memory statistic that appears at the end of the listing. It shows the available memory remaining for memory variables (out of a total of 6000 bytes available).

```
LIST MEMORY
M_TODAY      Pub    D    07/18/90
M_NAME       Pub    C    "Watterson"
M_SALARY     Pub    N    12.50  (            12.50000000)
M_MEMBER     Pub    L    .T.

    4 variables defined,        16 bytes used
  252 variables available,    5984 bytes available
```

In the list produced by DISPLAY MEMORY or LIST MEMORY, the first column shows the names of the memory variables. The second column indicates "Pub" for public variables, or "Priv" for private variables. (The difference between private and public variables is covered later in this chapter.) The third column shows the type of variable—"C" for character, "N" for numeric, "L" for logical, "D" for date, or "A" for array. To the right of the type column will appear the contents of the memory variable.

Releasing Variables from Memory

Memory variables are normally cleared when a program finishes and control returns to the Command window or to DOS, or when the subroutine where they were created terminates. Public variables must specifically be cleared from memory. The RELEASE command can be used to clear specific variables from memory, while the CLEAR MEMORY command can be used to clear all existing variables from memory. The RELEASE command with the ALL option can be used to clear all variables at the current level or in lower-level subroutines. Variables created in routines at higher levels of the program remain unaffected by RELEASE ALL. The syntax for the RELEASE command is

RELEASE *memory-variable list*/ALL [LIKE/EXCEPT *wildcards*]

In many cases, you list the name of one or more variables to be cleared from memory as part of the memory variable list. For example, you could clear memory variables named TAXRATE and PAYRATE from memory with a command like

```
RELEASE TAXRATE, PAYRATE
```

You can also use the LIKE or EXCEPT options, along with the asterisk (a wildcard signifying any number of characters) or the question mark (a wildcard signifying a single character) to release a group of memory variables. For example, the following command would release all memory variables beginning with the letter "S":

```
RELEASE ALL LIKE S*
```

And the following command could be used to clear all memory variables except those starting with the letters "TAX":

```
RELEASE ALL EXCEPT TAX*
```

Programmers should note an important difference between RELEASE ALL and CLEAR MEMORY (or CLEAR ALL). The RELEASE ALL command deletes only private variables that have been created *at or below* the current program level. CLEAR MEMORY and CLEAR ALL will clear all memory variables, whether private or public, with the exception of the printer-system memory variables. (Printer-system memory variables, used in FoxPro to control various printer settings, are detailed in Chapter 24.)

Memory Variable Files

Memory variables can be saved to and restored from disk files. You save memory variables to disk with the SAVE TO *filename* command, where *filename* is the name of the file the variables will be saved under. An extension of .MEM is added to the filename. The RESTORE FROM *filename* command can be used to restore variables from disk. For example, the following program stores variables to disk. Later, they are restored for use in setting parameters within the program.

```
INPUT "Left margin (a value from 1 to 10)? " TO L_MARGIN
INPUT "Width of memo fields (from 20 to 50)? " TO W_MEMOS
SAVE TO SETTINGS
QUIT


CLEAR
USE MYFILE INDEX NAMES
RESTORE FROM SETTINGS
SET MARGIN TO L_MARGIN
SET MEMOWIDTH TO W_MEMOS
<...more commands...>
```

NOTE: When variables are restored from a disk file, the restored variables will overwrite all existing variables. If you want to keep existing variables in memory while loading additional variables that were saved to a disk file, use the RESTORE FROM filename ADDITIVE variation of the command.

Hiding and Showing Variables with PRIVATE and PUBLIC

FoxPro provides two commands, PRIVATE and PUBLIC, that are used to classify memory variables. The names PRIVATE and PUBLIC refer to how variables will be treated within a large program that has one or more submodules. *Private variables* are available only to the program in which they are created and programs called by that program. Variables that you create in one program are considered private by default. If you do not use the PUBLIC command, FoxPro assumes that all the variables you create are private variables. This means that if you create a variable in a program that is called by another program and then transfer control back to the calling program with the RETURN command, the contents of that memory variable will be lost. You may or may not want those contents to be discarded, so you can use the PRIVATE and PUBLIC commands to specifically tell FoxPro how to handle your variables.

The PUBLIC command tells FoxPro that a memory variable is a *public variable*, to be made available to all programs, regardless of where the memory variable is created. The PRIVATE command tells FoxPro that the variable will be available only to the program that created the variable and all programs that are called by that specific program. Declaring a variable public requires two steps: using the PUBLIC command (the format is PUBLIC *variable name*) and declaring the actual variable with the STORE command or with an assignment (=) symbol. An example follows:

```
PUBLIC YEARSRENTS
STORE RENTAMT * 12 TO YEARSRENTS
```

In this example, the variable YEARSRENTS will be available to all parts of the program, even if program control returns from the part of the program containing these commands to a higher-level (or calling) program.

There is normally little need to declare a memory variable private, since FoxPro sets all memory variables to private by default. However, there may be times that you want to declare a variable private that was previously declared public. To do this, you can use the PRIVATE command in a format (PRIVATE *variable name*) similar to that used by the PUBLIC command. For example,

```
PRIVATE STAFFER
STORE Lastname + Firstname TO STAFFER
```

As an example of the problems that can occur if variables are not declared private or public, consider the following programs. The first program, named FIRST.PRG, passes control to the second program, called SECOND.PRG. The second program declares a variable (NAME), and then passes control back to the calling program, FIRST.PRG. The calling program then tries to display the contents of the memory variable, NAME.

```
*FIRST.PRG is first program CLEAR
? "This program will call the second program."
WAIT
DO SECOND
CLEAR
? "Control has returned to first program."
? "The name is: " + NAME
? "End of first program."


*SECOND.PRG is second program
CLEAR
STORE "Smith" TO NAME
? "The name is: " + NAME
WAIT "Press any key to return to first program."
RETURN
```

When the program is run with DO FIRST, an error message results after program control returns from the second program. FoxPro reports an error because the variable NAME was private to the second program. When control was passed back to the first program, the contents of the variable were lost. This problem can be solved by declaring the variable public, as in the following example:

```
*SECOND.PRG is second program
CLEAR
PUBLIC NAME
STORE "Smith" TO NAME
? "The name is: " + NAME
WAIT "Press any key to return to first program."
RETURN
```

When the first program is run after the change is made, the program completes successfully without an error.

You can use the ALL, LIKE, and EXCEPT options with PRIVATE to cover more than one variable at a time. These options operate in the manner previously described in this chapter. Examples of the use of the ALL, LIKE, and EXCEPT options with PRIVATE would include

```
PRIVATE ALL EXCEPT ???NAMES
PRIVATE ALL LIKE *RENT
PRIVATE ALL EXCEPT YEARSRENTS
```

You can use the accepted DOS wildcards, asterisk (*) and question mark (?), as part of a variable name. The asterisk represents any sequence of characters, and the question mark represents any single character.

Arrays

FoxPro, like its predecessor FoxBASE+, provides support for memory-variable arrays. An array is a matrix of variables arranged in a pattern of rows and columns. Memory-variable arrays are either one dimensional or two dimensional. A *one-dimensional array* contains a single column having a single type of data. By comparison, a *two-dimensional array* has multiple columns (each column having a single data type). Each item in an array is called an *element*, and the total number of elements is always equal to the number of rows multiplied by the number of columns. Figure 15-1 shows examples of a one-dimensional array and a two-dimensional array.

By declaring array-type memory variables, you can store multiple elements of data to the array. To create an array variable, use the DECLARE command or its

One-dimensional array | Two-dimensional array

Jan
Feb
Mar
Apr
May
Jun
Jul
Aug
Sep
Oct
Nov
Dec

Jan-90	Jan-91	Jan-92
Feb-90	Feb-91	Feb-92
Mar-90	Mar-91	Mar-92
Apr-90	Apr-91	Apr-92
May-90	May-91	May-92
Jun-90	Jun-91	Jun-92
Jul-90	Jul-91	Jul-92
Aug-90	Aug-91	Aug-92
Sep-90	Sep-91	Sep-92
Oct-90	Oct-91	Oct-92
Nov-90	Nov-91	Nov-92
Dec-90	Dec-91	Dec-92

Figure 15-1. *Two types of arrays*

equivalent, the DIMENSION command. Both commands perform the same function, but the DECLARE version of the command is compatible with dBASE IV, while the DIMENSION version of the command is compatible with FoxBASE+. The syntaxes of the commands are

DECLARE *array name [number of rows[, number of columns]]*

and

DIMENSION *array name [number of rows[, number of columns]]*

For example, you could declare a one-dimensional array containing 12 elements, named MONTHS, by using the following statement:

```
DECLARE MONTHS[12]
```

You could declare a two-dimensional array named YEARS, containing 36 elements in 12 rows by 3 columns, by using the following statement:

```
DECLARE YEARS[12,3]
```

After creating the array memory variable with the DECLARE command, you can store values to the arrays with the same STORE commands or assignment statements used to store values to other variables. Simply include a row and column reference, surrounded by square brackets, when referring to the array element. For example, to store a numeric value of 23.58 to the array element at row 8, column 2, you could use the following statement:

```
STORE 23.58 TO YEARS[8,2]
```

As an example of the use of arrays, consider the program shown below. The data entry program shown here uses DECLARE to create a one-dimensional array. The array is then used to store data for editing before that data is transferred to the fields of a database file. The program uses the APPEND FROM ARRAY command, which automatically copies each row from an array into each field of the current record in a database file.

```
CLEAR
DECLARE M_DATA[6]
M_DATA[1] = SPACE(15)
M_DATA[2] = SPACE(15)
M_DATA[3] = SPACE(25)
M_DATA[4] = SPACE(15)
M_DATA[5] = SPACE(2)
M_DATA[6] = SPACE(5)
*display prompts, store data to array.*
@  5,5 SAY " Last name:" GET M_DATA[1]
@  6,5 SAY "First name:" GET M_DATA[2]
@  7,5 SAY "   Address:" GET M_DATA[3]
@  8,5 SAY "      City:" GET M_DATA[4]
@  9,5 SAY "     State:" GET M_DATA[5]
@ 10,5 SAY "  ZIP Code:" GET M_DATA[6]
READ
*open database, add new record, store data.*
USE MAILER INDEX Zipcodes
APPEND FROM ARRAY M_DATA
CLOSE DATABASES
RETURN
```

NOTE: If you initialize a memory variable with the same name as an existing array, you will overwrite the array definition.

Macro Substitution

FoxPro provides *macro substitution*, a programming feature that lets you use a special macro character, the ampersand (&), to replace a variable name with the contents of the variable. This feature should not be confused with FoxPro macros, described in Chapter 9, which are used to record keystrokes. Macro substitution is invaluable in cases where FoxPro would normally interpret a variable name as a character string. By placing an ampersand in front of the variable name, you tell FoxPro to use the contents of the variable, and not the name of the variable.

The usefulness of macro substitution can be seen in the case of displaying a list of index filenames and selecting an index for use based on the list. Consider the following short program:

```
USE MYFILE
CLEAR
? "Here are all index files in the directory."
DIR LIKE *.IDX
ACCEPT " Name of the index file to use? " TO THISONE
SET INDEX TO THISONE
```

This program may look practical in theory, but in practice, it would not work. The last line, SET INDEX TO THISONE, would tell FoxPro to open an index file specifically named THISONE.IDX, rather than the name entered by the user in response to the ACCEPT statement.

To solve the problem, the last line of the program could be changed to read as follows:

```
SET INDEX TO &THISONE
```

The program would then operate correctly because the ampersand tells FoxPro to substitute the contents of the variable THISONE when processing the SET INDEX command.

Note that if you use macro substitution to directly control the execution of a loop such as DO WHILE (detailed further in Chapter 16), you must be careful not to change the value of the variable interpreted by the macro while inside the loop. This is because FoxPro evaluates the macro once, at the start of the loop, and does not reevaluate the macro before the loop ends. The following is an example of program code that would cause this type of problem:

```
USE MYFILE
STORE "CUSTOMERID = 1001" TO CONDITIONS
DO WHILE &CONDITIONS
    ? Name
    ? Address
    <...more commands...>
    STORE "CUSTOMERID = 1002" TO CONDITIONS
    SKIP
ENDDO
<...more commands...>
```

This kind of coding will result in loops that don't end when they are supposed to.
The value interpreted by the macro is changed within the loop, but FoxPro does
not check that value once the loop has started.

Chapter *16*

Process Control in a FoxPro Program

Complex applications typically use *modular* programming techniques, which break applications down into manageable parts. Such modular programming techniques would not be possible without the ability to control program flow throughout a complex application. FoxPro offers specific commands and functions that control program flow. The effective use of these commands and functions is detailed in this chapter.

Sequential Processing with DO, RETURN, RUN, and CALL

FoxPro provides four commands that can be used for various means of *sequential program flow* (when commands in a program must be executed in sequence). With sequential processing, you can call individual procedures within a program or you can call an external program outside of FoxPro. The DO command is used to call a *subroutine*, or lower-level procedure, from a higher level within a FoxPro program. When the subroutine completes its execution, the RETURN command can be used to return to the higher-level, or *calling*, program. While DO and RETURN are the most commonly used tools for managing sequential processing, there are jobs for which RUN and CALL are also needed. The RUN command lets you run another program from within the FoxPro environment (within limits of available memory), while the CALL command lets you call an assembly language routine that was previously loaded into memory with the LOAD command.

In a complex application, various menu choices will normally result in different subroutines being called, depending on the design of the application. As noted in Chapter 14, "The Basics of FoxPro Programming," the DO command is used to run a FoxPro program. In sequential processing, the DO command can also be used to call a separate program, a subroutine, from within a program that is already executing. When the FoxPro compiler processes the DO command, FoxPro calls the subroutine and passes program control to it. (The calling program is sometimes referred to as a higher-level program, while the subroutine is considered a lower-level program.) When a RETURN command is encountered in the subroutine, program control returns to the calling program. If there is no RETURN command, program control returns when all statements in the subroutine have been executed. You commonly run subroutines as a result of choices from a main menu in an application. The following program, designed to display a pulldown menu, shows an example of this common technique.

```
* Program:  APPMENU.PRG
@  7,18 CLEAR TO 14,40
@  7,18 TO 14,40 PANEL
@  8,19 PROMPT " Add Applicant        "
@  9,19 PROMPT " Edit Applicant       "
@ 10,19 PROMPT " Delete Applicant     "
@ 11,19 PROMPT " Print Reports        "
@ 12,19 PROMPT " Hire Applicant       "
@ 13,19 PROMPT " Quit to Main Menu    "
MENU TO CHOOSER
DO CASE
     CASE CHOOSER = 1
          DO ADDAPP
     CASE CHOOSER = 2
          DO EDITAPP
     CASE CHOOSER = 3
          DO DELAPP
     CASE CHOOSER = 4
          DO PRINTAPP
     CASE CHOOSER = 5
          DO MOVEAPP
     CASE CHOOSER = 6
          RETURN
ENDCASE
* EOF: APPMENU.PRG
```

In this program, a menu with six possible choices is displayed using @...SAY commands (which are further detailed in Chapter 17, "Programming for Data

Entry, Editing, and Reporting"). Depending on the user's response, a value of 1 to 6 will be stored by the MENU TO command to the memory variable called CHOOSER. The appropriate CASE command tells DO to call a particular subroutine. (Those unfamiliar with DO CASE and CASE statements will find these detailed shortly.)

You can pass parameters to a program you are calling with the DO command by including the WITH clause as part of the statement. You then use the PARAMETERS command within the called program to assign variable names to data items that are passed from the calling program. The PARAMETERS command must be the first executable command in the called program or the first executable statement after the PROCEDURE statement in a procedure file.

The calling program uses the syntax

DO *program name/procedure name* WITH *list of values*

The called program or procedure receives the data specified by *list of values* using the PARAMETERS statement, with the syntax

PARAMETERS *parameter list*

In *parameter list*, you specify the memory-variable names to be assigned to the data items.

Parameter passing can be very useful when you repeatedly perform the same type of task at numerous locations within a program and only the input data changes from task to task. In such cases, you can save considerable effort by coding the tasks as procedures and passing the values that change in the form of parameters. This technique is commonly used to display error messages to users, often where a message box with an error message is presented, with only the wording of the message changing between tasks.

For example, to call a procedure named ERRORS.PRG and pass a parameter containing the text string "Account number" to that procedure, the following command could be used.

```
DO ERRORS WITH "Account number"
```

The called procedure would use the PARAMETERS statement to receive the text string and display it within a message box, as shown in the following example:

```
PROCEDURE ERRORS
PARAMETERS SayIt
CLEAR
@ 4,3 TO 7,50 DOUBLE
@ 5,5 SAY "Cannot find " + SayIt
@ 6,5 SAY "in this database. Please try again."
```

```
WAIT
CLEAR
RETURN
```

Keep in mind that the number, order, and data types of the items in the *parameter list* must match the *list of values* included in the WITH option of the DO command that has called the program or procedure.

Using RUN to Run Other Programs

Sometimes an application presents such a demand that your first thought, once the need becomes evident in the design stage, is "How am I going to do that?" For many tasks that can't be done in FoxPro at all, a favored command is the RUN command. FoxPro can't be expected to do everything, flexible programming language or not. FoxPro is still a database manager, so you run into major design constraints when you try to make it imitate a spreadsheet, word processor, or communications program.

At times, you must have a door to the outside world, and you must be able to move information in and out of that door. One effective way to do this without being a whiz at assembly language is to write external programs using the tool of your choice, be it Turbo Pascal, C, or simply the DOS batch file feature.

Common uses of the RUN command within programs include performing DOS disk backup and formatting blank disks without leaving an application. For example, consider the following program:

```
***BACKIT.PRG***
**Backup program using DOS backup function.
**Last update 07/23/91
CLEAR
CLOSE DATABASES
? "This option backs up the data. You will need"
? "FORMATTED floppy disks to proceed."
? "Press C to CANCEL, any other key to proceed."
WAIT "" TO JUNK
IF UPPER(JUNK) = "C"
     RETURN
ENDIF
ACCEPT "Would you like to format floppy disks first? (Y/N): " TO ANS
IF UPPER(ANS) = "Y"
     RUN FORMAT A:
ENDIF
RUN BACKUP *.* A: /S
CLEAR
? "Backup process complete. Remove last disk from Drive A."
```

```
?
? "To return to main menu,"
WAIT
RETURN
* End of BACKIT.PRG*
```

In this case, the program uses the RUN command to run the DOS FORMAT command, if needed, to format blank floppy disks on drive A. Then the RUN command is used to run the DOS BACKUP program on drive A, allowing for a backup of data files to floppy disks. After the backup process is completed, program control returns to FoxPro.

Obviously, unless your task matches this one precisely, your approach must be different. This is just one example of how FoxPro can be used along with other programs for more complete performance. One caveat to keep in mind is that you may need plenty of memory for elaborate tasks. If you are attempting to run a program with large memory needs, such as a word processor or a spreadsheet, test the RUN command from the command level within FoxPro to make sure you have sufficient memory to accomplish the task before including the RUN command as an option within your application.

LOAD and CALL

Two FoxPro commands that do much toward tapping power not normally present in FoxPro are the LOAD and CALL commands, used to access assembly language programs written in binary (.BIN) format. You can transfer control to an assembly language routine and, assuming the program is written to move data, you can pass data from the routine back to FoxPro. The LOAD command tells FoxPro that the assembly language routine exists and that it is to be loaded into memory for future use.

The syntax for the command is

LOAD *binary filename*[.*ext*]

The extension is optional. If omitted, it is assumed to be .BIN.

Up to five binary files can be loaded into memory at once, each up to 32K in size. Unneeded modules that have been loaded into memory can be released with the RELEASE MODULE *module name* command.

Once the binary file has been loaded into memory, it can be executed at any time by using the CALL command, which has the syntax

CALL *module name* [WITH *expression/memory variable*]

where *module name* is the name of the binary file (the extension is omitted). The optional WITH clause lets you specify a character expression or a memory variable to be passed to the assembly language routine. When your FoxPro program processes the CALL command, control is passed to the binary routine, and execution begins at the first byte of the routine. Once control passes to the routine, the data segment (DS and BX registers) will contain the address for the first byte of the memory variable or character expression that has been passed from FoxPro.

FoxPro treats binary files loaded and executed with the LOAD and CALL commands differently than it treats external program files executed with RUN. When you use RUN, FoxPro creates a DOS shell and transfers control over to the program called with RUN. Because you are building a duplicate of COMMAND .COM in memory and loading the external program, RUN can consume significant amounts of memory. By comparison, with LOAD and CALL, FoxPro treats the binary files as subroutines or "modules" and not as external programs. As a result, FoxPro needs considerably less additional memory to use LOAD and CALL. You may encounter problems on a 512K machine, but any system with 640K or more should allow FoxPro and your external assembly language routines to coexist without difficulty.

Assembler Guidelines and a Warning

Certain guidelines must be followed if you are designing your own binary files to be accessed from FoxPro with the LOAD and CALL commands. If you do write your own binary files, the guidelines that follow will make sense. If you don't, the guidelines that follow become someone else's problem; however, that person should be aware of these rules.

1. Your binary routine must begin (ORG) its first executable instruction at offset zero.

2. Leave the stack pointer and the contents of the stack *alone*. Violating this rule is a sure way to wreak havoc when attempting to exit from the binary routine back to FoxPro. At worst, you will crash your system, requiring a complete reboot. If you must play around with the stack within your routine, you should restore both the stack segment (SS) and code segment (CS) registers to their original states before returning control to FoxPro.

3. Do not design routines that consume additional RAM beyond the size of the program. The LOAD command uses the file size to allocate memory, and you may overwrite portions of FoxPro in RAM if the program dynamically increases its memory needs.

4. Make sure that the binary routine ends with a FAR RETURN. This ensures that program control will return to the address which was pushed

onto the stack before the routine began its execution. If someone else is writing a BIN routine for you to use in FoxPro, this is an important point to stress. Many binary routines are written to end with an EXIT rather than a FAR RETURN. Assembly language programs that end with an EXIT should be assembled into fully executable files and called with RUN rather than with LOAD and CALL.

WARNING: If you commonly use binary routines accessed with LOAD and CALL along with external programs accessed with RUN, you can paint yourself into a corner with memory-allocation conflicts that are very, very difficult to debug. If you use LOAD to load a series of binary files and then use RUN to run an external program before you get around to using the binary files with CALL commands, the effects of the RUN command may overwrite the binary files in memory. When your program later tries a CALL command, it will jump to a point in memory where the expected routine no longer exists. To avoid the bizarre results that may ensue, remove unneeded binary files from memory with the RELEASE binary-module name *command before running external programs with the RUN command.*

FoxPro's Conditionals: IF, ELSE, and ENDIF

In any complex program, FoxPro must perform various operations that depend on a user's response to an option, on a prior calculation, or on different values stored in the fields of a database. For example, when a user is given the option of displaying a report on the screen or printing it on a printer, the program must have some way of responding to the user's desires. In FoxPro, you use the IF, ELSE, and ENDIF commands to branch to the part of the program that performs the desired operation. IF and ENDIF are decision-making commands that will execute other commands when certain conditions are true.

The syntax is

```
IF condition
    commands...
[ELSE]
    [commands...]
ENDIF
```

The IF and ENDIF commands make up a matching set of commands—for each IF statement, there must be a corresponding ENDIF statement. The ELSE command is optional; use it to provide an alternative execution path within the program.

When the IF statement is first encountered, the condition following the IF command is evaluated. If the IF condition is true, the commands between IF and

ENDIF will be executed. If the IF condition is false and there is an ELSE, the commands between ELSE and ENDIF will be executed. If the IF condition is false and there is no ELSE, program control will jump to the ENDIF statement without executing any commands. An example of the use of IF and ENDIF appears below; in this example, if the user presses the letter "C" in response to the prompt provided by the WAIT statement, the RETURN command is executed. If the user presses any other key in response, program control continues with the REPORT FORM command, which is part of the next statement that follows the ENDIF statement.

```
WAIT "Press C to CANCEL, any other key to print: " TO ANS
IF UPPER(ANS) = "C"
      RETURN
ENDIF
REPORT FORM STAFFERS TO PRINT
```

Nesting of multiple IF...ENDIF statements is also permitted. In the following example, whether the innermost IF...ENDIF is ever processed is determined by the response supplied to the outermost IF...ENDIF statement. If the user does not press the "P" key (Printer), program control skips ahead to the ELSE statement, and the REPORT FORM command is output to the screen. If the user does press "P" for printer, the "Ready printer" message is displayed, and the innermost IF...ENDIF tests for a response and takes appropriate action, sending the report to the printer if the user does not cancel by pressing the "C" key.

```
ACCEPT "Display report on (S)creen or (P)rinter?" TO ANS
IF UPPER(ANS) = "P"
    *send report to default printer.
    ACCEPT "Ready printer, press Enter, or type C then;
    press ENTER to cancel report." TO ANS2
    IF UPPER(ANS2) = "C"
         *user cancelled print run.
         RETURN
    ENDIF
    REPORT FORM MEMBERS TO PRINT
    EJECT
ELSE
    *display report on screen only.
    REPORT FORM MEMBERS
ENDIF
```

The Immediate IF( ) Function

The immediate IF function, IIF( ), can often be used to replace a simple pair of IF...ENDIF statements. The syntax for this function is

IIF(*condition*, *expression1*, *expression2*)

If the specified condition is true, FoxPro returns the first expression; if the condition is false, FoxPro returns the second expression.

For example, the following IF...ENDIF statements

```
IF INCOME >= 20000
    CREDIT = "yes"
ELSE
    CREDIT = "no"
ENDIF
```

could be written in a single-line statement with the IIF() function, as shown in the following example:

```
CREDIT = IIF(INCOME >= 20000,"yes","no")
```

This shows the obvious advantage of the immediate IF() function; it requires less coding to accomplish the same results. The immediate IF() function is also useful as part of an expression in stored reports or labels.

Evaluating Multiple Choices with DO CASE

Process flow within a program will often need to take one of several possible paths, depending on the circumstances. You could handle this need with a series of IF...ENDIF statements. However, when you have a number of choices, the corresponding number of IF...ENDIF statements becomes cumbersome to follow. The DO CASE command is specifically designed to handle such a task.

The DO CASE command selects one course of action from a number of choices. The conditions following the CASE statements are evaluated until one of the conditions is found to be true. The syntax for the command is

DO CASE
　CASE *logical expression 1*
　　commands...
　[CASE *logical expression 2*]
　　[*commands...*]
　[OTHERWISE]
　　[*commands...*]
　ENDCASE

When the condition defined by *logical expression 1* is true, the commands between the CASE statement and the next CASE, or OTHERWISE and ENDCASE, will be executed. Then the command following the ENDCASE statement will be executed. If none of the conditions in the CASE statements is found to be true, any commands following the optional OTHERWISE statement will be executed. If the OTHERWISE statement is not used and no conditions are found to be true, program control proceeds to the command following the ENDCASE statement.

NOTE: *When using the DO CASE structure to choose among alternatives, only the first CASE statement to match the specified condition will be chosen, even if more than one meets the specified condition. If you need to design a system where multiple options can result in multiple selections, use IF...ENDIF commands instead.*

In the following example of the use of DO CASE, FoxPro chooses from among three possible alternatives: executing a command file named MENU, appending records to the database, or exiting from the program.

```
INPUT "Enter a number from 1 to 3:" TO CHOICE
DO CASE
    CASE CHOICE = 1
        DO MENU
    CASE CHOICE = 2
        APPEND
    CASE CHOICE = 3
        QUIT
ENDCASE
```

Use DO CASE whenever you need to process a selection that involves a number of possible choices.

Repetitive Processing with DO WHILE...ENDDO and SCAN...ENDSCAN

There will often be times, particularly in the design of reports under program code, when a program must perform the same task repeatedly. FoxPro offers the DO WHILE and ENDDO commands as a matched pair, enabling you to repeat a series of commands for as long as needed. Another matched pair of commands, SCAN and ENDSCAN, are provided for repetitive processing of records in a database file.

The DO WHILE command repeatedly executes commands between DO WHILE and ENDDO as long as the expression defined by the logical expression is true. The syntax for this command is

DO WHILE *logical expression*
    [*commands...*]
    [LOOP]
    [*commands...*]
    [EXIT]
    [*commands...*]
ENDDO

When a DO WHILE command is encountered, the condition in that command statement is evaluated. If the condition is false, program control proceeds to the command following the ENDDO command. If the condition is true, the commands following the DO WHILE command are executed until the ENDDO command is reached. When the ENDDO command is reached, the condition in the DO WHILE statement is again evaluated. If it is still true, the commands between DO WHILE and ENDDO are again executed. If the condition is false, program control proceeds to the command immediately following the ENDDO command.

The LOOP option may be used to transfer program control to the start of the loop. The EXIT option may be used to terminate the loop, transferring program control to the first statement following the ENDDO command.

In the following example, a DO WHILE loop is used to produce an onscreen report using a REPORT FORM command. Each repetition of the DO WHILE loop causes another 20 records to be displayed on the screen until the end of the file is reached. If the user presses the "C" key (Cancel) after a screenful of records is displayed, the EXIT command terminates the loop and control passes to the RETURN command.

```
USE MEMBERS INDEX NAMES
CLEAR
WAIT "Press C to CANCEL, any other key to view members."
CLEAR
DO WHILE .NOT. EOF()
    REPORT FORM MEMBERS NEXT 20
    WAIT TO KEEPGOING
    IF UPPER(KEEPGOING) = "C"
        EXIT
    ENDIF
ENDDO
RETURN
```

NOTE: *A macro can be used in the conditional portion of a DO WHILE loop only if the value of the macro does not change within the loop. Macros are evaluated only during the first pass through the loop.*

The SCAN...ENDSCAN commands are simplified alternatives to the DO WHILE...ENDDO commands. The SCAN...ENDSCAN commands cause the file in use to be scanned, processing all records that meet the specified conditions. SCAN is similar to DO WHILE in that SCAN moves the record pointer to each successive record, testing for the condition specified by the FOR or WHILE clause. This process continues until the end of the file is reached or until the SCAN is terminated by the presence of an EXIT clause. The syntax for the commands is

```
SCAN [scope] [FOR condition] [WHILE condition]
    [commands...]
    [LOOP]
    [commands...]
    [EXIT]
ENDSCAN
```

Scope is used to set a scope (number of records) to be scanned. If no scope is identified, all records are scanned. The FOR option is used to identify the condition that a record must meet before the statements between SCAN and ENDSCAN will be executed. If you use the WHILE option, the statements between SCAN and ENDSCAN will be executed while the specified condition is true.

The EXIT and LOOP commands may be used anywhere between SCAN and ENDSCAN. EXIT halts the process, and program control then proceeds to the command immediately following the ENDSCAN statement. LOOP causes program control to jump back to the first statement following the SCAN statement. The LOOP and EXIT commands are normally placed within an IF...ENDIF conditional structure, inside the SCAN...ENDSCAN structure. If the condition defined by IF...ENDIF is evaluated as true, the LOOP or EXIT command is executed, changing the program flow within the SCAN...ENDSCAN structure.

The following program uses SCAN...ENDSCAN commands to print a renewal notice for every record of a membership database in which the member's expiration date is within 60 days of the current date (indicated by the computer's system clock).

```
USE MEMBERS
SCAN FOR EXPIREDATE <= DATE() + 60
    SET PRINT ON
    ? "Dear: "
    ?? TRIM(Firstname) + " " + Lastname
```

```
      ?
      ? "Your membership expires within the next 60 days."
      ? "Please call 555-1212 to renew your membership."
      EJECT
      SET PRINT OFF
ENDSCAN
```

FoxPro automatically skips to the next successive record whenever it encounters ENDSCAN unless the pointer has reached the end of the database file. Once the end of the file is reached, program control drops out of the loop and moves on to the command following the ENDSCAN command. Of course, you can cause program control to exit from the loop at any time before the end of the file is reached by including a WHILE clause as a part of the SCAN statement.

Chapter 17

Programming for Data Entry, Editing, and Reporting

This chapter details the commands and programming techniques used to handle data entry, editing, and reporting operations in a FoxPro application. The first half of the chapter covers how data can be displayed on screen for users, how responses can be obtained from users, and how the adding and editing of records can be handled within an application. The second half of the chapter details how reports can be generated.

ACCEPT, INPUT, and WAIT

The ACCEPT, INPUT, and WAIT commands are commonly used to obtain data from users. These commands are particularly useful when you need to get a single response, as opposed to a screenful of fields, from a user. All three commands will cause a program to come to a temporary halt, giving the user time to make a response. Once a response is made, it is stored to a memory variable and your program can then act upon the contents of the variable.

ACCEPT

The ACCEPT command uses the syntax

ACCEPT [*character expression*] TO *memvar*

ACCEPT stores a character string of up to 254 characters to the memory variable *memvar*. If the memory variable already exists, its contents are replaced by the response provided to the ACCEPT statement. If the variable does not exist, it is created by the response to the ACCEPT statement. If the user presses the ENTER key without entering a response, a null string (ASCII 0) is stored to the variable.

ACCEPT can be followed by an optional *character expression*. If this expression is included, its contents will appear on the screen when the ACCEPT command is executed.

For example, to display the prompt "Enter owner name:" and store to the memory variable, OWNER, the character string that the user enters in response to the prompt, the following statement could be used:

```
ACCEPT "Enter owner name:" TO OWNER
```

ACCEPT is particularly useful when you need to store a character string to a memory variable and you cannot determine in advance what the length of the string will be. Since ACCEPT lets you enter up to 254 characters in response to the prompt, the supplied length can vary greatly. If you have a more concrete idea of the length of the response, you may want to use the @...SAY...GET commands, discussed later in this chapter, instead. A disadvantage to the ACCEPT command is that you cannot validate data as easily as with the @... SAY...GET and READ commands, and the prompt appears at the current cursor position.

INPUT

The INPUT command stores a numeric, date, or character entry, entered by the user, to a memory variable. The command uses the syntax

INPUT [*character expression*] TO *memvar*

where *character expression* denotes an optional onscreen prompt. When used, it is displayed as a message to the user during keyboard entry. The expression can be a memory variable or a literal character string surrounded by quotes.

For example, to display the prompt "Enter new salary amount:" and store the response to the memory variable NEWAMT, the following command could be used:

```
INPUT "Enter new salary amount:" TO NEWAMT
```

NOTE: INPUT differs significantly from ACCEPT in that INPUT can create different types of memory variables, depending on what the user types as a response. While ACCEPT will always create a character variable, INPUT will create a numeric variable if a number is entered, a character variable if a character string surrounded by quotes is entered, and a date variable if a date string enclosed in curly braces or a CTOD function (such as CTOD("12/10/91")) is entered. INPUT works well when you need to store numeric variables supplied by a user. If you need to prompt a user for a character string, use ACCEPT instead.

WAIT

The WAIT command halts operation of a program until a key is pressed. If the optional character expression is defined, it will be displayed on the screen. If no character expression is defined, a default message of "Press any key to continue" appears. When the TO *memvar* option is used, the key pressed is stored as a memory variable of character type.

Consider the following program. In this program, a WAIT statement is used to pause a program's execution until the user is ready to print a report. The memory variable stored by means of the WAIT statement provides the user with an option for canceling the print run. If the user presses the letter "C" in response to the WAIT prompt, the print run is canceled.

```
CLEAR
? " Ready to print the Video Rentals Report."
WAIT "Press C to CANCEL, any other key to start..." TO DOIT
IF UPPER(DOIT) = "C"
     *user wants out, so...
     RETURN
ENDIF
REPORT FORM VIDEOS TO PRINT
EJECT
RETURN
```

Remember that the use of a variable is optional with WAIT. You can use WAIT without any variable, simply to pause the program and put a message on the screen. When you use WAIT in this manner, the program halts until the user presses a key; then the program continues.

The @...SAY...GET Command

The @...SAY...GET command can be used to display data and get user responses at a specific screen location. FoxPro divides the screen into 25 lines and 80 columns, as shown in Figure 17-1.

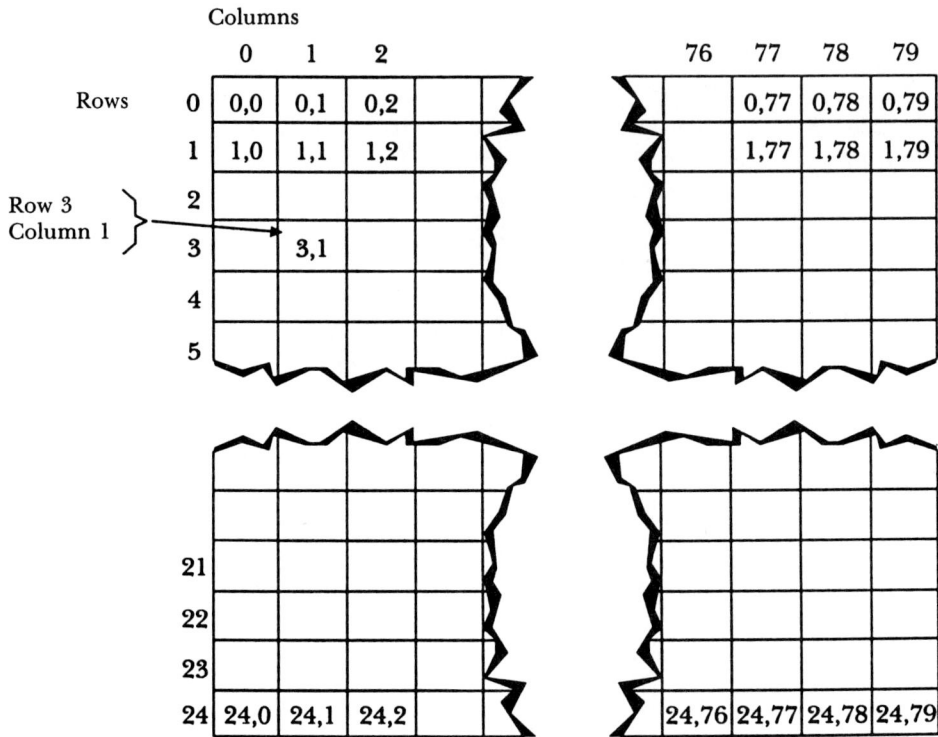

Figure 17-1.   *Screen coordinates*

Rows are numbered from 0 to 24, while columns are numbered from 0 to 79. Row 0, column 0 is in the upper-left corner, and row 24, column 79 is in the lower-right corner of the screen.

Once the cursor has been placed in the proper position with the @ command, messages can be displayed with the SAY option. The SAY option causes the text or the contents of a variable that follows the command to appear on the screen. The SAY option can be used with the @ command in one of two ways:

@ row,column SAY *"message"*

or

@ row,column SAY *varname*

In the first format, SAY is followed by a character string, enclosed in double or single quotes. (Use double quotes whenever there is an apostrophe in the text string itself.)

In the second format, a *varname* is a variable name. Any value that your application stores in that variable will be displayed.

The GET option is used as a part of the @...SAY...GET command. When this option is used, a READ command follows one or more @...SAY commands with GET options. The information displayed with GET can be an existing memory variable or a database field. The READ command then tells FoxPro to enter the editing mode which, much like EDIT, allows the user to move the cursor around the screen or to accept responses from the keyboard for any of the preceding GET options and store the responses in memory. A READ command applies to all GET statements since the last READ command or since the start of the program, if there have been no other READ commands used.

A GET option does not have to be immediately followed by a READ option; it can be the last command in a series of GETs. But if you use GET without READ, you cannot enter any responses from the keyboard. READ commands are only used following GET options.

Consider the following short program:

```
@  5,10 SAY "Enter name." GET Lastname
@  7,10 SAY "Enter address." GET Address
@  9,10 SAY "Enter city." GET City
@ 11,10 SAY "Enter state." GET State
READ
```

Assuming the use of a database with fields called Lastname, Address, City, and State (or existing memory variables by those names) when the program is run, the screen display shown in Figure 17-2 appears, with the cursor awaiting data entry or editing of the first field. The prompts appear at the locations defined by the @...SAY statements. As data is entered, FoxPro stores all of the entries in memory under the field names or variable names used. The name would be stored in Lastname, the address in Address, the city in City, and so on. Once a READ occurs, data entered under the field names is written to the database file itself.

Using Colors with @...SAY...GET Commands

In FoxPro, you can also use COLOR and COLOR SCHEME options with @...SAY...GET commands to control the hues of the data displayed or edited. Use the format

> @ *row,col* SAY *expression* GET *variable* COLOR *standard, enhanced*

or

> @ *row,col* SAY *expression* GET *variable* COLOR SCHEME *number*

where COLOR *standard, enhanced* is a color-pair combination for standard and enhanced foreground and background colors, or COLOR SCHEME *number* is a number from 1 to 11, representing one of FoxPro's 11 color schemes. For example, the statement

```
@ 5,5 SAY "Enter last name:" GET Lastname COLOR R/B, B/W
```

would cause the words, "Enter last name:" to appear in red on a blue background. The reverse-video entry for the data would appear as blue on a white background.

By comparison, the statement

```
@ 5,5 SAY "Are you SURE you want to do that?" COLOR SCHEME 1
```

would display the statement using the same colors as FoxPro's color scheme 1, which is the color scheme used for the windows under FoxPro. By default, this would be white on a blue background, unless you have modified the color set in use.

Using @...CLEAR to Selectively Clear Screens

You can erase any part of the screen with the @...CLEAR command. The format is @ *row,column* CLEAR, and the command erases the screen from the named cursor location to the lower-right corner. For example, the command

```
@ 12,5 CLEAR
```

would erase a rectangular area of the screen beginning at 12,5 and extending to the lower-right corner.

Enter name: Saeedi

Enter address: 1200 Laurence Avenue

Enter city: Rockville

Enter state: MD

Figure 17-2.   Results of the @...SAY...GET commands

Working with Memo Fields

If memo fields are included as part of your screen displays for adding or editing records, you can use the MODIFY MEMO command to display the memo fields in a sizable window. This is usually more desirable than simply using an @...SAY...GET command, because an @...SAY...GET command that names a memo field as part of the GET will display the memo field as the small rectangle containing the word "memo." Your users will then have to use the editing techniques described in Chapter 3, "Creating and Adding Information to Databases," to get into and out of the memo field.

By comparison, the use of the MODIFY MEMO command causes FoxPro to automatically open a window containing the contents of the memo field. The syntax for the command is

MODIFY MEMO *field1*[, *field2*...] [NOWAIT]

The command causes a window to open for every named memo field, with the contents of the current record appearing in each window.

The NOWAIT option, which is only used within programs, tells FoxPro to continue program execution after opening the window. If NOWAIT is omitted, the program pauses, allowing the user to edit the memo field. Program execution then continues when the memo window is closed with the usual methods.

Consider the following program:

```
SET TALK OFF
CLEAR
USE APPOINTS INDEX APPOINTS
STORE DATE() TO THEDAY
@ 5,5 SAY "Edit appointments for what day?"
GET THEDAY
READ
SEEK THEDAY
IF FOUND()
    @ 10,1 CLEAR TO 22,65
    DEFINE WINDOW JText FROM 12,3 TO 21,64
    MODIFY MEMO APTEXT WINDOW JText
    DEACTIVATE WINDOW JText
ELSE
    CLEAR
    ? "No appointments exist for that day!"
    WAIT
ENDIF
```

The program opens a file of appointments, indexed on a date field. When a desired appointment date is located in the file, the DEFINE WINDOW statement is first used to define a window to display the memo field. Then the MODIFY MEMO statement causes the contents of the memo field to appear in the window.

Using TEXT...ENDTEXT to Display Messages

You can use the TEXT and ENDTEXT commands to write large blocks of text to the screen. While you cannot get user input with these commands, they are useful for displaying lengthy messages, introductory screens, or simple menu options. The syntax is

TEXT
text to be displayed
ENDTEXT

All text that appears between the TEXT and ENDTEXT statements appears on the screen, beginning at the current cursor location. The TEXT...ENDTEXT commands work well when you want to present messages in a program and their precise positioning is relatively unimportant.

The following program uses TEXT...ENDTEXT to display a short message before presenting the program's main menu.

```
SET TALK OFF
SET BELL OFF
SET CONFIRM ON
CLEAR
TEXT
***********************************************
*        Program copyright (C) 1990 by     *
*      Integrity Software of Sausalito, CA  *
*             all rights reserved          *
***********************************************
ENDTEXT
WAIT "Press a key for main menu..."
<...more commands...>
```

Data Entry and Editing Under Program Control

A combination of APPEND BLANK commands or search routines and multiple @...SAY...GET commands is commonly used to build routines for adding and editing data. While APPEND and EDIT can be directly used within an application, programmers routinely avoid these commands because of the direct access they afford users to databases. With the use of @...SAY...GET commands and memory variables, you can validate data before additions or changes are allowed. If you are writing a network application, stay away from the APPEND command in particular, because the APPEND command under FoxPro/LAN locks the entire database, denying other users simultaneous use of the file.

Adding Data Under Program Control

To add data while under the control of a program, you can use memory variables and the @...SAY...GET commands. With this common programming technique, you first initialize a set of memory variables to store the data. You then display the variables using @...SAY...GET commands followed by a READ command, allowing the user to enter the desired data. As the entry fields are filled, you can perform any necessary validation of the data. Once the data has been validated, you can use an APPEND BLANK command to add a blank record and transfer the contents of the memory variables into the fields of the database. Network users would use this method because APPEND BLANK under FoxPro/LAN locks the database header, but not the entire file. Hence, other users could not modify a database structure while you were adding records with APPEND BLANK, but they could make simultaneous use of the file. An example of this technique appears in the program that follows:

```
* Program..: ADDER.PRG
USE EMPLOYEE INDEX NAMES
DO WHILE .T.
    STORE SPACE(20) TO M_LAST
    STORE SPACE(20) TO M_FIRST
    @ 4,3 CLEAR TO 7,51
    @ 4,3 TO 7,51 PANEL
    @ 5,6 SAY "Last name of employee? " GET M_LAST
    @ 6,5 SAY "First name of employee? " GET M_FIRST
    READ
    STORE M_LAST + M_FIRST TO FINDIT
    SEEK FINDIT
```

```
      IF FOUND()
         CLEAR
         @ 2,1 TO 14,60 DOUBLE
         @ 3,2 SAY [Last Name  ]
         @ 3,16 SAY Lastname
         @ 5,2 SAY [First Name ]
         @ 5,16 SAY Firstname
         @ 8,2 SAY [Employee ID:]
         @ 8,15 SAY Empid
         @ 9,2 Say [Department]
         @ 9,15 SAY Workgroup
         ? CHR(7)
         @ 14,20 SAY "This employee is already on file!"
         @ 15,2
         ACCEPT "Add new name anyway? Y/N:" TO ADDANS
         IF UPPER(ADDANS) = "N"
            RETURN
         ENDIF
      ENDIF
      STORE SPACE(5) TO M_EMPID
      STORE SPACE(10) TO M_WORKGRP
      CLEAR
      @ 2,1 TO 14,60 PANEL
      @ 3,2 SAY [Last Name  ] GET M_LAST
      @ 5,2 SAY [First Name ] GET M_FIRST
      @ 8,2 SAY [Employee ID:] GET M_EMPID
      @ 9,2 SAY [Department] GET M_WORKGRP
      READ
      APPEND BLANK
      REPLACE Lastname WITH M_LAST
      REPLACE Firstname WITH M_FIRST
      REPLACE Empid WITH M_EMPID
      REPLACE Workgroup WITH M_WORKGRP
      ?
      ACCEPT "[Add another new employee? Y/N] " TO YN
      IF UPPER(YN) = "N"
         CLOSE DATABASES
         EXIT
      ENDIF
   ENDDO
RETURN
* End of ADDER.PRG
```

This example includes a validation routine that checks to see if an employee's name already exists in a personnel file before it can be added as a new entry. All data is initially stored in memory variables, then the APPEND BLANK command is used to add a new record. Finally, the REPLACE commands move the data from the variables into the fields of the database.

Editing Records Under Program Control

You have a choice of doing things two ways when editing records. You can use the EDIT command (or its equivalent, the CHANGE command) or you can use a series of variables combined with @...SAY...GET commands. In either case, you must design some sort of search routine to find the desired record for editing, then display the contents of the fields of that record. This is usually done by searching an existing index with a SEEK or FIND command. You can use LOCATE, but with large database files, the LOCATE command can be terribly slow. The following program demonstrates the simple approach of finding a record, setting a format file, and using the EDIT command to edit the record.

```
*EDITOR.PRG edits employee file.*
CLEAR
STORE SPACE(20) TO M_LAST
STORE SPACE(20) TO M_FIRST
USE EMPLOYEE INDEX NAMES
@ 5,10 SAY "Editing a record."
@ 8,10 SAY "Last name: " GET M_LAST
@ 10,10 SAY "First name: " GET M_FIRST
READ
STORE M_LAST + M_FIRST TO FINDIT
IF FINDIT = " "
      RETURN
ENDIF
SEEK FINDIT
IF .NOT. FOUND()
      CLEAR
      @5,10 SAY "No such name in the database."
      WAIT
      *wait command causes a pause.
      RETURN
ENDIF
EDIT
CLOSE DATABASES
RETURN
```

The first part of the program finds the desired record by searching an index file which, in this example, is built on a combination of the Lastname and Firstname fields. When the desired record is found, the EDIT command allows editing of the record. When the user completes editing with CTRL-W, the CLOSE DATABASES statement closes the file and program control returns to the calling program.

If you prefer to stick with the approach of using variables and @...SAY...GET commands, your program for editing records might resemble the following example:

```
*Editor edits employee file.*
USE EMPLOYEE INDEX NAMES
DO WHILE .T.
    STORE SPACE(20) TO M_LAST
    STORE SPACE(20) TO M_FIRST
    @ 4,3 CLEAR TO 7,51
    @ 4,3 TO 7,51 PANEL
    @ 5,6 SAY "Last name? " GET M_LAST
    @ 6,5 SAY "First name? " GET M_FIRST
    READ
    STORE M_LAST + M_FIRST TO FINDIT
    SEEK FINDIT
    IF .NOT. FOUND()
        CLEAR
        ? "There is no such name in this database!"
        WAIT "Press any key to return to menu..."
        CLOSE DATABASES
        EXIT
    ENDIF
    STORE Lastname TO M_LAST
    STORE Firstname TO M_FIRST
    STORE Empid TO M_EMPID
    STORE Workgroup TO M_WORKGRP
    CLEAR
    @ 2,1 TO 14,60 PANEL
    @ 3,2 SAY [Last Name  ] GET M_LAST
    @ 5,2 SAY [First Name ] GET M_FIRST
    @ 8,2 SAY [Employee ID:] GET M_EMPID
    @ 9,2 SAY [Department] GET M_WORKGRP
    READ
    REPLACE Lastname WITH M_LAST,
    REPLACE Firstname WITH M_FIRST
    REPLACE Empid WITH M_EMPID
    REPLACE Workgroup WITH M_WORKGRP
    ?
    ACCEPT "[Edit another employee? Y/N] " TO YN
```

```
       IF UPPER(YN) = "N"
            CLOSE DATABASES
            EXIT
       ENDIF
ENDDO
RETURN
* End of EDITOR.PRG
```

In this program, the desired record is first found using a SEEK command. Once the record has been located, the contents of the existing fields are moved into memory variables with a series of STORE commands. A series of @...SAY...GET commands, along with a READ command, allow editing of the variables. Once the editing is complete, the contents of the variables are moved back into the record of the database file.

Deleting Records Under Program Control

You can provide a routine for deleting records by using an approach similar to the one shown above for editing records. The major difference is that instead of allowing changes, you display the contents, ask the user for confirmation, and then delete the record. The previous routine could be modified as follows to delete records:

```
*Eraser deletes employees.*
USE EMPLOYEE INDEX NAMES
DO WHILE .T.
    STORE SPACE(20) TO M_LAST
    STORE SPACE(20) TO M_FIRST
    @ 4,3 CLEAR TO 7,51
    @ 4,3 TO 7,51 PANEL
    @ 5,6 SAY "Last name? " GET M_LAST
    @ 6,5 SAY "First name? " GET M_FIRST
    READ
    STORE M_LAST + M_FIRST TO FINDIT
    SEEK FINDIT
    IF .NOT. FOUND()
       CLEAR
       ? "There is no such name in this database!"
       WAIT "Press any key to return to menu..."
       CLOSE DATABASES
       EXIT
    ENDIF
    CLEAR
    @ 2,1 TO 14,60 PANEL
    @ 3,2 SAY [Last Name   ]
```

```
    @ 3,17 SAY Lastname
    @ 5,2 SAY [First Name ]
    @ 5,17 SAY Firstname
    @ 8,2 SAY [Employee ID:]
    @ 8,19 SAY Empid
    STORE .F. TO ANSWER
    @ 12,10 SAY "DELETE employee? Y/N:" GET ANSWER PICTURE "Y"
    READ
    IF ANSWER
        DELETE
    ENDIF
    STORE .F. TO ANOTHER
    @ 14,10 SAY "Delete another? Y/N:" GET ANOTHER PICTURE "Y"
    READ
    IF .NOT. ANOTHER
        CLOSE DATABASES
        EXIT
    ENDIF
ENDDO
RETURN
* End of ERASER.PRG
```

If your application uses a SET DELETED ON statement at or near the start of the application, the use of DELETE alone will make the records appear to be nonexistent. This eliminates the need for a time-consuming PACK command after every series of deletions. If you do not use SET DELETED ON, you might want to include a PACK command just before closing the database file and exiting the subroutine.

Using BROWSE for Data Entry and Editing

The powerful features of the BROWSE command in FoxPro can and should be taken advantage of in an application. As detailed in Chapter 3, there are various BROWSE options that allow flexible display of records in the BROWSE tabular format.

In programming, BROWSE has been universally avoided by programmers using the dBASE language for the same reasons EDIT and APPEND have been avoided. However, the options provided by the BROWSE command in FoxPro offer much tighter control and validation than was possible in earlier variants of the dBASE language. The NOAPPEND clause can be added to prevent the addition of records while in Browse mode. In similar fashion, changes and deletions can be prevented with the NOEDIT, NOMODIFY, and NODELETE clauses. You can also use the NOWAIT clause to display the database in Browse mode and continue with program execution. Normally, program execution halts when a BROWSE command is executed.

As an example of the use of the BROWSE command within an application, consider the common problem of finding the correct record to edit, when all the user knows (or wants to enter) is the last name, and when the file contains multiple entries by that last name. Rather than making the user press PGDN to move through multiple records, you could display numerous records while in Browse mode, allowing the user to pick a desired record for editing.

The following program demonstrates this technique by offering a "point-and-shoot" approach to editing. The user points at the desired record while in the Browse mode, presses ESC, and then can edit the chosen record in a full-screen (Edit-style) display.

```
*BROWSER.PRG edits employee file using BROWSE.*
CLEAR
STORE SPACE(15) TO FINDIT
USE STAFF INDEX LASTNAME
@ 5,10 SAY "Editing a record."
@ 8,10 SAY "Last name: " GET FINDIT
READ
IF FINDIT = " "
     RETURN
ENDIF
SEEK FINDIT
IF .NOT. FOUND()
     CLEAR
     @5,10 SAY "There is no such name in the database."
     WAIT
     *WAIT command causes a pause.
     RETURN
ENDIF
DEFINE WINDOW LOOKIT FROM 8,4 TO 18,70 PANEL COLOR SCHEME 3
@ 6,4 SAY "Highlight the record to edit, and press ESC."
BROWSE NOEDIT NOAPPEND NODELETE NOCLEAR WINDOW LOOKIT
@ 2,1 CLEAR TO 7,50
@ 2,1 TO 7,50 PANEL
@ 3,2 SAY [Last Name  ] GET Lastname
@ 4,2 SAY [First Name ] GET Firstname
@ 5,2 SAY [Employee ID] GET Empid
@ 6,2 SAY [Department ] GET Department
READ
CLOSE DATABASES
CLEAR
RETURN
```

When the program runs, the user is prompted for a last name. After the name is entered, a SEEK command finds the first occurrence of that name in the index. The DEFINE WINDOW command defines a window for the Browse display, and the BROWSE command then displays the found record and successive records in the window. When the user presses ESC, a series of @...SAY...GET commands, followed by a READ command, allow editing of the record chosen through the Browse display.

Producing Reports Under Program Control

Of course, getting accurate data into a database is only half the battle. For most users, the end result will be the reports that your application is able to produce. When it comes to reports, FoxPro is no slouch; the program offers a very flexible report generator and label generator that allow a variety of custom reports and labels. Chapters 7 and 8 detail how you can design custom reports and labels. Being familiar with the design techniques outlined in those chapters can save you significant amounts of programming time. While you can write reports or labels entirely from program code, there is rarely a need to do so, given the flexibility of stored reports and labels in FoxPro.

LIST and DISPLAY

To display or print very basic listings, you may be able to get by with the DISPLAY or LIST command. For example, the program

```
USE RENTALS
LIST TO PRINT OFF
```

produces the following simple listing:

```
SOCIAL      TITLE                     DAYRENTED RETURNED
123-44-8976 Star Trek IV              03/05/91  03/06/91
121-33-9876 Lethal Weapon II          03/02/91  03/06/91
232-55-1234 Who Framed Roger Rabbit   03/06/91  03/09/91
901-77-3456 Beverly Hills Cop II      03/04/91  03/05/91
121-90-5432 Dirty Rotten Scoundrels   03/01/91  03/06/91
495-00-3456 Young Einstein            03/04/91  03/09/91
343-55-9821 When Harry Met Sally      03/06/91  03/12/91
876-54-3210 Lethal Weapon II          03/07/91  03/08/91
123-44-8976 Friday 13th Part XXVII    03/14/91  03/16/91
121-33-9876 Licence To Kill           03/15/91  03/17/91
232-55-1234 When Harry Met Sally      03/17/91  03/19/91
```

```
901-77-3456 Coming To America        03/14/91  03/18/91
121-90-5432 When Harry Met Sally     03/16/91  03/17/91
495-00-3456 Star Trek V              03/18/91  03/18/91
343-55-9821 Young Einstein           03/19/91  03/20/91
876-54-3210 Licence To Kill          03/16/91  03/18/91
```

The TO PRINT clause added to the LIST command causes the listing to be sent to the printer as well as to the screen. The OFF clause added to the LIST statement causes the listing to appear without the usual record numbers.

You can enclose the statement needed to produce a listing like this one in a routine with other statements that perform necessary housekeeping, such as sorting or indexing the records before printing a report, or producing a selective group of records from a large database. This works well when little or no formatting is needed. If any formatting, such as grouping, page breaks, or headers and footers, is needed, the report is a candidate for the report generator.

Using Stored Reports and Labels in Programs

Once you have designed a report form or a label form as outlined in Chapters 7 and 8, you can easily include such reports in your applications with the REPORT FORM and LABEL FORM commands. The REPORT FORM command uses the following syntax:

REPORT FORM *filename*/? [ENVIRONMENT] [*scope*] [FOR *condition*]
[WHILE *condition*] [PLAIN] [HEADING *character string*]
[SUMMARY] [NOEJECT] [TO PRINT/TO FILE *filename*] [OFF]

And as detailed in Chapter 7, "Reports," the REPORT FORM command uses a report-form file, previously created with the CREATE REPORT command, to produce the report. The FOR option can be used to specify a condition to be met before a record will be included in the report. If you use the WHILE option, records will be included until the condition is no longer true. If *scope* is not included, ALL is assumed.

The PLAIN option omits page headings (date, page number, and pagination). The HEADING option, followed by a character string, provides a header in addition to any header that was specified when the report was created with CREATE REPORT. The NOEJECT option cancels the initial form feed. The SUMMARY option causes a summary report to be printed. In summary reports, only group, subgroup, and total lines appear; detail lines are suppressed. TO PRINT directs output to the screen and the printer, while TO FILE directs output to a disk file. If the question mark is substituted in place of a filename, a list of all report files appears. The user may then select the report to print from the list. The ENVIRONMENT option may be used when a view file with the same name as the report file exists. When used, the view file settings will be placed into effect before the report is printed. The optional OFF clause, when used along with TO PRINT, turns off the normal screen output while the report is being printed.

For example, to print a report named STAFF with a heading of "Room 300" and the initial page eject suppressed, the following command could be used.

```
REPORT FORM STAFF TO PRINT HEADING "Room 300" NOEJECT
```

In a similar fashion, the LABEL FORM command (covered in Chapter 8, "Designing Labels") can be used to produce labels. The syntax for the command is

LABEL FORM *label filename*/? [*scope*] [SAMPLE] [FOR *condition*]
[WHILE *condition*] [TO PRINT] [TO FILE *filename*]
[ENVIRONMENT] [OFF]

The SAMPLE option allows a sample label to be printed. This is helpful for checking proper alignment and feeding of labels before actual printing of the labels begins.

The FOR, WHILE, ENVIRONMENT, OFF, and TO PRINT options operate in the same manner as they do with the REPORT FORM command.

You may also want to build selective indexes or set some sort of filter before generating the report, and it is a good idea to give users a way to cancel the report just before it starts. A simple report-producing program, called from one of the options in the main menu, might resemble the following:

```
*REPORTS.PRG provides menu of reports program.*
DO WHILE .T.
    CLEAR
    ANSWER = "0"
    @ 3,5 SAY "For Sales report-     1"
    @ 4,5 SAY "For Customer report-  2"
    @ 5,5 SAY "For Customer Labels-  3"
    @ 6,5 SAY "Return to prior menu- 4"
    @ 8,5 SAY "Enter desired choice:" GET ANSWER
    READ
    DO CASE
        CASE ANSWER = "1"
            WAIT " Ready printer, press a key."
            REPORT FORM SALES TO PRINT
            EJECT
            RETURN
        CASE ANSWER = "2"
            WAIT " Ready printer, press a key."
            REPORT FORM CUSTOMER TO PRINT
```

```
                EJECT
                RETURN
        CASE ANSWER = "3"
                WAIT " Insert labels, press a key."
                LABEL FORM CUSTOMER TO PRINT
                RETURN
        CASE ANSWER = "4"
                EXIT
        OTHERWISE
                CLEAR
                WAIT "Invalid answer! Enter 1-4."
    ENDCASE
ENDDO
RETURN
*End of REPORTS.PRG*
```

This is by far the easiest way to provide users of an application with a variety of reports and labels. You will probably want to add statements that allow users to select specific records, and possibly a sort order or the use of a particular index, before the reports are produced with the REPORT FORM or LABEL FORM command. One common technique is to use the SET FILTER command to limit the available records before using the REPORT FORM statement.

WARNING: When using FoxPro 1.x, the use of SET FILTER with large, indexed databases can cause a tremendous speed penalty, particularly with slower hardware, such as 8088/8086-based computers.

The following program uses SET FILTER to allow for the selection of specific records before a mailing list is printed.

```
*REPORTER.PRG produces the mailing list.*
CLEAR
@ 5,5 PROMPT "All customers    "
@ 6,5 PROMPT "By State         "
@ 7,5 PROMPT "By ZIP code range"
@ 4,4 TO 8,23 DOUBLE
MENU TO CHOICE
DO CASE
    CASE CHOICE = 1
    WAIT "All customers chosen. Press a key."
    CASE CHOICE = 2
    STORE SPACE(2) TO MSTATE
    @ 12,10 SAY "For which state? " GET MSTATE
    READ
    SET FILTER TO UPPER(State) = UPPER(MSTATE)
```

```
        GO TOP
        CASE CHOICE = 3
        STORE SPACE(10) TO STARTZIPS
        STORE SPACE(10) TO ENDZIPS
        @ 12,10 SAY "Starting ZIP code? " GET STARTZIPS
        @ 13,10 SAY "  Ending ZIP code? " GET ENDZIPS
        @ 15,10 SAY "(enter same ZIP code for a single ZIP.)"
        READ
        SET FILTER TO Zipcode >= STARTZIPS .AND. Zipcode <= ENDZIPS
        GO TOP
ENDCASE
CLEAR
TEXT
***************************************************
Ready to print the customer report. Make sure that
the printer is turned on and that paper is loaded.

Press C to CANCEL, any other key to start printing.
****************************************************
ENDTEXT
WAIT TO DOIT
IF UPPER(DOIT) = "C"
    *user cancelled option, so...
    SET FILTER TO
    *above line needed to clear effects of filter.*
    RETURN
ENDIF
REPORT FORM MEMBERS TO PRINT
SET FILTER TO
*above line needed to clear effects of filter.*
RETURN
```

In this program, depending on the menu choice selected, one of two filters may be set to limit the records printed. The SET FILTER TO statement near the end of the program is needed to clear any existing filter. If a filter is not cleared after the report is produced, records not meeting the filter condition will suddenly appear to be missing from the database.

Writing Reports with Program Code

If you must write reports by tediously entering program code rather than using stored reports, there are two common devices you can use: SET PRINT ON, followed by a series of ? statements, or SET DEVICE TO PRINT, followed by a series of @...SAY statements. Both these approaches are primarily holdovers from the days of FoxBASE+ and dBASE III PLUS, when you did not have as much flexibility as you do now when designing stored reports. With both approaches, you use one or more repetitive (DO WHILE) loops to print the contents of a record for each record within a group of records. The general techniques behind such reports are as follows

```
OPEN the database and index files
FIND the first record in the desired group or SET FILTER and GO TOP
Initialize any memory variables for page and line counters
Route output to the printer
Print report headings
DO WHILE not at the end of the file or desired data group
        Print the desired fields or expressions for one record
        Update the counter for page position
        IF the formfeed counter exceeds maximum lines per page
            Print footers, if any
            EJECT the paper
            Print headers, if any
        ENDIF
        SKIP to the next record in logical sequence
ENDDO
```

For example, the following two simple programs use both approaches described to produce reports with program code.

```
*MEMLIST.PRG prints membership roster.*
CLEAR
STORE 1 TO LINES
STORE 1 TO PAGES
USE MEMBERS INDEX NAMES
SET PRINT ON
? "*******************************************"
? "      Membership Address and Phone Roster      "
? "*******************************************"
DO WHILE .NOT. EOF()
    ? "Name: " + TRIM(Firstname) + " " + Lastname
    ? "Phone: " + Phone
    ?? "Expiration Date: " + DTOC(Expiredate)
    ? "Home address: " + Address
    ? SPACE(15) + TRIM(City) + " " + State + " " + Zipcode
    ? "*****************************"
    STORE LINES+ 5 TO LINES
    IF LINES > 55
        ?
        ? SPACE(40) + "Page" + LTRIM(STR(PAGES))
```

```
            EJECT
            STORE 1 + PAGES TO PAGES
            STORE 1 TO LINES
            ? "**************************************************"
            ? "          Membership Address and Phone Roster          "
            ? "**************************************************"
        ENDIF
        SKIP
ENDDO
IF LINES > 1
    EJECT
ENDIF
SET PRINT OFF
RETURN
```

This first example uses a SET PRINT ON statement to echo all successive screen output to the printer, followed by a series of ? commands to display the data. This technique gets the job done, but it is not always easy to place the data at a precise location when you are using ? commands.

The other method, using a SET DEVICE TO PRINT followed by a series of @...SAY statements, is demonstrated in the following program:

```
CLEAR
STORE 5 TO LINES
STORE 1 TO PAGES
USE MEMBERS INDEX NAMES
SET DEVICE TO PRINT
@ 2,15 SAY "MEMBERSHIP EXPIRATION REPORT"
@ 3,10 SAY "***************************"
@ 4,10 SAY "Name                 City"
@ 4,50 SAY "Tape Limit     Exp.Date"
DO WHILE .NOT. EOF()
    @ LINES, 5 SAY TRIM(Firstname) + " " + Lastname
    @ LINES, 30 SAY City
    @ LINES, 50 SAY Tapelimit
    @ LINES, 60 SAY Expiredate
    STORE LINES + 1 TO LINES
    IF LINES > 50
        @ LINES + 2,40 SAY "PAGE " + TRIM(STR(PAGES))
        EJECT
        STORE PAGES + 1 TO PAGES
        STORE 5 TO LINES
        @ 2,15 SAY "MEMBERSHIP EXPIRATION REPORT"
        @ 3,10 SAY "***************************"
        @ 4,10 SAY "Name                 City"
```

```
          @ 4,50 SAY "Tape Limit    Exp.Date"
      ENDIF
      SKIP
ENDDO
IF LINES > 5
      EJECT
ENDIF
SET DEVICE TO SCREEN
RETURN
```

Neither approach is more correct than the other for a given application—it's mostly a matter of preference on the part of the programmer. Using either method, you can implement reports from related files by selecting appropriate work areas and including filenames and pointers to find the related data. (This process is detailed further in Chapter 10, "The Relational Powers of FoxPro.") In one-to-many relationships where one record in the controlling database may have dozens or hundreds of records in a related file, you can add program code to monitor the page count and line count, eject pages, and print new headings when appropriate.

While we're on the subject of page numbers and line counts, note that both the examples of report code shown above use memory variables incremented by the program to keep track of page numbers and line counts. This approach was also common in FoxBASE+ and other earlier dBASE-compatible languages. In FoxPro, however, there are system memory variables (detailed in Chapter 24, "FoxPro System Memory Variables") that can be used to keep track of page numbers and line positions. These system memory variables work with the stored reports, and you may want to consider using them if you need reports that begin with a specific page number other than 1.

Sending Escape Codes to the Printer

In its default mode, FoxPro treats the printer as a simple device capable of receiving ASCII code and sends information in that format. This saves you the worry of trying to get a particular printer to match the output of FoxPro, but it also means that FoxPro, by default, will not use any special effects that your printer has to offer. You can take advantage of printer special effects by sending *escape codes* to your printer, using the CHR() function to send the applicable code. For example, the code for compressed print on Epson-compatible printers is the ASCII value 27, followed by the ASCII value 15. You can therefore switch an Epson-compatible printer into compressed mode with commands like

```
SET PRINT ON
??? CHR(27) + CHR(15)
SET PRINT OFF
```

The printer will remain in this mode until you send another escape code that clears the prior one or selects a different font, or until you manually reset the printer.

Note the use of the ??? command, ideal for sending data to the printer. Unlike the ? commands, ??? does not add a carriage return or linefeed code. Consult your printer manual for a listing of your escape codes.

Chapter *18*

Programming with the FoxPro User Interface

This chapter will detail the various types of menus, the use of colors, and the use of windows in FoxPro. A wide range of options and a high degree of compatibility with competing products (such as dBASE IV and Clipper) mean that you can often accomplish the same task, such as setting colors or displaying a menu, by using any of several different commands in FoxPro. The variety of commands available provides the power to design an interface for an application that offers mouse-sensitive menus, "point-and-shoot" pick lists, data and text in windows, and a wide range of color settings.

Building Effective Menus

In FoxPro, you can easily implement bar menus, popup menus, or pulldown menus. An important point to remember is that with menus in FoxPro, there are different groups of commands that can provide the same type of menu. This is because the command syntax of FoxPro is 100 percent compatible with its predecessor, FoxBASE+, and also highly compatible with Clipper (Summer 87 version) and dBASE IV. Because FoxBASE+, Clipper, and dBASE IV all implement menus using different commands, FoxPro offers menu commands that are compatible with all three. It is up to you to decide which commands you want to use to implement menus. If you don't need compatibility with an earlier product, use the style of command syntax you prefer.

Users of FoxPro 2 should keep in mind that the Menu Builder utility that is a part of version 2 can also be used to quickly design effective menus. See Chapter 13, "The Project Manager and FoxPro's Power Tools," for a description of the use of the Menu Builder.

Bar Menus

A *bar menu* (also called a menu pad or menu bar) is a menu with options arranged along a horizontal bar. This type of menu was originally popularized on the PC by Lotus 1-2-3. In Figure 18-1, the upper menu is an example of a bar menu. You can use the DEFINE MENU, DEFINE PAD, and ACTIVATE MENU commands to build a bar menu that is also compatible with dBASE IV, or you can use the @...PROMPT and MENU TO commands to build a bar menu that is also compatible with Clipper.

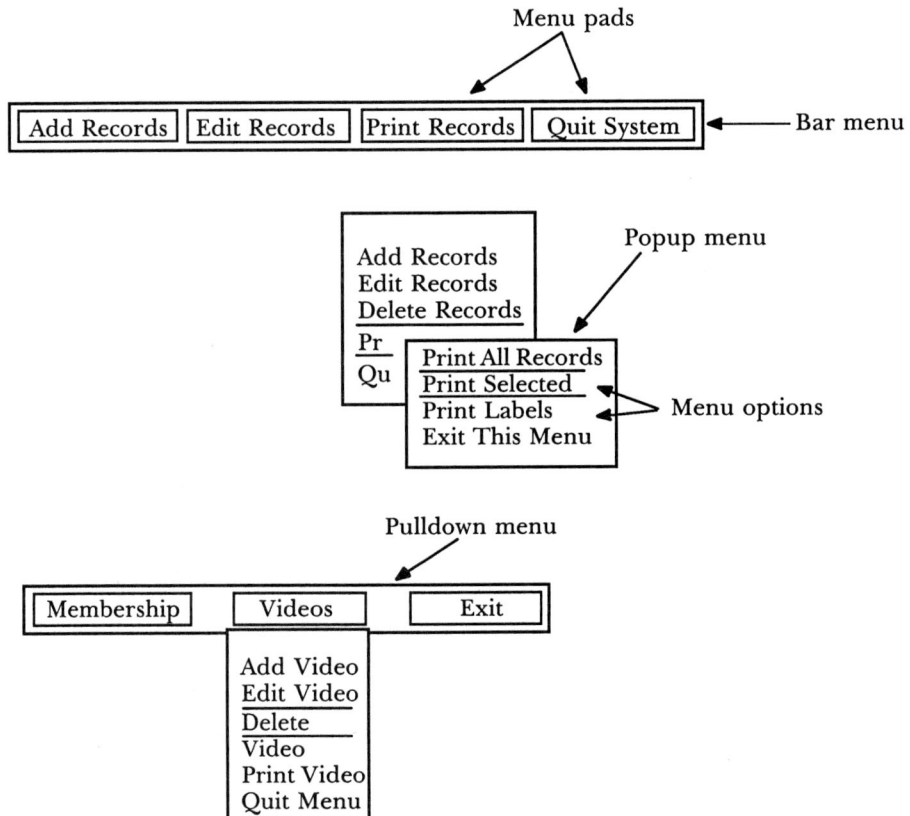

Figure 18-1.   *The components of a menu system*

Popup Menus

A popup menu is a menu that appears in a rectangular box with options arranged one below another. Some programmers refer to this type of menu as a *light-bar menu*. Popup menus that maintain program compatibility with Clipper can also be constructed using the @...PROMPT and MENU TO commands. If you prefer the dBASE IV method of programming, you'll use DEFINE POPUP, ACTIVATE POPUP, and ON SELECTION POPUP commands to implement popup menus. If you need program compatibility with FoxBASE+, you should use the @...MENU and READ MENU TO commands for building popup menus. In the center of Figure 18-1, two popup menus are shown, one overlaid on the other.

Pulldown Menus

A pulldown menu (called a *drop-down menu* by some programmers) is a combination of the bar menu and popup menu styles. With a pulldown menu, a particular selection from a bar menu causes a popup menu to appear with additional choices. Because the popup menu appears to "pull down" from the bar, the name "pulldown menu" applies. In Figure 18-1, the bottom menu is a pulldown menu. Since this type of menu is a combination of bar and popup, you'll use commands that are a combination of the commands used for bar and popup menus to implement the pulldown menu.

A Note About User Friendliness...

Regardless of the commands you use, FoxPro will allow the user to make menu selections with either the mouse or the cursor keys, or by pressing the first letter of a menu selection. Since many users like the first-letter approach, you may want to take care to give your options in each menu bar or popup names with different first letters, or to precede the menu options with numbers. For example, a menu with choices labeled "Edit customer," "Erase customer," and "Exit System" would not be friendly to a user who preferred the first-letter approach; pressing the E key would always bring up the first choice that starts with "E," which might not be what the user had in mind. If you labeled those same options as "Edit customer," "Delete customer," and "Quit System," the user could make successful use of the first-letter approach.

Also, if you plan to implement pulldown menus, and program compatibility does not matter, you may want to use the FoxBASE+ compatible syntax of @...MENU and READ MENU TO, or the dBASE IV syntax of DEFINE POPUP and ACTIVATE POPUP, for the popup menus. The reason is that these work better in cases where the user opens a pulldown menu, decides that he or she wants to be at another menu, and presses LEFT ARROW or RIGHT ARROW. With @...MENU and READ MENU TO or DEFINE and ACTIVATE POPUP, pressing LEFT ARROW or RIGHT ARROW causes an exit from the menu and a selection of the left or right option. With the Clipper-compatible commands like @...PROMPT and MENU TO, LEFT ARROW causes the same response as UP ARROW, and RIGHT ARROW causes the same response as DOWN ARROW.

Implementing Popup Menus in FoxPro

You have three choices when implementing popup menus in FoxPro. You can use the @...MENU and READ MENU TO commands, popularized by FoxBASE+; you can use @...PROMPT and MENU TO, originally implemented by Clipper; or you can use DEFINE POPUP and ON SELECTION POPUP, which are compatible with dBASE IV.

Popups Using @...PROMPT and MENU TO

For compatibility with Clipper and FoxBASE+, or when compatibility is not an issue, you can use @...PROMPT and MENU TO to implement your popup menus. You use a series of @...PROMPT commands to display the menu options, at the coordinates named. The MENU TO command invokes the popup menu, and the user response is controlled by the cursor keys, the first letter of the option, or the mouse. You can include an optional message with each menu option defined by the @...PROMPT command. When you do so, the message appears in the message area (usually the bottom of the screen, unless you have changed this with the SET MESSAGE command).

The following example program uses a series of @...PROMPT commands to place the choices of a popup menu on the screen. The MENU TO command is used to activate the menu and wait for a user response.

```
@ 4,4 TO 10,22
@ 5,5 PROMPT "1. Add records   "
@ 6,5 PROMPT "2. Edit records  "
@ 7,5 PROMPT "3. Delete records"
@ 8,5 PROMPT "4. Print records "
@ 9,5 PROMPT "5. Quit System   "
MENU TO MyChoice
DO CASE
     CASE MyChoice = 1
          DO ADDER
     CASE MyChoice = 2
          DO EDITOR
     CASE MyChoice = 3
          DO ERASER
```

```
        CASE MyChoice = 4
                DO REPORTER
        CASE MyChoice = 5
                QUIT
ENDCASE
```

The menu produced looks like this:

```
┌─────────────────┐
│1. Add records   │
│2. Edit records  │
│3. Delete records│
│4. Print records │
│5. Quit System   │
└─────────────────┘
```

A major difference in programming style between these commands and those that are compatible with dBASE IV is that with these commands, you must position the options with row and column coordinates supplied as a part of the PROMPT statement and include an @...TO command to draw the border around the menu (assuming you desire the usual menu border). With the dBASE IV style of menu syntax, you need not perform these tasks.

Popups Using DEFINE POPUP and ON SELECTION POPUP

With advantages there come disadvantages. The disadvantages of the dBASE IV style of syntax is that the menu commands are slightly more complex than @...PROMPT and MENU TO. The following program implements the same popup menu as in the previous example using the dBASE IV-compatible commands.

```
DEFINE POPUP MAINMENU FROM 4,4 TO 10,22
DEFINE BAR 1 OF MAINMENU PROMPT "1. Add records   "
DEFINE BAR 2 OF MAINMENU PROMPT "2. Edit records  "
DEFINE BAR 3 OF MAINMENU PROMPT "3. Delete records"
DEFINE BAR 4 OF MAINMENU PROMPT "4. Print records "
DEFINE BAR 5 OF MAINMENU PROMPT "5. Quit System   "
ON SELECTION POPUP MAINMENU DO THEMENU
ACTIVATE POPUP MAINMENU

*THEMENU.PRG*
*This is a subroutine called from the popup program.*
DO CASE
    CASE BAR() = 1
            DO ADDER
    CASE BAR() = 2
```

```
        DO EDITOR
    CASE BAR() = 3
        DO ERASER
    CASE BAR() = 4
        DO REPORTER
    CASE BAR() = 5
        QUIT
ENDCASE
```

In this example, the DEFINE POPUP command defines the location of the upper-left corner of the popup menu. Since no coordinates are specified for the lower-right corner, the menu will automatically be sized as large as necessary to fit all of the options. The DEFINE BAR commands are used to indicate the options that will appear in the menu. The ON SELECTION POPUP command displays the menu, and upon the user's selection, causes the subroutine, called THEMENU.PRG, to be called. In that subroutine, the BAR() function, which stores the number of the option chosen from the last popup menu, is used with a series of CASE statements to make the appropriate choice, depending on the user's response. As for visual appearance, the menu created by the above program is identical in appearance to the menu shown earlier with the @...PROMPT and MENU TO commands.

Popups Using @...MENU and READ MENU TO

The third method of implementing popup menus in FoxPro is to use the @...MENU and READ MENU TO commands. These are compatible with FoxBASE+, but not with other variants of the dBASE language. These commands offer the advantage of better operation with the LEFT ARROW and RIGHT ARROW keys when you use them as a part of a pulldown menu system.

You use the READ MENU command with the @ *row,col* MENU command to create the popup. First, use the DIMENSION command to create an array of memory variables, and store the menu choices to that array. Next, use the @ *row,col* MENU statement to position the popup on the screen. Then, use READ MENU to activate the menu and get the user's response. After the option has been chosen, the menu option is stored to the variable named by the READ MENU TO command. You can then use CASE statements to take action, depending on the value of that variable. Keep in mind that if a user exits the menu by pressing ESC, a value of zero is stored to the variable; you may or may not want to design your program to deal with this possibility.

The following program uses @...MENU and READ MENU TO to create the same menu that was illustrated in the prior two examples.

```
SET TALK OFF
STORE 0 TO MyChoice
DIMENSION Choices(5,1)
```

```
STORE "1. Add records   " TO Choices[1]
STORE "2. Edit records  " TO Choices[2]
STORE "3. Delete records" TO Choices[3]
STORE "4. Print records " TO Choices[4]
STORE "5. Quit System   " TO Choices[5]
@ 4,4 MENU Choices,5 TITLE "Data Menu"
READ MENU TO MyChoice
DO CASE
    CASE MyChoice = 1
        DO ADDER
    CASE MyChoice = 2
        DO EDITOR
    CASE MyChoice = 3
        DO ERASER
    CASE MyChoice = 4
        DO REPORTER
    CASE MyChoice = 5
        QUIT
ENDCASE
```

If the user were to press ESC in this program, the menu would simply be redisplayed, since a value of 0 is not handled by the CASE statements.

Implementing Bar Menus in FoxPro

You can implement bar menus in one of two ways in FoxPro. One of the ways is basically identical to the method described earlier with popup menus—the use of the Clipper-compatible @...PROMPT and MENU TO commands. Whether a series of @...PROMPT commands creates a popup menu or a bar menu is determined by the row and column coordinates you specify for the menu options.

Bar Menus Using DEFINE MENU, DEFINE PAD, and ACTIVATE MENU

The DEFINE MENU, DEFINE PAD, and ACTIVATE MENU commands let you implement bar menus using the dBASE IV programming syntax. You first define a menu by name in memory with the DEFINE MENU command, then you use the DEFINE PAD command to indicate what the names of the options, or pads, displayed on the bar menu will be.

In the following example, the DEFINE MENU command is used to define a bar menu called MainMenu. The optional message clause is added so that the message "Press letter of desired option" will appear in the message area when the menu is active. The DEFINE PAD commands are used to add four choices to the bar menu: Add records, Edit records, Print records, and Quit System. The ON SELECTION statements define which actions shall be taken when a particular menu option is chosen by the user. To keep the example simple, each ON SELECTION statement calls a particular command, such as APPEND or EDIT. In most applications, the ON SELECTION statements would be used to call another routine for adding or editing records or performing some other task. The ACTIVATE MENU statement that follows the ON SELECTION statement activates the menu, and the program then awaits the user's response.

```
USE MEMBERS INDEX NAMES
DEFINE MENU MainMenu MESSAGE "Press letter of desired option"
DEFINE PAD Addit OF MainMenu PROMPT "Add records"
DEFINE PAD Change OF MainMenu PROMPT "Edit records"
DEFINE PAD Print OF MainMenu PROMPT "Print records"
DEFINE PAD Quit OF MainMenu PROMPT "Quit System"
ON SELECTION PAD Addit OF MainMenu APPEND
ON SELECTION PAD Change OF MainMenu EDIT
ON SELECTION PAD Print OF MainMenu REPORT FORM MYFILE TO PRIN
ON SELECTION PAD Quit OF MainMenu QUIT
ACTIVATE MENU MainMenu
```

The example program produces a bar menu like that shown in the following illustration.

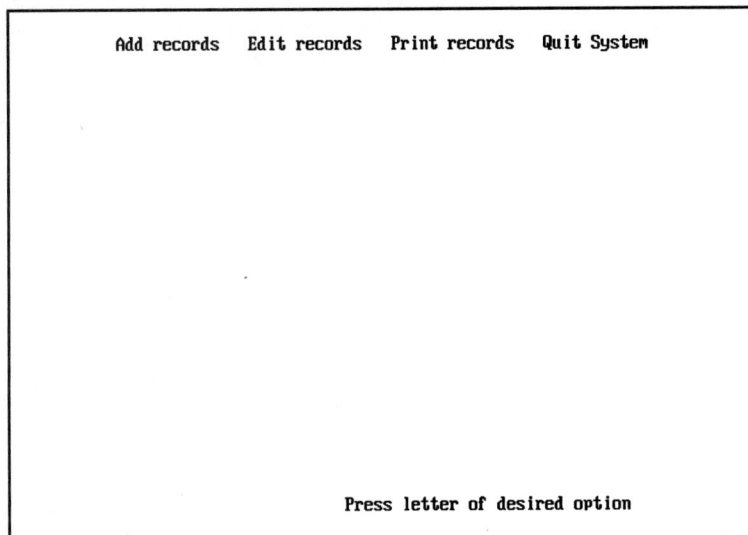

Bar Menus Using @...PROMPT and MENU TO

If you prefer the command syntax popularized by Clipper, use the @...PROMPT and MENU TO commands to implement your bar menus. These are used in the same manner as in implementing popup menus; you simply arrange the row and column coordinates so that the menu options appear along a horizontal bar instead of in a vertical popup. The following program uses @...PROMPT and MENU TO to produce a bar menu very similar in design to the one shown in the previous illustration.

```
SET TALK OFF
STORE 0 TO MyChoice
@ 0,1 TO 2,75
@ 1, 4 PROMPT "Add records    "
@ 1,23 PROMPT "Edit records   "
@ 1,40 PROMPT "Print records "
@ 1,58 PROMPT "Quit System    "
MENU TO MyChoice
DO CASE
     CASE MyChoice = 1
          APPEND
     CASE MyChoice = 2
          EDIT
     CASE MyChoice = 3
          REPORT FORM MYFILE TO PRINT
     CASE MyChoice = 4
          QUIT
ENDCASE
```

This time, because the @...PROMPT commands all place the menu options on line 1 of the screen, the menu appears as a horizontal, or bar, menu.

Implementing Pulldown Menus in FoxPro

To implement pulldown menus, simply combine the methods of your choosing for bar and popup menus into a pulldown menu system. The dBASE IV style of programming means more complicated coding when designing a pulldown menu. However, you need not be concerned with positioning all of the menu elements and drawing all of the needed borders. On the other hand, if you use a combination of @...PROMPT and MENU TO or READ MENU commands, the programming will be simpler in nature, but you will have to be careful to use the correct row and column coordinates to place all the menu elements in the right places and draw all the lines for the borders.

The first example program uses the dBASE IV syntax to display a pulldown menu. Note the combination of commands. The bar portion of the menu is defined and displayed with the DEFINE MENU, DEFINE PAD, and ON SELECTION PAD commands, as explained earlier. If the user chooses either of the first two pads from the bar menu, a popup appears, created with the DEFINE POPUP, DEFINE BAR, and ON SELECTION POPUP commands.

```
*Example of menuing functions*
CLEAR
*define horizontal bar menu to activate popups*
DEFINE MENU MAIN
DEFINE PAD MEMBER OF MAIN PROMPT "View Members" AT 1,10
DEFINE PAD VIDEO OF MAIN PROMPT "View Videos" AT 1,25
DEFINE PAD BYE OF MAIN PROMPT "Exit System" AT 1,40
ON PAD MEMBER OF MAIN ACTIVATE POPUP MVIEW
ON PAD VIDEO OF MAIN ACTIVATE POPUP VVIEW
ON SELECTION PAD BYE OF MAIN DEACTIVATE MENU MAIN
*popup to go with first menu prompt*
DEFINE POPUP MVIEW FROM 2,10
DEFINE BAR 1 OF MVIEW PROMPT "Short Browse"
DEFINE BAR 2 OF MVIEW PROMPT "Full Browse "
DEFINE BAR 3 OF MVIEW PROMPT "------------"
DEFINE BAR 4 OF MVIEW PROMPT "Edit Records"
*this line automatically deactivates popup temporarily*
ON SELECTION POPUP MVIEW DO PSEL WITH POPUP(), BAR()
*popup to go with second menu prompt*
DEFINE POPUP VVIEW FROM 2,25
DEFINE BAR 1 OF VVIEW PROMPT "Window Browse"
DEFINE BAR 2 OF VVIEW PROMPT "Full Browse  "
ON SELECTION POPUP VVIEW DO PSEL WITH POPUP(), BAR()
*activate main menu now.*
ACTIVATE MENU MAIN
*control returns here from 3rd prompt
RETURN

PROCEDURE PSEL
PARAMETERS POP, BAR
    CLEAR
    @ 10,10 SAY "popup is: " + POP
    @ 12,10 SAY "bar is: " + STR(BAR)
    * Your program code to perform various tasks,
    * depending on the values returned by the
    * POPUP() and BAR() functions would go here.
RETURN
```

The following illustration shows what the menu created by this program would look like on the screen if the user selected the second option of the bar menu.

```
View Members   View Videos   Exit System
┌─────────────┐
│Short Browse │
│Full Browse  │
│─────────────│
│Edit Records │
└─────────────┘
```

In the second example program, a menu very similar to that in the previous illustration is produced with a combination of @...PROMPT and MENU TO commands for the bar portion of the menu and @...MENU and READ MENU commands for the popups.

```
SET TALK OFF
STORE 0 TO MyChoice
@  0,1 TO 2,54
@  1,2 PROMPT "Members "
@ 1,22 PROMPT "Videos   "
@ 1,42 PROMPT "Quit System "
MENU TO MyChoice
DO CASE
    CASE MyChoice = 1
         DO MEMBERS
    CASE MyChoice = 2
         DO VIDEOS
    CASE MyChoice = 3
         QUIT
ENDCASE

PROCEDURE MEMBERS
STORE 0 TO MyChoice
DIMENSION Choices(5,1)
STORE "1. Add members    " TO Choices[1]
STORE "2. Edit members   " TO Choices[2]
STORE "3. Delete members" TO Choices[3]
STORE "4. Print members " TO Choices[4]
STORE "5. Quit System    " TO Choices[5]
@ 1,2 MENU Choices,5 TITLE "Member Menu"
READ MENU TO MyChoice
DO CASE
    CASE MyChoice = 1
         DO ADDMEMB
```

```
        CASE MyChoice = 2
            DO EDITMEMB
        CASE MyChoice = 3
            DO ERASEMEM
        CASE MyChoice = 4
            DO PRINMEMB
        CASE MyChoice = 5
            RETURN
ENDCASE
RETURN

PROCEDURE VIDEOS
STORE 0 TO MyChoice
DIMENSION Choices(5,1)
STORE "1. Add videos    " TO Choices[1]
STORE "2. Edit videos   " TO Choices[2]
STORE "3. Delete videos " TO Choices[3]
STORE "4. Print videos  " TO Choices[4]
STORE "5. Quit System   " TO Choices[5]
@ 1,19 MENU Choices,5 TITLE "Video Menu"
READ MENU TO MyChoice
DO CASE
        CASE MyChoice = 1
            DO ADDVID
        CASE MyChoice = 2
            DO EDITVID
        CASE MyChoice = 3
            DO ERASEVID
        CASE MyChoice = 4
            DO PRINTVID
        CASE MyChoice = 5
            RETURN
ENDCASE
RETURN
```

With all the menu commands supported by FoxPro, you could undoubtedly find other ways to implement a complete menu system. These examples are meant to provide building blocks for your applications. Any combination of commands that gets the job done in your case is appropriate.

Implementing Pick Lists

Before leaving the subject of popup menus and the DEFINE POPUP command entirely, you should know that you can use special options of the DEFINE

POPUP command to create *pick lists*. Pick lists add a "point-and-shoot" approach to your application's interface, by presenting lists of options based on database records, fields, or other types of files. The DEFINE POPUP command offers PROMPT FIELD, PROMPT FILE, and PROMPT STRUCTURE clauses that let you display a list of field names, filenames, or items from a database field. For example, perhaps you have a database of parts provided by eight possible suppliers. You want to allow data entry operators to pick a supplier name from a list of the eight authorized suppliers when they are entering new parts into the database. In this example, the database of parts is named PARTFILE, and it contains fields called Partno, Descript, Quantity, and Supplier. A second database, called SUPPLY, contains a field called Thename with names of the approved suppliers. The program below uses both databases to provide a pick list for entering the supplier's name during data entry of new parts.

```
*ADDER.PRG adds records to parts inventory.*
SELECT 1
USE PARTFILE
APPEND BLANK
CLEAR
@ 5,10 SAY "Part number:" GET Partno
@ 6,10 SAY "Description:" GET Descript
@ 7,10 SAY "  Quantity:" GET Quantity
READ
SELECT 2
USE SUPPLY
DEFINE POPUP SNAMES FROM 8,12 PROMPT FIELD Thename
ON SELECTION POPUP SNAMES DEACTIVATE POPUP
ACTIVATE POPUP SNAMES
GOTO BAR()
STORE THENAME TO M_SUPPLIER
SELECT 1
REPLACE SUPPLIER WITH M_SUPPLIER
@ 8,10 SAY "  Supplier:" GET Supplier
READ
RETURN
*End of ADDER.PRG.*
```

After the data entry operator enters the part number, description, and quantity, a pick list appears containing all the authorized suppliers (based on the entries in the Thename field of the SUPPLY.DBF database). The user picks a choice from the pick list, and that choice is automatically stored to the Supplier field of the PARTFILE database. Figure 18-2 shows what the screen looks like when this program is run.

```
           Part number: 1001
           Description: Keyboard
              Quantity: 3
           ┌─────────────────┐
           │Integrity Co.    │
           │NOVA Software    │
           │Chips N Disks    │
           │CompuWare        │
           │Island Graphics  │
           │Mean Screens     │
           │Electrical Hut   │
           │ABC Supply       │
           └─────────────────┘
```

Figure 18-2. *The results of a pick list*

FoxPro and Windows

One of FoxPro's claims to fame is its support of windows. (Here, "windows" refers to rectangular areas displayed on screen, and not to a trademarked software environment produced by Microsoft Corporation.) A *window*, once defined and activated, is a rectangular area where all screen output appears until that window is deactivated. In FoxPro, windows can be sized, moved, zoomed to full screen, and layered upon other windows. FoxPro users are already familiar with windows through the use of the Command window and the BROWSE and EDIT commands.

For your applications, FoxPro provides a number of commands that let you open windows and place them at desired screen locations; you can also assign your windows the colors of your choice. Common uses for windows in an application include using BROWSE and EDIT while under program control, displaying @...SAY...GETs, displaying help screens and messages, and performing text applications that make use of memo fields.

Three commonly used commands that control windows are DEFINE WINDOW, ACTIVATE WINDOW, and DEACTIVATE WINDOW. These commands are described as follows.

- DEFINE WINDOW *windowname* is used to define the screen coordinates (location) and the display attributes for a window.

- ACTIVATE WINDOW *windowname* [ALL] is used to activate a window that has been defined. Once a window is activated, all screen output appears in that window until another window is activated, or until the current window is deactivated. The ALL option, when used, activates all previously defined windows; current screen output appears in the window most recently defined.

- DEACTIVATE WINDOW *windowname* [ALL] is used to deactivate, or turn off, an active window. The ALL option, when used, deactivates all active windows.

To use windows in your application, first use the DEFINE WINDOW command to define as many windows as will be needed. One DEFINE WINDOW command is used for each window. Window names can be up to ten characters in length. Then, when you need to display data in a window, use the ACTIVATE WINDOW command to make the window active. When you have finished with the window, use the DEACTIVATE WINDOW command to close the window.

Defining the Window

The DEFINE WINDOW command provides a wide range of options. The syntax for this command is

DEFINE WINDOW *windowname* FROM *row1,col1* TO *row2,col2*
[TITLE *character expression*] [DOUBLE/PANEL/NONE]
[SHADOW/NOSHADOW] [COLOR *standard/enhanced*[,*border*]]
[COLOR SCHEME *n*]

The *row1,col1* numbers indicate the row and column coordinates for the upper-left corner of the window. The *row2,col2* values indicate the row and column coordinates of the lower-right corner of the window. The TITLE option, followed by a character expression, defines an optional title. If used, the expression appears as a title at the top of the window.

The DOUBLE, PANEL, or NONE option can be used to define a different border for the window. The default border, if no option is specified, is a single-line box. DOUBLE causes the window to have a double-line box. PANEL gives the window a panel border, like that used by FoxPro when editing and browsing. NONE specifies no border.

The SHADOW/NOSHADOW option determines whether a shadow will appear beneath the window. By default, FoxPro windows don't have shadows.

The FLOAT/NOFLOAT and ZOOM/NOZOOM options determine whether the window can be moved (in the case of FLOAT) or zoomed (in the case of ZOOM). If you omit the options, or specify the NOFLOAT or NOZOOM option, the window may not be moved or zoomed.

The GROW/NOGROW option specifies whether the user is permitted to resize the window. The GROW option allows resizing, and the NOGROW option (the default) prohibits resizing.

You can use the COLOR or COLOR SCHEME option to specify colors for the window. By default, windows take on the colors of Color Scheme 1, which is the scheme used for user windows in FoxPro. (A complete discussion of colors and color schemes can be found later in this chapter.)

As an example of a window definition, the command

```
DEFINE WINDOW Samples FROM 6,6 TO 18,70 PANEL SHADOW COLOR SCHEME 2
```

would define a window, with a panel border and a shadow underneath, with its upper-left corner at row 6, column 6 of the screen. The window's lower-right corner would be at row 18, column 70 of the screen. The window colors would be the same as those of color scheme 2, which is used by the FoxPro user menus. Since no FLOAT, GROW, or ZOOM options were used, the user would not be able to move, resize, or zoom the window.

Activating and Using the Window

After defining the window, use the ACTIVATE WINDOW *windowname* command to activate, or open, the window. When you activate a window, all screen output appears inside the window. When using @...SAY commands to place data inside a window, note that the coordinates are now *relative to the window*. In other words, row 0, column 0 is no longer the upper-left corner of the screen; it is now the upper-left corner of the *window*. You must be aware of this to avoid program errors in your applications. If, for example, you activate a window that is seven rows deep in size and you try to display data at row 14, your program will halt with a "Position is off the screen" error message, because the window you are using has no row 14.

After activating a window, you can use LIST or DISPLAY commands without being concerned with screen locations, and the data will appear completely contained within the window. If the data wraps around lines in an unattractive manner, you can either change the size of the window to fit more data or include fewer fields in the LIST or DISPLAY command. Figure 18-3 shows statements that define and activate a window and the results of a LIST command within that window.

If you are using BROWSE or EDIT within an application, you can use the WINDOW *windowname* clause, along with the BROWSE or EDIT command, to specify that the Browse mode or Edit mode will take effect within a predefined window. This is useful when, for one reason or another, you want a Browse or Edit window to assume a specific size or position. Figure 18-4 shows statements that define and activate a window; also shown are the results of a BROWSE command within that window.

```
System  File  Edit  Database  Record  Program  Window
```

```
    3   Jackson        Phillip        Rockville      MD
    4   Ballou         Joseph         Reston         VA
    5   Shelorson      Mildred        Leesburg       VA
    6   Murray         John           Leesburg       VA
    7   Tahan          Joseph         Fairfax        VA
    8   Lord           Scott          Reston         VA

              ACTIVATE WINDOW Samples
              LIST
              LIST LASTNAME, FIRSTNAME, CITY, STATE
```

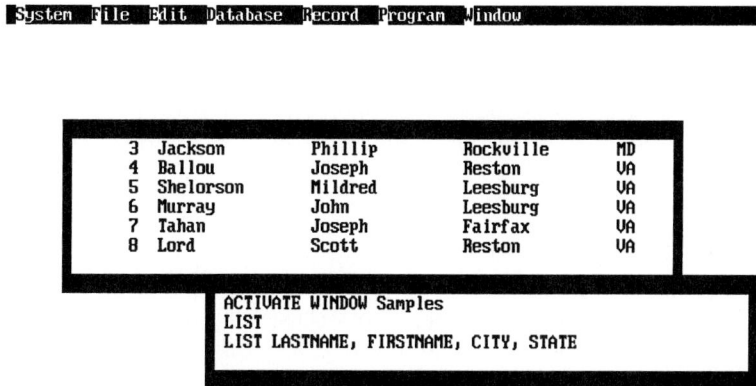

Figure 18-3.   *Window definition and the results of a LIST command*

Deactivating the Window

Once you have finished with the window, use the DEACTIVATE WINDOW *windowname* command to turn off the window. Screen output is then restored to the normal screen. If you have activated a number of windows, you can use the ALL clause in place of a window name with the command, and all active windows will be deactivated.

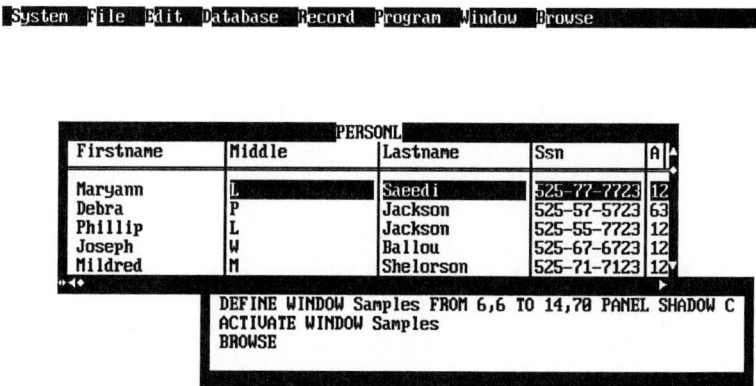

```
System  File  Edit  Database  Record  Program  Window  Browse
```

```
                         PERSONL
   Firstname     Middle       Lastname      Ssn          A

   Maryann       L            Saeedi        525-77-7723  12
   Debra         P            Jackson       525-57-5723  63
   Phillip       L            Jackson       525-55-7723  12
   Joseph        W            Ballou        525-67-6723  12
   Mildred       M            Shelorson     525-71-7123  12

              DEFINE WINDOW Samples FROM 6,6 TO 14,70 PANEL SHADOW C
              ACTIVATE WINDOW Samples
              BROWSE
```

Figure 18-4.   *Window definition and the results of a BROWSE command*

An Example of the Use of Windows

In the following program, a help screen is displayed within a window whenever the user presses the Help key (F1) during the process of editing a particular field. While this shows a simple way to provide help in your programs, note that a more flexible method of providing custom help is detailed at the end of this chapter.

```
ON KEY LABEL F1 DO HELP1
CLEAR
STORE 0 TO CNUMB
@ 3,10 SAY "Customer account number:" GET CNUMB
READ
ON KEY
RETURN


*HELP1.PRG*
DEFINE WINDOW HELPER FROM 5,5 TO 20,70 PANEL SHADOW
ACTIVATE WINDOW HELPER
@  3,2 SAY "Enter the four digit customer account number."
@  4,2 SAY "The most common account numbers are shown"
@  5,2 SAY "below. See the customer directory, for"
@  6,2 SAY "additional account numbers."
@  8,2 SAY "Press any key when done..."
@ 10,5 SAY "ABC Plumbing- 1001         Johnson Wallpaper- 1002"
@ 11,5 SAY "DJ's Improvements- 1003    Ace Auto- 1004"
@ 12,5 SAY "Klose Communications- 1005  Lee Accounting-1006"
WAIT " "
DEACTIVATE WINDOW HELPER
RETURN
```

Figure 18-5 shows the display that results when the program runs and the user presses the Help key (F1).

IN WINDOW

If you have FoxPro 1.02 or later, you can use the IN WINDOW *windowname* clause along with a number of commands, including ACTIVATE WINDOW, BROWSE, and EDIT, to open a window inside of an existing window. When this is done, the inside window is called the *child window*, and the outside window is called the *parent window*. If the parent window is moved, the child moves with it, and if the parent window is closed, the child closes with it. The child can be moved only within the boundaries of the parent, and a child cannot be larger than the parent (very unlike real life). As an example, the following short program displays a child window inside of a parent window, and moves the parent and child simultaneously to different locations on the screen.

```
CLEAR ALL
SET TALK OFF
DEFINE WINDOW bigger FROM 7,5 TO 16,60 PANEL COLOR SCHEME 3 ;
TITLE "the parent"
DEFINE WINDOW smaller FROM 1,1 TO 5,40 PANEL COLOR SCHEME 1 ;
TITLE "the child"
ACTIVATE WINDOW bigger
ACTIVATE WINDOW smaller IN WINDOW bigger
? "This shows a child in a parent."
MOVE WINDOW bigger BY 5,5
FOR MCOUNT = 1 TO 10000
    STORE MCOUNT + 1 TO MCOUNT
ENDFOR
MOVE WINDOW bigger BY 5,-5
? "parent and child on the move..."
FOR MCOUNT = 1 TO 8000
    STORE MCOUNT + 1 TO MCOUNT
ENDFOR
MOVE WINDOW bigger BY -10,10
? "family still on the move..."
FOR MCOUNT = 1 TO 8000
    STORE MCOUNT + 1 TO MCOUNT
ENDFOR
MOVE WINDOW bigger BY -5,5
WAIT " -Press any key."
DEACTIVATE WINDOWS ALL
CLEAR
RETURN
```

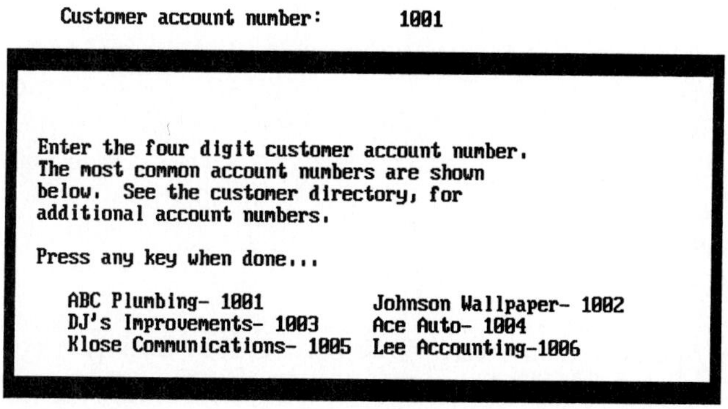

```
Customer account number:        1001

┌──────────────────────────────────────┐
│                                        │
│  Enter the four digit customer account number.
│  The most common account numbers are shown
│  below.  See the customer directory, for
│  additional account numbers.
│
│  Press any key when done...
│
│     ABC Plumbing- 1001      Johnson Wallpaper- 1002
│     DJ's Improvements- 1003 Ace Auto- 1004
│     Klose Communications- 1005 Lee Accounting-1006
│
└──────────────────────────────────────┘
```

Figure 18-5. A Help window created by the example program

Drawing Boxes

For those occasions when all you need is a rectangle containing some text (like a warning message to a user), it may be overkill to define and activate a window. You can draw a box with the @...TO command, which uses the syntax

@ *row1,col1* TO *row2,col2* [DOUBLE/PANEL] [COLOR *standard/enhanced*] [COLOR SCHEME *n*]

where the first set of row and column coordinates specifies the upper-left corner of the box, and the second set of row and column coordinates specifies the lower-right corner of the box.

The optional DOUBLE clause specifies a double-line border, and the PANEL option specifies a panel border.

You can use the COLOR or COLOR SCHEME option to specify colors for the box. (Color options will be detailed later in this chapter.)

Once you draw the box, you can use @...SAY...GET commands to place text or the contents of fields or variables within the box.

For example, the following statements produce the boxes shown in Figure 18-6.

```
@   3,1 TO 7,40
@   5,5 SAY "This is a single-line box."
@   9,20 TO 14,60 DOUBLE
@  11,30 SAY "This is a double-line box."
@  16,3 TO 20,50 PANEL SHADOW
@  18,5 SAY "This panel box has a shadow."
```

Using Colors in FoxPro

The dBASE language has for some time provided control of colors with the SET COLOR TO statement, familiar to many dBASE programmers. FoxPro, however, takes this flexibility to new heights with its use of color pairs, color schemes, and color sets (and commands that affect all three). Color pairs are familiar to most who have programmed in FoxBASE+ or dBASE III PLUS. However, color sets and color schemes are new to FoxPro. To avoid confusion, it may help to understand how FoxPro manages colors.

- A set of codes called a *color pair* can be used to define colors for the entire screen, or for a portion of a screen.

- A group of color pairs can be used to define colors for a FoxPro object, such as a Browse window; a group of color pairs defining colors for an object is called a *color scheme*.

- A collection of color schemes to define colors for all objects in FoxPro is called a *color set*.

Figure 18-7 illustrates the relationship between color pairs, color schemes, and color sets.

Color Pairs

Color pairs are pairs of codes used to specify foregrounds and backgrounds for standard and enhanced colors. The color codes consist of the letters that represent the colors, as indicated in Tables 18-1 and 18-2. You can use color pairs with the SET COLOR command to set colors for the entire screen, or as clauses along with numerous commands to set the colors for each specific screen area or object.

The codes are used with the SET COLOR command, or with the COLOR clause of numerous commands. The codes are arranged in pairs, separated by a slash—hence the name color pairs. With each color pair, the first letter indicates the foreground color, and the second letter indicates the background color. For example, the entire screen could be set to a white foreground on a blue

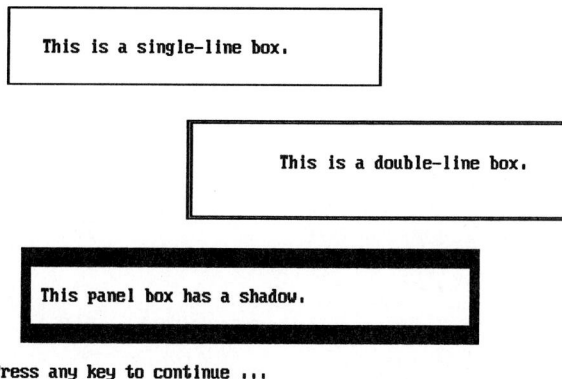

```
┌─────────────────────────────────┐
│ This is a single-line box.      │
│                                 │
└─────────────────────────────────┘
        ╔═════════════════════════════════╗
        ║                                 ║
        ║       This is a double-line box.║
        ║                                 ║
        ╚═════════════════════════════════╝
    ┌─────────────────────────────────┐
    │ This panel box has a shadow.    │
    └─────────────────────────────────┘

    Press any key to continue ...
```

Figure 18-6.   Various boxes drawn with the @...TO command

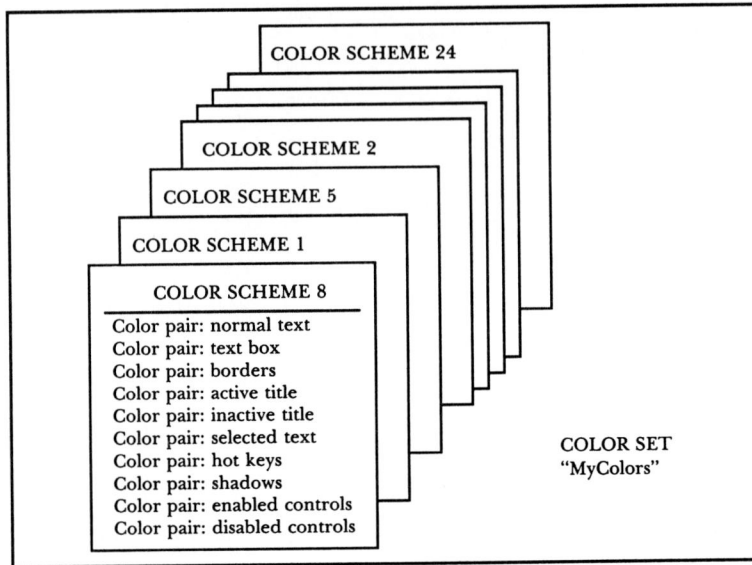

Figure 18-7.   *The relationship between colors in FoxPro*

Color	Code
Black	N
Blank	X
Blue	B
Brown	GR
Cyan	BG
Green	G
Grey	N+
Magenta	RB
Red	R
White	W
Yellow	GR+
Blinking	*
Enhanced (brightened)	+

Table 18-1.   *Color Codes for Color Monitors*

Color	Code
Black	N
Reverse video	I
Underlined	U
White	W

Table 18-2. *Color Codes for Monochrome Monitors*

background in standard mode, and a black foreground on a green background in enhanced mode, with the following statement:

```
SET COLOR TO W/B, N/G
```

You can use similar color pairs along with COLOR clauses for various commands to affect specific objects displayed on the screen. One common example is the @...SAY...GET command. The following statements would display a message asking for a name along with a data entry field. The message text would appear as red letters on a green background, and the data entry field would appear as green letters against a red background.

```
STORE SPACE(20) TO M_NAME
@ 5,5 SAY "Name?" GET M_NAME COLOR R/G, G/R
```

You can refer to a specific command you may have in mind to see if a COLOR clause can be used with that command to change the colors for a specific screen area or object. The commands that do allow the COLOR clause to be used include @...FILL, @...SAY...GET, @...TO, BROWSE, DEFINE WINDOW, CHANGE, and EDIT.

Color Schemes

A color scheme is a collection of up to ten color pairs that applies to a specific object or set of objects in FoxPro. For example, Color Scheme 10 refers to all the colors used by the Browse window, while Color Scheme 5 applies to dialog boxes. You can change any or all of the colors used throughout a color scheme with the SET COLOR OF SCHEME command. This command sets the colors of the desired scheme to the colors in the list you provide. The syntax for the command is

SET COLOR OF SCHEME *expN* TO [*color pairs list*]

where *expN* is a numeric expression from 1 to 11, or from 17 to 24. (Schemes 12 through 16 are reserved by FoxPro.) Schemes 17 through 24 can be user defined. Schemes 1 through 11 apply to the following FoxPro objects:

Scheme 1	User windows
Scheme 2	User menus
Scheme 3	Menu bar
Scheme 4	Popup menus
Scheme 5	Dialog boxes
Scheme 6	Dialog popups
Scheme 7	Alert boxes
Scheme 8	Windows
Scheme 9	Window popups
Scheme 10	Browse window
Scheme 11	Report layout window

Before using SET COLOR OF SCHEME, you should remember that this command is not compatible with FoxBASE+ or with other dBASE dialects.

The *color pairs list* consists of one to ten color pairs, with the foreground (standard) and background (enhanced) values separated by a slash and each color pair separated by commas. As an example, the following string of characters is a color pairs list for a color scheme:

W/B, B/W, GR+/B, GR+/RB, R+/B, N/GR, GR/B, BG/RB, W/N+, B/R

Each of the ten pairs of colors represents a different item within the designated color scheme. As an example of the SET COLOR OF SCHEME command, the following command would redefine all ten color pairs for Color Scheme 5 (dialog boxes):

```
SET COLOR OF SCHEME 5 TO ;
W/B, B/W, GR/B, GR/RB, R/B, N/GR, GR/B, BG/RB, W/N+, B/R
```

It is not necessary to specify all of the color pairs; you can specify only select pairs, and the others will remain unchanged. For example, to change only color pair 4 of a user-defined menu (Color Scheme 2) to blue and grey while leaving the remaining colors in Color Scheme 2 unchanged, you could use a command like the following:

```
SET COLOR OF SCHEME 2 TO , , , B/N+
```

Note that the preceding commas must be included for each color pair that remains unchanged. In this example, the first three color pairs are unchanged, as indicated by the commas.

While a maximum of ten color pairs can be changed for a color scheme, note that some color schemes do not make use of all ten color pairs. For example, Color Scheme 4 (popup menus) makes use of color pairs 1, 2, 3, 6, 7, and 8.

Color Sets

A *color set* is a named collection of all 24 color schemes used throughout FoxPro. You can use the SET COLOR SET TO command to put a color set different than the default color set into place. The syntax for this command is

SET COLOR SET TO [*color set name*]

The command loads a color set that was defined and saved previously.

The easiest way to create and save a color set is to use the Color Picker, available through the Color option of the Window menu. If you choose Color from the Window menu in FoxPro, the Color Picker appears, as in Figure 18-8.

You can tab to or click on the pulldown menu at the upper-right corner of the Color Picker and open the menu to reveal the names of all the color schemes. Choose each color scheme that you want to modify, one by one. Then tab to or click on the various options in the Color Picker, and choose the desired foreground and background colors from the list of colors at the bottom of the

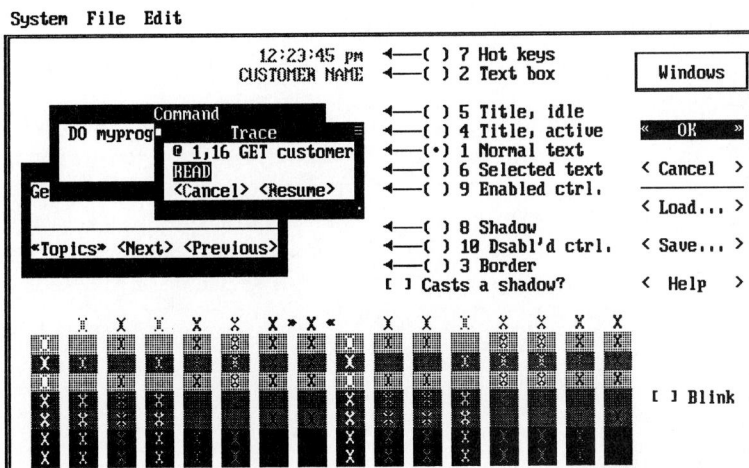

Figure 18-8.   The FoxPro Color Picker

screen. When you have the desired colors chosen, tab to or click on the Save option and provide a name for the new color set in the dialog box that appears. Once you have saved the color set, you can put it into effect at any time with the SET COLOR SET TO command.

With the variety of color controls that FoxPro offers, how you control colors within your application is up to you. You may prefer the easy way out, which is to leave the default FoxPro color set in place, or you can use the Color Picker to create and save a color set to control all objects displayed throughout your entire application, use the SET COLOR SET TO command to put that color set into place, and make no further changes to the colors. You may prefer instead to use SET COLOR TO statements and the COLOR clause along with @...SAY...GET commands throughout your application as the need arises. Regardless of your methods, FoxPro provides the tools needed for a colorful application.

Remember the Users...

If you are designing applications for use on different machines, remember that what you see on your monitor may be very different from what someone else sees. Applications developed with extensive use of colors can cause problems when those applications are moved to other computers with graphic cards and monochrome monitors. The hardware "looks" like a color system to FoxPro, but because the monitor displays everything in shades of amber or green, color settings like red on green or yellow on brown may make the screen difficult to read. This problem is especially apparent with most laptop computers. If you know that your application will be used on a system that does not have a color monitor, you may want to use clearly defined colors like white on black or white on blue. At the least, you should test the application on a machine that lacks a color monitor.

If you are designing an application and you do not know what hardware it will be running on, you can use the ISCOLOR() function to test for the presence of a color graphics card. You can then set colors as you wish, depending on the response. The ISCOLOR() function returns a value of true if a graphics adapter card is detected and a value of false if a monochrome adapter is detected. For example, the following portion of a program sets colors to white on blue if a graphics card is detected in the hardware.

```
*Myfile.PRG*
IF ISCOLOR()
    SET COLOR TO W/B
ENDIF
...more commands...
```

If you want to provide the users with the flexibility to make their own decisions regarding colors, you can provide menu options that let them choose from among various colors. The following example program provides a menu of color choices.

```
* Program..: COLORS.PRG
* Date.....: 11/8/90
IF .NOT. ISCOLOR()
    ? "  Can't do this on a monochrome monitor!"
    WAIT "  Press any key."
RETURN
ENDIF
CLEAR
@ 2,15 TO 17,61 DOUBLE
*display different possible color pairs.*
SET COLOR TO
@ 3,16 SAY [  1. This is an example of black on white    ]
SET COLOR TO N/W, W/N
@ 4,16 SAY [  2. This is an example of white on black    ]
SET COLOR TO W/B, B/W
@ 5,16 SAY [  3. This is an example of white on blue    ]
SET COLOR TO B/W, W/B
@ 6,16 SAY [  4. This is an example of blue on white    ]
SET COLOR TO R/W, W/R
@ 7,16 SAY [  5. This is an example of red on white    ]
SET COLOR TO R/N, N/R
@ 8,16 SAY [  6. This is an example of red on black    ]
SET COLOR TO G/W, W/G
@ 9,16 SAY [  7. This is an example of green on white    ]
SET COLOR TO W/G, G/W
@ 10,16 SAY [  8. This is an example of white on green    ]
SET COLOR TO GR+/W, W/GR+
@ 11,16 SAY [  9. This is an example of yellow on white    ]
SET COLOR TO W/R, R/W
@ 12,16 SAY [  10. This is an example of white on red    ]
SET COLOR TO BR/B, B/BR
@ 13,16 SAY [  11. This is an example of magenta on blue  ]
SET COLOR TO B/BR, BR/B
@ 14,16 SAY [  12. This is an example of blue on magenta  ]
SET COLOR TO N/BG, BG/N
@ 15,16 SAY [  13. This is an example of black on cyan    ]
SET COLOR TO BG/N, N/BG
@ 16,16 SAY [  14. This is an example of cyan on black    ]
SET COLOR TO
@ 19,12 SAY [Use arrow keys, Return to select your choice.]
```

```
* use PROMPT commands to point to color options shown.*
@  3,63 PROMPT [<===]
@  4,63 PROMPT [<===]
@  5,63 PROMPT [<===]
@  6,63 PROMPT [<===]
@  7,63 PROMPT [<===]
@  8,63 PROMPT [<===]
@  9,63 PROMPT [<===]
@ 10,63 PROMPT [<===]
@ 11,63 PROMPT [<===]
@ 12,63 PROMPT [<===]
@ 13,63 PROMPT [<===]
@ 14,63 PROMPT [<===]
@ 15,63 PROMPT [<===]
@ 16,63 PROMPT [<===]
MENU TO SelectNum
DO CASE
    CASE SelectNum = 1
        SET COLOR TO
    CASE SelectNum = 2
        SET COLOR TO N/W, W/N
    CASE SelectNum = 3
        SET COLOR TO W/B, B/W
    CASE SelectNum = 4
        SET COLOR TO B/W, W/B
    CASE SelectNum = 5
        SET COLOR TO R/W, W/R
    CASE SelectNum = 6
        SET COLOR TO R/N, N/R
    CASE SelectNum = 7
        SET COLOR TO G/W, W/G
    CASE SelectNum - 8
        SET COLOR TO W/G, G/W
    CASE SelectNum = 9
        SET COLOR TO GR+/W, W/GR+
    CASE SelectNum = 10
        SET COLOR TO W/R, R/W
    CASE SelectNum = 11
        SET COLOR TO BR/B, B/BR
    CASE SelectNum = 12
        SET COLOR TO B/BR, BR/B
    CASE SelectNum = 13
        SET COLOR TO N/BG, BG/N
    CASE SelectNum = 14
        SET COLOR TO BG/N, N/BG
```

```
ENDCASE
RETURN
* End of COLORS.PRG
```

Figure 18-9 shows the menu that results when the program runs. When the user with a color monitor selects a color by moving the cursor to that color and pressing ENTER, the screen is set to that color setting.

If you want to get really fancy, you can store the chosen color pair to a memory variable, and read that variable into memory whenever the application is started. Then you can use the SET COLOR command to set the colors to those values.

Implementing Custom Help

A powerful advantage to the way that FoxPro maintains its Help system is that you can use the system to implement customized Help in a FoxPro application. FoxPro's extensive Help system provides an indexed set of screens that normally appears whenever F1 is pressed. These Help screens are actually memo fields in a database file called FOXHELP.DBF. However, this complex set of Help screens does little good when an application is running, as the standard FoxPro Help screens will not tell your users about your application. What is significant about FoxPro is that, with the SET HELP TO command, you can change the Help database normally used by FoxPro to a database of your choosing. By storing text of your own in memo fields of the database, you can have that text appear when a user presses F1 in your application.

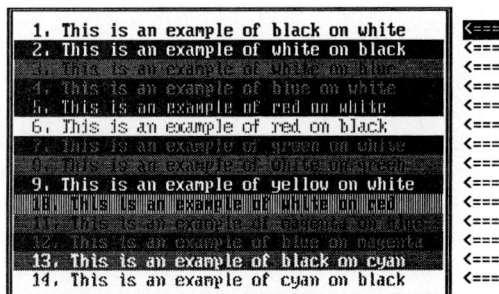

Figure 18-9.   *The Custom Colors menu*

The Help database you create can have any name other than FOXHELP .DBF, but you must keep two points in mind when creating the database.

1. The first field of the database must be a character field. This field will contain your Help topics, and you can call the field by any field name you like.

2. The second field must be a memo field. This field will contain the text that appears on your Help screens when the application is running.

You can have other fields in the Help database as well. Users won't see the contents of any fields other than the second (memo) field, but you may want to use additional fields to select records containing more detailed Help or to provide notes to yourself. Only the two fields described above are mandatory in a Help database.

To provide the Help in your application, use the SET HELP TO *Helpfilename* command early in the application, so that FoxPro knows to use your Help file instead of the default Help file, FOXHELP.DBF. Also, include an ON KEY statement to tell FoxPro to call up the Help system when F1 is pressed, since Help is not normally available when a program is running. You can handle both these tasks with statements like the following:

```
SET HELP TO MYHELP.DBF
ON KEY = 315 HELP
```

The ON KEY statement tells FoxPro to call up the Help system when the key with a code of 315 (the F1 key) is pressed.

These statements alone will result in the Help system appearing, using your chosen database. However, to get true context-sensitive Help, you will also need to use the SET TOPIC TO *Helptopicname* statement at various points in your program. This statement tells FoxPro which Help screen in your system to display at a given time. For example, if your Help database contains a record where the word "editor" is in the first field, and your program executes a SET TOPIC TO EDITOR statement, the text of the memo field for that record will appear when F1 is pressed.

For example, the following simple application implements customized Help using the FoxPro Help system, along with the SET HELP TO, SET TOPIC TO, and ON KEY statements. First, note the custom Help database, called HELPER .DBF. This file has two fields, a character field named Topics and a memo field named Helptext. The contents of these fields are shown. In this simple example, there will be only four Help screens for the application, so the Help database contains the following four records:

Topics	Helptext
ADDER	Enter the name, social security number, salary, and date of hire in the fields shown. When you are done, press CTRL-W to save the new employee.
EDITOR	Enter the social security number of the employee to edit at the prompt. When the form is visible, use PGUP or PGDN keys to view other employees. When done, press CTRL-W to save changes and return to the menu.
ERASER	Enter the social security number of the employee to delete at the prompt. You must confirm the deletion (when asked) before the record will be deleted.
REPORTER	Make sure your printer is turned on, then when prompted, press a key to print the report.

The application itself, shown here, uses the ON KEY statement to allow the use of F1 for Help and the SET HELP TO statement to specify the custom Help database as the default Help file. Notice that in each of the CASE choices, a different SET TOPIC TO statement is used, to tell FoxPro that a different record in the Help file should be accessed if F1 is pressed at that point.

```
*MYAPP.PRG is simple application with custom Help.*
SET HELP TO HELPER
SET TALK OFF
ON KEY = 315 HELP
DO WHILE .T.
CLEAR
USE STAFF INDEX SOCIAL
STORE 0 TO MyChoice
DIMENSION Choices(5,1)
STORE "1. Add records    " TO Choices[1]
STORE "2. Edit records   " TO Choices[2]
STORE "3. Delete records" TO Choices[3]
STORE "4. Print records " TO Choices[4]
STORE "5. Quit System    " TO Choices[5]
@ 4,4 MENU Choices,5 TITLE "Staff System"
READ MENU TO MyChoice
DO CASE
```

```
        CASE MyChoice = 1
            SET FORMAT TO STAFF
            SET TOPIC TO ADDER
            APPEND
        CASE MyChoice = 2
            SET NEAR ON
            SET TOPIC TO EDITOR
            CLEAR
            FINDIT = "999-99-9999"
            @ 5,5 SAY "Soc. sec. no to edit?" GET FINDIT
            READ
            SEEK FINDIT
            SET FORMAT TO STAFF
            EDIT
            SET NEAR OFF
        CASE MyChoice = 3
            CLEAR
            SET TOPIC TO ERASER
            FINDIT = "999-99-9999"
            THEANS = "N"
            @ 5,5 SAY "Soc. sec. no to delete?" GET FINDIT
            READ
            SEEK FINDIT
            IF FOUND()
                @ 6,5 SAY Lastname
                @ 6,30 SAY Firstname
                @ 8,5 SAY "DELETE this record? Y/N:" GET TheAns
                IF UPPER(TheAns) = "Y"
                    DELETE
                ENDIF
            ELSE
                @ 6,5 SAY "Can't find any such record!"
                WAIT WINDOW
            ENDIF
            CLEAR
        CASE MyChoice = 4
            SET TOPIC TO REPORTER
            WAIT WINDOW "Press a key to print report..."
            REPORT FORM STAFF TO PRINT
        CASE MyChoice = 5
            QUIT
    ENDCASE
ENDDO
```

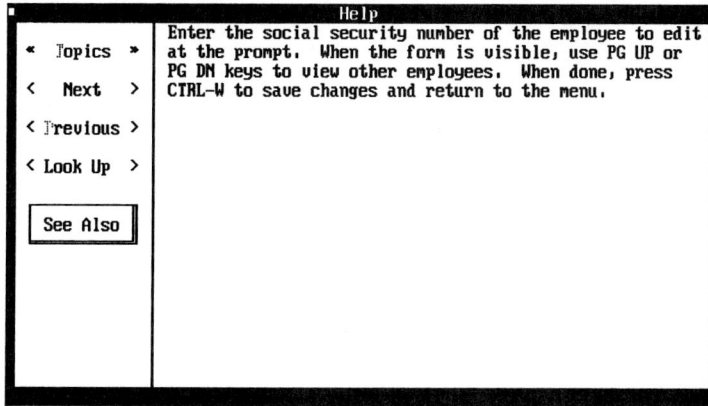

Figure 18-10. A custom Help screen

Figure 18-10 shows the Help screen that appears within the application if a record is being edited when F1 is pressed. As your application grows more complex, you can add SET TOPIC TO statements throughout and add corresponding records to the custom Help database. When such a scheme is implemented with care, you can significantly reduce the training and support time needed by novice users of your applications.

Chapter **19**

Advanced Topics

This chapter covers an assortment of programming commands and techniques that you will find useful when developing applications with FoxPro.

Debugging Applications

A truth of life as a programmer is that you will encounter bugs in programs that you write. Any program simple enough to be written perfectly the first time is rarely worth writing at all. With care in the design process, you can minimize the number of errors in a complex application, but there will undoubtedly be need for corrections and refinements. Fortunately, FoxPro offers a number of aids to streamline the debugging process. Some of these aids are in the form of commands that have long been a part of the dBASE programming language, such as the SET ECHO, SUSPEND, and RESUME commands. Other aids, such as the Trace and Debug windows, are significant additions that are available only in FoxPro.

When an error is detected in a FoxPro program, the program halts, and a dialog box is displayed with a message regarding the type of error. The dialog box also contains a menu with three options: Cancel, Suspend, and Ignore. Figure 19-1 shows the screen display in a program where an error has caused the program to halt.

Choosing Suspend suspends the program but leaves it active in memory, so that you can use commands within the Command window to test the values of variables or fields or to perform other desired tasks. Entering **RESUME** in the Command window starts the program running again.

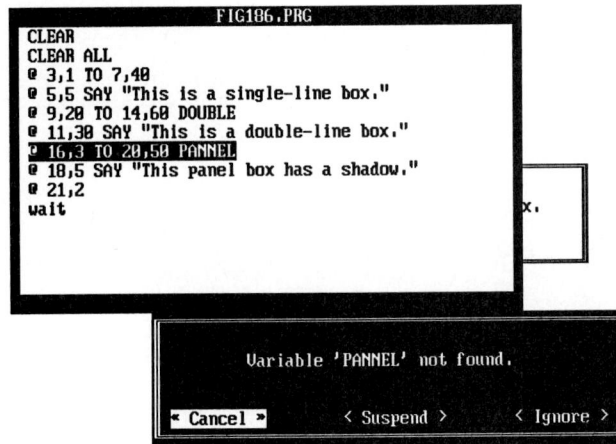

Figure 19-1.   A display in a halted program

The Ignore option tells FoxPro to ignore the error and continue. Depending on the cause of the error and your program's design, this can produce bizarre results.

The Cancel option stops the program and returns control to the Command window.

You may have already noticed a prime source of assistance provided by FoxPro for debugging programs—the close interaction of the FoxPro Editor when an error occurs. When a program error occurs in many other dBASE-compatible products, an error message appears, and you are simply given a choice of ignoring the error, temporarily suspending execution of the program, or canceling execution of the program. FoxPro offers more than this; it provides the same choices to cancel execution, suspend execution, or ignore the error, but it also displays the program that was running within the Editor, with the cursor highlighting the point where the error was detected. If you choose Cancel from the dialog box that appears, FoxPro places the cursor in the Editor at the highlighted line. This line often (but not always) contains the cause of the error. You can proceed to make the desired changes to the program, save it with CTRL-W, and run the program again.

SET ECHO and the Trace Window

You can use the SET ECHO command to follow the execution of a program. FoxPro provides a Trace window that lets you trace program execution. You can activate the Trace window by using the SET ECHO ON or SET STEP ON command, by selecting Echo or Step from the Program menu, or by choosing Trace from the Window menu. The Trace window lets you follow the program by showing the highlighted line in the window as it is executing. As the program runs, the source code of your program appears in the Trace window, with the line currently being executed shown by the highlight. Figure 19-2 shows the Trace window during the execution of a program.

NOTE: You can slow down the speed of execution while the Trace window is active to no more than four statements per second by pressing either SHIFT or CTRL or by pressing one mouse button. (You must hold the key or mouse button depressed to maintain the slower speed.) Pressing any two of these (CTRL and SHIFT, CTRL and a mouse button, SHIFT and a mouse button, or both mouse buttons) will cause the speed of execution to slow to no more than two statements per second while both buttons are down.

To stop the trace, press ESC to halt the program and choose Suspend or Cancel from the dialog box that appears. Then enter **SET ECHO OFF**, click on the Close box in the Trace window, or press CTRL-F1 to make the Trace window the active window and choose Close from the File menu.

SET STEP

You can also slow the execution of a program with the SET STEP command. This command causes FoxPro to execute each line of a program and wait for your OK before proceeding to execute the next line. You can enter **SET STEP ON** in the Command window or within your program, and the Trace window appears, but this time there are two options, Cancel and Resume, at the bottom of the window. When you start the program with the DO command, the first line

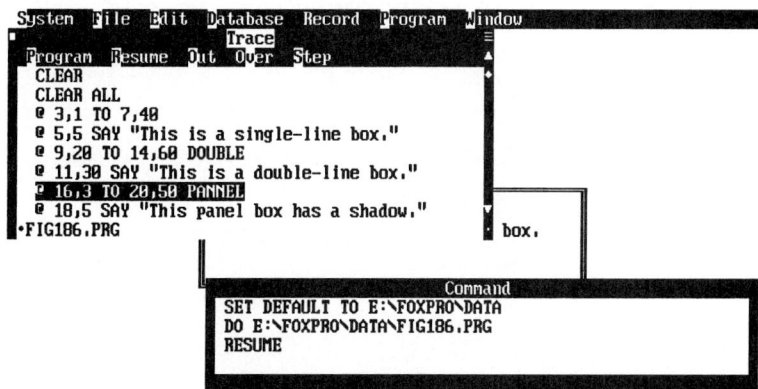

Figure 19-2. A Trace window

of the program is executed, and FoxPro pauses until you choose Resume by clicking on the Resume button or by pressing R. Each time you choose the Resume option, the next statement is executed. If you choose the Cancel option, program execution is canceled.

Using the Debug Window

For debugging purposes, it is often helpful to monitor the contents of memory variables, the location of the record pointer, or other statistics during program execution. FoxPro's Debug window can be used for these tasks. To display the Debug window, choose Debug from the Window menu. The Debug window will appear, with the cursor flashing at the left side of the window. You can enter desired expressions in the left pane of the window, as in Figure 19-3, and then use CTRL-F1 or the mouse to get back to the Command window to start your program running. As the program executes, the values of the expressions that you entered in the Debug window appear in the right pane of the window, as shown in Figure 19-3.

Setting Breakpoints in the Trace or Debug Windows

You can set breakpoints in either the Trace window or the Debug window. For those who may not have used debuggers with other programming languages, *breakpoints* are places in a program where you tell the program to halt (usually so you can examine variables or modify the values of variables before continuing program execution).

To set a breakpoint in the Trace window, you must suspend a program that is running. (You can do this by pressing ESC while the program is running, and then choosing Suspend from the dialog box.) Once a program is suspended, it will appear in the Trace window. Scroll the program within the window (with the mouse or the cursor keys) until you reach the line where you want to place the

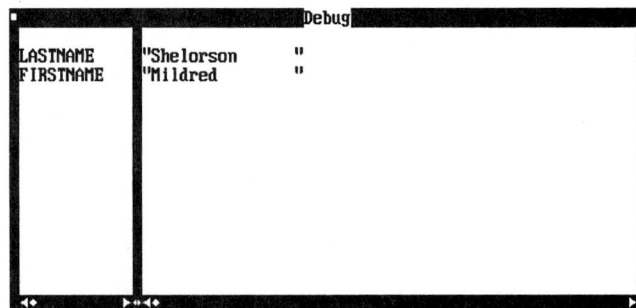

Figure 19-3.   *A Debug window with sample expressions entered*

breakpoint. Then click the mouse or press the SPACEBAR. A bullet will appear at the start of the line, marking the breakpoint. (You can press the mouse button or the SPACEBAR again to remove the bullet.) Each bullet marks a breakpoint. You can switch back to the Command window and enter **RESUME** or choose Resume from the Program menu to start the program going again. Whenever the program reaches a breakpoint, it will be suspended.

To set a breakpoint in the Debug window, press the SPACEBAR or click the mouse on the desired column separating the left and right panes of the Debug window. A bullet will appear in the column for that expression, indicating the presence of a breakpoint. Breakpoints set in the Debug window will suspend a program whenever the value of that expression changes.

When using the Trace and Debug windows, keep in mind that your application may open its own windows, which might make the Trace or Debug window difficult to see at times. When this is the case, you can use the mouse or the Move and Size options of the Window menu to change the location and size of the Debug window, the Trace window, or your application's windows (assuming that you allow window resizing in your application). If you have an EGA or VGA monitor, you may also find it helpful to switch to an extended display mode during debugging so that you have more screen space to work with. The SET DISPLAY TO EGA43 or SET DISPLAY TO VGA50 statement can be used for this purpose.

Handling Errors Within the Application

Even after you have spent time thoroughly testing and debugging a complex application, errors may still occur when the application is put into general use. This can prove confusing to end users, who may have no idea what to do when the program suddenly halts and the dialog box with the Cancel, Ignore, and Suspend options appears on the screen. Worse yet, a novice user might select the Cancel option, unknowingly get into the program through the Editor, and make destructive changes. To prevent this from happening, and to provide users with a friendly interface if an error should halt a program, you should always have an *error-trapping routine* if your application is to be used by others.

An error-trapping routine makes use of the ON ERROR command, placed at or near the start of the application. The ON ERROR command tells FoxPro what should be done in case an error occurs. The syntax for this command is

ON ERROR *command*

and if an error is detected in a FoxPro program, the specified command is carried out. Usually, the specified command is DO *programname*, where *program-name* is the name of your error-trapping routine. The error-trapping routine can be a short and simple program that informs the user that an error has occurred, and gracefully returns to the main menu or the DOS prompt. On the other hand, the routine can contain a series of CASE statements to analyze the error and try to take corrective action within the program. (This may save you a frantic phone call from a user someday.) As an example of a simple use of ON ERROR, consider the following programs:

```
*MENU.PRG displays main menu.*
SET TALK OFF
ON ERROR DO PROBLEMS
DO WHILE .T.
CLEAR
USE STAFF INDEX SOCIAL
...more commands to display menu and act on choices...


*PROBLEMS.PRG handles program errors.*
CLEAR
? "A program error has occurred. Record the message,"
? "and call the computer support department."
? MESSAGE()
?
WAIT WINDOW
QUIT
```

In this simple case of error handling, MENU.PRG, the second statement in the main program is an ON ERROR statement. It tells FoxPro that if a program error occurs, the subroutine named PROBLEMS.PRG should be called. The second program shown is the subroutine; it displays a message reporting the error to the user, uses the MESSAGE() function to display the error message for the type of error that occurred, and after the user presses a key, exits to DOS.

A more complex error-trapping routine appears below. The advantage of this kind of complexity is that the routine may be able to correct the cause of the error within the program, when the error is caused by something such as corrupted index files or a printer not being turned on. Even when the routine cannot correct for the error, it will give the user a more precise idea of what happened if the messages included in the CASE statements are fairly descriptive.

```
*MENU.PRG displays main menu.*
SET TALK OFF
ON ERROR DO PANIC
DO WHILE .T.
CLEAR
USE STAFF INDEX SOCIAL
...more commands to display menu and act on choices...
```

```
***PANIC.PRG is error trapping.
**Last update 8/14/91
CLEAR
DO CASE
  CASE ERROR() = 1
    ? "Cannot find a file. Record this message,"
    ? "and contact program developer for assistance."
    CLEAR ALL
    WAIT
    QUIT
  CASE ERROR() = 3
    USE
    RETRY
  CASE ERROR() = 20 .OR. ERROR() = 26 .OR. ERROR() = 114
    ? "The index file seems to be missing a record."
    ? "please wait while I repair the index."
    SET TALK ON
    REINDEX
    SET TALK OFF
    CLEAR
    RETRY
  CASE ERROR() = 9 .OR. ERROR() = 134 .OR. ERROR() = 143
    ? CHR(7)
    ? "The expression you entered does NOT match the"
    ? "database you are using, OR it contains an"
    ? "invalid term. Make sure you are using the"
    ? "right expression."
    WAIT
    CLEAR ALL
    RETURN TO MASTER
  CASE ERROR() = 56
    ? "Disk full!  Exit this system and erase"
    ? "unneeded files from the disk."
    WAIT
    CLEAR ALL
    RETURN TO MASTER
  CASE ERROR() = 125
    ? "Printer not ready. Reset printer, then"
    WAIT
    RETRY
  CASE ERROR() = 6
    ? "Failure to read configuration file."
    ? "System was not started from the hard disk."
    ? "Press a key to exit, and restart computer."
    WAIT
```

```
      QUIT
    OTHERWISE
      SET ESCAPE ON
      ? "A program error has occurred. Record the
      ? "message, and inform your program developer."
      ?
      ? MESSAGE()
      ?
      ?
      ? "After noting above message, press any key."
      WAIT
      SET CONSOLE OFF
      SET ALTERNATE TO ERRORS.TXT
      SET ALTERNATE ON
      LIST MEMORY
      LIST STATUS
      ? "Error message reported was: "
      ?? MESSAGE()
      CLEAR ALL
      QUIT
ENDCASE
*End of PANIC.PRG.
```

Also note that if the program cannot handle the error, statements called by the OTHERWISE statement use SET ALTERNATE to open a text file, and various data, such as the contents of memory, system status, and the type of error message reported are stored to the file. This will provide you with some details on what happened when you get back to the machine. Hopefully, this information will aid in pinpointing the source of the error.

Keep in mind that most low-level operating system errors, such as lack of a disk in the drive, errors reading data files, foul-ups in printer handshaking, and so forth, cannot be handled within FoxPro. You will have to go to the operating system to correct these.

Using Low-Level File Functions

FoxPro offers low-level file functions that can be used for manipulating any type of file. While these can be dangerous in the hands of the untrained, you should consider using them if you are writing serious applications. The low-level file functions are designed to work with files that are not created by FoxPro, such as text files created by word processors or files downloaded from mainframe computers. You can use the low-level file functions to read from or write to any file, regardless of its format. C Programmers will notice strong similarities between the FoxPro file functions and those found in most C compilers. The low-level file functions offered by FoxPro are summarized in Table 19-1. For a complete explanation of the syntax of each of these functions, refer to Chapter 23.

As an example of the use of low-level file functions, consider the problem of reading documents prepared with WordStar, a word processor, into memo fields of a FoxPro database. While most word processors have the ability to save files as plain ASCII text, early versions of WordStar lacked this ability. WordStar files commonly use ASCII values above 127 for the last character of each word, and to indicate the ends of lines. As a result, if you were to create a document with WordStar 3.3 or earlier and then use the APPEND MEMO FROM *filename* command to read the document into a memo field, the contents of the memo field would contain the text in WordStar's native format, as illustrated by the memo window in Figure 19-4.

If each character in a WordStar file having an ASCII value of more than 127 is replaced with a character having an ASCII value of 128 less than the original

---

Function	Purpose
FCHSIZE()	Changes the size of a file and returns the final size in bytes.
FCLOSE()	Closes a file and returns a logical true. If the file cannot be closed due to a hardware error, returns a logical false.
FCREATE()	Creates a new file, returns a numeric value as a handle for the file, and opens the file for use.
FEOF()	Returns a logical true if the pointer is at the end of the file, and a logical false if the pointer is not at the end of the file.
FERROR()	Tests whether a low-level file function was successful. Returns a zero if the last file function was successful, and a value other than zero if the function was not successful.
FFLUSH()	Writes all data currently in the buffers to disk.
FGETS()	Returns a series of bytes from the file until a carriage return is encountered.
FOPEN()	Opens a file and returns a numeric file handle assigned by DOS.
FPUTS()	Writes a character string to a file and returns the number of bytes written to the file. FPUTS() differs from FRWITE() in that FPUTS() adds a carriage return and linefeed to the character string.
FREAD()	Reads a character string from a file and returns the character string.
FSEEK()	Moves the pointer to a specified position in the file and returns a numeric value indicating the position of the pointer in the file.
FWRITE()	Writes a character string to a file and returns the number of bytes written to the file.

Table 19-1. FoxPro Low-Level File Functions

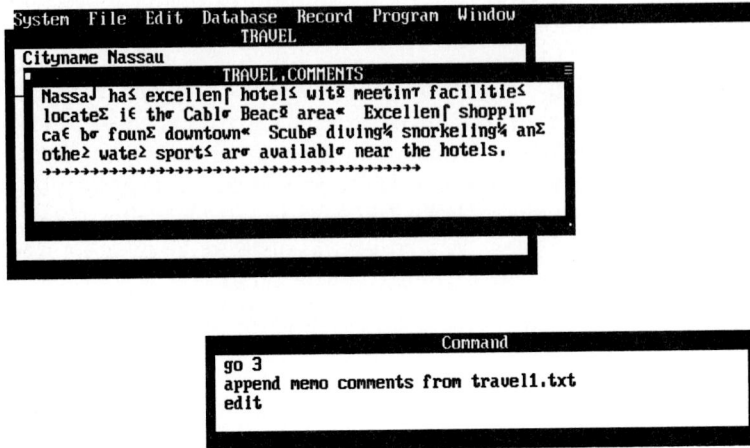

Figure 19-4. A memo field containing a WordStar document

character, the result is a normal ASCII text file. This type of conversion of a WordStar file from WordStar format to normal ASCII text can be done with the FoxPro low-level file functions. The following program opens a database file containing a memo field, prompts the user for the name of the WordStar file, and uses the low-level file functions to convert the WordStar file to ASCII text. The ASCII text file is then read into the memo field of a database record with the APPEND MEMO FROM *filename* command.

```
*WS2FP converts WordStar to ASCII.*
CLEAR
SET TALK OFF
USE BOOKS
?
INPUT " Record number to add WordStar text to memo? " TO THISREC
GOTO THISREC
ACCEPT " WordStar file to convert to text? " TO WSFILE
ACCEPT " Name for converted file? " TO OUTFILE
OLDFILE = FOPEN(WSFILE)
NEWFILE = FCREATE(OUTFILE)
IF OLDFILE < 0
    ? " Can't find WordStar file."
    ? " Check spelling, try again."
    WAIT WINDOW
    RETURN
ENDIF
DO WHILE .NOT. FEOF(OLDFILE)
```

```
        REC = FREAD(OLDFILE,1)
        IF ASC(REC) > 127
              REC = CHR(ASC(REC)-128)
        ENDIF
        IF ASC(REC) = 26
              REC = ""
        ENDIF
        WRITEOUT = FWRITE(NEWFILE,REC,1)
ENDDO
=FCLOSE(OLDFILE)
=FCLOSE(NEWFILE)
CLEAR
? " Converted text. Now adding to memo..."
APPEND MEMO Comments FROM &OUTFILE
RETURN
```

The program uses the FOPEN() function to open the WordStar file and uses the FCREATE() function to create a new file. Statements within a DO WHILE loop then translate the file from WordStar to ASCII format a character at a time, reading each character with the FREAD() function and writing a character to the new file with the FWRITE() function. After the translation is complete (when the end of the WordStar file is reached, as reported by the FEOF() function), the files are closed using the FCLOSE() function. Finally, the converted (ASCII text) version of the file is read into a memo field with the APPEND MEMO command. Figure 19-5 shows the memo field after the converted file is read into the field.

You can also use the low-level file functions to access communications ports on your computer. By using one of the DOS devices COM1 or COM2 in place of a filename, you can read from or write to that port. One important point to remember is to initialize the communications port before attempting to read from or write to it. An easy way to do this is with the DOS MODE command, which can be called from within FoxPro with a RUN statement. For example,

```
RUN MODE COM1 1200,N,8,1
```

initializes the COM1 port at 1200 baud, no parity, with eight data bits and one stop bit. Once you have initialized the port, you can use the low-level file functions described earlier to read and write to the port as if it were a file.

An example of this technique appears in the following program, which accepts a phone number from a user and then dials that phone number using a Hayes-compatible modem connected to the COM1 communications port.

```
SET TALK OFF
*Initialize COM port first.*
RUN MODE COM1 1200,N,8,1
*Get number to dial from user.*
```

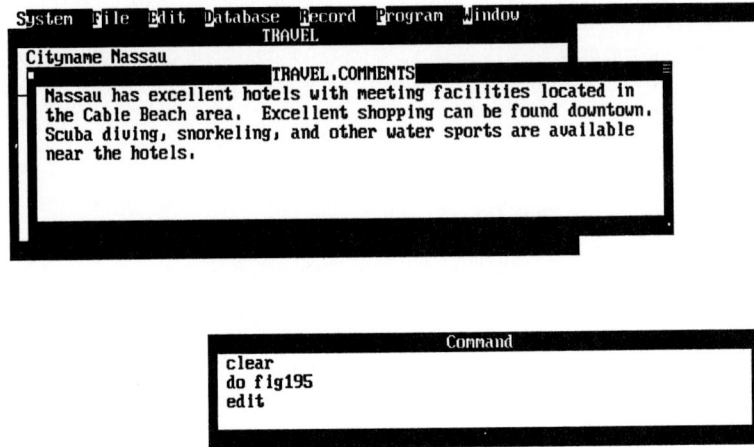

Figure 19-5. *The memo field containing the converted WordStar document*

```
STORE SPACE(12) TO PhoneNum
CLEAR
@ 5,5 SAY "Number to dial?" GET PhoneNum PICTURE "999-999-9999"
READ
*open COM1 port as file.*
MODEM = FOPEN('COM1',2)
IF (MODEM < 0)
    WAIT WINDOW 'Error raising Modem on COM1!'
    RETURN
ENDIF
*Store Hayes ATDT prefix to activate modem.*
PREFIX = 'ATDT'
DIALIT = FPUTS(modem, prefix + phonenum)
WAIT WINDOW "Wait for ringing, pick up the phone, press a key."
*Hang up and reset the modem.*
DIALIT = FPUTS(MODEM, 'ATH')
DIALIT = FPUTS(MODEM, 'ATZ')
= FCLOSE(MODEM)
RETURN
```

One point that you may want to keep in mind if you are reading data from a modem is that FoxPro uses *unbuffered I/O* when getting data from communications ports; in effect, this means that FoxPro will accept data a character at a time. This will limit the speed at which you can operate through the communications port. You probably will be unable to write fancy 9600-baud terminal emulators in FoxPro. You can minimize data errors from Hayes-compatible modems by turning off the Echo option of your modem with the Hayes ATE0 command. In a program,

```
MODEM = FOPEN('COM1',2)
DIALIT = FPUTS(modem,"ATE0")
```

sends the ECHO OFF command to the modem (assuming that it is connected to the COM1 port).

INKEY() and READKEY()

The INKEY() and READKEY() functions are useful for detecting and acting on single keystrokes in complex applications. These functions differ from WAIT, ACCEPT, and INPUT in that the program can continue performing other tasks while the keyboard is being monitored with INKEY() or READKEY(). For example, the WAIT command halts the execution of the program; the program can do nothing else while awaiting a response. The INKEY() function, on the other hand, can monitor the keyboard as a part of a loop, during which time other commands can be carried out. Consider the following excerpt from a program:

```
STORE 0 TO KEYS
@ 5,5 SAY "Printing. Press any key to halt."
DO WHILE .NOT. EOF() .AND. KEYS = 0
    ? PATIENT, ROOMNO, DIAGNOSED, ADMITTED, INSURED
    KEYS = INKEY()
    SKIP
ENDDO
...more commands...
```

Any key that is pressed is stored in the keyboard buffer, and the INKEY() function will act upon it when the statement containing INKEY() next executes.

Another important difference is that INKEY() can be used to test for keys that aren't normally monitored by ACCEPT, INPUT, or WAIT. The cursor keys, control-key combinations, and function keys fall into this category. When a key is pressed, the INKEY() function returns an integer matching the ASCII value of that key if it is an alphanumeric key, and a special value if it is a function or cursor key. For example, the value of the F10 key is −9. If you wanted to encourage the use of F10 as a universal "quit" key, you could rewrite the prior example to look like the following:

```
STORE 0 TO KEYS
@ 5,5 SAY "Printing. Press F10 to abort and exit."
DO WHILE .NOT. EOF() .AND. KEYS # -9
    ? PATIENT, ROOMNO, DIAGNOSED, ADMITTED, INSURED
    KEYS = INKEY()
    SKIP ENDDO
...more commands...
```

In a similar fashion, the INKEY() function could be used to trap function keys used to execute menu options, or the UP ARROW and DOWN ARROW keys used to move between screens. The values returned by the INKEY() function for the more unusual keys are listed in Table 19-2.

A similarly useful function is the READKEY() function. The READKEY() function can be used to tell a program which key has been used to exit from a full-screen operation, such as READ or EDIT. You can use READKEY() to detect noncharacter keys such as CTRL-END, ESC, PGUP, PGDN, and the other keys that will let you exit from a full-screen operation.

F1	28	CTRL-F1	94	ALT-F1	104
F2	−1	CTRL-F2	95	ALT-F2	105
F3	−2	CTRL-F3	96	ALT-F3	106
F4	−3	CTRL-F4	97	ALT-F4	107
F5	−4	CTRL-F5	98	ALT-F5	108
F6	−5	CTRL-F6	99	ALT-F6	109
F7	−6	CTRL-F7	100	ALT-F7	110
F8	−7	CTRL-F8	101	ALT-F8	111
F9	−8	CTRL-F9	102	ALT-F9	112
F10	−9	CTRL-F10	103	ALT-F10	113
PGUP	18	CTRL-PGUP	31		
PGDN	3	CTRL-PGDN	30		
HOME	1	CTRL-HOME	29		
END	6	CTRL-END	23		
RIGHT ARROW	4	CTRL-RIGHT ARROW	2		
LEFT ARROW	19	CTRL-LEFT ARROW	26		
UP ARROW	5				
DOWN ARROW	24				
DEL	7				
INS	22				
TAB	9				
BACKSPACE	127				

Table 19-2.   Values Returned By INKEY()

READKEY() also has a split personality, in that it returns different values depending on whether or not changes have been made to the record. For example, when using the REPLACE command to replace the contents of fields with the contents of memory variables, you may wish to perform a long, time-consuming string of REPLACE commands only if the user has not tried to abort the process by pressing ESC. You can do so by including commands like these in your edit routine:

```
...@...SAY...GET commands to get data...
READ
IF READKEY() <> 268 .AND. READKEY() <> 12
   *Escape not pressed.
   REPLACE LAST WITH M_LAST, FIRST WITH M_FIRST
   ...more REPLACE commands...
ENDIF
```

The replacements will take place as long as the ESC or equivalent CTRL-Q keys have not been used to exit the full-screen operation. Table 19-3 shows the values returned by the READKEY() function for common keys. Note that the value returned when the data has changed as a result of the operation is always 256 more than if the value had not changed. For example, if a user makes no changes to an edit screen and exits with CTRL-END, the READKEY() function returns a value of 14. However, if the user makes changes and then exits with CTRL-END, the READKEY() function returns a value of 270, equivalent to the unchanged value of 14 plus 256.

NOTE: The F1 function key can return a value to the READKEY() function. This technique is often used by programmers to implement Help routines, although FoxPro offers ways of providing more sophisticated help (as detailed in Chapter 18, "Programming with the FoxPro User Interface").

User-Defined Functions

FoxPro supports *user-defined functions*, or *UDFs*. Ordinary functions (covered in Chapter 14, "The Basics of FoxPro Programming") can be used to accept values, perform a calculation or an evaluation, and return a value. However, there may be times when you need to use a function that FoxPro does not provide. User-defined functions let you get around this limitation by constructing custom functions with the FUNCTION command. You use the FUNCTION command, along with the PARAMETERS command, to pass data from your program to the UDF. The UDF performs the desired calculation using the data received and

Key Combination	Value Returned (no data change)	Value Returned (data change)
CTRL-END or CTRL-W	14	270
ESC or CTR-Q	12	268
CTRL-S, CTRL-H, or BACKSPACE	0	256
CTRL-D or RIGHT ARROW	1	257
CTRL-A or HOME	2	258
CTRL-F or END	3	259
CTRL-E or UP ARROW	4	260
CTRL-X or DOWN ARROW	5	261
CTRL-R or PGUP	6	262
CTRL-C or PGDN	7	263
CTRL-Z or CTRL-LEFT ARROW	8	264
CTRL-B or CTRL-RIGHT ARROW	9	265
CTRL-U	10	266
CTRL-N	11	267
CTRL-M (or type past end of field)	15	271
RETURN	16	272
CTRL-HOME	33	289
CTRL-PGUP	34	290
CTRL-PGDN	35	291
F1	36	292

Table 19-3.   *READKEY() Values*

returns a value to the calling program. Since UDFs return a single value, you should use subroutines or procedures instead of UDFs if you want to return multiple values or no value at all.

UDFs differ from subroutines or procedures in that UDFs are not called with a DO command. Instead, you refer to a UDF by name as part of an expression, just as you would with any function. For example, if you assigned a UDF the name VALSTATE(), you could then use the function VALSTATE() within a program statement. When FoxPro encounters this function, it passes the desired values to the function, and the result is returned to the calling program. The syntax for the FUNCTION command is

```
FUNCTION UDFname
PARAMETERS parameter list
        ...commands...
RETURN value
```

User-defined functions can be placed at the end of the currently executing program or in a procedure file. If the functions are stored in a procedure file, be sure to include a SET PROCEDURE TO *filename* statement, to identify where the UDFs are stored, before calling a UDF. Also, note that UDF names must be eight characters or less, and that *parameter list* is a list of one or more memory-variable names representing values that the calling program supplies to the function.

As an example, the following UDF receives a date value and returns a character string that is the date spelled out in *Month day, year* form. Such a function can be useful when printing checks or invoices.

```
FUNCTION DAYWORDS
PARAMETERS Thedate
DateOut = CMONTH(Thedate) + " " +
LTRIM(STR(DAY(Thedate))) + ; ", " +
LTRIM(STR(YEAR(Thedate)))
RETURN DateOut
```

The following statements and responses show the results of the function's use within FoxPro.

```
STORE DATE() TO TODAY
? TODAY

11/22/90

? DAYWORDS(TODAY)

November 22, 1990
```

Keep in mind that every UDF must return a value to the calling program. If a value is not returned, a syntax error will occur in your program.

Part *III*

Networking with FoxPro

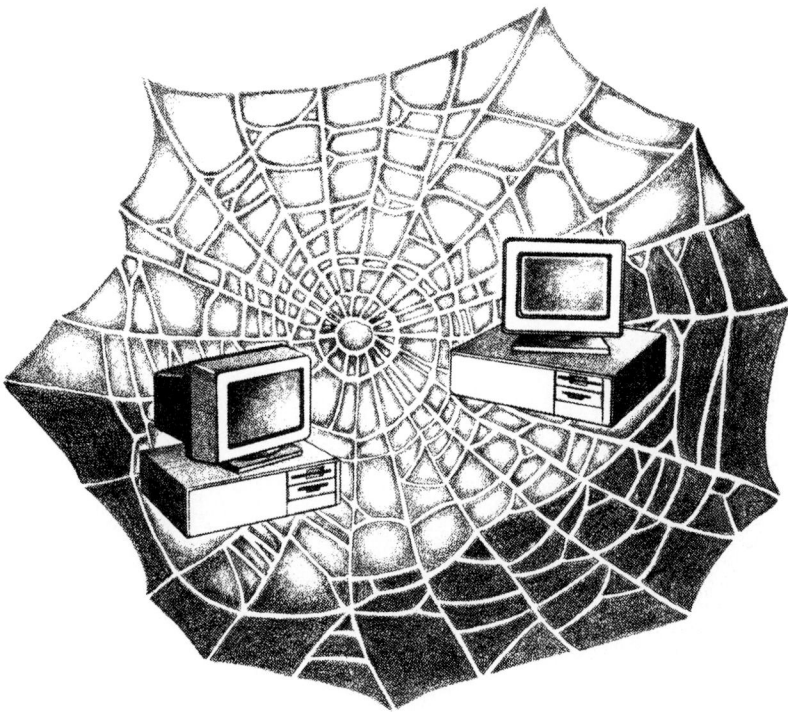

Chapter *20*

Using FoxPro on a Network

This chapter provides useful information for using FoxPro on a local area network (LAN). Included in this chapter are requirements for network use, hints for installing and using FoxPro/LAN on a network, and general hints for effective network use. Chapter 21, "Network Programming," examines programming considerations for effective design of network applications.

FoxPro/LAN and Compatible Networks

FoxPro/LAN is compatible with networks that support the standard NETBIOS interface and are compatible with DOS 3.1 or later. At the time of this writing, networks that are FoxPro/LAN-compatible include

- Novell Netware 286
- Novell Netware 386
- Novell Advanced Netware (revision 1.02 or above)
- Banyan Vines
- IBM PC Network
- 3 Com 3+
- Lantastic
- Invisible Net

This list is by no means all inclusive. If in doubt, check your network hardware and software documentation for compatibility with DOS 3.1 or later and with the NETBIOS interface.

NOTE: Some, but not all, networks require NETBIOS extensions to be loaded before NETBIOS compatibility is provided. In such cases, the NETBIOS module must be loaded before FoxPro/LAN will operate properly.

About SHARE

You may or may not need to load SHARE, provided with DOS, before loading FoxPro/LAN, depending on which network you are using. (SHARE is not required if you are using Novell network software.) When SHARE is loaded, files on the local drive can be opened by other users on the network. If SHARE is not loaded, files on the local drive are opened for exclusive use.

File Server Installation

FoxPro/LAN can be installed on the file server using the same procedure used to install the program on any computer; Fox Software uses the same installation routine both for single-user FoxPro and for FoxPro/LAN. To install the product, insert the FoxPro System Disk #1 into the source drive, enter

source drive:INSTALL

and follow the directions that appear on the screen. FoxPro will prompt you for the name of the directory in which the program should be installed. Note that the installation routine will provide you with options for installing either FoxPro or FoxPro Extended (assuming your hardware supports the use of FoxPro Extended). Both versions of FoxPro will automatically contain the LAN version, FoxPro/LAN. Hence, depending on your installation, you will be able to use either FoxPro/LAN or FoxPro/LAN Extended. (For simplicity, both versions are referred to in this chapter as FoxPro/LAN.) You can install FoxPro/LAN onto the file server's hard disk from a workstation or from the file server.

NOTE: The license agreement for the software allows you to install FoxPro/LAN on one machine only—typically, the file server. You can then provide access to the program from as many workstations as desired with the ADDUSER program provided with FoxPro.

Optimizing the FoxPro/LAN Installation

FoxPro/LAN installs its files under certain assumptions, which may or may not be most efficient on your particular network. Of significant importance in network performance is where certain files are stored. The installation process normally places FOXPROLN.EXE, FOXPROLN.OVL, and FOXPROLN.RSC on the file server. You can reduce network traffic and increase performance by placing copies of FOXPROLN.OVL and FOXPROLN.RSC at each local workstation. However, you should *not* delete any of these files from their original directory on the server hard disk.

Workstation Installation

Each workstation that will access FoxPro/LAN should have its own CONFIG.FP and FOXUSER.DBF files. The CONFIG.FP file contains options that control the default environment upon startup of FoxPro/LAN. The FOXUSER.DBF file contains specifications that control the operating environment of the local workstation under FoxPro/LAN, in a manner similar to that of the resource file under single-user FoxPro.

The easiest way to create CONFIG.FP and FOXUSER.DBF files is to run the ADDUSER.PRG program provided by Fox Software. The ADDUSER program will create customized CONFIG and FOXUSER files for each workstation. During the creation process, the ADDUSER program will let you configure the location of certain files for best operation.

To start ADDUSER and begin the process of creating files for the workstation, log onto the network at the workstation, start FoxPro/LAN and type **DO ADDUSER**.

Upon startup, ADDUSER presents an introductory screen describing the process that is about to occur. Note that the bottom of the screen shows the default directory in use. Make any desired changes to this directory and press ENTER. The ADDUSER program next lets you specify desired locations for six files used by FoxPro/LAN. The six files for which you specify the directory locations are as follows:

CONFIG.FP   This is the configuration file read at the startup of FoxPro/LAN. If more than one workstation on the network will access FoxPro/LAN, this file should have a unique name for each workstation. You can change the name of the file to any name you desire; whatever name you enter for the CONFIG.FP file is the name that the ADDUSER program will save the file under. The ADDUSER program will also add a SET statement to the workstation's AUTO-EXEC.BAT file, telling FoxPro/LAN where the CONFIG.FP file can be located.

FOXUSER.DBF   This is the resource file, which stores specifications that control operation of the workstation under FoxPro/LAN. For example, included in this file are settings for BROWSE and EDIT windows, calendar and diary entries, and color. Since each workstation will need its own unique resource file, Fox Software recommends that you specify a unique directory name or filename for the FOXUSER file. FOXUSER.DBF is the default filename, but you can specify any name you want.

Overlay Files, Editor Work Files, Sort Work Files, and Program Work Files
For these entries on the screen, you need only specify a directory name. If possible, you should specify a directory that exists on the workstation. Doing so will reduce network traffic between the workstation and the server.

   Once you have entered the desired filenames and/or directory names, press PGDN. You will be presented with four options, which appear at the bottom of the screen:

```
MODIFY    PROCEED    ABORT    FILER
```

   If your entries are correct, choose PROCEED. To change any entries, choose MODIFY. If you want to abort the entire installation process, choose ABORT. You can visually examine the directory structure of your drives on the workstation or on the server by choosing FILER.

   If you choose PROCEED, the ADDUSER program will create the needed configuration and resource files and will change the workstation's AUTOEXEC .BAT file as needed. You are now ready to run FoxPro/LAN from the workstation. You will want to repeat this process for every workstation on the network that will use FoxPro/LAN.

Running FoxPro/LAN

Once installed on a server, FoxPro/LAN becomes a shared application that can be loaded into memory on individual workstations of the network. To start FoxPro/LAN, first log onto the server from the workstation in the usual manner. Switch to the directory containing FoxPro/LAN, and enter the following from the DOS prompt:

```
FOXL
```

This command invokes the FoxPro/LAN loader, which then loads the most powerful version of FoxPro/LAN that will run within your network configuration. If there is sufficient free memory, FoxPro/LAN Extended will be loaded. If there is not sufficient free memory to load FoxPro/LAN Extended, the FoxPro/LAN Standard Edition will be loaded.

You can also load a specific version of FoxPro/LAN. To load FoxPro/LAN Extended, for example, enter

FOXPROLX

or to load FoxPro/LAN Standard Edition specifically, type

FOXPROL

at the DOS prompt.

Exclusive Versus Shared Use

On a network, files can be opened in one of two modes: Exclusive or Shared. As implied by the terms, *Exclusive mode* means that a file, once opened, can only be used by the network user who opened it. That file will not be available to others until the user closes the file. *Shared mode*, on the other hand, means that other users can make simultaneous use of the file.

By default, FoxPro opens all files in Exclusive mode. Of course, this defeats many of the benefits of operating on a network in the first place, so you will probably want to turn off the Exclusive mode. The SET EXCLUSIVE ON and SET EXCLUSIVE OFF commands, detailed later in the chapter, can be used to turn Exclusive mode on or off. Keep in mind that FoxPro is in Exclusive mode by default, so if you want multiple users to be able to share files, you will need to use the SET EXCLUSIVE OFF command.

Database Integrity

Users of database software on any local area network must consider database integrity. *Database integrity*—the completeness of the database—is threatened whenever two users attempt to modify the same database record at the same time. If the software is not designed to operate on a network, serious problems can occur. One user might overwrite the other's changes, or in more serious cases, the network's operating software might crash and bring the entire network down. To prevent such problems, FoxPro/LAN offers two features: file locking and record locking. *File locking* causes a database file being accessed by one user to be made unavailable to any other users on the network. *Record locking* performs the same type of safeguard, but does so for an individual record within a file. FoxPro/LAN will automatically perform record locking and file locking as needed, to maintain data integrity, for any database that you use. Commands that change data, such as CHANGE/EDIT, APPEND, and INDEX ON will cause FoxPro/LAN to lock the file or record automatically. In addition to automatic file and record locking, you can use specific programming commands to turn file and record locking off or on.

Automatic Versus Manual Locking

FoxPro/LAN's automatic file and record locking create a significant advantage to users who perform database work with the FoxPro menus or with direct commands (as opposed to writing programs). If you manage your databases by selecting menu options or by entering commands in the Command window, FoxPro/LAN will guard the integrity of your databases by automatically locking records or files when necessary. Basically, FoxPro/LAN locks records or files whenever it must perform write operations. For example, when you make changes to a record using a BROWSE or CHANGE/EDIT command, FoxPro automatically locks the record you are changing. Table 20-1 shows the FoxPro/LAN commands that perform automatic locking.

   In addition to automatic file and record locking, FoxPro/LAN provides commands and functions that you can use to lock a record or a file manually. These commands and functions are typically used within programs when you desire more explicit control over locking than is provided by the automatic locking of FoxPro/LAN. The next section of this chapter describes these and other network-specific commands in detail. In Chapter 21 you'll find specifics on using locking commands and functions in your FoxPro programs.

Network Commands and Functions

In FoxPro/LAN, certain commands and functions can be used to protect the integrity of data on a network. Certain other commands provide you with additional information regarding the status of records and files. These additional commands and functions are needed to prevent trouble when users try to share files. Collisions between users, caused when users try to access the same file or record at the same time, can cause problems for the network programmers because the program must be provided with enough "intelligence" to sense such collisions and find a solution. The commands and functions available for such tasks include the SET EXCLUSIVE and UNLOCK commands and the LOCK(), FLOCK(), and RLOCK() functions.

Command	Area Locked
APPEND	Entire database
APPEND BLANK	Database header (for a short period of time)
APPEND FROM	Entire database
APPEND FROM ARRAY	Database header
APPEND MEMO	Current record
BROWSE, CHANGE, and EDIT	Current record and all records in related databases
DELETE	Current record
DELETE NEXT 1	Current record
DELETE RECORD *n*	Record *n*
DELETE *(scope greater than one)*	Entire database
GATHER	Current record
INSERT − SQL	Database header
MODIFY MEMO	Current record, when editing starts
READ	Current record and all records in aliased fields
RECALL	Current record
RECALL NEXT 1	Current record
RECALL RECORD *n*	Record *n*
RECALL *(scope greater than one)*	Entire database
REPLACE	Current record and all records in aliased fields
REPLACE NEXT 1	Current record and all records in aliased fields
REPLACE RECORD *n*	Record *n* and all records in aliased fields
REPLACE *(scope greater than one)*	Entire database and all files from aliased fields
SHOW GETS	Current record and all records from aliased fields
UPDATE	Entire database

Table 20-1. Automatic Locking Performed by FoxPro/LAN

SET EXCLUSIVE

The SET EXCLUSIVE command controls whether files are available on a shared basis or only for the exclusive use of the first user to access each file. The format for this command is

SET EXCLUSIVE ON/OFF

Entering **SET EXCLUSIVE OFF** from the Command window will make files under FoxPro/LAN available for shared use. Entering **SET EXCLUSIVE ON** will make each file accessible for exclusive use by the first person opening the file.

As an alternative, you can also add the word "EXCLUSIVE" after the USE command when a file is opened to open that file for exclusive use only. For example, entering the command

```
USE PERSONL EXCLUSIVE
```

would open the named file, PERSONL.DBF, for exclusive use.

Keep in mind that if a program opens a file with SET EXCLUSIVE turned off, it is the responsibility of the program to guard against potential collisions by checking the status of files and records with the locking functions, FLOCK(), RLOCK(), and LOCK(). Chapter 21 provides hints for using the SET EXCLUSIVE command within your FoxPro programs.

The Locking Functions

In FoxPro/LAN, *locking functions* can be used to prevent collisions and occurrences of deadly embrace. Locking functions let you know whether a file or a record has been locked by another user on the network. Locking functions operate in a slightly different manner than other functions. Where other FoxPro/LAN functions usually return a value, such as true or false, the locking functions can perform an action—the locking of a file or a record—as well as returning a value.

There are three locking functions within FoxPro/LAN: FLOCK(), RLOCK(), and LOCK(). The RLOCK() and LOCK() functions perform the same task: attempting to lock the current record and return a value. If the lock is successful, a logical truc is returned. If the record is already locked, a logical false is returned. The FLOCK() function performs a similar task, but for the entire file. The FLOCK() function attempts to lock the file, and if the lock is successful, FLOCK() returns a value of true. If the attempt to lock the file fails, FLOCK() returns a logical false.

These functions can be used in an interactive mode (from the Command window) or from within a program. For example, the commands

```
USE PERSONL
? FLOCK()
```

will cause FoxPro/LAN to respond with true (.T.), assuming that no other users are using the PERSONL file. The FLOCK function causes the PERSONL file to be locked and reports the file-lock status as true. If another user then logs on to the system and enters the same commands, FoxPro/LAN will respond with false (.F.), which indicates that the PERSONL file is already locked.

UNLOCK

Once you have completed operations with a record or a file, the UNLOCK command can be used to clear all locks. The format of the command is simply UNLOCK.

You can type **UNLOCK ALL** to clear all record or file locks in all work areas of FoxPro. You can also type **UNLOCK IN** *expression* to release locks in another work area, where *expression* is the work area number or alias name.

As an alternative method of clearing a lock, you can lock a different record or file or close the database with a CLEAR ALL, USE, or QUIT command. Any of these operations will release a previous lock on a record or file.

SET REPROCESS

The SET REPROCESS command sets the number of times FoxPro/LAN attempts to open a previously locked file or record before it displays an error message. The command is valid either included in programs or stored in the CONFIG.DB file as REPROCESS = *n*. The default number is 0, which means that if FoxPro/LAN tries to open a locked file or record, it immediately displays an error message. You can use the command

SET REPROCESS TO *n*

where *n* is a number from 1 to 32,000, and FoxPro/LAN will then retry the operation the specified number of times before the error condition is reported. Note that you can also specify a value of −1, in which case FoxPro will perform retries indefinitely.

An alternative form of the command is

SET REPROCESS TO *n* SECONDS

If you use this form of the command, FoxPro/LAN will retry the operation for the specified number of seconds.

SET LOCK and SET MULTILOCKS

You can use the SET LOCK and SET MULTILOCKS commands to control different aspects of network locking under FoxPro/LAN. The SET LOCK command enables or disables automatic file and record locking, and the SET MULTILOCKS command enables or disables the ability of FoxPro to lock multiple records at the same time.

Normally, FoxPro/LAN does not lock a database file or record if a command requiring a read-only operation (such as a COUNT, LIST, REPORT FORM, or LABEL FORM command) is used. There may be times when you want to change this normal behavior of FoxPro; for example, during the printing of reports, you may want to ensure that the database the report is based on does not change while the report is printed. You can use the SET LOCK ON command, which will cause FoxPro/LAN to lock files or records, even for read-only operations like LIST and REPORT FORM.

When SET LOCK is ON, FoxPro/LAN automatically locks files or records in response to commands that require read-only access to a database file. If SET LOCK is OFF (the default), commands that perform read-only access of the data do not lock files or records.

Use the SET MULTILOCKS command to determine whether you can lock more than one record in a database file at the same time. Normally, you can lock only one record at a time. If you use the LOCK() or RLOCK() function to lock a record and then use the same function on another record, the existing record lock will be released before the new lock is set. However, once you use the SET MULTILOCKS ON command, you can use the LOCK() or RLOCK() function successively to lock multiple records. Each record you lock will remain locked until you use the UNLOCK command, at which time all locked records will be unlocked.

The default value of SET MULTILOCKS is OFF. Whenever you change the status of SET MULTILOCKS, FoxPro/LAN releases any existing record locks.

DISPLAY STATUS and LIST STATUS

The DISPLAY STATUS and LIST STATUS commands provide the same information in network FoxPro/LAN as they do in the single-user versions of FoxPro/LAN: the name of the database in use, the status of most SET commands, and the status of the programmable function keys. In addition to this information, the DISPLAY STATUS and LIST STATUS commands also indicate whether database files are locked and whether individual records within a file are locked.

SET PRINTER

The SET PRINTER command is used to specify whether print output should be sent to a local printer (one attached to a workstation) or to a printer attached to a server. The normal syntax of the SET PRINTER command is

SET PRINTER TO *computer name*\ *printer name* = *destination*

where *computer name* is the name of the workstation as assigned by the network operating software, *printer name* is the network name assigned to the desired printer, and *destination* is the DOS device that identifies the printer (LPT1, LPT2, and so on). If no destination is specified, the default destination will be the first parallel port (LPT1).

For example, to redirect printer output to parallel printer port 1 (LPT1) connected to a workstation named Chicago, where an attached laser printer has been named LASER by the network operating system software, you would use the command

```
SET PRINTER TO \\CHICAGO\LASER=LPT1
```

To redirect output to a printer attached to a file server that has been named PUBLIC by the network software, you would use the command

```
SET PRINTER TO \\PUBLIC
```

To redirect output to a printer attached to your workstation and choose LPT1 for the printer port, you would enter

```
SET PRINTER TO LPT1
```

General Network Hints

There are several points you should keep in mind to make the most effective use of FoxPro/LAN on a network:

- In any multi-user environment, large numbers of files tend to clutter the working space in the file server. To hold such clutter to a minimum, heavy users should be provided with individual subdirectories on the file server. The FoxPro SET PATH command can be used to cause all FoxPro commands that read files to search private subdirectories. See Chapter 22 for information on the SET PATH command.

- If users are going to create smaller files that will not be used by other users of the network, encourage those users to store such files at their workstations, rather than on the file server.

- Back up all databases regularly to floppy disks or tapes.

- Create new applications and databases at a workstation, in a single-user mode, and thoroughly test those applications before placing the files in shared space on the file server. A multi-user environment is not the best place to get all the bugs out of a system's design.

Chapter 21

Network Programming

As mentioned in Chapter 20, "Using FoxPro on a Network," sharing databases on a network introduces a range of concerns that may not have existed in a single-user situation. Database integrity is of prime concern when writing programs for a network; your programs must be written to ensure that collisions (when multiple users contend for the same file or record) are handled in an orderly fashion. Another common problem is *file deadlock*, which occurs when two programs contend for the same files and the program's design results in an unconditional retry of the file access.

Since FoxPro/LAN performs automatic file and record locking, programmers who are not experienced in network programming may wonder why the use of additional commands and functions in a program is necessary. Fine-tuning of programs is needed because, while FoxPro's automatic locking does much to keep users out of trouble, it may not be the most efficient way to share resources. You may prefer to institute your own manual locks at various points within a program. The RLOCK(), LOCK(), and FLOCK() functions and the UNLOCK command, detailed in Chapter 20, can be used within programs to explicitly control file and record locking.

The basic concept behind writing or modifying programs for network use is to lock records or files only when necessary and to provide a planned way out of a program if a needed resource (record or file) cannot be made available. The ways in which this can be accomplished will, of course, vary greatly with programming styles. This chapter presents some common methods for implementing programs on a network. You can base your style on the examples shown here or implement your own designs using the network commands and functions available in FoxPro/LAN.

Using the Locking Functions Within Programs

The locking functions described in Chapter 20 can be used within programs as part of conditional tests. Programs can allow a process, such as editing a record, to proceed if a locking function returns one value, and can display an error message or make a timed repeat attempt if the locking function returns a different value. As noted in Chapter 20, the FLOCK() function attempts a file lock and returns a logical true if the lock is successful; correspondingly, the RLOCK() function attempts a lock on the current record and returns a logical true if the lock is successful.

The following program demonstrates the use of the RLOCK() function and the UNLOCK command to ensure that a record can be locked before editing is allowed.

```
*Editor edits employee file.*
SELECT 2
*work area 2 has EMPLOYEE file and corresponding index
*already opened at start of program.
DO WHILE .T.
    STORE SPACE(20) TO M_LAST
    STORE SPACE(20) TO M_FIRST
    @ 4,3 CLEAR TO 7,51
    @ 4,3 TO 7,51 PANEL
    @ 5,6 SAY "Last name? " GET M_LAST
    @ 6,5 SAY "First name? " GET M_FIRST
    READ
    STORE M_LAST + M_FIRST TO FINDIT
    SEEK FINDIT
    IF .NOT. FOUND()
       CLEAR
       ? "There is no such name in this database!"
       WAIT "Press any key to return to menu..."
       EXIT
    ENDIF
    IF RLOCK()
       STORE Lastname TO M_LAST
       STORE Firstname TO M_FIRST
       STORE Empid TO M_EMPID
       STORE Workgroup TO M_WORKGRP
       CLEAR
       @ 2,1 TO 14,60 PANEL
       @ 3,2 Say [Last Name  ] GET M_LAST
       @ 5,2 Say [First Name ] GET M_FIRST
       @ 8,2 Say [Employee ID:] GET M_EMPID
```

```
        @ 9,2 Say [Department] GET M_WORKGRP
        READ
        REPLACE Lastname WITH M_LAST
        REPLACE Firstname WITH M_FIRST
        REPLACE Empid WITH M_EMPID
        REPLACE Workgroup WITH M_WORKGRP
        UNLOCK
        ?
        ACCEPT "  Edit another employee? Y/N " TO YN
        IF UPPER(YN) = "N"
              EXIT
        ENDIF
     ELSE
        @ 6,10 SAY "Sorry... record is in use."
        @ 7,10 SAY "Try your request later."
        WAIT
        EXIT
     ENDIF
ENDDO
RETURN
* End of EDITOR.PRG
```

The program uses the RLOCK() function to determine whether the record to be edited has been locked. If the RLOCK() function returns a logical true, editing of the record is allowed. Once editing is completed, the record is unlocked with the UNLOCK command. If the record is already locked when the editing process is attempted, control passes to the ELSE statement, and an error message alerts the user that the record is in use by another network user.

Generally, the most efficient strategy when programming for a network involves locking records during individual updates and locking files only when absolutely necessary (during global updates or reindexing, for example). You should also keep in mind that access to records and files granted by your programs can be overridden by the read/write attributes set by the network operating system software.

When to Open Files Exclusively

When writing programs, note that the following FoxPro commands require a database to be opened in Exclusive mode. Your program will crash with an

Code	Meaning
111	Attempt made to write to a read-only file
110	Attempted operation requires that file be opened for exclusive use
108	File in use by another
124	Invalid printer redirection
109	Record in use by another

Table 21-1.   *Network Error Codes*

"Exclusive open of file is required" error if you do not open the file in Exclusive mode before attempting any of the following commands:

- INSERT BLANK
- MODIFY STRUCTURE
- PACK
- REINDEX
- ZAP

Error Handling for Networks

Your error-trapping routines (detailed in Chapter 19, "Advanced Topics") should be expanded to cover the specific error codes returned when a network resource is not available. Table 21-1 shows the error codes returned by FoxPro/LAN that relate to network-specific errors.

If an error calls an error-trapping routine through the use of the ON ERROR statement, detailed in Chapter 19, the program can interpret the error code and take appropriate action. The following is an example of such a routine.

```
**NETPANIC.PRG is error trapping for network use.
**Last update 8/20/91
CLEAR
DO CASE
  CASE ERROR() = 111
    ? "Attempt made to write to a read-only file."
    ? "Contact network administrator for help."
    CLEAR ALL
    WAIT
    QUIT
  CASE ERROR() = 20 .or. ERROR() = 26 .or. ERROR() = 114
    ? "The index file seems to be missing a record."
```

```
  ? "please wait while I repair the index."
  IF FLOCK()
     REINDEX
     UNLOCK
  ELSE
     CLEAR
     ? "Cannot gain exclusive use of needed file."
     ? "Contact administrator, report failure of"
     ? "main index file."
     WAIT
     QUIT
  ENDIF
  CLEAR
  RETRY
CASE ERROR() = 108
  ? "Desired file is in use by someone else."
  ? "Try your request again later."
  WAIT
  CLEAR ALL
  RETURN TO MASTER
CASE ERROR() = 109
  ? "Desired record is in use by someone else."
  ? "Try your request again later."
  WAIT
  CLEAR ALL
  RETURN TO MASTER
CASE ERROR() = 125
  ? "Printer not ready. Reset printer, then"
  WAIT
  RETRY
OTHERWISE
  SET ESCAPE ON
  ? "A program error has occurred. Record the
  ? "message, and inform the system administrator."
  ?
  ? MESSAGE()
  ?
  ?
  ? "After noting above message, press any key."
  WAIT
  SET CONSOLE OFF
  SET ALTERNATE TO ERRORS.TXT
  SET ALTERNATE ON
  LIST MEMORY
  LIST STATUS
  ? "Error message reported was: "
```

```
   ?? MESSAGE()
   CLEAR ALL
   QUIT
ENDCASE
*End of NETPANIC.PRG.
```

Performing Automated Retries

The SET REPROCESS command is a valuable aid in network programming, as you can use it to specify how long FoxPro/LAN will attempt a record lock or a file lock. As mentioned in Chapter 20, the syntax for the command is

SET REPROCESS TO *n*

where *n* is a numeric value specifying how many times FoxPro will reattempt the locking operation. You can specify any value from 1 to 32,000. If you use SET REPROCESS TO −1, FoxPro will continue a locking attempt indefinitely. You can also use the format SET REPROCESS TO *n* SECONDS, in which case FoxPro will repeat attempts to set the lock for the determined number of seconds.

Early in the program, you can include a statement like SET REPROCESS TO 5 SECONDS so that users will not have to wait too long for FoxPro to gain access to a locked record. If the attempt to lock is unsuccessful after your preferred period of time (as indicated by a logical false returned by the FLOCK(), LOCK(), or RLOCK() function), you can display an appropriate error message asking the user to try the operation later.

Testing for Networks

Many programs (particularly those developed for commercial resale) may be used either on a network or on single-user systems. If you are faced with writing one program that might be used in either environment, you can use the NETWORK() function to determine whether the software is running on a network, and the program can then operate accordingly. The NETWORK() function returns a logical true if you are running under FoxPro/LAN. If you are running in single-user mode, the function returns a logical false.

You can write portions of a program to run in a single-user or in a network environment, as illustrated in the following example.

```
IF NETWORK()
   SET REFRESH TO 10
   SET REPROCESS TO 5
```

```
        SET BELL OFF
        SET TALK OFF
ELSE
        SET BELL OFF
        SET TALK OFF
ENDIF
...more commands...
```

File Deadlock and How to Avoid It

Many programs written for a single-user environment must be rewritten to contend adequately with the demands of the network environment. A very common fault of single-user FoxBASE+ and FoxPro programs running on a network is an inability to guard against file deadlock (also known as *deadly embrace*). File deadlock occurs when two or more programs running on different workstations contend for the same files exclusively, and become locked in an endless loop. Consider the following example, where two users are running the programs shown, which contend for the same files.

Program A	**Program B**
| ```
SELECT 1
USE PERSONL
DO WHILE .NOT. FLOCK()
       ...commands...
ENDDO
SELECT 2
USE HOURS
DO WHILE .NOT. FLOCK()
       ...commands...
ENDDO
UNLOCK ALL
``` | ```
SELECT 1
USE HOURS
DO WHILE .NOT. FLOCK()
       ...commands...
ENDDO
SELECT 2
USE PERSONNL
DO WHILE .NOT. FLOCK()
       ...commands...
ENDDO
UNLOCK ALL
``` |

In the scenario illustrated by this example, the first user's program opens the PERSONL database file in work area 1, and immediately locks the file. At the same time, the second user's program opens the HOURS database file in work area 1 on the other workstation and locks that file. The first user's program now tries to open the HOURS file, but cannot do so because the second user has that file locked. Meanwhile, the second user's program is trying to open the PERSONL file, but the first user's program has that file locked. If SET REPROCESS were by chance set to −1 (infinite retries), both workstations would lock up, and the only solution would be to reboot one of the machines—hardly an effective solution!.

This example illustrates the planning that is necessary when programming applications that will be used on a network. You can avoid file deadlock with a number of techniques. One is to always open files in a specific order and to assign specific files to specific work areas. Another common technique for avoiding file deadlock is to open all files for shared use at the start of the program and lock any records that must be locked near the start of the program. A final approach involves using the SET REPROCESS command to limit the maximum amount of time that FoxPro/LAN spends trying to access a file or a record. Remember that in most applications, a SET REPROCESS TO −1 statement is dangerous, as it opens a wide door to your hardware getting caught in infinite loops.

Part *IV*

Reference

Chapter **22**

Command Reference

This chapter contains a listing of FoxPro commands. Each command name is followed by the syntax of the command and a description of how the command works. Examples of command use are provided where appropriate.

Symbols and Conventions

1. All commands are printed in UPPERCASE letters, although you can enter them in either upper- or lowercase letters.

2. All parameters of the command are listed in italics.

3. Any part of a command or parameter that is surrounded by left and right brackets—[ ]—is optional.

4. When a slash separates two choices in a command, such as ON/OFF, you specify one choice but not both.

5. Ellipses (...) following a parameter or command mean that the parameter or command can be repeated "infinitely"—that is, until you reach the FoxPro limit of 1024 characters per command line.

6. The *scope* parameter, which is always an option, can have four different meanings depending upon the command: ALL for all records; NEXT *n* for *n* number of records beginning at the current position of the record

pointer; REST for all records from the pointer position to the end of the file; and RECORD *n*, for record number *n*.

7. The term *"expC"* indicates a character expression, *"expN"* indicates a numeric expression, and *"expL"* indicates a logical expression. Where data type does not matter, the term *"expression"* or *"expr"* is used.

\ (or) \\

Syntax

\ *<<text line>>*
\\ *<<text line>>*

The \ and \\ commands are used in implementing the textmerge capability of FoxPro 2. The \ and \\ commands send a line of text to the current output device. If the \ command is used, a carriage return and linefeed are sent before the contents of the text line are evaluated. If the \\ command is used, a carriage return and linefeed are not sent.

Expressions (including field names), variables, and functions placed within delimiters in the text line will be evaluated if SET TEXTMERGE is ON (see SET TEXTMERGE). If SET TEXTMERGE is OFF, the expressions, variables, or functions appear as literal characters. For example, if SET TEXTMERGE were ON, the command,

```
\ <<Lastname>>
```

which consists of the \ command followed by a field name called Lastname, would output the contents of that field for the current record of the active database. If SET TEXTMERGE were OFF, the same command would output the name of the field surrounded by the double angle brackets (in this case, Lastname).

? or ??

Syntax

?/?? [*expression*] [PICTURE *"clause"*] [FUNCTION *"functionlist"*] [AT *expN*]

The ? command displays the value of a FoxPro expression. If a single question mark (?) is used, the cursor executes a carriage return and linefeed, and then the value of the expression is displayed. If the double question mark (??) is used, the cursor is not moved before the value of the expression is displayed. The PICTURE and FUNCTION options may be used to customize the appearance of the displayed information. The AT option may be used to place the expression at a specific column location.

By default, the ?/?? commands direct the output to the screen. To simultaneously route the output to the default printer, issue a SET PRINT ON command, then use the ? or ?? commands. When routing output to a printer, also note that you can use SET CONSOLE OFF to disable the screen display during reports (see SET CONSOLE).

Example

Use the ? command to display the contents of database fields for the current record or of memory variables. You can provide a simultaneous display of more than one expression by including the names of each expression after the ? or ?? command, with the expressions separated by commas. The example below shows a display of four fields from a database, using the ? command.

```
? Lastname, Firstname, Grade, Salary
Robertson       Henry          G-08  1534.60
```

The PICTURE and FUNCTION options may be used to customize the appearance of the displayed information. Use the PICTURE or FUNCTION options by adding the word PICTURE or FUNCTION followed by the letters or symbols that specify the picture template or function. The function or picture templates are surrounded by quotes. For example, to use the ? command to display the contents of a Lastname field, ten characters in width, in uppercase letters, you could use either command shown below. (The first uses ten picture symbols, while the second uses a function to accomplish the same task.)

```
? Lastname PICTURE "!!!!!!!!!!"
? Lastname FUNCTION "!"
```

???

Syntax

   ??? *expC*

The ??? command sends characters to the printer without changing the current row and column positions. Use this command to send control codes or escape sequences to the printer. To specify control codes, enclose the ASCII code in curly braces.

HINT: Refer to your printer manual for a listing of control codes appropriate to your printer.

Example

All three lines shown below perform the same task, sending a CTRL-O code to switch an Epson-compatible printer into compressed mode. The first line uses the CHR() function, along with the ASCII code for CTRL-O. The second line uses control-code brace delimiters, surrounding the mnemonic for CTRL-O. The third line uses the ASCII code for CTRL-O enclosed within curly braces.

```
??? CHR(15)
??? "{CTRL-O}"
??? "{15}"
```

@

Syntax

@ *row,col* [SAY *expression*] [PICTURE *expression*] [FUNCTION *list*]
[GET *variable*] [PICTURE *expression*] [FUNCTION *list*] [RANGE]
[VALID *condition*] [ERROR *expC*] [COLOR *standard/enhanced*]
[COLOR SCHEME *expN*]

The @ command places the cursor at a specific screen location, which is identified by *row,col*. The @ command can be used with one or more of the named options. The SAY option displays the value of the *expression* following the word SAY. The GET option allows editing of the variable (which can be a field). The PICTURE option allows the use of templates, which specify the way data will be displayed or accepted in response to the GET option. The RANGE option is used with the GET option to specify a range of acceptable entries. The VALID option specifies acceptable entries for GET using a *condition*. ERROR displays a custom error message if VALID is not met. COLOR defines new color settings for the @...SAY...GET command. COLOR SCHEME is a numeric value from 1 to 11, denoting colors based on the corresponding color scheme (see SET COLOR OF SCHEME). Note that a READ command must follow the use of GET commands to achieve full-screen editing.

Example

To place the message "Enter member name:" at screen location 12,2 and allow full-screen editing of the value contained in the variable M_NAME, enter

```
@ 12,2 SAY "Enter member name:" GET M_NAME
```

To change data in a database field named SALARY, and to restrict entries to a range between 4.75 and 20.00, the following command could be used.

```
@ 5,5 GET SALARY RANGE 4.75, 20
```

FoxPro 2 users should note that there are some additional options of the @...GET command that are covered in the commands that follow. These options are used to create check boxes, radio buttons, list boxes, popups, and pushbuttons within programs.

@...BOX

Syntax

@ *row1,col1,row2,col2* BOX *expC*

This command draws a box between the specified coordinates. (Note that this command is compatible with FoxBASE+. If compatibility with dBASE IV is desired, use the @ *row, col* TO *row, col* command.) An optional character expression, *expC*, containing up to nine different characters may be specified, in which case those characters are used to construct the box. The first four characters define the four corners, starting from the upper-left corner and moving clockwise. The next four characters define the four sides, starting from the top and moving clockwise. The last character, if specified, is used as the background. If no character expression is provided, a single-line box is drawn.

Example

To draw a single-line box, with the upper-left corner at row 4, column 1, and the lower-right corner at row 18, column 70, enter

```
@ 4,1,18,70 BOX
```

To draw a box with the corners composed of # symbols, the top composed of hyphens, the sides composed of asterisks, and the bottom composed of equal signs, the following command could be used.

```
@ 2,2,15,60 BOX "#" + "-" + "#" + "*" + "#" + "=" + "#" + "*"
```

To draw a box composed of double lines on the top and bottom, single lines on the sides, and filled with a graphic pattern, the following commands could be used.

```
STORE CHR(211) TO LLC
STORE CHR(214) TO ULC
STORE CHR(183) TO URC
STORE CHR(189) TO LRC
STORE CHR(186) TO SIDE
STORE CHR(196) TO TOP
STORE CHR(196) TO BOTTOM
STORE CHR(176) + CHR(178) TO FILLER
@ 2,2,15,60 BOX ;
ULC+TOP+URC+SIDE+LRC+BOTTOM+LLC+SIDE+FILLER
```

@...CLEAR TO

Syntax

@ *row,col* CLEAR/CLEAR TO *row,col*

This variation of the @ command clears a portion of the screen. If @ *row, col* CLEAR is used, the screen is cleared to the right and below the coordinates provided. If @ *row, col* CLEAR TO *row, col* is used, the screen is cleared within a rectangular area, with the first coordinate indicating the upper-left corner, and the second coordinate indicating the lower-right corner.

Example

To erase a rectangular area from row 4, column 5 to row 12, column 70 while leaving the remainder of the screen unchanged, enter

```
@ 4,5 CLEAR TO 12,70
```

@...EDIT

Syntax

@ *row,col* EDIT *variable* [FUNCTION *expC2*] [DEFAULT *expr*] SIZE *expN1*,
expN2[, *expN3*] [ENABLE/DISABLE] [MESSAGE *expC3*]
[VALID *expL1* [ERROR *expC4*]] [WHEN *expL2*] [NOMODIFY] [SCROLL]
[TAB/NOTAB] [COLOR SCHEME *expN4*/COLOR *color-pair list*]

The @...EDIT command is used to allow editing of text in a rectangular area.
The text to be edited can be a field (referenced by the field name), a memo field,
a variable, or an array element. All standard FoxPro editing features are
available, wordwrap occurs normally, and text can be scrolled vertically.

Use *row, col* to specify the upper-left corner for the text editing region. Use
variable to specify the variable, array element, database field, or memo field that
will be edited. Note that *variable* must be a character type or memo field type. If
the ESC key is pressed to terminate the editing, the variable will be unchanged.

Use FUNCTION *"expC2"* to center text in the editing region or to justify the
text. The function codes are I to center text or J to right-justify text.

You can use the DEFAULT *expr* option to create the memory variable if the
variable specified by *variable* does not already exist. Use SIZE *expN1*, *expN2*
[,*expN3*] to change the size of the editing region; *expN1* specifies the height of the
editing region in rows, and *expN2* specifies the width of the editing region in
columns. *ExpN3* specifies the number of characters that can be edited. Use the
ENABLE/DISABLE options to allow or prevent editing of the variable when the
corresponding READ is issued. Use the MESSAGE *expC3* option to display the
message specified as *expC3* when the READ command activates the editing
region.

You can use the VALID *expL1* option to perform validation when the editing
region is activated. Typically, *expL1* is a user-defined function. Use ERROR *expC4*
to specify an error message that should appear if the logical expression tested by
the VALID clause evaluates to false. The optional WHEN clause permits or
prohibits editing of the edit region. The logical expression following the WHEN
option must evaluate to a logical true before editing will be allowed.

Use the NOMODIFY option to display the text editing region but not permit
editing. If the SCROLL clause is added, a scroll bar is placed to the right of the
text editing region. The TAB/NOTAB options can be used to specify the default
behavior of the TAB key. If the TAB clause is added, the use of the TAB key inserts
a tab at the current cursor location. If the NOTAB clause is included, the use of
the TAB key saves changes, exits the text editing region, and proceeds to the next
GET field or object.

Use the COLOR SCHEME or COLOR *color-pair list* options to change the
default colors for the list.

Example

The following program defines an editing region 5 lines down and 40 columns across, and the editing within the region appears justified.

```
STORE "This is text to be edited" TO M_TEXT
@ 5,10 EDIT M_TEXT FUNCTION "J" SIZE 5,40
READ
```

@...FILL TO

Syntax

@ *row1,col1* FILL TO *row2,col2* [COLOR *standard/enhanced*]
[COLOR SCHEME *expN*]

The @...FILL command changes the color of the screen within the defined area. The *standard/enhanced* is *X/Y*, where *X* is the code for the standard color, and *Y* is the code for the enhanced color. (See SET COLOR for a listing of color codes.) If the COLOR option is omitted, the screen is cleared within the defined area. COLOR SCHEME is a numeric value from 1 to 11, denoting a color based on the corresponding color scheme (see SET COLOR OF SCHEME).

Example

```
@ 5,5 FILL TO 10,40 COLOR B/R
```

@...GET to Make Check Boxes

Syntax

Version 2

@ *row,col* GET *variable* FUNCTION "*C *expC1*"/PICTURE "@*C *expC2*"
[DEFAULT *expr*] [SIZE *expN1, expN2*] [ENABLE/DISABLE]
[MESSAGE *expC3*] [VALID *expL1*] [WHEN *expL2*]
[COLOR SCHEME *expN3*/COLOR *color-pair list*]

This variation of the @...GET command is used to create check boxes. Check boxes appear as a pair of square brackets followed by a text string prompt, as in the following example:

```
[X] Married?
```

The user can turn on or off the check mark within the brackets. Check boxes provide your user interface a simple way to obtain yes/no or true/false decisions from users. The check box specification code of *C along with a function, or @*C as a picture, is what causes the @...GET command to display a check box.

Use *row, col* to specify the coordinates for the check box. Use *variable* to specify the variable that stores the user's response. (Note that *variable* can be a memory variable, the name of a database field, or an array element.) Variable must be a numeric or a logical type. If *variable* is numeric, 0 corresponds to the check box not being checked, and 1 corresponds to being checked. If *variable* is logical, then false (.F.) corresponds to not being checked, and true (.T.) corresponds to being checked.

Use FUNCTION "*C *expC1*" or PICTURE "@*C *expC2*" to cause the @...GET command to display a check box. You must include the *C specification to force the display of a check box. If PICTURE is used instead of FUNCTION, you must precede the *C specification with an at sign (@). For example, both of the following groups of statements create a check box with the "Married?" prompt:

```
STORE .F. TO MARRIED
@ 5,5 GET MARRIED FUNCTION "*C Married?"
READ

STORE .F. TO MARRIED
@ 5,5 GET MARRIED PICTURE "@*C Married?" READ
```

Immediately following the *C specification, you can add the optional N or T specifications. N indicates that checking the box will not terminate the corresponding READ. T indicates that checking the box will terminate the corresponding READ. If N or T is not included, by default the check box does not terminate the corresponding READ.

You can use the DEFAULT *expr* option to create the memory variable if the variable specified by *variable* does not already exist. Use SIZE *expN1, expN2* to change the size of the check box; *expN1* specifies the height of check box, and *expN2* specifies the width. Use the ENABLE/DISABLE options to allow or prevent activation of the check box when the corresponding READ is issued. Use the MESSAGE *expC3* option to display the message specified as *expC3* when the check box is selected.

You can use the VALID *expL1* option to perform validation when the check box is chosen. Typically, *expL1* is a user-defined function. The optional WHEN clause permits or prohibits selection of the check box. The logical expression *expL2* following the WHEN option must evaluate to a logical true before the check box can be selected. If the expression evaluates as false, the check box cannot be selected, and it will be skipped over if it is placed between other GET fields.

Use the COLOR SCHEME or COLOR *color-pair list* options to change the default colors for the check box.

Example

The FUNCTION clause looks like this:

```
STORE 1 TO MYCHOICE
@ 5,12 GET MYCHOICE FUNCTION "*C In stock?"
READ

STORE .T. TO MYCHOICE
STORE "*C In stock?" TO MYPROMPT
@ 5,12 GET MYCHOICE FUNCTION MYPROMPT
READ
```

The PICTURE clause looks like this:

```
STORE 1 TO MYCHOICE
@ 5,12 GET MYCHOICE PICTURE "@*C In stock?" READ
```

@...GET to Make Invisible Buttons

Syntax

Version 2

@ *row,col* GET *variable* FUNCTION "*I *expC1*"/PICTURE "@*I *expC2*"
[DEFAULT *expN1*] [SIZE *expN2, expN3*[, *expN4*]] [ENABLE/DISABLE]
[MESSAGE *expC3*] [VALID *expL1*] [WHEN *expL2*]
[COLOR SCHEME *expN5*/COLOR *color-pair list*]

This variation of the @...GET command is used to create invisible buttons. Invisible buttons are rectangular regions of the screen or of a window that can be selected. Use @...SAY commands to place characters over the region defined by the invisible button. When the button is selected, the characters in the region appear highlighted.

The invisible button specification code of *I along with a function or @*I as a picture, is what causes the @...GET command to display an invisible button.

Use *row,col* to specify the upper-left corner for the first invisible button. Use *variable* to specify the variable that stores the user's response. (Note that *variable* can be a memory variable, the name of a database field, or an array element.) *Variable* must be a numeric type. The value stored to *variable* corresponds to the invisible button that is selected. For example, if you create four invisible buttons on the screen and a user selects the third button, a value of 3 is stored to the variable.

Use FUNCTION *expC1* or PICTURE *expC2* to cause the @...GET command to display an invisible button. You must include the *I specification to force the display of an invisible button. To create additional invisible buttons, add a semicolon for each additional button. If PICTURE is used instead of FUNCTION, you must precede the *I specification with an at sign (@). The function or picture specification is enclosed in quotes.

Immediately following the *C specification, you can add the optional N, T, H, or V specifications. N indicates that selecting the button will not terminate the corresponding READ. T indicates that selecting the button will terminate the corresponding READ. (If N or T is not included, by default behavior the button does not terminate the corresponding READ.) H indicates that the buttons are arranged horizontally, and V indicates that the buttons are arranged vertically. (If H or V is not included, the default arrangement is a vertical one.)

You can use the DEFAULT *expr* option to create the memory variable if the variable specified by *variable* does not already exist. Use SIZE *expN2*, *expN3* [,*expN4*] to change the size of the invisible button. *ExpN2* specifies the height of the button, *expN3* specifies the width of the button, and *expN4* specifies spacing between buttons. Use the ENABLE/DISABLE options to allow or prevent activation of the button when the corresponding READ is issued. Use the MESSAGE *expC3* option to display the message specified as *expC3* when the button is selected.

You can use the VALID *expL1* option to perform validation when the button is chosen. Typically, *expL1* is a user-defined function. The optional WHEN clause permits or prohibits selection of the button. The logical expression following the WHEN option must evaluate to a logical true before the button can be selected. If the expression evaluates as false, the button cannot be selected, and it will be skipped over if it is placed between other GET fields.

Use the COLOR SCHEME or COLOR *color-pair list* options to change the default colors for the button.

Example

To display five invisible buttons using the FUNCTION clause, use statements like these:

```
STORE 1 TO MYCHOICE
@ 5,2 GET MYCHOICE FUNCTION "*I ;;;;" SIZE 2,8,1
READ
```

To display five invisible buttons using the PICTURE clause, use statements like these:

```
STORE 1 TO MYCHOICE
@ 5,2 GET MYCHOICE PICTURE "@*I ;;;;" SIZE 2,8,1
READ
```

@...GET to Make List Boxes

Syntax

@ *row,col* GET *variable* FROM *array*[RANGE *expN1*[, *expN2*]]
/POPUP *popupname* FUNCTION *expC1*/PICTURE *expC2* [DEFAULT *expr*]
[SIZE *expN2, expN3*] [ENABLE/DISABLE] [MESSAGE *expC3*] [VALID *expL1*]
[WHEN *expL2*] [COLOR SCHEME *expN5*/COLOR *color-pair list*]

This variation of the @...GET command is used to create list boxes. Like the list boxes used in FoxPro's dialog boxes, lists can provide users with a choice of options. The presence of the FROM *array* or POPUP *popupname* clauses are what cause the @...GET command to display a list. The items that appear in the list are taken from an array variable or from an existing popup menu. You use either FROM *array* or POPUP *popupname*, but not both.

Use *row, column* to specify the upper-left corner for the list. Use *variable* to specify the variable that stores the user's response. (Note that *variable* can be a memory variable, the name of a database field, or an array element.) *Variable* must be a numeric type or a character type. If *variable* is numeric, the chosen item's position in the list is stored. If *variable* is character, the item's prompt is stored.

Use FROM *array* if you want to build the list based on the contents of an array. The first element of the array becomes the first option in the list; the second element of the array becomes the second option in the list; and so on. Note that if the array is two-dimensional, only the elements in the first column of the array are used. Any elements in remaining columns are ignored. The optional RANGE clause can be used to limit the items in the list to a range of the array elements. Normally, items begin with the first element of the array and continue to the last element of the array. Use *expN1* to designate a different starting element in the array and *expN2* to designate a different ending element in the array.

Use POPUP *popupname* if you want to build the list based on the contents of an existing popup. Each item that appears in the popup will also appear in the list. (You must first use DEFINE POPUP to create the popup.)

Use FUNCTION *expC1* or PICTURE *expC2* along with the optional N or T specifications. N indicates that selecting a choice in the list will not terminate the corresponding READ. T indicates that selecting a choice will terminate the corresponding READ. (If N or T is not included, by default the choice does not terminate the corresponding READ.)

You can use the DEFAULT *expr* option to create the memory variable if the variable specified by *variable* does not already exist. Use SIZE [*expN2, expN3*] to change the size of the list; *expN2* specifies the height of the list box, and *expN3* specifies the width of the list box. (By default, the list box is made just large enough to contain all of the items in the list.) Use the ENABLE/DISABLE options to allow or prevent activation of the list when the corresponding READ is issued. Use the MESSAGE *expC3* option to display the message specified as *expC3* when the list is selected.

You can use the VALID *expL1* option to perform validation when a list option is chosen. Typically, *expL1* is a user-defined function. The optional WHEN clause permits or prohibits selection of a list option. The logical expression following the WHEN option must evaluate to a logical true before the item can be selected from the list. If the expression evaluates as false, the item cannot be selected.

Use the COLOR SCHEME or COLOR *color-pair list* options to change the default colors for the list.

Example

The following program creates a list that contains databases in the current directory.

```
CLEAR
SET TALK OFF
STORE 1 TO CHOOSER
DEFINE POPUP Bases FROM 4,5 PROMPT FILES LIKE *.DBF
@ 8,10 GET CHOOSER POPUP Bases SIZE 9,9
```

@...GET to Make Popups

Syntax

@ *row,col* GET *variable* FUNCTION "^ *expC1*"/PICTURE "@^ *expC2*"   *Version 2*
[DEFAULT *expr*] FROM *array* [RANGE *expN1*[, *expN2*]] [SIZE *expN3, expN4*]
[ENABLE/DISABLE] [MESSAGE *expC3*] [VALID *expL1*] [WHEN *expL2*]
[COLOR SCHEME *expN5*/COLOR *color-pair list*]

This variation of the @...GET command is used to create popups. The presence of the caret (^) specification within the FUNCTION or PICTURE clause is what causes the @...GET command to display the popup.

Use *row, col* to specify the upper-left corner for the popup. Use *variable* to specify the variable that stores the user's response. (Note that *variable* can be a memory variable, the name of a database field, or an array element.) *Variable* must be a numeric type or a character type. If *variable* is numeric, the chosen item's position in the popup is stored. If *variable* is character, the item's prompt is stored.

Use FUNCTION *expC1* or PICTURE *expC2* along with the caret (^) to specify that a popup is to be displayed. You must include the caret specification to force the display of a popup. If PICTURE is used instead of FUNCTION, you must precede the caret specification with an at sign (@). Immediately after the caret, you can include either of the optional N or T specifications. N indicates that selecting a choice in the popup will not terminate the corresponding READ. T indicates that selecting a choice will terminate the corresponding READ. (If N or T is not included, by default the choice does not terminate the corresponding READ.)

Use FROM *array* if you want to build the popup based on the contents of an array. The first element of the array becomes the first option in the popup; the second element of the array becomes the second option in the popup; and so on. Note that if the array is two-dimensional, only the elements in the first column of the array are used. Any elements in remaining columns are ignored. The optional RANGE clause can be used to limit the items in the popup to a range of the array elements. Normally, items begin with the first element of the array and continue to the last element of the array. Use *expN1* to designate a different starting element in the array and *expN2* to designate a different ending element in the array.

You can use the DEFAULT *expr* option to create the memory variable if the variable specified by *variable* does not already exist. Use SIZE [*expN3, expN4*] to change the size of the popup; *expN3* is ignored, and *expN4* specifies the width of the popup. (The height of a popup will always be determined by the number of items, regardless of what value you store to *expN3*.) Use the ENABLE/DISABLE options to allow or prevent activation of the popup when the corresponding READ is issued. Use the MESSAGE *expC3* option to display the message specified as *expC3* when an item from the popup is selected.

You can use the VALID *expL1* option to perform validation when a popup option is chosen. Typically, *expL1* is a user-defined function. The optional WHEN clause permits or prohibits selection of a popup option. The logical expression following the WHEN option must evaluate to a logical true before the item can be selected from the list. If the expression evaluates as false, the option cannot be selected.

Use the COLOR SCHEME or COLOR *color-pair list* option to change the default colors for the popup.

Example

The following example presents a popup with four choices (M/C, Visa, Amex, and Discover) available from the popup.

```
CLEAR
SET TALK OFF
STORE 1 TO CHOOSER
@ 8,10 GET CHOOSER FUNCTION "^ M/C;Visa;Amex;Discover"
READ
```

@...GET to Make Pushbuttons

Syntax

@ *row,col* GET *variable* FUNCTION "* *expC1*"/PICTURE "@* *expC2*"
[DEFAULT *expr*] [SIZE *expN1*, *expN2*[, *expN3*]] [ENABLE/DISABLE]
[MESSAGE *expC3*] [VALID *expL1*] [WHEN *expL2*]
[COLOR SCHEME *expN4*/COLOR *color-pair list*]

Version 2

This variation of the @...GET command is used to create pushbuttons. The presence of the asterisk (*) specification within the FUNCTION or PICTURE clause is what causes the @...GET command to display the pushbutton.

Use *row, column* to specify the location for the first button in a set of pushbuttons. Use *variable* to specify the variable that stores the user's response. (Note that *variable* can be a memory variable, the name of a database field, or an array element.) *Variable* must be a numeric type or a character type. If *variable* is numeric, the chosen item's position in the group of pushbuttons is stored. If *variable* is character, the pushbutton's prompt is stored.

Use FUNCTION *expC1* or PICTURE *expC2* along with the asterisk (*) to specify that a pushbutton is to be displayed. You must include the asterisk specification to force the display of a pushbutton. If PICTURE is used instead of FUNCTION, you must precede the asterisk specification with an at sign (@). Immediately after the asterisk, you can include either of the optional N, T, H, or V specifications. N indicates that selecting a choice in the popup will not terminate the corresponding READ. T indicates that selecting a choice will terminate the corresponding READ. (If N or T is not included, by default the choice does not terminate the corresponding READ.) H indicates that the buttons are arranged horizontally, and V indicates that the buttons are arranged vertically. (If H or V is not included, the default arrangement is a vertical one.) Following the optional specifications, you list the prompts needed for each pushbutton separated by semicolons, as shown by the example. A pushbutton will be created for each prompt you list.

You can use the DEFAULT *expr* option to create the memory variable if the variable specified by *variable* does not already exist. Use SIZE *expN1*, *expN2*[,*expN3*] to change the size of the pushbutton. As all pushbuttons are one row in height, *expN1* is ignored, but you must include a value if you wish to specify *expN2* or *expN3*. The value of *expN2* controls the width of the prompt (by default, prompts are as wide as needed to display all the characters). The value of *expN3* controls the spacing between the pushbuttons; by default, pushbuttons have no space between them when arranged vertically and are one space apart when arranged horizontally.

Use the ENABLE/DISABLE options to allow or prevent activation of the pushbutton when the corresponding READ is issued. Use the MESSAGE *expC3* option to display the message specified as *expC3* when an item from the pushbutton is selected.

You can use the VALID *expL1* option to perform validation when a pushbutton is chosen. Typically, *expL1* is a user-defined function. The optional WHEN clause permits or prohibits selection of a pushbutton. The logical expression following the WHEN option must evaluate to a logical true before the button can be selected. If the expression evaluates as false, the button cannot be selected.

Use the COLOR SCHEME or COLOR *color-pair list* options to change the default colors for the pushbuttons.

Example

The following example presents four pushbuttons with the prompts shown (M/C, Visa, Amex, or Discover) adjacent to the pushbuttons.

```
CLEAR
SET TALK OFF
STORE 1 TO CHOOSER
@ 8,10 GET CHOOSER FUNCTION "* M/C;Visa;Amex;Discover"
READ
```

@...GET to Make Radio Buttons

Syntax

Version 2

@ *row,col* GET *variable* FUNCTION "*R *expC1*"/PICTURE "@*R *expC2*"
[DEFAULT *expr*] [SIZE *expN1, expN2*[, *expN3*]] [ENABLE/DISABLE]
[MESSAGE *expC3*] [VALID *expL1*] [WHEN *expL2*]
[COLOR SCHEME *expN4*/COLOR *color-pair list*]

This variation of the @...GET command is used to create radio buttons. The presence of the asterisk and letter "R" (*R) specification within the FUNCTION or PICTURE clause is what causes the @...GET command to display the radio button.

Use *row, column* to specify the location for the first button in a set of radio buttons. Use *variable* to specify the variable that stores the user's response. (Note that *variable* can be a memory variable, the name of a database field, or an array element.) *Variable* must be a numeric type or a character type. If *variable* is numeric, the chosen item's position in the group of radio buttons is stored. If *variable* is character, the radio button's prompt is stored.

Use FUNCTION "*R *expC1*" or PICTURE "@*R *expC2*" to specify that a radio button is to be displayed. You must include this specification to force the display of a radio button. If PICTURE is used instead of FUNCTION, you must precede the specification with an at sign (@). Immediately after the specification, you can include either of the optional N, T, H, or V specifications. N indicates that selecting a choice from the radio buttons will not terminate the corresponding READ. T indicates that selecting a choice will terminate the corresponding READ. (If N or T is not included, by default the choice does not terminate the corresponding READ.) H indicates that the buttons are arranged horizontally, and V indicates that the buttons are arranged vertically. (If H or V is not included, the default arrangement is a vertical one.) Following the optional specifications, you'list the prompts needed for each radio button separated by semicolons, as shown by the example. A radio button will be created for each prompt you list.

You can use the DEFAULT *expr* option to create the memory variable if the variable specified by *variable* does not already exist. Use SIZE *expN1*, *expN2*[,*expN3*] to change the size of the radio button. As all radio buttons are one row in height, *expN1* is ignored, but you must include a value if you wish to specify *expN2* or *expN3*. The value of *expN2* controls the width of the prompt (by default, prompts are as wide as needed to display all the characters). The value of *expN3* controls the spacing between radio buttons; by default, radio buttons have no space between them when arranged vertically, and are one space apart when arranged horizontally.

Use the ENABLE/DISABLE options to allow or prevent activation of the radio button when the corresponding READ is issued. Use the MESSAGE *expC3* option to display the message specified as *expC3* when a radio button is selected.

You can use the VALID *expL1* option to perform validation when a radio button is chosen. Typically, *expL1* is a user-defined function. The optional WHEN clause permits or prohibits selection of a radio button. The logical expression following the WHEN option must evaluate to a logical true before the button can be selected. If the expression evaluates as false, the button cannot be selected.

Use the COLOR SCHEME or COLOR *color-pair list* options to change the default colors for the radio buttons.

Example

The following example presents four radio buttons, with four choices (M/C, Visa, Amex, and Discover) shown as prompts for the buttons.

```
CLEAR
SET TALK OFF
STORE 1 TO CHOOSER
@ 8,10 GET CHOOSER FUNCTION "*R M/C;Visa;Amex;Discover"
READ
```

@...MENU

Syntax

@ *row,col* MENU *array, expN1*[, *expN2*] [TITLE *expC*]

This command creates a popup menu. Note that the DEFINE BAR and DEFINE POPUP commands can accomplish the same result. DEFINE BAR and DEFINE POPUP are compatible with dBASE IV programs, while @ *row, col* MENU is compatible with FoxBASE+ programs. The row and column locations specify the left-corner location of the menu. *Array* contains a one-dimensional array that contains the menu items. *ExpN1* is the number of items in the menu. *ExpN2* is an optional number of menu items to be displayed on the screen at one time, to a maximum of 17 items. TITLE is an optional menu title that appears at the top of the menu window.

Example

The program shown below uses the @ *row,col* MENU command to create a popup menu with three options.

```
DIMENSION CHOICES(3,1)
STORE "Add records" TO CHOICES[1]
STORE "Edit records" TO CHOICES[2]
STORE "Delete record" TO CHOICES[3]
STORE 0 TO MCHOICE
@ 10,15 MENU CHOICES,3 TITLE "Data Menu"
READ MENU TO MCHOICE
```

@...PROMPT

Syntax

@ *row,col* PROMPT *expC* [MESSAGE *expC*]

This command, along with the MENU TO command, is used to create light-bar menus. (These commands for menu design are compatible with FoxBASE+ and Clipper; if compatibility with dBASE IV is desired, use the DEFINE POPUP and DEFINE BAR commands instead.) A series of PROMPT commands are used to display the options on the screen at the positions indicated by the *row, col* coordinates. The MENU TO command invokes the light-bar menu, and the user response is controlled by the cursor keys. A maximum of 128 prompts can be displayed on the screen at a time. If an optional message is included, the message appears at the row defined with the SET MESSAGE TO command when that particular option is highlighted in the menu.

Example

```
@ 5,5 PROMPT "1. Add records    "
@ 6,5 PROMPT "2. Edit records   "
@ 7,5 PROMPT "3. Delete records"
@ 8,5 PROMPT "4. Print records  "
@ 9,5 PROMPT "5. Quit System    "
MENU TO MYCHOICE DO CASE
        CASE MYCHOICE = 1
                DO ADDER
        CASE MYCHOICE = 2
                DO EDITOR
        CASE MYCHOICE = 3
                DO ERASER
        CASE MYCHOICE = 4
                DO REPORTER
        CASE MYCHOICE = 5
                QUIT
ENDCASE
```

@...TO

Syntax

@ *row,col* TO *row,col* [DOUBLE/PANEL/*border string*]
[COLOR *standard*[, *enhanced*]] [COLOR SCHEME *expN*]

Version 2

This variation of the @ command draws a line or a rectangular border (box) on the screen. The first value represents the upper-left screen coordinate, and the second value represents the lower-right screen coordinate. If both coordinates share a horizontal or vertical coordinate, a line is drawn; otherwise, a

rectangular border is drawn. When used with the DOUBLE options, the @ command draws double lines or borders (or a combination) on the screen. The PANEL option causes the line or border to be drawn with the panel character used by the default FoxPro windows COLOR *standard [,enhanced]* denotes a color pair combination for the foreground and background colors for the line or box. COLOR SCHEME is a numeric value from 1 to 11, denoting colors based on the corresponding color scheme (see SET COLOR OF SCHEME).

Example

To draw a single line from row 3, column 5 to row 3, column 50, enter the following:

```
@ 3,5 TO 3,50
```

To draw a double-line box, with the upper-left corner at row 4, column 1, and the lower-right corner at row 18, column 70, enter

```
@ 4,1 TO 18,70 DOUBLE
```

ACCEPT

Syntax

ACCEPT [*expC*] TO *memvar*

The ACCEPT command stores a character string to the memory variable *memvar*. ACCEPT can be followed by an optional character expression, *expC*. If this expression is included, its contents will appear on the screen when the ACCEPT command is executed.

Example

To display the prompt "Enter owner name:" and store to the memory variable OWNER the character string that the user enters in response to the prompt, the following command could be used.

```
ACCEPT "Enter owner name:" TO OWNER
```

ACTIVATE MENU

Syntax

ACTIVATE MENU *menuname* [PAD *padname*]

The ACTIVATE MENU command activates a predefined menu, and displays that menu on the screen. If the PAD option is specified, the highlight bar appears at the named pad; otherwise, the first pad in the menu is highlighted.

While more than one menu may be visible on the screen, the last menu activated is the currently active menu. The pads of the menu can be accessed either by highlighting the desired pad with the cursor keys and pressing ENTER or by using ALT plus the first letter of the pad name and pressing ENTER. You can deactivate a menu by pressing ESC or by using the DEACTIVATE MENU command.

HINT: *The main difference between ACTIVATE MENU and ACTIVATE POPUP is the type of menu displayed. Use ACTIVATE MENU if you want a horizontal (bar) menu; use ACTIVATE POPUP if you want a vertical menu.*

Example

In the section of program code shown below, the DEFINE MENU and DEFINE PAD commands are used to set up a bar menu with four choices: Add Records, Edit Records, Print Records, and Exit System. The ON SELECTION statements define which actions shall be taken when a particular menu option is chosen by the user. (To keep the example simple, each ON SELECTION statement calls a particular command, such as APPEND or EDIT. In most applications, the ON SELECTION statements will be used to call another routine for adding or editing records or performing some other task.) The ACTIVATE MENU statement that follows the ON SELECTION statement activates the menu, and the program awaits the user's response.

```
USE MEMBERS
SET INDEX TO NAMES
DEFINE MENU MainMenu MESSAGE "Press letter for desired option"
DEFINE PAD Addit OF MainMenu PROMPT "Add records"
DEFINE PAD Change OF MainMenu PROMPT "Edit records"
DEFINE PAD Print OF MainMenu PROMPT "Print records"
DEFINE PAD Quit OF MainMenu PROMPT "Exit System"
ON SELECTION PAD Addit OF MainMenu APPEND
ON SELECTION PAD Change OF MainMenu EDIT
ON SELECTION PAD Print OF MainMenu REPORT FORM MYFILE TO PRINT
```

```
ON SELECTION PAD Quit OF MainMenu DEACTIVATE MENU
ACTIVATE MENU MainMenu
QUIT
```

ACTIVATE POPUP

Syntax

ACTIVATE POPUP *popupname*

The ACTIVATE POPUP command activates a predefined popup menu and displays that popup on the screen. (Popup menus are vertical menus, with each successive choice under the prior choice.) To implement a popup menu, first define the menu with the DEFINE POPUP and DEFINE BAR commands. Then use the ACTIVATE POPUP command to activate the menu.

While more than one popup may be visible on the screen, the last popup activated is the currently active menu. The bars of the menu can be accessed in the order in which they were defined. You can deactivate a menu by pressing ESC or by using the DEACTIVATE MENU command.

Example

In the section of program code shown below, the DEFINE POPUP and DEFINE BAR commands are used to set up a popup menu with four choices: Add records, Edit records, Print records, and Exit System. In this example, the ON SELECTION statement executes a DEACTIVATE POPUP command. This is done so that the menu is not continually redisplayed, since in this case the rest of the program is enclosed in a DO WHILE .T. loop. The ACTIVATE MENU statement at the start of the DO WHILE .T. loop activates the menu, and the program awaits the user's response.

```
USE RENTALS
SET INDEX TO STOCKNO
DEFINE POPUP MainMenu FROM 3,15 TO 8,30
DEFINE BAR 1 OF MainMenu PROMPT " Add records"
DEFINE BAR 2 OF MainMenu PROMPT " Edit records"
DEFINE BAR 3 OF MainMenu PROMPT " Print records"
DEFINE BAR 4 OF MainMenu PROMPT " Exit System"
ON SELECTION POPUP MainMenu DO MainMenu
ACTIVATE POPUP MainMenu
RETURN
PROCEDURE MAINMENU DO CASE
```

```
      CASE BAR() = 1
      APPEND

      CASE BAR() = 2
      EDIT

      CASE BAR() = 3
      REPORT FORM RENTALS TO PRINT

      CASE BAR() = 4
      QUIT
   ENDCASE
   RETURN
```

ACTIVATE SCREEN

Syntax

ACTIVATE SCREEN

The **ACTIVATE SCREEN** command switches screen display from an active window to the full screen. The active window remains on the screen, and you can later use the ACTIVATE WINDOW command to redirect screen output to the window. While the ACTIVATE SCREEN command does not clear the window, it is possible to overwrite the window by successive screen operations. The program is responsible for maintaining any desired appearance of a window once the ACTIVATE SCREEN command has been used.

Keep in mind that when you use ACTIVATE SCREEN, you are returning from virtual screen coordinates to physical screen coordinates. In other words, the *row,col* positioning used with @...SAY commands was relative to the upper-left corner of the window; once you restore full-screen display with ACTIVATE SCREEN, the *row,col* positioning is now relative to the upper-left corner of the screen. This may call for different values for your cursor positioning in successive operations.

Example

The short data entry program below provides a help key (FI), implemented with the ON KEY command. When FI is pressed, the second program shown is run; in the program, ACTIVATE WINDOW is first used to display a window containing help text. Then, ACTIVATE SCREEN is used to switch output to the screen, so a series of often-used customer numbers can be displayed at the bottom of the screen while the help window remains in view.

```
ON KEY LABEL F1 DO HELP1
CLEAR STORE 0 TO CNUMB
@ 7,10 SAY "Customer account number:" GET CNUMB
READ
ON KEY
RETURN


*Help1.PRG*
DEFINE WINDOW HELPER FROM 3,5 TO 14,70 DOUBLE
ACTIVATE WINDOW HELPER
@  3,2 SAY "Enter the four digit customer account number."
@  4,2 SAY "The most common account numbers are at the"
@  5,2 SAY "bottom of the screen. See the customer directory"
@  6,2 SAY "for other account numbers."
@  8,2 SAY "Press any key..."
ACTIVATE SCREEN
@ 18,5 SAY "ABC Plumbing- 1001        Johnson Wallpaper- 1002"
@ 19,5 SAY "DJ's Improvements- 1003     Ace Auto- 1004"
@ 20,5 SAY "Klose Communications- 1005  Lee Accounting- 1006"
@ 21,0
WAIT " Press any key to continue..."
DEACTIVATE WINDOW HELPER
RETURN
```

ACTIVATE WINDOW

Syntax

ACTIVATE WINDOW *windowname list*/ALL [BOTTOM/TOP/SAME]
[NOSHOW] [IN WINDOW *windowname*/IN SCREEN]

The ACTIVATE WINDOW command activates a predefined window from memory. After the ACTIVATE WINDOW command is used, all screen output is directed to that window. If the ALL option is used, all defined windows in memory are displayed in the order in which they were defined. Use BOTTOM or TOP to place a window at the bottom or top of a stack of existing windows. The SAME option applies only to windows previously hidden with DEACTIVATE WINDOW or HIDE WINDOW. Use SAME to put the previously hidden window back in the same position it occupied earlier. Use the NOSHOW option to send output to a window without changing the window's status (for example, if it was hidden, output goes to the window but it remains hidden).

In FoxPro 1.02 and later, you can place desk accessories on the screen by naming the desk accessory in *windowname*. Use the names CALCULATOR,

CALENDAR, SPECIAL, ASCII, or PUZZLE to place the calculator, calendar, special characters, ASCII table, or puzzle in a window. Note that the desk accessory will be usable only when your program is awaiting input (as when a READ, BROWSE, MODIFY MEMO, or similar command has been executed).

In FoxPro 1.02 and later, the command also supports an optional [IN WINDOW *windowname*/IN SCREEN] clause. This clause lets you have background windows within windows or on the background screen.

When you include this clause, the inner window is dependent on the outer window. When the outer window is moved, the inner window moves with it. The inner window cannot be larger than the outer window and can be moved only within the confines of the outer window. If the outer window is closed, the inner window is closed with it. If the outer window is deactivated, the inner window is deactivated with it.

Example

The following program demonstrates how multiple windows can be used to highlight an application visually. The program asks for a user's name, displays a corresponding videotape limit value and video club membership expiration date, and then displays a list of videotapes rented by that member. The program shown below presents the information inside of multiple windows.

```
*WINDOWS.PRG shows off window use.*
STORE SPACE(15) TO MLAST
DEFINE WINDOW members1 FROM 5,5 TO 9,50
DEFINE WINDOW rentals1 FROM 8,8 TO 22,75
DEFINE WINDOW askthem FROM 3,15 TO 6,45
USE MEMBERS INDEX NAME
ACTIVATE WINDOW askthem
@ 1,1 SAY "Last name? " GET MLAST
READ
SEEK MLAST
IF .NOT. FOUND()
     @ 1,1 SAY "NAME NOT FOUND IN DATABASE!"
     WAIT
     DEACTIVATE WINDOW askthem
     CLOSE DATABASES
     RETURN
ENDIF
STORE SOCIAL TO FINDER
ACTIVATE WINDOW members1
@  1,2 SAY "Name: " + TRIM(Firstname) + " " + Lastname
@  2,2 SAY "Exp. date:"
@ 2,15 SAY EXPIREDATE
@ 2,25 SAY "Tape limit:"
```

```
@ 2,38 SAY TAPELIMIT
WAIT "Press a key to see rentals..."
SET ESCAPE OFF ACTIVATE WINDOW rentals1
SELECT 2
USE RENTALS
DISPLAY ALL OFF FOR SOCIAL = FINDER
WAIT "Press a key when done viewing..."
DEACTIVATE WINDOW ALL
CLOSE DATABASES
SET ESCAPE ON
RETURN
```

APPEND

Syntax

APPEND [BLANK]

The APPEND command appends records to a database. When the APPEND command is executed, a blank record is displayed, and FoxPro enters full-screen editing mode. The layout of the screen form matches the structure of the database currently in use, unless a format file is active or you used a SET FIELDS command. The cursor keys can be used to navigate between the various fields, and the BACKSPACE and DEL keys can be used for correcting errors. The APPEND process will be terminated if the user presses ESC, moves the cursor past the last field of an empty record, or presses ENTER without adding any data into the first field.

If the BLANK option is used, a blank record is added to the end of the database, but full-screen editing mode is not entered. The BLANK option is normally used within programs; first, an APPEND BLANK command adds a blank record, then a series of @...SAY...GET commands allow data to be entered into the fields of the new record.

APPEND FROM

Syntax

APPEND FROM *filename* [FIELDS *fieldlist*] [FOR *condition*] [TYPE *file type*] [DELIMITED [WITH *delimiter*/BLANK/TAB]]

APPEND FROM copies records from *filename* and appends them to the active database. The FOR/WHILE option specifies a *condition* that must be met before any records will be copied. If the filename containing the data to be copied is not a FoxPro database, an acceptable type option must be used. Valid type options in FoxPro 1.*x* are DELIMITED, DELIMITED WITH BLANK, DELIMITED WITH TAB, DELIMITED WITH *delimiter*, or SDF.

Example

The APPEND FROM command can be useful for merging the contents of multiple database files with the same structure. The commands listed below demonstrate the use of the APPEND FROM command to copy records from a small database file on a floppy disk into the active database file.

```
USE MEMBERS
APPEND FROM A:TEMP
```

With foreign files, the APPEND command is often used to transfer data into the database file format. For example, the following command could be used to append records from a Lotus spreadsheet into a database with a matching structure.

```
USE PAYROLL
APPEND FROM 123FILE.WK1 TYPE WK1
```

APPEND FROM ARRAY

Syntax

APPEND FROM ARRAY *array* FOR *condition*

The APPEND FROM ARRAY command appends records to a database file from a named array. (Note that APPEND FROM ARRAY is compatible with dBASE IV; if you need compatibility with FoxBASE+, use the GATHER FROM command instead.) The contents of each row in the array are transferred to a new record in the database file. The first column in the array becomes the first field, the second column in the array becomes the second field, and so on. If there are more elements in the array than fields in the database, the extra elements are ignored. If there are more fields in the database than there are elements in the array, the extra fields remain empty. The FOR clause, which is optional, lets you define a condition that must be met before data in the array will be added to a new record. An array must exist (be defined with DECLARE and filled with data using STORE) before you can successfully use the APPEND FROM ARRAY command.

Example

The data entry program shown below uses an array to store responses to @...SAY...GET commands. The values stored to the elements of the array are then transferred to the fields of the database. In operation, this example performs the same task as the example shown with the APPEND BLANK command. Note, however, that the use of APPEND FROM ARRAY eliminates the need for the usual REPLACE statements.

```
CLEAR
DECLARE M_DATA[1,6]
M_DATA[1,1] = SPACE(15)
M_DATA[1,2] = SPACE(15)
M_DATA[1,3] = SPACE(25)
M_DATA[1,4] = SPACE(15)
M_DATA[1,5] = SPACE(2)
M_DATA[1,6] = SPACE(10)
*display prompts, store data to variables.
@    3,5 SAY " LAST NAME:" GET M_DATA[1,1]
@    4,5 SAY "FIRST NAME:" GET M_DATA[1,2]
@    8,5 SAY "ADDRESS:" GET M_DATA[1,3]
@   10,5 SAY "    CITY:" GET M_DATA[1,4]
@ 10,35 SAY "STATE:" GET M_DATA[1,5]
@ 10,45 SAY "ZIP CODE:" GET M_DATA[1,6]
READ
*open database, make new record, store variables.
USE NAMES INDEX NAMES
APPEND FROM ARRAY M_DATA
CLOSE DATABASES
RETURN
```

APPEND MEMO

Syntax

APPEND MEMO *memofield* FROM *filename* [OVERWRITE]

The APPEND MEMO command imports a file into a memo field. If the OVERWRITE option is not used, the contents of the file are added to the end of any existing text in the memo field. If the OVERWRITE option is used, the contents of the file will overwrite any existing text in the memo field. FoxPro assumes that the file has an extension of .TXT. If this is not the case, the extension must be specified along with the filename. If the file has no extension, include a period at the end of the filename.

Example

Assuming the current database contains a memo field called COMMENTS, and a text file created with a word processor called LETTER.DOC is to be read into the memo field of the current record, the following command could be used.

```
APPEND MEMO COMMENTS FROM LETTER.DOC
```

AVERAGE

Syntax

> AVERAGE *fieldlist* [*scope*] [FOR *condition*] [WHILE *condition*]
> [TO *memvarlist*/TO ARRAY *array*]

The AVERAGE command computes an average of a specified numeric field listed in *fieldlist*. If the TO option is not used, the average is displayed onscreen. If TO is used, the average of the first field is assigned to the first memory variable, the average of the second field to the second memory variable, and so on down the list; and the average is stored as the memory variable specified. If the *scope* option is not used, the quantifier of ALL is assumed, meaning all records in the database will be averaged, unless you use the FOR or WHILE options. The FOR option can be used to specify a condition that must be met for the fields to be averaged. If you use the WHILE option, records will be averaged until the condition is no longer true.

Example

The following commands demonstrate the use of the AVERAGE command.

```
USE SALES
LIST OFF
```

```
SALESREP        REPNUMB AMTSOLD
Jones, C.         1003   350.00
Artis, K.         1008   110.00
Johnson, L.       1002   675.00
Walker, B.        1006  1167.00
Keemis, M.        1007    47.00
Williams, E.      1010   256.00
Smith, A.M        1009   220.00
Allen, L.         1005   312.00
Smith, A.         1001   788.50
Jones, J.         1011   875.00
Shepard, F.       1004  1850.00
Robertson, C.     1013   985.50
Keemis, M.        1007   362.00
Jones, J.         1011   519.00

AVERAGE

    AMTSOLD
    608.36     14 records averaged.

AVERAGE FOR SALESREP = KEEMIS, M.

    AMTSOLD
    204.50      2 records averaged.
```

BROWSE

Syntax

BROWSE FIELDS [*fieldlist*] [FORMAT] [FREEZE*field*] [LAST] [NOAPPEND]
[NOCLEAR] [NODELETE] [NOEDIT/NOMODIFY] [NOMENU]
[NOFOLLOW] [NORMAL] [NOWAIT] [SAVE] [WIDTH *expN*]
[WINDOW *windowname*] [COLOR [*standard*][, *enhanced*][, *border*]]/
[COLOR SCHEME *expN*] [IN WINDOW *windowname*/IN SCREEN]

Syntax for FoxPro 2

BROWSE FIELDS [*fieldlist*] [FOR *clause*] [FORMAT] [FREEZE *field*] [LAST]
[NOAPPEND]   [NOCLEAR]   [NODELETE]   [NOEDIT/NOMODIFY]
[NOMENU] [NOFOLLOW] [NORMAL] [NOWAIT] [SAVE] [WIDTH *expN*]

[WINDOW *windowname*] [PREFERENCE *expC*] [COLOR [*standard*]
[, *enhanced*][, *border*]]/[COLOR SCHEME *expN*] [NOOPTIMIZE] [NOLINK]
[NOLGRID] [NORGRID] [LEDIT] [LPARTITION] [PARTITION *n*]
[REDIT] [TIMEOUT *n*]

The BROWSE command displays records from a database in a tabular format. If the database contains too many fields to fit on the screen, BROWSE displays only the fields that fit. More fields can be viewed by scrolling to the left or right with the mouse or the TAB key. (If you have an EGA or VGA monitor, you can also fit more fields and records on the screen by using the SET DISPLAY command; see SET DISPLAY TO.) The contents of any field can be edited while in BROWSE mode. To save changes made during BROWSE, press CTRL-W; to exit BROWSE, press ESC. The FIELDS option will display only the fields listed in *fieldlist*. FORMAT tells the Browse window to assume any settings of an active format file. FREEZE *field* freezes the cursor within the named field. LAST tells FoxPro to use the most recent configuration (window size, column sizes) of Browse, as stored in the FOXUSER configuration file. NORMAL causes the Browse window to assume normal color attributes, rather than those of a previously defined window.

If NOFOLLOW is included, changes to a field that is part of an index expression will not cause the Browse display to follow the record to its new location in the database. The NOWAIT option is used within programs; when included, program control continues immediately after the Browse window is opened, rather than waiting for the user to exit the Browse mode. The SAVE option is also used only in programs; it keeps both the Browse window and any memo field window that is active both open after editing is completed.

The NOAPPEND, NOEDIT, and NODELETE options restrict the use of appending, editing, or deleting when in the BROWSE mode. The WIDTH option lets you adjust the width of columns. The WINDOW option causes the BROWSE display to appear in a previously defined window. NOMENU prevents user access to the Browse menu. NOCLEAR leaves the Browse window visible on the screen after the Browse Mode is exited. The COLOR or COLOR SCHEME options may be used to specify colors for the Browse window.

HINT: *The NOAPPEND, NOEDIT, NOMODIFY, and NODELETE options are powerful tools for controlling the use of BROWSE within programs.*

If the FOR clause is included, only records matching the logical expression specified in the FOR clause will be included in the Browse window. The LEDIT and REDIT clauses cause the Browse window to be split, with one side in the Change (or Edit) mode. Use LEDIT to place the left half of the window in Edit mode; use REDIT to place the right half of the window in Edit mode. *Version 2* The PARTITION *n* clause forces the Browse window to split into partitions; the numeric value *n* specifies the column where the window is split. Use LPARTITION along with the PARTITION clause; when LPARTITION is

included, the cursor is placed in the first field of the left partition. The PREFERENCE clause lets you save the various attributes and options used by the Change window for later reuse. The attributes and options for the window are saved to the FOXUSER resource file.

Version 2

The NOLGRID and NORGRID clauses remove the field lines from the left or right partitions of a split Browse window. Use NOLGRID to remove the field lines from the left partition, and use NORGRID to remove the field lines from the right grid. The NOLINK clause breaks the normal link between the two sides of a split Browse window, allowing independent movement in each side. The NOOPTIMIZE clause turns off FoxPro's internal optimization techniques. The TIMEOUT *n* clause lets you specify how long a Browse window will wait for input; the value of *n* (in seconds) controls the length of time the window remains on the screen without any user input before the window closes. Note that the TIMEOUT clause can only be used in programs; it has no effect when used from the Command window.

The complete format for the FIELDS clause when used along with the BROWSE command is as follows

BROWSE FIELDS *fieldname1* [/R] [/*expN1*] [/V = *expr1* [:E = *expC1*] [:F]]
[:B = *expr2, expr3*] [:W = *expL1*] [, *fieldname2*] [/R]...

The optional switches perform the following functions:

/R	Read-only: Specifies field as a read-only field; no changes will be permitted in that field.
/*expN1*	Specifies the width of a field in the Browse window. This does not affect the actual size of the field, only the width of the column display in Browse mode.
/V	Verify: This option lets you perform data validation within a Browse window. The contents of the field are compared to *expr1*, which can be a numeric or a logical expression.
:F	Forced validation: This controls how validation is performed. If this option is omitted, comparisons caused by the /V option are made only if the contents of the field are changed. If this option is included along with the /V option, the comparison is made whether the field contents are changed or not.
:E	Error: Normally, if the validation expression (*expr1*) evaluates to true, a normal exit from the field is allowed. If the expression evaluates to false, an exit is not allowed, and an error message "Invalid Input" appears. When you include the :E option, then the contents of the expression *expr1* are displayed instead of the "Invalid Input" error message, and the bell sounds (if SET BELL is ON).

:B   Bounds: Use this option to specify a set of boundaries, or range, between which the data entered in the field must fall. *Expr2* specifies the lower limit, and *expr3* specifies the upper limit. You can use this option with numeric, string, or date expressions, but not within a user-defined function.

:W   When: This option prohibits entry into a field based on the value of the logical expression *expL1*. The :W option causes the expression to be evaluated when the BROWSE command is executed. If the expression evaluates to a logical false, data entry into the named field is prohibited.

Versions of FoxPro 1.01 and later offer a KEY clause that can be used with the BROWSE command. The syntax for this option is BROWSE KEY *expr*, where *expr* represents an index key expression. The KEY clause can only be used when an index file is active, and it causes the available records in the Browse window to be limited to those which match the key expression in the index. For example, assuming a database contains a State field that is indexed, the command BROWSE KEY "OH" would limit the Browse display to only those records with "OH" (Ohio) in the STATE field. Check your FoxPro documentation to see whether your version supports this option or not.

In FoxPro 1.02 and later, the command also supports an optional [IN WINDOW *windowname*/IN SCREEN] clause. This clause lets you have background windows within windows or on the background screen.

When you include this clause, the inner window is dependent on the outer window. When the outer window is moved, the inner window moves with it. The inner window cannot be larger than the outer window and can be moved only within the confines of the outer window. If the outer window is closed, the inner window is closed with it. If the outer window is deactivated, the inner window is deactivated with it.

Example

The various options can be used with the BROWSE command to provide a display suited to your editing needs. For example, the following command selectively limits a browse display to those fields named, with the width of each column set at 15 spaces, and the cursor frozen in the Salary field.

```
BROWSE FIELDS Last, First, Salary FREEZE Salary WIDTH 15
```

BUILD APP

Syntax

BUILD APP *expC1* FROM *expC2*

Version 2

The BUILD APP command is used to convert information stored in a project file into a complete application. This command is typically used by programmers in building applications for mass distribution.

Use *expC1* to specify the filename for the application. Use *expC2* to specify the name of the existing project database file from which the application will be built. Before using the BUILD APP command, make sure that the project file contains all objects needed for the application.

For more details on the process of building applications, refer to Chapter 13.

BUILD PROJECT

Syntax

Version 2

BUILD PROJECT *expC1* FROM *expC2*

The BUILD PROJECT command is used to create a project database by opening and processing one or more database, program, screen, report, label, or library files, named as *expC2*. The project database can then be used along with the BUILD APP command to build a complete application. This command is typically used by programmers in building applications for mass distribution.

The BUILD PROJECT command automatically creates a project database, *expC1*, a special type of FoxPro database with a .PJX extension. The project database maintains a record of all files required to build the application, as well as any dependencies and references between the files. The project file can later be used to create two types of files: an application, which requires FoxPro to run, or a freestanding executable (.EXE) file, which does not require FoxPro to run.

For more details on the process of building projects, refer to Chapter 13.

CALCULATE

Syntax

CALCULATE [*scope*] *options* [FOR *condition*] [WHILE *condition*]
[TO *memvarlist*/TO ARRAY *array* >]

Syntax for FoxPro 2

CALCULATE [*scope*] *options* [FOR *condition*] [WHILE *condition*]
[TO *memvarlist*/TO ARRAY *array* >] [NOOPTIMIZE]

The CALCULATE command calculates amounts using standard financial and statistical functions. The functions are defined as part of the options list, shown below. All records are processed until the *scope* is completed or the *condition* is no longer true. The following financial and statistical functions can be used within the options list:

AVG(*expN*) Calculates the numerical average of value *expN*.

CNT() Counts the records in a database file. If a condition has been specified with the FOR clause, the condition must be met before the record will be counted.

MAX(*expr*) Determines the maximum value in a field. *Expr* is usually a field name or an expression that translates to a field name.

MIN(*expr*) Determines the minimum value in a field. *Expr* is usually a field name or an expression that translates to a field name.

NPV(*rate, flows,initial*) Calculates the net present value, where *rate* is the discount rate, *flows* is a series of signed periodic cash flow values, and *initial* is the initial investment.

STD(*expr*) Determines the standard deviation of values stored in a database field. *Expr* is usually a field name or an expression that translates to a field name.

SUM(*expr*) Determines the sum of the values in a database field. *Expr* is usually a field name or an expression that translates to a field name.

VAR(*expr*) Determines the variance of the values in a database field. *Expr* is usually a field name or an expression that translates to a field name. The value supplied by VAR(*expr*) is a floating-point number.

The TO ARRAY option can be added to the CALCULATE command. This option causes the results of the command to be stored in the elements of a one-dimensional array. (Use the DECLARE command first to create the array.) The results are stored in order, beginning with the first array element and continuing until all the results of the AVERAGE command have been stored. If there are too many results to fit in the array, the extra results are discarded. If there are extra array elements left over after the results are stored, the extra elements remain unchanged.

The NOOPTIMIZE clause is used to disable the normal internal optimization technology (Rushmore) present in FoxPro 2.

Example

The listing below shows a database containing currency amounts for various business expenses. In the statements shown after the listing, the CALCULATE command is used, first to obtain a count of records and the average, maximum, and minimum values of the Amount field, and secondly to obtain an average value of all records where "Office Supplies" is stored in the Category field.

```
USE FINANCE
LIST

DATES      AMOUNT CATEGORY            DESCRIBE
04/09/86    17.77 Office Supplies     Ribbon, envelopes
05/02/86    17.00 Travel              Cab fare to courthouse
05/15/86     0.63 Office Supplies     Copying costs
07/09/86    26.72 Office Supplies     Office Supplies
08/15/86    15.85 Office Supplies     Printer ribbon
09/18/86    10.61 Office Supplies     Office Supplies
10/07/86    25.90 Office Supplies     Ribbon and paper
10/10/86     9.95 Office Supplies     Ribbon
10/20/86     8.27 Office Supplies     Printer ribbon
12/11/86    12.00 Travel              Cab fare to courthouse
01/19/87   197.00 Travel              Shuttle fare to NY
01/28/87    10.66 Postage             Express mail shipment
01/28/87    62.70 Office Supplies     Office table for copier
02/06/87     5.25 Office Supplies     Folders, envelopes
02/11/87     3.24 Office Supplies     Folders

CALCULATE CNT(), AVG(Amount), MAX(Amount), MIN(Amount)

    CNT()    AVG(Amount) MAX(Amount)   MIN(Amount)
      15         28.24         197          0.63

CALCULATE AVG(Amount) FOR CATEGORY = "Office Supplies"

  AVG(Amount)
      16.99
```

CALL

Syntax

CALL *modulename* [WITH *expC/memvar*] [SAVE/NOSAVE]

The CALL command executes a binary (assembly language) program that was previously loaded into memory with the LOAD command (see LOAD).

Modulename is the name of the binary file; the usual .BIN extension may be omitted. The WITH option is used to pass the value of the expression or memory variable to the binary program. When a program processes the CALL command, control is passed to the binary routine, and execution begins at the first byte of the routine. Once control passes to the routine, the data segment (DS and BX registers) will contain the address for the first byte of the memory variable or character expression that was passed from the dBASE language program.

Binary files loaded and executed with the CALL command are treated differently than external program files executed with RUN. When the RUN command is used, a DOS shell is created, and control is transferred to the program called with RUN. By comparison, with CALL, the binary files are treated as subroutines or "modules," and not as external programs. As a result, considerably less additional memory is needed to use CALL. Up to 16 binary files can be loaded into memory at once, and each binary file can be up to 32K in size.

The SAVE and NOSAVE clauses are used with binary routines that write to the screen. If you include the SAVE clause, FoxPro copies the contents of video RAM into FoxPro's desktop when control returns from the binary routine; hence, data written by the binary routine becomes known to FoxPro and will not be overwritten by the appearance of the FoxPro screen. The NOSAVE clause (which is the default) causes FoxPro to ignore (and overwrite) any video changes made by the binary routine.

The CALL command should only be used with external programs designed as binary modules. (Normal executable programs should be accessed with the RUN/! command.)

Example

To call a binary routine named CURSOR.BIN and pass to that routine the value of ASCII 18, the following statement could be used.

```
CALL CURSOR WITH CHR(18)
```

CANCEL

Syntax

CANCEL

The CANCEL command halts execution of a program and returns control to the command window. All open program files are closed. However, other open files (such as database and index files) remain open, and existing public memory variables remain active in memory. (Private memory variables are cleared by CANCEL.)

CHANGE

Syntax

CHANGE [*scope*] [FIELDS *fieldlist*] [FOR *condition*] [WHILE *condition*]
[NOAPPEND] [NOCLEAR] [NOEDIT] [NODELETE]
[IN WINDOW *windowname*/IN SCREEN]

Syntax for FoxPro 2

CHANGE [*scope*] [FIELDS *fieldlist*] [FOR *condition*] [WHILE *condition*]
[FREEZE *field*] [KEY *expr1*[, *expr2*]] [LAST] [LEDIT] [REDIT]
[LPARTITION] [NOAPPEND] [NOCLEAR] [NODELETE]
[NOEDIT/NOMODIFY] [NOLINK] [NOMENU] [NOOPTIMIZE]
[NORMAL] [NOWAIT] [SAVE] [TIMEOUT *expN*] [TITLE *expC*]
[VALID [:F] *expL* [ERROR *expC*]] [WHEN *expL*] [WIDTH *expN*]
[WINDOW *windowname*] [IN WINDOW *windowname*/IN SCREEN]
[PREFERENCE *expC*] [COLOR [*standard*][, *enhanced*][, *border*]]/
[COLOR SCHEME *expN*]

The CHANGE command permits editing of fields listed in *fieldlist*. If the *scope* option is absent, the quantifier ALL is assumed. The FOR/WHILE option allows editing to only those records satisfying the condition. The NOAPPEND, NOEDIT, and NODELETE options restrict appending, editing, or deleting of records. The NOCLEAR option leaves the display on the screen after the user exits the CHANGE process. The WIDTH option specifies a maximum width for fields in the Change window. Note that the CHANGE command is operationally identical to the EDIT command.

In FoxPro 1.02 and later, the command also supports an optional [IN WINDOW *windowname*/IN SCREEN] clause. This clause lets you have background windows within windows or on the background screen.

When you include this clause, the inner window is dependent on the outer window. When the outer window is moved, the inner window moves with it. The inner window cannot be larger than the outer window and can be moved only within the confines of the outer window. If the outer window is closed, the inner window is closed with it. If the outer window is deactivated, the inner window is deactivated with it.

In FoxPro 2, the FREEZE clause is used to freeze a field; changes can then be made only to the specified field. The KEY clause is used to specify an index key value. Use *expr1* to specify a single value matching one found in the index; use *expr1,expr2* to specify a range of values. The CHANGE command will then allow editing only of those records which match the index key values. Use LEDIT to place the left half of the window in Edit mode; use REDIT to place the right half of the window in Edit mode. By default, the cursor appears in the first field of the

Version 2

right partition when the window is split; when LPARTITION is included, the cursor is placed in the first field of the left partition. LAST tells FoxPro to use the most recent configuration (window size, column sizes) of Browse, as stored in the FoxUser configuration file. NORMAL causes the Browse window to assume normal color attributes, rather than those of a previously defined window. The NOWAIT option is used within programs; when included, program control continues immediately after the Browse window is opened, rather than waiting for the user to exit the Browse mode. The SAVE option is also used only in programs; it keeps both the Browse window and any memo field window that is active open after editing is completed. The NOOPTIMIZE clause turns off FoxPro's internal optimization techniques.

The PREFERENCE clause lets you save the various attributes and options used by the Change window, for later reuse. The attributes and options for the window are saved to the FOXUSER resource file. The TIMEOUT *n* clause lets you specify how long the window will wait for input; the value of *n* (in seconds) controls the length of time the window remains on the screen without any user input before the window closes. Note that the TIMEOUT clause can only be used in programs; it has no effect when used from the Command window. Use the TITLE clause to specify a title that may appear in the top border of the Change window. Use the VALID clause to perform record-by-record validation. If a change is made to the record and the logical expression returned by the VALID clause evaluates to false, the error message "Invalid Input" is displayed. (You can change the default error message by including your own character expression along with the optional ERROR clause.) Include the optional :F parameter after the VALID clause to force validation even if the cursor is not moved to the next record. When this parameter is included, validation takes place even when the record is unchanged.

Use the WHEN clause to control whether or not changes can be made to a record. If the logical expression specified by WHEN evaluates to false, changes cannot be made to a record. If the logical expression evaluates to true, changes are permitted.

Example

To edit a database while limiting the available fields to Lastname and Firstname fields in a database, the following command could be used.

```
CHANGE FIELDS Lastname, Firstname
```

CLEAR

Syntax

```
CLEAR
```

The CLEAR command erases the screen. CLEAR can also be used as an option of the @ command to clear the screen below and to the right of the location specified by the @ command.

Example

To erase the entire screen, the following command could be used.

```
CLEAR
```

To erase the screen below and to the right of the cursor at 12,20, the following command could be used.

```
@ 12,20 CLEAR
```

CLEAR ALL

Syntax

CLEAR ALL

The CLEAR ALL command closes all open database, memo, index, and format files, and resets the current work area to 1.

CLEAR FIELDS

Syntax

CLEAR FIELDS

The CLEAR FIELDS command clears the list of fields specified by the SET FIELDS command. The CLEAR FIELDS command has no effect if SET FIELDS was not previously used to specify fields (see SET FIELDS) or if a view file has not established a list of fields. The CLEAR FIELDS command automatically performs a SET FIELDS OFF; this makes all fields of the current database available for use.

NOTE: A SET FIELDS TO command, without a list of fields, can also clear the field list from memory. The major difference between a SET FIELDS TO command and a CLEAR FIELDS command is that CLEAR FIELDS will clear any fields lists in effect in all work areas. By comparison, a SET FIELDS TO command without a field list will clear the field list in the current work area only.

CLEAR GETS

Syntax

CLEAR GETS

The CLEAR GETS command clears all pending GETS or all GETS that have not yet been accessed by a READ command. Use CLEAR GETS to prevent the next READ command in the program from invoking full-screen editing of the fields or variables named in the previous GETS.

The CLEAR GETS command can be useful for editing routines when you want to display all fields in reverse video (or in a color as chosen by the SET COLOR commands), but you do not want to permit editing in all fields. The CLEAR GETS command can be used, and any GETS prior to the CLEAR GETS command will be visible on the screen, but editing will be permitted only in the fields named after the CLEAR GETS command.

Example

In the following editing program, the Lastname and Firstname fields appear in reverse video, but cannot be edited. The CLEAR GETS command clears the GETS, causing the cursor to first appear in the Grade field.

```
SET TALK OFF
STORE "N" TO ANSWER
USE EMPLOYED
DO WHILE .NOT. EOF()
    CLEAR
    @  5,5 SAY "Name:"
    @ 5,10 GET Firstname
    @ 5,32 GET Lastname
    CLEAR GETS
    @  7,5 SAY "Grade:" GET GRADE
    @  9,5 SAY "Salary:" GET SALARY
    @ 11,5 SAY "Date of hire:" GET HIREDATE
    READ
```

```
    CLEAR
    @ 5,5 SAY "Edit another? Y/N:" GET ANSWER
    READ
    IF UPPER(ANSWER) = "N"
        EXIT
    ENDIF
    SKIP
ENDDO
```

CLEAR MACROS

Syntax

CLEAR MACROS

The CLEAR MACROS command releases all keyboard macros from memory.

CLEAR MEMORY

Syntax

CLEAR MEMORY

The CLEAR MEMORY command erases all current memory variables. If any array elements are in memory, they are also released by CLEAR MEMORY.

NOTE: CLEAR MEMORY and RELEASE ALL have different results when used within programs. CLEAR MEMORY clears all existing memory variables. By comparison, RELEASE ALL clears only private memory variables or those variables created within the subroutine where RELEASE ALL was used.

Example

The following commands demonstrate the effect of the CLEAR MEMORY command.

```
STORE "Johnson" TO NAME
STORE 105 TO AMOUNT
STORE DATE() TO TODAY
```

```
LIST MEMORY

NAME        pub   C   "Johnson"
AMOUNT      pub   N         105  (       105.00000000)
TODAY       pub   D   02/19/90
     3 variables defined,        27 bytes used
   253 variables available,    5973 bytes available

CLEAR MEMORY
LIST MEMORY

     0 variables defined,         0 bytes used
   256 variables available,    6000 bytes available
```

CLEAR MENUS

Syntax

    CLEAR MENUS

The CLEAR MENUS command clears all menus from the screen and erases all menus from memory. Any memory used by any bar menus is again available for program use after the CLEAR MENUS command has been used.

CLEAR POPUPS

Syntax

    CLEAR POPUPS

The CLEAR POPUPS command clears all popup menus from the screen and erases all popup menus from memory. Any memory used by any popup menus is again available for program use after the CLEAR POPUPS command has been used.

CLEAR PROGRAM

Syntax

CLEAR PROGRAM

The CLEAR PROGRAM command clears the buffer of any compiled program. You may need to use CLEAR PROGRAM when modifying FoxPro programs with your own editor. FoxPro stores programs that are running in memory. If you run a program, edit that program with your own editor, and run the program again, FoxPro will run the program from memory, rather than running the modified program from disk. To prevent this from happening, use the CLEAR PROGRAM command to clear the buffer after editing a program with your own editor (or you can also use the SET DEVELOPMENT ON command; see SET DEVELOPMENT).

CLEAR PROMPT

Syntax

CLEAR PROMPT

The CLEAR PROMPT command releases all menu prompts created with the @...PROMPT command from a screen or a window. Any memory used by any prompts is again available for program use after the CLEAR PROMPT command has been used.

CLEAR READ

Syntax

CLEAR READ [ALL]

The CLEAR READ command is used to terminate the current READ. When CLEAR READ is used, program control returns to the previous READ command (if any). If the optional ALL clause is included, all reads at all levels are cleared. The CLEAR READ command may be useful when multiple data entry screens are displayed by using nested levels of @...SAY...GET commands followed by multiple READ statements.

CLEAR TYPEAHEAD

Syntax

CLEAR TYPEAHEAD

The CLEAR TYPEAHEAD command clears the contents of the typeahead buffer (see SET TYPEAHEAD). The command can be useful as a part of operator input routines, when you want to ensure that an accidental keypress is not interpreted as an intentional key. You can use CLEAR TYPEAHEAD to clear the buffer of any previously received keystrokes, then use your ACCEPT, INPUT, or @..SAY..GET command to interpret any new input from the keyboard.

Example

In the following program, the CLEAR TYPEAHEAD command is used to clear the keyboard buffer before a WAIT command is used to acknowledge that a printer is ready. This prevents the report from being printed due to an accidental extra keypress.

```
*REPORT.PRG*
USE RENTALS
CLEAR TYPEAHEAD
WAIT "Press C to cancel, any other key for report." TO DOIT
IF UPPER(DOIT) = "C"
    RETURN
ENDIF
REPORT FORM RENTALS TO PRINT
RETURN
```

CLEAR WINDOWS

Syntax

CLEAR WINDOWS

The CLEAR WINDOWS command clears all active windows from the screen and erases all windows from memory. (See DEFINE WINDOW.) Any screen operations that take place after the CLEAR WINDOWS command will be written to the full screen, unless another window is defined and activated with the

DEFINE WINDOW and ACTIVATE WINDOW commands. Also, note that any text that was underlying a window when that window was activated will again be visible after the CLEAR WINDOWS command.

If you have not saved any defined windows to a disk file, they will be lost when you use CLEAR WINDOWS. If you are going to make use of the same windows often throughout a program, you can save programming time (and speed up the program slightly) by saving the windows to a disk file with the SAVE WINDOWS command. Then use CLEAR WINDOWS when the windows are no longer desired; later, you can use RESTORE WINDOWS to restore the windows to active memory, rather than defining them all over again.

CLOSE

Syntax

CLOSE *filetype*/ALL

The CLOSE command closes all file types listed in *filetype*. *Filetype* can be one of five: ALTERNATE, DATABASES, FORMAT, INDEX, or PROCEDURE. If the ALL option is used, all open files are closed, including any that may have been opened using low-level file functions of FoxPro.

CLOSE MEMO

Syntax

CLOSE MEMO *memofield1*[, *memofield2*...]/ALL

The CLOSE MEMO command closes an open memo field window. You can specify the memo window by name (using the name of the memo field, as shown in the syntax). Or, you can use the ALL option to close all open memo windows.

Any edits made to the memo field will be saved when the memo window is closed. Note that closing a database with the CLOSE DATABASES, CLOSE ALL, or USE commands will also result in any memo window for that associated database being closed.

COMPILE

Syntax

COMPILE *filename/skeleton* [ENCRYPT] [NODEBUG]

The COMPILE command reads a FoxPro program (or command) file and creates an object (.DBO) file, which is an execute-only FoxPro program file. A skeleton composed of wildcards can be used in place of the filename. For example, entering **COMPILE M*.PRG** would compile all .PRG files beginning with the letter "M."

The ENCRYPT option, when added, causes the compiled file to be encrypted. This is useful for added security, and it prevents others from examining your program code. The NODEBUG clause, when added, reduces the compiled program's size. If you use this option, note that you will not be able to see each line of the program highlighted in the Trace Window during debugging.

The DO command will also compile any program file that has not yet been compiled. The main purpose of the COMPILE command is to provide a way to compile program files without executing those files. Note that since the compilation process checks the program code for syntax errors and missing control structures, using COMPILE can be helpful when debugging a program.

Example

Entering the first command shown here would compile a file named MAIN.PRG. Entering the second command shown would compile all .PRG files beginning with the letter "M."

```
COMPILE MAIN.PRG
COMPILE M*.PRG
```

CONTINUE

Syntax

CONTINUE

The CONTINUE command resumes a search started by the LOCATE command. After LOCATE finds the record matching the criteria specified in the command, you can find additional records that meet the same criteria by entering CONTINUE. When a record is found by the CONTINUE command, the record pointer is moved to that record, the record number is displayed (if SET TALK is ON), and the EOF() function will return a logical false (.F.). If a matching record is not found, the message "End of LOCATE scope" is displayed, and the EOF() function will return a logical true (.T.). The FOUND() function will return a logical .T. if the CONTINUE is successful, and a logical .F. if the CONTINUE is unsuccessful.

HINT: *The CTRL-K key can be used as a substitute for the CONTINUE command.*

When using multiple databases, note that LOCATE and CONTINUE work in the work areas where you issued the commands. You can use a separate LOCATE or CONTINUE command in different work areas.

Example

The commands below show the use of CONTINUE to locate all records with a specific name in the Title field.

```
USE RENTALS
LIST TITLE, DAYRENTED
```

```
Record#  TITLE                    DAYRENTED
      1  Star Trek IV             03/05/90
      2  Lethal Weapon II         03/02/90
      3  Who Framed Roger Rabbit  03/06/90
      4  Beverly Hills Cop II     03/04/90
      5  Dirty Rotten Scoundrels  03/01/90
      6  Young Einstein           03/04/90
      7  When Harry Met Sally     03/06/90
      8  Lethal Weapon II         03/07/90
      9  Friday 13th Part XXVII   03/14/90
     10  Licence To Kill          03/15/90
     11  When Harry Met Sally     03/17/90
     12  Coming To America        03/14/90
     13  When Harry Met Sally     03/16/90
     14  Star Trek V              03/18/90
     15  Young Einstein           03/19/90
     16  Licence To Kill          03/16/90
```

```
LOCATE FOR TITLE = "When Harry Met Sally"

   Record = 7


CONTINUE
```

```
    Record = 11

CONTINUE

    Record = 13

CONTINUE

    End of Locate scope.
```

COPY

Syntax

COPY TO *filename* [*scope*] [FIELDS *fieldlist*] [FOR *condition*] [WHILE *condition*]
[TYPE SDF/DBMEMO3/FOXPLUS/DELIMITED [WITH *delimiter*]]

Syntax for FoxPro 2

COPY TO *filename* [*scope*] [FIELDS *fieldlist*] [FOR *condition*] [WHILE *condition*]
[[WITH] CDX | PRODUCTION] [NOOPTIMIZE] [TYPE]
[DBMEMO3/FOXPLUS/DIF/MOD/SDF/SYLK/WK1/WKS/WR1/WRK/XLS/
DELIMITED [WITH *delimiter*/WITH BLANK/WITH TAB]]

The COPY command copies all or part of the active database to *filename*. If
scope is not listed, ALL is assumed. The FIELDS option is used to pinpoint the
fields to be copied. The FOR option copies only those records meeting the
condition. The WHILE option copies records as long as the condition is true.
Specifying SDF will copy the file in System Data format; specifying DELIMITED
will copy the file in Delimited format. The DBMEMO3 or FOXPLUS type is used
when databases with memo fields must be copied out to FoxBASE+/dBASE
III+ file format.

Additional TYPE options can be used with FoxPro 2 to copy to foreign files.
The additional type options are DIF, MOD, SYLK, WK1, WKS, WR1, WRK, and
XLS. DIF is Data Interchange Format; MOD is Microsoft Multiplan version 4.01;
SYLK is Microsoft SYLK format; XLS is Microsoft Excel format; and WK1, WKS,
WR1, and WRK are Lotus 1-2-3 formats.

Use the WITH CDX or WITH PRODUCTION clauses to specify whether a
new structural compound-index file should be created along with the new
database. (Both options perform the same task; include WITH CDX or WITH

PRODUCTION if you want the .CDX file created with the database file.) The NOOPTIMIZE clause is used to disable the normal internal optimization technology (Rushmore) present in FoxPro 2.

Example

To copy Lastname, Firstname, and City fields from the active database MEMBERS to TOWNS, the following commands could be used.

```
COPY TO TOWNS Lastname, Firstname, City
```

COPY FILE

Syntax

COPY FILE *sourcefile* TO *destinationfile*

The COPY FILE command creates an identical copy of a file. You must supply the extension in both *sourcefile* and *destinationfile*. Note that you can include a drive and path designation along with the destination, if desired.

You cannot copy open files with the COPY FILE command. Also, because COPY FILE does a block-by-block copy, you may find that with large files it is much faster to access the DOS COPY command by using RUN.

Example

To copy a file named REPORTER.FRX to a new file named TESTER.FRX, the following commands could be used.

```
COPY FILE REPORTER.FRX TO TESTER.FRX
```

COPY INDEXES

Syntax

Version 2

COPY INDEXES *indexfile* list/ALL [TO .*CDXfilename*]

The COPY INDEXES command converts single-entry index files (.IDX files) into index tags within a compound-index file (.CDX file). If you omit the TO clause, the .IDX index file information is added as tags to the structural compound-index file. If you omit the TO clause and no structural compound-index file exists, a new one is created with the same name as the database, and the tags are added to that file.

If you include the TO clause, the .IDX-file index information is added as tags to the .CDX file specified as part of the option.

Example

To copy to the structural compound-index file three .IDX files called NAMES, STATES, and ZIPS, you could use the following command:

```
COPY INDEXES NAMES, STATES, ZIPS
```

COPY MEMO

Syntax

COPY MEMO *memofieldname* TO *filename* [ADDITIVE]

The COPY MEMO command is used to copy the contents of a memo field for the current record to a text file. A drive name and path can be included as a part of the filename. If the ADDITIVE option is used, the text of the memo field will be added to the end of an existing filename; if the ADDITIVE option is omitted, any existing file with the same name will be overwritten.

Example

The commands shown below could be used to open a database file, move the record pointer to a desired record, and copy the contents of the memo field named PREFERENCE for that record to a text file named COMMENTS.TXT.

```
USE MEMBERS
GO 4
COPY MEMO preference TO A:COMMENTS.TXT
```

By including the ADDITIVE option, the following example copies the contents of the memo field named Describe in a database where the Type field contains the entry, "Westerns" to a file called SUMMARY.TXT.

```
USE VIDEO
COPY MEMO Describe FOR Type = "Westerns" TO SUMMARY ADDITIVE
```

COPY STRUCTURE

Syntax

COPY STRUCTURE TO *filename* [FIELDS *fieldlist*]

The COPY STRUCTURE command copies the structure of an active database to *filename*, creating a new, empty database file. Specifying FIELDS with *fieldlist* will copy only those fields to the new structure.

The COPY STRUCTURE command can be particularly useful for creating empty copies of a database on multiple floppy disks, which others can use at their machines to add records. Later, the records can be combined at a single site with the APPEND FROM command.

Example

The commands shown below would copy an empty database containing the structure of an existing file called MEMBERS to a file called REMOTE.DBF on the disk in drive A. If the file contains memo fields, both a database file and a memo field file will be copied under the new name.

```
USE MEMBERS
COPY STRUCTURE TO A:REMOTE
```

COPY STRUCTURE EXTENDED

Syntax

COPY TO *filename* STRUCTURE EXTENDED

The COPY STRUCTURE EXTENDED command creates a new database with records that contain information about the fields of the old database. The new database contains the fields Field_name, Field_type, Field_len, and Field_dec. One record in the new database is added for each field in the old database.

The COPY STRUCTURE EXTENDED command can be used to create a new database while under program control. Using a combination of the COPY STRUCTURE EXTENDED and the CREATE FROM commands, you can create or modify database files from within a program, as shown in the example.

Example

The program shown allows a user to add a field to an existing database, while under control of the program.

```
SET SAFETY OFF
SET TALK OFF
CLEAR
DISPLAY FILES LIKE *.DBF
ACCEPT "Name of file to modify? " TO THISFILE
USE &THISFILE
COPY TO TEMP STRUCTURE EXTENDED
USE
CLEAR
ACCEPT "New field's name? " TO FNAME
ACCEPT "New field's type- C, N, L, D, or M?" TO FTYPE
INPUT "Length of new field? " TO FLONG
INPUT "No. of decimal places (enter zero if none)? " TO FDEC
USE TEMP
APPEND BLANK
REPLACE Field_name WITH FNAME, Field_type WITH FTYPE
REPLACE Field_len WITH FLONG, Field_dec WITH FDEC
USE
CREATE TEMP2 FROM TEMP
APPEND FROM &THISFILE
USE
DELETE FILE &THISFILE
USE TEMP2
COPY TO &THISFILE
USE
DELETE FILE TEMP.DBF
DELETE FILE TEMP2.DBF
RETURN
```

COPY TAG

Version 2

Syntax

COPY TAG *tagname* [OF *.CDX filename*] TO *indexfile*

The COPY TAG command converts a compound-index (.CDX) file's tag information into a single-index (.IDX) file. If you omit the OF clause, the index information is copied from the tag of the structural compound-index file.

Example

To copy the index tag named NAMES from the structural compound-index file to an .IDX index file called LASTNAME.IDX, you could use the following command:

```
COPY TAG names TO LASTNAME.IDX
```

COPY TO ARRAY

Syntax

COPY TO ARRAY *array* [FIELDS *fieldlist*] [*scope*] [FOR *condition*]
[WHILE *condition*]

The COPY TO ARRAY command copies data from the fields of a database into an array. (Note that the COPY TO ARRAY command is compatible with dBASE IV; if you need compatibility with FoxBASE+, use the SCATTER command instead.) For each record in the database, the first field is stored in the first element of the array, the second field in the second element, and so on. (You must first declare the array with the DECLARE command.) If the database has more fields than the array has elements, the contents of extra fields are not stored to the array. If the array has more elements than the database has fields, the extra elements in the array are not changed. Note that memo fields are not copied into the array.

Example

The following commands define a two-dimensional array and copy the next five records from a database into the elements of that array.

```
USE HOURS
DECLARE ThisWeek [6,5]
COPY TO ARRAY ThisWeek NEXT 5
```

COUNT

Syntax

COUNT [*scope*] [FOR *condition*] [WHILE *condition*] [TO *memvar*]

The COUNT command counts the number of records in the active database that meet a specific condition. The *scope* option quantifies the records to be counted. The FOR option can be used to specify a condition that must be met before a record will be counted. If you use the WHILE option, counting will take place until the condition is no longer true. The TO option can be used to store the count to the memory variable *memvar*.

Example

To count the number of records containing the letters "MD" in the State field, and to store that count as the memory variable MTEMP, the following command could be used.

```
COUNT FOR State = "MD" TO MTEMP
```

CREATE

Syntax

CREATE *filename*

The CREATE command creates a new database file and defines its structure. If CREATE is entered without a filename, FoxPro will prompt you for one when the structure is saved. If CREATE is followed by a filename, a database with that filename will be created. The filename extension .DBF is added automatically to the filename unless you specify otherwise.

When you create a database, a database definition screen appears. The database definition screen will have four columns, used to define the field name, field type, field size, and number of decimal places (if any).

Example

To create a new database called STAFF.DBF, the following command could be used.

```
CREATE STAFF
```

CREATE FROM

Syntax

CREATE *file1* FROM *file2*

The CREATE FROM command creates a new database whose structure is based on a file created earlier with the COPY STRUCTURE EXTENDED command (see COPY STRUCTURE EXTENDED).

Example

See COPY STRUCTURE EXTENDED for an example of the use of CREATE FROM.

CREATE LABEL

Syntax

CREATE LABEL [*filename*] [IN WINDOW *windowname*/IN SCREEN]

The CREATE LABEL command creates a label-form file. This file can be used with the LABEL FORM command to produce mailing labels. Once the label form has been outlined with the CREATE LABEL command, mailing labels can be displayed or printed with the LABEL FORM command. If you omit a filename, you will be prompted for one at some point during the design process.

In FoxPro 1.02 and later, the command also supports an optional [IN WINDOW *windowname*/IN SCREEN] clause. This clause lets you have background windows within windows or on the background screen.

When you include this clause, the inner window (containing the label design screen) is dependent on the outer window. When the outer window is moved, the inner window moves with it. The inner window cannot be larger than the outer window and can be moved only within the confines of the outer window. If the outer window is closed, the inner window is closed with it. If the outer window is deactivated, the inner window is deactivated with it.

Example

To create a label form called MAILER, you could use the command

```
CREATE LABEL MAILER
```

CREATE MENU

Syntax

Version 2

> CREATE MENU [*filename/?*] [WINDOW *windowname1*]
> [IN [WINDOW] *windowname2*/IN SCREEN]

The CREATE MENU command activates the FoxPro Menu Builder. After the desired menu is created, information about the menu is stored in a special database with an .MNX extension. If the CREATE MENU command is issued without a filename, the Menu Builder opens a menu layout window, with UNTITLED as the name supplied in the window. If a filename is included, the menu is assigned that filename, with an .MNX extension. If the question mark option is used in place of the filename, the Open File dialog box appears, and you can choose an existing file or enter a new filename.

The optional [IN WINDOW *windowname*/IN SCREEN] clause lets you have background windows within windows or on the background screen. When you include this clause, the inner window (containing the menu design screen) is dependent on the outer window. When the outer window is moved, the inner window moves with it. The inner window cannot be larger than the outer

window and can be moved only within the confines of the outer window. If the outer window is closed, the inner window is closed with it. If the outer window is deactivated, the inner window is deactivated with it.

For more details on using the Menu Builder, see Chapter 13.

CREATE PROJECT

Syntax

Version 2

CREATE PROJECT [*filename*/?] [WINDOW *windowname1*]
[IN [WINDOW] *windowname2*/IN SCREEN]

The CREATE PROJECT command opens a project window, used for the creation of a project database. A project database is a special database used to keep track of all parts of a FoxPro project. If the CREATE PROJECT command is issued without a filename, a project window opens, with UNTITLED as the name supplied in the window. If a filename is included, the project is assigned that filename, with a .PJX extension. If the question mark option is used in place of the filename, the Open File dialog box appears, and you can choose an existing file or enter a new filename.

The optional [IN WINDOW *windowname*/IN SCREEN] clause lets you have background windows within windows or on the background screen. When you include this clause, the inner window (containing the project design screen) is dependent on the outer window. When the outer window is moved, the inner window moves with it. The inner window cannot be larger than the outer window and can be moved only within the confines of the outer window. If the outer window is closed, the inner window is closed with it. If the outer window is deactivated, the inner window is deactivated with it.

For more details on building projects, see Chapter 13.

CREATE QUERY

Syntax

Version 2

CREATE QUERY [*filename*/?]

The CREATE QUERY command is used to display the RQBE Window, allowing the creation of a query. The command is equivalent to choosing New from the File menu and selecting Query in the dialog box. If the CREATE QUERY command is issued without a filename, the RQBE Window opens, with

UNTITLED as the name supplied in the window. If a filename is included, the query is assigned that filename with a .QPR extension. If the question mark option is used in place of the filename, the Open File dialog appears, and you can choose an existing file or enter a new filename.

For more details on queries and the use of the RQBE Window, refer to Chapter 6.

CREATE REPORT

Syntax

CREATE REPORT [*filename*] [IN WINDOW *windowname*/IN SCREEN]

The CREATE REPORT, or as an alternative, MODIFY REPORT, command creates or allows the user to modify a report form file for producing reports. Once the report has been outlined with the CREATE REPORT command, the report can be displayed or printed with the REPORT FORM command. As with CREATE LABEL, if you omit a filename, FoxPro will ask for one when you save the report.

In FoxPro 1.02 and later, the command also supports an optional [IN WINDOW *windowname*/IN SCREEN] clause. This clause lets you have background windows within windows or on the background screen.

When you include this clause, the inner window (containing the report design screen) is dependent on the outer window. When the outer window is moved, the inner window moves with it. The inner window cannot be larger than the outer window and can be moved only within the confines of the outer window. If the outer window is closed, the inner window is closed with it. If the outer window is deactivated, the inner window is deactivated with it.

Example

To create a report called SALES, you could use the command

```
CREATE REPORT SALES
```

CREATE REPORT FROM

Syntax

CREATE REPORT *filename1*/? FROM *filename2* [FORM/COLUMN]
[FIELDS *fieldlist*] [ALIAS] [NOOVERWRITE] [WIDTH *expN*]

Version 2

The CREATE REPORT FROM command creates a Quick Report, without opening the Report Design Window. This command is the equivalent of using the CREATE REPORT command, and choosing the Quick Report option from the Report Design Window. Use *filename1* to assign a name to the report. Use *filename2* to specify the database name on which the quick report will be based. (Note that the database does not need to be opened.) If a question mark is used in place of *filename1*, the Open File dialog appears, and you can choose an existing name or enter a new name.

Use the FORM or COLUMN options to specify a form-oriented report or a column-oriented report. If neither option is specified, the report defaults to a form-oriented report. Use the FIELDS clause followed by a list of fields to limit the fields included in the report. Use the ALIAS option if you wish to include the database alias along with the fields in the report. The NOOVERWRITE clause, when included, prevents overwriting an existing report name with the new report; if a report by the same name as *filename1* already exists, the new report is not created. Use the WIDTH clause to specify the width of the report page, where *expN* is a numeric value indicating the number of columns in the report.

CREATE SCREEN

Syntax

Version 2

CREATE SCREEN [*filename*/?] [WINDOW *windowname1*]
[IN [WINDOW *windowname2*/IN SCREEN]

The CREATE SCREEN command activates the FoxPro Screen Creation utility, used to design custom screen forms in FoxPro 2. The WINDOW and IN WINDOW clauses may be used to place the screen within a window or within the child window of a parent window. The IN SCREEN command places the screen within the full screen (this is also the default). For more details on the Screen Creation utility, see Chapter 11.

CREATE VIEW [FROM ENVIRONMENT]

Syntax

CREATE VIEW [FROM ENVIRONMENT]

The CREATE VIEW command saves the current environment to a view file. The command operates in the same manner, whether or not the FROM

ENVIRONMENT clause is specified. The optional clause is supported for compatibility with dBASE, which uses the CREATE VIEW command to display a menu used for designing view files. A view file will contain a record of any open database and index files, any relationships between multiple files, and any screen format file in use at the time the view file was created. A view file may be considered to be a "snapshot" of open database files, index files, a filter condition, and any screen format file in use. Once you have opened the appropriate database and index files, placed any desired format file into use, and set a filter condition with a SET FILTER command, you can enter the command

CREATE VIEW *filename* FROM ENVIRONMENT

where *filename* is the name for the view file. Once you have done this, you no longer need to repeat the same set of commands for the opening of files and the setting of the filter during a later session. Instead, simply use the SET VIEW command, using the syntax

SET VIEW TO *filename*

where *filename* is the name of the view file saved earlier, and the same database, index files, and screen format file will be opened. Any filter condition that was in effect when the view file was created will be placed back into effect, as will any relationship between multiple files.

Example

The following commands open two database files in work areas 1 and 2, create an associated index file, establish a relationship between the database files, and save the environment to a view file.

```
SELECT 1
USE RENTALS
SELECT 2
USE MEMBERS
INDEX ON SOCIAL TO SOCIALS
SELECT 1
SET RELATION TO SOCIAL INTO MEMBERS
CREATE VIEW RELATE1 FROM ENVIRONMENT
```

DEACTIVATE MENU

Syntax

DEACTIVATE MENU

The DEACTIVATE MENU command deactivates the active menu and clears the menu from the screen. The menu remains in memory and can be recalled with the ACTIVATE MENU command.

DEACTIVATE MENU is designed for use within programs; the command has no effect if used at the command level. Any screen text or images underneath the menu will reappear when the DEACTIVATE MENU command is used.

Example

In the following program, the DEACTIVATE MENU command is used to deactivate a menu display if the "Exit System" option is chosen by the user.

```
USE STAFF INDEX NAMES
CLEAR
DEFINE MENU MainMenu MESSAGE "Press letter of desired option"
DEFINE PAD Addit OF MainMenu PROMPT "Add records"
DEFINE PAD Change OF MainMenu PROMPT "Edit records"
DEFINE PAD Print OF MainMenu PROMPT "Print records"
DEFINE PAD Quit OF MainMenu PROMPT "Exit System"
ON SELECTION PAD Addit OF MainMenu APPEND
ON SELECTION PAD Change OF MainMenu EDIT
ON SELECTION PAD Print OF MainMenu REPORT FORM MYFILE TO PRINT
ON SELECTION PAD Quit OF MainMenu DEACTIVATE MENU
ACTIVATE MENU MainMenu
QUIT
```

DEACTIVATE POPUP

Syntax

DEACTIVATE POPUP

The DEACTIVATE POPUP command deactivates the active popup menu, and erases it from the screen. The popup menu remains in memory, and can be recalled to the screen with the ACTIVATE POPUP command.

DEACTIVATE POPUP is designed for use within programs; the command has no effect if used at the command level. Any screen text or images underneath the popup will reappear when the DEACTIVATE MENU command is used.

Example

In the following program, DEACTIVATE POPUP is used by the ON SELECTION POPUP statement to deactivate the popup menu after a selection is made. A series of CASE choices then use the BAR() function to determine which menu item was chosen, and the appropriate command is executed within the program.

```
*This is an example of a simple menu and application*
USE STAFF INDEX NAMES
DEFINE POPUP MainMenu FROM 5, 20
DEFINE BAR 1 OF MainMenu PROMPT " Select desired option " SKIP
DEFINE BAR 2 OF MainMenu PROMPT "  Add new employees      "
DEFINE BAR 3 OF MainMenu PROMPT "  Edit/Delete employees"
DEFINE BAR 4 OF MainMenu PROMPT "  Print Staff Report     "
DEFINE BAR 5 OF MainMenu PROMPT "  Quit System            "
ON SELECTION POPUP MainMenu DEACTIVATE POPUP
DO WHILE .T.
ACTIVATE POPUP MainMenu
DO CASE
     CASE BAR() = 2
     APPEND

     CASE BAR() = 3
     EDIT

     CASE BAR() = 4       CLEAR
     WAIT "ready printer, then press a key..."
     REPORT FORM MyFile TO PRINT

     CASE BAR() = 5
     QUIT
ENDCASE
ENDDO
```

DEACTIVATE WINDOW

Syntax

DEACTIVATE WINDOW *windowname*/ALL

The DEACTIVATE WINDOW command deactivates the window or windows named within the command and erases them from the screen. The windows remain in memory and can be restored to the screen with the ACTIVATE WINDOW command. If no options are used, the most recently activated window is deactivated. If a window is underlying the most recent window, it becomes the active window. If the ALL option is included, all active windows are deactivated.

Example

To deactivate a series of windows currently displayed on the screen, the following command could be used.

```
DEACTIVATE WINDOW ALL
```

DECLARE

Syntax

DECLARE *array1* [*rows,columns*] [*array2*] [*rows,columns*]

The DECLARE command creates an array. (Note that the DECLARE command is compatible with dBASE IV. If you desire compatibility with FoxBASE+, use the DIMENSION command instead.) In the definition list, you enter the array name and the dimensions of the array. Array names may be up to ten characters in length. Array dimensions consist of the row and column numbers. If a column number is omitted, FoxPro creates a one-dimensional array. If row and column numbers are used, they must be separated by a comma, and FoxPro creates a two-dimensional array. Arrays declared within programs are private unless declared public with the PUBLIC command. Up to 3600 array elements can be declared at one time.

Example

To declare a private array, enter

```
DECLARE ARRAY Finance[10,4]
```

To declare an array as public within a program, enter

```
PUBLIC ARRAY Finance[10,4]
```

NOTE: *The prior example both declares an array and makes it public. You can make a previously declared array public with the syntax, PUBLIC array.*

The data entry program shown below uses the DECLARE command to create an array used to store data in a database. The values stored to the elements of the array are edited using @...SAY...GET statements and are then transferred to the fields of the database.

```
CLEAR
DECLARE M_DATA[1,6]
M_DATA[1,1] = SPACE(15)
M_DATA[1,2] = SPACE(15)
M_DATA[1,3] = SPACE(25)
M_DATA[1,4] = SPACE(15)
M_DATA[1,5] = SPACE(2)
M_DATA[1,6] = SPACE(10)
*display prompts, store data to variables.
@   3,5 SAY " LAST NAME:" GET M_DATA[1,1]
@   4,5 SAY "FIRST NAME:" GET M_DATA[1,2]
@   8,5 SAY "ADDRESS:" GET M_DATA[1,3]
@  10,5 SAY "   CITY:" GET M_DATA[1,4]
@ 10,35 SAY "STATE:" GET M_DATA[1,5]
@ 10,45 SAY "ZIP CODE:" GET M_DATA[1,6]
READ
*open database, make new record, store variables.
USE NAMES INDEX NAMES
APPEND FROM ARRAY M_DATA
CLOSE DATABASES
RETURN
```

DEFINE BAR

Syntax

DEFINE BAR *linenumber* OF *popupname* PROMPT *expC* [MESSAGE *expC*] [SKIP [FOR *condition*]]

Syntax for FoxPro 2

DEFINE BAR *linenumber/System option name* OF *popupname* PROMPT *expC* [BEFORE *expN*/AFTER *expN*] [KEY *key label*] [MARK *expC*] [MESSAGE *expC*] [SKIP [FOR *expL*]] [COLOR *color-pair list*/COLOR SCHEME *expN*]

The DEFINE BAR command defines one bar option within a popup menu. *Popupname* must have been previously defined with the DEFINE POPUP command. *Linenumber* specifies the line number within the popup menu; line 1 appears on the first line of the popup, line 2 on the second line of the popup, and so on. The text specified with PROMPT appears as text in the bar of the menu. The MESSAGE option can be used to specify text that will appear at the bottom of the screen when the specified menu bar is highlighted. The SKIP option causes the bar to appear, but not be selectable within the menu.

The System Option Name clause can be used to place items that are available from the System menu in your popups. The BEFORE and AFTER clauses determine the physical location of an option, relative to the option number specified by *expN*. The KEY clause is used to assign another key to a popup option. The MARK clause, when used along with the SET MARK command, allows the placement of a check mark besides the popup option. The SKIP FOR clause lets you skip a bar of the popup based on the logical condition specified by *expL*. If the condition evaluates to a logical true, the bar is skipped. Use the COLOR or COLOR SCHEME option to change the colors of the popup.

Version 2

Example

In the portion of program code shown below, DEFINE PAD and ON PAD commands are used to set up a menu with two popups linked to the pads by means of ACTIVATE POPUP.

```
*Example of menuing functions*
CLEAR
*define horizontal bar menu to activate popups*
DEFINE MENU MAIN
DEFINE PAD MEMBER OF MAIN PROMPT "View Members" AT 1,10
DEFINE PAD VIDEO OF MAIN PROMPT "View Videos" AT 1,25
DEFINE PAD BYE OF MAIN PROMPT "Exit System" AT 1,40
***
ON PAD MEMBER OF MAIN ACTIVATE POPUP MVIEW
ON PAD VIDEO OF MAIN ACTIVATE POPUP VVIEW
ON SELECTION PAD BYE OF MAIN DEACTIVATE MENU MAIN
*popup to go with first menu prompt*
DEFINE POPUP MVIEW FROM 2,10
DEFINE BAR 1 OF MVIEW PROMPT "Short Browse"
DEFINE BAR 2 OF MVIEW PROMPT "Full Browse "
DEFINE BAR 3 OF MVIEW PROMPT "------------"
DEFINE BAR 4 OF MVIEW PROMPT "Edit Records"
*this line automatically deactivates popup temporarily*
ON SELECTION POPUP MVIEW DO PSEL WITH POPUP(), BAR()
*popup to go with second menu prompt*
DEFINE POPUP VVIEW FROM 2,25
```

```
DEFINE BAR 1 OF VVIEW PROMPT "Window Browse"
DEFINE BAR 2 OF VVIEW PROMPT "Full Browse  "
ON SELECTION POPUP VVIEW DO PSEL WITH POPUP(), BAR()
*activate main menu now.*
ACTIVATE MENU MAIN
*control returns here from 3rd prompt with deactivate menu main
RETURN


PROCEDURE PSEL
PARAMETERS POP, BAR
    CLEAR
    @ 10,10 SAY "popup is: " + POP
    @ 12,10 SAY "bar is: " + STR(BAR)
RETURN
```

DEFINE BOX

Syntax

DEFINE BOX FROM *printcolumn1* TO *printcolumn2* HEIGHT *expr*
[AT LINE *print line*] [SINGLE/DOUBLE/*border definition string*]

The DEFINE BOX command lets you define a box that appears around printed text. Use the specified options in the command to define the starting column on the left, the ending column on the right, the height of the box, and the starting line for the top of the box. The *border definition string* option lets you specify a character that will be used as the box border; the default, if this option is omitted, is a single line. Note that the printer system variable, _BOX, must be set to true to enable the printing of boxes. If _BOX is false, boxes will not be printed.

REMINDER: *DEFINE BOX works only with printers. Do not confuse the DEFINE BOX command with methods for drawing boxes with @...SAY commands. DEFINE BOX is only valid for printed output; it does not appear on the screen.*

Example

To define a box to appear around printed text measuring from print column 4 to print column 76, beginning at line 5 and extending 45 lines down the page, the following command could be used.

```
DEFINE BOX FROM 4 TO 76 HEIGHT 45 AT LINE 5
```

DEFINE MENU

Syntax

DEFINE MENU *menuname* [MESSAGE *expC*]

Syntax for FoxPro 2

DEFINE MENU *menuname* [BAR [AT LINE *expN*]]
[IN [WINDOW *windowname*/IN SCREEN] [KEY *key label*] [MARK *expC*]
[MESSAGE *expC*] [NOMARGIN] [COLOR *color-pair list*/COLOR SCHEME
expN]

The DEFINE MENU command defines a bar menu. If the MESSAGE option is added, the text of the message appears at the bottom of the screen when the menu is displayed. (See ACTIVATE MENU.) The DEFINE MENU command assigns a name to the bar menu; the DEFINE PAD commands then identify the options (or pads) that will appear within the bar menu.

If the MESSAGE option is added, the text of the message appears at the position specified by SET MESSAGE TO when the menu is displayed.

The BAR clause is used to create a bar-style menu that imitates the style of the FoxPro System menus. Use the IN WINDOW or IN SCREEN clauses to define whether the defined menu is in a window or in the full screen. (If the clause is omitted, the window appears in the full screen.) The KEY clause is used to assign another key to a popup option. The MARK clause, when used along with the SET MARK command, allows the placement of a check mark beside the popup option. The NOMARGIN clause, when used, omits the extra space that normally appears to the left of each menu pad. Use the COLOR or COLOR SCHEME options to change the colors of the popup.

Version 2

Example

In the portion of program code shown below, the DEFINE MENU command is used to define a bar menu called MainMenu. The optional message clause is added, so that the message "Press letter of desired option" will appear in the message area when the menu is active. The DEFINE PAD commands are used to add four choices to the bar menu; Add records, Edit records, Print records, and Exit System. The ON SELECTION statements define which actions shall be taken when a particular menu option is chosen by the user. (To keep the example simple, each ON SELECTION statement calls a particular command, such as APPEND or EDIT. In most applications, the ON SELECTION statements will be used to call another routine for adding or editing records or performing some other task.) The ACTIVATE MENU statement that follows the ON SELECTION statement activates the menu, and the program awaits the user's response.

```
USE MEMBERS
SET INDEX TO NAMES
DEFINE MENU MainMenu MESSAGE "Press letter of desired option"
DEFINE PAD Addit OF MainMenu PROMPT "Add records"
DEFINE PAD Change OF MainMenu PROMPT "Edit records"
DEFINE PAD Print OF MainMenu PROMPT "Print records"
DEFINE PAD Quit OF MainMenu PROMPT "Exit System"
ON SELECTION PAD Addit OF MainMenu APPEND
ON SELECTION PAD Change OF MainMenu EDIT
ON SELECTION PAD Print OF MainMenu REPORT FORM MYFILE TO PRINT
ON SELECTION PAD Quit OF MainMenu QUIT
ACTIVATE MENU MainMenu
```

DEFINE PAD

Syntax

DEFINE PAD *padname* OF *menuname* PROMPT *expC* [AT *row,col*] [MESSAGE *expC*]

Syntax for FoxPro 2

DEFINE PAD *padname* OF *menuname* PROMPT *expC* [AT *row,col*] [BEFORE *padname*/AFTER *padname*] [KEY *key label* [MARK *expC*] [MESSAGE *expC*] [SKIP [FOR *expL*]] [COLOR *color-pair list*/COLOR SCHEME *expN*]]

The DEFINE PAD command defines one pad of a bar menu. Use a separate statement containing this command for each desired pad within the menu. The text specified with PROMPT appears inside the menu pad. If the AT *row, col* option is omitted, the first pad appears at the far left, and each successive pad appears one space to the right of the previous pad. Any text that accompanies the MESSAGE option appears on the message line (see SET MESSAGE TO) when that pad is highlighted within the menu.

The KEY clause is used to assign another key to a popup option. The BEFORE and AFTER clauses determine the physical location of a pad, relative to the pad number specified by *expN*. The MARK clause, when used along with the SET MARK command, allows the placement of a check mark beside the popup option. The SKIP clause, when used, causes a pad to be skipped if the logical expression evaluates as true. Use the COLOR or COLOR SCHEME options to change the colors of the menu pad.

Example

See DEFINE MENU for an example of the use of the DEFINE PAD command, along with the DEFINE MENU command.

DEFINE POPUP

Syntax

DEFINE POPUP *popupname* FROM *row1,col1* [TO *row2,col2*]
[PROMPT FIELD *fieldname*/PROMPT FILES [LIKE *skeleton*]/
PROMPT STRUCTURE] [MESSAGE *expC*] [COLOR *standard*[, *enhanced*]/
COLOR SCHEME *expN*] [SHADOW]

Syntax for FoxPro 2

DEFINE POPUP *popupname* [FROM *row1,col1* [TO *row2,col2*]
[IN [WINDOW *windowname*/IN SCREEN] [FOOTER *expC*]
[KEY *key label*] [MARGIN] [MARK *expC*] [MESSAGE *expC*] [MOVER]
[MULTI] [PROMPT FIELD *field*/PROMPT FILES [LIKE *skeleton*]/
PROMPT STRUCTURE] [RELATIVE] [SCROLL] [SHADOW] [TITLE *expC*]
[COLOR *color-pair list*/COLOR SCHEME *expN*]

Use the DEFINE POPUP command to define a popup menu. The FROM and TO row and column coordinates define the upper-left and lower-right corners of the popup. If the TO coordinate is omitted, FoxPro will make the menu as large as needed to contain the prompts within the menu.

The PROMPT FIELD, PROMPT FILE, and PROMPT STRUCTURE clauses are optional. These allow you to display selection lists of field contents, filenames, or field names from a database structure. The COLOR or COLOR SCHEME options may be used to specify colors for the popup. By default, popups take on the colors of color scheme 2. If the optional SHADOW clause is included, a shadow appears beneath the popup.

The IN WINDOW and IN SCREEN clauses can be used to define whether the popup appears in a window or in the full screen. (If the clause is omitted, the default is the full screen.) The FOOTER clause assigns a text footer, centered in the bottom border of the popup. The KEY clause is used to assign another key as a hotkey for the popup. The MARGIN clause causes an extra space to appear to the left and the right of each popup option. The MARK clause, when used along with the SET MARK command, allows the placement of a check mark beside the popup option. The MESSAGE clause displays the specified message, in the position specified by the SET MESSAGE command.

Version 2

The MOVER clause, when included, allows the movement of popup options, using the double-headed arrow that appears at the left edge of the popup. The MULTI option allows multiple choices from a single popup option. The RELATIVE clause lets you change the order in which items appear in the popup. If a menu popup is created using the RELATIVE clause, menu options appear in the order that they were defined. The SCROLL clause, when included, adds a scroll bar at the right edge of the popup; mouse users can use the scroll bar to scroll through the menu options. The TITLE clause adds a title to the border of the popup. Use the COLOR or COLOR SCHEME options to change the colors of the popup.

Example

Two popup menus are desired. One will be called MainMenu and will measure from row 5, column 5 to row 14, column 40. The second will be called PrintMen, and will measure from row 15, column 12 to row 22, column 17. To define these menus, the following commands could be used.

```
DEFINE POPUP MainMenu FROM 5,5 TO 14,40
DEFINE POPUP PrintMen FROM 15,12 TO 22,17
```

Also, see the DEFINE BAR command for an example of DEFINE POPUP used along with DEFINE BAR to create a menu.

DEFINE WINDOW

Syntax

DEFINE WINDOW *windowname* FROM *row1,col1* TO *row2,col2*
[DOUBLE/PANEL/NONE/*border definition string*] [CLOSE/NOCLOSE]
[SHADOW/NOSHADOW] [GROW/NOGROW] [FLOAT/NOFLOAT]
[ZOOM/NOZOOM] [COLOR [*standard*][, *enhanced*][, *border*]]/
[COLOR SCHEME *expN*] [IN WINDOW *windowname*/IN SCREEN]

Syntax for FoxPro 2

> DEFINE WINDOW *windowname* FROM *row1,col1* TO *row2,col2*
> [FOOTER*expC*][TITLE*expC*][DOUBLE/PANEL/NONE/*borderdefinition string*]
> [CLOSE/NOCLOSE] [SHADOW/NOSHADOW] [GROW/NOGROW]
> [FLOAT/NOFLOAT] [ZOOM/NOZOOM] [MINIMIZE] [FILL *expC*]
> [COLOR [*standard*][, *enhanced*][, *border*]]/[COLOR SCHEME *expN*]
> [IN WINDOW *windowname*/IN SCREEN]

The DEFINE WINDOW command defines display attributes and screen coordinates for a window. The FROM and TO coordinates define the upper-left and lower-right corners of the window. The default border is a single-line box; you can use the DOUBLE, PANEL, NONE, or border definition character options to specify a different border for the window. (Use ASCII codes for the border definition option.) By default, windows use the colors of color scheme 1.

The CLOSE/NOCLOSE option specifies whether the window may be closed with the System menu or by clicking on the Close box. If the option is omitted or NOCLOSE is specified, the window may not be closed (other than by deactivating it). The SHADOW/NOSHADOW option determines whether a shadow will appear beneath the window. By default, windows do not have shadows. The FLOAT/NOFLOAT and ZOOM/NOZOOM options determine whether the window can be moved (in the case of FLOAT) or zoomed (in the case of ZOOM). If the options are omitted or if the NOFLOAT or NOZOOM options are specified, the window may not be moved or zoomed. The GROW/NOGROW options specify whether the user will be permitted to resize the window. If GROW is included, the user can resize the window. If NOGROW is included, the user cannot resize the window.

In FoxPro 2 and later, the TITLE and FOOTER options specify a title that appears centered at the top border of the window or a footer that appears centered at the bottom border of the window. The MINIMIZE option causes the window to be reduced to its minimum size. The FILL option causes the window to be filled with the character specified by *expC*.

HINT: The added options in FoxPro are useful for controlling what users can and cannot do to windows within your programs. Use NOFLOAT, NOZOOM, and NOGROW to prevent users from modifying the appearance of your windows at will.

In FoxPro 1.02 and later, the command also supports an optional [IN WINDOW *windowname*/IN SCREEN] clause. This clause lets you have background windows within windows or on the background screen.

When you include this clause, the inner window is dependent on the outer window. When the outer window is moved, the inner window moves with it. The inner window cannot be larger than the outer window and can be moved only within the confines of the outer window. If the outer window is closed, the inner window is closed with it. If the outer window is deactivated, the inner window is deactivated with it.

Example

The following lines of a program define a window with the upper-left corner at row 5, column 5 and the lower-right corner at row 7, column 52. The window is then activated, and a message to the user is displayed within the window.

```
DEFINE WINDOW MyWindow FROM 5,5 TO 7,52 DOUBLE COLOR B/W
ACTIVATE WINDOW MyWindow
@ 1,6 SAY "Are you SURE you want to do this?"
```

The following program uses the DEFINE WINDOW command to define three windows. The windows are used to prompt a user for information and to display data from separate files in response. The program asks for a video club member's name, displays a corresponding tape limit value and membership expiration date, and displays a list of videotapes rented by that member.

```
*WINDOWS.PRG shows off window use.*
STORE SPACE(15) TO MLAST
DEFINE WINDOW members1 FROM 5,5 TO 9,50
DEFINE WINDOW rentals1 FROM 8,8 TO 22,75
DEFINE WINDOW askthem FROM 3,15 TO 6,45
USE MEMBERS INDEX NAME
ACTIVATE WINDOW askthem
@ 1,1 SAY "Last name? " GET MLAST
READ
SEEK MLAST
IF .NOT. FOUND()
    @ 1,1 SAY "NAME NOT FOUND IN DATABASE!"
    WAIT
    DEACTIVATE WINDOW askthem
    CLOSE DATABASES
    RETURN
ENDIF
STORE SOCIAL TO FINDER
ACTIVATE WINDOW members1
@  1,2 SAY "Name: " + TRIM(Firstname) + " " + Lastname
@  2,2 SAY "Exp. date:"
@ 2,15 SAY EXPIREDATE
@ 2,25 SAY "Tape limit:"
```

```
@ 2,38 SAY TAPELIMIT
WAIT "Press a key to see rentals..."
SET ESCAPE OFF
ACTIVATE WINDOW rentals1
SELECT 2
USE RENTALS
DISPLAY ALL OFF FOR SOCIAL = FINDER
WAIT "Press a key when done viewing..."
DEACTIVATE WINDOW ALL
CLOSE DATABASES
SET ESCAPE ON
RETURN
```

DELETE

Syntax

DELETE [*scope*] [FOR *condition*] [WHILE *condition*]

Syntax for FoxPro 2

DELETE [*scope*] [FOR *condition*] [WHILE *condition*] [NOOPTIMIZE]

The DELETE command marks specific records for deletion. (Note that you can also use the Delete option of the Records menu to delete records.) If DELETE is used without a record number, the current record is marked for deletion. The *scope* option is used to identify the records to be deleted. The FOR option can be used to specify a condition that must be met before a record will be deleted. If you use the WHILE option, records will be deleted until the condition is no longer true. DELETE marks a record for deletion; the PACK command actually removes the record. In FoxPro versions 2 and later, the NOOPTIMIZE clause, when added, turns off FoxPro's internal optimization techniques (Rushmore).

Example

In the commands shown below, a database file is listed with the LIST command, then the DELETE command is used to delete certain records. A listing performed after the deletions shows that the records are still in the database, but are marked for deletion as shown by the asterisk to the left of the deleted records. After a PACK command is executed, another listing shows that the records marked for deletion have been removed.

```
USE COSTS
LIST
Record#  DATE      CATEGORY         CHECKNO PAIDTO           AMOUNT
      1  08/03/88 SUPPLIES          1516    Hub Disks Co.      37.00
      2  08/17/88 PROF. FEES        1524    C & P Telephone   385.34
      3  08/24/88 ADVERTISING       1528    C.U.Pers. Assoc.  150.00
      4  08/30/88 DUES/SUBSCRIP     1534    RNR Patterns        8.95
      5  09/05/88 TYPEWRITER PMT    1537    IBM Credit Corp.   62.00
      6  02/23/88 PROF. FEES        1445    Minuteman Press    92.00
      7  02/23/88 POSTAGE/MAILING 1447    Federal Express    20.00
      8  02/23/88 POSTAGE/MAILING 1448    Federal Express    17.50
      9  02/23/88 POSTAGE/MAILING 1449    MCI Mail           10.00
     10  03/01/88 LICENSE FEES      1450    Fairfax County     81.84
     11  03/01/88 LICENSE FEES      1451    Fairfax County    176.07

GO 7
DELETE
     1 record deleted
GO 8
DELETE
     1 record deleted
GO 10
DELETE
     1 record deleted
LIST

Record#  DATE      CATEGORY         CHECKNO PAIDTO           AMOUNT
      1  08/03/88 SUPPLIES          1516    Hub Disks Co.      37.00
      2  08/17/88 PROF. FEES        1524    C & P Telephone   385.34
      3  08/24/88 ADVERTISING       1528    C.U.Pers. Assoc.  150.00
      4  08/30/88 DUES/SUBSCRIP     1534    RNR Patterns        8.95
      5  09/05/88 TYPEWRITER PMT    1537    IBM Credit Corp.   62.00
      6  02/23/88 PROF. FEES        1445    Minuteman Press    92.00
      7 *02/23/88 POSTAGE/MAILING 1447    Federal Express    20.00
      8 *02/23/88 POSTAGE/MAILING 1448    Federal Express    17.50
      9  02/23/88 POSTAGE/MAILING 1449    MCI Mail           10.00
     10 *03/01/88 LICENSE FEES      1450    Fairfax County     81.84
     11  03/01/88 LICENSE FEES      1451    Fairfax County    176.07

PACK
     8 records copied
```

```
LIST

Record#  DATE      CATEGORY         CHECKNO PAIDTO            AMOUNT
      1  08/03/88  SUPPLIES         1516    Hub Disks Co.      37.00
      2  08/17/88  PROF. FEES       1524    C & P Telephone   385.34
      3  08/24/88  ADVERTISING      1528    C.U.Pers. Assoc.  150.00
      4  08/30/88  DUES/SUBSCRIP    1534    RNR Patterns        8.95
      5  09/05/88  TYPEWRITER PMT   1537    IBM Credit Corp.   62.00
      6  02/23/88  PROF. FEES       1445    Minuteman Press    92.00
      7  02/23/88  POSTAGE/MAILING  1449    MCI Mail           10.00
      8  03/01/88  LICENSE FEES     1451    Fairfax County    176.07
```

As a further example, to mark records within the next 24 records for deletion beginning with the current record and specifying that they have an entry of VA in the State field in order to be deleted, the following command could be used.

```
DELETE NEXT 24 FOR State = "VA"
```

DELETE FILE

Syntax

DELETE FILE *filename.ext*/[?]

The DELETE FILE command deletes a file from the disk. If an extension is present, it must be specified. If the optional question mark is used in place of a filename, a list box of all files in the current directory appears. The user can then select the file to be deleted from the list box.

DELETE TAG

Syntax

Version 2

DELETE TAG *tagname1* [OF .*CDXfile1*][, *tagname2* [OF .*CDXfile2*]].../ALL

The DELETE TAG command removes the named tag from a compound-index file. If the OF clause is omitted, FoxPro looks in the structural compound-index file for the tags to be deleted. The ALL clause causes all tags to be deleted from the compound-index file, and the file itself is also deleted.

Example

To delete an index tag named ZIPS stored in a compound-index file named ABCSTAFF.CDX, you could use the command

```
DELETE TAG ZIPS OF ABCSTAFF
```

DIMENSION

Syntax

DIMENSION *array1* [*rows,columns*] [*array2*] [*rows,columns*]...[< *arrayX*] [*rows,columns*]

The DIMENSION command creates an array. (Note that the DIMENSION command is compatible with FoxBASE+ and with Clipper. If you desire compatibility with dBASE IV, use the DECLARE command instead.) In the definition list, you enter the array name and the dimensions of the array. Array names may be up to 10 characters in length. Array dimensions consist of the numbers of rows and columns. If a column number is omitted, FoxPro creates a one-dimensional array. If row and column numbers are used, they must be separated by a comma, and FoxPro creates a two-dimensional array.

Example

To declare a two-dimensional array containing ten rows and four columns, the following command could be used.

```
DIMENSION ARRAY Finance[10,4]
```

NOTE: *The DECLARE command operates in an identical manner to the DIMENSION command. See DECLARE for additional examples detailing the use of arrays.*

DIR

Syntax

DIR [*drive:*] [*filename/skeleton*] [TO PRINT/TO FILE *filename*]

The DIR command displays the directory of all database files or files of a specific type if a file extension is specified. *Drive* is the drive designator and *filename* is the name of a file with or without an extension. *Skeletons* composed of wildcards, which are asterisks or question marks, can be used as part of or as a replacement for *filename*. In the case of database files, the display produced by DIR includes the number of records contained in the database, the date of the last update, and the size of the file (in bytes). The TO PRINT and TO FILE options may be used to route the directory display to the printer or to a filename.

Example

The following commands and the results shown demonstrate various uses of the DIR command.

```
DIR

Database Files    # Records    Last Update    Size
FINANCE.DBF          15         02/16/90       1152
SICK.DBF              2         02/23/90        668
ILLNESS.DBF           2         02/25/89        668
PERSONS.DBF           6         01/17/90        598
HOURS.DBF            12         07/17/89        414
BOOKS.DBF             3         01/17/90        386

   3886 bytes in      6 files
7499776 bytes remaining on drive

DIR *.FRM

BOOKS.FRM

   2077 bytes in      1 files
7499776 bytes remaining on drive

DIR LIKE *.IDX
ILLNESS.IDX        PERSONS.IDX        BOOKS.IDX

  12289 bytes in      3 files
7499776 bytes remaining on drive

DIR D:\DBASE

Database Files    # Records    Last Update    Size
DBASE.DBF             8         09/10/89       1530
```

```
    1530 bytes in      1 files
4677632 bytes remaining on drive

DIR D:\DBASE\*.*

DBASE.EXE        CONFIG.SYS       EMPLOYED.DBF      DBASEINL.OVL
DBASE.MSG        DBASE.OVL        HELP.DBS          ASSIST.HLP
DBASE.PIF        JAREL.DBF        JAREL.DBT         CONFIG.DB
GO.BAT           FOXMEMB.DBF      LOTUS.PRG         FOXFILE.DBT
FOXMEMB.DBT      FINANCE.NDX      MILAGE.PRG        MILAGE.FMT
READYSET.COM     MENU             SIMPLE.BAK        CHECKS.DBF
TEMP1.DBF        TEMP2.DBF        CHECKS.FRM        MEMBERS.DBF


 802874 bytes in     74 files
4677632 bytes remaining on drive
```

DISPLAY

Syntax

DISPLAY [*scope*] [*fieldlist*] [FOR *condition*] [WHILE *condition*] [OFF]
[TO PRINT/TO FILE *filename*]

Syntax for FoxPro 2

DISPLAY [*scope*] [*fieldlist*] [FOR *condition*] [WHILE *condition*] [OFF]
[TO PRINT/TO FILE *filename*] [NOOPTIMIZE]

The DISPLAY command displays a record from the active database. You can display more records by including the *scope* option. The FOR option limits the display of records to those satisfying the condition. If you use the WHILE option, records will be displayed until the condition is no longer true. Only the fields listed in *fieldlist* will be displayed; if *fieldlist* is absent, all fields will be displayed. The OFF option will prevent the record number from being displayed. The TO PRINT and TO FILE options may be used to route the display to the printer or to a file called *filename*. Note that when the TO FILE option is used, the default extension for the file is .TXT. In FoxPro 2 only, the NOOPTIMIZE clause, when added, turns off FoxPro's internal optimization techniques (Rushmore).

REMINDER: *DISPLAY will display only the current record unless you include a scope.*

Example

To display the Lastname, Firstname, City, and State fields for all records where the State field begins with the letters "DC," the following command could be used.

```
DISPLAY ALL Lastname, Firstname, City, State FOR State = "DC"
```

In the example shown below, the DISPLAY command is used along with specified field names and a NEXT 5 clause to display the next five records in a database file, listing only those fields named.

```
USE COSTS
DISPLAY DATE, CATEGORY, PAIDTO, AMOUNT NEXT 5

Record#  DATE      CATEGORY       PAIDTO             AMOUNT
      1  08/03/88  SUPPLIES       Hub Disks Co.       37.00
      2  08/17/88  PROF. FEES     C & P Telephone    385.34
      3  08/24/88  ADVERTISING    C.U.Pers. Assoc.   150.00
      4  08/30/88  DUES/SUBSCRIP  RNR Patterns         8.95
      5  09/05/88  TYPEWRITER PMT  IBM Credit Corp.   62.00
```

DISPLAY FILES

Syntax

DISPLAY FILES [ON *drive/dir*] [LIKE *skeleton*] [TO PRINT/TO FILE *filename*]

The DISPLAY FILES command displays the directory of all database files or files of a specific type if a file extension is specified. The DISPLAY FILES command and the LIST FILES command produce the same result, except that DISPLAY FILES pauses each screenful, while LIST FILES produces a continuous display. If the LIKE option is omitted, database files are shown. DISPLAY FILES is an alternative form of the DIR command, used to display all files or all files of a specific type. *Drive* is the drive designator, and *dir* is the path name. *Skeletons* composed of wildcards, which are asterisks or question marks, can be used to identify specific file types. In the case of database files, the display produced by DISPLAY FILES includes the number of records contained in the database, the date of the last update, and the size of the file (in bytes). The TO PRINT and TO FILE options may be used to route the directory display to the printer or to a filename.

Example

The following commands and the resulting listings show the effects of the DISPLAY FILES command.

```
DISPLAY FILES

Database Files    # Records    Last Update    Size
EMPLOYED.DBF          9        09/19/88        870
MEMBERS.DBF          18        06/21/87       2608
BOOKS.DBF             3        01/09/90        386
MILEAGE.DBF         409        10/08/89      16899
STAFF.DBF             3        01/15/90        456
SALES.DBF           289        01/03/80      51539
VIDEO.DBF             8        02/19/90       1530
MEDIA.DBF            58        08/12/88      13952
ILLNESS.DBF           2        07/09/88        648
COSTS.DBF             8        02/23/90        799
JUNK.DBF              6        02/23/90        524
FINANCE.DBF         692        10/08/89      45834

   59261 bytes in     18 files.
4677632 bytes remaining on drive.

DISPLAY FILES LIKE M*.*

MILEAGE.PRG     MILEAGE.FMT     MENU            MEMBERS.DBF
MILEAGE.DBF     MILEAGE.FRM     MILEAGE.IDX     MEDIA.IDX
MEDIA.FMT       MEDIA.DBF

   52098 bytes in     10 files.
4677632 bytes remaining on drive.
```

DISPLAY MEMORY

Syntax

DISPLAY MEMORY [LIKE *skeleton*] [TO PRINT/TO FILE *filename*]

The DISPLAY MEMORY command displays all active memory variables, their sizes, and their contents. The numbers of active variables and available variables are listed along with the numbers of bytes consumed and bytes available. Wildcards may be used as skeletons, for example, entering **DISPLAY MEMORY LIKE MEM∗** would display all variables beginning with the letters "MEM." The TO PRINT and TO FILE options may be used to route the display to the printer or to a filename. Note that when the TO FILE option is used, the default extension for the file is .TXT.

As part of the listing produced by DISPLAY MEMORY, FoxPro will also display the print system memory variables. Below the print system memory variables appear any existing menu and menu pad definitions, popup definitions, and window definitions.

Example

The short program shown below stores four memory variables, then defines one variable as public and stores the text string "BLUE" to the public variable. The DISPLAY MEMORY command, used after the program is run, produces the listing of the memory variables. (To save space, the Print System Memory Variables are not shown in this listing. See Chapter 24 for examples and explanations of the print system memory variables.)

```
STORE "Johnson" TO Firstname
STORE "Nathan" TO Lastname
STORE CTOD("05/05/52") TO DATEBORN
STORE 10.50 TO SALARY
PUBLIC COLORDEFS
STORE "BLUE" TO COLORDEFS
SUSPEND
WAIT
RETURN

DISPLAY MEMORY

COLORDEFS   Pub    C   "BLUE"
FIRSTNAME   Priv   C   "Johnson"
LASTNAME    Priv   C   "Nathan"
DATEBORN    Priv   D   05/05/52
SALARY      Priv   N   10.50  (        10.50000000)

     5 variables defined,      38 bytes used
   251 variables available,   5962 bytes available
```

DISPLAY STATUS

Syntax

DISPLAY STATUS [TO PRINT/TO FILE *filename*]

The DISPLAY STATUS command displays, for every active work area, the name and alias of the currently open database, any filter condition currently in effect, and the expressions used in any open index files. The current drive designator, function-key settings, and settings of SET commands are also displayed. The TO PRINT and TO FILE options may be used to route the display to the printer or to a filename. Note that when the TO FILE option is used, the default extension for the file is .TXT.

DISPLAY STRUCTURE

Syntax

DISPLAY STRUCTURE [IN *alias*] [TO PRINT/TO FILE *filename*]

The DISPLAY STRUCTURE command displays the structure of the active database, unless the IN *alias* option is used. The complete filename, along with the current drive designator, number of records, date of last update, and name of fields, including their statistics (type, length, and decimal places), are listed. Under FoxPro 2 or later, index tags are also displayed.

If you have established a field list with SET FIELDS, a > symbol appears to the left of the selected fields in the structure list. The IN ALIAS option causes the structure of a file open in another work area (as specified by the alias) to be displayed. The TO PRINT and TO FILE options may be used to route the display to the printer or to a filename. Note that when the TO FILE option is used, the default extension for the file is .TXT.

Example

The following commands demonstrate the use of the DISPLAY STRUCTURE command.

```
USE MEMBERS
DISPLAY STRUCTURE
```

```
Structure for database: E:\FOXPRO\FOXDATA\MEMBERS.DBF
Number of data records:        8
Date of last update   : 02/13/90
Field  Field Name  Type        Width    Dec
    1  SOCIAL      Character     11
    2  LASTNAME    Character     15
    3  FIRSTNAME   Character     15
    4  ADDRESS     Character     25
    5  CITY        Character     15
    6  STATE       Character      2
    7  ZIPCODE     Character     10
    8  PHONE       Character     12
    9  BIRTHDAY    Date           8
   10  EXPIREDATE  Date           8
   11  TAPELIMIT   Numeric        2
   12  BETA        Logical        1
   13  PREFERENCE  Memo          10
** Total **                     135
```

DO

Syntax

DO *filename* [WITH *parameter-list*]

Syntax for FoxPro 2

DO *filename* [WITH *parameter-list*] [IN *filename*]

The DO command starts execution of a FoxPro program. The filename extension of .PRG is assumed unless otherwise specified. If the WITH option is specified and followed by a list of parameters in *parameter-list*, those parameters are transferred to the program. The program must contain a PARAMETERS statement at the start of the file, and that statement must list the names of the variables that the parameters passed should be stored under. Under FoxPro 2 or later, the IN *filename* clause can be used to run a procedure that is stored in another program file.

Once a program called with the DO command finishes execution, program control returns to the calling program. If the program last executed was the highest level program, program control returns to the command window.

FoxPro supports multiple nesting of subroutines or programs called from programs. Such nesting takes place whenever one program uses a DO command to run another program that uses a DO command to run another program.

Example

To run a program named MENU.PRG, the following command could be used.

```
DO MENU
```

To run a program called ERRORS.PRG, and pass a parameter containing the text string "employee name" to that program, the following command could be used,

```
DO ERRORS WITH "employee name"
```

and the called program ERRORS.PRG would use the PARAMETERS statement to receive the text string, as shown in the following example:

```
*ERRORS.PRG is error display routine.*
PARAMETERS SayIt
CLEAR
@ 5,5 SAY "Cannot find " + SayIt
@ 7,5 SAY "in this database. Please try again."
WAIT
RETURN
```

DO CASE

Syntax

```
DO CASE
    CASE condition
        commands...
    [CASE condition]
        [commands...]
    [OTHERWISE] [commands...]
ENDCASE
```

The DO CASE command selects one course of action from a number of choices. The conditions following the CASE statements are evaluated until one of the conditions is found to be true. When a condition is true, the commands between the CASE statement and the next CASE or OTHERWISE and ENDCASE, will be executed. FoxPro then executes the command following the ENDCASE statement. If none of the conditions in the CASE statements are found to be true, any commands following the optional OTHERWISE statement will be executed. If the OTHERWISE statement is not used and no conditions are found to be true, FoxPro proceeds to the command following the ENDCASE statement.

Example

In the following DO CASE commands, FoxPro chooses from among three possible alternatives: (1)executing a command file named MENU, (2) appending records to the database, or (3) exiting from FoxPro.

```
DO CASE
 CASE SELECT = 1
 DO MENU
 CASE SELECT = 2   APPEND
 CASE SELECT = 3
 QUIT
ENDCASE
```

DO WHILE

Syntax

> DO WHILE *condition*
>   *commands...*
> ENDDO

The DO WHILE command repeatedly executes commands between DO WHILE and ENDDO as long as *condition* is true. When FoxPro encounters a DO WHILE command, the condition in that command statement is evaluated. If *condition* is false, FoxPro proceeds to the command following the ENDDO command; but if *condition* is true, FoxPro executes the commands following the DO WHILE command until the ENDDO command is reached. When the ENDDO command is reached, the condition in the DO WHILE statement is again evaluated. If it is still true, the commands between DO WHILE and ENDDO are again executed. If the condition is false, FoxPro proceeds to the command below the ENDDO command.

Example

In the following program, a DO...WHILE loop is used to produce an onscreen report using a REPORT FORM command. Each repetition of the DO...WHILE loop causes another 20 records to be displayed on the screen, until the end of the file is reached. If the user presses C (for cancel) after a screenful of records is displayed, the EXIT command terminates the loop, and control passes to the RETURN command.

```
USE MEMBERS INDEX NAMES
CLEAR
WAIT "Press C to CANCEL, any other key to view members."
CLEAR
DO WHILE .NOT. EOF()
     REPORT FORM MEMBERS NEXT 20
     WAIT TO KEEPGOING
     IF UPPER(KEEPGOING) = "C"
          EXIT
     ENDIF
ENDDO
RETURN
```

EDIT

Syntax

EDIT [*scope*] [NOAPPEND] [NOCLEAR] [NOEDIT] [NODELETE]
[NOMENU] [FIELDS *list*] [FOR *condition*] [WHILE *condition*]
[IN WINDOW *windowname*/IN SCREEN]

Syntax for FoxPro 2:

EDIT [*scope*] [FIELDS *fieldlist*] [FOR *condition*] [WHILE *condition*]
[FREEZE *field*] [KEY *exp1*[, *exp2*]] [LAST] [LEDIT] [REDIT] [LPARTITION]
[NOAPPEND] [NOCLEAR] [NODELETE] [NOEDIT/NOMODIFY]
[NOLINK] [NOMENU] [NOOPTIMIZE] [NORMAL] [NOWAIT] [SAVE]
[TIMEOUT *expN*] [TITLE *expC*] [VALID [:F] *expL* [ERROR *expC*]]
[WHEN *expL*] [WIDTH expN] [WINDOW *windowname*]
[IN WINDOW *windowname*/IN SCREEN] [PREFERENCE *expC*]
[COLOR [*standard*][, *enhanced*][, *border*]]/[COLOR SCHEME *expN*]

The EDIT command invokes the FoxPro full-screen editor. If no record number is specified in the *scope*, the current record, which is identified by the current position of the record pointer, will be displayed for editing. Note that the EDIT command is functionally equivalent to the CHANGE command.

The FIELDS option will display only the fields listed in *fieldlist*. The NOCLEAR option causes the edit display to remain on the screen after the changes are completed. The NOAPPEND, NOEDIT, and NODELETE options restrict the use of appending, editing, or deleting when in the EDIT mode. The NOMENU option prevents access to the Edit menu. The FOR and WHILE options let you specify conditions that must be met before a record will appear in the edit screen.

To save changes made during EDIT, press CTRL-W; to exit EDIT without saving changes to the current record, press ESC. Mouse users can use the scroll bars at the right edge of the Edit window (triangular in shape) to scroll the database vertically. Other mouse features work the same with Edit as they do with other windows; you can resize the window by dragging on the size indicator (lower-right corner), and you can zoom the window to full-screen and back by repeated clicking on the zoom indicator (upper-right corner).

Records can be added to a database while in Edit mode by opening the Browse menu with ALT-B and choosing Append Record. Note that there is a CTRL-key equivalent, CTRL-P for this menu option. When you choose the option (or press CTRL-P), a new blank record appears at the end of the file, and the cursor appears in the first field of that record. You can enter the desired information, and exit the Edit Mode when done with CTRL-W, by choosing Close from the File menu, or clicking on the Close Box.

While in Edit mode, an additional menu, the Browse menu, is available. Most options in this menu pertain to the use of FoxPro's Browse mode; see BROWSE for additional details. The menu options which will have an effect while in Edit mode are detailed here:

BROWSE	Shows the database in the Edit Window, but in tabular (browse) format, similar to the display that appears with the Browse command.
TOGGLE DELETE	This lets you mark a record for deletion while in the Browse mode. Place the cursor at the desired record, then choose Toggle Delete to mark the record for deletion.
APPEND RECORD	This adds a blank record to the end of the database.

In FoxPro 1.02 and later, the command also supports an optional [IN WINDOW *windowname*/IN SCREEN] clause. This clause lets you have background windows within windows or on the background screen.

When you include this clause, the inner window (containing the Edit screen) is dependent on the outer window. When the outer window is moved, the inner window moves with it. The inner window cannot be larger than the outer window and can be moved only within the confines of the outer window. If the outer window is closed, the inner window is closed with it. If the outer window is deactivated, the inner window is deactivated with it.

In FoxPro 2, the FREEZE clause is used to freeze a field; changes can then be made only to the specified field. The KEY clause is used to specify an index key value. Use *expr1* to specify a single value matching one found in the index; use *expr1, expr2* to specify a range of values. The CHANGE command will then allow editing only of those records which match the index key values. Use LEDIT to place the left half of the window in Edit mode; use REDIT to place the right half of the window in Edit mode. By default, the cursor appears in the first field of the right partition when the window is split; when LPARTITION is included, the cursor is placed in the first field of the left partition. LAST tells FoxPro to use the most recent configuration (window size, column sizes) of Browse, as stored in the FOXUSER configuration file. NORMAL causes the Browse window to assume normal color attributes, rather than those of a previously defined window. The NOWAIT option is used within programs; when included, program control continues immediately after the Browse window is opened, rather than waiting for the user to exit the Browse mode. The SAVE option is also used only in programs; it keeps both the Browse window and any memo field window that is active both open after editing is completed. The NOOPTIMIZE clause turns off FoxPro's internal optimization techniques.

The PREFERENCE clause lets you save the various attributes and options used by the Edit window for later reuse. The attributes and options for the window are saved to the FOXUSER resource file. The TIMEOUT *n* clause lets you specify how long the window will wait for input; the value of *n* (in seconds) controls the length of time the window remains on the screen without any user input before the window closes. Note that the TIMEOUT clause can only be used in programs; it has no effect when used from the Command window. Use the TITLE clause to specify a title that may appear in the top border of the Edit window. Use the VALID clause to perform record-by-record validation. If a change is made to the record and the logical expression returned by the VALID clause evaluates to false, the error message "Invalid Input" is displayed. (You can change the default error message by including your own character expression along with the optional ERROR clause.) Include the optional :F parameter after the VALID clause to force validation even if the cursor is not moved to the next record. When this parameter is included, validation takes place even when the record is unchanged.

Use the WHEN clause to control whether or not changes can be made to a record. If the logical expression specified by WHEN evaluates to false, changes cannot be made to a record. If the logical expression evaluates to true, changes are permitted.

Example

To edit a database while limiting the available fields to Lastname and Firstname fields in a database, the following command could be used.

```
EDIT FIELDS Lastname, Firstname
```

EJECT

Syntax

EJECT

The EJECT command causes the printer to perform a form feed, advancing the paper to the top of the next page. The EJECT command normally sends a formfeed code (ASCII 12) to the printer.

> *NOTE: The EJECT command resets the printhead position to the top-left corner; the PCOL() and PROW() functions will both return a zero after an EJECT command is issued. Also note that if the printer is not ready when an EJECT is issued, the computer may lock up. Bringing the printer to a ready state will normally cause the computer to resume proper operation.*

Example

In the program shown below, an EJECT command is used to eject the current page after a LABEL FORM command causes 18 names and addresses to be printed on the sheet.

```
SET TALK OFF
USE MEMBERS INDEX NAMES
STORE 1 TO PAGES
SET DEVICE TO PRINT
DO WHILE .NOT. EOF()
    @ 3,50 SAY "Page: " + LTRIM(STR(PAGES))
    @ 4,50 SAY DATE()
    @ 5,20 SAY "Generic Videos Membership Address Roster"
    @ 7,0
    LABEL FORM MEMBERS NEXT 18 TO PRINT
    STORE PAGES + 1 TO PAGES
    EJECT
ENDDO
SET DEVICE TO SCREEN
```

EJECT PAGE

Syntax

EJECT PAGE

The EJECT PAGE command causes the printer to perform a form feed. Use the EJECT PAGE command along with the ON PAGE command to handle page ejects for printed reports. The EJECT PAGE command invokes any end-of-page routines you have established with the ON PAGE command, and it increments _ PAGENO and resets _ PLINENO to zero. Note that the output of the EJECT PAGE command is made available to a disk file or screen if output is being sent to a disk file or screen instead of to the printer.

The EJECT PAGE command performs a similar task as the EJECT command, but EJECT PAGE offers more flexibility. If all you need to do is send a form feed to the printer, use the EJECT command. The EJECT PAGE command works in combination with the printer system memory variables, and the precise effects of the EJECT PAGE command depend on the settings of the printer system memory variables. Assuming you have established an end-of-page routine using ON PAGE, the EJECT PAGE command checks to see if the value of the current line number (_ PLINENO) is before or after the ON PAGE line. If _ PLINENO is before ON PAGE, the EJECT PAGE command sends the needed number of linefeeds. Otherwise, EJECT PAGE either sends a form feed (if SET PRINTER is ON and _ padvance is "FORMFEED") or sufficient line feeds to eject the page (if SET PRINTER is ON and _ padvance is "LINEFEED").

When EJECT PAGE forces a new page, it also increments the _ PAGENO printer system variable, and it resets the _ PLINENO printer system variable to zero.

ENDCASE

Syntax

ENDCASE

The ENDCASE command is the ending command used within the DO CASE construction. See DO CASE for complete details on the ENDCASE command.

ENDDO

Syntax

ENDDO

The ENDDO command is the ending command used within the DO WHILE...ENDDO loop. See DO WHILE for complete details on the ENDDO command.

ENDIF

Syntax

ENDIF

The ENDIF command is the ending command used within the IF...ENDIF construction. See IF for complete details on the ENDIF command.

ENDPRINTJOB

Syntax

ENDPRINTJOB

The ENDPRINTJOB command identifies the end of a print job, as specified with the PRINTJOB command. See PRINTJOB/ENDPRINTJOB for complete details on ENDPRINTJOB.

ENDSCAN

Syntax

ENDSCAN

The ENDSCAN command is the ending command used within the SCAN...ENDSCAN loop. See SCAN for complete details on the ENDSCAN command.

ENDTEXT

Syntax

ENDTEXT

The ENDTEXT command identifies the end of text that is displayed with the TEXT command. See TEXT for complete details on ENDTEXT.

ERASE

Syntax

ERASE *filename.ext*/[?]

The ERASE command erases the named file from the directory. The name must include the file extension. You can also use the command DELETE FILE *filename.ext* to erase a file. If the file is on a disk that is not in the default drive, you must include the drive designator. If the optional question mark is used in place of a filename, a list box appears. The user can select the file to be deleted from the list box.

EXIT

Syntax

EXIT

The EXIT command exits a DO WHILE, FOR, or SCAN loop and proceeds to the first command following the end of the loop (that is, the command after the ENDDO, ENDFOR, or ENDSCAN command).

Example

The following command-file portion uses EXIT to exit the DO WHILE loop if a part number of 9999 is entered.

```
DO WHILE .T.
    ? "Enter part number to add to inventory."
    ? "Enter 9999 to exit."
    INPUT TO PARTNO
    IF PARTNO = 9999
        EXIT
    ENDIF
    APPEND BLANK
    REPLACE PARTNUMB WITH PARTNO
    EDIT
ENDDO
```

EXPORT

Syntax:

Version 2

EXPORT TO *filename* [FIELDS *fieldlist*] [*scope*] [FOR *condition*]
[WHILE *condition*] [NOOPTIMIZE] [TYPE]
DIF/MOD/SYLK/WK1/WKS/WR1/WRK/XLS

The EXPORT command exports a database file to a foreign file of the type specified with the TYPE option, where DIF is Data Interchange Format; MOD is Microsoft Multiplan version 4.01; SYLK is Microsoft SYLK format; XLS is Microsoft Excel format; and WK1, WKS, WR1, and WRK are Lotus 1-2-3 formats.

Use the FIELDS clause to limit the fields that are copied to the foreign file. The FOR and WHILE clauses can be used to limit records that are copied to the other file. Use the NOOPTIMIZE clause to disable the normal optimization techniques (Rushmore) used by FoxPro 2.

EXTERNAL

Syntax

Version 2

EXTERNAL ARRAY/LABEL/LIBRARY/MENU/PROCEDURE/REPORT/
SCREEN *filename/arrayname*

The EXTERNAL command is used to make the FoxPro project manager aware of an undefined reference. The EXTERNAL command is ignored by FoxPro during normal execution of a program, as it is used only by the FoxPro Project Manager. The EXTERNAL command is needed if you use the Project Manager to maintain your applications. Use the command EXTERNAL, followed by the appropriate keyword (ARRAY, LABEL, LIBRARY, MENU, PROCEDURE, REPORT, or SCREEN), followed by the filename. This tells the Project Manager to include the specified file in the project database.

FILER

Syntax

FILER [LIKE *skeleton*] [NOWAIT] [IN WINDOW *windowname*/IN SCREEN]

The FILER command displays the FoxPro Filer, a utility for managing the hard disk. (See Chapter 12 for details on the use of the Filer.) An optional file skeleton can be included with the LIKE clause, which brings up the Filer with only those file types showing in the List Files box.

The NOWAIT option works only within programs. If the NOWAIT option is added, the Filer is displayed, and program execution continues. If the option is omitted, program execution halts when the Filer is displayed from within a program, and program execution continues when the Filer window is closed.

In FoxPro 1.02 and later, the command also supports an optional [IN WINDOW *windowname*/IN SCREEN] clause. This clause lets you have background windows within windows or on the background screen.

When you include this clause, the inner window is dependent on the outer window. When the outer window is moved, the inner window moves with it. The inner window cannot be larger than the outer window and can be moved only within the confines of the outer window. If the outer window is closed, the inner window is closed with it. If the outer window is deactivated, the inner window is deactivated with it.

FIND

Syntax

FIND *character-string*

The FIND command positions the record pointer at the first record containing an index key that matches *character-string*. If there are leading blanks in *character-string*, *character-string* must be surrounded by single or double quotes; otherwise, no quotes are necessary. If the specific character string cannot be found, the EOF() value is set to true, and a NO FIND message is displayed on the screen (if FoxPro is not executing a command file). An index file must be open before you use the FIND command.

You can use a memory variable containing a character expression with the FIND command, but must use a macro ahead of the variable name. For example, if the variable SEARCHER contains the character string "Robinson," you could enter **FIND &SEARCHER** to find the string "Robinson" in the index.

NOTE: The FIND command searches for an exact match, in terms of capitalization. In FoxPro, uppercase and lowercase letters are considered to be different characters. When performing a search with the FIND command, "Moore" and "moore" would be considered different names. One method of preventing problems with the case-significance of FoxPro is to use the UPPER function when performing searches. Another method is to design entry forms that store character data as all uppercase letters (see SET FORMAT).

When searching for a character string, FIND allows you to search on only the beginning of the string if SET EXACT is OFF (the default for SET EXACT is OFF). For example, assuming the string "Williams" exists in the index, the command

```
FIND Will
```

would find the record if SET EXACT is OFF. If you use the command SET EXACT ON, the search shown above would not be successful; SET EXACT, when ON, requires the search expression provided with FIND to precisely match the contents of the index.

The FIND command offers the advantage of speed over the LOCATE command. LOCATE is simple to use but slow. In a database containing thousands of records, a LOCATE command can take several minutes. A FIND command can accomplish the same task in a matter of seconds.

Example

In the example below, the FIND command is used to search an index file based on the Lastname field of the database. When the FIND is unsuccessful, the EOF() function returns a logical true, and the FOUND() function returns a logical false.

```
USE EMPLOYED
INDEX ON Lastname TO EMPLOYED
```

```
LIST OFF

LASTNAME    FIRSTNAME    GRADE HIREDATE  SALARY CITY       STATE
Johnson     Linda        G-12  04/30/81 2890.30 Carrollton TX
Johnson     Martin       G-11  07/01/77 2495.00 Fort Worth TX
Klein       Samuel       G-09  11/01/84 1775.00 Carrollton TX
Martin      Lydia        G-07  02/05/84 1390.00 Fort Worth TX
Roberts     Jerry        G-09  09/13/84 1740.00 Dallas     TX
Robertson   Henry        G-08  03/01/86 1534.60 Garland    TX
Sanders     Anette       G-06  12/01/87 1170.20 Dallas     TX
Smith       Karen        G-10  03/18/75 2075.40 Dallas     TX
Williams    Greg         G-09  10/18/83 1890.50 Arlington  TX

FIND Robertson
DISPLAY

Record#  LASTNAME       FIRSTNAME       GRADE HIREDATE  SALARY
CITY          STATE
      7  Robertson      Henry           G-08  03/01/86 1534.60
Garland       TX

FIND Martin
DISPLAY

Record#  LASTNAME       FIRSTNAME       GRADE HIREDATE  SALARY
CITY          STATE
      8  Martin         Lydia           G-07  02/05/84 1390.00
Fort Worth    TX

FIND Wilson
No find.

? EOF()
.T.

? FOUND()
.F.
```

FLUSH

Syntax

FLUSH

The FLUSH command flushes all active buffers to disk without closing the files. During processing, data is normally retained in memory; FoxPro realizes major speed gains by keeping large amounts of data in memory. Data is normally written from memory to disk when the buffers are full or when you use a command that closes a file (such as CLOSE DATABASES, USE, CLOSE ALL, or SET INDEX). To protect data integrity or to free up available memory for other use, you can use the FLUSH command to empty the buffers to disk.

FOR

Syntax

FOR *memvar* = *expN1* TO *expN2* [STEP *expN3*] commands...
ENDFOR

The FOR and accompanying ENDFOR statements set up a repetitive loop, which repeats a set number of times, as defined by the numeric expressions. The value of *expN1* marks the starting point, and the value of *expN2* marks the ending point. The loop repeats the number of times specified between *expN1* and *expN2*, unless an incremental value other than 1 is specified with the optional STEP clause. Once the set number of repetitions has been accomplished, FoxPro proceeds to the command below the ENDFOR command. If a STEP clause is used, *memvar* is incremented (or, if the value of STEP is negative, decremented) every time the ENDFOR is encountered until *memvar* equals or exceeds *expN2*.

Example

To use the FOR...ENDFOR commands to print Lastname, Firstname, City, and State fields for a specified number of records, you could use the following program:

```
USE MEMBERS
INPUT "Print how many records? " TO COUNTERS
STORE 1 TO BEGIN
FOR BEGIN = 1 TO COUNTERS
    ? Lastname, Firstname, City, State
    SKIP
ENDFOR
```

FUNCTION

Syntax

FUNCTION *procedurename* [PARAMETERS *list* RETURN *expression*]

The FUNCTION command identifies a procedure that serves as a user-defined function, or UDF. UDFs are functions you design. Like the standard functions, they can be provided with values, and they return values. Use UDFs to accomplish specialized tasks that are outside the range of the standard functions provided with FoxPro.

Functions may be placed within the currently executing program or within a procedure file, along with any other procedures the program may be using. If the functions are placed in a procedure file, the SET PROCEDURE TO statement must be used to identify where the UDFs can be found before a UDF is called. All UDFs start with the FUNCTION command and contain the commands and parameters needed to return the desired values. The names given to UDFs must be eight characters or less. Note that *list* of parameters is a list of one or more memory-variable names representing the values you will supply to the function. *Expression* is the value to be returned by the function. For example, perhaps you often need to convert temperature readings in centigrade stored in a scientific database to Fahrenheit. You could define a function for this purpose, which could resemble

```
FUNCTION FARENHT
PARAMETERS CTEMP
FTEMP = 9/5 * (CTEMP+32)
RETURN FTEMP
```

At any location in the program, you would call the function. If the database field containing the temperature readings were named Temp, you might use a statement like

```
? FARENHT(Temp)
```

and the function FARENHT() would return the value contained in the Temp field, converted to Fahrenheit.

You can also specify that UDFs return a true or false value, depending on how the commands within your UDF evaluate a particular condition. An example of this technique follows.

Example

In this example, the UDF checks to see if a two-letter code for a state entered by a user is actually a valid state.

```
FUNCTION ValState
PARAMETERS State
IF UPPER(state) $ "AK AL AR AZ CA CO CT DC DE FL GA " + ;
"HI IA ID IL IN KA KY LA MA MD ME MI MN MO MS MT NB " + ;
"NC ND NH NJ NM NY OH OK OR PA RI SC SD TN TX UT VA " + ;
"VT WA WI WV WY"
     RETURN .T.
ENDIF
RETURN .F.
```

A portion of a data entry program could use the function to verify for proper entries:

```
@ 7, 5 SAY "State: " GET MSTATE VALID ValState(MSTATE)
READ
...rest of program...
```

GATHER FROM

Syntax

GATHER FROM *array* [FIELDS *fieldlist*]

The GATHER FROM command is used to move data from an array of memory variables into a database file. (Note that GATHER FROM is compatible with FoxBASE+; if you need compatibility with dBASE IV, use APPEND FROM ARRAY instead.) The elements of the array are transferred, beginning with the first element of the array, into the corresponding records of the database file. If there are more elements in the array than fields in the database, the extra elements are ignored. If there are more fields in the database than there are elements in the array, the extra fields remain empty. Note that memo fields are ignored during the data transfer process, as there is no memo-type memory variable.

The FOR clause, which is optional, lets you define a condition that must be met before data in the array will be added to a new record. The condition specified with the FOR clause must include a field name from a database. If the condition evaluates as true, a row of the array gets appended to the database. If the condition evaluates as false, the row of the array is skipped and the next row is evaluated.

Example

The following data entry program uses an array to store responses to @...SAY...GET commands. The values stored to the elements of the array are then transferred to the fields of the database. In operation, this example performs the same task as the example shown with the APPEND BLANK command. Note, however, that the use of GATHER FROM eliminates the need for the usual REPLACE statements.

```
CLEAR
*open files, create memory variables.
USE MAILER INDEX NAMES
ACCEPT "Enter last name to edit:" TO FINDIT
SEEK FINDIT
IF .NOT. FOUND()
     WAIT "Can't find that record. Press a key..."
     RETURN
ENDIF
SCATTER TO M_DATA
DEFINE WINDOW Changes FROM 5,5 TO 15,70 PANEL
ACTIVATE WINDOW Changes
*display prompts, store data to variables.
@    3,5 SAY " LAST NAME:" GET M_DATA[1,1]
@    4,5 SAY "FIRST NAME:" GET M_DATA[1,2]
@    8,5 SAY "ADDRESS:" GET M_DATA[1,3]
@   10,5 SAY "   CITY:" GET M_DATA[1,4]
@ 10,35 SAY "STATE:" GET M_DATA[1,5]
@ 10,45 SAY "ZIP CODE:" GET M_DATA[1,6]
READ
*store variables.
GATHER FROM M_DATA
DEACTIVATE WINDOW Changes
RETURN
```

GETEXPR

Syntax

GETEXPR [*expC*] TO *memvar*

The GETEXPR command displays the FoxPro Expression Builder. The expression constructed by the user with the Expression Builder is then stored to the memory variable specified as part of the GETEXPR command. The GETEXPR command can be used within a program to allow the user to define selection criteria for printing a report or a set of labels.

The character expression *expC1* is an optional message; if used, it will appear within the Expression Builder. The TYPE clause, along with *expc2*, can be used to limit the acceptable response to a specific type: "C" for character, "N" for numeric, "D" for date, and "L" for logical. When used, *expc3* contains an optional error message that appears if the type supplied by the user does not match the type defined by *expc2*. Use the *expc4* optional expression to define a default expression; that expression appears automatically in the Expression Builder when it appears.

Example

The GETEXPR command is used within the following program to allow the user to enter a search expression to perform a LOCATE search on the database.

```
USE MEMBERS
GETEXPR "Enter desired locate condition." TO FINDER TYPE "L"
LOCATE FOR &FINDER
IF .NOT. FOUND()
     CLEAR
     WAIT " Can't find this record. Press a key..."
     RETURN
ENDIF
EDIT
RETURN
```

GO or GOTO

Syntax

GO or GOTO BOTTOM/TOP/*expn* [IN *alias*]

The GO and GOTO commands position the record pointer at a record. GO TOP will move the pointer to the beginning of a database, while GO BOTTOM will move it to the end of a database. If a numeric value is provided, the pointer moves to that record number. The IN *alias* clause can be used to move the record pointer in a database that is open in another work area. *Alias* can be either the file alias or a work area number.

NOTE: The GO[TO] command will override the effects of a SET FILTER command or of a SET DELETED command. If SET DELETED is ON and GO[TO] is used to move to a deleted record, the record pointer will be at the deleted record. Likewise, if a record is hidden by the effects of the SET FILTER command, GO[TO] can be used to move the record pointer to that record, although it remains hidden from use by other commands such as BROWSE and EDIT.

When you have established a relationship to other file(s) using SET RELATION, any movement of the record pointer with the GO[TO] command will cause a corresponding movement of the record pointer in the related database. In the related database, the record pointer moves to the matching record according to the expression specified by the SET RELATION command (see SET RELATION). If no matching record can be found, the record pointer in the related database is moved to the end of the file, and the value of EOF() is set to true.

Example

In the following example the GO command is used to position the record pointer to a particular record. Note that when an attempt is made to position the record pointer past the end of the file, an error is reported, and the value of the end-of-file function, EOF(), is set to a logical true.

```
USE EMPLOYED
LIST Lastname, Firstname, Salary, City, State OFF
```

LASTNAME	FIRSTNAME	SALARY	CITY	STATE
Smith	Karen	2075.40	Dallas	TX
Williams	Greg	1890.50	Arlington	TX
Johnson	Linda	2890.30	Carrollton	TX
Johnson	Martin	2495.00	Fort Worth	TX
Sanders	Anette	1170.20	Dallas	TX
Roberts	Jerry	1740.00	Dallas	TX
Robertson	Henry	1534.60	Garland	TX
Martin	Lydia	1390.00	Fort Worth	TX
Klein	Samuel	1775.00	Carrollton	TX

```
GO TOP
DISPLAY Lastname, Firstname
```

```
Record#  LASTNAME      FIRSTNAME
      1  Smith         Karen

GO BOTTOM
DISPLAY Lastname, Firstname

Record#  LASTNAME      FIRSTNAME
      9  Klein         Samuel

INDEX ON Lastname TO NAMES
GO TOP
DISPLAY Lastname, Firstname

Record#  LASTNAME      FIRSTNAME
      3  Johnson       Linda

GO BOTTOM
DISPLAY Lastname, Firstname

Record#  LASTNAME      FIRSTNAME
      2  Williams      Greg

GO 5
DISPLAY Lastname, Firstname

Record#  LASTNAME      FIRSTNAME
      5  Sanders       Anette

GO 12

Record is out of range.
```

HELP

Syntax

HELP [*commandname or functionname*]
[IN WINDOW *window name*/IN SCREEN]

The HELP command provides instructions on using FoxPro commands and functions, as well as other information. Entering the HELP command alone causes the display of a menu of help topics, contained within a help window. You can use the cursor keys and the PGUP and PGDN keys to move within the help window; you can also use the mouse scroll bars or press the first letter or letters of the command; then, press ENTER, and the help text for that command will appear in the window.

If HELP is followed by a command or function, information about that command or function will be displayed.

In FoxPro 1.02 and later, the command also supports an optional [IN WINDOW *windowname*/IN SCREEN] clause. This clause lets you have background windows within windows or on the background screen.

When you include this clause, the inner window (containing the Help screen) is dependent on the outer window. When the outer window is moved, the inner window moves with it. The inner window cannot be larger than the outer window and can be moved only within the confines of the outer window. If the outer window is closed, the inner window is closed with it. If the outer window is deactivated, the inner window is deactivated with it.

HIDE MENU

Syntax

HIDE MENU [[*name1*][, *name2*...]]/[ALL] [SAVE]

The HIDE MENU command hides the named menu bar(s) or all menu bars from the screen or a window. HIDE MENU is useful for when you want to remove the appearance of a menu from the screen, but you intend to use the menu later. If you want to remove the menu and don't need it at a later time, use DEACTIVATE MENU instead to free the memory used by the menu. As long as a menu is hidden, it remains in memory, and you can redisplay it at any time with the SHOW MENU or ACTIVATE MENU commands.

To hide a specific menu bar, include its name. To hide a set of menu bars, include a list of menu bar names. You can hide all menus currently on the screen by using the ALL option with the HIDE MENU command.

Use the SAVE option to place an image of a menu bar on the screen or in a window. This technique can be useful when you are developing and testing programs.

HIDE POPUP

Syntax

HIDE POPUP [[*name1*][, *name2*...]]/[ALL] [SAVE]

The HIDE POPUP command hides the named popup(s) or all popup menus from the screen or a window. HIDE POPUP is useful when you want to remove the appearance of a popup from the screen, but you intend to use the popup later. If you want to remove the popup and don't need it at a later time, use DEACTIVATE POPUP instead to free the memory used by the popup. As long as a popup is hidden it remains in memory, and you can redisplay it at any time with the SHOW POPUP or ACTIVATE POPUP commands.

To hide a specific popup, include its name. To hide a set of popups, include a list of popup names. You can hide all popups currently on the screen by using the ALL option with the HIDE POPUP command.

Use the SAVE option to place an image of a popup on the screen or in a window. This technique can be useful when you are developing and testing programs.

HIDE WINDOW

Syntax

HIDE WINDOW [[*name1*][, *name2*...]]/[ALL]
[IN WINDOW *windowname*/IN SCREEN]

The HIDE WINDOW command hides a current window while retaining the window in memory. To hide a specific window, include its name. To hide a set of windows, include a list of window names. To hide all defined windows, include the ALL option. If the ALL option is omitted and no name is provided, the currently active window is hidden.

NOTE: *Hiding a window is not the same as deactivating a window. Hidden windows remain active in memory, and screen output can still be directed to a hidden window; the window simply remains invisible. By comparison, deactivating a window removes it from memory, and screen output can no longer be sent to that window.*

You can also hide windows by selecting the Hide option of the Window menu. To redisplay the window, select it by name from the Window menu.

In FoxPro 1.02 and later, the HIDE WINDOW command also supports an optional [IN WINDOW *windowname*/IN SCREEN] clause. This clause lets you have background windows within windows or on the background screen.

When you include this clause, the inner window is dependent on the outer window. When the outer window is moved, the inner window moves with it. The inner window cannot be larger than the outer window and can be moved only within the confines of the outer window. If the outer window is closed, the inner window is closed with it. If the outer window is deactivated, the inner window is deactivated with it.

Example

The example shown below defines a help window called MyWind. The ACTIVATE WINDOW command is used to display the window, then the HIDE WINDOW command is used (after the WAIT statement) to hide the window, and the previous display appears underneath. After the user responds to the second WAIT statement, the help window is redisplayed.

```
ACCEPT "Enter company name:" TO FINDER
SEEK FINDER
DEFINE WINDOW MyWind FROM 4,2 TO 11,65;
TITLE "SystemHelp" CLOSE GROW FLOAT ZOOM PANEL
ACTIVATE WINDOW MyWind
@ 2,3 SAY "Get the customer number from the Edit screen."
@ 3,3 SAY "Enter all digits, including the hyphen."
WAIT
HIDE WINDOW MyWind
@ 2,3 SAY "The customer number you just read must be entered"
@ 3,3 SAY "in the transactions screen which will appear next."
WAIT
SHOW WINDOW MyWind
```

IF

Syntax

> IF *condition*
>   *commands...*
> [ELSE]
>   *commands...*
> ENDIF

IF is a decision-making command that will execute commands when certain conditions are true. If the condition for the IF statement is true, the commands between the IF and ENDIF will be executed. Should the condition be false and there is an ELSE, the commands between ELSE and ENDIF will be executed. On the other hand, if the condition for IF is not true and there is no ELSE, FoxPro will drop to the ENDIF statement without executing any commands.

NOTE: IF...ENDIF can only be used within programs. However, you can obtain the same type of decision-based qualifying from the command level by using the IIF() function. See IIF() in Chapter 23 for additional details.

Nesting of multiple IF...ENDIF statements is permitted, as demonstrated in the example.

Example

In the following example, whether the innermost IF...ENDIF is ever processed is determined by the response supplied to the outermost IF...ENDIF statement. If the user does not input **P** for printer, program control skips ahead to the ELSE statement, and the report is output to the screen with the REPORT FORM command. If the user does respond with **P** for printer, the "Ready printer" message is displayed, and the innermost IF...ENDIF tests for a response, and takes appropriate action (that of running the report to the printer if the user does not cancel by typing **P**).

```
ACCEPT "Display report on (S)creen or (P)rinter?" TO ANS
IF UPPER(ANS) = "P"
     *send report to default printer.
     ACCEPT "Ready printer, press ENTER or type C then;
     press ENTER to cancel report." TO ANS2
     IF UPPER(ANS2) = "C"
          *user cancelled print run.
          RETURN
     ENDIF
     REPORT FORM MEMBERS TO PRINT
     EJECT
ELSE
     *display report on screen only.
     REPORT FORM MEMBERS
ENDIF
```

IMPORT

Syntax:

Version 2

IMPORT FROM *filename*
[TYPE] DIF/FW2/MOD/PDOX/RPD/SYLK/WK1/WK3/WKS/WR1/WRK/XLS

The IMPORT command imports a foreign file of the type specified with the TYPE option and creates an equivalent database file. Use the TYPE option to specify the format of the foreign file where DIF is Data Interchange Format; FW2 is Framework II; MOD is Microsoft Multiplan version 4.01; PDOX is Paradox; RPD is RapidFile; SYLK is Microsoft SYLK format; XLS is Microsoft Excel format; and WK1, WK3, WR1, and WRK are Lotus 1-2-3 formats.

INDEX

Syntax

INDEX ON *expC* TO *filename* [DESCENDING] [UNIQUE]

Syntax for FoxPro 2

INDEX ON *expr* TO *.IDX file*/TAG *tagname* [OF *.CDXfile*] [FOR *expL*] [COMPACT] [ASCENDING/DESCENDING] [UNIQUE] [ADDITIVE]

The INDEX command creates an index file based on an expression, *expr*, (which is usually a field name or a combination of fields) from the active database. Depending on the expression, the index file will be indexed alphabetically, numerically, chronologically, or logically. If an index based on the first field of an expression has duplicate entries, the duplicates are indexed according to additional fields in the expression, provided additional fields have been listed. When the UNIQUE option is used, duplicate entries are omitted from the index. The indexing occurs in ascending order unless you add the DESCENDING option.

The TAG *tagname* and OF *.cdx filename* options can be used to specify that the index should be a tag of a compound-index file. If the OF clause is omitted and the TAG clause is included, the tag is added to the structural compound-index file; if none exists, one with the same name as the database is created. The COMPACT clause forces the creation of an index file in the compact format, *Version 2* compatible only with FoxPro 2 and later. The ASCENDING clause specifies an index in ascending order; this is also the default if no ASCENDING or DESCENDING clause is used.

During the indexing process, the record number is used to reference the record in the parent database. In effect, an index file is a virtual sort of the parent database, since none of the records in the parent database are sorted. When the database file is opened along with the index file, the first record to be retrieved

is not the first record in the parent database; instead, it is the first record listed in the index. The next record retrieved will be the second record listed in the index, and so on. Indexing does not affect the order of the records in the database.

A simple use of the syntax INDEX ON *fieldname* TO *index file* name creates an index file based on the named field, with all records included in the index. The UNIQUE clause, if added, causes a "unique" index to be constructed. Such an index will not contain any duplicates of the index expression. You would use this type of index to intentionally hide any accidental duplicate records. For example, if a social security field were used to build the index and two records contained the same social security number, the second occurrence would be omitted from the index.

Indexes are normally arranged in ascending order. You can use the DESCENDING clause to specify that an index should be arranged in descending order. To index on multiple fields of different types, use functions to convert the fields to a common type. For example, to build an index file that is indexed in alphabetical order based on the contents of a State field, and in numeric order by the contents of the Salary field within each group of states, the following command could be used.

```
INDEX ON State + STR(Salary) TO MYFILE
```

Multiple index files can be open at the same time, although only one index file will be the controlling (or active) index. To change the active index when more than one index file is open, use the SET ORDER command (see SET ORDER).

After an index has been created, it can be put into use with a number of different commands. A newly created index is immediately active after its creation, but is closed when you close the database. Thereafter, the index file may be reopened with the SET INDEX TO command or by specifying the keyword INDEX followed by the index name along with the USE command. (See USE and SET INDEX for full descriptions of these command options.)

Example

The INDEX commands and the resulting listings shown below demonstrate the effects of the INDEX command.

```
USE EMPLOYED
LIST Lastname, Firstname, Salary, City, State OFF
```

LASTNAME	FIRSTNAME	SALARY	CITY	STATE
Smith	Karen	2075.40	Dallas	TX
Williams	Greg	1890.50	Arlington	TX
Johnson	Linda	2890.30	Carrollton	TX
Johnson	Martin	2495.00	Fort Worth	TX

```
Sanders        Anette         1170.20 Dallas         TX
Roberts        Jerry          1740.00 Dallas         TX
Robertson      Henry          1534.60 Garland        TX
Martin         Lydia          1390.00 Fort Worth     TX
Klein          Samuel         1775.00 Carrollton     TX
```

INDEX ON Lastname + Firstname TO NAMES
LIST Lastname, Firstname, Salary, City, State OFF

```
LASTNAME       FIRSTNAME      SALARY CITY            STATE
Johnson        Linda          2890.30 Carrollton     TX
Johnson        Martin         2495.00 Fort Worth     TX
Klein          Samuel         1775.00 Carrollton     TX
Martin         Lydia          1390.00 Fort Worth     TX
Roberts        Jerry          1740.00 Dallas         TX
Robertson      Henry          1534.60 Garland        TX
Sanders        Anette         1170.20 Dallas         TX
Smith          Karen          2075.40 Dallas         TX
Williams       Greg           1890.50 Arlington      TX
```

INDEX ON SALARY TO COSTS
LIST Lastname, Firstname, Salary, City, State OFF

```
LASTNAME       FIRSTNAME      SALARY CITY            STATE
Sanders        Anette         1170.20 Dallas         TX
Martin         Lydia          1390.00 Fort Worth     TX
Robertson      Henry          1534.60 Garland        TX
Roberts        Jerry          1740.00 Dallas         TX
Klein          Samuel         1775.00 Carrollton     TX
Williams       Greg           1890.50 Arlington      TX
Smith          Karen          2075.40 Dallas         TX
Johnson        Martin         2495.00 Fort Worth     TX
Johnson        Linda          2890.30 Carrollton     TX
```

INDEX ON State + City TO TOWNS
LIST Lastname, Firstname, Salary, City, State OFF

```
LASTNAME       FIRSTNAME      SALARY CITY            STATE
Williams       Greg           1890.50 Arlington      TX
Johnson        Linda          2890.30 Carrollton     TX
Klein          Samuel         1775.00 Carrollton     TX
Smith          Karen          2075.40 Dallas         TX
Sanders        Anette         1170.20 Dallas         TX
Roberts        Jerry          1740.00 Dallas         TX
Johnson        Martin         2495.00 Fort Worth     TX
Martin         Lydia          1390.00 Fort Worth     TX
Robertson      Henry          1534.60 Garland        TX
```

INPUT

Syntax

INPUT [*expC*] [TO *memvar*]

The INPUT command stores a numeric entry that is entered by the user to a memory variable. An optional character expression can display a message to the user during keyboard entry. The expression can be a memory variable or a character string.

Example

To display the prompt "Enter new salary amount:," and store the response to the memory variable NEWAMT, the following command could be used.

```
INPUT "Enter new salary amount:" TO NEWAMT
```

INSERT

Syntax

INSERT [BLANK] [BEFORE]

The INSERT command adds a new record below the record pointer's position and renumbers the records below the insertion. Specifying BEFORE causes the record to be inserted at the record pointer; thus, if the pointer is at record 3, the new record will be 3 and the records below it renumbered. If the BLANK option is omitted, FoxPro allows immediate editing of the new record; otherwise, the record will be blank, but editing mode will not be entered.

WARNING: The INSERT command has been provided for backward compatibility with programs written in the dBASE language, but its use is not highly recommended. With large databases, the use of the INSERT command can be very time consuming. It is generally better to use the APPEND or APPEND BLANK commands.

Example

To insert a new record at position 10 in the active data base, you could use the following command:

```
GO 10
INSERT BEFORE
```

JOIN

Syntax

JOIN WITH *alias* TO *filename* FOR *condition* [FIELDS *fieldlist*] [FOR *condition*]

The JOIN command creates a new database by combining specific records and fields from the active database and another database, listed as *alias*. The combined database is assigned the name filename. When the joining process begins, the record pointer is placed at the start of the active file. Each record in the alias database is then evaluated to see if any specified FOR condition is true. If the specified condition is true (or if no condition was specified), a new record with the combined information from the active database and the alias database will be added to the new database. This process is repeated for every record in the active file.

You can limit the choice of records from the active database by specifying a FOR condition. All fields from both files will be copied if you do not include a *fieldlist*; but if you do, only those fields specified in *fieldlist* will be copied. Specify fields from the alias database by including the alias name and pointer (*filename -> fieldname*). Note that field lists used in a JOIN operation may not contain memo fields.

Exercise care when using JOIN. The command processes an amount equal to the number of records in the active database times the number of records in the alias database. If you accidentally or intentionally define a JOIN statement where every record is processed, the created database will contain a number of records equal to the records in the active file times the records in the alias file. Assuming an active file of 300,000 records and an alias file of 300,000 records, this would attempt to create a database of 90 billion records, far beyond the capacity of FoxPro (not to mention most hard disks).

HINT: SET RELATION generally works faster, and with less trouble, than JOIN.

The JOIN command is very much a holdover from the days of dBASE II and does not provide the power of the SET RELATION command. It has been included in current versions of FoxPro to provide compatibility with programs originally written in dBASE II. JOIN should be avoided, however, as it is time consuming and can use large amounts of disk space. In most cases, the same results can be accomplished faster and with less disk space needed by using a SET RELATION command (see SET RELATION).

Example

Two databases contain listings of a parts inventory and of customer orders for specific parts, as follows. The JOIN command is used in the example to create a third file showing the names of parts ordered by specific customers. Note that the three lines making up the JOIN command are shown as three lines due to printing limitations. At the command level, these could be entered as a single line without the semicolons.

```
USE PARTS
LIST OFF

PARTNO         DESCRIPT        COST
1001           keyboard        175.80
1002           disk drive      192.55
1003           memory chip       6.15
1004           power supply    128.32
1005           microprocessor   24.74

USE ORDERS
LIST OFF

CUSTNO         CUSTNAME        PARTNO    QUANTITY
0001           Smith           1003      9
0002           Johnson         1005      2
0003           Mills           1002      2
0004           Reynolds        1001      1

CLEAR ALL
SELECT 2
USE ORDERS
SELECT 1
USE PARTS
JOIN WITH ORDERS TO FINALS FOR Partno = Orders->Partno ;
FIELDS Orders->Custname, Orders->Partno, Orders->Quantity, ;
PARTS->Cost, Parts->Descript
```

```
USE FINALS
LIST

CUSTNAME  PARTNO    QUANTITY      COST    DESCRIPTION
Smith     1003         9          6.15    memory chip
Johnson   1005         2         24.75    microprocessor
Mills     1002         2        192.55    disk drive
Reynolds  1001         1        175.80    keyboard
```

KEYBOARD

Syntax

KEYBOARD *expC* [PLAIN]

The KEYBOARD command stuffs the keyboard buffer with a character string. The data will remain in the keyboard buffer until the program seeks input from the keyboard. The KEYBOARD command can be very useful for creating self-executing demonstrations that showcase your programs. (Note that the PLAY MACRO command can also be used to emulate keystrokes for self-running demos or other purposes (see PLAY MACRO).)

The PLAIN option, when used, tells FoxPro to ignore any keyboard assignments made by macros and to stuff the literal characters specified by *expC* into the keyboard buffer.

Example

To fill a data entry field with the name "San Jose" followed by a carriage return, the following command could be used.

```
KEYBOARD "San Jose" + CHR(13)
```

LABEL FORM

Syntax

LABEL FORM *label-filename/?* [*scope*] [SAMPLE] [FOR *condition*]
[WHILE *condition*] [TO PRINT] [TO FILE *filename*] [NOCONSOLE]
[ENVIRONMENT] [OFF]

Syntax for FoxPro 2

> LABEL FORM *label-filename*/? [*scope*] [SAMPLE] [FOR *condition*]
> [WHILE *condition*] [TO PRINT] [TO FILE *filename*] [ENVIRONMENT]
> [OFF]
> [NOCONSOLE] [NOOPTIMIZE] [PREVIEW]

The LABEL FORM command is used to print mailing labels from a label form file (extension .LBX). The SAMPLE option allows a sample label to be printed. The FOR option can be used to specify a condition that must be met before a label for a record will be printed. If you use the WHILE option, records will be printed until the condition is no longer true. The TO PRINT option sends output to the printer, while the TO FILE option sends output to a named disk file. The NOCONSOLE option suppresses the appearance of the labels on the screen. The ENVIRONMENT option causes a view file with the same name as the label file to be used before printing begins. If the question mark is substituted for a filename, a box containing a list of all label files appears. The user may then select the label to print from the list. The OFF option causes the display of labels on the screen to be suppressed while the labels are printed or sent to a file.

In FoxPro 2 and later, the NOOPTIMIZE clause, when added, turns off FoxPro's internal optimization techniques (Rushmore). The PREVIEW option sends the labels to screen in Page Preview mode, and the labels are not printed.

Example

To print mailing labels, using a label form named MAILERS, for records with State fields containing "NM", and to restrict printing to the next 25 records beginning at the current record-pointer position, enter

```
LABEL FORM MAILERS NEXT 25 FOR STATE = "NM" TO PRINT
```

LIST

Syntax

> LIST [OFF] [*scope*] [*fieldlist*] [FOR *condition*] [WHILE *condition*]
> [TO PRINT/TO FILE *filename*]

Syntax for FoxPro 2

LIST [OFF] [*scope*] [*fieldlist*] [FOR *condition*] [WHILE *condition*]
[TO PRINT/TO FILE *filename*] [NOOPTIMIZE]

The LIST command provides a list of database contents. The *scope* option is used to quantify the records to be listed. If *scope* is absent, ALL is assumed. The FOR option specifies a *condition* that must be met before a record will be listed. If you use the WHILE option, records will be listed until the condition is no longer true. The OFF option will prevent the record number from being listed. If the TO PRINT option is used, the listing will be printed on the printer. TO FILE directs the list to a disk file. In FoxPro 2 and later, the NOOPTIMIZE clause, when added, turns off FoxPro's internal optimization techniques (Rushmore).

REMINDER: *Contents of memo fields are not shown with LIST unless you name the memo field(s) as part of a field list.*

Example

To list the fields Lastname, Firstname, Salary, Hired, and Grade from a personnel file, showing only those records containing an amount greater than $10.00 in the SALARY field, the following command could be used.

```
LIST Lastname, Firstname, Salary, Hired, Grade FOR Salary > 10
```

LIST FILES

Syntax

LIST FILES [ON *drive/dir* [LIKE *skeleton*] [TO PRINT/TO FILE *filename*]

The LIST FILES command displays a list of disk files. Use the ON option to specify a drive and/or directory. Wildcards may be used as skeletons. For example, entering **LIST FILES LIKE *.IDX** would display all files with the extension of .IDX. The TO PRINT and TO FILE options may be used to route the list to the printer or to the named disk file.

The LIST FILES command is identical to DISPLAY FILES, except that the screen display does not pause between each screenful. For additional details and specific examples, see DISPLAY FILES.

LIST MEMORY

Syntax

LIST MEMORY [LIKE *skeleton*] [TO PRINT/TO FILE *filename*]

The LIST MEMORY command lists the names, sizes, and types of memory variables. Wildcards may be used to define skeletons. For example, entering **LIST MEMORY LIKE MEM*** would display all variables beginning with "MEM". If the TO PRINT option is used, the listing will be printed on the printer. If the TO FILE option is used, the listing will be directed to the named disk file.

The LIST MEMORY command is identical to DISPLAY MEMORY, except that the screen display does not pause between each screenful. For additional details including an explanation of memory variable types along with specific examples, see DISPLAY MEMORY.

LIST STATUS

Syntax

LIST STATUS [TO PRINT/TO FILE *filename*]

The LIST STATUS command lists information on currently open work areas, the active file, and system settings. All open files and open index filenames are displayed, along with work area numbers, any expressions used in index files, the default disk drive, function-key settings, and settings of the SET commands. If the TO PRINT option is used, the listing will be printed on the printer.

The LIST STATUS command is identical to DISPLAY STATUS, except that the screen display does not pause between each screenful. For additional details along with specific examples, see DISPLAY STATUS.

LIST STRUCTURE

Syntax

LIST STRUCTURE [TO PRINT/TO FILE *filename*] [IN ALIAS *alias*]

The LIST STRUCTURE command lists the structure of the database in use, including the name, number of records, all names of fields, and the date of the last update. If the TO PRINT option is used, the listing will be printed on the printer. The TO FILE option may be specified to redirect the output to a file. LIST STRUCTURE does not pause during the listing, which is the only difference between LIST STRUCTURE and DISPLAY STRUCTURE. The IN ALIAS option may be used to list the structure of a file in another work area. *Alias* may be either an alias name or a work area number.

The LIST STRUCTURE command is identical to DISPLAY STRUCTURE, except that the screen display does not pause between each screenful. For additional details and specific examples, see DISPLAY STRUCTURE.

LOAD

Syntax

LOAD *binary filename*

The LOAD command is used to load binary (assembly language) programs into memory for future use with the CALL command. An extension is optional; if omitted, it is assumed to be .BIN. Up to 16 binary files can be loaded at once. (Unneeded modules that have been loaded into memory can be released with the RELEASE MODULE *modulename* command.) Binary routines loaded with LOAD must be designed to begin the first executable instruction at offset zero and end with a FAR RETURN.

Once the binary file has been loaded into memory, it can be executed at any time with the CALL command (see CALL).

Assembly language programmers should also note that, when saving a string address between calls, you should reset the string address you are storing to just before using the string variable. This is particularly important if you are using Tom Rettig's dBASE Tools for C software utility, as some of the binary routines in dBASE Tools for C will move string variables around in RAM due to the memory management systems in FoxPro.

Example

To load a binary file named DISKSTAT.BIN into memory, the following command could be used.

```
LOAD DISKSTAT
```

LOCATE

Syntax

LOCATE [*scope*] [FOR *condition*] [WHILE *condition*]

Syntax for FoxPro 2

LOCATE [*scope*] [FOR *condition*] [WHILE *condition*] [NOOPTIMIZE]

The LOCATE command finds the first record that matches *condition*. Unless you specify otherwise with a NEXT *scope*, the LOCATE operation begins with the first record in the database. The *scope* option can be used to limit the number of records that will be searched, but if *scope* is omitted, ALL is assumed. The LOCATE command ends when a record matching *condition* is found, after which the location of the record is displayed (if SET TALK is ON) but the record itself is not displayed. If the LOCATE operation is successful, the value of EOF() will be false, and the value of FOUND() is set to true. If the LOCATE operation is not successful, the value of EOF() is set to true, and the value of FOUND() is set to false. If SET TALK is ON, an unsuccessful LOCATE will display the message "End of LOCATE scope." With FoxPro 2 and later, the NOOPTIMIZE clause, when added, turns off FoxPro's internal optimization techniques (Rushmore).

Use the CONTINUE command after a LOCATE command to locate additional records meeting the same condition (see CONTINUE). The FOR option specifies a condition that must be met before a record will be located. If you use the WHILE option, a record will be located until the condition is no longer true.

REMINDER: *With indexed files, SEEK and FIND work much faster than LOCATE.*

Example

To locate a record containing the character string Smith in the Lastname field, enter

```
LOCATE FOR Lastname = "Smith"
```

LOOP

Syntax

LOOP

The LOOP command causes a jump back to the start of a DO WHILE loop. The LOOP command is normally executed conditionally within a control structure such as DO WHILE...ENDDO. Complete details on the use of LOOP, along with examples, are provided with the descriptions of the control structures (DO WHILE, FOR...ENDFOR). For additional details, see DO WHILE, FOR, or SCAN.

MENU

Syntax

MENU BAR *array1, expN1*
MENU *expN2, array2, expN3[, expN4]*
READ MENU BAR TO *var1, var2* [SAVE]

The MENU BAR, MENU, and READ MENU BAR TO commands are used to create a menu bar system, where the menu bar appears in a horizontal format across the top of the screen, and each option of the menu, when chosen, displays a list of associated choices in a popup menu. (Before creating a menu bar, you must use the DIMENSION command to initialize an array for each list of menu options.)

Users of FoxPro 2 and later can also use the Menu Builder utility to create menus; see Chapter 13 for details.

Use the MENU BAR command to insert the character expressions contained in *array1* into the menu bar. *Array1* is a two-dimensional array of character strings. *Array1(i,1)* becomes the menu pad that is displayed on the menu bar at position *i*. *Array1(i,2)* can be used to define an optional message that will appear at the SET MESSAGE TO location when the pad is selected. *ExpN1* defines the number of pads that appear on the menu bar.

Use the MENU command to insert menu popups into a menu bar. *ExpN2* defines the position on the menu bar where the popup being defined will appear. *ExpN3* defines the number of options on the popup menu. *ExpN4*, which is optional, limits the number of menu options shown on the screen at any time. If there are more options in the menu than this limit, the options scroll within the popup menu. *Array2* is a one-dimensional array containing the character strings that are used as menu options. Use a backslash (\) as the first character to make an option nonselectable. Use a backslash followed by a hyphen (\-) to draw a graphics bar in place of a menu item.

Use the READ MENU BAR TO command to activate the menu bar defined by the previous commands. Use *var1* and *var2* to control which menu bar pad and menu options are selected by default when the menu is initially displayed. Once a selection has been made by the user, *var1* and *var2* will contain values that correspond to the menu selection. These values may then be acted on by the program. Use the optional SAVE clause to cause the menu bar to remain on the screen after a menu option has been chosen.

Example

The following program uses the MENU BAR command to define and display a menu. The menu displays a horizontal bar with three menu options; when chosen, each option results in the display of a pulldown menu with additional choices.

```
*MAINMENU.PRG displays main menu.*
SET TALK OFF
SET MESSAGE TO 24 CENTER
*Initialize arrays used for menu bar.
DIMENSION TOPBAR(3,2)
TOPBAR(1,1) = "  ADD  "
TOPBAR(2,1) = "  EDIT  "
TOPBAR(3,1) = "  PRINT "
TOPBAR(1,2) = "Add data to file"
TOPBAR(2,2) = "Edit data in file"
TOPBAR(3,2) = "Print data in file"
*Initialize array used for Add popup.
DIMENSION Adder(4)
Adder(1) = "Add Members    "
Adder(2) = "Add Rentals    "
Adder(3) = "Add Purchases "
Adder(4) = "Exit this menu"
*Initialize array used for Edit popup.
DIMENSION Edits(4)
Edits(1) = "Edit Members    "
Edits(2) = "Edit Rentals    "
Edits(3) = "Edit Purchases "
Edits(4) = "Exit this menu"
*Initialize array used for Print popup.
DIMENSION Print(4)
```

```
Print(1) = "Print Members   "
Print(2) = "Print Rentals   "
"Print(3) = "Print Purchases "
Print(4) = "Exit this menu"
*Insert the popups into the menu bar.
MENU BAR TOPBAR,3
MENU 1,Adder,4
MENU 2,Edits,4
MENU 3,Print,4
*Activate the menu system.
READ MENU BAR TO 1,1
```

MENU TO

Syntax

MENU TO *memvar*

The MENU TO command is used along with the @...PROMPT command to implement light-bar menus. See @...PROMPT for a complete explanation of the use of the MENU TO command.

MODIFY COMMAND/MODIFY FILE

Syntax

MODIFY COMMAND/FILE *filename* [*skeleton*] [NOEDIT] [NOWAIT]
[RANGE *expN1*[, *expN2*] [WINDOW *windowname*]
[IN WINDOW *windowname*/IN SCREEN] [SAVE]

MODIFY COMMAND or MODIFY FILE starts the FoxPro editor, which can be used for editing command files or ASCII text files. If MODIFY COMMAND is used, the filename will be given the extension .PRG unless a different extension is named. If MODIFY FILE is used, no extension is added unless one is specified in *filename*.

The WINDOW option may be used to open the file in a previously defined window. The [*skeleton*] option may be used to open windows for all files that match the file skeleton supplied. The NOEDIT option causes the text to be displayed, but editing is not allowed. The NOWAIT option causes program execution to continue as soon as the window is opened. The RANGE option may be used to open an editing window with a range of characters selected for editing. The characters selected begin with the position specified in *expN1* and continue for *expN2* characters. If *expN2* is omitted, editing begins at the character position specified by *expN1*. The SAVE option causes the window to remain visible after editing is completed.

In FoxPro 1.02 and later, the command also supports an optional [IN WINDOW *windowname*/IN SCREEN] clause. This clause lets you have background windows within windows or on the background screen.

When you include this clause, the inner window is dependent on the outer window. When the outer window is moved, the inner window moves with it. The inner window cannot be larger than the outer window and can be moved only within the confines of the outer window. If the outer window is closed, the inner window is closed with it. If the outer window is deactivated, the inner window is deactivated with it.

MODIFY LABEL

Syntax

MODIFY LABEL *filename*/? [IN WINDOW *windowname*/IN SCREEN]

Syntax for FoxPro 2

MODIFY LABEL *filename*/? [[WINDOW *windowname1*]
[IN [WINDOW] *windowname2*/IN SCREEN]] [NOENVIRONMENT]
[NOWAIT] [SAVE]

The MODIFY LABEL command creates or allows editing of a label form file. This file can be used with the LABEL FORM command to produce mailing labels. Filename will be given the extension .LBX. If the question mark is used in place of a filename, FoxPro displays a list containing all label files in the current directory. The user may then select a label file for editing from the list.

In FoxPro 1.02 and later, the command also supports an optional [IN [WINDOW] *windowname*/IN SCREEN]] clause. This clause lets you have background windows within windows or on the background screen.

In FoxPro 2, the WINDOW and IN WINDOW clauses can be used to specify that the label design should take place in a window or in the child window of a parent window. The IN SCREEN clause forces label design to use the full screen; this is also the default if no WINDOW clause is used. The NOENVIRONMENT clause is used when you do not want to restore the environment that was in place when you originally created the labels. The NOWAIT clause, used within programs, causes program execution to continue after the label design screen or window has appeared.

When you include this clause, the inner window (containing the label design screen) is dependent on the outer window. When the outer window is moved, the inner window moves with it. The inner window cannot be larger than the outer window and can be moved only within the confines of the outer window. If the outer window is closed, the inner window is closed with it. If the outer window is deactivated, the inner window is deactivated with it.

MODIFY MEMO

Syntax

MODIFY MEMO *memofield1*[, *memofield2*...] [NOEDIT] [NOWAIT]
[RANGE *expN1*[, *expN2*]] [WINDOW *windowname*] [SAVE]
[IN WINDOW *windowname*/IN SCREEN]

MODIFY MEMO places the contents of a memo field in the FoxPro Editor. The WINDOW option may be used to open the memo field in a previously defined window. The NOEDIT option causes the text to be displayed, but editing is not allowed. The NOWAIT option causes program execution to continue as soon as the window is opened. The RANGE option may be used to edit a memo field with a range of characters selected for editing. The characters selected begin with the position specified in *expN1* and continue for *expN2* characters. If *expN2* is omitted, editing begins at the character position specified by *expN1*. The SAVE option causes the memo window to remain visible after editing is completed.

In FoxPro 1.02 and later, the command also supports an optional [IN WINDOW *windowname*/IN SCREEN] clause. This clause lets you have background windows within windows or on the background screen.

When you include this clause, the inner window (containing the memo field) is dependent on the outer window. When the outer window is moved, the inner window moves with it. The inner window cannot be larger than the outer window and can be moved only within the confines of the outer window. If the outer window is closed, the inner window is closed with it. If the outer window is deactivated, the inner window is deactivated with it.

Example

The following short program is used to search an index to find a record by name and to modify the memo field named COMMENTS once the desired record has been found.

```
CLEAR
STORE SPACE(20) TO TITLE
@ 5,5 SAY "Title? " GET TITLE
```

```
READ
STORE TITLE TO FINDIT
USE BOOKS INDEX NAMES
*File of books is indexed on book title.*
SEEK FINDIT
IF .NOT. FOUND()
    CLEAR
    WAIT "Can't find that book! Check spelling..."
    RETURN
ENDIF
CLEAR
@  5,5 SAY "Title:" @ 5,13 SAY TITLE
@  7,5 SAY "Author:"
@ 7,14 SAY AUTHOR
DEFINE WINDOW MYMEMOS FROM 9,5 TO 18,70 PANEL
MODIFY MEMO COMMENTS WINDOW MYMEMOS
DEACTIVATE WINDOW MYMEMOS
CLOSE DATABASES
RETURN
```

MODIFY MENU

Syntax

Version 2

MODIFY MENU [*filename*/?] [[WINDOW *windowname1*]
[IN [WINDOW] *windowname2*/SCREEN]] [NOWAIT] [SAVE]

The MODIFY MENU command is used to modify an existing menu. The command brings up the FoxPro menu creation utility. See CREATE MENU for additional details.

MODIFY PROJECT

Syntax

Version 2

MODIFY PROJECT [*filename*/?] [[WINDOW *windowname1*]
[IN [WINDOW] *windowname2*/SCREEN]] [SAVE]

The MODIFY PROJECT command is used to modify an existing project. The command opens the project window. See CREATE PROJECT for additional details.

MODIFY QUERY

Syntax

MODIFY QUERY [*filename*/?] [NOWAIT]

Version 2

The MODIFY QUERY command is used to modify an existing query. The command causes the RQBE window to be displayed, containing the previously stored query. For more details on designing and saving queries, see Chapter 6.

MODIFY REPORT

Syntax

MODIFY REPORT *filename*/? [IN WINDOW *windowname*/IN SCREEN]

Syntax for FoxPro 2

MODIFY REPORT *filename*/? [[WINDOW *windowname1*]
[IN [WINDOW] *windowname2*/IN SCREEN]] [NOENVIRONMENT]
[NOWAIT] [SAVE]

The MODIFY REPORT command allows you to use FoxReport, the report generator, to create or modify a report form file for producing reports. The filename produced will be given an extension of .FRX. If the question mark is used in place of a filename, FoxPro displays a list containing all report form files in the current directory. The user may then select a report file for editing from the list.

In FoxPro 1.02 and later, the command also supports an optional [IN WINDOW *windowname*/IN SCREEN] clause. This clause lets you have background windows within windows or on the background screen.

When you include this clause, the inner window is dependent on the outer window. When the outer window is moved, the inner window moves with it. The inner window cannot be larger than the outer window and can be moved only within the confines of the outer window. If the outer window is closed, the inner window is closed with it. If the outer window is deactivated, the inner window is deactivated with it.

In FoxPro 2, the NOENVIRONMENT clause is used when you do not want to restore the environment that was in place when you originally created the report. The NOWAIT clause, used within programs, causes program execution to continue after the report design screen or window has appeared.

MODIFY SCREEN

Syntax

Version 2

MODIFY SCREEN [*filename*/?] [[WINDOW *windowname1*]
[IN [WINDOW] *windowname2*/IN SCREEN]] [NOENVIRONMENT]
[NOWAIT] [SAVE]

The MODIFY SCREEN command modifies an existing screen form, created with the CREATE SCREEN command. See CREATE SCREEN for additional details.

MODIFY STRUCTURE

Syntax

MODIFY STRUCTURE

The MODIFY STRUCTURE command allows you to alter the structure of the active database. After the structure has been modified, a backup copy containing the original data remains on disk with the same filename but with a different extension of .BAK. (If there is already a file with the .BAK extension, it gets overwritten by the newer backup.)

A database must be in use before the MODIFY STRUCTURE command is entered. If no database is open in the current work area, you will be prompted for a database name upon entering the MODIFY STRUCTURE command. After entering MODIFY STRUCTURE, the database definition screen appears. The database definition screen will have four columns containing the existing field names, field types, field sizes, and number of decimal places (if any).

When you modify a database, data is first copied into a temporary database, and the permanent database is then changed to meet your new design. Finally, data is copied back from the temporary file into the modified database. Note that data will be returned from the fields of the temporary file to the fields in the modified database automatically only if the field names and field types match. If you change the type of a field, data may not be restored to that particular field since the program doesn't always know how to convert the data type. The conversion will be made where possible. For example, if you change a character field into a numeric field, all valid numeric entries will be converted. However, if you were to change a numeric field into a logical field, the data in the numeric field would be lost, as the two field types have nothing in common.

If you rename a field and change its location in the database structure at the same time by inserting or deleting fields, the data in that field will be lost. The software uses either the field name or the position of the field in the database structure to transfer existing data. If both are changed, the existing data is discarded. If you need to change both the name of a field and its existing location in a database structure, perform the task in two steps. Change the field name, and exit the MODIFY STRUCTURE process; then, repeat the MODIFY STRUCTURE command, and make any other changes to the file structure.

Example

To modify a database called STAFF.DBF, the following commands could be used.

```
USE STAFF
MODIFY STRUCTURE
```

MOVE POPUP

Syntax

MOVE POPUP *popupname* TO *row,col*/BY *rows,cols*

Version 2

The MOVE POPUP command moves a popup to a different screen location.

Examples

To move a popup to the starting position of row 14, column 18, you could use the command

```
MOVE POPUP MyPop TO 14,18
```

To move the popup 6 lines down and 4 lines to the right, you could use the command

```
MOVE POPUP MyPop BY 6,4
```

MOVE WINDOW

Syntax

MOVE WINDOW *windowname* TO *row,col*/BY *rows,cols*

The MOVE WINDOW command moves a predefined window to a new location on the screen.

Example

To move the window to the starting position of row 15, column 20 enter

```
MOVE WINDOW MYWINDOW TO 15,20
```

To move the window six lines down and two lines to the right enter

```
MOVE WINDOW MYWINDOW BY 6,4
```

NOTE or * or &&

Syntax

NOTE/*/&&

The NOTE or * or && command is used to insert comments in a command file. Use && to add a comment at the end of an existing statement. Use NOTE or * at the beginning of a line, when the entire line is to be a comment. Text after the * or the && or the word NOTE in a command file will be ignored by FoxPro.

ON BAR

Syntax

Version 2

ON BAR *expN* OF *popup1*
[ACTIVATE POPUP *popup2*/ACTIVATE MENU *menuname*]

The ON BAR command activates a popup or a bar menu when a particular bar of a popup is selected. Use *expN* to specify the desired bar that, when chosen, will activate the other popup or menu. The corresponding ACTIVATE POPUP or ACTIVATE MENU clause specifies the popup or the menu that is activated as the result of the choice.

ON ERROR

Syntax

ON ERROR *command*

The ON ERROR command executes a specified command when a program error occurs. Use ON ERROR at or near the start of a program to provide a specific path the program should take if an error occurs. Note that the specified command can be DO *filename*, where *filename* is another program that should be called if an error occurs.

ON ERROR is commonly used to call error-handling routines, which can provide detailed messages of your own design when an error occurs. You can use the ERROR() and MESSAGE() functions in your error-handling routines to display the cause of the error number and the error message. Also, note that the RETRY command can be used to repeat the line that caused the error after an error-handling routine has corrected the cause of the error. When a program called by ON ERROR completes, program execution normally continues on the line immediately following the line which caused the error. To resume execution on the line that originally caused the error, use RETRY in the error-handling routine.

The ON ERROR statement remains in effect until you issue another ON ERROR statement. To disable the effects of ON ERROR, issue ON ERROR without specifying a command.

Example

To cause the program to display a customized error message if an error occurs, the following command could be used near the start of the program:

```
ON ERROR ? "Call tech support, report this error-" + MESSAGE()
```

As a more complex example, the following program demonstrates the use of ON ERROR to call an error-handling routine.

```
*ACCOUNTS.PRG is accounting system.*
SET SAFETY OFF
SET BELL OFF
ON ERROR DO ERRTRAP WITH ERROR(), MESSAGE(), PROGRAM()
SELECT 1
USE ACCOUNTS INDEX CUSTOMER
...more commands...

PROCEDURE ERRTRAP
PARAMETERS errors, messages, programs
DO CASE
    CASE errors = 125
        *printer not ready error code.
        ? "Printer is not ready. Correct problem, then"
        WAIT
        RETRY
```

```
CASE errors = 1
    *file not found error code.
    ? "Cannot find a file. Record this message,"
    ? "and contact tech support immediately."
    CLEAR ALL
    WAIT
    QUIT
CASE errors = 20 .OR. errors = 26 .OR. errors = 114
    *index key missing or index corrupted error code.
    ? "An index file seems to have a minor problem."
    ? "Please wait while I repair the index."
    SET TALK ON
    INDEX ON Lastname + Firstname TO NAMES
    SET TALK OFF
    CLEAR
    RETRY
OTHERWISE
    *unknown error. Notify user to record it.
    ? "Call tech support. Report the following:"
    ? "Error number is: " + LTRIM(STR(errors))
    ? "Error message is: " + messages
    ? "Program in use during error is: " + programs
    WAIT "Write above messages down, press a key..."
    QUIT
ENDCASE
```

ON ESCAPE

Syntax

ON ESCAPE *command*

The ON ESCAPE command executes a specified command when ESC is pressed. Use ON ESCAPE at or near the start of a program to provide a specific path the program should take if ESC is pressed. Note that the specified command can be DO *filename*, where *filename* is a program that should be run if ESC is pressed.

Normally, pressing ESC while a program is running causes the program to halt, and the user is returned to the command level. This can be confusing to novice users. One commonly-used solution to this problem is to disable the ESC key (however, when a user is pressing ESC, it is generally for a good reason). A better method of handling the ESC key within a program is to use ON ESCAPE to display a message and possibly provide alternative courses of action for the user.

If ON ESCAPE and ON KEY have both been specified, ON ESCAPE takes priority over ON KEY; when ESC is pressed, the action taken will be dependent on the ON ESCAPE statement, not the ON KEY statement.

Example

In the following printing routine, a press of ESC displays a customized message, and the user is given the option of continuing with the printing operation or canceling the operation.

```
*PRINTER.PRG prints mailing list.*
SET PROCEDURE TO BACKOUT
SET ESCAPE ON
USE MAILER INDEX NAMES
SET PRINT ON
ON ESCAPE DO BACKOUT
DO WHILE .NOT. EOF()
    ? "Name: " + TRIM(Firstname) + " " + Lastname
    ? "Address: " + Address
    ? TRIM(City) + ", " + State + " " + Zipcode
    ?
    SKIP
ENDDO
SET PRINT OFF
RETURN


PROCEDURE BACKOUT
SET PRINT OFF
STORE "N" TO ANSWER
CLEAR
@ 5,5 SAY "ESC key pressed. CANCEL print run? Y/N:" GET ANSWER
READ
IF UPPER(ANSWER) = "Y"
    RETURN TO MASTER
ENDIF
*Continue print run with Retry command.
SET PRINT ON
RETRY
```

ON KEY

Syntax

ON KEY command

The ON KEY command executes a specified command when any key is pressed. ON KEY is commonly used while a self-executing process, such as a print run, is occurring to monitor for possible interruptions. Use ON KEY followed by the desired command to monitor for a keypress.

The use of ON KEY will result in the key that is pressed being stored in the keyboard buffer. Be sure to use a READ command or an INKEY() function to clear the buffer after calling another program with the ON KEY statement. If you don't clear the buffer, the ON KEY statement may repeat indefinitely.

If ON KEY and ON ESCAPE are used in the same program, the ON ESCAPE statement takes priority over the ON KEY statement; if the first key pressed is ESC, the command that is executed is defined by the ON ESCAPE statement and not by the ON KEY statement. You can use SET ESCAPE OFF to disable a prior ON ESCAPE statement, and the ON KEY statement will then act on the ESC key like any other key.

When a program called by ON KEY completes, program execution continues on the line immediately following the ON KEY statement. To resume program execution at the ON KEY statement, use RETRY at the end of the program called by ON KEY.

Example

In the following demonstration program, a series of screens are continually displayed for advertising purposes. If any key is pressed, the display is interrupted and a menu of choices appears.

```
*DEMO.PRG is demo program.*
CLEAR
ON KEY DO MAINMENU
DO WHILE .T.
    CLEAR
    @ 3,3 TO 6,20 DOUBLE
    @ 4,5 SAY "Press any key."
    COUNTER = 1
    DO WHILE COUNTER < 1000
        COUNTER = COUNTER + 1
    ENDDO
    @ 5,15 CLEAR TO 8,32
    @ 5,15 TO 8,32 DOUBLE
    @ 6,17 SAY "Press any key."
    COUNTER = 1
    DO WHILE COUNTER < 1000
        COUNTER = COUNTER + 1
    ENDDO
ENDDO
```

```
*MAINMENU.PRG is sales demo menu.*
CLEAR
@ 3,5 SAY "Welcome to the ABC Realty Showcase of Homes."
@ 4,5 SAY "Pick a menu choice."
...rest of commands...
```

ON KEY =

Syntax

ON KEY = *expN* [*command*]

The ON KEY = *expN* command executes a specified command when a certain key is pressed during a READ operation. The key is specified by *expN*, which is the ASCII code for the character. You can name nonprintable keys (function keys, control keys, cursor keys, or key combinations) by using the IBM-key scan code plus 256.

The ON KEY = *expN* command is commonly used to redefine the Fi key to serve as a context-sensitive help key during READ operations. Because ON KEY = *expN* works with the READ command, you can also use it to perform certain operations based on which cursor key is pressed; for example, at the start of a screenful of @...SAY...GETs, you could test for the UP ARROW key, and use it to redisplay a prior page of @...SAY...GETs. Note that you can also use the VARREAD() function along with ONKEY to return the name of the field being entered when the key was pressed.

Example

In the following program, an ONKEY statement is used to branch to a help routine if the Fi key is pressed.

```
ON KEY = 315 DO HELPER WITH VARREAD()
USE STAFF INDEX SOCIAL
ACCEPT "Enter social security number of employee: " TO FINDER
SEEK FINDER
IF .NOT. FOUND()
    WAIT "No such record found. Press a key..."
    RETURN
ENDIF
CLEAR
DEFINE WINDOW Edits FROM 5,5 TO 15,70 DOUBLE
```

```
ACTIVATE WINDOW Edits
@  2,2 SAY "Lastname: " GET Lastname
@  3,2 SAY "Firstname: " GET Firstname
@  4,2 SAY "Soc. Sec. No: " GET Social
@  5,2 SAY "Grade: " GET Grade
@  6,2 SAY "Salary: " GET Salary
@  8,10 SAY "F1 for Help, ESC cancels editing."
READ
DEACTIVATE WINDOW Edits
RETURN
```

ON KEY LABEL

Syntax

ON KEY LABEL *key label command*

The ON KEY LABEL command executes a specified command when a certain key is pressed. The key is specified by *key label*, which is the letter or digit of the key surrounded by quotes. Note that you can have multiple ON KEY LABEL statements in a single program or procedure with different responses assigned to different keys.

In FoxPro 1.02 and later, you can specify SPACEBAR, LEFTMOUSE, RIGHTMOUSE, and MOUSE as key labels. The specified command will then be executed when the SPACEBAR or appropriate mouse button is pressed. (The MOUSE label responds to either mouse button.)

Example

In the following program, an ON KEY LABEL statement allows the display of a help screen if F1 is pressed.

```
USE MAILER INDEX NAMES
ON KEY LABEL "F1" DO HELPER
DO WHILE .T.
    @  3,5 SAY "Last name: " GET Lastname  \
    @  4,5 SAY "First name: " GET Firstname
    READ
    CLEAR
    @  3,5 SAY TRIM(Firstname) + " " + Lastname
```

```
@ 5,5 SAY "Address: " GET Address
@ 7,5 SAY "City: " GET City
@ 9,5 SAY "State: " GET State
@ 9,18 SAY "Zip: " GET Zipcode
READ
CLEAR
FINIS = "Y"
@ 3,5 SAY "Done editing? Y/N:" GET FINIS PICTURE '!'
READ
IF FINIS = 'Y'
     EXIT     ENDIF
SKIP
ENDDO
RETURN


PROCEDURE HELPER
DEFINE WINDOW HELPER FROM 14,20 TO 20,70 DOUBLE
ACTIVATE WINDOW HELPER
@ 2,2 SAY "Enter member name, address in desired fields."
@ 3,2 SAY "Press CTRL-END when done."
@ 4,2 SAY "Press ESC to exit without saving changes."
WAIT "...press any key to exit Help."
RELEASE WINDOW HELPER
RETURN
```

ON PAD

Syntax

ON PAD *padname* OF *menuname* [ACTIVATE POPUP *popupname*]

Syntax for FoxPro 2

ON PAD *padname* OF *menuname*
[ACTIVATE POPUP *popupname*/ACTIVATE MENU *menuname*]

The ON PAD command links a popup menu to a specific pad within a bar menu. When the pad named in pad name is highlighted within the menu, the associated popup menu appears. Use ON PAD as part of a series of commands for building pulldown menus. In pulldown menus, a series of choices within a horizontal (bar) menu each reveal individual vertical (popup) menus. (Note that in FoxPro 2 and later, you can also use the command to link a pad name to another bar menu.)

To link the popup menu to a specific menu pad, include the name of the menu pad (specified by *padname*) on the menu bar (specified by *menuname*). Remember to define the popup menus with DEFINE POPUP before calling the popups with the ACTIVATE POPUP clause of ON PAD.

You cannot use ON PAD and ON SELECTION PAD for the same menu pads. Use ON SELECTION PAD if you want the popup to appear only after a menu pad option has been selected. With ON PAD, the popup appears as soon as you highlight the pad; you need not select it. Also, ON PAD is limited to use with menus; ON SELECTION PAD can be used to activate menus or perform other commands (see ON SELECTION PAD for details).

Example

In the following example, a series of DEFINE BAR and DEFINE POPUP commands define a bar menu with three pads, along with three popup menus that will be linked with each of the three pads. The ON PAD command is then used to link each of the three popup menus to a particular pad of the bar menu.

```
*MENU.PRG creates pulldown main menu for system.*
DEFINE MENU MainMenu MESSAGE "Select the desired option"
DEFINE POPUP AddMenu FROM 2, 4
DEFINE POPUP EditMenu FROM 2, 12
DEFINE POPUP PrinMenu FROM 2, 20
DEFINE BAR 1 OF AddMenu PROMPT "Add to customer file"
DEFINE BAR 2 OF AddMenu PROMPT "Add to sales file"
DEFINE BAR 3 OF AddMenu PROMPT "Add to inventory"
DEFINE BAR 1 OF EditMenu PROMPT "Edit customer file"
DEFINE BAR 2 OF EditMenu PROMPT "Edit sales file"
DEFINE BAR 3 OF EditMenu PROMPT "Edit inventory"
DEFINE BAR 1 OF PrinMenu PROMPT "Print customer list"
DEFINE BAR 2 OF PrinMenu PROMPT "Print sales list"
DEFINE BAR 3 OF PrinMenu PROMPT "Print inventory"
DEFINE PAD Adder OF MainMenu PROMPT "Add Items"
DEFINE PAD Editor OF MainMenu PROMPT "Edit Items"
DEFINE PAD Printer OF MainMenu PROMPT "Print Items"
DEFINE PAD Exit OF MainMenu PROMPT "Quit System"
ON PAD Adder OF MainMenu ACTIVATE POPUP AddMenu
ON PAD Editor OF MainMenu ACTIVATE POPUP EditMenu
ON PAD Printer OF MainMenu ACTIVATE POPUP PrinMenu
ON SELECTION PAD Exit OF MainMenu QUIT
ACTIVATE MENU MainMenu
```

ON PAGE

Syntax

ON PAGE [AT LINE *expN command*]

The ON PAGE command executes the command named after the ON PAGE command whenever FoxPro reaches the designated line number or encounters an EJECT PAGE command. The ON PAGE command is generally used to call a procedure that prints a footer, ejects a page, and prints a header. Also note that using ON PAGE without any clauses will cancel the effects of the previous ON PAGE command.

Example

In the following example, the ON PAGE command is used to call a subroutine that produces footers at the bottom of a report produced with the LIST command.

```
ON PAGE AT LINE 58 DO FOOTERS
SET PRINT ON
LIST Lastname, Firstname, Salary, Hiredate
...more commands...

PROCEDURE FOOTERS ?
? " Salary listing- for personnel use only."
EJECT PAGE
? " SALARY LISTING "
?
? DATE()
RETURN
```

ON READERROR

Syntax

ON READERROR [*command*]

The ON READERROR command runs a program or executes a named command or procedure after testing for an error in input. The ON READER-ROR command is called in response to invalid dates, improper responses to a

VALID clause, or improper entries when a RANGE clause is in effect. ON READERROR without the *command* clause is used to cancel the previous ON READERROR command.

Example

In the following program, the ONREADERROR statement is used to display a custom help screen if a user makes an invalid entry.

```
ON READERROR DO Mistakes
USE STAFF INDEX SOCIAL
@   3,5 SAY "  LAST NAME:" GET Lastname
@   4,5 SAY " FIRST NAME:" GET Firstname
@   8,5 SAY "     SALARY:" GET Salary
@  10,5 SAY "DATE HIRED:" GET Hired
@ 10,40 SAY "DATE OF BIRTH:" GET Dateborn
READ
...more commands...

PROCEDURE Mistakes
DEFINE WINDOW Mistakes FROM 14,10 TO 20,70 DOUBLE
ACTIVATE WINDOW Mistakes
@ 2,2 SAY "Salaries MUST be more than 4.50, less than 20.00."
@ 3,2 SAY "Also check that all dates entered are valid dates."
WAIT
RELEASE WINDOW Mistakes
RETURN
```

ON SELECTION BAR

Syntax

Version 2

ON SELECTION BAR *expN* OF *popupname* [*command*]

The ON SELECTION BAR command links a program, a procedure, or a command to a specific bar of a bar menu. When the bar identified by the value of *expN* is chosen from the menu, the command, procedure, or program named will be executed.

ON SELECTION BAR without the rest of the expression is used to cancel the effects of the previous ON SELECTION BAR command.

Example

```
ON SELECTION BAR 2 OF MyPop DO REPORTER
```

ON SELECTION MENU

Syntax

ON SELECTION MENU *menuname*/ALL [*command*]

Version 2

The ON SELECTION MENU command links a program, a procedure, or a command to any pad of a bar menu. When any pad is chosen from the menu, the command, procedure, or program named will be executed.

ON SELECTION MENU without the rest of the expression is used to cancel the effects of the previous ON SELECTION MENU command.

Example

```
ON SELECTION MENU OF MyPop DO SUBMENU2
```

ON SELECTION PAD

Syntax

ON SELECTION PAD *padname* OF *menuname* [*command*]

The ON SELECTION PAD command links a program, procedure, or a command to a specific pad of a bar menu. When the named pad is chosen from the menu, the command, procedure, or program named within the ON SELECTION statement will be executed. ON SELECTION PAD without the *padname* clause is used to cancel the previous ON SELECTION PAD command.

Example

In the section of program code shown below, the ON SELECTION PAD statements define which actions shall be taken when a particular menu option is chosen by the user. (To keep the example simple, each ON SELECTION statement calls a particular command, such as APPEND or EDIT. In most applications, the ON SELECTION statements will be used to call another routine for adding or editing records or performing some other task.) The ACTIVATE MENU statement that follows the ON SELECTION statement activates the menu, and the program awaits the user's response.

```
USE STAFF INDEX NAMES
CLEAR
DEFINE MENU MainMenu MESSAGE "Press letter of desired option"
DEFINE PAD Addit OF MainMenu PROMPT "Add records"
DEFINE PAD Change OF MainMenu PROMPT "Edit records"
DEFINE PAD Print OF MainMenu PROMPT "Print records"
DEFINE PAD Quit OF MainMenu PROMPT "Exit System"
ON SELECTION PAD Addit OF MainMenu APPEND
ON SELECTION PAD Change OF MainMenu EDIT
ON SELECTION PAD Print OF MainMenu REPORT FORM MYFILE TO PRINT
ON SELECTION PAD Quit OF MainMenu DEACTIVATE MENU
ACTIVATE MENU MainMenu
QUIT
```

ON SELECTION POPUP

Syntax

ON SELECTION POPUP *popupname*/ALL [*command*]

The ON SELECTION POPUP command executes a program, procedure or a command when any option of a popup menu is chosen. Note the significant difference between ON SELECTION POPUP and ON SELECTION PAD; the ON SELECTION POPUP command is not tied to a specific option of the menu, but executes when any option is chosen. You can use the BAR() function to determine which popup menu item was selected, and your program can act accordingly, as demonstrated in the example.

Use *popupname* to name the popup menu that the action is to be assigned to. Use command to identify the action taken when any option from that popup menu is chosen; it may be DO *filename* or DO *procedurename* to call a routine, or it may be a DEACTIVATE POPUP statement to clear the menu from the screen.

Example

In the following program, ON SELECTION POPUP is used to deactivate the popup menu after a selection is made. A series of CASE choices then use the

BAR() function to determine which menu item was chosen, and the appropriate command is executed within the program.

```
*This is an example of a simple menu and application*
USE STAFF INDEX NAMES
DEFINE POPUP MainMenu FROM 5, 20
DEFINE BAR 1 OF MainMenu PROMPT " Select desired option " SKIP
DEFINE BAR 2 OF MainMenu PROMPT "  Add new employees      "
DEFINE BAR 3 OF MainMenu PROMPT "  Edit/Delete employees"
DEFINE BAR 4 OF MainMenu PROMPT "  Print Staff Report    "
DEFINE BAR 5 OF MainMenu PROMPT "  Quit System           "
ON SELECTION POPUP MainMenu DEACTIVATE POPUP
DO WHILE .T.
ACTIVATE POPUP MainMenu
DO CASE
    CASE BAR() = 2
    APPEND

    CASE BAR() = 3
    EDIT

    CASE BAR() = 4
    CLEAR
    WAIT "ready printer, then press a key..."
    REPORT FORM MyFile TO PRINT

    CASE BAR() = 5 .OR. BAR() = 0
    EXIT
ENDCASE
ENDDO
```

PACK

Syntax

```
PACK
```

Syntax for FoxPro 2

```
PACK [MEMO] [DBF]
```

The PACK command removes records that have been marked for deletion by the DELETE command (see DELETE). After a pack operation, all records in the database are renumbered, and disk space consumed by the database is minimized. If any index files are open when the PACK command is issued, those index files will be reindexed upon completion of the PACK operation. The ESC key will not interrupt a pack operation, regardless of the status of SET ESCAPE.

In FoxPro 2, you can add the MEMO or DBF clauses to specifically pack just the database file without packing the memo fields or to pack just the memo-field file without packing the database. The MEMO clause causes a pack of the memo-field file, but the database file is not packed. The DBF clause causes a pack of just the database file, but the memo-field file is not packed. If you omit both clauses under FoxPro 2, both the database file and the memo-field file are packed.

The larger the file, the longer it takes to perform a pack operation. Because the command involves recopying much of the active database, it can be quite time consuming with very large files. It is a wise idea to use PACK only on occasion, and certainly not after each deletion of a record. Deleted records can be hidden from further processing with the SET DELETED ON command (see SET DELETED).

PARAMETERS

Syntax

PARAMETERS *parameter-list*

The PARAMETERS command is used within a program or procedure to assign variable names to data items that are passed to the program or procedure from another program or procedure. The PARAMETERS command must be the first executable command in the called program or the first executable statement after the PROCEDURE statement in a procedure file. The calling program uses the syntax

DO *program name or procedure name* WITH *list of values*

and the called program or procedure receives the data specified by *list of values* using the PARAMETERS statement.

In *parameter-list*, specify the memory variable names to be assigned to the data items. Note that the number, order, and data types of the items in the parameter list must match the list of parameters included with the WITH option of the DO command that called the program or procedure or FoxPro will halt and display a program error.

Parameter passing can be very useful when you repeatedly perform the same type of task at numerous locations within a program, and only the input data changes from task to task. In such cases, you can save considerable coding effort by coding the tasks as procedures and passing the values that change in the form of parameters. In the example, this technique is used to handle error messages to users, where often a display in the form of a message box with an error message is presented to the user, and only the wording of the message changes between tasks.

Example

To call a procedure named ERRORS.PRG and pass a parameter containing the text string "Account number" to that procedure, the following command could be used

```
DO ERRORS WITH "Account number"
```

The called procedure would use the PARAMETERS statement to receive the text string and display it within a message box, as shown in the following example:

```
PROCEDURE ERRORS
PARAMETERS SayIt
CLEAR
@ 4,3 TO 7,50 DOUBLE
@ 5,5 SAY "Cannot find " + SayIt
@ 6,5 SAY "in this database. Please try again."
WAIT
CLEAR
RETURN
```

PLAY MACRO

Syntax

PLAY MACRO *macroname*

The PLAY MACRO command plays a previously stored macro. Any series of keystrokes can be recorded as a macro; a collection of macros currently in memory can be stored to a macro file. Macros that are created from the FoxPro menus are assigned key combinations and macro names. The macro names are used along with the PLAY MACRO command to replay the macro. (Macros can also be played by pressing the key combination assigned to the macro.)

To record a macro, press SHIFT-F10, press the key to be assigned as the macro key, and enter the keystrokes to be stored to the macro. To save all macros in memory to a file, choose Macros from the System menu and choose Save. Macros can be restored from a saved macro file with the RESTORE MACROS *filename* command. You can play a macro by entering **PLAY MACRO macroname**, where *macroname* is the name that the macro was saved under.

POP MENU

Syntax

Version 2

POP MENU *menuname*

The POP MENU command is used to pull a menu bar off a stack of menus. The POP MENU command can be used along with the PUSH MENU command to save a menu to memory, modify that menu, and later restore the menu to its original design. Note that menus are added to and taken from the stack of menus in last-in, first-out order.

POP POPUP

Syntax

Version 2

POP POPUP *popupname*

The POP POPUP command is used to pull a popup off a stack of menus. The POP POPUP command can be used along with the PUSH POPUP command to save a popup to memory, modify that popup, and later restore the popup to its original design. Note that popups are added to and taken from the stack of popups in last-in, first-out order.

PRINTJOB/ENDPRINTJOB

Syntax

```
PRINTJOB
...commands...
ENDPRINTJOB
```

The PRINTJOB command places stored print-related settings into effect for the duration of a printing job. Desired values must be stored to print-system memory variables before the PRINTJOB command is encountered. When PRINTJOB is executed, starting codes stored to _PSCODES are sent to the printer; a form feed is sent if _PEJECT contains "BEFORE" or "BOTH"; _pcolno is initialized to zero; and _PLINENO and ON PAGE are activated. When the printing process is complete and the ENDPRINTJOB command is encountered, any ending print codes stored to _PECODES are sent to the printer; a form feed is sent if _PEJECT contains "AFTER" or "BOTH"; FoxPro returns to the PRINTJOB command if the _PCOPIES variable contains a value greater than 1 (set to more than one copy of the report). _PLINENO and ON PAGE are deactivated.

Example

In the following program, a list of checks is printed using compressed print on an Epson FX printer, with page ejects at the end of each page and a page length of 54 lines.

```
USE CHECKS INDEX DATES
STORE "AFTER" TO _PEJECT
STORE 54 TO _PLENGTH
STORE CHR(18) TO _PSCODE
STORE CHR(15) TO _PECODE
ON PAGE AT LINE _PLENGTH EJECT PAGE
SET PRINT ON
PRINTJOB
    LIST ALL FOR CATEGORY = "Office Supplies"
ENDPRINTJOB
```

PRIVATE

Syntax

PRIVATE ALL [LIKE/EXCEPT *skeleton/memvarlist*/ARRAY *array definition list*]

The PRIVATE command sets specified variables to private, hiding values of those variables from all higher-level parts of a program. Skeletons are filename patterns that include the acceptable DOS wildcards of asterisk (*) or question mark (?).

While memory variables are normally private by default, the PRIVATE command is useful when you want to explicitly name variables as private to prevent conflicts with other variables assigned the same names elsewhere in a program. For example, one program may establish certain memory variables, and later that program calls another program. If you want to assign new memory variables within the called program the same variable names as those used in the calling program, you'll need to use the PRIVATE command to declare the variables as private to the current program.

NOTE: PRIVATE differs from PUBLIC in that the PRIVATE command does not create and initially assign a value; it must be used with a variable that already exists. In contrast, the PUBLIC command creates the named variable and assigns it an initial logical value of false.

Example

To hide all variables, excluding BILLPAY, from higher-level parts of the program, you could use the following command:

```
PRIVATE ALL EXCEPT BILLPAY
```

To hide all variables with eight-character names that end in "TEST" from higher-level parts of the program, you could use the following command:

```
PRIVATE ALL LIKE ????TEST
```

To hide only the variable named PAYOUT from higher-level parts of the program, you could use the following command:

```
PRIVATE PAYOUT
```

PROCEDURE

Syntax

PROCEDURE *procedurename*

The PROCEDURE command identifies the start of each separate procedure within a procedure file. Procedure files are files that contain procedures, which are separate routines called by your programs. To identify procedures, you enclose each group of program statements between a PROCEDURE statement and a RETURN statement. (In FoxPro, the RETURN statement is optional; however, it is a wise idea to include it as a clear indication of the end of the procedure.) When procedures are placed in a separate procedure file, that file must be identified (before any procedure is called) with the SET PROCEDURE TO statement. Note that you can place procedures in the main program file, eliminating the need for a SET PROCEDURE statement. Placing routines within a single procedure file speeds execution of your program, since the program will not need to go to disk to load each routine as it is called from the main program.

Procedure names may be up to eight characters long. The names may contain underscores, letters, or numbers, but they must start with a letter. Be careful not to assign the same name to a program file and to a procedure contained within that program file.

A maximum of 1170 procedures can be contained in a procedure file. FoxPro searches for procedures in the following order:

1. The current compiled object (.FXP) file is searched.

2. The object file named by SET PROCEDURE is searched.

3. Program files are searched, beginning with the most recently executed program and continuing to the first executed program.

4. Last, a stand-alone program file having the same name as the procedure file is searched.

If you decide to place procedures in the main program file, put them at the end of the file. This should be done, because any statements that follow a PROCEDURE statement will not be called unless they are directly referenced with a DO command; in other words, if you were to put a PROCEDURE statement, a group of commands, and a RETURN statement in the middle of an existing program, none of the program statements following the RETURN statement would ever be executed.

Example

The following menu routine uses the SET PROCEDURE command to name a procedure file. Then, depending on the menu option chosen, a particular procedure in the procedure file is called.

```
*REPORTS.PRG is main menu of reports program.*
SET TALK OFF
SET PROCEDURE TO PRINTER
DO WHILE .T.
   CLEAR
   ANSWER = "0"
   @  3,5 SAY "For Sales report-     1"
   @  4,5 SAY "For Customer report-  2"
   @  5,5 SAY "For Customer Labels-  3"
   @  6,5 SAY "Return to prior menu- 4"
```

```
    @ 8,5 SAY "Enter desired choice:" GET ANSWER
    READ
    DO CASE
        CASE ANSWER = "1"
            DO PRINSALE
        CASE ANSWER = "2"
            DO PRINCUST
        CASE ANSWER = "3"
            DO CLABELS
        CASE ANSWER = "4"
            RETURN
        OTHERWISE
            CLEAR
            WAIT "Invalid answer! Enter 1-4."
    ENDCASE
ENDDO

*PRINTER.PRG is procedure file for reports.*
PROCEDURE PRINSALE
WAIT " Ready printer, press any key..."
REPORT FORM SALES TO PRINT
EJECT
RETURN
********
PROCEDURE PRINCUST
WAIT " Ready printer, press any key..."
REPORT FORM CUSTOMER TO PRINT
EJECT
RETURN
********
PROCEDURE CLABELS
WAIT " Load mailing labels, ready printer, press any key..."
LABEL FORM CUSTOMER TO PRINT
RETURN
*End of PRINTER.PRG*
```

PUBLIC

Syntax

PUBLIC *memvarlist*/ARRAY *array definition list*

The PUBLIC command sets the named variables or arrays to public, making the values of those variables or arrays available to all levels of a program. Unlike the PRIVATE command, the PUBLIC command will create memory variables and define them as public at the same time. However, note that memory variables created with PUBLIC are initially assigned the logical type, with a value of false. You can store a different type value to the variable after creating it with the PUBLIC command. For example, if you wanted to create a public logical variable named PRINTIT with an initial value of false, you could use the command

```
PUBLIC PRINTIT
```

to accomplish the task. However, if you wanted to create a public numeric variable named AGE containing a value of 18, you would need to use a PUBLIC statement followed by an assignment statement, as in this example:

```
PUBLIC AGE
STORE 18 TO AGE
```

NOTE: You must declare the variable as public before assigning it a value. If you assign a value to a variable and then try to declare that variable as public, an error will occur.

Any variables created at the command level are public by default. Also note that system memory variables are always public variables. If you save variables to a memory variable file and later restore them with the RESTORE command, they are restored as public if you restore them from the command level. If restored from within a program, they are restored as private to all levels above the program level they were restored from. If you want to restore saved variables as public to all levels within a program, first create and declare the variables with the PUBLIC command, and then use RESTORE FROM *filename* ADDITIVE to restore the variables as public variables. Another easy way to restore variables as public within a program is to restore them at the highest level of the program (usually the main menu); this in effect makes the variables public to all other levels of that program.

You can use also the PUBLIC command to define arrays and specify that the contents of those arrays are public variables. Simply use the keyword ARRAY followed by the names and the dimensions of the arrays. The PUBLIC statement will then create the arrays, and fill the elements with logical false values. You can then use commands of your choosing to store the desired values to the arrays.

Example

To make the variables named BILLPAY, DUEDATE, and AMOUNT available to all modules of a program, the following command could be used.

```
PUBLIC BILLPAY, DUEDATE, AMOUNT
```

PUSH MENU

Syntax

Version 2

PUSH MENU *menuname*

The PUSH MENU command is used to push a menu bar onto a stack of menus. The PUSH MENU command can be used along with the POP MENU command to save a menu to memory, modify that menu, and later restore the menu to its original design. Note that menus are added to and taken from the stack of menus in last-in, first-out order.

PUSH POPUP

Syntax

Version 2

PUSH POPUP *popupname*

The PUSH POPUP command is used to push a popup onto a stack of menus. The PUSH POPUP command can be used along with the POP POPUP command to save a popup to memory, modify that popup, and later restore the popup to its original design. Note that popups are added to and taken from the stack of popups in last-in, first-out order.

QUIT

Syntax

QUIT

The QUIT command closes all open files, leaves FoxPro, and returns you to the operating system prompt.

The QUIT command is the only safe means of exiting from FoxPro. Turning off the system without entering **QUIT** leaves files open and accessible to possible damage; also, changes to records may not be fully written to disk unless QUIT is used.

READ

Syntax

> READ [SAVE]

Syntax for FoxPro 2

> READ [CYCLE] [ACTIVATE *expL1*] [DEACTIVATE *expL2*] [MODAL]
> [WITH *window title list*] [SHOW *expL3*] [VALID *expL4/expN1*] [WHEN *expL5*]
> [OBJECT *expN2*] [TIMEOUT *expN3*] [SAVE] [NOMOUSE]
> [LOCK/NOLOCK] [COLOR [*color-pair list*]/COLOR SCHEME *expN4*]

The READ command allows entry and editing of a memory variable or field displayed using an @...GET statement. The value(s) that you enter are then stored as the new values in the variables or fields.

The READ statement starts the editing for all @...GET statements encountered since the last READ statement. The cursor appears at the location specified by the first @...GET statement, and the cursor may be moved throughout all fields created by the @...GET statements with the same cursor movement and editing keys as are used in full-screen operations like BROWSE and EDIT.

In FoxPro 2, the CYCLE clause is used to leave the READ active when moving past the last or first GET. The ACTIVATE clause is executed when READ is issued and whenever the current READ window changes. (ACTIVATE can be considered to be a window-level WHEN clause.) The DEACTIVATE clause is executed if you bring another window forward (or, whenever the value of WONTOP() changes). DEACTIVATE can be considered to be a window-level VALID clause. The SHOW clause is used along with the SHOW GETS command (see SHOW GETS). The SHOW clause will be executed whenever the SHOW GETS command is issued.

The optional VALID clause is evaluated when you exit from the READ. The WHEN clause can be used to determine whether the READ will take place, depending on the value of the logical expression. The OBJECT specifies which object is initially selected within the READ. Use the TIMEOUT clause to specify how long (in seconds) a READ will be in effect if no key is pressed. Normally, all GETs are cleared following a READ; use the SAVE statement to reissue a READ without reissuing the GETs. The NOMOUSE option prevents objects from being selected with the mouse, and the COLOR and COLOR SCHEME options can be used to specify colors for the READ.

Version 2

NOTE: *READ can also be used immediately after a SET FORMAT TO filename statement, and the screen defined by the format file will appear, with the cursor in the first field. You can use this technique to limit editing through a format file to a single record; use the commands of your choosing to locate the desired record, then issue a SET FORMAT TO filename statement followed by a READ statement.*

Normally, a READ command clears all GETs when all data entry or editing is completed. The SAVE option can be used to avoid clearing all GETs after completion of data entry or editing. This causes the GETs to retain their prior values for the next READ. Such a technique can be useful for repetitive editing, where the data entered into certain fields of successive records is the same as that entered into prior records.

Example

The following program adds a blank record to a database and displays the fields for data entry, using a combination of @...SAY...GET statements. The READ command is used to activate the GETs, allowing data entry of the named fields. After the editing of all fields is complete, the screen is cleared, and another @...SAY...GET statement questions the user as to whether another record should be added; a second READ command is used to accept a user response.

```
USE MEMBERS
CLEAR
DO WHILE .T.
    APPEND BLANK
    @  1,0 SAY "    Social Sec." GET Social
    @  2,0 SAY "      Lastname:" GET Lastname
    @  3,0 SAY "     Firstname:" GET Firstname
    @  4,0 SAY "       Address:" GET Address
    @  5,0 SAY "          City:" GET City
    @  6,0 SAY "         State:" GET State
    @  7,0 SAY "      ZIP Code:" GET Zipcode
    @  8,0 SAY "     Telephone:" GET Phone
    @  9,0 SAY "    Birth date:" GET Birthday
    @ 10,0 SAY "Expiration Date:" GET Expiredate
    @ 11,0 SAY "    Tape limit:" GET Tapelimit
    @ 12,0 SAY "         Beta?:" GET Beta
    READ
    AGAIN = "N"
    CLEAR
    @ 5,5 SAY "Add another? Y/N:" GET AGAIN PICTURE '!'
    READ
    IF AGAIN = "N"
```

```
        EXIT
      ENDIF
  ENDDO
  RETURN
```

READ MENU

Syntax

READ MENU TO *memvar* [SAVE]

The READ MENU command is used in combination with the @ *row,col* MENU command to create popup menus. The @ *row,col* MENU statement is first used to position the popup menu on the screen, then READ MENU is used to activate the menu and accept a user response. After a menu option has been chosen, the menu option number gets stored to *memvar*; hence, if the user chooses the fourth menu option, a value of 4 gets stored to *memvar*. You can then use CASE statements to take action depending on the value of the variable. Note that if the user exits the menu by pressing the ESC key, a value of zero gets stored to the variable.

Example

The program shown below uses the @ *row,col* MENU command to create a light-bar menu with three options, and READ MENU is then used to pass the value of the selected option on to the CASE statements in the program.

```
DIMENSION Choices(3,1)
STORE "Add records" TO choices[1]
STORE "Edit records" TO choices[2]
STORE "Delete record" TO choices[3]
STORE 0 TO mchoice
@ 10,15 MENU Choices,3 TITLE "Data Menu"
READ MENU TO mchoice
DO CASE
    CASE mchoice = 1
        APPEND
    CASE mchoice = 2
        EDIT
    CASE mchoice = 3
        DELETE
ENDCASE
```

RECALL

Syntax

RECALL [*scope*] [FOR *condition*] [WHILE *condition*]

Syntax for FoxPro 2

RECALL [*scope*] [FOR *condition*] [WHILE *condition*] [NOOPTIMIZE]

The RECALL command unmarks records that have been marked for deletion. If *scope* is not listed, ALL is assumed. The FOR option can be used to specify a condition that must be met before a record will be recalled. If you use the WHILE option, deleted records will be recalled until the condition is no longer true. Note that conditionally recalling records with a *scope*, FOR, or WHILE option is only possible if SET DELETED is OFF (the default). If SET DELETED is ON, a RECALL command will only affect the current record. In FoxPro 2 and later, the NOOPTIMIZE clause, when added, turns off FoxPro's internal optimization techniques (Rushmore).

You can use RECALL to unmark (undelete) records that have been marked for deletion but not yet permanently removed with PACK. Once a PACK or a ZAP command has been used, records cannot be recovered with a RECALL command.

Example

The following statements demonstrate the effects of the RECALL command.

```
USE DONATION
LIST OFF
```

LASTNAME	FIRSTNAME	EXPDATE	CONTRIBUTE
Askew	Lonnie	03/01/88	25.00
Baker	Benjamin	09/08/87	20.00
Baker	Jeanette	06/22/87	10.00
Block	Paul	03/08/87	20.00
Brown	Nicole	08/15/87	25.00
Harris	Charles	02/22/87	10.00
Hayes	Cynthia	08/15/88	100.00
Johnson, Jr.	Lamar	12/01/87	40.00
*Jones	Renee	05/15/87	30.00
Mills	Ernest	04/30/87	20.00
*Roberts	James	05/06/87	25.00

```
*Roberts        Norma           03/08/87        20.00
*Roberts        Terry           05/06/87        25.00
 Sand           Lucy            01/01/99       500.00
 Schultz        Bobby           11/17/87        10.00
 Shaw           Michael         07/21/87        35.00
 Sloan          Wanda           10/15/86        25.00
 Smith          Larry           01/12/88       100.00
```

DISPLAY RECORD 9

```
Record#  LASTNAME        FIRSTNAME        EXPDATE        CONTRIBUTE
      9 *Jones           Renee           05/15/87           30.00
```

RECALL RECORD 9
         1 record recalled

DISPLAY RECORD 9

```
Record#  LASTNAME        FIRSTNAME        EXPDATE        CONTRIBUTE
      9  Jones           Renee           05/15/87           30.00
```

RECALL ALL FOR LASTNAME = "Roberts"
         3 records recalled

LIST OFF

```
    LASTNAME        FIRSTNAME       EXPDATE       CONTRIBUTE
    Askew           Lonnie          03/01/88         25.00
    Baker           Benjamin        09/08/87         20.00
    Baker           Jeanette        06/22/87         10.00
    Block           Paul            03/08/87         20.00
    Brown           Nicole          08/15/87         25.00
    Harris          Charles         02/22/87         10.00
    Hayes           Cynthia         08/15/88        100.00
    Johnson, Jr.    Lamar           12/01/87         40.00
    Jones           Renee           05/15/87         30.00
    Mills           Ernest          04/30/87         20.00
    Roberts         James           05/06/87         25.00
    Roberts         Norma           03/08/87         20.00
    Roberts         Terry           05/06/87         25.00
    Sand            Lucy            01/01/99        500.00
    Schultz         Bobby           11/17/87         10.00
    Shaw            Michael         07/21/87         35.00
    Sloan           Wanda           10/15/86         25.00
    Smith           Larry           01/12/88        100.00
```

REINDEX

Syntax

REINDEX

Syntax for FoxPro 2

REINDEX [COMPACT]

The REINDEX command rebuilds all open index files in the current work area. If any changes have been made to the database while its index file was closed, you can update the index file with REINDEX.

If an index file was originally created with the UNIQUE clause included as part of the INDEX command or with a SET UNIQUE ON statement in effect, a REINDEX will reconstruct the same unique index. In FoxPro 2 and later, the COMPACT option causes the reindexed file to be stored in FoxPro's compact index format.

REMINDER: *If an index file has been damaged, REINDEX may not work. Use the INDEX command to rebuild the index file.*

Example

In the example shown below, the REINDEX command is used to rebuild three open index files. Whenever SET TALK is ON (as in the example), messages indicating the status of the reindexing will appear.

```
USE FINANCE
SET INDEX TO DATES, AMOUNTS, CATS
SET TALK ON
REINDEX

Rebuilding index - D:DATES.ndx
   00% indexed-  100% indexed          692 Records indexed
Rebuilding index - D:AMOUNTS.ndx
   00% indexed-  100% indexed          692 Records indexed
Rebuilding index - D:CATS.ndx
   00% indexed-  100% indexed          692 Records indexed
```

RELEASE

Syntax

> RELEASE *memvarlist*/ALL [LIKE/EXCEPT *wildcards*]

> RELEASE MODULE *modulename*/MENUS *menuname list*/POPUP *popupname list*/WINDOW *windowname list*

The RELEASE command removes all or specified memory variables from memory. Wildcards, which are asterisks or question marks, are used with the LIKE and EXCEPT options. The asterisk can be used to represent one or more characters, the question mark to represent one character. The RELEASE MENUS, RELEASE POPUP, and RELEASE WINDOW variations of the command release the named objects from active memory. The RELEASE MODULE command releases any binary files loaded with the LOAD command from memory.

From the command level, RELEASE ALL will release all variables (with the exception of system memory variables used by FoxPro). When used in a program, RELEASE ALL releases all variables at the current level or in lower-level routines. Variables created in routines at higher levels of the program remain unaffected by RELEASE ALL.

Example

To release all memory variables except those ending with the characters TAX, the following command could be used.

```
RELEASE ALL EXCEPT ???TAX
```

To release a memory variable named LINECOUNT, the following command could be used.

```
RELEASE LINECOUNT
```

RENAME

Syntax

> RENAME *oldfile.ext* TO *newfile.ext*

The RENAME command changes the name of a file. The name must include the file extension. If the files are on drives other than the default drive, the drive designator must be included in *oldfile.ext* and *newfile.ext*.

NOTE: *A file must be closed before it can be renamed, and the new filename cannot be an existing file. Also, if you rename a database containing memo fields, remember to rename the corresponding memo field file.*

Example

To rename a database file named STAFF.DBF to EMPLOYED.DBF, the following command could be used.

```
RENAME STAFF.DBF TO EMPLOYED.DBF
```

REPLACE

Syntax

REPLACE [*scope*] *field* WITH *expression* [ADDITIVE]
[...*field2* WITH *expression2*...] [ADDITIVE] [FOR *condition*] [WHILE *condition*]

Syntax for FoxPro 2

REPLACE [*scope*] *field* WITH *expression* [ADDITIVE]
[...*field2* WITH *expression2*...] [ADDITIVE] [FOR *condition*] [WHILE *condition*]
[NOOPTIMIZE]

The REPLACE command replaces the contents of a specified field with new values. You can replace values in more than one field by listing more than one field WITH *expression*; be sure to separate each field replacement with a comma. The FOR option can be used to specify a condition that must be met before a field in a record will be replaced. If you use the WHILE option, records will be replaced until the condition is no longer true. If the *scope*, FOR, or WHILE options are not used, the current record (at the current record pointer location) will be the only record replaced. The ADDITIVE option can be used when replacing a memo field to add the expression to the existing text in the field. FoxPro will automatically insert a carriage return between the old text and the new. With FoxPro 2 and later, the NOOPTIMIZE clause, when added, turns off FoxPro's internal optimization techniques (Rushmore).

Care should be exercised when making global replacements from the command level, as an improperly structured REPLACE statement can wreak havoc on a database. If you have doubts as to whether a REPLACE statement will have the desired effect on a database, make a copy of the database with COPY TO and experiment on the copy instead of the original.

Example

To replace the contents of a field called Salary at the current record with a new amount equal to the old amount multiplied by 1.05, the following command could be used.

```
REPLACE Salary WITH Salary * 1.05
```

In programs, REPLACE statements are commonly used to transfer data from memory variables into the fields of a database. The following program, designed for editing a database record, uses REPLACE statements to transfer user responses stored in GETs into the fields of a database file.

```
CLEAR
MLAST = SPACE(15)
MFIRST = SPACE(15)
MADDRESS = SPACE(25)
MCITY  = SPACE(15)
MSTATE = SPACE(2)
MZIP = SPACE(10)
*display prompts, store data to variables.
@   3,5 SAY " LAST NAME:" GET MLAST
@   4,5 SAY "FIRST NAME:" GET MFIRST
@   8,5 SAY "ADDRESS:" GET MADDRESS
@  10,5 SAY "   CITY:" GET MCITY
@ 10,35 SAY "STATE:" GET MSTATE
@ 10,45 SAY "ZIP CODE:" GET MZIP
READ
*open database, make new record, store variables.
USE NAMES INDEX NAMES
APPEND BLANK
REPLACE Lastname WITH MLAST, Firstname WITH MFIRST
REPLACE Address WITH MADDRESS, City WITH MCITY
REPLACE State WITH MSTATE, Zip WITH MZIP
CLOSE DATABASES
RETURN
```

REPORT FORM

Syntax

REPORT FORM *filename*/? [*scope*] [FOR *condition*] [WHILE *condition*] [PLAIN]
[HEADING *expC*] [SUMMARY] [NOEJECT] [TO PRINT/TO FILE *filename*]
[OFF]

Syntax for FoxPro 2

REPORT FORM *filename*/? [*scope*] [FOR *condition*] [WHILE *condition*] [PLAIN]
[HEADING *expC*] [SUMMARY] [NOEJECT] [TO PRINT/TO FILE *filename*]
[OFF] [NOCONSOLE] [NOOPTIMIZE] [PREVIEW]

The REPORT FORM command uses a report form file (previously created
with the CREATE REPORT command) to produce a report. A filename with the
extension .FRX is assumed unless otherwise specified. The FOR option can be
used to specify a condition to be met before a record will be printed. If you use
the WHILE option, records will be printed until the condition is no longer true.
If *scope* is not included, ALL is assumed.

The PLAIN option omits page headings. The HEADING option (followed by
a character string, *expC*) provides a header in addition to any header that was
specified when the report was created with CREATE REPORT. The NOEJECT
option cancels the initial form feed. The SUMMARY option causes a summary
report to be printed. TO PRINT directs output to the screen and the printer,
while TO FILE directs output to a disk file. If the question mark is substituted in
place of a filename, a list of all report files appears. The user may then select the
report to print from the list. The optional OFF clause, when used, turns off the
normal screen output while the report is being printed.

In FoxPro 2 and later, the NOOPTIMIZE option, when added, turns off
FoxPro's internal optimization techniques (Rushmore). The NOCONSOLE
option suppresses the display of the records on the screen. The PREVIEW
option sends the labels to screen in page preview mode, and the labels are not
printed.

Version 2

Example

To print a report named MEMBERS with a heading of "For Management" and
the initial page eject suppressed, the following command could be used.

```
REPORT FORM MEMBERS TO PRINT HEADING "For Management" NOEJECT
```

RESTORE

Syntax

RESTORE FROM *filename*/MEMO *memofield* [ADDITIVE]

The RESTORE command reads variables into memory from a memory variable file. RESTORE FROM assumes that *filename* has an extension of .MEM; if it does not, you should include the extension. If the ADDITIVE option is used, current memory variables will not be deleted; the new variables occupy memory space along with existing variables. If ADDITIVE is not used, any existing variables will be deleted when the RESTORE command is used.

If RESTORE is used within a program, variables are restored as private variables. If you need to restore the variables as public to all levels of the program, first declare the variable names as PUBLIC, and then restore the variables with the RESTORE command. If you restore variables from the command level, the variables are restored as public variables.

The RESTORE FROM MEMO memo field syntax may be used to restore variables that were stored to a memo field of a database. (The corresponding SAVE TO command can be used with a MEMO option to save variables to a memo field; see SAVE for details.) The ability to save and restore variables from a memo field can be useful if you want to associate a set of variables to a particular record in a database.

Example

The following statements demonstrate the effects of the RESTORE command, used to restore variables from a file called MEMFILE.

```
STORE 25 TO QUANTITY
SET TALK OFF
STORE "Jefferson" TO NAMES
STORE TIME() TO CLOCK
DISPLAY MEMORY


QUANTITY      pub   N         25  (        25.00000000)
NAMES         pub   C   "Jefferson"
CLOCK         pub   C   "00:19:52"
    3 variables defined,        30 bytes used
  253 variables available,    5970 bytes available


SAVE TO MEMFILE
RELEASE ALL
DISPLAY MEMORY
```

```
    0 variables defined,         0 bytes used
  256 variables available,    6000 bytes available

RESTORE FROM MEMFILE
DISPLAY MEMORY

QUANTITY    pub   N          25 (          25.00000000)
NAMES       pub   C   "Jefferson"
CLOCK       pub   C   "00:19:52"
    3 variables defined,        30 bytes used
  253 variables available,    5970 bytes available
```

RESTORE MACROS

Syntax

RESTORE MACROS FROM *macroname*/MEMO *memofieldname*

The RESTORE MACROS command restores keyboard macros that were saved in a macro file. Normally, any keyboard macros that you create are lost when you exit from FoxPro. To reuse keyboard macros during a later session, you can save them to a macro file with the SAVE MACROS command (see SAVE MACROS). Once macros have been saved to a file, you can restore them to memory at any time with the RESTORE MACROS command. Note that the MEMO clause can be used to restore macros that were saved to a memo field. (Macros can be saved to a memo field of the current record with the SAVE MACROS TO MEMO *memofieldname* statement.)

Any macros existing in memory that are assigned to the same keys when you use the RESTORE MACROS command will be overwritten.

Example

To restore the macros in a file named MYMACROS, the following command could be used.

```
RESTORE MACROS FROM MYMACROS
```

RESTORE SCREEN

Syntax

RESTORE SCREEN [FROM *memvar*]

The RESTORE SCREEN command restores a screen from the buffer or from the named memory variable. (The corresponding command, SAVE SCREEN, is used to store the screen in the memory buffer or to a memory variable.)

RESTORE SCREEN, along with the corresponding command SAVE SCREEN, can be useful when you want to display messages over screen displays, and you want to avoid having to redraw the screen display after the message is removed. Use SAVE SCREEN TO *memvar* to save the screen image to a variable, then display the message. When the message has been viewed, clear the message, and use RESTORE SCREEN FROM *memvar* to redisplay the original screen.

RESTORE WINDOW

Syntax

RESTORE WINDOW *windowname list*/ALL FROM *filename*/MEMO *memofield*

The RESTORE WINDOW command restores window definitions that were saved to a file with the SAVE WINDOW command. One or more windows can be defined with DEFINE WINDOW and then saved to a window file for later use with the SAVE WINDOW command. Window files are assigned an extension of .WIN. Once the window(s) have been saved, you can use the RESTORE WINDOW command to restore the windows.

NOTE: You can selectively restore windows from a window file; you need not restore all of the windows contained in a file. Specify one or more windows in window name list. If you want to restore all windows from the file, use the ALL keyword in place of window name list.

There are two points to remember when restoring windows from a file: First, if a window currently in memory has a name identical to a window stored in the file, the window currently in memory will be overwritten by the one restored from the file. Second, the window's status when saved to disk (active, hidden, etc.) will be its status once restored from disk.

The MEMO clause can be used to restore windows that were saved to a memo field. (Windows can be saved to a memo field of the current record with the SAVE WINDOW TO MEMO *memofieldname* statement.)

Example

In the following program, two windows are defined and saved to a window file named MYWINDOW.WIN. The window definitions are cleared from memory, and then restored to memory with the RESTORE WINDOW statement. Next, ACTIVATE WINDOW statements are used to activate the restored windows for use by BROWSE operations.

```
CLEAR
DEFINE WINDOW members FROM 3,3 TO 12,70
DEFINE WINDOW rentals FROM 14,8 TO 22,75
SAVE WINDOW ALL TO MYWINDOW
CLEAR WINDOWS
RESTORE WINDOW ALL FROM MYWINDOW
ACTIVATE WINDOW members
USE MEMBERS
BROWSE
ACTIVATE WINDOW rentals
SELECT 2
USE RENTALS
BROWSE
```

RESUME

Syntax

RESUME

The RESUME command causes program execution to continue at the line following the line at which program operation was suspended, either with the SUSPEND command or with the ESC key and the Suspend menu option (if SET ESCAPE is ON). RESUME is normally used when debugging programs to restart the program where it was halted after you have had a chance to examine or modify memory variables or field values.

Use RESUME along with SUSPEND to track down the cause of errors in your program. You can insert a SUSPEND command in a program in an area where errors are occurring, and when the program halts, you can use DISPLAY STATUS and DISPLAY MEMORY to examine the contents of memory variables or environmental settings. Entering **RESUME** will then restart the program at the point it was halted.

RETRY

Syntax

RETRY

The RETRY command returns control to a calling program and executes the same line that called the program containing the RETRY command. The function of RETRY is similar to the function of the RETURN command; however, where RETURN executes the next successive line of the calling program, RETRY executes the same line of the calling program. RETRY can be useful in error-recovery situations, where an action can be taken to clear the cause of an error and the command repeated.

Example

In the following printing program, an ON ERROR statement will cause a branch to an error-trapping routine if a printer not ready error occurs. The error-trapping routine posts a message to the user to correct the problem with the printer and uses a RETRY statement to return control to the point in the calling program where the error occurred.

```
*printing program includes error recovery.*
WAIT "Press a key to start the report."
ON ERROR DO PROBLEMS
REPORT FORM MYFILE TO PRINT
ON ERROR
RETURN
...more commands...

*PROBLEMS.PRG*
*error trapping for printer program.*
CLEAR
? "Printer is NOT READY."
? "Take corrective action, then press any key."
WAIT
RETRY
RETURN
```

RETURN

Syntax

RETURN [TO MASTER/*expression*/TO *procedurename*]

The RETURN command ends execution of a command file or procedure. If the command file was called by another command file, program control returns to the other command file. If the command file was not called by another command file, control returns to the command level. If the TO MASTER option is used, control returns to the highest level command file. If the TO *procedurename* option is used, control returns to the named procedure. The *expression* option is used to return the value in a user-defined function to another procedure or command file.

RUN

Syntax

RUN [FOXSWAP] [/N [K]] *filename*

or

! [FOXSWAP] [/N [K]] *filename*

The RUN command executes a non-FoxPro program from within the FoxPro environment, provided there is enough available memory. The program must be an executable file (having an extension of .COM, .EXE, or .BAT). When the program completes its execution, control is passed back to FoxPro. You can also execute DOS commands with RUN. The exclamation point (!) can be substituted for the word RUN. To use the RUN command, the DOS file COMMAND.COM must be in the current directory or locatable through either a PATH statement or the DOS COMSPEC parameter.

The /N or /NK options can be used to specify an amount of memory to be freed, where N is a numeric value in kilobytes (K). If N is omitted, RUN frees a standard amount of memory (which varies depending on your system). If N is zero, RUN frees as much memory as possible, swapping large portions of FoxPro out to disk. Any value other than zero is interpreted as memory needed in kilobytes, and as much of FoxPro as is needed is swapped out to disk to provide the memory.

The FOXSWAP option causes FoxPro to use the FoxSwap utility, which makes as much memory as is possible available. (FoxSwap is also invoked if you specify a zero value for the N parameter.)

WARNING: *You should not run programs that modify memory or disk allocation tables, such as CHKDSK or memory-resident programs, with the RUN command. Doing so may cause unpredictable results and possible loss of data when you return to FoxPro.*

Example

To run the DOS DATE command to change the system date from within FoxPro, the following command could be used.

```
RUN DATE
```

SAVE

Syntax

SAVE TO *filename*/MEMO *memofieldname* [ALL LIKE/EXCEPT *skeleton*]

The SAVE command copies memory variables to a disk file or to the contents of a memo field. Wildcards, which are asterisks or question marks, are used with parts of variable names as skeletons along with the LIKE and EXCEPT options. The asterisk can be used to represent one or more characters, the question mark to represent one character.

The SAVE TO MEMO *memofieldname* syntax can be used to save variables to a memo field of the current record of the active database. (The corresponding RESTORE FROM command can be used with a MEMO option to restore variables from a memo field; see RESTORE for details.) The ability to save and restore variables from a memo field can be useful if you want to associate a set of variables to a particular record in a database.

Example

To save all existing six-letter memory variables ending in the letters "TAX" to a disk file named FIGURES, enter

```
SAVE TO FIGURES ALL LIKE ???TAX
```

SAVE MACROS

Syntax

SAVE MACROS TO *macroname*/MEMO *memofieldname*

The SAVE MACROS command saves macros currently in memory to the macro file specified by *macroname*. Normally, any keyboard macros that you create are lost when you exit from FoxPro. To reuse keyboard macros during a later session, you can save them to a macro file with the SAVE MACROS command. Once macros have been saved to a file, you can later restore them to memory with the RESTORE MACROS command. (To record macros, press SHIFT-F10, press the key to be assigned as the macro key, and enter the keystrokes to be stored to the macro.)

FoxPro saves macro files with a default extension of .FKY. You can specify a different extension by including it along with the filename; if you do, be sure to include the extension with the RESTORE MACRO command.

Example

To save all macros currently in memory to a file called MYMACROS, the following command could be used.

```
SAVE MACROS TO MYMACROS
```

SAVE SCREEN

Syntax

SAVE SCREEN [TO *memvar*]

The SAVE SCREEN command saves a screen to the buffer or to the named memory variable. (The corresponding command, RESTORE SCREEN, is used to restore the screen currently in the memory buffer or from a memory variable.)

SAVE SCREEN, along with the corresponding command RESTORE SCREEN, can be useful when you want to display messages over screen displays, and you want to avoid having to redraw the screen display after the message is removed. Use SAVE SCREEN TO *memvar* to save the screen image to a variable and then display the message. When the message has been viewed, clear the message, and use RESTORE SCREEN FROM *memvar* to redisplay the original screen. This presents less programming work than redrawing the original screen, and with complex screens it is considerably faster.

SAVE WINDOW

Syntax

SAVE WINDOW *windownamelist*/ALL TO *windowname*/MEMO *memofield*

The SAVE WINDOW command saves the windows named in *windownamelist* to a disk file. If the ALL option is used, all windows in memory are saved to a file. If the MEMO option is used, the windows are saved to the named memo field of the current record. The windows can be restored to memory using the RESTORE WINDOW command. (See RESTORE WINDOW for an example of the use of the SAVE WINDOW command along with the RESTORE WINDOW command.)

SCAN

Syntax

SCAN [*scope*] [FOR *condition*] [WHILE *condition*]
[*commands*...]
   [LOOP]
   [*commands*...]
   [EXIT]
ENDSCAN

Syntax for FoxPro 2

SCAN [*scope*] [FOR *condition*] [WHILE *condition*] [NOOPTIMIZE]
[*commands*...]
   [LOOP]
   [*commands*...]
   [EXIT]
ENDSCAN

The SCAN and ENDSCAN commands are simplified alternatives to the DO WHILE and ENDDO commands. The SCAN...ENDSCAN commands cause the file in use to be scanned, processing all records that meet the specified conditions. SCAN is similar to DO WHILE in that SCAN moves the record pointer to each successive record, testing for the condition specified by the FOR or WHILE clauses. This process continues until the end of the file is reached or the SCAN is terminated by the presence of an EXIT clause.

The *scope* option is used to set a scope (or set number of records) to be scanned. If no *scope* is identified, all records are scanned. The FOR option is used to identify the condition that a record must meet before the statements between SCAN and ENDSCAN will be executed. If you use the WHILE option, the statements between SCAN and ENDSCAN will be executed while the specified condition is true.

The EXIT and LOOP commands may be used anywhere between SCAN and ENDSCAN; EXIT halts the process, and program control proceeds to the command immediately following the ENDSCAN statement. LOOP causes program control to jump back to the first statement following the SCAN statement. The LOOP and EXIT commands are normally placed in an IF...ENDIF conditional structure inside of the SCAN...ENDSCAN structure. If the condition defined by IF...ENDIF evaluates as true, the LOOP or EXIT command is executed, changing the program flow within the SCAN...ENDSCAN structure.

In FoxPro 2 only, the NOOPTIMIZE clause, when added, turns off FoxPro's internal optimization techniques (Rushmore).

Example

The following program uses a group of statements between SCAN and END-SCAN statements to print all records in a database where the membership date is greater than or equal to the date indicated by the computer's system clock.

```
USE MEMBERS
SCAN FOR EXPIREDATE <= DATE()+60
   SET PRINT ON
   ? "Dear: "
   ?? trim(Firstname) + " " + Lastname
   ?
   ? "Your membership expires within the next 60 days."
   ? "Please call 555-1212 to renew your membership."
   EJECT
   SET PRINT OFF
ENDSCAN
```

SCATTER TO

Syntax

SCATTER [FIELDS *fieldlist*] TO *array* [BLANK]

The SCATTER TO command is used to move data from the current record of a database file into memory variables. (Note that SCATTER TO is compatible with FoxBASE+; if you need compatibility with dBASE IV, use COPY TO ARRAY instead.) The fields of the current record are transferred, beginning with the first field of the record, into the corresponding elements of the array. If the database has more fields than the array has elements, the contents of extra fields are not stored to the array. If the array has more elements than the database has fields, the extra elements in the array are not changed. Note that memo fields are ignored during the data transfer process.

The BLANK option will create an empty set of memory variables. They will be of the same type and size as the database fields, and they will have the same name. You can include the optional FIELDS *fieldlist* clause to specify the memory variables that should be created; if you use this option, one variable is created for each field you name in the field list.

Example

The data entry program shown below moves existing data from a database into an array for editing. The values stored to the elements of the array are edited with a series of @...SAY...GET statements and are then transfered back to the fields of the database. Note that the use of SCATTER eliminates the need for the usual STORE or assignment (=) statements to fill the variables with existing data from the database fields.

```
CLEAR
*open files, create memory variables.
USE MAILER INDEX NAMES
ACCEPT "Enter last name to edit:" TO FINDIT
SEEK FINDIT
IF .NOT. FOUND()
    WAIT "Can't find that record. Press a key..."
    RETURN
ENDIF
SCATTER TO M_DATA
*display prompts, store data to variables.
@   3,5 SAY " LAST NAME:" GET M_DATA[1,1]
@   4,5 SAY "FIRST NAME:" GET M_DATA[1,2]
@   8,5 SAY "ADDRESS:" GET M_DATA[1,3]
@  10,5 SAY "   CITY:" GET M_DATA[1,4]
@ 10,35 SAY "STATE:" GET M_DATA[1,5]
@ 10,45 SAY "ZIP CODE:" GET M_DATA[1,6]
READ
*store variables.
GATHER FROM M_DATA
RETURN
```

SCROLL

Syntax

SCROLL *row1,col1,row2,col2,expN*

The SCROLL command causes a rectangular portion of the screen to scroll. The upper-left corner of the portion is designated by *row1,col1*, and the lower-right corner is designated by *row2,col2*. The numeric expression *expN* indicates the number of lines of the area to scroll. A negative number forces a scroll downward, while a positive number forces a scroll upward.

Example

To scroll a portion of the screen measuring from row 4, column 4 to row 8, column 20 down five lines, the following command could be used.

```
SCROLL 4,4,8,20,-5
```

SEEK

Syntax

SEEK *expression*

The SEEK command searches for the first record in an indexed file whose field matches a specific expression. If *expression* is a character string, it must be surrounded by single or double quotes.

If *expression* cannot be found and FoxPro is not executing a command file, the EOF() value is set to true and a "No find" message is displayed on the screen.

An index file must be open before you can use the SEEK command. Also note the use of two related commands, SET EXACT and SET NEAR. Use SET EXACT to tell FoxPro to find a precise match. Use SET NEAR to tell FoxPro that if a match cannot be found, to position the record pointer to the closest record rather than the end of the file.

Example

The following commands are used from the command level to search an index file for a particular name.

```
USE MEMBERS
SET INDEX TO Lastname
STORE "Johnson" TO FINDIT
SEEK FINDIT
DISPLAY
```

Record 4	LASTNAME	FIRSTNAME	AGE	SALARY
	Johnson	Wendy	27	750.00

SELECT

Syntax

SELECT *n*
SELECT *alias*

The SELECT command chooses from among ten possible work areas for database files. When FoxPro is first loaded into the computer, it defaults to a work area of 1. To use multiple files at once, you can select other work areas with the SELECT command; other files can then be opened in those areas. Acceptable work areas are the numbers 1 through 10.

Once a database has been opened in a work area, you can also select it by referring to the database name rather than a work area number.

The SET RELATION command is often used along with the SELECT command to establish relationships between files. See SET RELATION for additional details.

Example

To open a file named PAYROLL in work area 1, a file named TAXES in work area 2, and switch back to work area 1, the following commands could be used.

```
SELECT 1
USE PAYROLL
SELECT 2
USE TAXES
SELECT PAYROLL
```

SELECT - SQL

Syntax

Version 2

SELECT [ALL/DISTINCT] [*alias.*] *selectitem* [AS *columnname*]
[, [*alias.*] *selectitem* [AS *columnname*]...] FROM *database* [*local_alias*]
[, *database* [*local_alias*]...] [[INTO *destination*]/[TO FILE *filename*
[ADDITIVE]/TO PRINTER]] [NOCONSOLE] [PLAIN] [NOWAIT]
[WHERE *joincondition* [AND *joincondition*...] [AND/OR *filtercondition*
[AND/OR *filtercondition*...]]] [GROUP BY *groupcolumn*
[, *groupcolumn*...]] [HAVING *filtercondition*] [UNION [ALL] *SELECTcommand*]
[ORDER BY *order_item* [ASC/DESC] [, *orderitem* [ASC/DESC]...]]

This variation of the SELECT command is used to retrieve data from a table (made up of fields from one or more FoxPro database files). SELECT commands can be entered manually in the Command window or they can be created by designing a query in the RQBE window. The use of the SQL SELECT statement is a topic beyond the scope of this text; for more information, refer to your FoxPro documentation or to a text on the SQL Data Retrieval language.

SET

Syntax

SET

The SET command causes the View window to be displayed. The View Window options (at the left edge of the window) can then be used to view and modify most available SET parameters within FoxPro. The options displayed by SET can be used to set most of the environmental variables that are also accessible through individual SET commands, like SET BELL, SET COLOR, and SET MARGINS. Margins, decimals, date formats, and function key assignments are some of the environmental variables that can be set with the SET menus.

SET ALTERNATE

Syntax

SET ALTERNATE ON/OFF and SET ALTERNATE TO *filename* [ADDITIVE]

The SET ALTERNATE TO command creates a text file with extension .TXT and, when activated by SET ALTERNATE ON, stores all keyboard entries and screen displays to the file. The SET ALTERNATE OFF command halts the process, after which CLOSE ALTERNATE is used to close the file. (You can SET ALTERNATE OFF temporarily, and turn it on again later before using CLOSE ALTERNATE to resume sending output to the file.) If the ADDITIVE option is used, SET ALTERNATE appends to the end of any existing file.

SET ALTERNATE can be used to have a print file and an alternate file open at the same time, allowing the creation of two reports on disk at the same time. SET ALTERNATE can also be very useful when debugging problems that occur only when you are not around and someone else is using the program. In such cases, use the SET ALTERNATE commands to save a record of operations to a disk file. When the SET ALTERNATE ON command is used, everything that appears on your screen, with the exception of full-screen editing operations, will be stored in the text file in ASCII format. You can later examine the contents of the text file to see what replies to the program were typed and what program responses occurred as a result. Using these commands can quickly consume disk space, so consider available disk space before using the SET ALTERNATE commands for an extended period of time.

Example

To store the actions of the LIST command to a text file, the following commands could be used.

```
SET ALTERNATE TO CAPTURE
SET ALTERNATE ON
LIST Lastname, Firstname
SET ALTERNATE OFF
CLOSE ALTERNATE
```

SET ANSI

Syntax

SET ANSI ON/OFF

Version 2

The SET ANSI command is used to determine how comparisons of strings of different length are made with FoxPro's SQL commands. When SET ANSI is ON, character strings are compared for the full length of the string. Hence, "Derek " and "Derek" do not match if SET ANSI is ON. When SET ANSI is OFF, strings are compared character by character only until the shorter string ends. Hence, "Derek " and "Derek" match if SET ANSI is OFF.

SET AUTOSAVE

Syntax

SET AUTOSAVE ON/OFF

The SET AUTOSAVE command, when turned on, causes FoxPro to save changes to disk after each I/O operation. This reduces the chances of data loss due to power or hardware failure. The default for SET AUTOSAVE is OFF.

NOTE: It is important to use SET AUTOSAVE ON in programs that operate on local area networks to ensure timely updates to shared data.

SET BELL

Syntax

SET BELL ON/OFF

The SET BELL command controls whether audible warnings will be issued during certain operations. SET BELL ON enables the bell, while SET BELL OFF disables the bell. The default for SET BELL is ON.

SET BELL TO

Syntax

SET BELL TO *frequency/duration*

The SET BELL TO command controls the frequency and duration of the bell. The frequency is the desired tone in Hertz (cycles per second), and each unit of duration is approximately .0549 seconds. Available frequency is from 18 to 10,001, and available duration is from 2 to 20. The default for SET BELL TO is a frequency of 512 Hz, and a duration of 2.

Example

To play a series of tones using the computer's speaker, the following commands could be used.

```
SET BELL TO 440,8
? CHR(7)
SET BELL TO 880,5
? CHR(7)
SET BELL TO 440,8
? CHR(7)
SET BELL TO 880,5
? CHR(7)
SET BELL TO 880,5
? CHR(7)
```

SET BLINK

Syntax

SET BLINK ON/OFF

The SET BLINK command determines whether screen elements (borders, shadows, text) can be made to blink on EGA or VGA monitors. Note that SET BLINK ON enables blinking of selected elements, but does not actually cause the elements to blink. Use the Color option of the Window menu or the SET COLOR command to change the actual elements to blinking. The default for SET BLINK is ON.

If SET BLINK is OFF, background colors can be set to the high resolution or "bright" setting. This doubles the number of available colors.

SET BLOCKSIZE

Syntax

SET BLOCKSIZE TO *expN*

The SET BLOCKSIZE command changes the block size used to store data in memo fields. The value of *expN* can be any number from 1 to 32. The value multiplied by 512 represents the actual size of the blocks, in bytes. The default value for SET BLOCKSIZE is 64.

With large amounts of text, larger blocks often increase performance, but only up to a point. Large blocks offer faster string manipulation, but often slow down disk reads and writes. Smaller blocks may offer better performance with disk reads and writes, but may slow down string manipulation. If your memo fields are large, you may want to experiment with the value of SET BLOCKSIZE to determine the effect on overall speed of your application.

Once you change the value of SET BLOCKSIZE, new databases with memo fields that are created will use the new blocksize. To make the change effective with an existing database, use SET BLOCKSIZE to establish the new value, then use COPY TO to copy the existing database to a new file. The new file will have the new block size.

Example

To set the block size to 4, or 2K (2048 bytes) per block, the following command could be used.

```
SET BLOCKSIZE TO 4
```

SET BORDER

Syntax

SET BORDER TO
[SINGLE/DOUBLE/PANEL/NONE/*border-definition string1*]
[, *border-definition string2*]

The SET BORDER command redefines the border, which is a single line. The SINGLE option defines a single line; the DOUBLE option defines a double line; the PANEL option defines a panel built with the ASCII 219 character; and NONE defines no border. The border definition string option may contain up to 8 ASCII values separated by commas. Value 1 defines the top of the border; value 2 the bottom; values 3 and 4 the left and right edges; and values 5, 6, 7, and 8 the upper-left, upper-right, lower-left, and lower-right corners, respectively. By default, <*border-definition string1* is also used for the active window. The optional *border-definition string2* defines the appearance of the border if the window is not active.

Example

To change the default border to a double-line box, the following command could be used.

```
SET BORDER TO DOUBLE
```

To change the default border to a panel, the following command could be used.

```
SET BORDER TO PANEL
```

To change the default border to double lines on both sides, single lines on the top and bottom, and matching corners, and to draw a box from row 2, column 2 to row 15, column 50 using the new border, the following commands could be used.

```
SET BORDER TO 196,196,186,186,214,183,211,189
@ 2,2 TO 15,50
```

To change the default border back to a single line, the following command could be used.

```
SET BORDER TO
```

SET CARRY

Syntax

SET CARRY ON/OFF

The SET CARRY command controls whether data will be copied from the prior record into the next record when APPEND or INSERT is used. If SET CARRY is ON, the contents of all fields from the current record are passed to the fields of a new record. By default, SET CARRY is OFF.

The SET CARRY command is often useful when you are making a large number of additions, and many of the fields in the new record will be duplicates of fields in the existing records. Use SET CARRY to avoid typing the same data repeatedly into the fields of the new records.

SET CENTURY

Syntax

SET CENTURY ON/OFF

The SET CENTURY command enables or hides the century in the display of dates. For example, a date that appears as 12/30/90 will appear as 12/30/1990 after the SET CENTURY ON command is used. SET CENTURY affects both the display and the editing of data values. If SET CENTURY is OFF, the year portion of a date field will allow only two digits and the 20th century is assumed for the year. If SET CENTURY is ON, the year portion of a date field will permit the display or editing of four digits.

NOTE: Dates must be entered using a valid century while SET CENTURY is ON for a century (other than the current one) to appear when the dates are displayed or printed.

Example

The commands shown below demonstrate the use of the SET CENTURY command.

```
USE BONDS
LIST OFF

BONDNAME               MATURES   FACEVALUE
Lunar Power & Light    03/01/10  10000.00
Continental Space Co   06/30/05   5000.00
Alpha Omega Travel     12/01/90   1500.00
Uptown Computers Inc   03/31/95   5000.00
European Economics     06/01/01   5000.00
Moscow Manufacturing   10/01/30  10000.00
California Motors       06/01/95   3500.00
```

```
SET CENTURY ON
LIST OFF

BONDNAME              MATURES     FACEVALUE
Lunar Power & Light   03/01/2010  10000.00
Continental Space Co  06/30/2005   5000.00
Alpha Omega Travel    12/01/1990   1500.00
Uptown Computers Inc  03/31/1995   5000.00
European Economics    06/01/2001   5000.00
Moscow Manufacturing  10/01/2030  10000.00
California Motors      06/01/1995   3500.00
```

SET CLEAR

Syntax

SET CLEAR ON/OFF

The SET CLEAR command determines whether the screen should be cleared after executing a SET FORMAT command or a QUIT command. If SET CLEAR is OFF, the screen will not be cleared after a format screen has been displayed with SET FORMAT TO *filename*, and the screen will not be cleared after a QUIT command. The default value of SET CLEAR is ON.

Example

To exit a program and leave a message regarding backup of files on the screen, the following commands could be used.

```
SET CLEAR OFF
CLEAR
@ 5,5 SAY "Don't forget to BACK UP your data files!!!"
QUIT
```

SET CLOCK

Syntax

SET CLOCK ON/OFF

The SET CLOCK command defines whether the system clock will appear. SET CLOCK ON displays the clock, while SET CLOCK OFF hides the clock.

SET CLOCK TO

Syntax

SET CLOCK TO *row,col*

The SET CLOCK TO command defines the location of the system clock, as defined by the row and column coordinates provided. By default, the clock appears in the upper-right corner of the screen. Use SET CLOCK TO to change this location.

SET COLOR OF

Syntax

SET COLOR OF
NORMAL/MESSAGES/TITLES/BOX/HIGHLIGHT/INFORMATION/
FIELDS TO [*color-pair list*]

To better control a visual user interface, the SET COLOR OF command is provided to change colors between different objects. The SET COLOR OF command can be used to define colors for standard items, such as messages, titles, boxes, and highlights.

Note that color attribute is specified as a foreground and a background color code, separated by a slash. The color codes used for color attribute are as indicated in the table below. An asterisk denotes blinking or bright intensity (depending on the setting of SET BLINK), and a plus sign denotes high intensity. For example, the combination B+/W would indicate a high-intensity blue foreground with a white background.

Color	Code	Color	Code
Black	N	Green	G
Blank	X	Magenta	RB
Blue	B	Red	R
Brown	GR	White	W
Cyan	BG	Yellow	GR+
Grey	N+		

Monochrome monitors may use one of four codes: W for white, N for black, U for underlined, and I for inverse video.

Note that the SET COLOR OF command changes the color settings in Color Schemes 1 and 2, since these color schemes control the appearance of user menus and user windows. (For a detailed breakdown of which objects each of the 11 FoxPro color schemes affects, see SET COLOR OF SCHEME.)

On Compaq portable computers and on most laptop computers, the monochrome monitors appear to be color systems from a hardware standpoint; thus, the monochrome attributes of U and I will not generate underlining and inverse video. The normal color codes can be used on these systems, and the colors will appear as varying shades of black and green (on Compaq portables) or as varying shades of blue and grey (on most laptops).

Use the desired option (NORMAL, MESSAGES, TITLES, BOX, HIGH-LIGHT, INFORMATION, or FIELDS) to determine which objects you want to apply the color changes to. The objects include the following items:

- NORMAL @...SAY output, unselected fields in BROWSE, unselected and uncolored display-only field templates, static memo or window borders, and calculated field expressions.

- MESSAGES message-line bright messages, navigation-line messages, available, unselected menu and list choices (bright), unavailable list choices (dimmed); error box contents, file-window contents, help-box contents, prompt-box contents, unselected prompt, error, and help-box buttons (all bright).

- TITLES list headings, help-box headings, BROWSE field-name headings and table grids, database design column labels & field numbers, file headings, ruler lines, text that is underlined in Help screens.

- BOX menu borders, file and sorted-by information, file window border, list borders, prompt box borders, and label design-layout borders.

- HIGHLIGHT Highlighted menu and list choices, highlighted prompt-box buttons, selected text or fields on design surface, information-box borders and interiors, box or field under cursor in design surface.

- INFORMATION clock, error-box borders, help-box borders, status line, selected button in error or help boxes.

- FIELDS prompt-box data entry areas, selected field in BROWSE, editable fields in @...GET, selected field in database design, and editable-field design-surface templates.

Example

To change the colors of boxes (including list boxes, prompt boxes, menu borders, and file window borders) to blue on a magenta background, the following command could be used.

```
SET COLOR OF BOX TO B/RB
```

To change the colors of fields (which includes editable fields in @...GET, selected fields in BROWSE, and prompt box data entry areas) to green characters on a white background, the following command could be used.

```
SET COLOR OF FIELDS TO G/W
```

SET COLOR OF SCHEME

Syntax

SET COLOR OF SCHEME *expN* TO [*color-pair list*]

The SET COLOR OF SCHEME command sets the colors of the numbered scheme to the colors list identified in *color-pair list*. *ExpN* is a numeric expression from 1 to 11 or from 17 to 24. (Schemes 12 through 16 are reserved by FoxPro.) Schemes 17 through 24 can be user-defined; you can use these along with the SET COLOR OF SCHEME *expN1* TO [SCHEME *expN2*] command to transfer the colors in a custom color scheme into one of FoxPro's standard color schemes. Schemes 1 through 11 apply to the following objects:

Scheme 1 User windows
Scheme 2 User menus
Scheme 3 Menu Bar
Scheme 4 Popup Menus
Scheme 5 Dialog boxes
Scheme 6 Dialog popups
Scheme 7 Alert boxes
Scheme 8 Windows
Scheme 9 Window popups
Scheme 10 Browse window
Scheme 11 Report Layout window

The *color-pair list* consists of 1 to 10 color pairs, with the foreground (standard) and background (enhanced) values separated by a slash and each color pair separated by commas. For example, the following string of characters is a color pairs list:

W/B, B/W, GR+/B, GR+/RB, R+/B, N/GR, GR/B, BG/RB

The colors are as indicated in the table below. An asterisk denotes blinking or bright intensity (depending on the setting of SET BLINK), and a plus sign denotes high intensity.

Color	Code	Color	Code
Black	N	Green	G
Blank	X	Magenta	RB
Blue	B	Red	R
Brown	GR	White	W
Cyan	BG	Yellow	GR+
Grey	N+		

Monochrome monitors may use one of four codes: W for white, N for black, U for underlined, and I for inverse video.

Each of the ten pairs of colors represents a different item within the designated color scheme. Note that it is not necessary to specify all of the color pairs; you can specify only select pairs, and the others will remain unchanged. For example, to change just color pair 4 of a user-defined menu (COLOR SCHEME 2) to blue and grey, while leaving the remaining colors in color scheme 2 unchanged, you could use a command like the following:

```
SET COLOR OF SCHEME 2 TO , , , B/N+
```

The preceding commas must be included for each color pair that remains unchanged (in this example, the first three color pairs are unchanged and indicated by the commas).

Example

The following command would redefine all ten color pairs for color scheme 5 (Dialog Boxes):

```
SET COLOR OF SCHEME 5 TO ;
W/B, B/W, GR/B, GR/RB, R/B, N/GR, GR/B, BG/RB, W/N+, B/R
```

SET COLOR OF SCHEME TO

Syntax

SET COLOR OF SCHEME *expN1* TO *expN2*

The SET COLOR OF SCHEME TO command copies the colors of the first color scheme to the second color scheme. *ExpN* is a numeric expression from 1 to 11 or from 17 to 24. (Schemes 12 through 16 are reserved by FoxPro.) Schemes 17 through 24 can be user-defined. When you use the command, Scheme *expN1* takes on the color settings stored in Scheme *expN2*.

If the SCHEME *expN2* clause is omitted, color scheme *expN1* will copy its colors from the last color set to be loaded or saved, the last color set defined with the SET COLOR SET TO command or the FoxPro default color set.

Example

In an application, color scheme 20 was user-defined with the SET COLOR OF SCHEME command. To transfer the colors in color scheme 20 to color scheme 7 (Alert Boxes), the following command could be used.

```
SET COLOR OF SCHEME 7 TO SCHEME 20
```

SET COLOR ON/OFF

Syntax

SET COLOR ON/OFF

The SET COLOR ON/OFF command is used to change between color and monochrome monitors on systems that are equipped for both. SET COLOR ON switches to color mode, while SET COLOR OFF switches to monochrome mode. The default value of SET COLOR is determined by which graphics adapter is in use when FoxPro is initially loaded. If the monochrome adapter and monitor are in use, SET COLOR will be OFF at startup; if the color adapter and monitor are in use, SET COLOR will be ON at startup.

SET COLOR SET TO

Syntax

SET COLOR SET TO [*ColorSetname*]

The SET COLOR SET TO command lets you load colors from a previously defined color set *ColorSetname*. Color sets can be defined with the SET COLOR

OF SCHEME command or through the Color Picker dialog. The Color Picker dialog is accessed by choosing Color... from the Window menu popup. After a color set has been defined it must be saved in the Color Picker if it is to be used again.

If the optional COLOR SET *ColorSetname* clause is not included, color set *expN1* gets its colors from the last named color set. The last-named color set is the last color set loaded or saved, a color set defined with the SET COLOR SET TO command, a color set loaded from the CONFIG.FP configuration file on startup or the FoxPro default color set. If there is no last-named color set, the hardware default is restored.

SET COLOR TO

Syntax

SET COLOR TO *color-pair list*

The SET COLOR TO command is used to select screen colors and display attributes. The standard and enhanced settings are used to specify the foreground and background values separated by a slash, and each color setting is separated from the next one by a comma. The border attribute, when used, is represented by a single color code. (Border attributes can be specified only on color monitors.)

The color codes used are as indicated in the table below. An asterisk denotes blinking, and a plus sign denotes high intensity. For example, the combination B+/W would indicate a high-intensity blue foreground with a white background.

Color	Code	Color	Code
Black	N	Green	G
Blank	X	Magenta	RB
Blue	B	Red	R
Brown	GR	White	W
Cyan	BG	Yellow	GR+
Grey	N+		

Monochrome monitors may use one of four codes: W for white, N for black, U for underlined, and I for inverse video.

NOTE: *The SET COLOR TO command without a specified color setting resets the screen to the default colors of black and white.*

Example

To display standard text as blue over red background, enhanced text as green on a white background, and borders of magenta, the following command could be used.

```
SET COLOR TO B/R, G/W, RB
```

SET COMPATIBLE

Syntax

SET COMPATIBLE [ON/DB4]/[OFF/FOXPRO]

The SET COMPATIBLE command determines whether FoxPro will run FoxBASE+ programs unchanged. The FOXPLUS option and the OFF option are identical. The DB4 option and the ON option are identical. If you use a SET COMPATIBLE OFF statement or a SET COMPATIBLE FOXPLUS statement, FoxBASE+ programs can be run unchanged in FoxPro. If you use a SET COMPATIBLE ON statement or a SET COMPATIBLE DB4 statement, dBASE IV programs can be run in FoxPro with less changes than would be needed if SET COMPATIBLE were OFF. The default setting for SET COMPATIBLE is OFF.

SET COMPATIBLE affects how FoxPro handles the PLAY MACRO and STORE commands and the LIKE() and SELECT() functions.

In FoxPro 1.02 and later, SET COMPATIBLE also affects whether parameters passed by reference become hidden memory variables. When SET COMPATIBLE is set to FOXPLUS or OFF, parameters that are passed by reference are hidden. When SET COMPATIBLE is set to DB4 or ON, parameters that are passed by reference are not hidden.

SET CONFIRM

Syntax

SET CONFIRM ON/OFF

The SET CONFIRM command controls the behavior of the cursor during editing. When SET CONFIRM is ON, a terminating key (such as ENTER, PGDN, or TAB) must be pressed to move from one field to another when editing in a highlighted field, even if you completely fill the field. When CONFIRM is OFF, the cursor automatically advances to the next field when you fill a field. Also, the bell sounds (if SET BELL is ON). The default for SET CONFIRM is OFF.

SET CONFIRM OFF is useful when data entered into fields is always the same length, such as with ZIP codes, telephone numbers, social security numbers, and so on. When data of varying lengths is to be entered into a field, use SET CONFIRM ON. This helps ensure the integrity of the data entry.

SET CONSOLE

Syntax

SET CONSOLE ON/OFF

The SET CONSOLE command turns output to the screen on or off. SET CONSOLE ON directs output to the screen, while SET CONSOLE OFF turns off screen output. Note that @...SAY...GETs and error messages are not affected by SET CONSOLE. To accept responses to variables while hiding the display with SET CONSOLE OFF, use WAIT, ACCEPT, or INPUT rather than @...SAY...GETs.

SET CONSOLE does not control output to the printer. Use SET CONSOLE within a program when you want to hide any screen display while leaving the keyboard active (such as during the typing in of a user's password).

Example

In the following program, a password routine hides the display of the password with a SET CONSOLE OFF statement.

```
CLEAR
? " Enter the password now:"
SET CONSOLE OFF
ACCEPT TO PASS
SET CONSOLE ON
IF UPPER(PASS) <> "SKYWALKER"
    CLEAR
    WAIT " INVALID PASSWORD!  PRESS A KEY..."
    QUIT
ENDIF
USE STAFF INDEX NAMES
...more commands...
```

SET CURRENCY

Syntax

SET CURRENCY TO [*expC*]

The SET CURRENCY command changes the symbol used for currency. A character expression containing up to nine characters may be used as the currency symbol.

SET CURRENCY LEFT/RIGHT

Syntax

SET CURRENCY LEFT/RIGHT

The SET CURRENCY LEFT/RIGHT command changes the placement of the currency symbol, allowing the symbol to appear to the left or the right of the value.

SET DATE

Syntax

SET DATE AMERICAN/ANSI/BRITISH/ITALIAN/FRENCH/GERMAN/
JAPAN/USA/MDY/DMY/YMD

The SET DATE command sets the display format for the appearance of dates. American displays as mm/dd/yy; ANSI displays as *yy.mm.dd*; British displays as *dd/mm/yy*; Italian displays as *dd-mm-yy*; French displays as *dd/mm/yy*; and German displays as *dd.mm.yy*. Japan displays as *yy/mm/dd*; USA displays as *mm-dd-yy*; MDY displays as *mm/dd/yy*; DMY displays as *dd/mm/yy*; and YMD displays as *yy/mm/dd*. The default value of SET DATE is American.

The SET DATE format provides increased flexibility when displaying dates. Note that entries into date fields or into variables having a data type of Date must be entered following the format established by SET DATE. Reports generated with the REPORT FORM command will automatically display dates using the format specified by SET DATE.

Example

The following statements and listings demonstrate the effects of the SET DATE command.

```
USE DONATION
SET DATE BRITISH
LIST NEXT 5
```

Record#	LASTNAME	FIRSTNAME	EXPDATE	CONTRIBUTE
1	Askew	Lonnie	01/03/88	25.00
2	Baker	Benjamin	08/09/87	20.00
3	Baker	Jeanette	22/06/87	10.00
4	Block	Paul	08/03/87	20.00
5	Brown	Nicole	15/08/87	25.00

```
GO TOP
SET DATE ANSI
LIST NEXT 5
```

Record#	LASTNAME	FIRSTNAME	EXPDATE	CONTRIBUTE
1	Askew	Lonnie	88.03.01	25.00
2	Baker	Benjamin	87.09.08	20.00
3	Baker	Jeanette	87.06.22	10.00
4	Block	Paul	87.03.08	20.00
5	Brown	Nicole	87.08.15	25.00

```
GO TOP
SET DATE GERMAN
LIST NEXT 5
```

Record#	LASTNAME	FIRSTNAME	EXPDATE	CONTRIBUTE
1	Askew	Lonnie	01.03.88	25.00
2	Baker	Benjamin	08.09.87	20.00
3	Baker	Jeanette	22.06.87	10.00
4	Block	Paul	08.03.87	20.00
5	Brown	Nicole	15.08.87	25.00

```
GO TOP
SET DATE AMERICAN
LIST NEXT 5
```

Record#	LASTNAME	FIRSTNAME	EXPDATE	CONTRIBUTE
1	Askew	Lonnie	03/01/88	25.00
2	Baker	Benjamin	09/08/87	20.00

```
3   Baker        Jeanette    06/22/87    10.00
4   Block        Paul        03/08/87    20.00
5   Brown        Nicole      08/15/87    25.00
```

SET DECIMALS

Syntax

SET DECIMALS TO *expN*

The SET DECIMALS command changes the number of decimal places that are normally displayed as a result of calculations or as values displayed by numeric functions. The default value of SET DECIMALS is 2. You can specify any value from zero to 18. Also, note that SET DECIMALS does not perform a rounding; internally, the numbers retain full precision. SET DECIMALS only affects how the numbers are displayed.

For SET DECIMALS to have an effect, SET FIXED must be ON. If SET FIXED is OFF, calculations will use as many decimal places as are needed to accurately display a value (up to the maximum internal precision).

REMINDER: *SET DECIMALS only affects numbers displayed as a result of a calculation or a numeric function. SET DECIMALS will not affect the display of numeric fields performed with a LIST or DISPLAY command.*

Example

The following statements and listings demonstrate the effects of the SET DECIMALS command.

```
USE SCIENCE
LIST

Record#  SPECIMEN       TEMPERATUR AGE COLOR
      1  Donatello       36.678213 3.5 green
      2  Michelangelo    87.923256 2.7 green
      3  Leonardo       102.323760 1.8 green
      4  Raphael         77.956423 5.4 green

SET DECIMALS TO 4
SET FIXED ON
GO 2
```

```
? TEMPERATUR * 4
  351.6930

SET DECIMALS TO 2
? TEMPERATUR * 4
  351.69

SET FIXED OFF
? TEMPERATUR * 4
  351.693024
```

SET DEFAULT

Syntax

SET DEFAULT TO *drive*: *directory*

The SET DEFAULT command changes the default drive used in file operations. When you specify a new default drive with SET DEFAULT, the default directory is the last directory used on that drive.

The named drive and current directory you specify with SET DEFAULT will be the first path searched for files. You can specify additional paths to be searched with the SET PATH command (see SET PATH).

Example

To specify drive D as the default drive, the following command could be used.

```
SET DEFAULT TO D:
```

SET DELETED

Syntax

SET DELETED ON/OFF

The SET DELETED command enables the hiding of deleted records from processing by other operations, such as COUNT, LIST, BROWSE, and REPORT

FORM. When SET DELETED is OFF (as it is by default), all records marked for deletion will be displayed when commands such as LIST and REPORT FORM are used. When SET DELETED is ON, deleted records are omitted from the output of LIST, DISPLAY, LABEL FORM, and REPORT FORM commands. They are also omitted from the EDIT and BROWSE displays, unless you explicitly move the record pointer to a deleted record with a GOTO command before issuing the EDIT or BROWSE command.

Use SET DELETED ON near the start of a program (or near the start of a series of deletions performed at the command level) to avoid the necessity of frequent PACKs. You can use SET DELETED ON to hide the deleted records from processing, and a PACK will be necessary only on an occasional basis to recover disk space.

Example

The following statements and listings demonstrate the effects of the SET DELETED command. Note that the records marked for deletion, as shown by the asterisk, are not visible when SET DELETED is ON.

```
USE DONATION
LIST
```

Record#	LASTNAME	FIRSTNAME	EXPDATE	CONTRIBUTE
1	Baker	Jeanette	06/22/87	10.00
2	Block	Paul	03/08/87	20.00
3	Harris	Charles	02/22/87	10.00
4	*Hayes	Cynthia	08/15/88	100.00
5	Johnson, Jr.	Lamar	12/01/87	40.00
6	Jones	Renee	05/15/87	30.00
7	*Roberts	James	05/06/87	25.00
8	Roberts	Norma	03/08/87	20.00
9	Roberts	Terry	05/06/87	25.00
10	Sand	Lucy	01/01/99	500.00
11	*Smith	Larry	01/12/88	100.00

```
SET DELETED ON
LIST
```

Record#	LASTNAME	FIRSTNAME	EXPDATE	CONTRIBUTE
1	Baker	Jeanette	06/22/87	10.00
2	Block	Paul	03/08/87	20.00
3	Harris	Charles	02/22/87	10.00
5	Johnson, Jr.	Lamar	12/01/87	40.00
6	Jones	Renee	05/15/87	30.00

```
 8  Roberts     Norma     03/08/87     20.00
 9  Roberts     Terry     05/06/87     25.00
10  Sand        Lucy      01/01/99    500.00

COUNT FOR Lastname = "Roberts"
     2 records

SET DELETED OFF
COUNT FOR Lastname = "Roberts"
     3 records
```

SET DELIMITER

Syntax

SET DELIMITER TO *"character-string"*
[DEFAULT] SET DELIMITER ON/OFF

The SET DELIMITER TO command assigns characters other than the default colon (:) to be used to mark the field area. Once assigned, SET DELIMITER ON activates the delimiters, and SET DELIMITER OFF deactivates the delimiters. DEFAULT restores the colon (:) as the delimiter.

Note that FoxPro normally leaves one space between the results of a SAY and a GET in an @...SAY...GET command. The presence of delimiters effectively increases the size of the GET field by 2, adding 1 to the left and 1 to the right of the field. As a result, the addition of delimiters to screen GETs can throw off your screen formatting. You should consider this when designing screens that will use delimiters, and reposition the @...SAY...GETs accordingly.

Example

To mark the beginning of a field with a left curly brace ({) and end the field with a right curly brace (}), the following commands could be used.

```
SET DELIMITERS ON
SET DELIMITERS TO "{}"
```

SET DEVELOPMENT

Syntax

SET DEVELOPMENT ON/OFF

The SET DEVELOPMENT command, when ON, tells FoxPro to compare creation dates of .PRG files and compiled (.FXP) files, so that when a program is run, an outdated .FXP file will not be used. The FoxPro Editor automatically deletes old .FXP files as programs are updated, so the SET DEVELOPMENT command is not needed if you use the FoxPro Editor. If you use another editor to create and modify program files, enter **SET DEVELOPMENT ON** at the command level before modifying and running your programs.

SET DEVICE

Syntax

SET DEVICE TO PRINTER/SCREEN/FILE *filename*

The SET DEVICE command controls whether @...SAY commands are sent to the screen or printer. SET DEVICE is normally set to SCREEN, but if PRINT is specified, output will be directed to the printer.

The SET DEVICE command is commonly used when designing reports based on program code, rather than a report form. You can use SET DEVICE TO PRINT to reroute output to the printer, and then use a combination of @...SAY commands to position the data on the printed page, as shown in the example.

NOTE: If you use SET DEVICE TO PRINT and later issue an @...SAY command with a lower number than a previous @...SAY command, the printer will perform a form feed (page eject). Also, on some printers, you may need to send a page eject to get the last line to appear or the last page to print.

Example

In the program below, a SET DEVICE TO PRINT statement is used to reroute screen output to the printer. A series of @...SAY commands then make use of a memory variable called LINES to print data on successive lines of a sheet of paper.

```
CLEAR
STORE 5 TO LINES
STORE 1 TO PAGES
USE MEMBERS INDEX NAMES
SET DEVICE TO PRINT
@ 2,15 SAY "MEMBERSHIP EXPIRATION DATES REPORT"
```

```
@ 3,10 SAY REPLICATE ("*",40)
@ 4,10 SAY "Name                    City"
@ 4,50 SAY "Tape Limit    Exp.Date"
DO WHILE .NOT. EOF()
    @ LINES, 5 SAY TRIM(Firstname) + " " + Lastname
    @ LINES, 30 SAY City
    @ LINES, 50 SAY Tapelimit
    @ LINES, 60 SAY Expiredate
    STORE LINES + 1 TO LINES
    IF LINES > 50
        @ LINES + 2,40 SAY "PAGE " + TRIM(STR(PAGES))
        EJECT
        STORE PAGES + 1 TO PAGES
        STORE 5 TO LINES
            @ 2,15 SAY "MEMBERSHIP EXPIRATION DATES REPORT"
            @ 3,10 SAY REPLICATE("*",40)
            @ 4,10 SAY "Name                    City"
            @ 4,50 SAY "Tape Limit    Exp.Date"
    ENDIF
    SKIP
ENDDO
IF LINES > 5
    EJECT
ENDIF
SET DEVICE TO SCREEN
RETURN
```

SET DISPLAY TO

Syntax

SET DISPLAY TO MONO/COLOR/CGA/EGA25/EGA43/MONO43/VGA25/
VGA43/VGA50

The SET DISPLAY command chooses a monitor type and sets the number of lines displayed. For the number of lines option to have effect, the graphics hardware must support the type chosen within the SET DISPLAY command. The MONO option supports monochrome graphics adapters. The COLOR option supports any color adapter. The EGA25 and EGA43 options support EGA adapters; using EGA25 puts the display into a 25-line per screen mode, while using EGA43 puts the screen into a 43-line per screen mode. The MONO43 option supports monochrome adapters that can display 43 lines per screen. The various VGA options support the three modes of VGA adapters (25-line, 43-line, and 50-line).

SET DOHISTORY

Syntax

SET DOHISTORY ON/OFF

The SET DOHISTORY command turns on (or off) the storage of commands from command files in the Command window. When DOHISTORY is ON, program file commands are stored in the Command window as they are executed. You can later edit and reexecute those commands as if they had been entered at the command level.

When DOHISTORY is OFF, program statements are not stored. Only those statements entered at the command level are stored in history. The default value for SET DOHISTORY is OFF.

SET ECHO

Syntax

SET ECHO ON/OFF

The SET ECHO command determines whether command lines will be displayed or printed during program execution. When SET ECHO is ON, the command lines appear in the Trace window as they are executed. To route the command lines to the printer instead of the screen, SET ECHO ON then SET DEBUG ON.

Setting ECHO to ON can be useful when debugging programs. The default for SET ECHO is OFF.

SET ESCAPE

Syntax

SET ESCAPE ON/OFF

The SET ESCAPE command determines whether the ESC key will interrupt a program during execution. If SET ESCAPE is OFF, pressing ESC during a program has no effect. The default for SET ESCAPE is ON.

SET EXACT

Syntax

SET EXACT ON/OFF

The SET EXACT command determines how precisely two character strings will be compared. With SET EXACT OFF, which is the default case, comparison is not strict: a string on the left of the test is equal to its substring on the right if the substring acts as a prefix of the larger string. Thus, "turnbull" = "turn" is true, even though it clearly is not. SET EXACT ON corrects for this lack of precision.

NOTE: SET EXACT determines whether you can FIND or SEEK the first part of an index key. If SET EXACT is OFF, you can search for the first part of the key; if SET EXACT is ON, you must search for the entire key expression.

Example

The following statements and the resultant listings demonstrate the effects of the SET EXACT command.

```
USE DONATION
LIST FOR Lastname = "Roberts"
```

Record#	LASTNAME	FIRSTNAME	EXPDATE	CONTRIBUTE
7	Roberts	James	05/06/87	25.00
8	Roberts	Norma	03/08/87	20.00
9	Roberts	Terry	05/06/87	25.00
10	Robertson	Linda	03/02/89	100.00

```
SET EXACT ON
LIST FOR Lastname = "Roberts"
```

```
Record#   LASTNAME      FIRSTNAME      EXPDATE     CONTRIBUTE
      7   Roberts       James          05/06/87         25.00
      8   Roberts       Norma          03/08/87         20.00
      9   Roberts       Terry          05/06/87         25.00
```

SET FIELDS

Syntax

SET FIELDS ON/OFF

The SET FIELDS command enables or disables a list of fields specified by the SET FIELDS TO command. Use the SET FIELDS TO command to specify a list of available fields. Once SET FIELDS TO has been used, the SET FIELDS ON command will make only those fields specified available to database operations. The SET FIELDS OFF command will restore all fields of the database to processing by commands.

Example

See SET FIELDS TO for a detailed example of the SET FIELDS command.

SET FIELDS TO

Syntax

SET FIELDS TO [*fieldlist*/ALL [LIKE/EXCEPT *skeleton*]] [ADDITIVE]

The SET FIELDS TO command sets a specified list of fields that will be available for use. Using SET FIELDS TO along with a list of field names automatically activates the *fieldlist*, and fields named in the list are now available for use. In effect, a SET FIELDS TO command will make the software behave as if only those fields named in the field list are in existence. After using SET FIELDS TO, you can use BROWSE, EDIT, LIST or similar commands, and only the fields named in SET FIELDS TO will appear when using those commands.

The ALL option causes all fields present in the active database to be made available. Entering **SET FIELDS TO** without specifying a field list or the ALL option will remove all fields present in the current database from the field list.

Example

In the example, a membership database contains nine fields, but only the Lastname, Firstname, Expdate, and Contribute fields are desired for inclusion in various operations, including a LIST command. The SET FIELDS TO command is used to make only those fields available to further operations.

```
USE MEMBERS
LIST STRUCTURE

Structure for database: D:MEMBERS.dbf
Number of data records:      18
Date of last update   : 06/21/87
Field  Field Name  Type       Width   Dec
    1  LASTNAME    Character     15
    2  FIRSTNAME   Character     15
    3  EXPDATE     Date           8
    4  CONTRIBUTE  Numeric       13     2
    5  ADDRESS     Character     15
    6  CITY        Character     15
    7  STATE       Character     15
    8  ZIP         Character     15
    9  TYPE        Character     15
** Total **                    127

SET FIELDS TO Lastname, Firstname, Contribute, Expdate
LIST OFF

    LASTNAME        FIRSTNAME       EXPDATE     CONTRIBUTE
    Askew           Lonnie          03/01/88        25.00
    Baker           Benjamin        09/08/87        20.00
    Baker           Jeanette        06/22/87        10.00
    Block           Paul            03/08/87        20.00
    Brown           Nicole          08/15/87        25.00
    Harris          Charles         02/22/87        10.00
    Hayes           Cynthia         08/15/88       100.00
    Johnson, Jr.    Lamar           12/01/87        40.00
    Jones           Renee           05/15/87        30.00
    Mills           Ernest          04/30/87        20.00
```

SET FILTER

Syntax

SET FILTER TO [*condition*]

The SET FILTER command permits a display of only those records in a database that meet a specific condition. Once SET FILTER has been used, successive records that are accessed must match the specified condition; records not matching the specified condition will be hidden from processing. Note that the current record is not affected by a SET FILTER command; the SET FILTER command does not take effect until the record pointer is moved. Issuing a SET FILTER followed by a GO TOP helps ensure that the filter is in effect.

The SET FILTER command is useful in limiting records made available to common database operations such as COUNT, LIST, or REPORT FORM. Note that a separate SET FILTER command may be issued in each work area where a database file is open.

Issuing SET FILTER without naming any condition cancels an existing filter condition.

Example

To display only those records in a database that contain an amount of more than 10.50 in the SALARY field, the following commands could be used.

```
SET FILTER TO SALARY > 10.50
GO TOP
LIST
```

To display only those records in a database that contain the name "Main St." in the ADDRESS field during a DISPLAY or LIST command, the following commands could be used (note the $ or "contains" operator is used here):

```
SET FILTER TO "Main St." $ ADDRESS
GO TOP
LIST
```

SET FIXED

Syntax

SET FIXED ON/OFF

The SET FIXED command switches on (or off) the control of decimal places displayed by calculations, according to the setting of SET DECIMALS. When SET FIXED is ON, numeric values that are a result of calculations are displayed with the number of decimal places set by the SET DECIMALS command. When

SET FIXED is OFF, calculations will use as many decimal places as are needed to accurately display a value (up to the maximum internal precision).

> ***REMINDER:*** *SET FIXED only affects numbers displayed as a result of a calculation or a numeric function. SET FIXED will not affect the display of numeric fields performed with a LIST or DISPLAY command. (See SET DECIMALS for an example of the use of the SET FIXED command along with the SET DECIMALS command.)*

SET FORMAT

Syntax

SET FORMAT TO *filename/*?

The SET FORMAT command lets you activate a format file called *filename* to control the format of the screen display used during EDIT, CHANGE, and APPEND operations. If filename has the extension .FMT, you need not supply the extension. The SET FORMAT command without a filename specified cancels the effects of the previous SET FORMAT command. If the optional question mark is used, a list box of all format files appears; the user can select the desired file from the list box.

A format file is a text file with the extension .FMT that contains @ commands with SAY and GET options that will display messages and prompts according to your arrangements. Once you have created the format file, you can implement it with the SET FORMAT TO command. Format files can be created with any text editor that writes ASCII files (including the FoxPro Editor). Format files can also be designed using FoxView, the screen-design utility provided with FoxPro.

You can create multiple-page format files by placing a READ statement at the end of each page of @...SAY...GET commands. When the user views data through the format file, the PGUP and PGDN keys may be used to move between the screens of the format file.

The SET FORMAT command without a filename specified cancels the effects of the previous SET FORMAT command.

Example

The following format file, named EMPLOYED.FMT, is named in the SET FORMAT TO statement. When APPEND or EDIT is used after the SET FORMAT TO statement is issued, records are viewed using the format of the format file.

```
*EMPLOYED.FMT*
@   3,5   SAY  "Lastname"
@   3,17  GET   EMPLOYED->Lastname
@   4,5   SAY  "Firstname"
@   4,17  GET   EMPLOYED->Firstname
@   6,5   SAY  "Grade"
@   6,17  GET   EMPLOYED->Grade
@   7,5   SAY  "Hiredate"
@   7,17  GET   EMPLOYED->Hiredate
@   8,5   SAY  "Salary"
@   8,17  GET   EMPLOYED->Salary
@  10,5   SAY  "City"
@  10,17  GET   EMPLOYED->City
@  11,5   SAY  "STATE"
@  11,17  GET   EMPLOYED->State
@   2,2   TO 12, 37    DOUBLE

USE EMPLOYED
SET FORMAT TO EMPLOYED
EDIT
```

SET FULLPATH

Syntax

SET FULLPATH ON/OFF

The SET FULLPATH command specifies whether full pathnames appear with filenames returned by the DBF() and NDX() functions. If SET FULLPATH is OFF, only the drive designator and filename are returned by the functions. If SET FULLPATH is ON, the drive designator, pathname, and filename are returned by the functions. The default for SET FULLPATH is ON.

SET FUNCTION

Syntax

SET FUNCTION *expN/key label* TO *"character-string"*

The SET FUNCTION command resets a function key to a command or

sequence of commands of your choice. The maximum width of a command
sequence is 75 characters. You can view the current settings with the
DISPLAY STATUS command.

Example

To change the function of the F5 key to open a file named MEMBERS and enter
Append mode, the following commands could be used.

```
SET FUNCTION "5" TO "USE MEMBERS;APPEND;"
```

The semicolon (;) represents a carriage return.

SET HEADING

Syntax

SET HEADING ON/OFF

The SET HEADING command determines whether column headings appear
when the LIST, DISPLAY, CALCULATE, AVERAGE, or SUM command is
used. Normally, a LIST or DISPLAY command shows the field names above the
fields. Entering **SET HEADING OFF** suppresses the display of field names above
the fields. The default setting for SET HEADING is ON.

The SET HEADING OFF statement can be useful when you are generating
your own reports from program code, making use of a LIST or DISPLAY
command. You can use the ? or @...SAY commands to place your own headings,
instead of the default headings that appear when SET HEADING is ON.

Example

The following statements and listings demonstrate the effects of the SET
HEADING command.

```
USE DONATION
LIST NEXT 5 OFF
```

LASTNAME	FIRSTNAME	EXPDATE	CONTRIBUTE
Baker	Jeanette	06/22/87	10.00
Block	Paul	03/08/87	20.00
Harris	Charles	02/22/87	10.00
Hayes	Cynthia	08/15/88	100.00

```
Johnson, Jr.  Lamar          12/01/87         40.00


SET HEADING OFF
GO TOP
LIST NEXT 5 OFF

    LASTNAME        FIRSTNAME     EXPDATE    CONTRIBUTE
    Baker           Jeanette      06/22/87        10.00
    Block           Paul          03/08/87        20.00
    Harris          Charles       02/22/87        10.00
    Hayes           Cynthia       08/15/88       100.00
    Johnson, Jr.    Lamar         12/01/87        40.00
```

SET HELP

Syntax

SET HELP ON/OFF or SET HELP TO *filename*

The SET HELP command turns on (or off) the FoxPro online help facility. When SET HELP is ON, pressing F1 or entering **HELP** as a command displays the Help window. When SET HELP is OFF, the Help window is not available.

All help commands are stored in a database file, named FOXHELP.DBF. You can use the SET HELP TO *filename* command to specify a different database file. This can be useful if you are designing your own custom help system for an application.

SET HELPFILTER

Syntax

SET HELPFILTER [AUTOMATIC] TO *expL*

Version 2

The SET HELPFILTER command permits the display of a subset of help topics in the Help window. Only those records in the help database that meet the logical condition specified by the expression will be available in the Help window. The AUTOMATIC clause will cause the filtering effect to be canceled after the help window is closed. (You can also cancel the filtering effects of SET HELPFILTER by issuing another SET HELPFILTER TO command, without specifying an expression.)

SET HOURS

Syntax

SET HOURS TO [12/24]

The SET HOURS command changes the clock to the desired format, 12 or 24 hours. If you choose the 12-hour clock, AM or PM is displayed along with the time. The clock normally appears at the upper-right corner of full-screen operations such as Browse and Edit.

NOTE: *The clock is off by default. Use SET CLOCK ON to turn on the clock.*

Example

To change the clock to a 24-hour display, the following command could be used.

```
SET HOURS TO 24
```

SET INDEX

Syntax

SET INDEX TO *filename*/?

Syntax for FoxPro 2

SET INDEX TO
[*indexfile list*/?] [ORDER *expN*/.*IDXfile*/[TAG] *tagname* [OF .*CDXfile*]]
[ASCENDING/DESCENDING] [ADDITIVE]

The SET INDEX command opens the index file or files listed in *indexfile list*. If the question mark is substituted in place of a filename, a list of all index files appears. You may then select the index file to activate from the list. You can open up to seven index files at the same time.

When *indexfile list* specifies more than one index file, the first index named is the controlling index (it controls the order in which records are displayed or printed). Once the index files have been opened, the SET ORDER command may be used to change the controlling index.

Under FoxPro 2, you can use the ORDER, TAG, and ASCENDING/ DESCENDING clauses. Use ORDER and TAG to specify a master index file or a master tag in a compound-index file. Use ASCENDING or DESCENDING to specify whether the records should be accessed in ascending or descending order. For example, if an index file was originally created in ascending order, you can use the DESCENDING option to force the records to be displayed or retrieved in descending order.

NOTE: The SET INDEX TO command, without any options specified, closes all open index files.

Example

To open three index files named ALLNAMES, DATES, and ZIPS, and to specify ZIPS as the controlling index, the following command could be used.

```
SET INDEX TO ZIPS, ALLNAMES, DATES
```

The statements and resulting listings shown here demonstrate the effects of the SET INDEX command used to activate three different index files individually. Each listing following the activating of the index shows that the records are now in order according to the index.

```
USE VIDEO
INDEX ON SOCIAL TO SOCIALS
INDEX ON ZIPCODE TO ZIPS INDEX ON STATE TO STATES
SET INDEX TO SOCIALS
LIST Lastname, Social
```

Record#	LASTNAME	SOCIAL
2	Martin	121-33-9876
5	Moore	121-90-5432
1	Miller	123-44-8976
3	Robinson	232-55-1234
7	Robinson	343-55-9821
6	Zachman	495-00-3456
8	Hart	876-54-3210
4	Kramer	901-77-3456

```
SET INDEX TO ZIPS
LIST Lastname, ZIPCODE
```

Record#	LASTNAME	ZIPCODE
7	Robinson	20009
1	Miller	20815-0988
2	Martin	20910-0124
5	Moore	20912

```
8  Hart        22025
3  Robinson    22043
6  Zachman     22043
4  Kramer      22203
```

```
SET INDEX TO STATES
LIST Lastname, State
```

```
Record#  LASTNAME      STATE
      7  Robinson      DC
      1  Miller        MD
      2  Martin        MD
      5  Moore         MD
      3  Robinson      VA
      4  Kramer        VA
      6  Zachman       VA
      8  Hart          VA
```

SET INTENSITY

Syntax

SET INTENSITY ON/OFF

The SET INTENSITY command determines whether reverse video is on or off during full-screen operations. SET INTENSITY is ON when you begin a session using a full-screen command such as BROWSE or EDIT. Whenever SET INTENSITY is ON, all @...SAY commands are displayed using standard screen attributes. All @...GET commands are displayed using enhanced screen attributes. Keep in mind that standard and enhanced screen attributes can be changed with the SET COLOR commands (see SET COLOR).

If you SET INTENSITY to OFF, you should generally turn on the delimiters to mark the boundaries of the data entry area for each field (see SET DELIMITER). Otherwise, it will be difficult to tell areas of data entry defined by @...GET apart from normal text.

SET LIBRARY

Syntax

Version 2

SET LIBRARY TO *filename* [ADDITIVE]

The SET LIBRARY command is used to open external API (Application Program Interface) libraries. Use *filename* to specify the name of the existing API library. Once the SET LIBRARY command has been used, functions stored in the API library can be used as if they were FoxPro functions. The ADDITIVE option can be used to open additional API libraries. To close all open API libraries, use the command SET LIBRARY TO without specifying a filename.

SET LOGERRORS

Syntax

SET LOGERRORS ON/OFF

The SET LOGERRORS command determines whether FoxPro stores compilation errors in a file. If SET LOGERRORS is OFF, program errors reported during compilation appear on the screen, but are not stored. If SET LOGERRORS is ON, program errors reported during compilation are stored to a text file with the same name as the program and an extension of .ERR. The default value for SET LOGERRORS is ON.

SET MARGIN

Syntax

SET MARGIN TO *expN*

The SET MARGIN command sets the left printer margin. Only printed output is affected by the SET MARGIN command; any screen display remains unaffected. Use *expN* to define the number of spaces from the left edge that you want to set the margin to. The default value is zero.

Note that the value specified by SET MARGIN is also stored to the printer-system memory variable, _ PLOFFSET. In a program, you can either use the SET MARGIN command or an assignment statement such as _ PLOFFSET = 10 to reset the margin.

Example

To set the left margin to ten spaces indented from the left edge, the following command could be used.

```
SET MARGIN TO 10
```

SET MARK

Syntax

SET MARK TO *expC*

The SET MARK command specifies the delimiter used to separate the month, day, and year of a date. The character expression must be a single character surrounded by quotes or a memory variable of the character type. The character that you specify will appear as a separator in all date fields and in date-type memory variables until you change it with another SET MARK command or a SET DATE command.

Example

The following statements and listings demonstrate the effects of the SET MARK command.

```
USE NETTIME
SET DATE AMERICAN
LIST NEXT 3 OFF

  IDNO WKENDING REGULAR OVERTIME
  1001 04/15/89    40.0
  1001 04/22/89    40.0       7.0
  1001 04/29/89    35.0

SET MARK TO "\"
LIST NEXT 3 OFF

  IDNO WKENDING REGULAR OVERTIME
  1001 04\29\89    35.0
  1002 04\15\89    36.0
  1002 04\22\89    40.0      12.0

SET MARK TO "@"
LIST NEXT 3 OFF

  IDNO WKENDING REGULAR OVERTIME
  1002 04@22@89    40.0      12.0
  1002 04@29@89    40.0       6.0
  1003 04@15@89    36.0
```

SET MARK OF

Syntax

Version 2

      SET MARK OF MENU *menuname*
          TO *expC1/expL1*

      SET MARK OF PAD *padname*
          OF *menuname*
          TO *expC2/expL2*

      SET MARK OF POPUP *popupname*
          TO *expC3/expL3*

      SET MARK OF BAR *expN*
          OF *popupname*
          TO *expC4/expL4*

The SET MARK OF command is used to place a check mark before each pad or option in user-defined menus. The character used for the check mark is specified by the character expression. The value of the logical expression may be used in the program to toggle the check mark on and off.

SET MEMOWIDTH

Syntax

      SET MEMOWIDTH TO *expN*

The SET MEMOWIDTH command is used to control the width of a memo field when it is displayed, such as with a LIST or DISPLAY command. The default value of memo fields shown with DISPLAY or LIST, if SET MEMO-WIDTH is not used, is 50 characters. Using SET MEMOWIDTH to narrow the default width of a memo field can result in a more attractive display of information.

Example

Without the use of SET MEMOWIDTH, the following commands for a particular database result in the display shown below. The display is unattractive because the words in the memo field wrap around the screen at the right margin.

```
USE MEMBERS
LIST Lastname, Firstname, Preference

Record#  LASTNAME        FIRSTNAME       PREFERENCE
    1 Miller          Karen           Prefers science
fiction, horror movies. Fan of Star Trek films.

    2 Martin          William         Enjoys Clint Eastwood,
John Wayne films.

    3 Robinson        Carol           Likes comedy, drama
films.

    4 Kramer          Harry           Big fan of Eddie
Murphy. Also enjoys westerns.
```

By comparison, the following statements include a SET MEMOWIDTH command to limit the width of the memo field column to 20 characters. The result is a much more attractive format for the display of the memo field, as shown in the example below.

```
SET MEMOWIDTH TO 20
USE MEMBERS
LIST Lastname, Firstname, Preference

Record#  LASTNAME        FIRSTNAME       PREFERENCE
    1 Miller          Karen           Prefers science
                                      fiction, horror
                                      movies. Fan of Star
                                      Trek films.

    2 Martin          William         Enjoys Clint
                                      Eastwood, John Wayne
                                      films.

    3 Robinson        Carol           Likes comedy, drama
                                      films.

    4 Kramer          Harry           Big fan of Eddie
                                      Murphy. Also enjoys
                                      westerns.
```

SET MESSAGE

Syntax

SET MESSAGE TO [*expC*/LEFT/CENTER/RIGHT]

The SET MESSAGE command can be used to define the row where a message should appear when that message is named in an @...PROMPT command. Hence, you can use SET MESSAGE to define a message that appears in the message line or to define a message that is used with menus only (see @...PROMPT for more details). FoxPro also lets you use the optional LEFT, RIGHT, and CENTER clauses with the SET MESSAGE TO *expN* statement. LEFT places the message flush left, CENTER centers the message, and RIGHT places the message flush right. If no clause is specified, the message is centered.

SET MOUSE

Syntax

SET MOUSE TO *expN*

The SET MOUSE command enables or disables the mouse and adjusts the sensitivity of the mouse. SET MOUSE ON enables the mouse, and SET MOUSE OFF disables the mouse. You can adjust mouse sensitivity by specifying the value of *expN*. The value controls how much pointer movement on the screen results from a given amount of mouse movement. Permissible values are from 1 to 10, with 1 being the least sensitive and 10 being the most sensitive. The default value for SET MOUSE is 5.

Example

To set the mouse to its most sensitive position, the following command could be used.

```
SET MOUSE TO 10
```

SET NEAR

Syntax

SET NEAR ON/SET NEAR OFF

The SET NEAR command can be used to position the record pointer at the nearest record when a FIND or a SEEK is unsuccessful. If SET NEAR is ON, the record pointer will be placed at the next record after the expression that could not be located. If SET NEAR is OFF, the record pointer is placed at the end of the file when the expression is not found.

Use SET NEAR ON to get as close as possible to a desired record if a search is not successful. SET NEAR ON can be useful when implementing a Browse operation after a search, as you can visually find the precise record once in the Browse mode.

Example

The following statements show the effects of the SET NEAR command. During the first search, SET NEAR is OFF. The desired record is not found, EOF() returns a value of true, and FOUND() returns a value of false. In the second search, SET NEAR is ON. The desired record is not found, but this time the record pointer is positioned at the closest record in the index matching the search term. The EOF() function returns a false, and FOUND() returns a false. The DISPLAY command shows the current record.

```
USE ABCSTAFF
SET NEAR OFF
FIND Mitchal

    Find not successful

? EOF()
.T.
? FOUND()
.F.

SET NEAR ON
FIND Mitchal

    Find not successful

? EOF()
.F.
? FOUND()
.F.
```

```
DISPLAY Lastname, Firstname

Record#  LASTNAME      FIRSTNAME
      4  Mitchell      Mary Jo
```

SET ODOMETER

Syntax

SET ODOMETER TO [*expN*]

The SET ODOMETER command determines how often commands that display a record count (such as COPY, SUM, AVERAGE, and COUNT) should update the screen display. The value named in *expN* represents the number of records that will be processed before the screen count is updated. For example, if SET ODOMETER is 100, the record count during an AVERAGE command will be updated every 100 records. The default value is 100, and the maximum value is 32,767.

SET OPTIMIZE

Syntax

SET OPTIMIZE ON/OFF

Version 2

The SET OPTIMIZE command is used to enable or disable the query-optimization techniques present in FoxPro 2, called Rushmore. FoxPro uses Rushmore and commands that support FOR clauses to enhance performance. FoxPro's Rushmore technology is turned on by default. SET OPTIMIZE ON turns on Rushmore, while SET OPTIMIZE OFF turns off Rushmore. In rare cases where Rushmore should be disabled, use the SET OPTIMIZE OFF command. Note that some commands in FoxPro 2 also support a NOOPTIMIZE option; this option disables Rushmore for the specific command.

SET ORDER

Syntax

SET ORDER TO *expN*

Syntax for FoxPro 2

SET ORDER TO [*expN*/.*IDXfile*/[TAG] *tagname* [OF .*CDXfile*]
[IN *work area*/*alias*] [ASCENDING/DESCENDING]] [ADDITIVE]

The SET ORDER TO command makes the specified index file the active index, without changing the open or closed status of other index files. The value of *expN* refers to the index files in the order in which they were opened. Hence, if you opened three index files at the same time as you opened the database with a command like USE MYFILE INDEX NAMES, PAY, ZIPS, a SET ORDER TO 2 statement would make the second index opened (in this case, PAY) the controlling index file.

Under FoxPro 2, you can use the TAG, IN, and ASCENDING/DESCENDING clauses. Use TAG to specify a master tag in a compound-index file. Use ASCENDING or DESCENDING to specify whether the records should be accessed in ascending or descending order. For example, if an index file was originally created in ascending order, you can use the DESCENDING option to force the records to be displayed or retrieved in descending order. Use the IN clause to designate the master index file or tag for a database that is open in another work area.

NOTE: SET ORDER TO can also be used with no value or with a value of zero. If this is done, index files remain open, but no index controls the order; the order reverts back to the natural order of the database (or by record number).

Example

The following statements and resultant listings demonstrate the use of the SET ORDER command. In the first example, SET ORDER TO 1 makes the NAMES index file the controlling index. In the second example, SET ORDER TO 2 makes the STATES index file the controlling index. In the third example, SET ORDER TO 3 makes the ZIPS index file the controlling index.

```
USE VIDEO
SET INDEX TO NAMES, STATES, ZIPS
SET ORDER TO 1
    Master index: D:NAMES.NDX

LIST Lastname, STATE, ZIPCODE

Record#  LASTNAME      STATE ZIPCODE
      8  Hart          VA    22025
      4  Kramer        VA    22203
      2  Martin        MD    20910-0124
      1  Miller        MD    20815-0988
```

```
    5   Moore          MD      20912
    3   Robinson       VA      22043
    7   Robinson       DC      20009
    6   Zachman        VA      22043

SET ORDER TO 2
    Master index: D:STATES.NDX

LIST Lastname, STATE, ZIPCODE

Record#   LASTNAME        STATE ZIPCODE
    7   Robinson       DC      20009
    1   Miller         MD      20815-0988
    2   Martin         MD      20910-0124
    5   Moore          MD      20912
    3   Robinson       VA      22043
    4   Kramer         VA      22203
    6   Zachman        VA      22043
    8   Hart           VA      22025

SET ORDER TO 3
    Master index: D:ZIPS.NDX

LIST Lastname, STATE, ZIPCODE

Record#   LASTNAME        STATE ZIPCODE
    7   Robinson       DC      20009
    1   Miller         MD      20815-0988
    2   Martin         MD      20910-0124
    5   Moore          MD      20912
    8   Hart           VA      22025
    3   Robinson       VA      22043
    6   Zachman        VA      22043
    4   Kramer         VA      22203
```

SET PATH

Syntax

SET PATH TO *pathname*

The SET PATH command identifies a search path that will be searched if a file is not found in the current directory. Note that the SET PATH command

does not alter an existing DOS path; it merely specifies a search path
for database and related FoxPro files. The existing DOS path will still be
searched, in addition to any path you specify with the SET PATH command.

Example

To change the path from the default path to a path named FoxPro on drive C,
the following commands could be used.

```
SET PATH TO C:\FOXPRO
```

For more information on search paths, read your DOS manual (DOS 2.1 or
later).

SET POINT

Syntax

SET POINT TO *"expC"*

The SET POINT command changes the character used as the decimal point.
The specified expression can be any single character surrounded by quotes.

Example

To change the symbol used as the decimal point to a comma, the following
command could be used.

```
SET POINT TO ","
```

SET PRINT

Syntax

SET PRINT ON/OFF

The SET PRINT command directs output to the printer as well as the screen.
The default for SET PRINT is OFF. (The SET PRINTER ON/OFF command is
identical to this command.) When SET PRINT is ON, all screen output (with the

exception of that produced with @...SAY...GET commands) is echoed to the printer. When SET PRINT is OFF, screen output is not echoed to the printer. The default for SET PRINT is OFF.

If you want to send screen output resulting from @...SAY commands to the printer, use SET DEVICE TO PRINT instead (see SET DEVICE).

SET PRINTER TO

Syntax

SET PRINTER TO LPT1/COM1/COM2/*other DOS device/filename* [ADDITIVE]

The SET PRINTER TO command reroutes printer output to the device or disk file specified. By default, the DOS print device is always PRN. Unless you have used DOS assignment commands to change the routing of printed output, the logical DOS device of PRN will be whatever printer is connected to LPT1. You can redirect output to a different printer connected to another port or to a disk file with the SET PRINTER command.

In FoxPro 1.02 and later, the ADDITIVE option can be used with a filename when output is rerouted to a disk file. This tells FoxPro to add to any existing disk file, rather than overwriting the file (the default).

Example

To redirect printer output to a laser printer connected to LPT2, the following command could be used.

```
SET PRINTER TO LPT2
```

To redirect printer output to a daisywheel printer connected to COM1, the following command could be used.

```
SET PRINTER TO COM1
```

SET PROCEDURE

Syntax

SET PROCEDURE TO *procedurefilename*

The SET PROCEDURE command opens the procedure file named in *procedurefilename*. SET PROCEDURE is placed in the command file that will reference the procedures contained in a procedure file. Note that SET PROCEDURE TO without a filename will close any open procedure file.

Procedures are program files containing groups of commands, identified by different group names. Procedures are useful for repeating often-used tasks, such as printing a report header or displaying a commonly used error message. You can store repetitive tasks (any programming task you perform at more than one place in the program) in a procedure. Then, rather than duplicate that program code in multiple places within the program, you can call the procedure within the procedure file.

Example

The following short program demonstrates the use of a procedure file, along with the SET PROCEDURE statement. In the main menu program (shown first), the SET PROCEDURE TO MYFILE statement identifies MYFILE.PRG as the procedure file. When any of the chosen menu options in the program calls another routine with a DO command, that routine is called from the procedure file, which is loaded into memory one time, and remains in memory as long as the procedure file is open.

```
*MENU.PRG is main menu.*
SET PROCEDURE TO MYFILE
USE MEMBERS
SET TALK OFF
STORE 0 TO CHOICE
DO WHILE CHOICE < 5
    CLEAR
    *Display main menu.
    @  5,5 SAY "Generic Videos Database System Menu"
    @  6,4 SAY "Highlight selection, and press Enter:"
    @  8,10 PROMPT "Add Members    "
    @  9,10 PROMPT "Edit Members   "
    @ 10,10 PROMPT "Print Report   "
    @ 11,10 PROMPT "Display Member"
    @ 12,10 PROMPT "Exit System    "
    @  7,8 TO 13,25 DOUBLE
    * above line draws double line box around menu.*
    MENU TO CHOICE
    * note "menu-to" compatible with Clipper, Fox products.*
    DO CASE
        CASE CHOICE = 1
            DO ADDER
        CASE CHOICE = 2
```

```
            DO EDITS
      CASE CHOICE = 3
            DO REPORTER
      CASE CHOICE = 4
            DO SHOWME
      CASE CHOICE = 5
            RETURN
     ENDCASE
ENDDO

*MYFILE.PRG contains procedures.*
PROCEDURE ADDER
USE MEMBERS
CLEAR
APPEND BLANK
@ 1,0 SAY "      Social Sec." GET Social PICTURE "999-99-9999"
@ 2,0 SAY "        Lastname:" GET Lastname
@ 3,0 SAY "       Firstname:" GET Firstname
@ 4,0 SAY "         Address:" GET Address
@ 5,0 SAY "            City:" GET City
@ 6,0 SAY "           State:" GET State
@ 7,0 SAY "        ZIP Code:" GET Zipcode
READ
RETURN

PROCEDURE EDITS
CLEAR
STORE SPACE(20) TO TEST
USE MEMBERS INDEX NAME
@  5,10 SAY "Editing a record."
@  7,10 SAY "Enter the last name of the member."
@ 10,10 SAY "Last name: " GET TEST
READ
FIND &TEST
IF EOF()
     CLEAR
     @5,10 SAY "There is no such name in the database."
     WAIT
     *wait command causes a pause.
     RETURN
ENDIF
EDIT
RETURN

PROCEDURE SHOWME
USE MEMBERS
```

```
SET TALK OFF
CLEAR
ACCEPT " Search for what last name? " TO SNAME
DO WHILE .NOT. EOF()
   IF Lastname = SNAME
      ? "Lastname is: "
      ?? Lastname
      ? "Firstname is: "
      ?? Firstname
      ? "Address is: "
      ?? ADDRESS
      ? City + State + " " + Zipcode
   ENDIF
   SKIP
ENDDO
WAIT
RETURN

PROCEDURE REPORTER
WAIT " -Press any key to begin printing..."
REPORT FORM MEMBERS TO PRINT
RETURN
```

SET RELATION

Syntax

SET RELATION TO [*expression1* INTO *alias*] [ADDITIVE]
[[, *expression2* INTO *alias*] [ADDITIVE]...]

The SET RELATION command links the active database to an open database in another area. The key expression is the common field present in both databases. The alias is the name of the other database that the active database is to be linked to. Note that ADDITIVE is an optional clause, needed only when you are setting a relation into more than one file at a time. The overall process of linking two databases using a common field involves the following steps:

1. Open the file from which you want to establish the relation in one work area.

2. In another work area, open the file that you wish to link to the first file.

3. Activate an index file based on the field (or expression) that is the basis of the relationship in the second work area.

    4. In the first work area, use the SET RELATION command to establish the link.

Once the link has been established, any movement of the record pointer in the active file will result in a corresponding movement of the pointer in the related file. The nature of such a relationship can be seen in the following example.

    If a key expression is used to establish the relationship, the active file must contain that key, and the other file must be indexed on that key. The ADDITIVE option may be used to specify multiple relations out of a single work area.

    FoxPro also lets you set a relation based upon a record number. The syntax for this variation of the SET RELATION command is

SET RELATION TO *expN*

ExpN defines the record number in the related file that the active file is to be linked to.

    Typically, the RECNO() function is used to supply the value of *expN*. This lets you link record 1 in the active database to record 1 in the related database, record 27 in the active database to record 27 in the related database, and so on. Note that if you are going to establish this type of relation, the related (child) database must not have an index active.

    If a matching record cannot be located in the related file, the record pointer in the related file is positioned at the end of the file, and the EOF() function returns a value of true.

Example

The following commands demonstrate the effects of the SET RELATION command, used to establish a link between a video rentals database and a video membership database. Once SET RELATION has been used to establish the link, the LIST command can be used to simultaneously display fields from both database files.

```
SELECT 1
USE RENTALS
SELECT 2
USE MEMBER INDEX SOCIALS
SELECT 1
SET RELATION TO Social INTO MEMBERS
LIST Member->Last, Title, Dayrented, Returned OFF
```

MEMBER->LAST	TITLE	DAYRENTED	RETURNED
Miller	Star Trek IV	03/05/90	03/06/90
Martin	Lethal Weapon II	03/02/90	03/06/90

Robinson	Who Framed Roger Rabbit	03/06/90	03/09/90
Kramer	Beverly Hills Cop II	03/04/90	03/05/90
Moore	Dirty Rotten Scoundrels	03/01/90	03/06/90
Zachman	Young Einstein	03/04/90	03/09/90
Robinson	When Harry Met Sally	03/06/90	03/12/90
Hart	Lethal Weapon II	03/07/90	03/08/90
Miller	Friday 13th Part XXVII	03/14/90	03/16/90
Martin	Licence To Kill	03/15/90	03/17/90
Robinson	When Harry Met Sally	03/17/90	03/19/90
Kramer	Coming To America	03/14/90	03/18/90
Moore	When Harry Met Sally	03/16/90	03/17/90
Zachman	Star Trek V	03/18/90	03/18/90
Robinson	Young Einstein	03/19/90	03/20/90
Hart	Licence To Kill	03/16/90	03/18/90

SET RELATION OFF

Syntax

SET RELATION OFF INTO *alias*

The SET RELATION OFF command breaks an existing relation between two databases (see SET RELATION). The parent database must be the currently selected database, and *alias* indicates the related (child) database. *Alias* may be the alias name or a work area number.

SET RESOURCE

Syntax

SET RESOURCE ON/OFF

The SET RESOURCE command tells FoxPro whether to save any changes made to the FoxPro environment when exiting the program. Changes are saved to the resource file (FOXUSER.DBF). If SET RESOURCE is OFF, changes will not be saved upon exiting FoxPro.

SET RESOURCE TO

Syntax

SET RESOURCE TO *filename*

The SET RESOURCE TO command tells FoxPro to use a different file as the resource file. By default, the resource file is a database named FOXUSER.DBF. You can provide another filename, along with the SET RESOURCE TO command to cause that file to be used as the resource file.

SET SAFETY

Syntax

SET SAFETY ON/OFF

The SET SAFETY command determines whether a confirmation message will be provided before existing files are overwritten by commands such as SORT or COPY or before a ZAP command is executed. SET SAFETY is normally set to ON.

SET SEPARATOR

Syntax

SET SEPARATOR TO "*expC*"

The SET SEPARATOR command specifies the symbol that should be used to separate hundreds in numeric amounts. The default is the comma, which is standard in U.S. currency. The expression may be any single character surrounded by quotes.

Example

To change the symbol used as the separator to a period, the following command could be used.

```
SET SEPARATOR TO "."
```

SET SHADOWS

Syntax

SET SHADOWS ON/OFF

The SET SHADOWS command enables or disables shadows underneath windows. SET SHADOWS ON enables the display of shadows under the windows, and SET SHADOWS OFF disables the shadows. The default for SET SHADOWS is ON.

SET SKIP

Syntax

Version 2

SET SKIP TO [*alias1*[, *alias2*...]]

The SET SKIP command, which you use along with SET RELATION, lets you access all records in the linked file that match a particular index-key value in the parent file. Use SET SKIP to identify one-to-many relationships, where one record in the parent file is related to many records in the related, or child, file. When you use SET SKIP, subsequent LIST, DISPLAY, REPORT FORM, and LABEL FORM commands will process all records that match the expression used to define the relation, rather than just the first matching record.

SET SPACE

Syntax

SET SPACE ON/OFF

The SET SPACE command determines whether a space appears between expressions displayed or printed with the ? and ?? commands. If SET SPACE is ON, a space will be added between expressions displayed or printed with ? and ?? commands. If SET SPACE is OFF, no space appears between the expressions. The default for SET SPACE is ON.

Example

The following statements demonstrate the effects of the SET SPACE command.

```
SET SPACE ON
USE MEMBERS
GO 1
? Lastname, Firstname
Morse Marcia
```

```
SET SPACE OFF
? Lastname, Firstname
MorseMarcia
```

SET STATUS

Syntax

SET STATUS ON/OFF

The SET STATUS command turns on or turns off the status display. When SET STATUS is ON, the status bar appears at the bottom of the screen. SET STATUS OFF hides the display.

FoxPro allows the SET STATUS command to maintain compatibility with FoxBASE+ and dBASE III PLUS. However, the status bar is off by default in FoxPro.

SET STEP

Syntax

SET STEP ON/OFF

The SET STEP command is a debugging command that determines whether processing will stop each time a command in a command file is executed. When SET STEP is ON and you run a program with the DO command, the program halts after each line is executed. SET STEP ON also causes the Trace window to appear. Each line of the program appears in the Trace window as the program executes. You can choose the Resume option in the window to continue stepping through the program, or you can choose the Cancel option to halt the program's execution.

Use SET STEP along with the SET DEBUG, SET ECHO, and SET TALK commands to debug your programs. The default of SET STEP is OFF.

SET STICKY

Syntax

SET STICKY ON/OFF

The SET STICKY command affects the operation of menu pads and menu popups when using the mouse. When SET STICKY is ON and a menu pad is selected with the mouse, the associated menu popup remains open on the screen until an option is selected (or ESC is pressed). When SET STICKY is OFF and a menu pad is selected with the mouse, the associated menu popup closes as soon as the mouse button is released.

SET SYSMENU

Syntax

Version 2

SET SYSMENU ON/OFF/AUTOMATIC/TO
[*System menu popup list/pad list*]/TO [DEFAULT]

The SET SYSMENU command controls access to the FoxPro System menus within a program. Use ON to enable menu access, and use OFF to disable menu access. The AUTOMATIC option makes the menus visible during program execution, and options are either enabled or disabled as appropriate, depending on the current command within your program. You can use the TO clause to specify that only certain menu pads or popups are available from the FoxPro System menus.

SET TALK

Syntax

SET TALK ON/OFF

The SET TALK command determines whether results of FoxPro commands (such as the current record number after a SKIP or LOCATE or the results of a SUM or AVERAGE command) are displayed on the screen. The default for SET TALK is ON.

SET TEXTMERGE

Syntax

Version 2

SET TEXTMERGE [ON/OFF] [TO [*filename*] [ADDITIVE]]
[WINDOW *windowname*] [SHOW/NOSHOW]

The SET TEXTMERGE command is used to enable or disable the evaluation of database fields, variables, or the results of expressions during a textmerge operation. If SET TEXTMERGE is ON, database fields, variables and expressions surrounded by the textmerge delimiters are evaluated and output when placed after the \ or \\ commands or when placed between TEXT and END-TEXT. If SET TEXTMERGE is OFF, the fields, variables, or expressions are not evaluated; instead, the actual names for the fields, variables, or expressions are output instead. Use the TO clause to direct the output of a textmerge operation to a file; use the ADDITIVE clause to add the output to an existing file. Use the WINDOW clause to direct output to the named window. To suppress visual output, use the NOSHOW clause; the SHOW clause may later be used to restore visual output.

SET TEXTMERGE DELIMITERS

Syntax

SET TEXTMERGE DELIMITERS [TO] [*expC1*[, *expC2*]]

Version 2

Use the SET TEXTMERGE DELIMITERS command to change the default textmerge delimiters. (The default delimiters are double sets of angle brackets.) If just *expC1* is specified, the specified character is used for both delimiters. If you specify *expC1* and *expC2*, *expC1* becomes the left delimiter, and *expC2* becomes the right delimiter. If the expressions are literal strings, be sure to surround them with quotes.

SET TOPIC

Syntax

SET TOPIC TO [*expC/expL*]

The SET TOPIC command determines how help topics are displayed. When help is selected, a list of available topics is normally displayed. By entering SET TOPIC TO *expC* where *expC* is the name of a help topic, that particular topic will be displayed whenever help is selected. The logical expression *expL* is used when creating a user-defined help system.

SET TYPEAHEAD

Syntax

SET TYPEAHEAD TO *expN*

The SET TYPEAHEAD command sets the size, in number of keystrokes, of the typeahead buffer. The default value is 20. The size of the typeahead buffer can be increased to prevent fast typists from outrunning the keyboard. Acceptable values are any number between 0 and 32,000.

You can use a SET TYPEAHEAD TO 0 statement to disable the typeahead buffer. This technique is common in programs during processes like sorting and indexing. Setting SET TYPEAHEAD to zero ensures that if a user types a series of characters while waiting for the process to finish, that series of characters does not get passed on to successive operations. Note that setting SET TYPEAHEAD to 0 also deactivates any ON KEY command, along with the INKEY() function.

SET UDFPARMS

Syntax

SET UDFPARMS TO VALUE/REFERENCE

The SET UDFPARMS command determines whether parameters passed to a user-defined function (UDF) are passed by value or by reference. By default, parameters passed to a UDF are passed by value. This means that the UDF may change the value of the parameter, but the changed value is not returned to the calling program. Use the SET UDF TO REFERENCE command to tell FoxPro to pass parameters by reference; this will allow changes made to the parameter within the UDF to be returned to the calling program.

SET UNIQUE

Syntax

SET UNIQUE ON/OFF

The SET UNIQUE command is used with the INDEX command to create lists of items with no duplicates. The list may not be indexed adequately if there are duplicates. When you build an index with UNIQUE set ON, there is only one index entry for each unique index key. (Note that an alternative way to achieve the same effect is to add the UNIQUE clause to the INDEX ON command.) The default setting for SET UNIQUE is OFF.

Example

The following statements and the resultant listings demonstrate the effects of the SET UNIQUE command. In the first listing, a database of employees contains a number of duplicate entries with slightly different first names but the same social security numbers for the duplicate records. In the second example, the SET UNIQUE command is used, and the index based on social security numbers is rebuilt with the INDEX command. The listing produced contains unique social security numbers only; no duplicate records appear, even though they are still contained in the database.

```
USE STAFF
INDEX ON Social TO PEOPLE
LIST OFF
```

LASTNAME	FIRSTNAME	SOCIAL	CITY	STATE
Martin	William	121-33-9876	Silver Spring	MD
Martin	Bill	121-33-9876	Silver Spring	MD
Moore	Ellen	121-90-5432	Takoma Park	MD
Moore	E.	121-90-5432	Takoma Park	MD
Miller	Karen	123-44-8976	Chevy Chase	MD
Miller	Karen W.	123-44-8976	Chevy Chase	MD
Robinson	Carol	232-55-1234	Falls Church	VA
Robinson	Karol	232-55-1234	Falls Church	VA
Robinson	Benjamin	343-55-9821	Washington	DC
Robinson	Benny	343-55-9821	Washington	DC
Zachman	David	495-00-3456	Falls Church	VA
Zachman	David	495-00-3456	Falls Church	VA
Hart	Wendy	876-54-3210	Fairfax	VA
Kramer	Harry	901-77-3456	Arlington	VA
Kramer	Harrison	901-77-3456	Arlington	VA

```
SET UNIQUE ON
INDEX ON Social TO PEOPLE
LIST OFF
```

LASTNAME	FIRSTNAME	SOCIAL	CITY	STATE
Martin	William	121-33-9876	Silver Spring	MD
Moore	Ellen	121-90-5432	Takoma Park	MD
Miller	Karen	123-44-8976	Chevy Chase	MD
Robinson	Carol	232-55-1234	Falls Church	VA
Robinson	Benjamin	343-55-9821	Washington	DC
Zachman	David	495-00-3456	Falls Church	VA
Hart	Wendy	876-54-3210	Fairfax	VA
Kramer	Harry	901-77-3456	Arlington	VA

SET VIEW

Syntax

SET VIEW ON/OFF

The SET VIEW command enables (or disables) the View window.

SET VIEW TO

Syntax

SET VIEW TO *filename*

The SET VIEW TO command activates the view file named in *filename*, placing all settings in that view file (open databases, indexes, relations, and filters) into effect. A view file will contain a record of all open database and index files, any filters set in the current work area, and any screen format file in use in the current work area at the time the view file was created. The view file can be created with the CREATE VIEW *filename* FROM ENVIRONMENT command. Once the view file exists, you no longer need to repeat the same set of commands for the opening of files and the setting of the filter during a later session. Instead, you can simply use the SET VIEW TO *filename* statement, and the same databases, index files, filter and screen format file (if any) will be opened.

View files can be useful in saving the tedious entry of a number of commands and can also be used with reports. Note that a view file will also contain any relations that have been established between multiple files (see SET RELATION for details).

Example

The following statements and resulting listings demonstrate the effects of the SET VIEW command. A database and accompanying index file is opened, and a filter is set. The environment is saved to a view file with the CREATE VIEW FROM ENVIRONMENT command. Then CLEAR ALL is used to close all files. The DISPLAY STATUS command entered after the CLEAR ALL command shows that no files are open.

After the SET VIEW TO statement is entered, another DISPLAY STATUS command reveals that the previously active database, index, and filter are back in effect.

```
USE CHECKS
SET INDEX TO DATES
SET FILTER TO CATEGORY = "POSTAGE/MAILING"
CREATE VIEW STAMPS FROM ENVIRONMENT
CLEAR ALL

DISPLAY STATUS

Alternate file: E:\PERFECT\FILES\FOO.txt
File search path:
Default disk drive: D:
Print destination:  PRN:
Margin =      0
Current work area =    1

Press any key to continue...
*** INTERRUPTED ***

SET VIEW TO STAMPS
DISPLAY STATUS

Currently Selected Database:
Select area:  1, Database in Use: D:CHECKS.DBF    Alias: CHECKS
    Master index file:  D:DATES.NDX  Key: date
Filter: CATEGORY = "POSTAGE/MAILING"

Alternate file: E:\PERFECT\FILES\FOO.txt
File search path:
Default disk drive: D:
Print destination:  PRN:
Margin =      0
Current work area =    1

Press any key to continue...
```

SET WINDOW OF MEMO

Syntax

SET WINDOW OF MEMO TO *windowname*

The SET WINDOW command sets a window for use when editing the contents of memo fields. The window named by the SET WINDOW statement will be used for editing memo fields whenever you are editing a database using a full-screen command, such as APPEND, BROWSE, EDIT, or READ. The window listed as *windowname* must have been defined previously with the DEFINE WINDOW command.

The SET WINDOW command provides you with one way to edit a memo field within a program and the optional WINDOW clause of the @...SAY...GET command provides another. Note that if a SET WINDOW statement is in effect and an @...SAY...GET statement with a WINDOW clause is used to access a memo field, the @...SAY...GET statement takes priority over the SET WINDOW statement for editing of the memo field.

Example

In the following example, a database containing a memo field is to be edited in Browse mode. To allow the display of a memo field near the bottom of the Browse window, the DEFINE WINDOW command is first used to establish the window size. Then, the SET WINDOW command sets aside the defined window for the use of memo fields in the database. Once Browse mode is entered, pressing CTRL-HOME while in the memo field of the Browse display causes the memo field text to appear in the defined window.

```
USE BOOKS
DEFINE WINDOW COMMENT FROM 15,10 TO 20,70 PANEL
SET WINDOW OF MEMO TO COMMENT
BROWSE
```

SHOW GET

Syntax

Version 2

SHOW GET *variable*[, *expN* [PROMPT *expC*]] [ENABLE/DISABLE]
[LEVEL *expN*] [COLOR *color-pair list*/COLOR SCHEME *expN*]

The SHOW GET command redisplays a single GET field or object. When the field or object is redisplayed, editing can be enabled or disabled with the ENABLE/DISABLE clauses. The PROMPT clause can be used to display a character expression as a prompt for the object. Use the LEVEL clause to display a field or object on a READ level other than the current one. Use the COLOR or COLOR SCHEME clauses to set the colors for the object.

SHOW GETS

Syntax

SHOW GETS *variable* [ENABLE/DISABLE] [LEVEL *expN*]
[WINDOW *windowname*] [COLOR *color-pair list*/COLOR SCHEME *expN*]

Version 2

The SHOW GET command redisplays all GET fields or objects. When the fields or objects are redisplayed, editing can be enabled or disabled with the ENABLE/DISABLE clauses. The WINDOW clause can be used to display the fields or objects in a window. Use the LEVEL clause to display fields or objects on a READ level other than the current one. Use the COLOR or COLOR SCHEME clauses to set the colors for the objects.

SHOW MENU

Syntax

SHOW MENU *menuname*/ALL [PAD *padname*] [SAVE]

The SHOW MENU command displays a menu without activating the menu. The command is primarily used in the program design process to check the visual appearance of a menu. The ALL option causes all menus to be shown. The SAVE option is used to cause the images of menus to remain on the screen. This option is normally used when testing and debugging programs.

SHOW OBJECT

Syntax

SHOW OBJECT *expN* [PROMPT *expC*] [ENABLE/DISABLE] [LEVEL *expN*]
[COLOR *color-pair list*/COLOR SCHEME *expN*]

Version 2

The SHOW OBJECT command redisplays a single GET field or object. The SHOW OBJECT command differs from SHOW GET in that SHOW OBJECT refers to the field or object by the object number, and SHOW GET refers to the

field or object by name (field name, variable name, or array element name). When the field or object is redisplayed, editing can be enabled or disabled with the ENABLE/DISABLE clauses. The PROMPT clause can be used to display a character expression as a prompt for the object. Use the LEVEL clause to display a field or object on a READ level other than the current one. Use the COLOR or COLOR SCHEME clauses to set the colors for the object.

SHOW POPUP

Syntax

SHOW POPUP *popupname*/ALL [SAVE]

The SHOW POPUP command displays a popup menu without activating the menu. The command is primarily used in the program design process to check the visual appearance of a menu. The ALL option causes all popups to be shown. The SAVE option is used to cause the images of popups to remain on the screen. This option is normally used when testing and debugging programs.

SHOW WINDOW

Syntax

SHOW WINDOW *windowname*/ALL [SAVE] [TOP/BOTTOM/SAME]
[IN WINDOW *windowname*/IN SCREEN]

The SHOW WINDOW command displays a window without activating the window. The command is primarily used in the program design process to check the visual appearance of a window. The ALL option causes all windows to be shown. Use BOTTOM or TOP to place a window at the bottom or top of a stack of existing windows. The SAME option applies only to windows previously hidden with DEACTIVATE WINDOW or HIDE WINDOW. Use SAME to put the previously hidden window back in the same position it occupied earlier. The SAVE option is used to cause the images of the window to remain on the screen. This option is normally used when testing and debugging programs.

In FoxPro 1.02 and later, the command also supports an optional [IN WINDOW *windowname*/IN SCREEN] clause. This clause lets you have background windows within windows or on the background screen.

When you include this clause, the inner window is dependent on the outer window. When the outer window is moved, the inner window moves with it. The inner window cannot be larger than the outer window and can be moved only within the confines of the outer window. If the outer window is closed, the inner window is closed with it. If the outer window is deactivated, the inner window is deactivated with it.

SIZE POPUP

Syntax

SIZE POPUP *popupname* TO *expN1*, *expN2*/BY *expN3*, *expN4*

Version 2

The SIZE POPUP command resizes a popup menu. If the TO clause is used, the popup will be changed to the new size, where *expN1* is the new size in rows, and *expN2* is the new size in columns. If the BY clause is used, the popup will be changed relative to its existing size, with *expN3* representing rows and *expN4* representing columns; for example, the command SIZE POPUP BY 4,3 would make an existing popup four rows larger and three columns wider.

SKIP

Syntax

SKIP *expN* [IN *alias*]

The SKIP command moves the record pointer. SKIP moves one record forward if no value is specified. Values can be expressed as memory variables or as constants. The IN *alias* option can be used to move the record pointer within a file in another work area.

Example

To skip two records back, the following command could be used.

```
SKIP -2
```

To prompt a user for a number, and to then move the record pointer by that number of records, the following statements could be used.

```
INPUT "Move record pointer by how many records? " TO THISMANY
SKIP THISMANY
```

SORT

Syntax

SORT TO *filename* ON *field1* [/A][/C][/D][, *field2* [/A][/C][/D]...]
[ASCENDING/DESCENDING] [*scope*] [FOR *condition*] [WHILE *condition*]
[FIELDS *fieldlist*]

Syntax for FoxPro 2

SORT TO *filename* ON *field1* [/A][/C][/D][, *field2* [/A][/C][/D]...] [ASCENDING/
DESCENDING] [*scope*] [FOR *condition*] [WHILE *condition*] [FIELDS *fieldlist*]
[NOOPTIMIZE]

The SORT command creates a rearranged copy of a database. The order of
the new database depends on the fields and options specified. The /C option
creates a sorted file in dictionary order, where there is no differentiation between
upper- and lowercase. Use /A for ascending order on a specific field and /D for
descending order on a specific field. Use the ASCENDING or DESCENDING
options to specify ascending or descending order for all fields. (The /A or /D
option can be used with any field to override the effects of the ASCENDING or
DESCENDING options.) The FIELDS option may be used to specify fields to be
included in the sorted file; if omitted, all fields are included. You can sort up to
ten fields in a single sort, and you cannot sort on memo fields or on logical fields.
With FoxPro 2 or above, the NOOPTIMIZE clause, when added, turns off
FoxPro's internal optimization techniques (Rushmore).

Sorting and indexing provide a similar result, that of being able to access
records in a specified order. However, there are notable differences between
SORT and INDEX. SORT always creates a new database, while INDEX creates
an index file associated with the original database. You must place the newly
created database in use to gain access to the sorted records. SORT tends to use
considerably more disk space than INDEX. Indexes are updated with the
database (as long as they are open), while sorts must be performed again after
records are added to maintain proper order. And the FIND and SEEK
commands require indexes; you cannot use FIND and SEEK with sorted files
unless you also index the files. As an advantage of SORT, you can use SORT to
arrange files based on fields of different types without having to resort to the use
of functions; for example, a database can be easily sorted on a combination of
character and numeric fields.

Example

The following statements and resultant listings demonstrate the effects of the
SORT command.

```
USE EMPLOYED
LIST Lastname, Firstname, Salary, City, State OFF

    LASTNAME      FIRSTNAME      SALARY CITY          STATE
    Smith         Karen          2075.40 Dallas        TX
    Williams      Greg           1890.50 Arlington     TX
    Johnson       Linda          2890.30 Carrollton    TX
    Johnson       Martin         2495.00 Fort Worth    TX
    Sanders       Anette         1170.20 Dallas        TX
    Roberts       Jerry          1740.00 Dallas        TX
    Robertson     Henry          1534.60 Garland       TX
    Martin        Lydia          1390.00 Fort Worth    TX
    Klein         Samuel         1775.00 Carrollton    TX

SORT ON Lastname, Firstname TO NAMES
USE NAMES
LIST Lastname, Firstname, Salary, City, State OFF

    LASTNAME      FIRSTNAME      SALARY CITY          STATE
    Johnson       Linda          2890.30 Carrollton    TX
    Johnson       Martin         2495.00 Fort Worth    TX
    Klein         Samuel         1775.00 Carrollton    TX
    Martin        Lydia          1390.00 Fort Worth    TX
    Roberts       Jerry          1740.00 Dallas        TX
    Robertson     Henry          1534.60 Garland       TX
    Sanders       Anette         1170.20 Dallas        TX
    Smith         Karen          2075.40 Dallas        TX
    Williams      Greg           1890.50 Arlington     TX

USE EMPLOYED
SORT ON Salary /D TO COSTS
USE COSTS
LIST Lastname, Firstname, Salary, City, State OFF

    LASTNAME      FIRSTNAME      SALARY CITY          STATE
    Johnson       Linda          2890.30 Carrollton    TX
    Johnson       Martin         2495.00 Fort Worth    TX
    Smith         Karen          2075.40 Dallas        TX
    Williams      Greg           1890.50 Arlington     TX
    Klein         Samuel         1775.00 Carrollton    TX
    Roberts       Jerry          1740.00 Dallas        TX
    Robertson     Henry          1534.60 Garland       TX
    Martin        Lydia          1390.00 Fort Worth    TX
    Sanders       Anette         1170.20 Dallas        TX

USE EMPLOYED SORT ON State, City TO TOWNS
```

```
USE TOWNS
LIST Lastname, Firstname, Salary, City, State OFF
```

LASTNAME	FIRSTNAME	SALARY	CITY	STATE
Williams	Greg	1890.50	Arlington	TX
Johnson	Linda	2890.30	Carrollton	TX
Klein	Samuel	1775.00	Carrollton	TX
Smith	Karen	2075.40	Dallas	TX
Sanders	Anette	1170.20	Dallas	TX
Roberts	Jerry	1740.00	Dallas	TX
Johnson	Martin	2495.00	Fort Worth	TX
Martin	Lydia	1390.00	Fort Worth	TX
Robertson	Henry	1534.60	Garland	TX

STORE

Syntax

> STORE *expression* TO *memvarlist/array element list*

The STORE command creates a memory variable and stores a value to that variable. Note that an alternative form of the command is the assignment (=) statement, where the variable name is placed to the left of the equal sign, and the value to be stored to the variable is placed to the right of the equal sign. Hence, the following two statements would accomplish the same task—storing a value of 23.5 to a variable named AMOUNT.

```
STORE 23.5 TO AMOUNT
AMOUNT = 23.5
```

The assignment statement and the STORE command perform the same task, but a single STORE command can assign a value to more than one variable at a time, while the ASSIGNMENT statement can assign a value to only one variable at a time. For example, the following three assignment statements

```
SALARY1 = 8.50
SALARY2 = 8.50
SALARY3 = 8.50
```

could be performed with the following STORE statement

```
STORE 8.50 TO SALARY1, SALARY2, SALARY3
```

If the memory variable does not exist, the STORE command (or an equivalent assignment statement) will create it. If a memory variable by the same name already exists, it will be overwritten by the new one.

Character variables may be created by enclosing character strings in quotes or by storing the contents of character fields to variables. For example, the statement

```
STORE "Johnson" TO FINDER
```

creates a character variable containing the name Johnson. Numbers may be stored directly, as shown in the earlier example or by storing the contents of a numeric field to a variable. Dates may be stored using the CTOD() function, by surrounding the date with curly braces or by storing the contents of a date field to a variable. For example, to store a date value of 12/20/90 to a variable, either of the following statements could be used.

```
STORE {12/20/90} TO MYDAY
STORE CTOD("12/20/90") TO MYDAY
```

Example

To multiply a field called Salary for the current record by 1.05 and store it in the new memory variable named NEWAMT, the following command could be used.

```
STORE SALARY * 1.05 TO NEWAMT
```

The following statements demonstrate the effects of the STORE command at the command level.

```
STORE "Johnson" TO NAME
STORE 105 TO AMOUNT
STORE DATE() TO TODAY
LIST MEMORY


NAME        pub  C  "Johnson"
AMOUNT      pub  N        105  (       105.00000000)
TODAY       pub  D  02/19/90
    3 variables defined,      27 bytes used
  253 variables available,   5973 bytes available
```

In the following portion of a program, a STORE command is used to initialize a character variable so it can be used by an @...GET command and a READ command to accept a social security number. The value entered is then used for a search of an indexed database.

```
STORE SPACE(11) TO M_SOCIAL
USE STAFF INDEX SOCIAL CLEAR
@  5,5 SAY "Social sec. no. of employee:"
@ 5,35 GET M_SOCIAL PICTURE "999-99-9999"
READ
SEEK M_SOCIAL
CLEAR
@  6,5 SAY "Name:"
@ 6,12 SAY TRIM(Firstname) + " " + Lastname
...more commands...
```

SUM

Syntax

SUM [*scope*] [*fieldlist*] [TO *memvarlist*] [TO ARRAY *array*] [FOR *condition*] [WHILE *condition*]

Syntax for FoxPro 2

SUM [*scope*] [*fieldlist*] [TO *memvarlist*] [TO ARRAY *array*] [FOR *condition*] [WHILE *condition*] [NOOPTIMIZE]

The SUM command provides a sum total of *fieldlist* involving numeric fields. If the TO option is not used, the sum is displayed (assuming SET TALK is ON), but not stored in memory. If the TO option is used, the sum is displayed (assuming SET TALK is ON), and the sum is stored as the memory variable specified. If the *scope* option is not used, ALL is assumed by FoxPro. The FOR option can be used to specify a condition that must be met before an entry in a field can be summed. If you use the WHILE option, records will be summed until the condition is no longer true. The TO ARRAY option stores the values summed to the elements of the named array. With FoxPro 2 and later, the NOOPTIMIZE clause, when added, turns off FoxPro's internal optimization techniques (Rushmore).

Example

The following statements and resulting listings demonstrate the effects of the SUM command. The SUM command is used without any conditions specified to sum the numeric fields of the database (Salary and FICA). Next, the SUM command is used with a condition of Lastname = "Johnson" to sum the fields for only those records containing Johnson in the Lastname field.

```
USE COSTS
LIST Lastname, Firstname, Salary, Fica OFF

LASTNAME       FIRSTNAME     SALARY   FICA
Johnson        Linda         2890.30 187.87
Johnson        Martin        2495.00 162.18
Smith          Karen         2075.40 134.90
Williams       Greg          1890.50 122.88
Klein          Samuel        1775.00 115.38
Roberts        Jerry         1740.00 113.10
Robertson      Henry         1534.60  99.75
Martin         Lydia         1390.00  90.35
Sanders        Anette        1170.20  76.06

SUM
     9 records summed
   SALARY       FICA
  16961.00    1102.47

SUM SALARY FOR Lastname = "Johnson"
     2 records summed
   SALARY
  5385.30
```

SUSPEND

Syntax

SUSPEND

The SUSPEND command suspends execution of a command file or procedure and returns program control to the command level while leaving current memory variables intact. Execution of the command file or procedure can be restarted where it was interrupted with the RESUME command.

TEXT

Syntax

TEXT
...text to be displayed...
ENDTEXT

The TEXT command displays blocks of text on the screen. All text that appears between the TEXT and the ENDTEXT statements appears on the screen. If SET PRINT is ON, the text will also be printed. The TEXT and ENDTEXT statements can be useful when you want to present messages in a program and precise positioning is relatively unimportant.

In FoxPro 2, note that expressions (including field names), memory variables, and functions placed between TEXT and ENDTEXT statements will be evaluated if SET TEXTMERGE is ON. If SET TEXTMERGE is OFF, expressions, variables, and functions are output as literal characters, including the textmerge delimiters. For example, a line between a TEXT and ENDTEXT statement containing the expression < <TIME()> > would appear as < <TIME()> > if SET TEXTMERGE was OFF. The same expression would appear as the current time according to the computer's clock if SET TEXTMERGE was ON.

Version 2

Example

In the following program, TEXT and ENDTEXT are used to display a copyright message at the start of a program.

```
SET TALK OFF
SET BELL OFF
SET CONFIRM ON
SET DELETED ON
CLEAR TEXT
*************************************************************
*                                                         *
*              Program copyright (C) 1990 by              *
*        Integrity Software of Mayaguez, Puerto Rico      *
*                  All rights reserved.                   *
*                                                         *
*************************************************************

ENDTEXT
...more commands...
```

TOTAL

Syntax

TOTAL TO *filename* ON *key* [*scope*] [FIELDS *fieldlist*] [FOR *condition*]
[WHILE *condition*]

Syntax for FoxPro 2

TOTAL TO *filename* ON *key* [*scope*] [FIELDS *fieldlist*] [FOR *condition*]
[WHILE *condition*] [NOOPTIMIZE]

The TOTAL command adds the numeric fields in a database and creates a new database containing the results. The file to be totaled must be indexed or sorted on the key field. If the FIELDS *fieldlist* option is used, fields totaled will be limited to those fields named in the list. If the *scope* option is not used, the quantifier of ALL is assumed, meaning all records in the database will be totaled, unless you use the FOR or WHILE options. The FOR option can be used to specify a condition that must be met for the fields to be totaled. If you use the WHILE option, records will be totaled until the condition is no longer true. With FoxPro 2 and later, the NOOPTIMIZE clause, when added, turns off FoxPro's internal optimization techniques (Rushmore).

Example

The following statements and resultant listings demonstrate the effects of the TOTAL command. The first listing shows part of a database of expenses with different records of expenses stored under various categories. For tax purposes, a total of expenses for each category is needed. The TOTAL command is used, and CATEGORY is used as the key expression. As the second listing shows, the resultant records stored in the file created by the TOTAL command contains a record for each category with a total amount in the Amount field.

```
USE CHECKS
INDEX ON CATEGORY TO TYPES
LIST NEXT 10 OFF
```

DATE	CATEGORY	CHECKNO	PAIDTO	AMOUNT
04/15/88	ADVERTISING	1461	Amer. Legal Assoc.	150.00
08/24/88	ADVERTISING	1528	C.U.Pers. Assoc.	150.00
06/01/88	COPIER PAYMT	1485	Xerox Corp.	208.00
09/05/88	COPIER PAYMT	1538	Xerox Corp.	208.00
04/26/88	DUES/SUBSCRIP	1470	DP Directory	65.00
08/30/88	DUES/SUBSCRIP	1534	ABC Patterns	8.95
03/01/88	LICENSE FEES	1450	Fairfax County	81.84
03/01/88	LICENSE FEES	1451	Fairfax County	176.07
01/04/88	PERSONAL	1396	M. Johnson	1174.00
01/04/88	PERSONAL	1397	J.P. Getty	120.83

```
TOTAL ON CATEGORY TO DOLLARS

    60 Record(s) totaled
    14 Records generated
```

```
USE DOLLARS
LIST OFF Category, Amount

CATEGORY          AMOUNT
ADVERTISING       300.00
COPIER PAYMT      416.00
DUES/SUBSCRIP      73.95
LICENSE FEES      257.91
PERSONAL         6551.02
POSTAGE/MAILING   438.15
PROF. FEES       2378.40
REFUND-SOFTWARE    30.00
SALARIES         4354.55
SUPPLIES          593.89
SOFTWARE          218.50
TYPEWRITER PMT     62.00
```

TYPE

Syntax

TYPE *filename.ext* [TO PRINT/TO FILE *filename*] [NUMBER]

The TYPE command displays the contents of a disk file on screen. If the TO PRINT option is used, the file will be printed. The TO FILE option directs the output of the TYPE command to a named disk file. The NUMBER option causes line numbers to be included.

Example

To type the contents of a file called LETTER.TXT, the following command could be used.

```
TYPE LETTER.TXT
```

UPDATE

Syntax

UPDATE [RANDOM] ON *keyfield* FROM *alias* REPLACE *field* WITH *expression*[, *field2* WITH *expression2*...]

The UPDATE command uses data from a database specified by *alias* to make changes to the database in the current work area. The UPDATE command lets you change the contents of fields in a database, based on a field or fields in another database. The file that is to be updated must be opened in the current work area, and the file containing the data that serves as a basis for the updating can be open in any other work area. The UPDATE command requires that the two files have a common field with the same field name. (You can also update on an expression that consists of more than one field, as long as both databases have the combination of fields you are using in the expression.)

Both files must be sorted or indexed on the key field or combination of fields unless the RANDOM clause is included, in which case only the file open in the other work area needs to be sorted or indexed.

Note that if there is not a unique key entry in the file being updated for every record having a match in the alias file, then only the first record that matches a record in the alias file will be updated. If more than one record in the alias file matches the key used in the current file, only the value from the last matching record in the alias file gets stored to the matching record in the updated file. It is important to understand this concept when using UPDATE. In other words, the UPDATE command supports one-to-one or one-to-many relationships between the current work area and the alias file. UPDATE does not support many-to-many relationships or many-to-one relationships between the current work area and the alias file. If your use of an UPDATE command results in a file where only the first record in a group of records with the same index key gets updated, you are trying to establish the type of relationship that UPDATE does not support. You should use SET RELATION with the ADDITIVE clause instead to obtain the needed data.

Example

The following statements demonstrate the effects of the UPDATE command. A database of sales items (ITEMS.DBF) is opened in work area 1 and indexed on the unique field of Stockno. Next, a database of customer orders (ORDERS.DBF) is opened in work area 2, and is also indexed on the Stockno field. The REPLACE command is used to store a value of zero in all TOTAL fields of the ORDERS database. Finally, the UPDATE command is used to replace the contents of the Total field with a total cost. This cost is calculated by multiplying the value of the Cost field for a record with a matching stock number in the ITEMS database by the value stored in the Quantity field of the ORDERS database.

```
SELECT 1
USE ITEMS
INDEX ON Stockno TO ITEMS
LIST OFF
```

```
STOCKNO DESCRIPT                    COST
2001    leather handbag, black     89.95
2002    attache case              139.95
2003    suitcase, overnighter     159.95
2004    carry on bag, leather      69.95


SELECT 2
USE ORDERS
INDEX ON Stockno TO ORDERS
REPLACE ALL Total WITH 0
LIST OFF

CUSTNO STOCKNO QUANTITY DATE       TOTAL
9001   2001           1 03/05/90   0.00
9002   2002           2 03/06/90   0.00
9003   2003           1 03/04/90   0.00
9001   2004           1 03/05/90   0.00


UPDATE ON Stockno FROM ITEMS REPLACE Total WITH ;
Quantity*Items->Cost
     4 records updated


LIST OFF

CUSTNO STOCKNO QUANTITY DATE       TOTAL
9001   2001           1 03/05/90    89.95
9002   2002           2 03/06/90   279.90
9003   2003           1 03/04/90   159.95
9001   2004           1 03/05/90    69.95
```

USE

Syntax

USE [*filename*/?] [IN *work area*] [INDEX *indexfile list*] [ORDER *expN*]
[ALIAS *alias*]

Syntax for FoxPro 2

USE [*filename*/?] [IN *work area*] [AGAIN] [INDEX *indexfile list*/?
[ORDER [*expN*/.*IDXfile*/[TAG] *tag name* [OF .*CDXfile*]
[ASCENDING/DESCENDING]]]] [ALIAS *alias*] [EXCLUSIVE] [NOUPDATE]

The USE command opens a database file and related index files in a work area. If the ? is used in place of the database filename, a list of available files appears. Use the INDEX and ORDER options to specify index files which will be open or active. Use the ALIAS option to open the file in a different work area. Entering the USE command without specifying a filename will close the file that is currently open.

Under FoxPro 2, use the AGAIN clause to open the same database simultaneously in a different work area. The ORDER and TAG clauses can be used to designate the master index file or the master tag of a compound-index file. The ASCENDING and DESCENDING clauses may be used to determine whether records are displayed and retrieved in ascending or descending order. For *Version 2* example, if the index file opened with the database was originally created in descending order, the ASCENDING clause would cause the records to be accessed in ascending order.

The ALIAS clause may be used to assign an alternate name, or *alias*, to the database. Work areas may then be selected by referring to the work area number, to the database name, or to the alias. The EXCLUSIVE clause has an effect only in FoxPro/LAN; it causes the database to be opened for exclusive use, and other network users cannot use the database until it is closed. The NOUPDATE clause prevents changes to the database file.

Example

To open a file called MEMBERS along with three index files named NAMES, PAYROLL, and DATES, with the NAMES index file as the controlling index, the following command could be used.

```
USE MEMBERS INDEX NAMES, PAYROLL, DATES
```

WAIT

Syntax

WAIT [*expC*] [TO *memvar*]

Syntax for FoxPro 2

WAIT [*expC*] [TO *memvar*] [WINDOW [NOWAIT]] [TIMEOUT *expN*]

The WAIT command halts operation of a command file until a key is pressed. If a character expression is included, it will be displayed on the screen. If no character expression is defined, a default message of "Press any key to continue" appears.

If the TO option is used, the key pressed will be stored as a memory variable.

Version 2

In FoxPro 2 and later, the WINDOW option causes the WAIT statement to appear within a window at the upper-right corner of the screen. The NOWAIT option can be added to make the window behave like FoxPro system messages; moving the mouse or pressing any key causes the window to disappear. The TIMEOUT option, followed by a value in seconds, causes the WAIT statement to terminate after the specified number of seconds.

Example

In the following program, a WAIT statement is used to pause a program's execution until the user is ready to print a report. The memory variable stored by means of the WAIT statement provides the user with an option for canceling the print run; if the user presses C in response to the WAIT prompt, the print run is canceled.

```
CLEAR
? " Ready to print the ABC Payroll Report."
WAIT "Press C to CANCEL, any other key to start..." TO DOIT
IF UPPER(DOIT) = "C"
    *user wants out, so...
    RETURN
ENDIF
REPORT FORM ABCPAY TO PRINT
EJECT
RETURN
```

ZAP

Syntax

ZAP

The ZAP command removes all records from the active database file. The ZAP command is equivalent to a DELETE ALL command followed by a PACK command.

WARNING: *A ZAP command, once executed, is not undoable. You cannot recall records removed with a ZAP command.*

ZOOM WINDOW

Syntax

Version 2

> ZOOM WINDOW *windowname* MIN/MAX/NORM
> [AT *row1,col1*/FROM *row1,col1* [SIZE *row2,col2*/TO *row2,col2*]]

The ZOOM WINDOW command is used to change the size of a window. Windows can be reduced to minimum size (minimized), enlarged to maximum size (maximized) or sized anywhere in between. The MIN clause minimizes the named window, and the MAX clause maximizes the named window. Note that if a window is a child window (a window within a window), the window can be maximized only up to the size of the parent window. The NORM clause can be used to return a window to its original size, after it was minimized or maximized.

The AT and FROM clauses can be used to restore a minimized or maximized window to a different location. The *row1, col1* coordinates specify the upper-left corner of the window. The optional *row2, col2* coordinates specify the lower-right corner of the window. The second set of coordinates is omitted, and the window takes on the same size as it had before it was minimized or maximized.

Chapter **23**

Function Reference

This chapter summarizes the FoxPro functions. Following the name of each function is the function's syntax and a description of its purpose. Where appropriate, examples of the use of the functions are included. For a similar summary of FoxPro commands, see Chapter 22.

Reference Symbols and Conventions

1. All functions are printed in UPPERCASE letters, although you can enter them in either upper- or lowercase letters.

2. The term "*expC*" indicates a character expression, "*expN*" indicates a numeric expression, "*expD*" represents a date expression, and "*expL*" indicates a logical expression. Where data type does not matter, the term "*expression*" or "*expr*" is used. Wherever an expression is a literal string, you must enclose it in single or double quotes. If the expression is a variable name, quotes are not used.

3. Whenever a function calls for or permits an alias argument, you can use the alias name (in quotes), or you can use the work-area number or letter.

4. Any part of a parameter that is surrounded by [] (left and right brackets) is optional.

5. Ellipses (...) following a parameter mean that the parameter can be repeated infinitely—that is, until you reach the limit of 1024 characters on a single program line.

ABS

Syntax

ABS(*expN*)

The ABS() function returns the absolute (positive) value of the specified numeric expression.

Example

```
? ABS(-40)
 40
 ? ABS(100-70)
  30
? ABS(70-100)    30
```

ACOPY

Syntax

ACOPY(*expC1*, *expC2*[, *expN1*[, *expN2*[, *expN3*]]])

The ACOPY() function copies elements of the first array, named in *expC1*, to the elements of the second array, named in *expC2*. The number of elements copied to the destination array is returned if the copy is successful; otherwise, a value of −1 is returned. *ExpN1*, which is optional, denotes the starting position in the source array. *ExpN2* is the number of elements to copy, beginning with *expN1*. If *expN1* is omitted, the copying begins at the first element of the array. *ExpN3*, which is also optional, denotes the starting element in the target array. If *expN3* is omitted, the copying begins at the first element in the target array.

ACOS

Syntax

ACOS(*expN*)

The ACOS() function returns the arc cosine of *expN*, as measured in radians between zero and +pi (3.14159). Allowable values for *expN* range from 0 to +1.

Example

```
MYCOS = 3/4
ANGLE=ACOS(MYCOS)
? ANGLE
        0.72
```

Related Functions

COS(), DTOR(), RTOD()

ADEL

Syntax

Version 2

ADEL (*expC, expN*[, 2])

The ADEL() function deletes a single element within an array, or it deletes a row or a column from a two-dimensional array. If the deletion is successful, a value of 1 is returned; otherwise, −1 is returned. *ExpC* denotes the name of the array, and *expN* identifies the element to delete. For example, if *expN* is 3, the third element in the array is deleted. Also note that when an array element is deleted with ADEL(), the element is not left blank; instead, the contents of all remaining elements after the deleted element are shifted forward by one element, leaving the last element unused and set to a logical false (.F.) value. The optional ,2 argument is used to delete a column from a two-dimensional array.

ADIR

Syntax

Version 2

ADIR(*expC1*[, *expC2*[, *expC3*]])

The ADIR() function fills array elements with information from a disk directory. *ExpC1* is the name of the array where the file information is to be stored. *ExpC2* is any DOS file skeleton. The array will be filled with filenames, sizes, creation dates and times, and DOS attributes for all files matching the skeleton. *ExpC3*, which is optional, specifies additional information that is to be returned; "D" for subdirectory information, "H" for hidden files, "S" for system files, and "V" for volume names.

AELEMENT

Syntax

Version 2

AELEMENT(*expC*, *expN1*[, *expN2*])

The AELEMENT() function returns the element number of an array element, based on the row and column location for that element. (Array elements can be referred to in one of two ways: by element number, or by row and column location. Use AELEMENT() to convert a row-and-column location to an element number.) *ExpC* is the name of the array. *ExpN1* is the row location, and *expN2*, which is used with two-dimensional arrays, is the column location.

AFIELDS

Syntax

Version 2

AFIELDS(*expC*)

The AFIELDS() function fills array elements with field attributes from the current work area. The array elements are filled with field names, field types, field lengths, and field decimal places.

The array, whose name is *expC*, is filled with the contents of the four columns that normally appear as a result of the LIST STRUCTURE command. Field names are stored in the first column, and the contents of the column will be character elements. Field types are stored in the second column, and the contents of the column will be character elements containing a single letter; "C" for character, "D" for date, "L" for logical, "M" for memo, "N" for numeric, or "F" for floating point. Field lengths are stored in the third column, and the contents of the column will be numeric elements. The number of decimal places for the fields are stored in the fourth column, and the contents of the column will be numeric elements.

AINS

Syntax

Version 2

AINS(*expC, expN*[, 2])

The AINS() function inserts a new element into an existing array. *ExpC* is the name of the array that receives the new element, and *expN* is an element number for one-dimensional arrays, or it is a row number or a column number for two-dimensional arrays. The optional ,2 argument indicates that *expN* is a column number.

NOTE: *When the new element is inserted, the last element of the array is discarded, and all remaining elements following the new element are moved back by one position. If the insertion is successful, a value of 1 is returned; otherwise, a value of −1 is returned.*

ALEN

Syntax

Version 2

ALEN(*expC*[, *expN*])

The ALEN() function returns the number of elements, rows, or columns in an array. *ExpC* is the array name, and *expN* denotes whether the function should return the number of elements, rows, or columns. If *expN* is 0 (or if *expN* is omitted), the number of elements is returned. If *expN* is 1, the number of rows is returned. If *expN* is 2, the number of columns is returned.

ALIAS

Syntax

ALIAS([*expN*])

The ALIAS() function returns the alias of the database open in the work area specified by *expN*. If *expN* is omitted, ALIAS() returns the alias of the current work area. Note that if *expN* is omitted and no database is open in the current work area, ALIAS() returns a null string ("").

Example

```
SELECT 1
USE STAFF
SELECT 2
USE VIDEO ALIAS FILMS
? ALIAS()
FILMS
? ALIAS(1)
STAFF
```

Related Functions

DBF(), SELECT()

ALLTRIM

Syntax

ALLTRIM(*expC*)

ALLTRIM() returns the character expression *expC* minus any leading and trailing blanks. ALLTRIM() is functionally equivalent to LTRIM(RTRIM(*expC*)).

Related Functions

LTRIM(), RTRIM(), TRIM()

ASC

Syntax

ASC(*expC*)

The ASC() function returns the decimal ASCII code for the leftmost character in *expC*.

Example

```
? ASC("U")
85
? ASC("hello")
104
```

Related Functions

CHR(), INKEY()

ASCAN

Syntax

Version 2

ASCAN(*expC, expression*[, *expN1*[, *expN2*]])

The ASCAN() function is used to scan an array, searching for a particular value. *ExpC* names the array to be scanned, and *expression* denotes the data to search for. The *expression* can be any data type. *ExpN1*, which is optional, denotes the starting element where the search will begin; if omitted, ASCAN() begins with the first element. *ExpN2*, which is also optional, denotes the number of elements that should be searched; if omitted, ASCAN() searches to the end of the array.

ASCAN() returns a numeric value, indicating the position of the data in the array. If ASCAN() cannot find the data, a value of 0 is returned.

NOTE: ASCAN() does respect the status of SET EXACT. If SET EXACT is ON, the contents of the array element must precisely match the contents of expression, in length and in content. If SET EXACT is OFF, the contents of expression are tested from left to right until a match is found; any remaining characters in the array element are ignored.

ASIN

Syntax

ASIN(*expN*)

The ASIN() function returns the arc sine of *expN*, as measured in radians between −pi/2 and +pi/2 (−1.57079 to 1.57079). To convert the value returned in radians to degrees, use the RTOD() function. Acceptable values for *expN* are from +1 to −1.

Example

```
? ASIN(.707)
       0.79
```

Related Functions

DTOR(), RTOD(), SIN()

ASORT

Syntax

Version 2

ASORT(*expC*[, *expN1*[, *expN2*[, *expN3*]]])

The ASORT() function sorts an array. The elements contained in the array are sorted in ascending order. *ExpC* denotes the name of the array. *ExpN1*, which is optional, is a numeric value that denotes the element at which to start the sort. If omitted, the sort begins with the first element. *ExpN2*, which is used along with *expN1*, is a numeric value that denotes the column where sorting starts; when *expN2* is used, *expN1* is then assumed to be the row where sorting starts. *ExpN3* denotes a sort order; 0 for ascending or 1 for descending.

ASUBSCRIPT

Syntax

ASUBSCRIPT(*expC, expN1, expN2*)

Version 2

The ASUBSCRIPT() function returns the row or column location of an array element, based on an element's number. Array elements can be referred to in one of two ways: by element number, or by row and column location. Use ASUBSCRIPT() to convert an element number to a row-and-column location. *ExpC* is the name of the array. *ExpN1* is the element number. *ExpN2*, which is used with two-dimensional arrays, must be 1 if the row location is desired or 2 if the column location is desired.

AT

Syntax

AT(*expC1, expC2*[, *expN*])

The AT() function finds *expC1* in *expC2*. (Note that *expC2* may be a memo field.) The function returns as an integer the starting position of *expC1*. If *expC1* is not found, the function returns a zero. If the optional *expN* is used, the *expN*th occurrence of *expC1* is searched for.

Example

```
LONGTEXT = "The quick brown fox jumps over"
SHORTEXT = "fox"
? AT(SHORTEXT, LONGTEXT)
      17
```

Related Functions

LEFT(), RAT(), RIGHT(), SUBSTR()

ATAN

Syntax

ATAN(*expN*)

The ATAN() function returns the arctangent of *expN*, as measured in radians between −pi/2 and +pi/2 (−1.57079 to 1.57079). To convert the value returned in radians to degrees, use the RTOD() function. *ExpN* can be any value.

Example

```
? ATAN(1.0)
        0.79
? ATAN(0.5)
        0.46
```

Related Functions

ATN2(), DTOR(), RTOD(), TAN()

ATC

Syntax

ATC(*expC1*, *expC2*[, *expN*])

The ATC() function searches a character string *expC1* for another character string *expC2*. If *expC1* is not found, the function returns a zero. If the optional *expN* is used, the *expN*th occurrence of *expC1* is searched for. The ATC() function operates just like the AT() function, but the ATC function is not case-sensitive.

Related Functions

AT(), LEFT(), RIGHT(), SUBSTR()

ATCLINE

Syntax

ATCLINE(*expC1*, *expC2*)

The ATCLINE() function finds *expC1* within *expC2*, and then returns the line number where it was found. ATCLINE is usually used with memo fields, to locate text within a memo field and return the line number containing the desired text. *ExpC2* is the name of the memo field or character variable. If *expC1* is not found in *expC2*, the function returns a zero.

The length, and consequently the number of lines, in a memo field is determined by SET MEMOWIDTH. Also, note that ATCLINE() is not case-sensitive; the ATLINE() function (see next entry) performs the same task, but is case-sensitive.

Related Functions

ATLINE(), MLINE()

ATLINE

Syntax

ATLINE(*expC1*, *expC2*)

The ATLINE() function finds *expC1* within *expC2*, and then returns (as an integer) the line number where it was found. ATLINE is usually used with memo fields to locate text within a memo field and return the line number containing the desired text. *ExpC2* is the name of the memo field or character variable. If *expC1* is not found in *expC2*, the function returns a zero. The case of the search string in *expC1* must match the case of the text to be found in *expC2*.

Related Functions

ATCLINE(), MLINE()

ATN2

Syntax

ATN2(*expN1*, *expN2*)

The ATN2() function returns the arctangent angle (as measured in radians) for all four quadrants. You specify the X and Y coordinates (or sine and cosine of the angle) instead of specifying the tangent value as with the ATAN() function. *ExpN1* is the X coordinate or sine of the angle, and *expN2* is the Y coordinate, or cosine of the angle.

Example

```
? ATN2(3,4)
     0.64
? RTOD(ATN2(3,4))
    36.87
```

Related Functions

ATAN(), DTOR(), RTOD(), TAN()

BAR

Syntax

BAR()

The BAR() function returns the number of the option most recently selected from the active popup menu. Use the DEFINE BAR command to assign each menu item a number. If no popup menu is active, the BAR() function returns a zero.

Related Functions

PAD(), PROMPT()

BETWEEN

Syntax

BETWEEN(*expr1*, *expr2*, *expr3*)

The BETWEEN() function returns a logical true (.T.) if *expr1* is greater than or equal to *expr2* and less than or equal to *expr3*; otherwise, the function returns a logical false (.F.). The expressions used must be of the same type.

Related Functions

MAX(), MIN()

BOF

Syntax

BOF([*alias*])

The BOF() function returns a logical true (.T.) if the record pointer is at the beginning of the file (above the first record in the database file). Use the optional *alias* to test for the beginning of the file in a different work area.

Example

```
USE STAFF
GO 2
? BOF()
.F.
GO TOP
? BOF()
.F.
SKIP -1
Record No. 1 ? BOF()
.T.
```

Related Function

EOF()

CAPSLOCK

Syntax

CAPSLOCK([*expL*])

The CAPSLOCK() function turns the Caps Lock keyboard mode on or off, or it returns the current state of Caps Lock. CAPSLOCK(.T.) turns the Caps Lock mode on, and CAPSLOCK(.F.) turns the Caps Lock mode off. If *expL* is omitted, the status of CAPSLOCK() is returned without changing the state of the keyboard.

Related Functions

INSMODE(), NUMLOCK()

CDOW

Syntax

CDOW(*expD*)

The CDOW() function returns the name of the day of the week for the given date expression.

Example

```
TODAY = DATE()
? CDOW(TODAY)
Sunday
```

Related Functions

DATE(), DAY(), DOW(), SYS()

CDX

Syntax

CDX(*expN*[, *alias*])

Version 2

The CDX() function returns the names of open compound-index (.CDX) files. Note that the CDX() function is identical in operation to the MDX() function. *ExpN* is a numeric value which identifies the desired compound-index file, according to the following possibilities: If the database has a structural compound-index file and *expN1* is 1, the name of the structural compound-index file is returned. If *expN1* is 2, the name of the first .CDX compound-index file (as identified by the INDEX clause of the USE command, or the SET INDEX command) is returned. If *expN1* is 3, the second .CDX compound-index file name is returned, and so forth. If *expN1* is greater than the number of open .CDX compound-index files, the function returns a null string.

If the database does not have a structural compound-index file and *expN1* is 1, the name of the first .CDX compound-index file (as identified by the INDEX clause of the USE command, or by the SET INDEX command) is returned. If *expN1* is 2, the second .CDX compound-index filename is returned, and so forth. If *expN1* is greater than the number of open .CDX compound-index files, the function returns a null string.

Use the *alias* option to return the names of compound-index files open in different work areas.

CEILING

Syntax

CEILING(*expN*)

The CEILING() function returns the nearest integer greater than or equal to *expN*. Positive numbers with decimals are rounded up to the next-highest number, and negative numbers with decimals are rounded up to the next number closest to zero.

Example

```
? CEILING(13.97)
      14
? CEILING(-13.97)
     -13
```

Related Functions

FLOOR(), ROUND()

CHR

Syntax

CHR(*expN*)

The CHR() function returns the character whose decimal ASCII code is equivalent to *expN*.

Example

```
? CHR(85)
U
? CHR(117)
u
```

Related Functions

ASC(), INKEY()

CHRSAW

Syntax

CHRSAW([*expN*])

The CHRSAW() function checks the keyboard buffer for the presence of a character and returns a logical true (.T.) if a character is found in the keyboard buffer. The optional *expN* specifies the number of seconds to wait for a keypress before returning the value.

Related Functions

INKEY(), READKEY()

CHRTRAN

Syntax

CHRTRAN(*expC1*, *expC2*, *expC3*)

The CHRTRAN() function translates the characters of *expC1*. The strings in *expC2* and *expC3* are used as a translation table. Any occurrences of the first character in *expC2* are replaced by the first character in *expC3*, the second character in *expC2* by the second character in *expC3*, and so forth.

CMONTH

Syntax

CMONTH(*expD*)

The CMONTH() function returns the name of the month that corresponds to the date expression.

Example

```
TODAY = DATE()
? CMONTH(TODAY)
April
```

Related Functions

DATE(), DMY(), MDY(), MONTH()

CNTBAR

Syntax

CNTBAR(*expC*)

Version 2

The CNTBAR() function returns the number of bars in the popup menu by *expC*.

CNTPAD

Syntax

Version 2

CNTPAD(*expC*)

The CNTPAD() function returns the number of menu pads in the menu bar named by *expC*.

COL

Syntax

COL()

The COL() function returns the current column location of the cursor.

Related Functions

PCOL(), PROW(), ROW()

COS

Syntax

COS(*expN*)

The COS() function returns the cosine of *expN* as measured in radians. To convert an angle from degrees to radians, use the DTOR() function.

Example

```
RADS = DTOR(45)
? COS(RADS)
         0.71
```

Related Functions

ACOS(), DTOR(), RTOD()

CTOD

Syntax

CTOD(*expC*)

The CTOD() function returns the date value which corresponds to *expC*, in the default date format (generally *MM/DD/YY*). Use the SET DATE and SET CENTURY commands to change the default format. Also, note that curly braces surrounding a date perform the equivalent of the CTOD() function; hence, CTOD("12/21/91") and {12/21/91} produce the same date value in FoxPro.

Example

```
STORE CTOD("12/22/79") TO ANNIVERSAR
STORE DATE() + 7 TO AWEEKAWAY
STORE DATE() + 31 TO NEXTMONTH
DISPLAY MEMORY
TODAY       Pub   D   04/15/90
ANNIVERSAR  Pub   D   12/22/79
AWEEKAWAY   Pub   D   04/22/90
NEXTMONTH   Pub   D   05/16/90
    4 variables defined,       0 bytes used
  252 variables available,   6000 bytes available
```

Related Functions

DATE(), DTOC()

CURDIR

Syntax

CURDIR([*expC*])

The CURDIR() function returns the current DOS directory on the drive identified by *expC*. If no such drive exists, CURDIR() returns a null string. If *expC* is omitted, the default drive is assumed. Note that SET DEFAULT and SET PATH do not affect the expression returned by CURDIR().

Related Function

FULLPATH()

DATE

Syntax

DATE()

The DATE() function returns the current system date, as measured by the system clock.

Example

```
? DATE()
04/15/90
STORE DATE() + 1 TO TOMORROW
? TOMORROW
04/16/90
```

Related Function

TIME()

DAY

Syntax

DAY(*expD*)

The DAY() function returns the numeric day of the month that corresponds to the date expression.

Example

```
? DATE()
04/15/90
? DAY(DATE())
  15
```

Related Functions

CDOW(), DATE(), DOW(), SYS()

DBF

Syntax

DBF([*alias*])

The DBF() function returns the database filename for the file open in the specified work area. If no *alias* is specified, the DBF() function returns the filename for the currently selected work area. If no file is open in the work area, the function returns a null string. Use the optional *alias* to return the filename for an open file in a different work area.

Example

```
USE BOOKS
? DBF()
D:\FOXBASE\BOOKS.DBF
```

Related Functions

FIELD(), NDX(), RECCOUNT(), RECSIZE()

DELETED

Syntax

DELETED([*alias*])

The DELETED() function returns a logical true (.T.) if the current record is marked for deletion; otherwise, it returns a logical false (.F.). Use the optional *alias* to test for deleted records in a different work area.

Example

```
USE MEMBERS
GO 5
DELETE
? DELETED()
.T.
SKIP
? DELETED()
.F.
SKIP -1
RECALL
? DELETED()
.F.
```

DIFFERENCE

Syntax

DIFFERENCE(*expC1*, *expC2*)

The DIFFERENCE() function returns a numeric value between 0 and 4, representing the phonetic difference between two character strings, *expC1* and *expC2*. The DIFFERENCE() function can be useful for searching databases when the precise spelling of an entry is not known.

Example

```
LIST Lastname, Firstname
Record#   LASTNAME        FIRSTNAME
     1    Morse           Marcia
     2    Westman         Andrea
     3    Jackson         David
     4    Mitchell        Mary Jo
     5    Robinson        Shirley
     6    Jackson         Cheryl
     7    Robinson        Wanda
     8    Hart            Edward
     9    Jones           Judi
    10    Jones           Jarel

LIST Lastname, Firstname FOR DIFFERENCE(Lastname,"Jonson")  1
Record#   LASTNAME        FIRSTNAME
     2    Westman         Andrea
     3    Jackson         David
     5    Robinson        Shirley
     6    Jackson         Cheryl
     7    Robinson        Wanda
     9    Jones           Judi
    10    Jones           Jarel

LIST Lastname, Firstname FOR DIFFERENCE(Lastname,"Jonson")  2
Record#   LASTNAME        FIRSTNAME
     3    Jackson         David
     6    Jackson         Cheryl
     9    Jones           Judi
    10    Jones           Jarel
```

Related Function

SOUNDEX()

DISKSPACE

Syntax

DISKSPACE()

The DISKSPACE() function returns the number of bytes available on the default drive.

Related Functions

HEADER(), RECCOUNT(), RECSIZE()

DMY

Syntax

DMY(*expD*)

The DMY() function returns a date expression in European format (*DD Month YY*) for the given date expression.

Example

```
? DATE()
04/15/90
? DMY(DATE())
15 April 90
```

Related Functions

DATE(), MDY()

DOW

Syntax

DOW(*expD*)

The DOW() function returns the numeric day of the week corresponding to the date expression. The value returned ranges from 1 (Sunday) to 7 (Saturday).

Example

```
? DATE()
09/15/91
? DOW(DATE())
 1
? CDOW(DATE())
Sunday
```

Related Functions

CDOW(), DATE(), DAY()

DTOC

Syntax

DTOC(*expD*[, 1])

The DTOC() function returns a character string containing the date that corresponds to the date expression. Use the SET DATE and the SET CENTURY commands to change the format of the string. The optional ,1 argument causes DTOC() to return the string in the *YYYYMMDD* format, similar to the DTOS() function.

Example

```
STORE "Today's date is: " TO MTEXT
? MTEXT + DTOC(DATE())
Today's date is: 04/15/90
```

Related Functions

CTOD(), DATE()

DTOR

Syntax

DTOR(*expN*)

The DTOR() function converts the angle specified by *expN* from degrees to radians.

Example

```
? DTOR(90)
        1.57
```

Related Functions

ACOS(), ATAN(), ATN2(), COS(), RTOD(), SIN(), TAN()

DTOS

Syntax

DTOS(*expD*)

The DTOS() function returns a character string in the format YYYYMMDD for the given date expression. This function is useful when indexing on a date field.

Example

```
? DATE()
04/15/90
? DTOS(DATE())
19900415
```

Related Functions

CTOD(), DATE(), DTOC()

EMPTY

Syntax

EMPTY(*expression*)

The EMPTY() function returns a logical true (.T.) if the *expression* is blank. The function will also return a value of true if the *expression* is a numeric expression with a value of zero or a logical expression with a value of false. Note that FoxPro will also return a value of true if the *expression* is a memo field, and the memo field contains no text.

Related Function

LEN()

EOF

Syntax

EOF([*alias*])

The EOF() function returns a logical true (.T.) if the end-of-file is reached (the record pointer passes the last record in the database or a FIND, LOCATE, or SEEK command was unsuccessful). You can use the optional *alias* to test for end-of-file in a different work area. Note that if you establish a relation with SET RELATION and the related file does not contain a record with the key matching the current record, the record pointer will be at the end-of-file in the related file.

Example

```
USE MEMBERS
GO 7
? EOF()
.F.
GO BOTTOM
? EOF()
.F.
SKIP
? EOF() .T.
```

Related Function

BOF()

ERROR

Syntax

ERROR()

The ERROR() function returns the number of the error causing the ON ERROR condition. An ON ERROR routine must be in effect for the ERROR() function to return a value other than zero.

Related Functions

CERROR(), MESSAGE()

EVALUATE

Syntax

EVALUATE(*expC*)

The EVALUATE() function evaluates a character expression, and returns the result. The expression must be a character string enclosed in quotes, and the character string may be a character expression, variable, or database field name.

EXP

Syntax

EXP(*expN*)

The EXP() function returns the value of e raised to *expN*th power. *ExpN* is the exponent, N, in the equation e^N. The value of e is roughly 2.71828 (the base of the natural logarithm).

Example

```
? EXP(2)
        7.39
? EXP(3)
       20.09
? EXP(0)
        1.00
```

Related Functions

LOG(), LOG10()

FCLOSE

Syntax

FCLOSE(*expN*)

The FCLOSE() function flushes the buffers for the file with the numeric file handle specified by *expN* to disk and closes the file. Use the FCREATE or FOPEN function to assign a file handle to the file. Once the file is closed, FCLOSE() will return a logical true (.T.). If a DOS or hardware failure prevents the file from being closed, FCLOSE() will return a logical false (.F.).

Related Functions

FCREATE(), FOPEN(), FREAD(), FSEEK(), FWRITE()

FCOUNT

Syntax

FCOUNT([*alias*])

The FCOUNT() function returns the number of fields in a database. Use the optional [*alias*] to return the number of fields in a database that is open in a different work area.

Example

```
USE STAFF
LIST STRUCTURE
Structure for database: E:\FOXPRO\STAFF.DBF
Number of data records:      3
Date of last update   : 01/23/90
Field  Field Name  Type        Width    Dec
    1  LASTNAME    Character      15
    2  FIRSTNAME   Character      15
    3  DEPARTMENT  Character      10
    4  AGE         Numeric         2
    5  SALARY      Numeric         5      2
    6  HIRED       Date            8
    7  PERFORMANC  Memo           10
** Total **                      66


? FCOUNT()
        7
```

Related Functions

DBF(), NDX(), RECCOUNT(), RECSIZE()

FCREATE

Syntax

FCREATE(*expC*[, *expN*])

The FCREATE() function creates a new file named *expC* and opens the file for use. If a file with the name *expC* already exists, the existing file is overwritten. FCREATE also assigns the file a numeric handle to identify the file when other low-level file functions are used. By default, the file will have a DOS read/write attribute assigned. The optional numeric expression can be used to specify the attribute of the file created, using one of the following values:

0	Read/write (default)
1	Read-only
2	Hidden
3	Read-only/hidden
4	System
5	Read-only/system
6	System/hidden
7	Read-only/system/hidden

If FCREATE() is unable to create the file, the function returns a value of −1.

Related Functions

FCLOSE(), FOPEN(), FREAD(), FSEEK(), FWRITE()

FEOF

Syntax

FEOF(*expN*)

The FEOF() function returns a logical true (.T.) if the file pointer is positioned at the end of the file (EOF). *ExpN* indicates the numeric handle of the file that you wish to test for the end-of-file.

Related Function

FSEEK()

FERROR

Syntax

FERROR()

The FERROR() function is used to test whether a low-level file function has been successful. FERROR() returns a zero if the last low-level function was successfully performed. If the last function was not successful, a nonzero value is returned.

Related Functions

FCREATE(), FCLOSE(), FOPEN(), FREAD(), FSEEK(), FWRITE()

FFLUSH

Syntax

FFLUSH(*expN*)

The FFLUSH() function flushes the file whose handle is *expN*. If the file was written to, FFLUSH() writes all data in the buffers to disk.

Related Function

FCLOSE()

FGETS

Syntax

FGETS(*expN1*[, *expN2*])

The FGETS() function returns a series of bytes from the file having the file handle specified by *expN1*. FGETS() returns a series of bytes from a file until a carriage return is encountered. The optional numeric argument *expN2* can be used to specify the number of bytes that the function will return, unless a carriage return is encountered first. The carriage return is never included in the string returned by FGETS().

Related Function

FREAD()

FIELD

Syntax

FIELD(*expN1*[, *alias*])

The FIELD() function returns the name of the field in the active database that corresponds to the numeric position specified in the expression. If there is no corresponding field in the active database, FIELD() returns a null string. Use the optional *alias* to return a field name from a database that is open in a different work area.

Related Functions

DBF(), FCOUNT(), NDX(), RECCOUNT(), RECSIZE()

FILE

Syntax

FILE(*expC*)

The FILE() function returns a logical true (.T.) if the character expression matches the name for an existing file in the default directory. If no such file can be found, the FILE() function returns a logical false (.F.).

Example

```
DIR
Database Files   # Records   Last Update   Size
FOXINST.DBF          8       11/10/88      2314
BOOKS.DBF            3       01/15/90       386
STAFF.DBF           3       01/23/90       456
VIDEO.DBF          88       03/28/90     12330
MEMBERS.DBF         8       04/15/90      1530

  17016 bytes in 5 files.
3749888 bytes remaining on drive.

? FILE("BOOKS.DBF")
```

```
.T.
? FILE("TRAVEL.DBF")
.F.
```

Related Function

FULLPATH()

FILTER

Syntax

FILTER([*alias*])

The FILTER() function returns the filter expression of the current work area. Use the optional *alias* to return a filter from a different work area. If no filter is in effect, a null string is returned.

FKLABEL

Syntax

FKLABEL(*expN*)

The FKLABEL() function returns the name of the function key that corresponds to *expN*.

Related Function

FKMAX()

FKMAX

Syntax

FKMAX()

The FKMAX() function returns the number of programmable function keys or programmable function key combinations available on your keyboard. If SET COMPATIBLE is set to FOXPLUS (the default), the number of function keys is returned. If SET COMPATIBLE is set to DB4, the number of function keys and function key combinations (such as F1, SHIFT-F1, CTRL-F1, ALT-F1, etc.) is returned.

Related Function

FKLABEL()

FLOOR

Syntax

FLOOR(*expN*)

The FLOOR() function returns the nearest integer value less than or equal to the numeric expression. All positive numbers with a decimal will be rounded down to the next-lowest number, and all negative numbers with a decimal will be rounded down to the next number farther from zero.

Example

```
STORE 13.995 TO NUMB
? FLOOR(NUMB)
        13
? FLOOR(-NUMB)
       -14
```

Related Functions

CEIL(), CEILING(), ROUND()

FOPEN

Syntax

FOPEN(*expC*[, *expN*])

The FOPEN() function opens the file named by *expC* for use. *ExpC* may include a full pathname for files on drives or in directories that are not in the current search path. The optional numeric expression can be used to specify an attribute of read-only, read/write, or write-only. Use 0 for read-only (the default), 1 for write-only, or 2 for read/write. If a file named by FOPEN is not found, the function returns a value of −1.

Related Functions

FCREATE(), FCLOSE(), FREAD(), FSEEK(), FWRITE()

FOUND

Syntax

FOUND([*alias*])

The FOUND() function returns a logical true (.T.) if the last CONTINUE, FIND, LOCATE, or SEEK command was successful. A logical false (.F.) is returned if the search command was unsuccessful. You can use the optional *alias* to test for a successful search in a different work area. Note that if you have established a relation with SET RELATION and you specify the related file with *alias*, the function returns a logical true if the pointer is on a record with a key value matching that of the current record in the active database.

Example

```
USE MEMBERS
LOCATE FOR Lastname = "Robinson"
? FOUND()
.T.
SKIP
? FOUND()
.F.
```

Related Functions

EOF(), SEEK()

FPUTS

Syntax

FPUTS(*expN1*, *expC*[, *expN2*])

The FPUTS() function writes the character string within *expC* to the file whose file handle is *expN1*. FPUTS() is different from FWRITE() in that FPUTS() adds a carriage return and line feed to the end of each line. The entire character string identified as *expC* is written, unless the optional numeric argument *expN2* is used. The value of *expN2* specifies the number of characters to write.

Related Function

FWRITE()

FREAD

Syntax

FREAD(*expN1*, *expN2*)

The FREAD() function returns as a character string a specified number of bytes from a file whose file handle is *expN1*. The numeric value of *expN2* is the number of bytes to read, starting from the current position of the file pointer. A character expression containing the characters read is returned by the function.

Use an assignment statement (=) to store the value returned by the function into the desired variable. The FOPEN() function can be used to open the file.

Related Functions

FCREATE(), FCLOSE(), FOPEN(), FREADSTR(), FSEEK(), FWRITE()

FSEEK

Syntax

FSEEK(*expN1*, *expN2*[, *expN3*])

The FSEEK() function moves the file pointer within a file. *ExpN1* is the file's handle (returned from the FOPEN function), and *expN2* is the number of bytes the file pointer must be moved. If *expN2* is positive, the file pointer is moved toward the end of the file. If *expN2* is negative, the file pointer is moved toward the beginning of the file. The number of bytes moved is normally relative to the beginning of the file. The optional argument specified in *expN3* can be used to change this relative position.

If *expN3* is 0, movement is relative to the start of the file (the default). If *expN3* is 1, movement is relative to the current position of the file pointer. If *expN3* is 2, movement is relative to the end of the file.

Related Functions

FREAD(), FREADSTR(), FWRITE()

FSIZE

Syntax

FSIZE(*expC*[, *alias*])

FSIZE() returns the size of *expC*, which represents the specified field, in bytes. Use the optional *alias* to select a field from a file in a different work area.

Related Function

LEN()

FULLPATH

Syntax

FULLPATH(*expC*[, 1])

FULLPATH() returns the full DOS pathname for the file named in *expC*. If the file is not found in the default directory, FULLPATH() will search the FoxPro path for the file. If the optional argument ,1 is added, the search will use the DOS path.

Related Functions
DBF(), NDX()

FV

Syntax

FV(*expN1*, *expN2*, *expN3*)

The FV() function returns the future value of an investment. FV() calculates the future value of a series of equal payments earning a fixed interest rate. The future value is the total of all payments plus the interest. *ExpN1* is the payment amount, *expN2* is the interest rate, and *expN3* is the number of periods. If the payments are compounded monthly and the interest rate is compounded yearly, divide the interest rate by 12 to get the proper results.

Example

```
STORE 120.00 TO PAYMENT
STORE .01 TO INTEREST
STORE 36 TO PERIODS
? FV(PAYMENT,INTEREST,PERIODS)
      5169.23
(3)Related Functions
PV()
```

FWRITE

Syntax

FWRITE(*expN1*, *expC*[, *expN2*])

The FWRITE() function lets you write to a file whose handle is *expN1*. The numeric value of *expN2* is the number of bytes to read, starting from the current position of the file pointer. (Use the FOPEN() function to open the file and assign a handle.)

Related Functions

FCREATE(), FCLOSE(), FOPEN(), FREAD(), FSEEK(), FWRITE()

GETBAR

Syntax

Version 2

GETBAR(*expC, expN*)

The GETBAR() function returns the number of a bar at a specific position in a popup menu. This function can be useful when popup options have been added, removed, or rearranged. *ExpC* denotes the popup name, and *expN* denotes a position within the popup.

GETENV

Syntax

GETENV(*expC*)

The GETENV() function returns a character string that contains the contents of the DOS environmental variable named as the character expression *expC*.

Example

```
? GETENV("path")
E:\PCWRITE;E:\PERFECT;E:\WINDOWS;E:\DOS;E:
```

Related Functions

DISKSPACE(), FULLPATH(), OS(), VERSION()

GETFILE

Syntax

GETFILE([*expC1*][, *expC2*])

The GETFILE() function causes the FoxPro Open File dialog box to be displayed. Using the dialog box, a file may be chosen. The function then returns the name of the chosen file. *ExpC1* is an optional extension; if used, only files with that extension will appear in the list box. *ExpC2* is an optional prompt that appears at the top of the Open File dialog box.

Related Functions

FULLPATH(), PUTFILE()

GETPAD

Syntax

GETPAD(*expC*, *expN*)

Version 2

The GETPAD() function returns the name of a menu pad at a specific position in a bar menu. This function can be useful when menu pads have been added, removed, or rearranged. *ExpC* denotes the menu name, and *expN* denotes a position within the menu.

GOMONTH

Syntax

GOMONTH(*expD*, *expN*)

The GOMONTH() function returns a date that is *expN* months before or after *expD*. If *expN* is positive, the date returned is *expN* months after *expD*. If *expN* is negative, the date returned is *expN* months before *expD*.

Related Function

DATE()

HEADER

Syntax

HEADER([*alias*])

The HEADER() function returns the number of bytes in the header of the database open in the current work area. If no database is open in the specified work area, zero is returned. Use the optional *alias* to return the bytes in the header of a file open in a different work area.

Related Functions

DISKSPACE(), FSIZE(), RECOUNT(), RECSIZE()

IIF

Syntax

IIF(*expL*, *expr1*, *expr2*)

The IIF() function (Immediate IF) returns the value of *expr1* if the logical expression is true and returns the value of *expr2* if the logical expression is false. *Expr1* and *expr2* must be of the same data type.

INKEY

Syntax

INKEY([*expN*])

The INKEY() function returns an integer value between 0 and 255. This value corresponds to the decimal ASCII code for the key that was pressed. A zero will be returned if no key has been pressed.

Related Functions

CHR(), LASTKEY(), NEXTKEY(), READKEY()

INLIST

Syntax

INLIST(*expr1*, *expr2*[, *expr3*...])

The INLIST() function determines if an expression is contained in a series of expressions. INLIST() returns a logical true (.T.) if *expr1* is contained in the list of expressions *expr2*, *expr3*, and so on. The expressions must all be of the same data type.

Related Functions

BETWEEN(), OCCURS()

INSMODE

Syntax

INSMODE([*expL*])

The INSMODE() function changes the Insert/Overwrite mode based on *expL*. INSMODE(.T.) turns on the Insert mode, and INSMODE(.F.) turns off the Insert mode. If *expL* is omitted, the function returns the Insert mode setting. If the Insert mode is on, .T. is returned. If the Insert mode is off, .F. is returned.

Related Functions

CAPSLOCK(), NUMLOCK()

INT

Syntax

INT(*expN*)

The INT() function returns the integer portion of *expN*. No rounding occurs; any decimal values are simply dropped.

Example

```
STORE 12.9957 TO NUMBER
12.9957
? NUMBER
        12.9957
? INT(NUMBER)
         12
STORE -11.878 TO NUMBER
-11.878
? NUMBER
        -11.878
? INT(NUMBER)
        -11
```

Related Functions

CEILING(), FLOOR(), ROUND()

ISALPHA

Syntax

ISALPHA(*expC*)

The ISALPHA() function returns a logical true (.T.) if the first character of *expC* is "a"-"z" or "A"-"Z." A logical false (.F.) is returned if *expC* begins with a nonalphabetic or a numeric character.

Example

```
? ISALPHA("words12345")
.T.
? ISALPHA("12345words")
.F.
```

Related Functions

ISLOWER(), ISUPPER(), LOWER(), UPPER()

ISCOLOR

Syntax

ISCOLOR()

The ISCOLOR() function returns a logical true (.T.) if the system has color capability (whether or not a color monitor is being used) and returns a logical false (.F.) if the system has only monochrome capability.

ISDIGIT

Syntax

ISDIGIT(*expC*)

The ISDIGIT() function returns a logical true (.T.) if the first character of *expC* is a digit (0 to 9).

Related Function

ISALPHA()

ISLOWER

Syntax

ISLOWER(*expC*)

The ISLOWER() function returns a logical true (.T.) if the first character in *expC* is a lowercase alphabetical character, or a logical false (.F.) if the first character is anything other than a lowercase alphabetical character.

Example

```
? Lastname
Moore
? ISLOWER(Lastname)
.F.
? ISLOWER("lowercase letters")
.T.
```

Related Functions

ISALPHA(), ISUPPER(), LOWER(), UPPER()

ISUPPER

Syntax

ISUPPER(*expC*)

The ISUPPER() function returns a logical true (.T.) if the first character in *expC* is an uppercase alphabetical character, and a logical false (.F.) if the first character is anything other than an uppercase alphabetical character.

Example

```
? Lastname
Moore
? ISUPPER(Lastname)
```

```
.T.
? ISUPPER("lowercase letters")
.F.
```

Related Functions

ISALPHA(), ISLOWER(), LOWER(), UPPER()

KEY

Syntax

KEY(*expN*[, *alias*])

The KEY() function returns the index expression of the specified index file. The numeric expression identifies the index file, where 1 is the first index file opened, 2 is the second index file opened, and so on. Use the *alias* option to return the key expression for an index file that is open in a different work area.

LASTKEY

Syntax

LASTKEY()

The LASTKEY() function returns the decimal ASCII value for the last key pressed. LASTKEY() can be useful for determining the key used to terminate a wait state. The LASTKEY() function returns the same ASCII values as the INKEY() function.

Related Functions

INKEY(), READKEY()

LEFT

Syntax

LEFT(*expC, expN*)

The LEFT() function returns the leftmost number of characters specified in *expN* from the character expression *expC,* starting with the first or leftmost character.

Example

```
USE MEMBERS
GO 5
? ADDRESS
270 Browning Ave #3C
? LEFT(ADDRESS,12)
270 Browning
```

Related Functions

AT(), LTRIM(), RTRIM(), RIGHT(), SUBSTR()

LEN

Syntax

LEN(*expC*)

The LEN() function returns the length of a character string expression specified in *expC. ExpC* can be a memo field name, in which case the length of the text stored within the memo field is returned. Note that in the case of character fields, LEN() returns the length of the field, not the length of the text within the field. With character fields, you must add a TRIM() function to get the length of the text stored in the field.

Example

```
? LEN("This text string has 35 characters.")
    35
```

Related Functions

ASC(), AT(), FSIZE(), TRIM()

LIKE

Syntax

LIKE(*expC1*, *expC2*)

The LIKE() function compares two character expressions and returns a logical true (.T.) if the character string in *expC2* contains the characters in *expC1*. The pattern can include the wildcard characters * (representing any sequence of characters) and ? (representing any single character).

Related Functions

AT(), ATC(), RAT()

LINENO

Syntax

LINENO()

The LINENO() function returns the line number of the next statement in the program that is currently running.

Related Functions

ERROR(), MESSAGE(), PROGRAM()

LOCFILE

Syntax

LOCFILE(*expC1*[, *expC2*][, *expC3*])

Version 2

The LOCFILE() function locates a disk file, and returns the filename along with the complete search path. To be found, the file must be in the current directory or somewhere in the FoxPro path. If the specified file cannot be found, the Open File dialog box appears so a manual search can be attempted. *ExpC1* indicates the filename. The optional *expC2* specifies extensions of files to be displayed in the Open File dialog box. The optional *expC3* is a prompt to be displayed at the top of the Open File dialog box.

LOG

Syntax

LOG(*expN*)

The LOG() function returns the natural logarithm of a number specified by *expN*. *ExpN* must be greater than zero. Use the SET DECIMALS command to specify the number of decimal places returned.

Example

```
? LOG(6)
1.79
? LOG(1)
0.00
? LOG(10)
2.30
```

Related Functions

EXP(), LOG10()

LOG10

Syntax

LOG10(*expN*)

The LOG10() function returns the common (base 10) logarithm of a number specified by *expN*. *ExpN* must be greater than zero. Use the SET DECIMALS command to specify the number of decimal places returned.

Related Functions

EXP(), LOG()

LOWER

Syntax

LOWER(*expC*)

The LOWER() function converts all uppercase letters in *expC* to lowercase. The function will not affect nonalphabetic characters. The LOWER() function does not change the way the data is stored unless you use it as part of a STORE or REPLACE command. The function is generally used for finding or comparing data, when you do not know the case of the original data.

Example

```
STORE "UPPERCASE LETTERS" TO TEXT
? TEXT
UPPERCASE LETTERS
? LOWER(TEXT)
uppercase letters
```

Related Functions

ISALPHA(), ISLOWER(), ISUPPER(), UPPER()

LTRIM

Syntax

LTRIM(*expC*)

The LTRIM() function trims all leading blanks from the character expression defined as *expC*.

Example

```
STORE "        TEN LEADING SPACES" TO TEXT
? TEXT
        TEN LEADING SPACES
? LTRIM(TEXT)
TEN LEADING SPACES
```

Related Functions

ALLTRIM(), LEFT(), RIGHT(), RTRIM(), SUBSTR(), TRIM()

LUPDATE

Syntax

LUPDATE([*alias*])

The LUPDATE() function returns the last update of the active database. Use the optional *alias* to return the last update for a file open in a different work area.

Example

```
USE BOOKS
? LUPDATE()
01/15/90
EDIT
CLOSE DATABASES
USE BOOKS ? LUPDATE()
11/18/90
```

Related Functions

DBF(), RECCOUNT()

MAX

Syntax

MAX(*expr1*, *expr2*[, *expr3*...])

The MAX() function returns the maximum value from the list of expressions. The expressions must all be of the same data type. The expressions can be numeric or date expressions; if date expressions are used, MAX() returns the later of the dates.

Example

```
STORE 87 TO A
STORE 95 TO B
? MAX(A,B)
        95
```

Related Function

MIN()

MCOL()

Syntax

MCOL([*expC*])

The MCOL() function returns a value representing the column location of the mouse pointer, in the screen or within a window. The optional *expC* denotes the name of the window. If *expC* is omitted, the column coordinate of the mouse pointer relative to the entire screen is returned by the function. If *expC* is used, the column coordinate of the mouse pointer relative to the named window is returned. If the mouse pointer lies outside a window and the window is named, MCOL() returns a value of −1.

Related Functions

COL(), MROW(), ROW(), WCOLS(), WROWS()

MDOWN()

Syntax

MDOWN()

The MDOWN() function returns a logical value representing the state of the left mouse button. If the left mouse button is pressed, MDOWN() returns a logical true (.T.); otherwise, MDOWN() returns a logical false (.F.).

Related Functions

MCOL(), MROW()

MDX()

Syntax

Version 2

MDX(*expN*[, *alias*])

The MDX() function returns the names of open compound index (.CDX) files. The MDX() function is identical in operation to the CDX() function. *ExpN* is a numeric value that identifies the desired compound-index file according to the following possibilities: If the database has a structural compound-index file and *expN1* is 1, the name of the structural compound-index file is returned. If *expN1* is 2, the name of the first .CDX compound-index file (as identified by the INDEX clause of the USE command, or the SET INDEX command) is returned. If *expN1* is 3, the second .CDX compound-index file name is returned, and so forth. If *expN1* is greater than the number of open .CDX compound-index files, the function returns a null string.

If the database does not have a structural compound-index file and *expN1* is 1, the name of the first .CDX compound-index file (as identified by the INDEX clause of the USE command, or by the SET INDEX command) is returned. If *expN1* is 2, the second .CDX compound-index file name is returned, and so forth. If *expN1* is greater than the number of open .CDX compound-index files, the function returns a null string.

Use the *alias* option to return the names of compound-index files open in different work areas.

MDY

Syntax

MDY(*expD*)

The MDY() function returns a *Month DD, YY* (or *Month DD, YYYY*) character string for a given date expression. The month is always spelled out, and the day always takes the *DD* format. If SET CENTURY is OFF, the year takes the *YY* format; otherwise, the year takes the *YYYY* format.

Example

```
? DATE()
04/15/90
? MDY(DATE())
April 15, 90
```

Related Functions

DATE(), DMY()

MEMLINES

Syntax

MEMLINES(*expC*)

The MEMLINES() function returns the number of lines in *expC*, the memo field for the current record. Note that the number of lines in the memo field will be affected by the current value of SET MEMOWIDTH.

Example

```
SET MEMOWIDTH TO 20
? COMMENTS
Discusses FoxBase
Plus, how to create
```

```
data files, how to
search for data,
print reports, build
simple applications.

? MEMLINES(COMMENTS)
        6

SET MEMOWIDTH TO 40
? COMMENTS
Discusses FoxBase Plus, how to create
data files, how to search for data,
print reports, build simple
applications.

? MEMLINES(COMMENTS)
        4
```

Related Function

MLINE()

MEMORY

Syntax

MEMORY()

The MEMORY() function returns the amount of free conventional memory as a numeric value in kilobytes.

Related Function

SYS()

MENU

Syntax

MENU()

The MENU() function returns the name of the currently active menu. If a menu is not active, MENU() returns a null string ("").

Related Function
PAD()

MESSAGE

Syntax

MESSAGE([1])

The MESSAGE() function returns the current error message, which is useful for situations in which FoxPro detects an error within a program. The MESSAGE() function can be used along with the ON ERROR command for error-trapping and recovery purposes. The optional argument of 1 tells FoxPro to return the actual program code for the last line that caused the ON ERROR condition.

Related Function
ERROR()

MIN

Syntax

MIN(*expr1*, *expr2*[, *expr3*...])

The MIN() function returns the minimum value expression from the list of expressions. The expressions must all be of the same data type. The expressions can be numeric or date expressions; if date expressions are used, MIN() returns the earlier of the dates.

Example

```
STORE 87 TO A
STORE 95 TO B
? MIN(A,B)
        87
```

Related Function

MAX()

MLINE

Syntax

MLINE(*expC*, *expN*)

The MLINE() function returns the specified line *expN* from *expC*, the memo field in the current record. Note that the value of SET MEMOWIDTH will affect the number of lines in a memo field.

Example

```
? COMMENTS
Discusses FoxBase Plus, how to create
data files, how to search for data,
print reports, build simple
applications.

? MLINE(COMMENTS,2)
data files, how to search for data,
```

Related Function

MEMLINES()

MOD

Syntax

MOD(*expN1*, *expN2*)

The MOD() function returns the remainder when *expN1* is divided by *expN2*. A positive number is returned if *expN2* is positive, and a negative number is returned if *expN2* is negative. If there is no remainder, a zero is returned.

Example

```
? MOD(22,5)
  2
```

Related Function

INT()

MONTH

Syntax

MONTH(*expD*)

The MONTH() function returns the numeric month (1 to 12) that corresponds to the date expression. The numbers 1 through 12 correspond to January through December.

Example

```
? DATE()
04/15/90
? MONTH(DATE())
  4
```

Related Functions

CMONTH(), DATE(), DMY(), MDY(), YEAR()

MRKBAR

Syntax

Version 2

MRKBAR(*expC, expN*)

The MRKBAR() function returns a logical value, indicating whether a specific bar of a popup menu is marked. (The SET MARK command can be used to mark or unmark a popup bar.) *ExpC* is the name of the popup menu. *ExpN* is the number that identifies the specific bar of the menu. If the bar is marked, the function returns a logical true (.T.); otherwise, the function returns a logical false (.F.).

MRKPAD

Syntax

Version 2

MRKPAD(*expC1, expC2*)

The MRKPAD() function returns a logical value, indicating whether a specific pad of a bar menu is marked. (The SET MARK command can be used to mark or unmark a menu pad.) *ExpC1* is the name of the menu bar. *ExpC2* is the pad name. If the pad is marked, the function returns a logical true (.T.); otherwise, the function returns a logical false (.F.).

MROW()

Syntax

MROW(*expC*)

The MROW() function returns a value representing the row location of the mouse pointer, in the screen or in a window. The optional *expC* denotes the name of the window. If *expC* is omitted, the row coordinate of the mouse pointer relative to the entire screen is returned by the function. If *expC* is used, the row coordinate of the mouse pointer relative to the named window is returned. If the mouse pointer lies outside a window and the window is named, MROW() returns a value of −1.

Related Functions

COL(), MCOL(), ROW(), WCOLS(), WROWS()

NDX()

Syntax

NDX(*expN*[, *alias*])

The NDX() function returns the name of an open index file in the current work area. The numeric expression *expN* specifies the order of the index file, 1 being the first index file opened, 2 the second index file opened, and so on. You can use the optional *alias* to return the name of an open index file in a different work area.

Example

```
USE MEMBERS INDEX NAMES, SOCIAL, ZIPS
? NDX(1)
D:\FOXPRO\NAMES.IDX
? NDX(2)
D:\FOXPRO\SOCIAL.IDX
? NDX(3)
D:\FOXPRO\ZIPS.IDX
```

Related Functions

DBF(), MDX(), SELECT()

NUMLOCK

Syntax

NUMLOCK([*expL*])

The NUMLOCK() function changes the Num Lock keyboard mode or returns the status of the Num Lock mode. NUMLOCK(.T.) turns on Num Lock, and NUMLOCK(.F.) turns off Num Lock. If the logical expression *expL* is omitted, NUMLOCK() returns the status of the Num Lock mode.

Related Functions

CAPSLOCK(), INSMODE()

OBJNUM

Syntax

Version 2

OBJNUM(*expC*[, *expN*])

The OBJNUM() function returns the object number of a GET object. (GET objects such as fields, check boxes, pushbuttons, and radio buttons are assigned object numbers, in the order in which they are created.) *ExpC* is the name of the variable used to create the GET object. When nested READs are used, the optional argument of *expN* can be used to specify an object at a different READ level.

OCCURS

Syntax

OCCURS(*expC1*, *expC2*)

The OCCURS() function returns an integer that represents the number of times *expC1* occurs in *expC2*. If *expC1* is not found in *expC2*, the function returns a zero.

Related Function

INLIST()

ORDER

Syntax

ORDER([*alias*])

ORDER() returns the name of the master (or active) index file in the current work area. Use the optional *alias* to return the name of the active index in a different work area.

Example

```
USE BOOKS
INDEX ON TITLE TAG TITLES
? ORDER()
TITLES
```

Related Functions

KEY(), NDX()

OS

Syntax

OS()

The OS() function returns the name and version of the current operating system.

Example

```
? "This computer is using: " + OS()
This computer is using: DOS 03.30
```

Related Functions

GETENV(), VERSION()

PAD

Syntax

PAD()

The PAD() function returns the name of the pad last chosen from the active menu bar. The function returns a null string if no menu is active.

Related Functions

BAR(), MENU(), PROMPT()

PADC, PADL, PADR

Syntax

PADC(*expression, expN[, expC]*)
PADL(*expression, expN[, expC]*)
PADR(*expression, expN[, expC]*)

These functions are used to pad the expression supplied as *expression* with a designated character on the left side, the right side, or on both sides. *ExpN* specifies the total length of the resulting string. The *expression* is padded with blanks unless an optional character is supplied as *expC*; if provided, the optional character is used to pad the expression. Use PADC() to pad an expression on both sides; use PADL() to pad an expression on the left side; and use PADR() to pad an expression on the right side. You can pad character, date, or numeric expressions with these functions; however, the returned value will always be a character string.

Related Functions
ALLTRIM(), LEFT(), LTRIM(), RIGHT(), STUFF(), TRIM()

PARAMETERS

Syntax

PARAMETERS()

The PARAMETERS() function returns a numeric value indicating the number of parameters passed to the procedure most recently called.

Related Function
PCOUNT()

PAYMENT

Syntax

PAYMENT(*expN1*, *expN2*, *expN3*)

The PAYMENT() function returns the amount of a loan payment. PAYMENT() assumes that the interest rate is constant and that payments are made at the end of each period. *ExpN1* is the principal amount, *expN2* is the interest rate, and *expN3* is the number of payments. If the payments are compounded monthly and the interest rate is compounded yearly, divide the interest rate by 12 to get the proper results.

Example

```
STORE 10000.00 TO PRINCIPAL
STORE .01 TO INTEREST
STORE 48 TO PERIODS
? PAYMENT(PRINCIPAL,INTEREST,PERIODS)
        263.34
```

Related Functions

FV(), PV()

PCOL

Syntax

PCOL()

The PCOL() function returns the current column position of the printer.

Related Functions

COL(), PROW(), ROW()

PI

Syntax

PI()

The PI() function returns the numeric constant pi (approximately 3.14159).

Example

```
? PI()
        3.14
SET DECIMALS TO 15
? PI()
        3.141592653589790
```

POPUP

Syntax

POPUP()

The POPUP() function returns the name of the active popup menu.

Related Function
BAR()

PRINTSTATUS

Syntax

PRINTSTATUS()

The PRINTSTATUS() function returns a logical true (.T.) if the printer is ready and a logical false (.F.) if it is not.

Related Functions
ISPRINTER(), PRINTER()

PRMBAR

Syntax

PRMBAR(*expC, expN*)

Version 2

The PRMBAR() function returns the prompt text for a specific option of a popup menu. *ExpC* denotes the popup name, and *expN* denotes the bar number of the popup menu.

PRMPAD

Syntax

Version 2

PRMPAD(*expC1*, *expC2*)

The PRMPAD() function returns the prompt text for a specific pad of a bar menu. *ExpC1* denotes the menu name, and *expC2* denotes the pad name in the bar menu.

PROGRAM

Syntax

PROGRAM([*expN*])

The PROGRAM() function returns the name of the program currently running or the program that was running when an error occurred. The optional *expN* can be used for nesting programs (calling a program from a program). When used, the value of *expN* indicates how many levels back FoxPro should go to get the program name.

Related Functions

ERROR(), LINENO(), MESSAGE(), PROCNAME()

PROMPT

Syntax

PROMPT()

The PROMPT() function returns the prompt for the last option chosen from the active menu pad or popup menu. The function returns a null string if no popup menu is active.

Related Functions

BAR(), POPUP()

PROPER

Syntax

PROPER(*expC*)

The PROPER() function returns the character expression specified in *expC* with initial capitals. Each word in the character string has the first letter capitalized and the remaining letters in lowercase.

Related Functions

LOWER(), UPPER()

PROW

Syntax

PROW()

The PROW() function returns the current row position of the printer. Note that when an EJECT command is issued, PROW() is reset to zero.

Related Functions

COL(), FCOL(), FROW(), PCOL(), ROW()

PUTFILE

Syntax

PUTFILE([*expC1*][, *expC2*][, *expC3*])

The PUTFILE() function displays the Save As dialog box. The user can enter or choose a filename, which is returned as a character expression by the function. The optional *expC1* argument is a prompt string that, if used, appears above the text box. The optional *expC2* argument is a default filename that appears in the text box. The optional *expC3* argument is a default file extension.

Related Function

GETFILE()

PV

Syntax

PV(*expN1*, *expN2*, *expN3*)

The PV() function returns the present value of an investment, or the amount that must be invested to earn a known future value. *ExpN1* is the payment made each period, *expN2* is the interest rate, and *expN3* is the number of periods. If the payments are compounded monthly and the interest rate is yearly, divide the interest rate by 12 to get the proper results.

Example

```
STORE 100 TO PAYMENT
STORE .2 TO RATE
STORE 12 TO PERIODS
? PV(PAYMENT,RATE,PERIODS)
      443.92
```

Related Functions

FV(), PMT()

RAND

Syntax

RAND([*expN*])

The RAND() function returns a random number between 0 and 1. The optional numeric expression, *expN*, can be used to provide a seed different than the default for generating the random number. A given seed will always produce the same sequence of random numbers. You can vary the sequence of random numbers by varying the seed. If *expN* is any negative value, the seed is taken from the system clock.

To obtain a random number in a particular range, multiply the result of the RAND() function by a chosen value. For example, you could get a random number between 50 and 100 by using INT((RAND()*50)+50).

Example

```
? RAND()
        0.83
? RAND()
        0.38
? RAND()
        0.26
? RAND()
        0.96
? RAND()
        0.45
```

RAT

Syntax

RAT(*expC1*, *expC2*[, *expN*])

The RAT() function (Reverse AT()) searches *expC2*, starting from the right, for the *expN*th occurrence of the character string *expC1*. The function returns as an integer the position where *expC1* is found. If *expC1* is not found in *expC2* the specified number of times, the function returns a zero. If *expN* is omitted, the default is 1.

Related Functions

AT(), LEFT(), RIGHT(), SUBSTR()

RATLINE

Syntax

RATLINE(*expC1*, *expC2*)

The RATLINE() function (Reverse ATLINE()) searches *expC2* for the last occurrence of *expC1*. The function returns the line number of the line where *expC1* was found. If *expC1* is not found in *expC2*, the function returns a zero. Note that *expC2* can be a memo field.

Related Functions

AT(), ATLINE(), LEFT(), RAT(), RIGHT(), SUBSTR()

RDLEVEL

Syntax

Version 2

RDLEVEL()

The RDLEVEL() function returns a numeric value representing the level of the current READ. (READs can be nested up to four levels deep in FoxPro 2.)

READKEY

Syntax

READKEY()

The READKEY() function returns an integer value that indicates the key pressed when exiting from the editing commands APPEND, BROWSE, CHANGE, CREATE, EDIT, INSERT, MODIFY, and READ. READKEY() provides a value between 0 and 36 if no changes were made to the data or a value between 256 and 292 if changes were made to the data.

Related Function

INKEY()

RECCOUNT

Syntax

RECCOUNT([*alias*])

The RECCOUNT() function returns the number of records in the database open in the current work area. If no database is open, RECCOUNT() returns a zero. Use the optional *alias* to return the number of records in a database open in a different work area.

Example

```
USE MEMBERS
? RECCOUNT()
        8
```

Related Function

RECSIZE()

RECNO

Syntax

RECNO([*alias*])

The RECNO() function returns the current record number. Use the optional *alias* to return the current record number in a database open in a different work area. Note that RECNO(0) can follow an unsuccessful SEEK to determine what record number to return. If a SEEK is unsuccessful, the use of RECNO(0) immediately after the SEEK returns the record number of the closest matching record.

Example

```
USE MEMBERS
? RECNO()
        1
GO 5
? RECNO()
        5
GO BOTTOM
? RECNO()
        8
```

Related Functions

LASTREC(), RECCOUNT()

RECSIZE

Syntax

RECSIZE([*alias*])

The RECSIZE() function returns the size of the database record in the current work area. Use the optional *alias* to return the size of the database record for a database open in a different work area. If no database is open, RECSIZE() returns a zero.

Example

```
USE MEMBERS
LIST STRUCTURE
Structure for database: D:\FOXPRO\MEMBERS.DBF
Number of data records:       8
Date of last update   : 04/15/90
Field  Field Name  Type      Width    Dec
    1  SOCIAL      Character    11
    2  LASTNAME    Character    15
    3  FIRSTNAME   Character    15
    4  ADDRESS     Character    25
    5  CITY        Character    15
```

```
 6  STATE       Character    2
 7  ZIPCODE     Character   10
 8  PHONE       Character   12
 9  BIRTHDAY    Date         8
10  EXPIREDATE  Date         8
11  TAPELIMIT   Numeric      2
12  BETA        Logical      1
13  PREFERENCE  Memo        10
** Total **                135

. ? RECSIZE()
      135
```

Related Function

RECCOUNT()

RELATION

Syntax

RELATION(*expN*[, *alias*])

The RELATION() function returns the relational expression for the *N*th relation of the work area identified by *alias*. Use the optional *alias* to specify a different work-area number, work-area letter, or alias name. If no relation exists, the function returns a null string.

Related Functions

FILTER(), TARGET()

REPLICATE

Syntax

REPLICATE(*expC, expN*)

The REPLICATE() function returns a character string consisting of *expC* repeated *expN* times. The maximum value of *expN* is 65,504 characters.

Example

```
? REPLICATE("*",25)
*************************
? REPLICATE("*",50)
** **************************************************
```

Related Function

SPACE()

RIGHT

Syntax

RIGHT(*expC or memvar, expN*)

The RIGHT() function returns the rightmost part of the character string *expC* or memory variable *memvar*. Use the numeric expression *expN* to specify the number of characters that will be returned.

Example

```
? RIGHT("a few words",5)
words
```

Related Functions

AT(), LEFT(), LTRIM(), RTRIM(), STUFF(), SUBSTR(), TRIM()

ROUND

Syntax

ROUND(*expN1*, *expN2*)

The ROUND() function rounds off the number supplied in *expN1*. Use *expN2* to specify the number of decimal places to round off to. If *expN2* is negative, the rounded number returned is a whole number.

Example

```
? ROUND(32.7567,2)
 32.7600
? ROUND(32.7567,1)
 32.8000
? ROUND(32.7567,-1)
 30.0000
```

Related Functions

CEILING(), FLOOR(), INT()

ROW

Syntax

ROW()

The ROW() function returns the current row location of the cursor.

Related Functions

COL(), FCOL(), FROW(), PCOL(), PROW()

RTOD

Syntax

RTOD(*expN*)

The RTOD() function converts radians to degrees. The numeric expression *expN* is the value in radians, and the value returned by the function is the equivalent value in degrees.

Example

```
? RTOD(3.14159)
      180.00
```

Related Functions

COS(), DTOR(), SIN(), TAN()

RTRIM

Syntax

RTRIM(*expC*)

The RTRIM() function strips the trailing spaces from the named character string, *expC*. The RTRIM() function is identical to the TRIM function.

Related Functions

ALLTRIM(), LEFT(), LTRIM(), STUFF(), SUBSTR(), TRIM()

SCHEME

Syntax

SCHEME(*expN1*[, *expN2*])

The SCHEME() function returns a color-pair list or a color pair from a color scheme. To return the complete color-pair listing for a color scheme, provide the color-scheme number as *expN1*. To return a single pair listing from a color scheme, provide the optional argument *expN2*, which is the position of the color pair in the color-pair list.

SCOLS

Syntax

SCOLS()

The SCOLS() function returns the number of columns available on the display screen. The SCOLS() function is useful when writing programs that will operate on systems with enhanced display adapters having more than 80 columns available; use SCOLS() to determine the number of available columns. On standard hardware, SCOLS() returns a value of 80.

Related Functions

COL(), ROW(), SROWS(), WCOLS(), WROWS()

SECONDS

Syntax

SECONDS()

The SECONDS() function returns the value of the system clock in the number of seconds past 12 o'clock midnight, using a *seconds.thousandths* format.

Related Function

TIME()

SEEK

Syntax

SEEK(*expression*[, *alias*])

The SEEK() function returns a logical true (.T.) if the search *expression* can be found in the active index. If the search *expression* is not found, the function returns a logical false (.F.), and the record pointer is placed at the end of the file. Use the optional *alias* to search an open index in a different work area.

Related Functions

EOF(), FOUND(), LOOKUP()

SELECT

Syntax

SELECT()

The SELECT() function returns the number of the current work area if SET COMPATIBLE is OFF. If SET COMPATIBLE is ON, the function returns the number of the highest unused work area.

Related Function

ALIAS()

SET

Syntax

SET(*expC*[, 1])

The SET() function returns the status of the various SET commands. The character expression *expC* contains the name of the desired SET command. Note that you need to use quotes around *expC* if it is a character string rather than a memory variable. Using SET without the optional argument returns the ON/OFF setting. Using SET() with the optional argument ([,1]) returns the SET TO setting.

Example

```
? SET("BELL")
ON
? SET("CONFIRM")
OFF
```

SIGN

Syntax

SIGN(*expN*)

SIGN() returns a numeric value that represents the sign of the numeric expression. If *expN* is positive, SIGN() returns a value of 1. If *expN* is negative, SIGN() returns a value of −1. If *expN* is zero, SIGN() returns a zero.

Example

```
? SIGN(32)
        1
? SIGN(-45.667)
       -1
? SIGN(0)
        0
```

Related Function

ABS()

SIN

Syntax

SIN(*expN*)

The SIN() function returns the sine of *expN*, where *expN* is an angle measured in radians. To convert degrees to radians, use the DTOR() function.

Example

```
? SIN((3.14159)/2)
       1.00
```

Related Functions

ASIN(), COS(), DTOR(), PI(), RTOD(), TAN()

SOUNDEX

Syntax

SOUNDEX(*expC*)

The SOUNDEX() function returns a four-character string that represents the phonetic SOUNDEX() code for the character expression *expC*. The four-character code returned by the SOUNDEX() function can be useful for finding similar-sounding names or for building an index to perform lookups based on the sound of a word.

Example

```
? SOUNDEX("Cathy")
C300 ? SOUNDEX("Kathy")
K300
? SOUNDEX("Sears")
S620
? SOUNDEX("Seers")
S620
```

Related Functions

DIFFERENCE(), LIKE()

SPACE

Syntax

SPACE(*expN*)

The SPACE() function returns a character string containing the specified number of blank spaces. The maximum number of spaces that can be specified by *expN* is 65,504.

Example

```
? SPACE(10) + "a few words..."
          a few words...
? SPACE(20) + "a few words..."
                    a few words...
? SPACE(30) + "a few words..."
                              a few words...
```

Related Functions

PADC(), PADL(), PADR(), REPLICATE()

SQRT

Syntax

SQRT(*expN*)

The SQRT() function returns the square root of the numeric expression *expN*. The numeric expression must be a positive number.

Example

```
? SQRT(9)
3.00
? SQRT(36)
 6.00
? SQRT(50)
 7.07
```

Related Function

ABS()

SROWS

Syntax

SROWS()

The SROWS() function returns a numeric value representing the number of rows available on the screen. The SROWS() function is useful for writing programs that will operate on systems with enhanced display adapters having more than 25 rows available; use SROWS() to determine the number of available rows. On standard CGA or monochrome monitors, SROWS() returns a value of 25.

Related Functions

COL(), ROW(), SCOLS(), WCOLS(), WROWS()

STR

Syntax

STR(*expN1*[, *expN2*[, *expN3*]])

The STR() function converts a numeric expression to a character expression, where *expN1* is the numeric expression to be converted to a character string. Use the optional *expN2* to specify a length (including the decimal point and decimal places), and use the optional *expN3* to specify a number of decimal places.

Example

```
STORE 987.65 TO NUMBER
987.65
? "The number is: " + STR(NUMBER)
The number is:        988
```

Related Function

VAL()

STRTRAN

Syntax

STRTRAN(*expC1*, *expC2*[, *expC3*][, *expN1*][, *expN2*])

The STRTRAN() function performs a search-and-replace operation on a character string. The function returns the given expression *expC1* with occurrences of *expC2* replaced with *expC3*. If *expC3* is omitted, the found text is replaced with a null string ("").

Replacements start at the *expN1*th occurrence and continue for a total of *expN2* replacements. If *expN1* is omitted, replacements start at the beginning of the string. If *expN2* is omitted, all needed replacements are made.

Related Functions

AT(), RAT(), SUBSTR()

STUFF

Syntax

STUFF(*expC1*, *expN1*, *expN2*, *expC2*)

The STUFF() function inserts or removes characters from any part of a character string. *ExpC1* is the existing character string, *expN1* is the starting position in the string, *expN2* is the number of characters to remove, and *expC2* is the character string to insert.

Example

```
STORE "This is missing words" TO TEXT1
STORE "a few " TO TEXT2
? STUFF(TEXT1,17,0,TEXT2)
This is missing a few words
```

Related Functions

AT(), LEFT(), PADC(), PADL(), PADR(), RAT(), RIGHT(), STRTRAN(), SUBSTR()

SUBSTR

Syntax

SUBSTR(*expC, expN1*[, *expN2*])

The SUBSTR() function extracts a portion of a string from a character expression. *ExpC* is the character expression to extract the string from, *expN1* is the starting position in the expression, and *expN2* is the number of characters to extract from the expression.

Example

```
USE MEMBERS
GO 6
? ADDRESS
1617 Arlington Blvd
? SUBSTR(ADDRESS,6,9)
Arlington
```

Related Functions

AT(), LEFT(), RAT(), RIGHT(), STRTRAN(), STUFF()

SYS

Syntax

SYS(*expN*)

The SYS() functions return character strings that contain various system data. *ExpN* is a numeric value that corresponds to the appropriate system function. The more commonly used system functions are shown here. Consult your FoxPro documentation for a complete listing.

SYS(1)	Returns the current system date
SYS(2)	Returns the number of seconds since midnight
SYS(3)	Returns a unique legal filename
SYS(5)	Returns the current default device
SYS(6)	Returns the current print device
SYS(7)	Returns the name of the current format file
SYS(9)	Returns your FoxPro serial number
SYS(12)	Returns the amount of free memory
SYS(13)	Returns the printer status
SYS(23)	Returns the amount of EMS memory used by FoxPro
SYS(24)	Returns the EMS limit specified in CONFIG.FP
SYS(2003)	Returns the current directory name
SYS(2006)	Returns the type of graphics hardware in use

Related Functions

GETENV(), MEMORY(), OS(), VERSION()

TAG

Syntax

TAG([*expC*,] *expN*[, *alias*])

Version 2

The TAG() function returns tag names from compound-index files (.CDX) or it returns the names of open index (.IDX) files. The optional .CDX filename argument, *expC*, when used, lets you return the tag names from a specific

compound-index file. *ExpN* denotes the order of the tag; if *expN* is 1, the name of the first tag in the compound-index file is retrieved; if *expN* is 2, the name of the second tag in the compound-index file is retrieved; and so on. Use the optional *alias* to return tag names from index files open in different work areas.

If the .CDX filename argument is omitted, the TAG function first returns names of the .IDX files (based on their order specified by the USE command or the SET INDEX command). Next, the function returns tag names from the structural compound-index file, if there is one. Finally, the function returns tag names from other compound-index files, in the order that the tags were created and in the order the compound-index files were identified with the USE and/or SET INDEX commands.

TAN

Syntax

TAN(*expN*)

The TAN() function returns the tangent of *expN*, where *expN* is measured in radians. To convert degrees to radians, use the DTOR() function.

Example

```
? TAN(PI())
        0
```

Related Functions

ACOS(), ASIN(), ATAN(), ATN2(), COS(), DTOR(), RTOD(), SIN()

TARGET

Syntax

TARGET(*expN*[, *expression*])

The TARGET() function returns the alias of the work area that is the target of the *N*th relation from the work area specified by *expression*. Use the optional *expression* to specify another work area by alias, number, or letter. If *expression* is omitted, the current work area is used. If the relation specified by the function does not exist, a zero is returned.

Related Functions
ALIAS(), RELATION()

TIME

Syntax

TIME([*expN*])

The TIME() function returns the current system time in the format of *HH:MM:SS* (if SET HOURS is set to 24) or in the format of *HH:MM:SS* am/pm (if SET HOURS is set to 12). If you include the optional numeric argument *expN*, the function's result includes hundredths of a second. (Note, however, that maximum accuracy of the clock is about 1/18th of a second.)

Related Functions
DATE(), SECONDS()

TRANSFORM

Syntax

TRANSFORM(*expression, expC*)

The TRANSFORM() function formats character strings or numbers with PICTURE options without using the @...SAY command. *Expression* is the variable or field to format; *expC* is a character expression that contains the PICTURE clause.

Example

```
USE STAFF
? Lastname, Salary
Jones           13.00
? TRANSFORM(Salary,"$$$.99")
$13.00
```

Related Functions

LOWER(), STR(), UPPER()

TRIM

Syntax

TRIM(*expC*)

The TRIM() function trims trailing spaces from a character string. If the character string is composed entirely of spaces, TRIM() returns a null string. The TRIM() function is identical to the RTRIM() function.

Example

```
USE STAFF
GO 2
? Lastname + " works here."
Jones            works here.
? TRIM(Lastname) + " works here."
Jones works here.
```

Related Functions

ALLTRIM(), LEFT(), LTRIM(), RTRIM(), STUFF(), SUBSTR()

TYPE

Syntax

TYPE(*expC*)

The TYPE() function returns a single character indicating the data type of the expression named in *expC*. The character "C" denotes character type, "L" denotes logical type, "N" denotes numeric type, "D" denotes date type, "M" denotes memo type, and "U" denotes an undefined type.

Example

```
STORE "some words" TO WORDS
STORE 123.456 TO NUMBERS
STORE DATE() TO TODAY
STORE .T. TO THISIS
? TYPE("WORDS")
C
? TYPE("NUMBERS")
N
? TYPE("TODAY")
D
? TYPE("THISIS")
L
? TYPE("NOTSTORED")
U
```

Related Function

FIELD()

UPDATED

Syntax

UPDATED()

The UPDATED() function returns a logical true (.T.) if any data was changed in the associated GETs when the last READ command was processed. It can be useful in data entry programs when you want to test whether data was changed before taking the time to open databases, add or find records, or execute a long series of REPLACE statements. The UPDATED() function can be particularly useful when you are programming for local area networks and you want to avoid opening files or locking records unless absolutely necessary.

Example

```
M_LAST = SPACE(20)
M_FIRST = SPACE(20)
M_AGE = 18
CLEAR
@ 10,4 SAY "Last name:" GET M_LAST
@ 11,3 SAY "First name:" GET M_FIRST
@ 13,10 SAY "Age:" GET M_AGE
READ
IF UPDATED()
    USE PERSONS INDEX NAMES
    APPEND BLANK
    REPLACE Lastname WITH M_LAST
    REPLACE Firstname WITH M_FIRST
    REPLACE Age WITH M_AGE
ENDIF
```

Related Functions

INKEY(), READKEY()

UPPER

Syntax

UPPER(*expC*)

The UPPER() function converts all alphabetic characters in *expC* to uppercase letters. The UPPER() function does not change the way the data is stored unless you use the function as part of a STORE or REPLACE command. It is generally used for finding or comparing data when you do not know in what case the data was originally entered.

Example

```
STORE "lowercase letters" TO WORDS
? WORDS
lowercase letters
? UPPER(WORDS)
LOWERCASE LETTERS
```

Related Functions
ISLOWER(), ISUPPER(), LOWER()

USED

Syntax

USED([*alias*])

The USED() function returns a logical true (.T.) if a database is open in the current work area. Use the optional *alias* to identify a different work area by its alias, number, or letter. If no database is open in the specified work area, a logical false (.F.) is returned.

Related Functions
ALIAS(), SELECT()

VAL

Syntax

VAL(*expC*)

The VAL() function converts a character expression, *expC*, containing numbers into a numeric value. Starting at the leftmost character and ignoring leading blanks, VAL() processes digits until a nonnumeric character is encountered. If the first character of *expC* is not a number, VAL() returns a value of zero.

Example

```
STORE 22 TO NUMA
STORE "44" TO NUMB
? NUMA + VAL(NUMB)
        66.00
```

Related Function

STR()

VARREAD

Syntax

VARREAD()

The VARREAD() function returns the name of the field or variable currently being edited. The function can be useful when designing context-sensitive help systems, so that different help messages can appear for different fields.

Example

In the following example, the VARREAD() function is used to test for the presence of the F1 (Help) key, through the use of the ON KEY statement. When F1 is pressed, a custom help window appears as a result.

```
ON KEY = 315 DO HELPER WITH VARREAD()
USE STAFF INDEX SOCIAL
ACCEPT "Enter social security number of employee: " TO FINDER
SEEK FINDER
IF .NOT. FOUND()
    WAIT "No such record found. Press a key..."
    RETURN
ENDIF
CLEAR
DEFINE WINDOW Edits FROM 5,5 TO 15,70 DOUBLE
ACTIVATE WINDOW Edits
@ 2,2 SAY "Lastname: " GET Lastname
@ 3,2 SAY "Firstname: " GET Firstname
@ 4,2 SAY "Soc. Sec. No: " GET Social
```

```
@ 5,2 SAY "Grade: " GET Grade
@ 6,2 SAY "Salary: " GET Salary
@ 8,10 SAY "F1 for Help, ESC cancels editing."
READ
DEACTIVATE WINDOW Edits
RETURN
```

VERSION

Syntax

VERSION()

The VERSION() function returns a character string indicating the version number of FoxPro.

Example

```
? VERSION()
FoxPro Rev. 1.02
```

Related Functions

GETENV(), OS()

WCHILD

Syntax

WCHILD([*expC/expN1*])

The WCHILD() function returns the number of child windows in a parent window, or the names of the child windows in a parent window. If the names are returned, they are returned in the order that they were stacked in the parent window. The window-name argument, *expC*, is the name of the desired window; if omitted, the function assumes the use of the current window. If a window name is specified, the optional numeric expression *expN1* can also be used. When

Version 2

expN1 is used, the name of the child window is returned. The value of *expN1* corresponds to the desired child window, varying from 0 (denoting the child window at the bottom of the stack) up to the number of child windows in the stack.

WCOLS

Syntax

WCOLS([*expC*])

The WCOLS() function returns the number of columns available in the active window. Use the optional *expC* to name a window other than the currently active window.

Related Functions

SCOLS(), SROWS(), WLCOLS(), WLROWS(), WROWS()

WEXIST

Syntax

WEXIST(*expC*)

The WEXIST() function returns a logical true (.T.) if the window named in *expC* has been previously defined.

Related Functions

WONTOP(), WOUTPUT(), WVISIBLE()

WLCOL

Syntax

WLCOL([*expC*])

The WLCOL() function returns a numeric value representing the column location of the upper-left corner of a window. Use the optional *expC* to identify the window by name. If *expC* is omitted, WLCOL() returns the column location of the upper-left corner of the currently active window.

Because windows can be positioned off the screen in FoxPro, it is possible to retrieve negative values from WLCOL(). If a window's upper-left corner is located above or below the screen, negative values will be returned by WLCOL().

Related Functions

WCOL(), WROW()

WLROW

Syntax

WLROW([*expC*])

The WLROW() function returns a numeric value representing the row location of the upper-left corner of a window. Use the optional *expC* to identify the window by name. If *expC* is omitted, WLROW() returns the row location of the upper-left corner of the currently active window.

Because windows can be positioned off the screen in FoxPro, it is possible to retrieve negative values from WLROW(). If a window's upper-left corner is located above or below the screen, the values returned by WLROW() will be negative.

Related Functions

WCOL(), WLCOL()

WONTOP

Syntax

WONTOP([*expC*])

The WONTOP() function returns the name of the window that is frontmost on the screen. If the optional *expC* is used to name a window, the function returns a logical true (.T.) if the named window is frontmost.

Related Functions

WEXIST(), WOUTPUT(), WVISIBLE()

WOUTPUT

Syntax

WOUTPUT([*expC*])

The WOUTPUT() function returns the name of the window currently receiving output. If the optional *expC* is used to name a window, the function returns a logical true (.T.) if output is currently being directed to the window named in *expC*. If output is not being directed to a window, the function returns a null string.

Related Functions

WEXIST(), WONTOP(), WVISIBLE()

WPARENT

Syntax

Version 2

WPARENT([*expC*])

The WPARENT() function returns the name of a parent window for a specific child window. The optional window-name argument, *expC*, denotes the child

window for which the name of the parent window is desired. If the argument is omitted, the function assumes the use of the current window. If the current window is not a child window, the function returns a null string.

WROWS

Syntax

WROWS([*expC*])

The WROWS() function returns the number of rows available in the active window. Use the optional *expC* to return the number of rows available in the window named in *expC*.

Related Functions

SCOLS(), SROWS(), WCOLS(), WLCOLS(), WLROWS()

WVISIBLE

Syntax

WVISIBLE(*expC*)

The WVISIBLE() function returns a logical true (.T.) if the window named in *expC* has been activated and is not hidden. The function returns a logical false (.F.) if the window has not been activated, has been deactivated, or is hidden.

Related Functions

WEXIST(), WONTOP(), WOUTPUT()

YEAR

Syntax

YEAR(*expD*)

The YEAR() function returns the numeric year corresponding to the date expression.

Example

```
? DATE()
04/15/90
? YEAR(DATE())
 1990
```

Related Functions

CMONTH(), CTOD(), DATE(), DMY(), MDY(), MONTH()

Chapter 24

FoxPro System Memory Variables

System memory variables are special memory variables that FoxPro uses to control its output, usually to the printer. The system memory variables affect settings like page length, page offset from the left margin, the number of pages printed within a report, and line spacing. By changing the system memory variables, you can control various settings used when stored report forms are generated with the REPORT FORM command. You can change the values of system memory variables by storing different values to the variables before running the report or generating screen output.

If you perform a LIST MEMORY command, you can see a list of the system memory variables. Names of the system memory variables start with an underline, as shown in the following.

System memory variables displayed by FoxPro version 2:

```
_ALIGNMENT   Pub    C    "LEFT"
_BOX         Pub    L    .T.
_INDENT      Pub    N          0  (          0.00000000)
_LMARGIN     Pub    N          0  (          0.00000000)
_PADVANCE    Pub    C    "FORMFEED"
_PAGENO      Pub    N          2  (          2.00000000)
_PBPAGE      Pub    N          1  (          1.00000000)
_PCOLNO      Pub    N         55  (         55.00000000)
_PCOPIES     Pub    N          1  (          1.00000000)
_PDRIVER     Pub    C    ""
_PECODE      Pub    C    ""
_PEJECT      Pub    C    "BEFORE"
```

```
_PEPAGE      Pub    N        32767  (      32767.00000000)
_PFORM       Pub    C    ""
_PLENGTH     Pub    N           66  (         66.00000000)
_PLINENO     Pub    N           16  (         16.00000000)
_PLOFFSET    Pub    N            0  (          0.00000000)
_PPITCH      Pub    C    "DEFAULT"
_PQUALITY    Pub    L    .F.
_PSCODE      Pub    C    ""
_PSPACING    Pub    N            1  (          1.00000000)
_PWAIT       Pub    L    .F.
_RMARGIN     Pub    N           80  (         80.00000000)
_TABS        Pub    C    ""
_WRAP        Pub    L    .F.
_DBLCLICK    Pub    N         0.49  (          0.49432944)
_CALCVALUE   Pub    N         0.00  (          0.00000000)
_CALCMEM     Pub    N         0.00  (          0.00000000)
_CLIPTEXT    Pub    C    ""
_DIARYDATE   Pub    D    08/11/91
_TEXT        Pub    N           -1  (         -1.00000000)
_PRETEXT     Pub    C    ""
_TALLY       Pub    N           24  (         24.00000000)
_CUROBJ      Pub    N           -1  (         -1.00000000)
_MLINE       Pub    N            0  (          0.00000000)
_THROTTLE    Pub    N         0.00  (          0.00000000)
_GENMENU     Pub    C    "E:\FOXPRO\GENMENU.FXP"
_GENSCRN     Pub    C    "E:\FOXPRO\GENSCRN.FXP"
_GENGRAPH    Pub    C    ""
_GENPD       Pub    C    "E:\FOXPRO\GENPD.APP"
_PDSETUP     Pub    C    ""
_GENXTAB     Pub    C    "E:\FOXPRO\GENXTAB.PRG"
_FOXDOC      Pub    C    "E:\FOXPRO\FOXDOC.EXE"
_FOXGRAPH    Pub    C    ""
```

System memory variables displayed by FoxPro version 1.01:

```
_ALIGNMENT   Pub    C    "LEFT"
_BOX         Pub    L    .T.
_INDENT      Pub    N            0  (          0.00000000)
_LMARGIN     Pub    N            0  (          0.00000000)
_PADVANCE    Pub    C    "FORMFEED"
_PAGENO      Pub    N            1  (          1.00000000)
_PBPAGE      Pub    N            1  (          1.00000000)
_PCOLNO      Pub    N           55  (         55.00000000)
_PCOPIES     Pub    N            1  (          1.00000000)
```

```
_PDRIVER    Pub   C   ""
_PECODE     Pub   C   ""
_PEJECT     Pub   C   "BEFORE"
_PEPAGE     Pub   N        32767  (    32767.00000000)
_PFORM      Pub   C   ""
_PLENGTH    Pub   N           66  (       66.00000000)
_PLINENO    Pub   N            2  (        2.00000000)
_PLOFFSET   Pub   N            0  (        0.00000000)
_PPITCH     Pub   C   "DEFAULT"
_PQUALITY   Pub   L   .F.
_PSCODE     Pub   C   ""
_PSPACING   Pub   N            1  (        1.00000000)
_PWAIT      Pub   L   .F.
_RMARGIN    Pub   N           80  (       80.00000000)
_TABS       Pub   C   ""
_WRAP       Pub   L   .F.
_DBLCLICK   Pub   N         0.49  (        0.49432944)
_CALCVALUE  Pub   N         0.00  (        0.00000000)
_CALCMEM    Pub   N         0.00  (        0.00000000)
_DIARYDATE  Pub   D   08/22/91
```

_ALIGNMENT

Syntax

_ALIGNMENT = *expC*

The _ALIGNMENT variable expression contains a character expression of either "LEFT", "CENTER", or "RIGHT". The contents of the expression determines how output appears; left-justified, centered, or right-justified. The default for text is left-justified. Note that the value of _ALIGNMENT has an effect only when the _WRAP variable is set to true.

_BOX

Syntax

_BOX = *expL*

The _BOX variable expression determines whether boxes specified with the DEFINE BOX command will be printed around areas of text. When _BOX = .T. (logical true), boxes are printed. If _BOX = .F. (logical false), boxes are not printed. The default for _BOX is .T.

_CALCMEM

Syntax

_CALCMEM = *expN*

The _CALCMEM variable expression contains the numeric value stored in the calculator's memory. After the calculator is used, the last value present in the memory will be stored in _CALCMEM. You can also initialize the memory value in the calculator by storing a value to _CALCMEM before allowing the use of the calculator in a program.

_CALCVALUE

Syntax

_CALCVALUE = *expN*

The _CALCVALUE variable expression contains the numeric value stored in the calculator. After the calculator is used, the last value present in the calculator will be stored in _CALCVALUE. You can also initialize the value in the calculator by storing a value to _CALCVALUE before allowing the use of the calculator in a program.

_CLIPTEXT

Syntax

_CLIPTEXT = *expC*

The _CLIPTEXT variable expression contains the character expression stored in the clipboard. After the clipboard is used, the last entry present in the clipboard will be stored in _CLIPTEXT. You can also initialize the value in the clipboard by storing a character string to _CLIPTEXT before allowing the use of the clipboard in a program.

_CUROBJ

Syntax

_CUROBJ = *expN*

The _CUROBJ variable expression contains the currently selected GET object number, *expN*. (Use @...GET to create GET objects such as check boxes, pushbuttons, invisible buttons, popups, and lists.) The GET object number is determined by the order in which the GET objects are supplied. (Keep in mind that each button in a set of buttons is considered to be an individual GET object.)

_DBCLICK

Syntax

_DBCLICK = *expN*

The _DBCLICK variable expression specifies the time interval, in seconds, between double mouse clicks or triple mouse clicks. The larger the value specified, the longer you can wait between mouse clicks and still have FoxPro interpret the action as a double click or a triple click. The value can range from 0.055 to 5.5, and the default is 0.5.

_DIARYDATE

Syntax

_DIARYDATE = *expD*

The _DIARYDATE variable expression contains the currently selected date stored in the calendar. By default, the current date (according to the computer's clock) is the selected date in the calendar, and is the value stored to _DIARYDATE. You can store a different date value to _DIARYDATE, in which case that will be the selected date when the calendar is opened.

_INDENT

Syntax

_INDENT = *expN*

The _INDENT variable expression specifies an indentation for the first line of text in each paragraph. The value specified can be negative, in which case the first line of text will be outdented. Note that the value has an effect only when the _WRAP variable is set to true.

_LMARGIN

Syntax

_LMARGIN = *expN*

The _LMARGIN variable expression specifies the position of the left margin for output generated with the ? command. The value can range from 0 to 254. The value will be added to any value specified for the current page offset (_PLOFFSET) variable. This value has an effect only when the _WRAP variable is set to true.

_MLINE

Syntax

_MLINE = *expN*

The _MLINE variable expression provides the memo field offset of the MLINE() function. Whenever the MLINE() function is used, MLINE() stores its memo field offset to the _MLINE system memory variable. You can use the value of _MLINE as the second numeric argument in the MLINE() function to improve the performance of the MLINE() function. (See MLINE() in Chapter 23.)

_PADVANCE

Syntax

_PADVANCE = *expC*

The _PADVANCE variable expression contains a character expression of either "LINEFEED" or "FORMFEED." Depending on the value of the expression, new pages are generated either with multiple line feeds or with form feeds. The default for _PADVANCE is "FORMFEED."

_PAGENO

Syntax

_PAGENO = *expN*

The _PAGENO variable expression indicates the page number to use on the first page of a report. The default is 1, but you can enter any value from 1 to 32,767.

_PBPAGE

Syntax

_PBPAGE = *expN*

The _PBPAGE variable expression indicates the beginning page of a report when you don't want to print the entire report. The default is 1, but you can enter any value from 1 to 32,767. The value of _PBPAGE must be less than or equal to _PEPAGE for any printing to occur.

_PCOLNO

Syntax

_PCOLNO = *expN*

The _PCOLNO variable expression indicates a new starting column position; it repositions the printer at the specified cursor location before the report begins.

_PCOPIES

Syntax

_PCOPIES = *expN*

The _PCOPIES variable expression indicates the number of copies of a report desired; the default is 1. You can enter any value from 1 to 32,767.

_PDRIVER

Syntax

_PDRIVER = *expC*

The _PDRIVER variable expression contains a character expression that is the name of the printer driver in use. If no printer has been specified, the default will be a null string (""). Note that FoxPro version 1.*x* does not support selectable printer drivers; hence, _PDRIVER has no effect in these versions. It is included in the language for compatibility with dBASE IV programs.

_PECODE

Syntax

_PECODE = *expC*

The _PECODE variable expression contains any ending escape codes that you want to send to the printer after the report is completed. Consult your printer for a list of valid escape codes. You can use any character expression up to 255 characters in length.

_PEJECT

Syntax

_PEJECT = *expC*

The _PEJECT variable expression contains a character expression of "NONE", "BEFORE", "AFTER", or "BOTH". The expression determines whether a form feed (page eject) is sent to the printer during output. NONE indicates that no form feed is needed (other than those that naturally occur inside a stored report); BEFORE indicates that a form feed should occur at the start of printing; AFTER indicates that a form feed should occur at the end of printing; BOTH indicates that a form feed is needed both before and after printing.

NOTE: _PEJECT only has an effect if the output is produced as the result of a PRINTJOB/ENDPRINTJOB command structure.

_PEPAGE

Syntax

_PEPAGE = *expN*

The _PEPAGE variable expression indicates the ending page of a report when you don't want to print the entire report. The value of _PEPAGE can be any value between 1 and 32,767, although it cannot be less than any value specified for _PBPAGE. The default is 32,767.

_PFORM

Syntax

_PFORM = *expC*

The _PFORM variable expression contains a character expression that evaluates to the name of a stored print form file. The CREATE REPORT and CREATE LABEL commands store various system memory variables to a print form (.PRF) file. This file is not automatically loaded when a stored report or label is printed; you must use the _PFORM variable to load the *expC* settings in the form file.

_PLENGTH

Syntax

_PLENGTH = *expN*

The _PLENGTH variable expression indicates the page length for the printed page. The default of 66 matches standard 11-inch (U.S.) paper; you can store 84 to this value for 14-inch (U.S. legal-size) paper. The value can range from 1 to 32,767.

_PLINENO

Syntax

_PLINENO = *expN*

The _PLINENO variable expression indicates a new starting line number. It repositions the printer at the specified row location before the output begins.

_PLOFFSET

Syntax

_PLOFFSET = *expN*

The _PLOFFSET variable expression indicates the left offset (distance from left edge) where printing will begin. Enter a desired numeric value, for example, 15 for a left offset of 15 spaces. Note that the use of _PLOFFSET is equivalent to the SET MARGIN command.

_PPITCH

Syntax

_PPITCH = *expC*

The _PPITCH variable expression contains a character expression that selects the printing type style. Valid choices are "PICA" (or 10 characters per inch), "ELITE" (or 12 characters per inch), "CONDENSED" (or 17 characters per inch), or "DEFAULT" (using the current printer settings). Note that in order for _PPITCH to be used successfully, your printer must support the option for the desired type style.

_PQUALITY

Syntax

_PQUALITY = *expL*

The _PQUALITY variable expression indicates whether near-letter-quality printing mode will be used. A logical false stored to this variable turns off near-letter-quality printing, while a logical true turns it on. Note that in order for this variable to have an effect, your printer must support near-letter-quality printing.

_PRETEXT

Syntax

_PRETEXT = *expC*

The _PRETEXT variable expression specifies a character expression that will be used to precede text-merge lines. The character expression identified as *expC* will be output before text lines output with the SET TEXTMERGE command. (See SET TEXTMERGE in Chapter 22.) Note that you can store tab characters to _PRETEXT to indent text that is output with SET TEXTMERGE.

_PSCODE

Syntax

_PSCODE = *expC*

The _PSCODE variable expression contains any starting escape codes you want to send to the printer before the report begins printing. Consult your printer manual for a list of valid escape codes. You can use any character expression up to 255 characters in length.

_PSPACING

Syntax

_PSPACING = *expN*

The _PSPACING variable expression contains a numeric value of 1, 2, or 3, indicating the line spacing to be used with printed output. The default value is 1. Note that _PSPACING also affects output produced with the LIST...TO PRINT or DISPLAY...TO PRINT command.

_PWAIT

Syntax

_PWAIT = *expL*

The _PWAIT variable expression indicates whether your printer should pause between each page. A logical value of false indicates no pause, while a logical value of true indicates a pause. When printing on single sheets of paper, use _PWAIT = .T. to allow for reinsertion of paper into the printer.

_RMARGIN

Syntax

_RMARGIN = *expN*

The _RMARGIN variable expression specifies the position of the right margin for output generated with the ? command. The value can range from a minimum of one more than the value of the left margin (plus any indent) to a maximum of 255. Note that the value has an effect only when the _WRAP variable is set to true.

_TABS

Syntax

_TABS = *expC*

The _TABS variable expression specifies where tabs will appear as part of the printed output. The character expression contains a series of numbers separated by commas indicating the tab stops; for example, five tabs at six-character intervals could be specified with an expression like "6,12,18,24,30." Note that if the value of _WRAP is a logical true, any tabs equal to or greater than the right margin are ignored.

_ TALLY

Syntax

_ TALLY = *expN*

The _ TALLY variable expression contains the number of records processed by the last database commands. Certain commands that include a count of records processed when SET TALK is ON (such as AVERAGE, COUNT, COPY, PACK, and REINDEX) will return the number of records processed when the command has finished. This value is stored to the _ TALLY system variable; the value is stored to _ TALLY whether or not SET TALK is ON.

_ TEXT

Syntax

_ TEXT = *expN*

The _ TEXT variable expression directs the output produced by \, \\, and TEXT...ENDTEXT text merge commands to a low-level file. *ExpN* is the file handle for the file created and opened with the FCREATE() and FOPEN() functions. Storing the file handle to the _ TEXT system variable causes all successive text output with text-merge commands to be directed to the file.

_ WRAP

Syntax

_ WRAP = *expL*

The _ WRAP variable expression determines whether automatic word wrap occurs. By default, _ WRAP is set to a logical false. Note that the value of _ WRAP must be true for _ ALIGNMENT, _ INDENT, _ LMARGIN, _ RMARGIN, _ TABS, or _ PADVANCE to have any effect.

Using System Memory Variables and Other Parameters

Many of the parameters that control printing can be set in other ways, such as making various selections when designing or printing a report, or entering other commands, such as SET MARGIN TO (the command equivalent of the left offset variable). The existence of these variables can be quite useful if you want to offer your users multiple options for printing reports while under program control. Depending on the user's response to various menu options, you could store certain values to different printer variables, then print the report with the REPORT FORM command or with program code contained within a PRINT-JOB...ENDPRINTJOB control structure.

Chapter 25

Optimizing FoxPro

FoxPro can be *optimized* in a number of ways to run most efficiently. This chapter covers tips and techniques for optimizing FoxPro, such as modifying the configuration file, including SET commands in applications, using printer drivers, and using additional memory.

Modifying the CONFIG.FP File

The working environment in FoxPro can be customized by making modifications to the configuration file. Users who are upgrading from FoxBase+ should note that the configuration file is named CONFIG.FP, and not CONFIG.FX as it was in FoxBase+. The configuration file is an ASCII text file containing commands that specify the operating parameters for the FoxPro environment. When you start FoxPro, the program tries to find a configuration file in the current directory. If the file is found, it is read into memory, and the environmental settings contained in the file are placed into effect.

Most of the environmental variables that can be changed with SET commands or from the View menu can also be specified in the configuration file. You can also modify the default editors used for editing programs and memo fields.

When SET commands are used in the configuration file, the syntax differs from that used at the command level. In the configuration file, the normal syntax is

option = desired setting

rather than the normal syntax for a SET command at the command level, which is

SET *option* TO *desired setting*

Keep in mind that if the desired setting is a character string, you must surround it with quotes.

Valid Options for CONFIG.FP

The possible options that can be placed in a configuration file are listed here. In the case of the SET options, no explanations are provided, as the options work in the same manner as the SET commands detailed in Chapter 22.

```
ALTERNATE = filename
ALTERNATE = ON/OFF
AUTOSAVE = ON/OFF
BELL = expN
BELL = ON/OFF
BLINK = ON/OFF
BLOCKSIZE = expN
BORDER = color attribute
BRSTATUS = ON/OFF
CARRY = ON/OFF
CENTURY = ON/OFF
CLEAR = ON/OFF
CLOCK = ON/OFF
CLOCK = row,col
COLOR = color attribute
COLOR OF BOX = color attribute
COLOR OF FIELDS = color attribute
COLOR OF HIGHLIGHT = color attribute
COLOR OF INFORMATION = color attribute
COLOR OF MESSAGES = color attribute
COLOR OF NORMAL = color attribute
COLOR OF SCHEME expN = color pairs list
COLOR OF TITLES = color attribute
COLOR SET = color-set name
COMMAND = command name
```

Use COMMAND to run a command upon startup of the FoxPro environment. The *command name* can be DO *filename*, where *filename* is the name of a program file to be called. If the program is not located in the current directory or along the path, be sure to include the path with the program name.

```
COMPATIBLE = [OFF/FOXPLUS] / [ON/DB4]
CONFIRM = ON/OFF
CONSOLE = ON/OFF
CURRENCY = expC
CURRENCY = LEFT/RIGHT
CURSOR = ON/OFF
DATE = date format
DEBUG = ON/OFF
DECIMALS = expN
DEFAULT = disk drive letter
DELETED = ON/OFF
DELIMITER = expC
DELIMITER = ON/OFF
DEVELOPMENT = ON/OFF
DEVICE = SCREEN/PRINT/FILE
DISPLAY = display type installed
ECHO = ON/OFF
EMS = expN
EMS = ON/OFF
```

Use EMS to determine whether FoxPro can take advantage of any expanded memory meeting the LIM (Lotus-Intel-Microsoft) memory specifications. If EMS = ON, FoxPro uses any available expanded memory. The default for EMS is OFF. Use the EMS = *expN* format to denote how much expanded memory should be made available. FoxPro allocates expanded memory in 16K allotments, so any value of *expN* that is not a multiple of 16 will be reduced to the nearest multiple of 16. You can specify any value from 0 up to the total allotment of expanded memory in your system.

```
ESCAPE = ON/OFF
EXACT = ON/OFF
EXCLUSIVE = ON/OFF
FULLPATH = ON/OFF
FUNCTION expN = expC
```

Use FUNCTION to specify a function key assignment. Note that the F1 key cannot be reassigned in FoxPro. *ExpN* is the number of the function key, and *expC* is the string of text to assign to the function key. If *expC* is a character string, rather than a character memory variable, remember to surround it with quotes. Also, note that a semicolon can be used within the character string to indicate the pressing of the ENTER key.

```
HEADING = ON/OFF
HELP = helpfile name
```

```
HELP = ON/OFF
HOURS = 12/24
INDEX = expC
```

Use INDEX to change the default file extension used for index files.

```
INTENSITY = ON/OFF
LABEL = expC
```

Use LABEL to change the default file extension used for label files.

```
LOGERROR = key name
MACKEY = key name
MARGIN = expN
MARK = expC
MEMOWIDTH = expN
MOUSE = expN
MVARSIZ = expN
```

Use MVARSIZ to denote the amount of memory (in kilobytes) that FoxPro will reserve for character strings stored in memory variables. You can specify any value from 1 to 64. The default, if none is specified, is 6.

```
MVCOUNT = expN
```

Use MVCOUNT to denote the maximum number of memory variables that can occupy memory during a FoxPro session. *ExpN* may be any value from 128 to 3,600. If no value is specified, FoxPro defaults to 256.

```
NEAR = ON/OFF
NOTIFY = ON/OFF
ODOMETER = expN
PATH = path names
PDSETUP = printer setup driver name
POINT = expC
PRINT = ON/OFF
RESOURCE = ON/OFF
RESOURCE = resource filename
SAFETY = ON/OFF
SCOREBOARD = ON/OFF
SEPARATOR = expC
SPACE = ON/OFF
STATUS = ON/OFF
```

```
STEP = ON/OFF
STICKY = ON/OFF
SYSMENU = ON/OFF
TALK = ON/OFF
TABS = ExpC
TEDIT = filename[/expN]
```

Use TEDIT to change the default text editor used for editing programs with MODIFY COMMAND. The *filename* is the name of your preferred editor, minus the extension. The desired program must be available in the current directory or through a DOS PATH command. The */expN* option may be added to specify the amount of memory to be freed for use by the external editor. If zero is supplied as a value, FoxPro will make as much memory as possible available to the editor.

```
TMPFILES = drive:
```

Use TMPFILES to change the default drive where FoxPro stores temporary files. Normally, temporary files are stored in the current drive. You can use TMPFILES to change the default drive, so that temporary files may be stored to a RAMdisk.

```
TIME = expN
```

Use TIME to specify a length of time (determined by the number of retries) to a print device before FoxPro displays a "Printer is not ready" message. *ExpN* may be any value from 1 to 1,000,000. If no value is specified, FoxPro defaults to 6,000 retries.

```
TYPEAHEAD = expN
UNIQUE = ON/OFF
```

Using SET Commands in Applications

If you are running multiple applications under the same copy of FoxPro, you may need to fine-tune FoxPro for each application. This is often the case with local area networks, which may have multiple users running different tasks. Rather than trying to make the settings in the CONFIG.FP file please everyone, you can include a series of SET commands at the start of each application to best modify the preferences for the users of that particular application.

FoxPro's Printer Drivers

The report design utility, FoxReport, provides options that allow the addition of printing styles (bold, italics, condensed print, and so on) to a report. In order for such characteristics to be available, your printer driver under FoxPro must support the styles. FoxPro provides a set of printer drivers and lets you create different printer setups (with differing page orientation or font styles) for use with FoxPro.

Choosing a Printer Driver

To specify a printer driver in FoxPro, open the File menu and choose Printer Setup. From the dialog box that appears, choose Printer Driver Setup. The Printer Driver Setups dialog box next appears, as shown in Figure 25-1.

The Printer Driver Setups dialog box provides options that let you create a new driver setup, edit an existing setup, delete an existing setup, set the default setup, or load (set) a setup.

To create a driver setup, choose New. The Printer Setup Editing dialog box appears, as shown in Figure 25-2.

First choose the desired printer by name from the Printers list box. Then make any desired adjustments to the print parameters shown. If you choose a PostScript printer, you can change the default font, the leading (space between

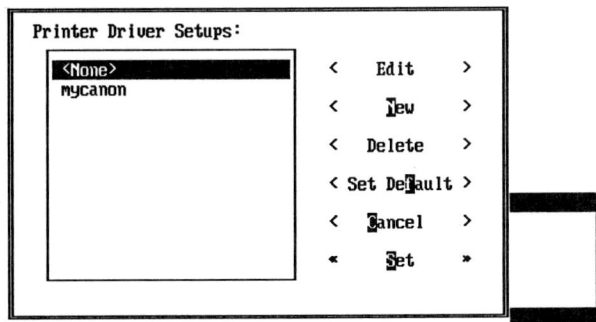

Figure 25-1.   *The Printer Driver Setups dialog box*

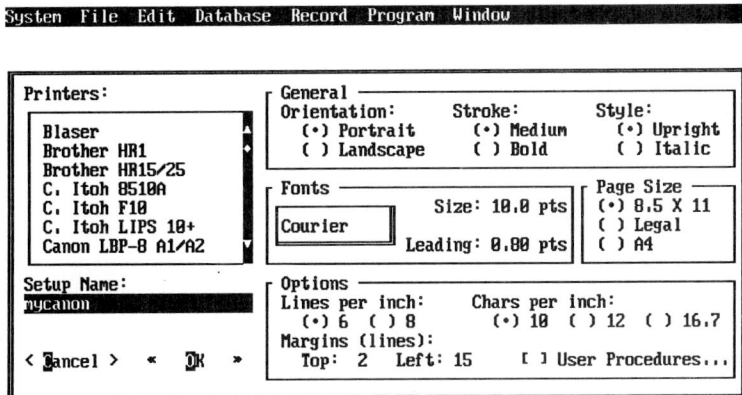

```
 System  File  Edit  Database  Record  Program  Window
```

```
┌─────────────────────┐ ┌ General ──────────────────────────────┐
│ Printers:           │ │ Orientation:      Stroke:      Style:  │
│ ┌─────────────────┐ │ │  (•) Portrait    (•) Medium   (•) Upright│
│ │ Blaser          ▲ │ │  ( ) Landscape   ( ) Bold     ( ) Italic│
│ │ Brother HR1     ▪ │ │                                        │
│ │ Brother HR15/25 │ │ └────────────────────────────────────────┘
│ │ C. Itoh 8510A   │ │ ┌ Fonts ──────────────────┐┌ Page Size ──┐
│ │ C. Itoh F10     │ │ │            Size: 10.0 pts ││ (•) 8.5 X 11│
│ │ C. Itoh LIPS 10+│ │ │ ┌───────┐               ││ ( ) Legal   │
│ │ Canon LBP-8 A1/A2 ▼│ │ │ │Courier│               ││ ( ) A4      │
│ └─────────────────┘ │ │ └───────┘  Leading: 0.00 pts│└─────────────┘
│ Setup Name:         │ └──────────────────────────┘
│ ▐mycanon            │ ┌ Options ──────────────────────────────┐
│                     │ │ Lines per inch:    Chars per inch:     │
│                     │ │  (•) 6  ( ) 8       (•) 10 ( ) 12 ( ) 16.7│
│  < Cancel >  «  OK  »│ │ Margins (lines):                       │
│                     │ │   Top:  2   Left: 15    [ ] User Procedures...│
└─────────────────────┘ └────────────────────────────────────────┘
```

Figure 25-2. *The Printer Setup Editing dialog box*

lines), and the top and left margins. If you choose a non-PostScript printer, you can change the number of vertical lines per inch and the number of characters horizontally per inch.

After choosing the desired printer and setting the desired parameters, enter a name of your choosing for the setup in the Setup Name text box and choose OK. The printer driver setup will be saved to the FOXUSER resource file, and the message "Setup saved" will appear.

The new printer driver setup now appears in the list box of the Printer Driver Setups dialog box, as you can see in Figure 25-1. To put this printer driver setup in effect for use in FoxPro, choose Set from the dialog box.

Changing or Deleting an Existing Printer Setup

To edit an existing printer driver setup, choose the driver setup by name from the list box and choose Edit. The Printer Setup Editing dialog box appears, as shown in Figure 25-2. You can make the desired changes to the setup and choose OK to store the changes. To delete a printer driver setup from the FoxPro resource file, select the setup by name in the list box and choose Delete.

Specifying the Default Printer Driver Setup

To specify a default printer driver setup that is automatically loaded along with FoxPro, choose the driver setup by name from the list box and choose Set Default. You can also specify the printer driver setup to be loaded at startup by modifying the CONFIG.FP file. Add the line

PDSETUP = *setup name*

where *setup name* is the name of the printer driver setup to be loaded. If you use both methods described to name a startup printer driver setup, the driver setup specified by the CONFIG.FP file takes precedence over the driver setup specified in the Printer Driver Setups dialog box.

Loading a Printer Driver Setup

You can temporarily load a printer driver setup in one of two ways: from the Printer Driver Setups dialog box or with the _PDSETUP system memory variable. From the Printer Driver Setups dialog box, choose the desired driver setup by name, then choose Set. The selected driver setup will be loaded into memory. You can also enter the statement

   _ PDSETUP = *setup name*

where *setup name* is the name of the printer driver setup to be loaded into memory.

FoxPro and Memory

One of the most effective means of improving FoxPro's performance is to add expanded memory, or memory meeting the Lotus-Intel-Microsoft (LIM) speci-fications. This type of memory can be added to any IBM PC-compatible computer having an expansion slot. Your computer may have plenty of memory, but it may not be the type FoxPro needs; for those unfamiliar with the different types of PC memory, the subject is worth considering.

Types of PC Memory

IBM PC-compatibles utilize three types of memory: conventional, expanded, and extended. *Conventional memory* includes the first 640K of RAM, which is a standard feature of most PC-compatibles on the market. FoxPro requires a minimum of 512K of installed RAM (with 400K remaining free after DOS is loaded). A full 640K of conventional RAM is not required, but is highly recommended. While FoxPro will run in 512K, you will suffer speed degrada-tion, because FoxPro will have to go to disk for a large number of operations.

   Expanded memory denotes additional memory above the conventional limits. This is the type of additional memory that FoxPro uses effectively. Expanded memory is accessed through a special software scheme, whereby the operating system looks at the added memory through a 64K "page" set aside in conventional memory. This scheme was jointly developed by Lotus, Intel, and Microsoft, primarily to cure the headaches of spreadsheet users who kept running into the 640K memory limit. Since then, many programs, FoxPro included, have been designed to take advantage of expanded memory. FoxPro can utilize any expanded memory meeting the LIM specifications of 3.2 or higher.

Extended memory also denotes additional memory above the conventional limits, but it is directly addressable through hardware, rather than through the page-swapping scheme used with expanded memory. Extended memory is a standard feature of machines based on 80386 (and higher) processors. (Due to hardware limitations, 8088- and 8086-based machines never have extended memory.) Unfortunately, DOS does not have the ability to directly address extended memory, so various software programs exist to utilize such memory. FoxPro cannot use extended memory in its natural state, but there is a fast and inexpensive way around this limitation. You can use memory-management software to make extended memory imitate expanded memory; FoxPro will then be able to use that memory.

Memory-management software is often available from computer bulletin board user groups. You can also purchase commercial packages; one popular example is QEMM, an expanded memory manager from Quarterdeck Office Systems. If you use Microsoft Windows, a memory manager is included on your Windows disks. You can install and use it to make all or part of your extended memory appear as expanded memory. (See your Windows documentation for details.)

If your computer has only conventional memory, you should strongly consider the addition of an expanded memory board meeting the LIM specifications. Such boards are relatively inexpensive and come with installation instructions and software. Adding one megabyte or more of expanded memory will boost FoxPro's performance, particularly with complex applications.

A Note About Conventional RAM

FoxPro can also benefit significantly from any conventional RAM that can be obtained beyond the normal 640K barrier. While DOS was never designed to make conventional RAM above 640K available to programs, some add-on cards and software do exist to make such memory available. FoxPro will sense the presence of such memory, and will make good use of it. Such RAM will speed performance, and will let FoxPro open more files, indexes, and windows without displaying the dreaded "insufficient memory" error message. If you are using XT-class hardware, this is a helpful way to go.

A Note for Users of Microsoft Windows

If you use Microsoft Windows, you probably have significant amounts of extended memory installed in your computer; hopefully, you are running an

80386SX or higher processor, as Windows is no speed demon on anything less. You are sure to run into a configuration dilemma when optimizing FoxPro for use on a Windows machine, because Windows wants to see lots of extended memory. As mentioned earlier, FoxPro can't use extended memory, but would like to see lots of expanded memory. The solution, like many things in life, is a compromise. You will have to decide how much of your system's extended memory can be put aside as simulated expanded memory. If you put too little aside, FoxPro's performance suffers. Set aside too much, and you may see Windows performance suffer. You will have to experiment with various values, depending on your available RAM, to find a compromise that works best with FoxPro and Microsoft Windows. You can refer to your Windows documentation for details on how to use the memory manager provided with Windows and how to allocate varying amounts of extended memory to simulate expanded memory.

Modifying the FoxPro Resource File

FoxPro keeps track of a significant number of settings through the resource file, FOXUSER.DBF, and its associated memo field file, FOXUSER.FPT. The resource file is a special database that FoxPro uses to keep track of color sets, window locations, Browse window configurations, label definitions, and other similar information. If you are designing applications and you want to protect certain default window placements or similar settings from being changed by users, you can change the value of the READONLY field in the resource file. Because the resource file contains important data needed by FoxPro, it's a wise idea to make a backup copy of the resource file before modifying it.

Because FoxPro normally uses the resource file, you will have to close it before you can open it as a database. Enter

```
SET RESOURCE OFF
```

to stop FoxPro's normal use of the default resource file. You can then open the resource file as a database with a USE FOXUSER statement. If you then list the structure of the resource file, you see something similar to this:

```
Structure for database: E:\FOXPRO\FOXDATA\FOXUSER.DBF
Number of data records:      47
Date of last update   : 11/29/90
Field  Field Name  Type       Width    Dec
    1  TYPE        Character    12
    2  ID          Character    12
    3  NAME        Character    24
    4  READONLY    Logical       1
```

```
   5  CKVAL        Numeric        6
   6  DATA         Memo          10
   7  UPDATED      Date           8
** Total **                      74
```

FoxPro uses the fields of the resource file for the following purposes.

TYPE	The type of information stored by the particular resource
ID	The record within the type of resource
NAME	The name given the resource
READONLY	When set to logical true, prevents changes to the resource
CKVAL	Verifies the data contained in the memo field
DATA	Data for the resource
UPDATED	Date of the last change to the resource

In addition to changes to the READONLY field, you can also delete unwanted records (resources) from the file and perform a PACK to conserve disk space. Changes to fields other than the READONLY field are not recommended. After any desired changes, type **SET RESOURCE ON** to place the resource file back in use.

You can use different resource files with different applications by entering **SET RESOURCE TO** *resource filename*. To create additional resource files, enter **SET RESOURCE OFF** and open the resource file with **USE FOXUSER**. Enter **COPY TO** *filename* to copy the resource file to a different filename. Use the new file and make any desired deletions or changes. Then enter **SET RESOURCE TO** *filename*, where *filename* is the name of the new resource file, to place it into effect.

Finally, a Note About Hardware

The speed of your hard disk will impact the performance of FoxPro (along with all your other software), so you should consider it when looking for performance gains. Speed increases can often be realized without replacing your hard disk. A directory that is cluttered with files will slow down FoxPro because DOS will take longer to search the directory for files. Move files that aren't needed by an application out of that application's directory and into other directories on the hard disk. Avoid keeping application files in the same directory as the FoxPro program; instead, place them in separate subdirectories, and set a path with the DOS PATH command back to the directory containing FoxPro. From time to time, you should use a "disk optimizer" like that included in PC Tools, Central Point Software's utility package, to defragment your hard disk.

One often overlooked solution to sluggish performance is to upgrade your hardware. Microcomputers have experienced major gains in computational power at least four times in their history: from the 8-bit machines that ran dBASE II under CP/M operating systems; to the 16-bit address, 8-bit data bus, 8088-based IBM-compatibles; to the true 16-bit, 80286-based, IBM/AT-compatibles; to the 32-bit, 80386-based machines. At the time of this writing, 80486-based machines with large cache memory banks are readily available, and the Intel 80586 is well on its way to release. If an application is becoming bogged down due to overwhelming size, it may be time to ask if your hardware is sufficient to handle the task. You can spend time structuring your commands in a more efficient manner, recoding program loops to minimize unnecessary repetition, and fine-tuning configuration files, and you may pick up a total of 25 to 50 percent performance increase. On the other hand, by adding an accelerator board to your existing computer, or by moving the application to a faster machine, you can easily double or triple the performance of FoxPro.

Part V

Appendixes

File Types Used by FoxPro

Database-Related File Types	Extension
Databases	.DBF
Database memo files	.FPT
Compact index files	.CDX
Single-entry index files	.IDX
Screen databases	.SCX
Screen memo files	.SCT
Menu databases	.MNX
Menu memo files	.MNT
Project databases	.PJX
Project memo files	.PJT

Program-Related File Types	Extension
Programs	.PRG
Compiled programs	.FXP
Generated screen programs	.SPR
Compiled screen programs	.SPX
Generated menu programs	.MPR
Compiled menu programs	.MPX
Generated query programs	.QPR

Program-Related File Types	Extension
Compiled query programs	.QPX
Generated applications	.APP
Executable programs	.EXE

Other File Types	Extension
Compilation error files	.ERR
Memory variable files	.MEM
Key macro files	.FKY
Window files	.WIN
Libraries	.PLB
FoxPro temporary files	.TMP
Temporary database files	.TBK
Backup files	.BAK

Appendix B

System Functions

The following list shows the values returned by the SYSTEM() functions. Values not shown in this list are not used by FoxPro.

Function	Value Returned
SYS(0)	Network machine number/name
SYS(1)	Julian system date
SYS(2)	Seconds since midnight
SYS(3)	Unique filename
SYS(5)	Default drive
SYS(6)	Printer device
SYS(7)	Format file
SYS(9)	FoxPro serial number
SYS(10)	String from day number
SYS(11)	Julian day number
SYS(12)	Remaining memory
SYS(13)	Printer status
SYS(14)	Index expression
SYS(15)	Character translation
SYS(16)	Executing program name
SYS(17)	Processor in use

Function	Value Returned
SYS(18)	Current field/object
SYS(21)	Master index number
SYS(22)	Master tag/index name
SYS(23)	EMS memory available
SYS(24)	EMS memory limit
SYS(100)	Console setting
SYS(101)	Device setting
SYS(102)	Printer setting
SYS(103)	Talk setting
SYS(1001)	FoxPro's memory
SYS(1016)	User-allocated memory
SYS(2000)	File wildcard match
SYS(2001)	SET command status
SYS(2002)	Turn cursor on/off
SYS(2003)	Current directory
SYS(2004)	FoxPro's directory
SYS(2005)	Resource file
SYS(2006)	Graphics card
SYS(2007)	Checksum
SYS(2008)	Cursor shape
SYS(2009)	Swap cursor shape
SYS(2010)	FILES in CONFIG.SYS
SYS(2011)	Lock status
SYS(2012)	Memo file blocksize
SYS(2013)	System menu name
SYS(2014)	Get minimum path name
SYS(2015)	Unique name
SYS(2016)	SHOW GETS window
SYS(2017)	Show sign-on screen
SYS(2018)	Error message
SYS(2019)	CONFIG.FP file
SYS(2020)	Disk size
SYS(2021)	Filtered index expression

Appendix *C*

dBASE Commands Not Supported by FoxPro

The following dBASE commands are not supported by FoxPro 2 at the time of this writing.

ASSIST	ROLLBACK
BEGIN TRANSACTION	SET CATALOG ON/OFF
CONVERT	SET CATALOG TO
CREATE APPLICATION	SET DEBUG
DEBUG	SET DESIGN
DELETE TAG	SET ENCRYPTION
DISPLAY HISTORY	SET HISTORY
DISPLAY USERS	SET INSTRUCT
END TRANSACTION	SET MENU
LOGOUT	SET PRECISION
MODIFY APPLICATION	SET REFRESH
MODIFY VIEW	SET SQL
PROTECT	SET TITLE
RESET	SET TRAP

FoxPro version 1.*x* does not support the dBASE commands just listed and, further, does not support the following dBASE commands:

COPY INDEXES	MODIFY SCREEN
COPY TAG	SET DELIMITERS
CREATE QUERY	SET REPROCESS
CREATE SCREEN	SET SCOREBOARD
EXPORT TO	SET SKIP
IMPORT FROM	UNLOCK
MODIFY QUERY	

Appendix D

ASCII Codes

Decimal Value	Hexadecimal Value	Control Character	Character
0	00	NUL	Null
1	01	SOH	☺
2	02	STX	●
3	03	ETX	♥
4	04	EOT	◆
5	05	ENQ	♣
6	06	ACK	♠
7	07	BEL	Beep
8	08	BS	◘
9	09	HT	Tab
10	0A	LF	Line feed
11	0B	VT	Cursor home
12	0C	FF	Form feed
13	0D	CR	Enter
14	0E	SO	♪
15	0F	SI	☼
16	10	DLE	►

Decimal Value	Hexadecimal Value	Control Character	Character
17	11	DC1	◀
18	12	DC2	↕
19	13	DC3	‼
20	14	DC4	¶
21	15	NAK	§
22	16	SYN	▬
23	17	ETB	↨
24	18	CAN	↑
25	19	EM	↓
26	1A	SUB	→
27	1B	ESC	←
28	1C	FS	Cursor right
29	1D	GS	Cursor left
30	1E	RS	Cursor up
31	1F	US	Cursor down
32	20	SP	Space
33	21		!
34	22		"
35	23		#
36	24		$
37	25		%
38	26		&
39	27		'
40	28		(
41	29		)
42	2A		*
43	2B		+
44	2C		,
45	2D		-
46	2E		.
47	2F		/
48	30		0
49	31		1
50	32		2
51	33		3

Decimal Value	Hexadecimal Value	Control Character	Character
52	34		4
53	35		5
54	36		6
55	37		7
56	38		8
57	39		9
58	3A		:
59	3B		;
60	3C		<
61	3D		=
62	3E		>
63	3F		?
64	40		@
65	41		A
66	42		B
67	43		C
68	44		D
69	45		E
70	46		F
71	47		G
72	48		H
73	49		I
74	4A		J
75	4B		K
76	4C		L
77	4D		M
78	4E		N
79	4F		O
80	50		P
81	51		Q
82	52		R
83	53		S
84	54		T
85	55		U
86	56		V

Decimal Value	Hexadecimal Value	Control Character	Character
87	57		W
88	58		X
89	59		Y
90	5A		Z
91	5B		[
92	5C		\
93	5D		]
94	5E		^
95	5F		—
96	60		`
97	61		a
98	62		b
99	63		c
100	64		d
101	65		e
102	66		f
103	67		g
104	68		h
105	69		i
106	6A		j
107	6B		k
108	6C		l
109	6D		m
110	6E		n
111	6F		o
112	70		p
113	71		q
114	72		r
115	73		s
116	74		t
117	75		u
118	76		v
119	77		w
120	78		x
121	79		y

Decimal Value	Hexadecimal Value	Control Character	Character
122	7A		z
123	7B		{
124	7C		¦
125	7D		}
126	7E		~
127	7F	DEL	⌂
128	80		Ç
129	81		ü
130	82		é
131	83		â
132	84		ä
133	85		à
134	86		å
135	87		ç
136	88		ê
137	89		ë
138	8A		è
139	8B		ï
140	8C		î
141	8D		ì
142	8E		Ä
143	8F		Å
144	90		É
145	91		æ
146	92		Æ
147	93		ô
148	94		ö
149	95		ò
150	96		û
151	97		ù
152	98		ÿ
153	99		Ö
154	9A		Ü
155	9B		¢

Decimal Value	Hexadecimal Value	Control Character	Character
156	9C		£
157	9D		¥
158	9E		Pt
159	9F		ƒ
160	A0		á
161	A1		í
162	A2		ó
163	A3		ú
164	A4		ñ
165	A5		Ñ
166	A6		ª
167	A7		º
168	A8		¿
169	A9		⌐
170	AA		¬
171	AB		½
172	AC		¼
173	AD		¡
174	AE		«
175	AF		»
176	B0		░
177	B1		▒
178	B2		▓
179	B3		│
180	B4		┤
181	B5		╡
182	B6		╢
183	B7		╖
184	B8		╕
185	B9		╣
186	BA		║
187	BB		╗
188	BC		╝
189	BD		╜

Decimal Value	Hexadecimal Value	Control Character	Character
190	BE		⌐
191	BF		┐
192	C0		└
193	C1		┴
194	C2		┬
195	C3		├
196	C4		─
197	C5		+
198	C6		╞
199	C7		╟
200	C8		╚
201	C9		╔
202	CA		╩
203	CB		╦
204	CC		╠
205	CD		═
206	CE		╬
207	CF		╧
208	D0		╨
209	D1		╤
210	D2		╥
211	D3		╙
212	D4		╘
213	D5		╒
214	D6		╓
215	D7		╫
216	D8		╪
217	D9		┘
218	DA		┌
219	DB		█
220	DC		▄
221	DD		▌
222	DE		▐
223	DF		▀

Decimal Value	Hexadecimal Value	Control Character	Character
224	E0		α
225	E1		β
226	E2		Γ
227	E3		π
228	E4		Σ
229	E5		σ
230	E6		μ
231	E7		τ
232	E8		φ
233	E9		Θ
234	EA		Ω
235	EB		δ
236	EC		∞
237	ED		∅
238	EE		ε
239	EF		∩
240	F0		≡
241	F1		±
242	F2		≥
243	F3		≤
244	F4		⌠
245	F5		⌡
246	F6		÷
247	F7		≈
248	F8		°
249	F9		•
250	FA		·
251	FB		√
252	FC		η
253	FD		²
254	FE		■
255	FF		(blank)

Index

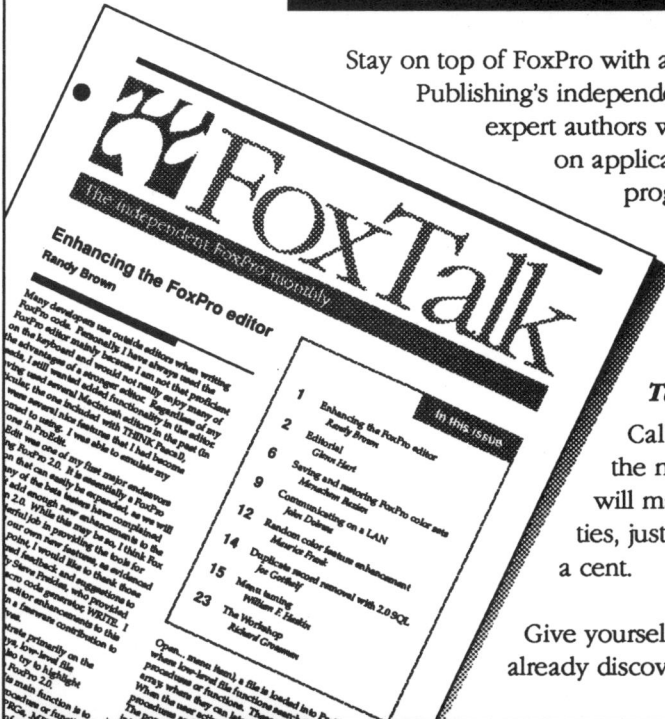

Osborne McGraw-Hill

Computer Books

(800) 227-0900

Bookmarker Design — Lance Ravella

Tear off for Bookmark

▼

You're important to us...

We'd like to know what you're interested in, what kinds of books you're looking for, and what you thought about this book in particular.

Please fill out the attached card and mail it in. We'll do our best to keep you informed about Osborne's newest books and special offers.

▶ *YES, Send Me a FREE Color Catalog of all Osborne computer books*
To Receive Catalog, Fill in Last 4 Digits of ISBN Number from Back of Book
(see below bar code) 0-07-881 _ _ _ — _

Name: _____ Title: _____

Company: _____

Address: _____

City: _____ State: _____ Zip: _____

I'M PARTICULARLY INTERESTED IN THE FOLLOWING *(Check all that apply)*

I use this software
- ☐ WordPerfect
- ☐ Microsoft Word
- ☐ WordStar
- ☐ Lotus 1-2-3
- ☐ Quattro
- ☐ Others _____

I use this operating system
- ☐ DOS
- ☐ Windows
- ☐ UNIX
- ☐ Macintosh
- ☐ Others _____

I rate this book:
- ☐ Excellent ☐ Good ☐ Poor

I program in
- ☐ C or C++
- ☐ Pascal
- ☐ BASIC
- ☐ Others _____

I chose this book because
- ☐ Recognized author's name
- ☐ Osborne/McGraw-Hill's reputation
- ☐ Read book review
- ☐ Read Osborne catalog
- ☐ Saw advertisement in store
- ☐ Found/recommended in library
- ☐ Required textbook
- ☐ Price
- ☐ Other _____

Comments _____

Topics I would like to see covered in future books by Osborne/McGraw-Hill include:

_____

IMPORTANT REMINDER
To get your FREE catalog, write in the last 4 digits of the ISBN number printed on the back cover (see below bar code) 0-07-881 _ _ _ — _

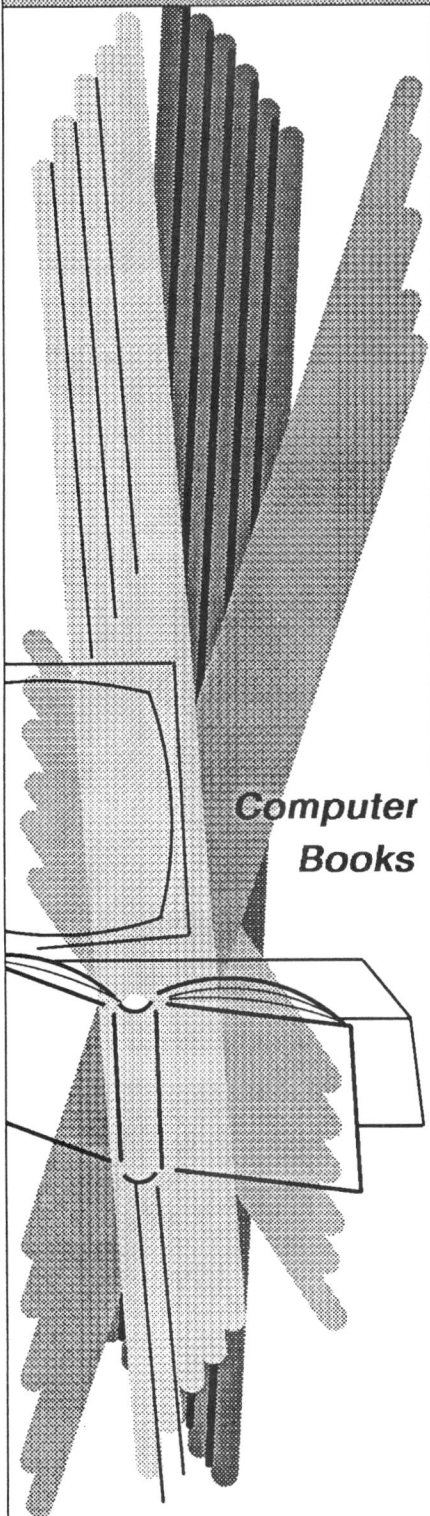

Osborne **McGraw-Hill**

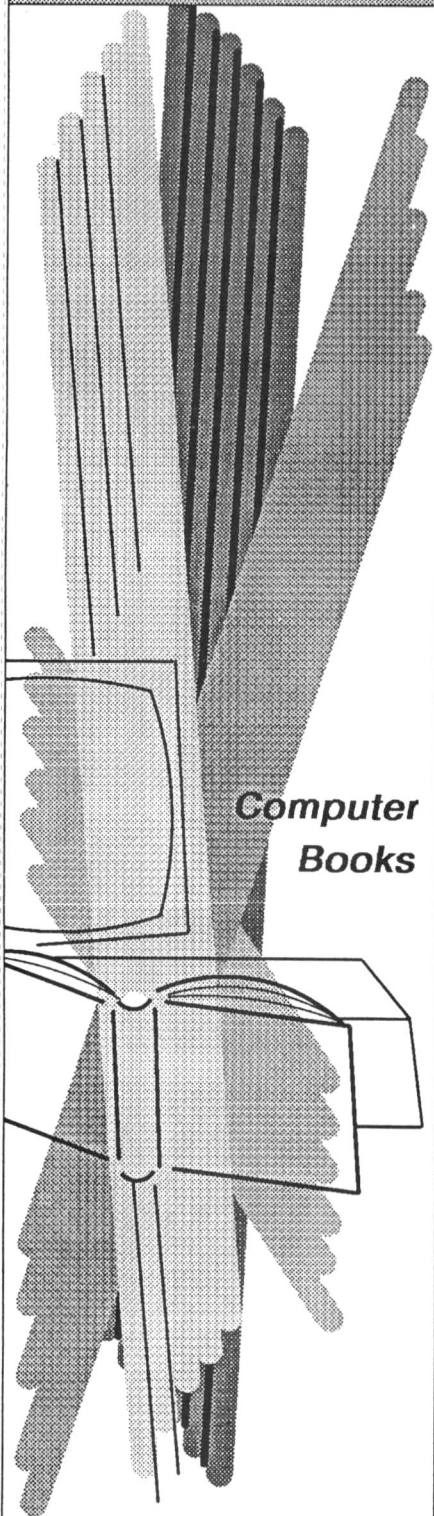

Computer
Books

(800) 227-0900